EUROPEAN
SOCIETY AND POLITICS:
BRITAIN, FRANCE AND GERMANY

*

EUROPEAN SOCIETY AND POLITICS:
BRITAIN, FRANCE AND GERMANY

STANLEY ROTHMAN
Smith College

HOWARD SCARROW
State University of New York at Stony Brook

MARTIN SCHAIN
New York University

WEST PUBLISHING CO.
St. Paul • New York • Boston • Los Angeles • San Francisco

Library of Congress Cataloging in Publication Data

Rothman, Stanley, 1927
    European Society and Politics
    Bibliography: p.
    Includes index.
      1. Europe—Politics and government. 2. Europe—Social conditions. 3. Comparative government.
  I. Scarrow, Howard, 1928–   joint author
 II. Schain, Martin, 1940–   joint author
III. Title.
JF51.R56 1976   309.1'4   75–43682
ISBN 0–8299–0068–3

    Rothman et al.–European Soc. & Pol.
    2nd Reprint—1976

Preface

This book is a revision of an earlier text (*European Society and Politics*) that was published in a clothbound edition in 1970. The present paperback edition has been shortened and brought up to date by Professors Howard Scarrow and Martin Schain, with assistance on the German section by Carl F. Lankowski, a graduate student in political science at Columbia University. In addition to their country responsibilities Professors Scarrow and Schain divided the special sections, such as education, family, and others which required a comparative perspective. Professor Scarrow assumed the major burden of reducing the length of various chapters by deciding what could be safely excised. The final editing of the material was completed by the senior author with assistance from both Professors Scarrow and Schain.

Material on the Soviet Union has been omitted, and the discussions of Britain, France, and Germany shortened. In addition, the theoretical sections of the book have been tightened; the material on public policy has been reduced in scope, and the chapters on foreign policy and local government have been dropped.

Our effort, in the light of comments by colleagues who used the earlier volume, has been to develop a text that would allow for more flexibility in teaching. Because of its shorter length, and lower price, this second edition can be used in either one-semester or two-semester courses, along with studies of other countries or in conjunction with theoretical introductions to the study of comparative politics.

In one key respect the text has not been changed. It remains the only volume available that deals with the politics of Britain, France, and Germany *within* a European framework. The overall approach is in terms of political development, yet the peculiar features of the developmental process in each of these three nations are seen as variations on common European themes. *European Society and Politics: Britain, France, and Germany* now boasts three authors rather than one; its approach, however, is still fully integrated and truly comparative.

Like the earlier edition, this one is an interpretation—or rather a series of interpretations—of the social and political life of the nations under study. The book begins with a discussion of the forces that have shaped European history and then turns to the particular fusion of these forces responsible for the different courses taken by Britain, France and Germany.

European social and political institutions are treated throughout the volume as patterns of relationships that have been continuously changing and will continue to change. The section on political parties, for example, relates the character of the party system to other institutions and emphasizes that contemporary patterns are part of an ever-evolving political process. Individual parties are also discussed in the order of their appearance on the political scene—the purpose here being to enable students to develop an understanding not only of the factors that led to their emergence at a particular moment, but also of the reasons for their particular configuration.

Other sections of the book are arranged in the same way, moving always from the general European experience to more specific national phenomena. This arrangement allows the reader to view contemporary European politics as the product of a complex interplay between indigenous cultural and social patterns and the forces that have transformed a specific type of traditional society into a number of modern industrial states. It also enables the reader to avoid confusing European political development with political development in general and to begin to understand why the European political experience has differed so markedly from that of other parts of the world.

As the explicitly theoretical sections of the book indicate, our approach to the study of politics is highly eclectic. We have drawn whatever ideas seemed useful from various functionalist approaches, but we have combined them with more traditional kinds of analysis. We have also tried to keep technical language at a minimum; whatever may be the advantages of a precise vocabulary, we think that an excessive emphasis on theoretical distinctions, in a text of this nature, would be more confusing than helpful.

In rewriting this book, we have again been keenly aware of the problem of not being able to say everything at once. The text, therefore, is quite deliberately organized, and it will best be read in the order in which the material is presented. We suspect that the relevance of the points made in early chapters cannot be fully appreciated by students until later on; similarly, much of the material in later chapters cannot be properly evaluated without reading the earlier chapters. In short, the text builds on itself.

Some of the conclusions we have reached are undoubtedly controversial. We have attempted to be as fair as we can, but we have not hesitated to evaluate the actions of men or the consequences of institutions where such evaluations seemed germane. Though ethical and factual propositions are analytically distinct, one's ethical position is necessarily related in important ways to one's empirical analysis; we believe that the social scientist can legitimately draw moral inferences from his understanding of politics.

We should especially like to thank the Press and Information Service of the French Embassy in New York for providing us with needed materials.

Stanley Rothman
Howard Scarrow
Martin Schain

Contents

†

EUROPEAN
SOCIETY AND POLITICS:
BRITAIN, FRANCE AND GERMANY

PART ONE

The European Inheritance

Page 2: Eglise de la Madeleine, Vezelay, France.
Page 3: Town of St. Pierre Entremont, France.
Both photos courtesy French Embassy Press &
Information Division. *Left:* Bishops in procession.

Above: The Bank of England. *Below:* Steelmills in Salzgitter, Germany. Courtesy German
Information Center.

1

The
Development
of
Modern Europe

1. INTRODUCTION

The present can be understood only in terms of the past—in terms of the forces that brought it into existence. The relevance of the past to an understanding of the present constitutes a major argument of this text. More specifically, it is argued that the most fruitful way of examining European nations is to deal with them in terms of their transformation from traditional to modern societies.

"Traditional" and "modern" are shorthand terms used by social scientists to describe two contrasting clusters of complex social phenomena. Traditional societies were characterized by relatively simple agricultural economies and rural living patterns; modern societies are largely industrialized and urbanized. Traditional societies were heavily imbued with religious or mystical values; modern societies are far more scientific and secular in orientation. In traditional societies, legal, political, and economic institutions were generally fused; in modern societies these institutions are more or less autonomous structures, each of which is charged with a particular set of functions. One consequence of such differentiation has been the emergence of large-scale bureaucratic organizations. Furthermore, in traditional societies rules of behavior may be applicable only to certain lineage groups, villages, or families, whereas in modern societies rules of law are universally applicable. Finally, in traditional societies the authority of various elites was accepted because it had always been accepted. In modern societies binding rules are accepted by individuals and groups not because of tradition, or because of religious sanction, but because these people have participated, even if only symbolically, in the political process.

The classification of political systems as traditional or modern has become rather commonplace among social scientists; so, too, has the analysis of social and political life in terms of the tensions produced by the transition from traditional to modern forms. This approach has enabled us to compare various political systems within a common framework. One of the dangers of such a method of comparison, however, is an implicit assumption that all traditional and all modern societies are alike, and that the process of development involves facing essentially the same problems and tensions. We disagree with this assumption. We would argue instead that while the pattern of European development shared some common features with development in other parts of the world, an understanding of contemporary European politics requires a recognition that traditional European society exhibited certain cultural and social configurations that were unique and that these in turn gave the process of European development a unique cast. The social and political life of the three European nations considered in this volume may be seen as representing variations on a common European theme.

Scholars of comparative history have always been aware of the uniqueness of Europe. As our awareness of the world has grown in recent years, the sharp contrasts between the common heritage of Western Europe and the civilizations of the Far and Middle East and Africa have become still more apparent. This common heritage derives largely from Greek and Roman sources that fused with Christianity. The institutional patterns that have developed on the Continent in the past thousand years are modifications of that basic inheritance. Consequently, while other areas of the world went through periods resembling European feudalism, the European pattern generated qualities that were specific to it; and while modern industrial societies seem to resemble one another more and more, significant cultural and social differences continue to exist between any European country and, say, Japan.

The scientific, industrial, and intellectual revolutions that created the modern world began in Europe. The question of why the process of modernization began there rather than in some other civilizations to which it has since been imported has long interested historians and sociologists. Aside from racial explanations, now largely discredited, the first answer usually advanced involves environmental variables: a temperate climate; a soil, especially in the north, that allows the intensive cultivation of any number of food crops; many large harbors and river systems that afford easy transportation of goods and easy access to the interior; coal and iron, crucial resources in the industrialization process, in convenient proximity.

These factors may help to explain why Europe industrialized more rapidly than did areas where a harsh climate and a lack of resources inhibited development; but they do not explain the primacy of Europe as a whole as against China, for example, or of Britain as against France and France as against Italy. The superiority of northern European soils became an advantage only when the special tools necessary to exploit them became available, and indeed, in the early years of British industrialization, iron ore was imported from Sweden. It may be well to remember also that northern Europe was inhabited by primitive migratory tribes long after civilizations of a very high order had flourished in other parts of the globe, and that northern Europe might have remained uncivilized for a long time had it not been for the influence of Rome. Further, it is difficult to argue that the European environment was far more conducive to industrialization than that of the Asiatic mainland. Though ecological conditions may have had some significance in setting the broad limits within which a modern civilization could grow, a full explanation of Europe's industrialization must take into account other factors.

It seems reasonable to suggest that what was primarily responsible for Europe's lead in modernization was its particular cultural heritage, including the Christian tradition. This heritage provided the underlying values for an industrial society; it also explains much of the contemporary structure of European social and political life. Part One of this book emphasizes this European cultural heritage.

2. EUROPEAN FEUDALISM

With the administrative collapse of the Roman Empire in the West following the barbarian invasions, the economic, social, and political life in most of Western Europe regressed to a more primitive level than that achieved under Roman influence. Large-scale commerce dropped off sharply; the heritage of classical thought and literature all but disappeared; and tribal Germanic law tended to replace the urban Roman legal system.

The major problem for society was that of controlling violence. Coastal areas were continually harassed by Viking invasions from the north and Muslim invasions from the south, and the marauders moved far inland; indeed the Mongols once crossed all of Russia from the north to the Black Sea. More importantly, the disappearance of Roman legal authority left a vacuum that could not be satisfactorily filled by the traditional tribal organization. Rather, a new form of political organization—European feudalism —evolved to provide rudimentary domestic peace and security.

The essence of feudalism was vassalage. The more powerful persons granted the use of land or the benefits of offices (fiefs) sufficient for decent livelihood to persons who in turn became their vassals and vowed homage and fealty. The relationship between lord and vassal was not simple; deemed honorable by both parties, it was fundamentally one involving mutual defense

and service. From its beginnings in Norman France as a series of local, petty arrangements, feudalism became in a few centuries a political or administrative device used by monarchs to extend their authority indirectly over larger and larger areas. The vassal, in addition to serving upon call and at his own expense in his lord's military forces and to paying the customary dues for his fief, also acted as his lord's administrative agent in dispensing justice and collecting taxes. When a lord's vassals granted the use of land or offices to other men, making them vassals of their own in a process we have come to call "subinfeudation," the patterns of authority and administration became more intricate—and security and order became less certain. For several centuries before the rise of the national monarchies, much of Europe was divided into feudalities with only tenuous obligations to any higher level of authority.

The basic elements of European economic life during the feudal period revolved about the manor of the lord. Physically, it consisted of lands, fields, streams, woods, the lord's great house, its mills and barns, its animals, and the persons attached to it in varying degrees of bondage. Psychologically, it represented the whole world to the peasants and laborers who were tied to it by customary law. Serfs, whose children were inherited as chattels by the manor, and even freemen, though custom protected their rights against abuse by the lord of the manor, could not leave without their lord's consent.

The manor was a comparatively self-sufficient unit. Life revolved about the land and its cultivation. Time was ordered about the seasons, religious feast days, and the cycle of birth and death. A person was born, lived, and died in a single community on a certain piece of land, the use of which was to be handed on to his heirs. Of all things, land was the most valuable because it was the immediate source of life itself.

Individuals were born into stations in life; they fulfilled the tasks of those stations and trained their children to fulfill them. Even after the revival of trade and the growth of towns that accompanied the High Middle Ages, tradesmen and artisans, theoretically at least, charged only a "just price" for their goods or services, and the production and distribution of goods were regulated by a specific set of customary rules enforced by the Roman Catholic Church, by guilds, and by local and regional—later, national—authorities. These regulations were derived from a conception of the community as an organic unit to which each person contributed according to his fixed station; each person's rights, obligations, and rewards were restricted to those appropriate to his station.

Social mobility, nevertheless, did not disappear completely. In the later Middle Ages, the aristocracy became a relatively closed class, but peasants and artisans could and did migrate to towns where social organization was more fluid. The Roman church always accepted men from any station, and occasionally the lowborn rose within it to heights of power and influence. Yet compared with the societies of nineteenth- and twentieth-century America and Europe, the most striking features of feudal Europe are the relatively static character of social classes, their differences before the law, and the rigidity of an individual's social status.

By the late Middle Ages, Europe, except for Spain, was Christian Europe. Spreading out from the center of the Roman Empire, Christianity had finally been adopted, although considerably modified, by the Germanic and Slavic peoples of the north. And as is true of all traditional societies, religious or magical ideas and customs dominated much of life. The Christian might find secular life meaningless or directionless, but secular history would some day terminate in the millennium.

The structure and content of Western Christianity had profound effects upon later European development; the elements of which it was composed provided European society with a dynamic impetus that was not present in other societies. First, Christianity was both universalistic and individualistic. The purpose of the Catholic Church was the salvation of all men, and man's relation to God was individual rather than communal. Western Christianity, therefore, was far less likely to become identified with a single community or state than were Judaism or Byzantine Christianity.

Out of Christianity sprang both the individualism that became an integral part of Western European culture and the tension between religious and secular authority that play so important a role in Europe's political development. Theocracy, or the fusion of religious and secular authority in the hand of a political figure (caesaropapism), has historically been far less characteristic of Western Europe than of other cultures, even during those periods when the papacy claimed substantial secular authority.

Further, Christianity paralleled many other religious creeds in stressing the sinfulness of the flesh and the corruption of the world. But its emphasis was on "practical" or "inner-worldly" asceticism, not on mystical or "other-worldly" asceticism. Rather than counseling withdrawal from the world, as did a number of Eastern religions, it called for fulfilling one's appointed function in the world by mastering and ordering it.

And finally, Christianity set God above the world as its creator and stressed the importance of human reason in enabling men to understand the laws by which God ruled the world. In this way, Christian doctrine officially discouraged belief in magic and contributed to the development of modern science in the West.

3. THE EMERGENCE OF MODERN EUROPE

In the centuries following the collapse of the Roman Empire, the population of Europe grew steadily, if slowly. New methods of plowing were discovered that permitted the more effective use of the heavier soils of northern Europe. Trade and commerce gradually expanded; and, after the eleventh century, towns increased rapidly in size and number. Elements of the classical heritage, including Roman law, were rediscovered and incorporated into Christian and secular thought, a process that culminated in the Italian Renaissance of the fifteenth century.

These changes contributed to a revolution that was to transform European society. The revolution consisted of four inter-related developments: the emergence of the modern nation-state; the schism of Christianity and the development of the Protestant sects; the growth of modern science and technology and an industrial civilization; and the secularization of European society.

THE NATION-STATE: Despite the decline of central authority during the early Middle Ages, the memory of the Roman Empire (later the Holy Roman Empire) did not disappear; nor did traditional conceptions of royal authority. European monarchs established their authority over more and more territory, and the peoples of Europe began severally to manifest a national consciousness. England was the first country to achieve the national unity that was crucial for its development; this process began in the eleventh century under William the Conqueror and was consummated by the Tudors in the sixteenth. France achieved effective nationhood by the late sixteenth century, and Germany in the late nineteenth century. In general, this awakening of national self-consciousness moved from west to east, with national boundaries tending to follow ethnic or linguistic lines. The growth of the nation-state resulted in a central authority replacing local authority; it also weakened the medieval sense of being part of a common Christian community coextensive with Europe. Moreover, the growth of the nation-state contributed to the secularization of political authority as individual rulers wrested power from the church.

The rise of the nation-state also helped to induce, and was supported by, economic changes. The unified nation-states constituted larger economic units in which, for the first time since the Roman Empire, centralized governments took some responsibility for establishing transportation networks, uniform systems of weights and coinage, and uniform systems of enforceable law. In return, the drive toward unity and centralized control won the endorsement of the new commercial strata of the cities, who saw in the destruction of the feudal order by the new monarchs, the best means of achieving their own ends.

The Protestant revolt, too, had a far-reaching effect upon the creation of nation-states by weakening the authority of a transnational church. Indeed, Protestantism was supported by secular authorities in some cases for just this reason.

THE REFORMATION: Whatever the degree of success, or failure, of the Reformation as a religious movement in the nations with which we are concerned—a subject that will be treated later—its consequences for Europe were enormous. Protestantism was a vital factor in the secularization of political authority and of life in general; it was instrumental to the development of an industrial society and to the origin and growth of political liberalism and the idea of democracy.

The contribution of Protestantism, especially of the Calvinist sects, to secularization reversed the intention of the reformers, who saw in their break with Rome a return to society dominated by religious values. In fact, however, the breakdown of a central religious authority and the extreme individualism of the Protestant sects helped to spawn a multiplicity of sects; and this very multiplicity undoubtedly diminished the influence of religious ideals, producing an ideological ferment that undermined the credibility of any particular doctrine. Social stability required toleration, and toleration, in the Christian world at least, entailed the gradual dilution of the content of Christian belief. Insofar as Protestantism fostered secularization, it also had an effect on the development of a scientific world view, at least by weakening the barriers inhibiting its acceptance. And to the extent that Protestantism furthered the growth of modern science, it was an important agent in the creation of an industrial technology. The relations between Protestantism and both science and industrialization were, however, more complex than this. Calvinism's insistence that one must fulfill one's calling, and its identification of salvation with success in rationally ordering the environment through hard work, are the core of the "Protestant ethic." Max Weber has argued that even though Calvin himself, and early Calvinists, were as antagonistic to commercialism as was the Catholic Church, the ethos of Protestantism provided the cultural basis for an industrial order, especially after the initial religious fervor had waned. Weber's hypothesis is by no means universally accepted; it has, on the contrary, provoked extensive study and debate. One can say, nonetheless, that Protestantism was *one* important factor in the growth of European capitalism.

The legacy of Protestantism to democracy and liberalism is even more difficult to delineate. Certainly the diversity of sects, along with the idea of toleration, was important; so, too, was the primacy assigned self-government in the Calvinist congregation.

Sectarian diversity and toleration abetted the fragmentation of religious and political authority; the idea of self-government for each congregation was closely associated with an individualism that stressed a personal relationship with God and rejected the idea of a governing religious hierarchy. Such views could easily be transformed into a demand for political institutions responsive to the wishes of the community.

SCIENCE, TECHNOLOGY, AND SECULARIZATION: After 1800, modern science and industry profoundly influenced European society. Because we are accustomed to vast and rapid changes in technology, we cannot appreciate fully the impact of science and technology in the nineteenth century; but though change was slower then, its effects were in some ways comparable to developments in India or Africa today. The material life of the European peasant had remained almost unchanged from Roman times to the nineteenth century. Then, in a period of several generations, his world was altered radically. In 1800 Britain was still basically a traditional agricultural society; by 1900 the nation was highly industrialized. In 1806 Britain produced less than 250,000 tons of pig iron; by 1910 it was producing more than 9 million tons—roughly thirty-six times as much in about one century. Britain's gross national product in 1913 was at least fifty times greater than it had been in 1800. Agricultural products made similar gains.[1]

The improvement of the material circumstances of life, the control of disease through advances in medical science and sanitation (and consequently the elimination of plagues), led to a sudden drop in the death rate and an astounding increase in population. It is estimated that in A.D. 500 the population of Europe was about 20 million persons. By 1600 Europe had some 100 million inhabitants, a general growth of approximately 1 percent a decade. By 1800 its population had risen to 200 million and by 1900 to 400 million. In other words, between 1700 and 1900 the rate of increase averaged 5 percent a decade.

This geometric rate of population increase (Table 1.2) revolutionized the Continent and ultimately the entire world. Urbanization and industrialization gave time and distance new meanings and produced highly significant changes in the class and power structure of Europe and in the content of European culture. The industrial middle and working classes replaced a landed gentry and a peasantry as the dominant social strata; increasingly, life became regulated by the rhythm of the machine and measured by the clock instead of the calendar. The development of new and faster means of communication and the growth of literacy brought new strata into politics. In 1850 daily pa-

[1] Estimates of production or population in earlier periods are only approximate. Data from W. S. Woytinsky and E. S. Woytinsky, *World Population and Production* (New York: The Twentieth Century Fund, 1953), and Colin Clark, *The Conditions of Economic Progress* (London: Macmillan & Co., 1950).

TABLE 1.1   THE GROWTH OF SELECTED EUROPEAN CITIES

Population in thousands

Country and city	1800	1850	1900	1930	1950's	1960's
United Kingdom						
London (excluding						
suburbs)	959	2,363	4,537	4,397	8,348 [1]	7,703
Birmingham	71	242	522	1,003	2,237 [1]	2,446
Manchester	77	336	544	766	2,422 [1]	2,451
Germany						
Berlin	172	419	1,889	4,243	2,146 [2]	2,135 [2]
Hamburg	130	132	706	1,129	1,605	1,818
Cologne	50	97	373	757	595	860
France						
Paris	547	1,053	2,714	2,830	4,823 [1]	8,197
Marseilles	111	195	491	914	661 [1]	964
Lyons	110	177	459	571	650 [1]	1,075
Other cities						
Moscow	250	365	612	3,100 [3]	4,847	7,061
Rome	153	175	423	931	1,651 [1]	2,706
Amsterdam	201	224	511	757	838 [1]	1,043
Warsaw	100	160	638	1,179	804	1,283

[1] For the 1950's and 1960's the figures are for urban agglomerates.

[2] Figures for West Berlin only for 1950 and 1962.

[3] Estimated.

[4] United Kingdom figures are for 1967; Germany, for 1969; France for 1968.
Sources: To 1930, W. S. and E. S. Woytinsky, *World Population and Production* (New York: Twentieth Century Fund, 1953), pp. 120–121, reprinted by permission of the publisher. Figures for 1950's and 1960's, *U.N. Demographic Yearbook, 1970* (New York, 1971), pp. 432–479.

pers were being read by one adult in eighty; in 1900 by one adult in five or six.[2]

More than any other single factor, the revolution in science and technology was responsible for the secularization of life. The scientific world view was inconsistent with substantial portions of Christian dogma. Protestantism accommodated itself to the new outlook far more easily than did the Catholic Church, whose rigidly structured organization and large body of well-defined

[2] Data from Raymond Williams, *Britain in the Sixties: Communications* (Baltimore: Penguin Books, 1962).

dogma made adaptation more troublesome. Reformers, therefore, especially in Catholic nations, saw the church as an obstacle not only to the reorganization of society but to the achievement of a personal happiness that increasing wealth seemed to promise.

4.   THE NINETEENTH CENTURY

The industrialization of Europe was accompanied by a series of social and political upheavals and an explosion of new ideologies, both of which reached their greatest intensity in the nineteenth century. The three most important ideologies that matured dur-

TABLE 1.2 COMPARATIVE POPULATION DATA:
EUROPE AND THE UNITED STATES

In millions

	France	Germany	United Kingdom	Italy	Russia	United States
Ca. 1800	27	25	11	18	39	5
Ca. 1850	36	35	27	23	62	23
Ca. 1900	38	56	37	32	129	76
Pre–World War I (1910–1913)	40	68	41	35	—	92
Pre–World War II (1936–1940)	41	70	46	43	170	132
Ca. 1950	42	70 [1]	49	47	201	151
Ca. 1972	50	78	55	54	242	203
Approximate increase						
1850–1950	6	35	22	24	139	128
1950–1972	8	8	6	7	41	52

[1] Includes Federal Republic and German Democratic Republic.

From *Regional Geography of the World* by Jesse H. Wheeler, Jr., J. Trenton Kost-bade and Richard S. Thoman. Copyright © 1955 by Holt, Rinehart and Winston, Inc. Reprinted by permission of Holt, Rinehart and Winston.

ing this period were liberalism, conservatism, and socialism. To a considerable, although decreasing, extent, these ideologies still dominate political rhetoric in Europe.

LIBERALISM: As a system of thought, liberalism, in its nineteenth-century context, is primarily associated with Adam Smith and with Jeremy Bentham and his followers, the Philosophical Radicals in England. Its source can be traced to John Locke, Thomas Hobbes, and the Protestant sects. In general, nineteenth-century liberals regarded the state as a watchman whose function was to enforce the basic rules necessary to permit the individual's power of self-government and self-control to produce a reasonable, just, and peaceful society. The removal of traditional restrictions upon behavior would enable individual energies to be channeled in directions that would contribute to th heightened well-being of all citizens.

The state was expected to perform only limited role in the economic sphere. Asid from keeping the peace, its major function were the protection of property rights an the defense of the nation. Within thi framework, and pushed and pulled by thei desires to achieve pleasure and avoid pain men would pursue their economic self-inter est. In so doing, however, they would through the mechanism of the marketplace contribute to the wealth of all, and the greater rewards would go to the more indus-trious and skillful. The state should by nc means regulate wages and prices as it had in the past; such policies, enforced by the re-strictive guild system as well as by the state, had only hampered the effective operation of the economy.

In a free market encouraged by the state, relations between employer and employee would be purely contractual, each using the other to his own advantage and hence to the mutual advantage of both. The employer would hire the worker at the lowest possible wage, and the worker would sell his labor as dearly as possible. In this contractual association, the authority of the employer and the obligations of the worker would extend no further than their specific economic relationship.

Institutions were to be judged by whether they served the interest of the majority of the community. All institutions that contributed to ordered liberty were of value because they permitted the individual the widest range of choice in his goals. All institutions that substituted rational principles for custom and tradition were of value, both because they were rational and because individuals should be evaluated on the basis of their actions rather than the accident of birth.

Representative government came to be considered superior to other forms. Men could be assured that their own interests would be furthered by their governors only if it was in the interest of the governors to do so—and the elective principle was the most effective means of achieving this assurance. While all men were not necessarily equal in talent, they were considered equally entitled to pursue their own interests, and each certainly knew this interest better than did any hereditary monarch or social class.

Liberal thought was characterized by a faith in man's burgeoning capacity to master the physical world and to take an enlightened and social view of his own interests. As poverty and superstition were eliminated, one could look forward to a world mastered by science, a world in which war and other conflicts would be reduced, if not eliminated altogether. This enlightened view would evolve from the free competition of ideas, a competition in which truth would eventually triumph. Restrictions on the expression of ideas, liberals believed, only inhibited innovation and prevented both the community and individuals from discovering where their true interests lay. Restrictions also deprived the individual not only of his right to choose how he would act, but of the chance to be responsible for that free choice —rights which were essential to his humanity.

Liberal intellectuals were often hostile to organized religion. As "reformers" who welcomed the new industrial society, they equated religion with superstition, arguing that science offers no evidence for the existence of God and that religious beliefs merely uphold erroneous customs. The Catholic Church particularly came under attack as authoritarian and intolerant, as fostering backwardness and inequality, and as representing all that was wrong with the religious outlook.

Liberal groups and, later, political parties, found membership and support in the urban commercial and industrial classes, and in those elements of the skilled working class that by the middle of the nineteenth century were beginning to obtain the vote.

This description of liberalism, like those of conservatism and socialism that follow, pertains to "ideal types" and deals only with the essential characteristics and implications of liberal thought.[3] In actuality, groups included under the generic term "liberal" held a variety of views depending, among other factors, upon the country and the period under consideration. English Whigs, for instance, were hesitant about extending the suffrage to the "masses"; in the middle of the nineteenth century it was only the "radicals" who favored such measures. The nature of some of the divisions among liberals and the reasons for them will be spelled out more fully in later chapters.

CONSERVATISM: European conservatism essentially represented an attempt to rationalize tradition—to justify retaining the customary arrangements of the past. Conservatism was a reaction against both indus-

[3] See "ideal type analysis" in Julius Gould and William L. Kolb, eds., A Dictionary of the Social Sciences (New York: Free Press, 1964), pp. 311–313.

trialization and liberalism, and in European intellectual history its foremost advocates were Edmund Burke in England, Louis de Bonald and Joseph de Maistre in France, and Georg Wilhelm Friedrich Hegel in Germany, although Hegel's position is, in some ways, quite ambiguous.

Conservatives de-emphasized the role of reason and assailed the individualistic and egalitarian premises of liberalism. They condemned the liberals' faith in science and reason as utopian, regarded the new conceptions of knowledge as restrictive and self-contradictory, and denied that one could successfully construct a society based on self-interest. Tradition and religion, they claimed, were necessary for cohesion. The emphasis upon man's rationality would only accentuate irrationality; reducing social life to a calculus of pains and pleasures would destroy the reality of life. Generally, conservatives supported established religion, hereditary (even absolute) monarchies, tradition for the sake of tradition, and the need for a society grounded in respect for authority.

Conservatives argued that the individualism of liberalism contributed to social dissolution and injustice. They re-emphasized that the purpose of the community was to achieve a just social order. And as a just social order involved the mutual responsibilities and rights of various estates, so it necessarily presupposed an ordered hierarchy. Again, the achievement of social justice—indeed of an ordered society—required a governing class that by inheritance and breeding was fit to govern. The emphasis on equality, they argued, could lead only to chaos. Thus, the conservatives rejected both the idea of the democratic state and the idea of the minimum state. The state, governed by the better elements in the community, would take an active part in social affairs in order to bring about social cohesion and justice.

The conservatives attacked industrialism and the values of capitalism as being egoistic and philistine. These attacks merged with the English and Continental Romantic movement, which contrasted the bucolic joys of an agricultural society with the filth, dirt, and general unhealthiness of industrial society, and the contentment and balance of rural society with the frenzied life of the masses in the growing industrial centers.

SOCIALISM: Another and equally sharp critique of the values of liberal capitalism was leveled in the nineteenth century. This time the attack came from Socialist intellectuals.

Socialist ideas can be traced back at least as far as the early Christian community, and throughout the medieval and early modern periods. Christian sects arose that espoused a communal ownership of property in accordance with Christian doctrine and scripture. Modern European socialism, however, is primarily associated with industrialization and forms an integral part of Europe's transition from a traditional to a modern industrial society. Whereas both peasants and aristocrats remained conservative because, for different reasons, they felt threatened by the new society and new ideas associated with industrialization, the working class, migrating to the cities from a peasant background, was drawn to Socialist parties by both class consciousness and the trauma of having to adjust to an urban industrial environment. Criticism of the new society by Socialist intellectuals was taken seriously because of the constant tensions involved in the transition to modernity—and because the new society could be contrasted (unfavorably) with an older one which, in retrospect, seemed to have placed much more stress on community life. As a consequence, Socialist movements of considerable size appeared almost simultaneously among the nations of Western Europe in the nineteenth century.

On the ideological level, socialism involved, first of all, a basic criticism of the values of capitalist society. Socialists condemned capitalism's egoistic individualism, its acquisitive materialism, its denial of mutual responsibility, its dehumanization of man into types identifiable with economic functions. On these points, the Socialist and the conservative critiques of capitalism were at one. The Socialist's solutions to the problems of industrialization, however, differed profoundly from those of the conservatives; for Socialists, on the whole, accepted the liberal faith in science, progress, and equality. Their critique of industrialism was directed solely against capitalist industrialization. They maintained that liberal capitalism worshipped false ideals, and that even those of its goals that were humane could not be achieved in a capitalistic society. Only under a Socialist organization of society was it possible to direct the fruits of science toward a fully human existence.

Karl Marx, whose towering genius dominated European political and social thinking during the latter part of the nineteenth century and whose work inspired every major European Socialist party except the British, drew upon both the conservative critique of capitalism and industrialization and upon the values of liberal capitalism. Marx regarded historical change as the result of the violent collision of social classes, each limited in its awareness by its specific class ideology. Hence, once the time was ripe, the transformation of a capitalist society into a communist society could be effected only through the revolutionary efforts of the working class. When Socialist parties developed on the Continent, the Marxist ones were usually the most militant and the most strongly committed to a violent course of action.

5. CONTEMPORARY EUROPE

The development of all Western European nations during the nineteenth century was in certain ways fundamentally similar. Industrial capitalist society was associated both with social stresses of varying intensity and with the birth of liberal democracy and more radical movements. By the end of the century, the alleviation of many of these stresses had begun. Liberal capitalist ideas were being amended as working-class demands, expressed through revolutionary action and the ballot box, combined with tradi-

tional concepts of the community to modify extreme individualism. Liberal parties were producing socially concerned programs, and conservative parties were slowly coming to accept democratic and industrial ideals. The aristocracy, as a class of landowners, was disappearing, and Socialist parties were becoming more moderate as they grew more popular.

Nineteenth-century Europe was also expanding beyond its borders. The motives underlying this expansion were mixed: they came partly from the desire for trading opportunities and for power and prestige, partly from missionary zeal. Europe's ability to expand its influence and the ability of European countries to control non-European countries of far greater size and population were based on technological superiority, one manifestation of which was the creation of ever more effective military weapons. Europe's political suzerainty, however, was short-lived; the European empire began to crumble no more than fifty or sixty years after it had achieved its maximum extent. Compared with the Roman attainment, it was fleeting indeed.

COMMUNISM: Contemporary Europe can probably best be dated from World War I, which, along with its aftermath, served to accelerate previous trends and to create new tensions that altered the direction of European development. One major political consequence of the war was the founding of the Soviet state.

By the end of the nineteenth century, Socialist parties in the West had begun to lose their revolutionary élan. Within almost all of them, however, powerful revolutionary factions remained, usually the more "orthodox" Marxists, though many who called themselves Marxists had accepted both gradualism and the democratic state. With the chaos and slaughter of World War I and a newly proclaimed revolutionary Marxist state in Russia, these factions grew quickly in strength. To the more radical Socialists, the war had been a capitalist enterprise and the slaughter it had entailed offered justification for their doctrines. The inflation and unemployment that accompanied postwar adjustments made the promises of radical Marxism even more appealing.

As a result of increasing factionalism, all Socialist movements of Western Europe, except the British, split, and powerful national Communist parties were created that owed allegiance to the Comintern, or Third International, which had been set up in Moscow. Although the Communists expected the immediate outbreak of revolutions throughout Western Europe, these did not occur, and the Socialist movements of the West continued to be divided between increasingly hostile Socialist and Communist parties. Only briefly, before the pall of fascism fell over Europe, did the left unite in France in the Popular Front to push through a series of long-overdue reform measures. The Communist parties of Western Europe eventually came under the domination of the Soviet Union, partly because of the prestige it enjoyed and partly because the Soviet Union provided financial aid upon which the Communist parties in the West depended.

The Communists were active in the Resistance during World War II, and in France and Italy they joined in the constituent assemblies and coalition governments of the immediate postwar years. Their resistance activities had brought them popular support while Europe was recovering from the war and the Nazi occupation, and because of their pervasive organizational network, they were prepared to take advantage of the fluid, postwar conditions. But as the disagreements between the Allies and the Soviet Union intensified and then became the Cold War, and with the predilection of the Communist parties, especially the French, to follow Moscow's lead, these coalition governments collapsed and the Communists went into opposition. They have remained in opposition ever since. However, changes in European politics since the middle 1960's, including the waning of the "Cold War," lead many observers to believe that coalition governments in which Communist parties participate are in the offing in the near future. The possibility of such participation by both the Italian and French Communist parties has been enhanced by their increasing independence from Moscow and their verbal acceptance of democratic norms.

FASCISM: A Second movement fashioned from the strains produced by World War I was European fascism, which reached its zenith during the 1930's in German National Socialism. Its origins are also to be found in the nineteenth century. Conservatism in Europe had been a reaction against both liberalism and industrialization. By the end of the nineteenth century, however, conservative parties in many countries were suffering a serious malaise. Based upon a landowning aristocracy, they were identified with monarchy and the church and a hierarchical society. As land became a less important source of wealth, as the tenets of aristocratic authority were weakened by the challenge of democratic ideologies, and as the participation of the mass of the people in political life increased, the power of the European aristocracy faded. In addition, the old attachments to both monarchy and church were slowly being undermined.

In Britain, and certain other countries, conservative parties adapted to the new epoch, established a mass political base, and continued to flourish. But for many reasons, conservative parties in some nations could not successfully adjust to the new conditions. Their decline did not necessarily mean, however, that hostility to industrial society had disappeared on the "ideological" right and in substantial segments of the peasantry. On the contrary, it was this hostility that gave rise to fascism. Though fascism appealed to the masses, claimed to speak for them, and used "pseudo-democratic" catch phrases, it was a movement that nevertheless represented a vehement reaction against modernity; its aim was to restore certain values of a vanishing, traditional society. Paradoxically, fascism based its censure of modernity on some of the slogans of modernity. A belief in the rule of the people's will—or in a ruling, racial elite issuing from and speaking for the people—was combined with an attack upon industrial society and its ramifications. Fascists thus rejected liberal capitalism because of the callousness and philistinism of bourgeois society; and they rejected Marxist socialism because, like liberalism, it denied traditional values and the concept of a heroic, disciplined social order. Fascists were at one with conservatives in calling for a society in which the community regulated economic activities for the common good; but they, particularly the German Fascists, discarded a hereditary class elite in favor of a racial elite.

For different reasons, then, fascism appealed to different types of people: those who deplored the "heartlessness" of urban, industrial society; those who had been displaced or who feared displacement; those who feared the destruction of traditional values; those who applauded the collapse of traditional society; and finally, those who felt personally threatened by the loosening of long-established controls.

The tensions and strains of these people were reflected also in the anti-Semitism of most fascist movements. The Jews served as a focus for the animosity of persons who believed that the old values of the society were being threatened, as well as those who, rebelling against traditional values, feared their own impulses and projected them upon the Jew.

Fascist movements reached their peak in the 1920's and 1930's, drawing their support primarily from the peasantry, small businessmen, and other lower-middle-class elements who, in many cases, deserted the liberal, anti-aristocratic parties they had supported earlier. Their switch in allegiance is understandable if one recognizes that fascism was a postdemocratic movement that contained genuine populist overtones. In fact, this populist appeal distinguishes fascism from traditional conservatism and from traditional dictatorships like that of Franco's Spain, which, despite some Fascist elements, lacked the populist and totalitarian character of Nazi Germany and, to a lesser extent, of Fascist Italy.

POSTWAR CHANGES: Fascism led to World War II—and another crucial turning point in European history. Again, some of the changes that have occurred since the defeat of Germany and Italy in 1945 are merely a continuation of earlier trends. In some cases, the changes were accelerated by the war itself; in other cases, the changes represent new directions.

Europe has by and large completed the transition to a "modern" society. The tech-

TABLE 1.3   THE AFFLUENT SOCIETY IN EUROPE
AND THE UNITED STATES, 1971

Number per thousand inhabitants

	Passenger cars	Television sets	Telephones	Persons per doctor
Germany	234	262	212	568
France	245	201	161	747
Britain	213	284	253	855
United States	432	399	567	669

Source: Press and Information Office of the Government of the Federal Republic of Germany, *The European Community* (Wiesbaden, 1972), pp. 135–136.

nological impetus provided by the war and the increasing rate of postwar technological development have contributed to rapid social change. Europe has now entered an age of affluence—an era of television sets, washing machines, and automobiles, an era that is closing the material gap between rural and urban existence. The destruction of old landmarks and the building of new ones— such as highways and supermarkets—are visible everywhere. It is also an age in which regional variations are declining and in which some of the superficial indications of class differences—language, dress, luxuries—are vanishing. Another sign of the times has been the disappearance of that traditional emblem of middle- or upper-class status, the domestic servant.

Despite growing affluence there are still substantial pockets of poverty in all European countries, especially in the rural areas and among the elderly. Housing conditions in Britain, France, and Germany are still inadequate. Furthermore, the distribution of income has not become noticeably more nearly equal. Yet compared with prewar Europe, it is the affluence, geographic mobility, and greater homogeneity of the population that are most striking. It is quite clear that Western Europe, has accepted modernity. The restoration of traditional institutions no longer seems even remotely possible.

Given these facts and the emergence and widespread acceptance of the "welfare state" after World War II, intellectuals in the West began speaking more frequently of Europe not only as a "postcapitalist" society, but also as a society in which ideology was on the decline. Liberal and conservative parties alike (the terms are no longer completely fitting) were accepting democracy and social-welfare policies. Socialist parties, too, were committed to parliamentary regimes; in fact, they tended to become parties of reform accepting the framework of a mixed economy with an ever-expanding public sector. True, the Communist parties of France and Italy remained quite power-

ful, but their commitment to electoral politics was clearly growing. There have been, however, despite these signs of moderation, new sources of ideological strain and conflict developing in Western countries— strains over demands for greater equality and greater political participation. Perhaps just as important are the demands for more emphasis upon community goals and less upon private affluence. As such, they are an assault, once again, upon the liberal "bourgeois" mentality. This renewal of ideological fervor has ignited bands of students in France and Germany, some French labor unions and many intellectuals. More importantly, a growing problem of inflation and unemployment has led to a new pessimism regarding the ultimate viability of democratic regimes.

World War II marked a turning point for Europe in another way—the sudden decline of its empires and of the power of its nations on the international scene. The disintegration of its empires was basically, and somewhat ironically, the consequence of two factors: the worldwide endorsement of Europe's own ideas of independence and self-determination and the far-reaching technological revolution induced by Europe's example. The power aggregated by Europe as a whole, and by the individual nations of Europe, was a temporary phenomenon based upon early industrialization. The loss of this advantage abetted the decline of the Western European nations to second-rank powers.

The forfeiture of empire and power involved severe dislocations and necessitated a readjustment of conceptions of national identity. These strains have been sharper in France than in Britain or Germany, but they have affected the politics of all three countries. While adjusting to the loss of their empires, Europeans have become increasingly self-conscious as Europeans. Contributing to this growing sense of being European was the need to face up to the awesome consequences of continuing to foster their national hatreds and rivalries—especially those between the Germans and the

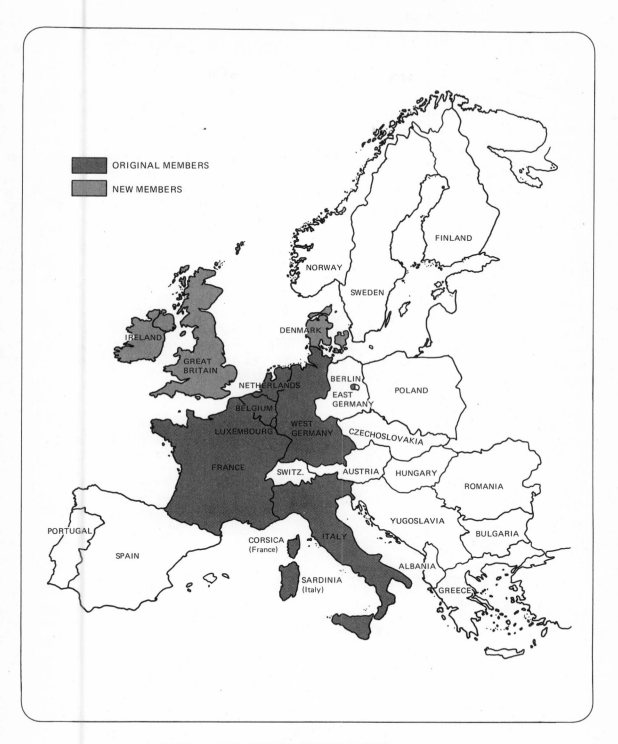

ORIGINAL MEMBERS

NEW MEMBERS

MAP 1.1 EUROPE'S COMMON MARKET—THE NINE

French. Europe could hardly afford another conflagration on the scale of World War II.

Since 1945 many organizations of a supranational type, among them the Western European Union, the European Coal and Steel Community, the Council of Europe, the Organization for European Economic Cooperation (now the Organization for Economic Cooperation and Development), the European Free Trade Association, Euratom, and, most recently and importantly, the European Economic Community (EEC, the Common Market), have been formed to promote economic and political cooperation among the nations on the Continent.

The movement toward European unification has been uneven, and politically "Europe" is still a fledgling. Nevertheless, the trend toward closer union seems clear. The initial six of the European Coal and Steel Community (France, Germany, Italy, Belgium, the Netherlands, Luxembourg), who then went on to forge the Common Market, made especially solid progress. They emphasized economic cooperation and unification because it was expected and hoped that economic agreement would "spill over" into

the political arena and also because they had shown themselves unable to deal with political unification directly. The speed with which "The Six" went about dismantling their national economic barriers and erecting a common protective wall toward the outside far exceeded their own expectations as well as those of observers on the outside. Within several years, the British government was having second thoughts and some regrets about not having joined the Common Market and by 1961 was seeking admittance. Britain's application for entry was denied by French President Charles de Gaulle in 1963 and again in 1967. But after de Gaulle's death and after prolonged negotiations, Britain was finally admitted as a full-fledged member on January 1, 1973, together with Denmark and the Republic of Ireland; "The Six" became "The Nine." (The Norwegian government had also negotiated for membership and was committed to joining, but the Norwegian electorate vetoed entry on a popular referendum on the issue.)

Despite the long wait, Britain's entry seemed to have come at an inauspicious time. Labor unrest and rampant inflation were being compounded by the international

TABLE 1.4   THE ENLARGED EUROPEAN COMMUNITY

EEC	Population (in 1,000s)	Area (in 1,000 sq. miles)	GNP [1] (in $1,000 millions)	
			1958	1970
The Six	189,787	450.8	163.4	485.2
The Nine	253,363	587.9	234.6	626.0
United States	205,395	3,614.1	455.0	993.3
U.S.S.R.	244,000	8,646.0	—	288 [2]

[1] At current prices and exchange rates.

[2] The expression "gross national product" does not exist in the Soviet Union; the comparable expression "net material product" represents, by and large, the sum total of goods and services produced in any one year.

Adapted from Press and Information Office of the Government of the Federal Republic of Germany, *The European Community* (Wiesbaden, 1972), pp. 127–128.

oil crisis, and many people in Britain continue to have second thoughts—despite a positive referendum result on the issue in 1974. At the same time other governments of the Common Market were also being sorely tried and were found to be not always able to resist the temptation to assert their national interests at the expense of their common interests.

6. CONCLUSIONS

Europe's role in introducing "modernity" to the world is to be explained in terms of a peculiar combination of social and cultural elements, including its Christian heritage and, particularly, Calvinist Protestantism. It is important to re-emphasize, however, that the religious influence was only one of the factors contributing to modernization, which, as a process, has taken different courses under different auspices at different times. Indeed, as we shall see, the British example induced the beginnings of modernization in France, while both the French and British examples spurred modernization in Germany, where nationalism was an additional important factor. The total Western European experience as a whole provided the impetus—whether by example or through colonial domination—for the spread of industrial society to the rest of the globe.

The next chapter explains why the three nations with which we are concerned took the particular paths they did toward modernization. In each, the significance of religious institutions, the problems of nation building, and the social and ideological conflicts kindled by industrialization are examined.

2

Great Britain,
France,
and Germany

1. THE PATTERN OF BRITISH DEVELOPMENT

INTRODUCTION: Great Britain is a group of islands just off the Eurasian mainland, about the size of the state of Oregon.[1] The climate benefits from the cool summers and relatively warm winters of the western coast of Europe; over most of the nation the temperature rarely falls below freezing. British soil is only moderately good, suited primarily to cereals, potatoes, and grazing. With the exceptions of coal, iron, and (be-

ginning in the 1970's) oil, the country is not well endowed with mineral resources; it has to import most of the other raw materials needed to sustain modern industry.

Although the best coal fields have long since been worked out, iron and coal were once plentiful enough, and conveniently found in the same general area near the ocean, to provide Britain with an economic windfall when Europe was creating a technology that required both. Despite its small size, Britain was among the dominant powers of the world for more than a century, ruler of the modern world's largest empire and center of its industrial and financial life. Britain's world position stemmed less from its resource base than from the fact that this small island introduced the world to modernity through its own commercial and industrial revolutions.

---

[1] Strictly used, *Great Britain* refers only to the major island, which is made up of the historic and cultural regions of England, Scotland, and Wales. The formally correct designation for the country is the United Kingdom of Great Britain and Northern Ireland. Following the usual convention *Britain* and *British* will be used throughout this text to refer to the entire country, except where *England* and *English* are historically or regionally appropriate.

It was in Britain, too, that the ideas of modern liberalism and liberal capitalism first developed. The British Parliament is among the oldest and most copied of all legislative assemblies, and the ideas of Bacon, Hobbes, and Locke provided much of the framework for contemporary political discourse.

Britain not only introduced modernity to the world, but is also one of the few countries that made comparatively peaceful transitions from a traditional agricultural society to a modern industrial society. The ideological conflicts that convulsed every other European nation in the wake of this process were echoed in Britain, but they never rent the social fabric. The fact is all the more surprising when one realizes that Britons today are as class-conscious as Frenchmen or Germans and that Britain retains more of her traditional past than does France or Germany, neither of which, for example, continues to support a monarchy or has a largely hereditary upper legislative house.

The British achievement has been explained in a multitude of ways. The early genesis of stable representative institutions has been credited to Britain's insular position which, it is argued, obviated the need for a large standing army for protection against invasion. The phlegmatic quality of British politics has been attributed to the climate, and the nation's industrial development to her resources. But while insularity, climate, and resources were significant, any or all of them are insufficient to explain the British experience. Japan and Java are also islands, but they evolved quite differently. There is little reason to draw a connection between climate and civilization, except at the extremes—or, for that matter, between climate and political culture. Why Britain modernized first, and why it was able to do so relatively peacefully, can be understood only by examining British development within a general European framework. Within that framework three factors appear to be crucial in explaining Britain's uniqueness: the time and manner in which Britain attained unity as a nation, the nature of the Protestant Reformation, and the pattern of British industrialization.

THE ACHIEVEMENT OF NATIONAL UNITY: In 1066 England was invaded successfully by William the Conqueror, duke of Normandy, who brought with him the feudal characteristics of his duchy. The Norman followers of William obtained their fiefs, the great earldoms, directly from him, so that he and his successors had the fealty of a greater number of powerful vassals than did any other European feudal monarch. Far more quickly and completely than their French and German counterparts, therefore, English barons developed a sense of being part of a single realm to which they owed a common allegiance. English isolation from Continental territorial conflicts also contributed to the relative facility with which English sovereigns asserted their prerogatives.

Far more easily than France or Germany, England was thus transformed from a collection of feudalities to a unified nation bound by a "common law," subject to a sovereign monarch, and infused with a sense of national identification. Whereas in France the destruction of feudal suzerainties required political absolutism, in England the creation of a national state proceeded almost naturally; and whereas in Germany late unification resulted in an exaggerated sense of national exclusiveness, Englishmen were able to take their nationality in stride.

THE ENGLISH REFORMATION: Compared with the violent religious wars of the Continent, the English revolt against Catholicism was relatively peaceful. The final break with the Roman Catholic Church in 1534 was accomplished by a strong and secure monarch, Henry VIII, who was not faced with the opposition of powerful baronial factions, as was Henry IV of France. So long as changes in doctrine and services were not too radical, Englishmen were willing to accept the idea of a national church.

In another respect, too, the Reformation had important consequences for the nation's transition to modernity. Soon after the break with Rome many Protestant sects appeared in England, including radical Calvinism, which was to be closely related to the founding of liberal capitalism. Although the Calvinist ethos did not become the dominant factor in English social history, as it did in America, it was integrated as one strand in an English culture that was to fuse modern and traditional elements.

SOCIAL CHANGE AND THE STATE: The pattern of industrialization in Britain was clearly related both to the early attainment of national unity and the emergence of the Calvinist sects. The existence of both a modern national state and a national system of law meant that industrialization was able to proceed with fewer hindrances in Britain than on the Continent. Little support existed for the kind of royal absolutism that the commercial strata in other nations, notably France, were willing to endorse in order to create a national community. The presence of indigenous values and orientations conducive to change also assured that industrialization could develop without the sharp ideological conflicts that engulfed the Continent. The disruption of previous patterns of life and ideas that industrialization usually entails was therefore not nearly so distinct as it was to be in other European nations. Instead of disruption, the British community retained much of the sense of class rights, duties, and mutual responsibility that had characterized the earlier feudal period; instead of a completely new value system, the tradition of class consciousness, deference, and noblesse oblige persisted, the last attitude originally characteristic of the aristocracy and later of the middle classes. Thus, from the seventeenth until the early nineteenth century the English gentry, under the supervision of the state, contributed to "poor rates" which provided basic subsistence for the indigent.

Largely for these reasons, then, Britain entered the modern era as a society in which the power of the monarchy was limited by customary or constitutional rules and usages —rules that evolved from the tradition of reciprocal obligations that was feudalism. The Magna Carta (1215), the feudal document designed to preserve the prerogatives of the nobility from encroachments and abuse by King John, became in the seventeenth century the symbol of English liberties.

FROM TRADITIONAL TO INDUSTRIAL SOCIETY: The changes in the distribution of wealth and population and in occupations, levels, and styles of living that industrialization incurred were accompanied by increasingly vociferous attacks upon what was left of the old social order. In the last half of the eighteenth century and the first half of the nineteenth, Parliament, under the influence of laissez-faire doctrines, repealed (or allowed to die) many of the old codes that had regulated apprenticeship, wages, and conditions of work because these contradicted liberal notions of the proper relationship between employers and employees. The corn laws were repealed in favor of a policy of free trade. Liberals also sought to reform the poor laws; thus, the new law of 1834 was a conscious attempt to encourage the able-bodied poor to seek work.

At the same time, liberals fought for a more representative and democratic parliament. They tried to reduce the powers of the House of Lords and of the monarchy, placing in the House of Commons alone the control of political power. The Reform Bill of 1832 provided a rational system of comparatively equal parliamentary representation, while the Reform Bill of 1867 extended the suffrage to the skilled workers of the cities. Other electoral reforms culminated in universal manhood suffrage in 1918.

All these goals were justified in terms of liberal political and economic values and assumptions. The constitutional shift in the control of political power from a balance among king, Lords, and Commons, to the House of Commons alone was accepted on the same grounds. So completely had liberal assumptions permeated British political life by the last quarter of the nineteenth century that a Conservative prime minister, Disraeli, could be instrumental in securing passage of the 1867 Reform Bill. Conservatives in other countries preferred to fight to the last ditch against reform.

The temperament of British liberalism was quite moderate, as compared to that of Continental liberals. British reformers settled for piecemeal change and were not, on the whole, interested in destroying all traditional institutions. They believed, also, that persuasion and rhetoric would serve to bring about needed reforms. Further, they did not share the anticlericalism of Continental liberals. For their part, British conservatives were not unalterably opposed to change, and they knew their opponents were also moderate men. In short, the broad feeling of community that underlay British life served to blur divisions and to take the edge off social conflict, while the traditional institutions did not prevent effective change.

The continued impact of traditional conceptions of community and mutual class responsibilities on liberals themselves is indicated by their willingness to support social-reform measures that violated their ideological position that the state should not interfere in the free workings of the market. Thus, the Parliament that enacted the new poor law also passed a law (in 1833) prohibiting the employment of children under nine in textile mills and limiting the work of children under thirteen to forty-eight hours a week. This legislation was partially the handiwork of Conservative landowners who wanted to strike back at the commercial interests for supporting measures that weakened their traditional authority, and who, though autocrats, believed in community responsibility. Many liberals opposed it, quoting the laissez-faire economists in arguing that the measure would pauperize Britain and in the long run serve all her people ill. The poor law was, however, supported by many reformers who, despite their belief (in theory) in liberal economics, thought that in practice the more fortunate members of

the community had a responsibility for the less fortunate.

Through the latter half of the nineteenth century, the pace of reform accelerated until in 1911 a Liberal government could sponsor legislation, The National Insurance Act, providing for universal unemployment insurance and extensive medical care for individuals in the lower income brackets. By the turn of the century, British liberals had so far accepted the state's responsibility for social welfare that even in the United States of the early 1960's their views would have been considered somewhat radical. In the United States, of course, the liberal idea represented the only tradition, while in Britain that tradition was joined with traditional concepts of mutual responsibility.[2]

These nineteenth-century conflicts of conservative and liberal ideologies were accompanied by a headlong growth in industry. In 1851, for example, agriculture accounted for 25 percent of the British labor force; by 1900 the percentage had dropped to 9. As the aristocracy's economic base—land—declined in value, so its power diminished as that of the commercial and industrial middle class rose. And as the peasantry swarmed to the cities, it was transformed as a class into an industrial proletariat increasingly attracted by radical—eventually Socialist—ideas.

But again in contrast with circumstances on the Continent, socialism in Britain took on a peculiarly British cast. It was usually moderate and reformist; both Socialist intellectuals and workers were convinced that reform could come through educating the com-

---

[2] Perhaps nothing indicates better the differences between British and American cultural values than the contrasting experience of the two countries with social-welfare policies on the one hand and public-education policies on the other. Britain accepted the idea that the community as a whole was responsible for social-welfare measures, though it retained until very recently a highly elite educational system. America, on the other hand, has poured money into a relatively democratic system of mass education designed to provide equality of opportunity, while at the same time holding onto the notion of "rugged individualism" and the virtues of an absolutely "free" economy.

munity, and they never engaged in a full-scale assault on the traditional institutions and values of British society. The comparative moderateness of British workers was the result of the easier transition to an industrial society in Britain than in France; but it also stemmed from the fact that the British working class never felt completely alienated from the community. Almost from the beginning British workers were part of a society whose leaders accepted some responsibility for the workers' welfare and provided for it by enacting social legislation and accepting the formation of trade unions.

The possibilities of social upheaval were further reduced by the renewed vigor of the Puritan temperament as it expressed itself in the spread of Methodism during the first half of the nineteenth century. Like the original Calvinism out of which it sprang, Methodism emphasized hard work and self-discipline as a religious duty; at the same time it provided emotional release at revivalist meetings. In these ways it helped to mitigate working-class discontent and violence. But if the Puritan ethic served to maintain social and political moderation in Britain, so, too, did traditional values. Because the British middle classes adopted many of the attitudes of the gentry, the British working class became more class-conscious than did the American. Bourgeois class consciousness was associated with a sense of noblesse oblige, however, which goes a long way toward explaining the acceptance by the British working class of the rule of its "betters."

Quite naturally, the transition from rural to urban life and from a traditional to an industrial society was an enormously traumatic experience for millions, especially for workers crowded into the spawning urban slums. For some former artisans, it meant lower living standards during the first half of the nineteenth century. Moreover, the limits of knowledge, as well as of liberal ideology, allowed the society as a whole to learn only slowly how best to deal with the problems of the new age. By modern standards,

the attempts made to ameliorate the tremendously disruptive conditions were feeble indeed, and the possibility of large-scale violence was, obviously, never completely absent. Yet in comparison with parallel events in France, it is still the docility of the British working class, and the sense of responsibility of other social classes, that are so striking.

Other factors contributed to the comparative tranquillity of British political life. Because Britain was the first nation to industrialize, it enjoyed a commercial supremacy during most of the nineteenth century that yielded a slow but continuing rise in the standard of living for most of its burgeoning population. There were no models of advanced societies, such as exist today, to make the gap between aspirations and accomplishments painfully apparent. Nor had literacy been so far extended or the media so widely disseminated that workers could become substantially more aware of possibilities for changing their lot. Finally, the British Empire offered an outlet for service, prestige, and power to the sons of an aristocracy whose social primacy was gradually being usurped by other classes; and large-scale emigration to North America, Australia, and later to South Africa gave Britain a means of providing the more "restless" members of the working class with an equivalent of the American frontier.

CONTEMPORARY BRITAIN: Many of these props to a stable social order began to fall away after World War I. By the 1920's Britain had plainly lost her commercial supremacy and as a result was plagued by a high rate of unemployment. Some 10 percent of the labor force was receiving relief payments ("the dole") during all of the 1920's, and during the Great Depression this figure rose to more than 20 percent. Combined with the loss of military dominance, the loss of commercial supremacy caused the British in the interwar decades to abandon the remnants of economic liberalism that had survived from the nineteenth century. Free trade went out the window in favor of imperial preference, and the state began to intervene more and more frequently in all aspects of the nation's economic and social life.

These changes were accelerated by World War II and have continued into the postwar era. Since the war, the British Empire has gradually been liquidated and Britain reduced to the status of a second-rank power. The markets and raw materials of British colonies are no longer available, and earlier investments in the empire have been disposed of. The British now find that other European countries, not to mention the United States, the Soviet Union, and Japan, are cutting more deeply into their share of the world's markets. Since 1945 the British growth rate has been slow compared with that of other European nations (Table 2.1), and the British have experienced several acute financial crises. The decline in Britain's ability to compete on the world market has forced her to relinquish her insular position and to join other European nations in supranational economic arrangements. These moves culminated in the historic decision by the Conservative Government in 1971–72 to bring Britain into the Common Market. Britain's economic plight was dramatically illustrated in the winter of 1973–74; a three-day work week, soaring inflation, and record balance-of-payment deficits added up to the most discouraging economic situation confronted by the country since World War II. The only bright spot was the continued exploitation of oil deposits which had been discovered off the coast of Scotland toward the end of the 1960's.

The postwar position of Britain has not, of course, been entirely desperate. In abso-

TABLE 2.1   GROWTH OF THE EUROPEAN AND
UNITED STATES ECONOMY

Movement in total volume of output (1913-100)

	France	Germany [1]	Britain	United States
1870	51.1	30.0	39.1	16.9 [2]
1900	87.9	68.4	85.8	60.4
1913	100.0	100.0	100.0	100.0
1920	77.6	—	—	114.5
1925	110.6	90.3	113.4	141.3
1938	109.4	149.9	158.3	163.3
1950	130.3	157.3	189.7	293.0
1955	162.0	242.5	218.8	360.9
1960	199.8	327.4	244.3	403.1
1965	265.4	418.4	287.9	510.5
1970	350.8	517.9	318.3	598.4

[1] Figures adjusted to eliminate the effect of territorial change.

[2] Figures for 1871.

Adapted from Angus Maddison, *Economic Growth in the West* (New York: Twentieth Century Fund, 1964), pp. 201, 202, reprinted by permission of the publisher; and the Committee for Economic Development, *The United States and the European Community* (New York, 1971), p. 75.

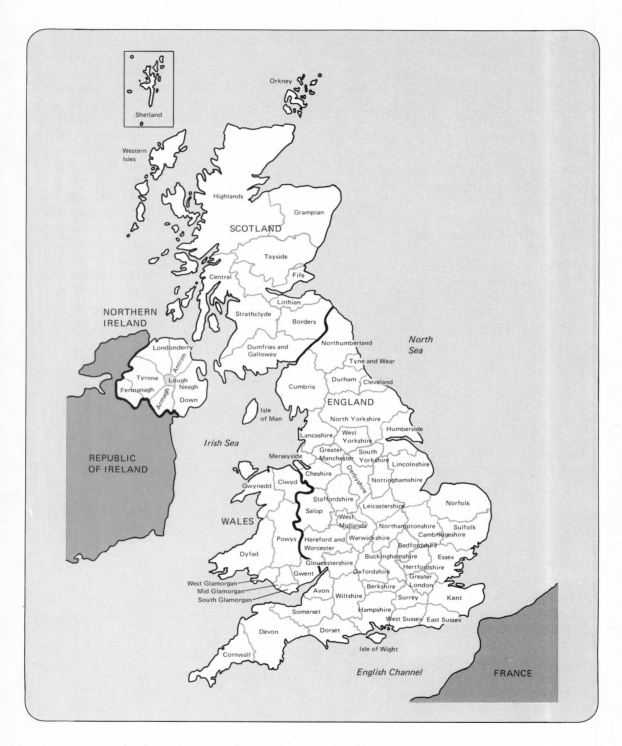

MAP 2.1   THE UNITED KINGDOM

28

lute terms, the British standard of living has continued to rise, and Britain led the Continent in making the breakthrough to the "consumer society." Also, governmental policies have managed to insure relatively full employment for most of the postwar years.

Meanwhile, signs of other changes are also omnipresent. Newly trained technical personnel are beginning to challenge some of the older values; another generation of intellectuals, stifled by the insularity of British culture, is making repeated attacks on traditional values; the inviolability of the police has been attacked, and there has been an abrupt increase in crime, particularly crimes of violence. All these facts indicate that ⌐traditional patterns are crumbling.⌐ There are other signs, too: the victory of architectural functionalism and modernism over those who wish to keep the old landmarks in cities like London; the easing of sexual mores; the changing ideals of British women as to what constitutes personal attractiveness; and the gradual erosion of both class and regional accents. All sides seem dedicated to change—from the Tory businessman who wanted to join the Common Market so as to have the opportunity to make the operation of his firm more rational by developing a lever against "excessive" trade-union demands, to the left-wing intellectual railing against the continued cant of an Establishment that he sees as refusing to adjust to the imperatives of modernity.

Some of these and other changes are the result simply of technical imperatives, as for example the decision finally to shift to a metric system of weights and measures and a decimal system of money. Others arise from greater contact with other cultural patterns, including American television, and the increasing opportunities of the middle and lower classes to travel to the Continent. The loss of empire and the reduction of Britain to a second-class power have also had their effect by removing the halo from institutions that somehow seemed associated with the claim that the sun never set on the British Empire.

2. THE PATTERN OF FRENCH DEVELOPMENT

INTRODUCTION: Although smaller than Texas, France is the largest country in Western Europe. The extent and location of the nation offer a variety of climates. The north and west share Britain's mists; in Alsace, winters are colder and summers warmer; and in the south the nation is warmed by the Mediterranean. France's temperate climate and rich soil have been conducive to the development of a highly diverse agriculture ranging from the production of oats and wheat to grapes. The nation does not possess a river system that penetrates the interior as the Rhine does in Germany, but even so the lack of mountain barriers could have permitted far more effective railway and canal systems had the French applied their resources to this end. France has less coal than Britain or Germany, but there are extensive reserves of iron ore and the world's largest deposits of bauxite, for the production of aluminum.

⌐France's wealth in natural resources, in other words, compares favorably with that of the other major West European countries.⌐ Yet French economic growth in the nineteenth century and the first half of the twentieth lagged far behind that of Britain and, later, Germany. As a consequence, the dominance that France had once held on the Continent declined steadily after Waterloo. French population stabilized, and in certain periods even declined, which further weakened the nation's industrial and military potential. And over a long interval,⌐political instability continually stymied efforts by the community to solve common problems.⌐ In 1958, when the Fifth Republic was established and Frenchmen adopted their twelfth constitution since 1789, the event prompted a good many anecdotes; one is told of the man who, in trying to buy a copy of the new constitution, was informed by his bookseller that he did not carry periodical literature.

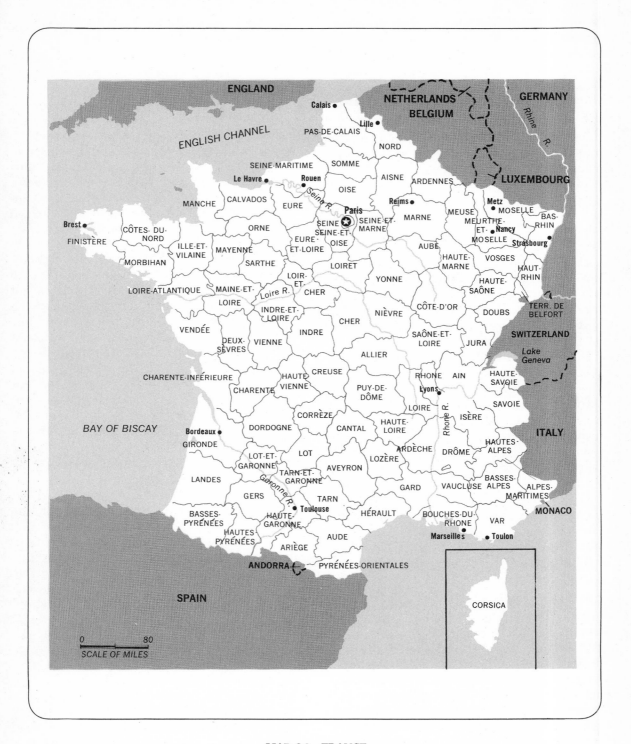

MAP 2.2 FRANCE

The Fifth Republic, however, has provided an effective government, even though under Charles de Gaulle it was also fairly authoritarian. Since the early fifties, the French economy has moved forward steadily and at a pace that has astonished economic analysts, despite some recent difficulties. (See Table 2.1, page 27.)

The history of France's industrial backwardness and political instability has long been examined and argued by students of French life. The causes have been said to lie in certain basic traits of French national character—for example—or in the unresolved tensions generated by the French Revolution that irreconcilably divided the French public. Political scientists have sought the sources of political instability in France's failure to develop a strong and stable executive under the Third and Fourth Republics, and they have blamed the weakness of the French executive at least partially on the particular constitutional arrangements adopted by the country. None of these explanations is completely satisfactory, though all contain elements of truth. Rather, the social and political patterns of contemporary France can best be understood as part of a European pattern; within that pattern, it was such crucial factors in French history as the nature of her feudal inheritance, the manner in which national unity was consummated, and the character of religious and industrial development that set the conditions under which France became a modern state—and also created her seemingly intractable social and political difficulties.

THE CREATION OF THE FRENCH STATE: The final destruction of the French nobility's power and the creation of a relatively modern state was the work of Louis XIV. The last attempt by the aristocracy to assert its prerogatives culminated in the rebellion of 1650–52, when the king was in his early teens. It was crushed by Cardinal Mazarin, the boy king's chief minister, who followed his victory with policies fashioned to make

sure challenges of this kind to the throne could never recur. Louis himself continued those policies, stripping the aristocracy of the remainder of its traditional authority and establishing his absolute political control over France in theory if not in practice.

The process of nation building had begun much earlier, in the tenth century under the Capetian kings, who gradually extended their authority from Paris and its environs until it encompassed all of France. Their efforts, and those of the Valois kings who succeeded them in the fourteenth century, to transform France into a nation had been effectively hindered, both by the complex territorial and dynastic struggles that Europe experienced during these centuries and by the religious wars that exploded after the Protestant Reformation. In contrast with Britain, political unity was imposed on France by a monarchy that was forced to rely upon its own centralized bureaucracy to create the framework of a modern state.

The French nobility lost its authority but not its privileges. It became a class largely composed of absentee landlords who spent their time at court and insisted resolutely upon their class prerogatives when the substance of their power was gone. Whereas the British aristocracy was sufficiently self-confident to permit a blurring of the lines between itself and the newer commercial strata of society, the French aristocracy accentuated traditional distinctions. The result was that the French monarchy was unable to carry its centralizing policies to a logical conclusion. In Britain a gentry that identified itself with the nation provided administrative personnel who engendered social and economic as well as political unity. But France remained in some sense a confederation of cities and provinces, each maintaining its own customs and, to a considerable extent, its own laws. In fact, France was not even a free-trade area within its own borders until the Revolution of 1789.

THE REFORMATION IN FRANCE: France also differed from Britain in her religious experiences. Calvinism gained a substantial foothold in France, but Protestants, mostly Huguenots, remained a minority. After a series of bitter religious wars, a compromise was effected in the Edict of Nantes (1598), which temporarily stabilized the religious situation; it granted the Protestant minority political rights equal to those of Catholics, and permission to retain fortified towns. Under Louis XIII and Louis XIV, however, the rights were gradually curbed, and finally, after the revocation of the Edict of Nantes in 1685, thousands of French Protestants emigrated.

France thus continued to be a Catholic nation. The intellectuals of the Enlightenment, drawing inspiration partly from their observation of the British scene, confronted in France a society still operating on the basis of highly traditional mores. The rigidity of French society was such that many reformers opted for a root change in its institutions and reacted against the existing regimes with millenarian fervor. Furthermore, because liberals believed that the most backward aspects of French culture were derived from the Catholic tradition and maintained by the Catholic Church, liberalism in France was strongly anticlerical.

POLITICAL REVOLUTION: The revolutionaries of 1789 had a multitude of aims. The peasants, for the most part, simply wanted land or the redress of certain grievances under the old law. The intellectuals, who drove and directed the Revolution, wanted to establish a representative republic of free men with a rational political and legal structure. They were supported by the commercial classes, who regarded the ancient privileges of the feudal, local rights and restrictions as inhibiting development of the good society.

The Revolution of 1789, which centered in Paris, achieved only some of these goals—and a rift in French society that still influences French politics. As authority disintegrated, the Revolution quickly slipped under the control of its most radical elements. The extreme radicals were abetted unwittingly by both the resistance of conservative elements in French society and the hostility of Europe. The increasing antipathy of the church and segments of both the aristocracy and bourgeoisie, plus the threat of invasion by other monarchs who denounced the Revolution, served only to create a climate in which the radicals could gain support for ever more extreme policies. Further, the breakdown of authority and the ferment of ideas produced a hypertrophy of political organizations, each dedicated to its own ideological vision.

The radicals could not remake France completely, despite—and partly because of —the bloodbath they started. They did not have the power to gain full control, and the great majority of the people were not sympathetic to the revolutionary changes they envisioned. The more conservative forces —the church, the aristocracy, large elements of the peasantry, and some elements of the middle classes—were unable, of course, to turn the clock back. Out of the resulting chaos emerged France's first "democratic despot": Napoleon. Promising to preserve the best of the Revolution and to restore order, Napoleon also sought to unify Europe under France, all in the name of the principles of the Enlightenment. His rule was based on both force and demagogic appeal.

The dynamism of Napoleon's dictatorship eventually led to its downfall, and the Bourbon monarchy was restored by France's enemies. Many of the émigrés, nobles who had fled France, especially during the Terror, returned hoping to restore the old regime. But a return to the times before the Bastille was impossible; the Revolution and Napoleon had made momentous, permanent changes in French life. For one thing, French administration had been unified and centralized. In decisive reaction against localism and diversity, the provinces had been replaced, administratively, with a set of eighty-three departments (which, by design, lacked any geographic or historical unity) responsible directly to the central government in Paris. For another, the traditional and confusing conglomeration of the three hundred local legal systems of the old regime had been superseded by a civil code that drew upon Roman law and systemized these local customs. The judicial reforms of Napoleon provided France with an integrated legal system based as nearly as possible upon a minimum number of general assumptions. The Napoleonic Code eliminated feudal privileges and modernized the law of property, satisfying those who wanted a legal system conducive to trade and commerce.

These issues of law and administration were settled by the Revolution; what had not been settled was who should rule and for what purposes. By the end of the Revolution, at least five ideological groupings in French politics could be distinguished, each with a different answer to these two questions. On the extreme right were the "ultras." They wanted to restore the old regime as nearly as possible. Composed of the émigré aristocracy, segments of the peasantry, and some elements of the middle class, this group was strongly supported by the dominant elements among the Catholic clergy and the more religious citizens. The Revolution, they argued, had attempted to destroy the Catholic Church; the church therefore would remain hostile to all ideas associated with the Revolution.

At the other extreme was the group of Jacobin remnants who, after the Bourbon restoration, still believed that the Great Revolution had yet to be consummated and who continued to hope and fight for an egalitarian, democratic, and secular republic. Because the attitude of the clergy remained conservative, this group was consistently anticlerical. On the left wing of the Jacobins there developed a third group, quite small, that carried Jacobinism to its ultimate egalitarian conclusions: it called for a Socialist republic and the communalization of property.

A variety of more "moderate" groups occupied intermediate positions between the ultra right and the Jacobin left. The two most important were the Doctrinaires and the Bonapartists. The Doctrinaires accepted some of the fruits of the Revolution and wished to see a constitutional monarchy established on the British model. They were primarily associated with the House of Orléans, which claimed, after the House of Bourbon, the right of succession to the throne. The Bonapartists, too, accepted a compromise between the Revolution and traditional institutions, but they rallied around the Napoleonic legend and extolled the greatness that Napoleon had brought to France.

Between 1815 and 1870, France went through three revolutions and one coup d'état. Frenchmen were governed successively by a semi-absolutist monarchy, a constitutional monarchy, a radical democratic republic, a presidential regime, an empire, and finally, in 1871, by a conservative and "temporary" republic—the Third Republic —that lasted until 1940. None of the political ideologies described above was strong enough to dominate the others, and because they were violently hostile to one another, no enduring compromise was possible. Advocates of various policies became more intransigent with the years, and attempts to strike a balance resulted only in new, divisive political tendencies. Frenchmen continued to slaughter Frenchmen in endless civic violence.

INDUSTRIAL CHANGE: In addition to political difficulties, France suffered the dilemmas concomitant with industrialization. In the cities an urban proletariat appeared largely alienated from the rest of the community and was attracted sporadically to sundry revolutionary movements. Working-class alienation was the result of most of the same factors that had already fragmented French society. The aristocracy had lost its authority and sense of responsibility under the Bourbons, and the Revolution had convinced the aristocracy that it had to resist any demands of the masses. France, then, unlike Britain, lacked a governing class that could stand as an exemplar of civic responsibility to be emulated by the bourgeoisie. Further, large segments of the bourgeoisie had become frightened by the

TABLE 2.2   LANDHOLDING IN FRANCE, 1862–1970

Number of holdings

Size of holding, in acres	1862	1882	1892	1908	1929	1955	1970
Very small: less than 2½	—	2,167,667	2,235,405	2,087,851	1,014,731	151,700	92,700
Small: 2½–25	2,435,401	2,635,030	2,617,558	2,523,713	1,863,867	1,125,500	574,800
Medium: 25–100 [1]	636,309	727,222	711,118	745,862	973,520	913,400	754,100
Large: 100–250 [1]	154,167	142,088	105,391	118,497	114,312	75,100	101,300
Very large: over 250	—	—	33,280	29,541		20,000	30,000

[1] 25–124 and 125–249 in 1929, 1955, and 1970.

Adapted in part from *The Economic Development of Western Civilization* by Shepherd C. Clough, p. 300.   Copyright © 1959 by McGraw-Hill, Inc.   Used with permission of McGraw-Hill Book Company.   Also adapted from Gordon Wright, *Rural Revolution in France* (Stanford, Calif.: Stanford University Press, 1964), p. 214; and Institut National de la Statistique et des Études Économiques, *Annuaire Statistique de la France, 1974* (Paris: INSEE, 1975), p. 130; reprinted by permission of the publishers.

mobs that seemed to spring up in the wake of reform movements.   Many felt that concessions to workers' demands would open the way for another revolution—and the loss of their property.   The radicalism of the French working class only confirmed and strengthened these suspicions, and the uncompromising attitude of the middle class, in turn, aggravated working-class disaffection.

In France industrialization proceeded far more slowly than it did in Britain, partly because of a less fortuitous combination of crucial resources.   Yet of greater importance were the traditional patterns of thought and action and the mutual animosities and suspicions of French social life. The French bourgeois lacked the confidence of his American, British, or German counterparts.   He hoarded cash or invested his money overseas, hampering the growth of capital resources necessary to industry.   The Revolution had divided agricultural estates into small peasant holdings that by French law descended equally to all children, not to the oldest son as in Britain; property was consequently divided into ever smaller parcels (Table 2.2), inhibiting the modernization of agriculture.   Only after 1892 did the number of French farms, which had been growing since the Revolution, begin to decline; and only in the Paris basin and the

northeast was this decline due to a consolidation of farm holdings.   Finally, to complete the circle, the French political stalemate inhibited the formulation of sound policies that might have contributed to economic growth.

During the nineteenth century, therefore, despite periods of dramatic growth, France slipped behind the other European nations. Its population increased by only 5 million between 1850 and 1940, while Britain's rose by 19 million and Germany's by 35 million.   In 1814 one out of every seven Europeans west of Russia was French; by 1914 the proportion was one in ten.[3]   As other European countries industrialized, France's economic importance also waned.   The French population until after World War I was predominantly small-town and rural.   As late as 1930, some 30 percent of the labor force worked in agriculture, and most industrial workers were employed by small establishments.

THE THIRD AND FOURTH REPUBLICS: The year after France's defeat in the Franco-Prussian War of 1870, a National Assembly was elected, and it convened to draft a new constitution.   Though the Monarchists domi-

[3] C. Gordon Wright, *France in Modern Times* (Chicago: Rand McNally & Co., 1960), p. 226.

nated the assembly, they were hopelessly divided into Bourbons and Orléanists, and the only thing their leaders could agree on was to establish temporarily a "conservative" republic with a strong president who would later be replaced by a king. The Monarchists never reached any larger agreement, primarily because the Count of Chambord, of the House of Bourbon, insisted upon the Bourbon flag and would not accept the tricolor. It is not without reason that Louis Adolphe Thiers, one of the architects of the Third Republic, ironically called Chambord "The George Washington of France."

The Third Republic was thus established *faute de mieux*. It maintained itself, nevertheless, against both the right and the left, gaining support as it grew older and more familiar. It survived also because it did very little to resolve the tensions inherent in French life. The divisions in the nation were so serious that systematic policies were difficult to implement. Even so, the achievements of the period from 1871 to 1914 should not be ignored. True, the French did fall further and further behind the British and the Germans economically, but the last quarter of the nineteenth century witnessed the creation of a modern banking system; substantial rail and road construction; the beginnings of a system of free, secular education; and, from 1880 to 1910, reasonably healthy economic growth. Indeed, by 1914 it seemed as if France might achieve political stability and social reconciliation. The Catholic Church had been disestablished and the important segments of the Catholic hierarchy had come to accept the legitimacy of the republican regime. The idea of restoring the monarchy had all but disappeared; even conservatives had come to accept the republic. And within the Socialist movement, despite the lack of social welfare measures, reformism was replacing revolutionary tendencies.

World War I and its aftermath, however, caused new disruptions, new problems, new tensions. France suffered more than any other Western European participant in the war. To the destruction of farms, homes, and factories and the loss of manpower were added the moral ferment of the 1920's, the Great Depression of the 1930's, and the emergence of a powerful and highly expansionist National Socialist regime in Germany. The Depression brought with it an intensification of radicalism particularly on the right, and semi-Fascist organizations dedicated to aping Italy or Germany grew in strength. The role of the Catholic Church in the Spanish Civil War once again brought to the surface the latent antagonism between French Catholics and anticlericals.

The polarization and fragmentation of French politics did not bring down the republic, but they weakened the regime, and they help explain why France collapsed so quickly in 1940. During the German occupation and the wartime Vichy French regime, conservative elements dominated politics in France; Marshal Pétain and Pierre Laval established a regime that substituted authority for liberty and sought to strengthen traditional institutions, including the Catholic Church.[4] The support that many elements of the business community, alarmed by the Communist Party's growth in the interwar years, gave to Pétain, and their collaboration with the Germans, compromised them seriously with other groups in France.

With the end of World War II, therefore, the ideological right was largely discredited. In the first postwar elections, left-wing parties (the Communists, the Socialists, and the *Mouvement républicain populaire*—MRP) dominated the scene. At first the three parties cooperated to draft a new constitution, a circumstance singular enough to cause a wave of optimism to sweep through France.

[4] Pétain was given credit for stopping the Germans at Verdun in World War I and later became chief of the French armies. A national hero, he was called upon to form a government at Vichy when France surrendered to the Germans in 1940. Laval, twice premier of France in the 1930's took over Pétain's Vichy government in 1942. He was tried and executed for treason after the war. Pétain was also convicted of treason; his sentence was commuted to life imprisonment, and he died in 1951.

The optimism did not last long. The three parties first collided with General Charles de Gaulle, then the temporary president, over the new constitution. De Gaulle wanted a strong executive, modeled after the American presidency. The left, on the other hand, associated a strong presidency with conservatism in general, and, in particular, with the personal dictatorship of Napoleon III.

After defeating de Gaulle on the constitutional issue, the tripartite coalition disintegrated under the pressures of the developing Cold War, the outbreak of a colonial war in Indochina, and an explosion of strikes among industrial workers. By the summer of 1947, the Communists had been forced from the government, and de Gaulle and his followers had created a new political party, *Rassemblement du peuple français*—RPF (Rally of the French People), dedicated to a basic revision of the constitution. In the 1951 elections the Communists and the RPF, both of which were committed to systematic opposition, received almost 49 percent of the vote (but only 35 percent of the seats in the new Assembly, because of the election law). As a result, the center and center-left parties were thrown together, not on the basis of any agreement on policy, but on the basis of a commitment to the preservation of the constitutional regime—a "third force" between the opposition of the right and the left.

The constitution was preserved, but at the price of political stagnation and instability. Under the Fourth Republic, as under the Third, the prime minister and the cabinet were responsible to the Parliament; that is, they could govern only if they had the support of a majority of the national legislature. The coalition majorities that could be arranged in the Assembly were always minimal majorities, so that no particular government lasted very long; and because opinions within any government were as diverse as the parties making up the coalition to support it, no government could act decisively. Between 1947 and 1958, no less than twenty-one cabinets governed the nation.

A NEW FRANCE?: Important changes were, nevertheless, taking place in France. The birth rate of the nation, which had remained fixed for one hundred years, began to rise; suddenly France was becoming one of the youngest in Western Europe. In 1946 responsibility for overhauling large segments of the French economy had been entrusted to a group of dedicated civil servants led by Jean Monnet, and despite recurring financial crises, Monnet's work was beginning to pay off: the French economy entered upon a period of rapid expansion, increasing as fast as that of any other nation in Europe.

By the late 1950's, this economic rejuvenation was yielding higher living standards. For the first time since 1913, the economic position of the working class improved materially; and consumer goods, such as automobiles and television sets, began to flood the market at prices that workers could afford. The nation's growth rate was aided by greater commercial cooperation between France and her neighbors. For example, the European Coal and Steel Community, consisting of France, Germany, the Benelux countries (Belgium, the Netherlands, and Luxembourg), and Italy, created a common market in iron and coal that benefited all six countries.

In the 1950's only one thing seemed to be keeping France from a real breakthrough in material prosperity: the colonial wars it was continually fighting to preserve the remnants of an empire. After the liquidation of the war in Indochina in 1954, French North Africa erupted in rebellion to renew the drain on French manpower and financial resources, though American aid alleviated this considerably. The Algerian situation constituted an especially difficult problem. The population of Algeria included some one million Europeans, many of them descendants of workers who had been exiled after the failure of revolutionary upheavals in the nineteenth century. Ties of sentiment, the influence of the European settler (the *colon*) in Algeria, and the possibility, after the discovery of huge oil reserves in the Sahara, of reducing French dependence upon Middle

East oil supplies combined with a misplaced pride to prevent a settlement of the explosive Algerian issue. To these troubles were added a genuine and legitimate fear for the safety of Europeans in an Arab-dominated state and the stiff-necked attitude of professional soldiers who were angered by losing a series of small wars in which, they believed, they had not received adequate moral and material support from the politicians. Tired of the government's vacillation and inability to make or implement effective decisions, and adamant in its insistence that Algeria was French, the army brought about the downfall of the Fourth Republic by supporting a rebellion of the Algerian *colons* in 1958. The rebellion ushered in the return to power of Charles de Gaulle.

Basing his authority upon a referendum which gave him overwhelming popular support, de Gaulle established the Fifth French Republic, a republic led by a president with the strong powers he had always advocated. He instituted a series of dramatic new policies, the most important of which were the liquidation of the French African empire and an international role for France independent of the North Atlantic Treaty Organization (NATO). Domestically, the Fifth Republic has been associated with many significant reforms, but its major contribution has been to provide France with a stable government capable of carrying through consistent policies.

By 1965 the euphoria that had marked the early years of the de Gaulle regime was beginning to wear off. And by the beginning of 1968, the regime's power was on the wane and traditional French political allegiances were reasserting themselves. Many commentators speculating on a post-Gaullist political scene believed that, despite a number of thorny problems, French politics would have considerably greater stability even without the general than it had in the years before the Fifth Republic.

In the spring of 1968 French students, hitherto relatively quiescent in comparison with their German and American counterparts, exploded in a mass confrontation with the government. Their action was closely followed by a massive general strike by French workers, who argued that their living standards had lagged behind growth in productivity. For a short time the government appeared on the verge of collapse. However, after making economic concessions to the workers and promising educational reform, de Gaulle called for new legislative elections, warning the populace that failure to support him would result in anarchy or worse. As a result of the "events" of 1968, the Gaullists won a massive electoral victory, and all the major left-wing parties, despite Communist attacks on student militancy, suffered serious losses.

De Gaulle's 1968 victory was a reaction to fears of chaos rather than the result of massive support for maintaining him in power. This was confirmed in the spring of 1969, when de Gaulle staked his presidency on the results of a national referendum on both replacing the Senate with a new body based on functional representation and establishing new regional institutions; he was decisively defeated. The presidential election that followed found the left in disarray and brought to power Georges Pompidou, one of de Gaulle's former premiers. Creating a government that combined Gaullists with members of center and conservative groupings, Pompidou continued the broad outlines of de Gaulle's policies, but with a rather less authoritarian hand.

With the legislative elections of 1973, the death of Pompidou, and the rather narrow victory of Giscard d'Estaing over a left-wing candidate in the presidential elections of 1974, France entered a new political phase, the fixed contours of which are difficult to discern.

The unity of the Gaullist movement has been weakened by the divisions engendered by the 1974 presidential election, and the Gaullist party no longer dominates the presidential cabinet. The new presidential majority in Parliament is both broader and less cohesive than those of de Gaulle and Pompidou. It is nevertheless held together by an underlying fear of the Socialist-Communist left. Thus, the first non-Gaullist president of the Fifth Republic has succeeded in reaffirming the presidential domination of the regime.

However, the two elections in 1973 and 1974 polarized the electorate between right and left, and the new government has done little to reduce this division, which is being fed by accelerating inflation, increasing unemployment, and numerous bitter strikes. Nevertheless, while conflict over government policies remains intense, the historical link between policy conflict and institutional structures seems to have been broken. The institutional framework was not an issue in either of the recent elections, and it is now accepted by all of the major contestants for political power.

3. THE PATTERN OF GERMAN DEVELOPMENT

INTRODUCTION: Germany's historical development has been considerably different from that of France. Although France did not acquire the political and administrative structures of a modern nation until after the Revolution of 1789, its national boundaries had reached their modern limits by the seventeenth century. Germany's geographic position—her location in the heart of Europe and her lack of easily defended natural boundaries—complicated the problem of nation-building. Germans, Slavs, and other ethnic and linguistic groups competed for the same territories in the Middle Ages, even as the German states competed for control of the entire German realm. The ethnic issue, in fact, was an important part of German foreign policy until after World War II. At least some of Hitler's territorial claims during the interwar years, including the Saar and parts of Poland (some of which had been taken from Germany after World War I) and Czechoslovakia, were based on the existence of large German populations in those areas. At the end of World War II the Germans were expelled from Poland and Czechoslovakia; and although there are still persons in Germany who talk about again incorporating some of the "Germanic" areas into the homeland, the West Germans have now signed peace treaties recognizing the postwar boundaries; thus it is scarcely imaginable that any regime in the foreseeable future would try to do so. As a result both of the Allies' postwar decision to divide Germany into zones of occupation and of the development of the Cold War, Germany today is divided into the Federal Republic of Germany (*Bundesrepublik Deutschland*), which comprises the former American, British, and French zones; and the German Democratic Republic (*Deutsche Demokratische Republik*), the former Soviet zone (Map 2.3).

Together, East and West Germany are smaller today than Montana; West Germany alone is about the size of Oregon. Before World War I the German empire was somewhat larger than the two states combined. Imperial Germany was traversed by five large rivers, the Rhine, the Weser, the Elbe, the Oder, and the Vistula; all were made navigable for long distances by dredging and the large-scale program of canal building that was initiated in the late nineteenth century. A variety of soils and temperate climatic conditions permit considerable agricultural diversity. The country also contains substantial deposits of high-grade coal, the most important of which, in the Ruhr Valley, is located close to river transportation. German reserves of iron ore have never been large, except between the end of the Franco-Prussian War in 1870, when the French province of Alsace-Lorraine was incorporated into the German Reich, and the beginning of World War I in 1914. Then as before, however, the Germans relied heavily upon Swedish ores for the production of iron and steel. Aside from potash, Germany possesses no other mineral resources of note.

In the dismemberment and partition of Germany after World War II, the nation lost the Oder River, which now forms the border between East Germany and Poland, as well as the croplands of Prussia. These territories contained some of the poorer German soils, however, and the production of certain

MAP 2.3 POSTWAR GERMANY

39

important crops, such as wheat, in West Germany alone now equals or surpasses the prewar production for all of Germany. The major coal resources of Germany and the center of German industrial production have always been located in the west.

Since the fall of the Nazi regime, studies of German history and politics have concentrated on two questions: What were the historical conditions and forces that permitted and gave rise to National Socialism? How firm and reliable is West Germany's commitment to democratic institutions? Both issues are best approached by examining German history within the European framework.

RELIGION AND THE FORMATION OF THE GERMAN STATE: In the Middle Ages, Germany, like France, was divided into many principalities, baronies (both religious and secular), and free cities, all of which asserted their independence. Theoretically, the Germans were ruled by the emperor of the Holy Roman Empire, a traditional fiction originating under Charlemagne and revived in the tenth century by Otto I, whose territories included what was to become the western part of Germany, Austria, and half of Italy. Theoretically, too, the empire was the successor of the Christian Roman Empire; and the emperor, who received his authority directly from God, was the supreme suzerain of Christian Europe even as the pope was its spiritual lord. Like Charlemagne before him, Otto was crowned emperor by the pope, (who had been previously nominated for the office by Otto).

Because the German monarchs were continually in conflict with the papacy and had to fight dynastic wars involving almost the entire continent, the myth of the Holy Roman Empire hindered the building of a German state. In the end the empire collapsed and the attempt by Otto and his successors to achieve universal dominion for it only thwarted the achievement of more modest goals.

The development of a national state in Germany was further delayed by the religious wars of the sixteenth and seventeenth centuries. These wars ravaged the countryside, left Germany divided into Protestant and Catholic states, and created a residue of bitterness that lasted well into the twentieth century. German Protestantism or Lutheranism—a product of the Reformation—shared with Calvinism an emphasis on order and a rigid puritanism. In its other aspects, however, including an insistence on respect for hierarchical authority, it was far more traditional.

Until the early nineteenth century, the German realm was broken up into 314 states and 1,475 estates—a total of 1,789 sovereignties. The two most powerful were the Protestant kingdom of Brandenburg-Prussia and the predominantly Catholic Austrian monarchy. Prussia had emerged as a state in the seventeenth century under the leadership of strong kings and a military aristocracy that had gradually expanded its borders. Its resources were limited and its ability to survive and enlarge, especially at the expense of the Slavs, was based on the disciplined military prowess of its landowning aristocracy, the Junkers. It was said of Prussia that the state was built around the army, not the army around the state.

The unity of Prussia had been achieved by the Hohenzollern dynasty—Frederick William of Brandenburg ("the Great Elector") and his grandson and great-grandson, Frederick William I and Frederick II ("The Great") who died in 1786. Together they welded Prussia into an important force in Europe. They broke the power of the barony but, unlike the Bourbons, brought the aristocracy into the service of the state somewhat on the English model.

The northern German princes had supported Luther in his struggles with the papacy, and Lutheranism became the established state religion of Prussia. The Prussian temperament and Luther's emphasis upon self-discipline and submission to secular authority combined to create a religious ethos that reinforced the authoritarian character of German society. In the nineteenth century the Prussian state was to unify Germany and impress its personality upon all of Germany. In England national unity had been achieved before the development of liberal ideologies, and in France the Jacobin liberals were nationalists responsible for the final centralized political order; but in Germany national unity was achieved in part as reaction against liberalism. In England liberalism was indigenous; in France (though imported) it was adopted by a native intelligentsia. In Germany, it came with a foreign invader and was always tainted as being fundamentally non-German.

The foreign invader was Napoleon. During France's seven-year domination of Germany, which began in 1806, the number of petty German principalities was sharply reduced. Also, the administrative and legal systems of many German states were overhauled. Local lords lost jurisdiction over their peasants, who became subjects of the state legally free to move, migrate, or marry, and entitled to bring suits in courts of law. Jews, too, were granted full citizenship rights and permitted to leave the ghetto. In several important ways, then, the principles of the Enlightenment were applied to the reordering of German social life.

Initially, many German intellectuals, including Immanuel Kant and the young Georg Wilhelm Friedrich Hegel, welcomed the French Revolution as the birth of a new freedom. In the aftermath of the Napoleonic Wars, however, the nationalism Napoleon had awakened became anti-French and anti-liberal. Many Germans thought their defeat was the result of weakness produced by disunity, and many considered the ideals of the French Revolution to be foreign ideals, inferior to traditional German values. To be a liberal was to be anti-German, and therefore anti-national. Consequently, German liberalism during the nineteenth century was fairly ineffective, and liberals tended to share the nationalism embraced by other segments of the population.

While the Prussians, especially, rejected many of the values of liberalism, they heartily embraced the techniques of the modern state. Napoleon's victories resulted from the use of a mass army, the fruits of science, and the rational administration of a national community. The Prussians, led by their great reformers of the nineteenth century, imitated Napoleon's accomplishments of statecraft within the framework of their highly authoritarian society.

When Bismarck finally united Germany in 1871, Austria was excluded; one reason was to insure Prussian predominance and another to guarantee that the new German state contained a Protestant majority. Prussia, which was responsible for the unification, was a hierarchical state dominated by traditional values. Only once, in 1848, had there seemed any chance that the Prussian monarchy would adopt a liberal outlook, but German liberalism was so fragile that the attempt to achieve reforms was completely squelched. That a conservative Prussia had brought about unification heightened the prestige of Prussian values, and they became the dominant German values.

INDUSTRIALIZATION AND ITS CONSEQUENCES: German national unity was followed by a tremendous upsurge in industrial growth. National unification and the goal of national greatness served the same function in Germany that the Calvinist ethic had in Britain, though, of course, the Germans' disciplined respect for authority was also an important factor in the nation's industrial development. Industrial progress was so rapid that by 1914 Germany was challenging Britain's leadership. In only two generations, the nation had transformed itself from a rural society to a predominantly urban one.

In Germany, however, industrialization was not accompanied by the ideology or practice of laissez-faire. On the contrary, the government was an active participant in the economy—subsidizing industries, imposing tariffs, and creating a state-owned transportation network and a state-controlled banking system. At the same time, the German state developed the earliest and broadest measures for social welfare of any of the industrial powers. At least initially, the bourgeoisie did not mount a challenge to the traditional elite. Instead, it adopted elite values and tried to emulate the aristocracy—thus rejecting, for the most part, the liberal ideology that in Britain had been so closely associated with the emergence of a commercial and industrial middle class.

Germany became a modern industrial state even as she retained much of her traditional culture and social structure. Though the clash between the old and the new was far more serious in Germany than in Britain or France, before World War I the tensions were masked both by increasing prosperity and the growth of national power. These tensions were a consequence of the speed with which Germany industrialized and of the widening gap between urban and peasant cultures; they also resulted from the repressiveness of traditional German society and the rigidity with which Germans organized their lives. In both Britain and France, rebellion against traditional institutions could be directed into liberal or radical channels; in Germany, these alternatives were not as openly available, and German rebellion sometimes took the direction of nihilism —the rejection of all values.

Virulent racism is one force often associated with nihilistic movements. In Germany, it was the product of several factors. One was a sense of national inferiority—the consequence of continually frustrated national ambitions. Another was the exposed position of the German Jew: because of the unique features of German development, the Jewish citizen's liberalism and his association with urban culture made him seem more of an alien in Germany than he did in most other Western countries. Anti-Semitism was a convenient rationalization that assuaged feelings of inferiority not only for members of the German Catholic minority but also for the German Protestant peasant and small businessman. Because they could not use liberal slogans to challenge the authority of the Junker class, they tried to establish their equality with the Junkers by emphasizing the "racial" equality of the German people and their superiority over other peoples, including, especially, the Jews.

These radical and racist tendencies remained at the periphery of German life until the end of World War I. At that time, however, succession of national catastrophes spread discontent and unrest to the point where the Nazi Party, with an ideology based on these elements, could obtain control of the German state. The first national catastrophe was defeat in World War I and the Treaty of Versailles; the second was the elimination of the monarchy and the establishment of a democratic republic with institutions for which many Germans were not ready and which was almost immediately forced to cope with the terms of the treaty; the third was the inflation of the early 1920's and the Great Depression that began in 1929, which ruined thousands of peasants, small businessmen, and white-collar workers. All these national ills, plus the general ferment of the twenties, produced a moral and intellectual turmoil that seemed to threaten all traditional standards.

Beset by the Fascists on the right and the Communists on the left, both movements hostile to a democratic state, the Weimar Republic floundered and failed. It could not make effective policy decisions, and it was incapable of action. It could not even control the violent street fighting that became typical of German civic politics. Governments rose and fell, and new elections were held without any issues having been decided; democracy became a beer-hall joke.

THE NAZI REGIME: Adolph Hitler came to power in part because some Germans hoped he would restore traditional institutions, including the monarchy; in part because many saw him as the only alternative to communism or chaos; and in part because many simply longed for a more stable and effective political order.

The secret of Hitler's great appeal, however, can be fully understood only if one recognizes that he himself reflected the contradictions rampant in German society. His fears were the fears of many Germans. His aspirations, their aspirations. His madness, their madness. In his own person he synthesized their rejection of old values and their fear of rejecting them. In himself he reflected their loss of bearings in the modern world, and their strong desire for order.

Hitler's aim was to create a new and mighty Germany, ruled by a heroic, disciplined, responsible racial elite—a racial community unified by blood and thriving in unit and harmony. He attacked the philistinism and egoistic individualism of capitalist civilization. His intention was to combine a modern technological society with the best of German tradition, although his view of this tradition was considerably distorted. Thus, the regime implemented programs designed to recapture the world of the past, to re-educate and re-dedicate the German people, to purify the Germans, and, finally, to bring Germany to a position of greatness. These programs required a political system that had unparalleled control over the entire life of the nation—in other words, a totalitarian political order. What these programs resulted in, of course, was World War II and the destruction of Nazi Germany.

Under the Third Reich, Hitler sought to create a corporate society. Both workers and employers were organized in a National Labor Front directed by the Nazi Party. All professional people were required to join guildlike organizations under the direction of the party and to form professional courts to insure competence and fair charges for services.

The Nazis extended their control over the universities and centralized education in the lower grades. Youth organizations were formed that placed great stress on ideological unity and on physical fitness. Indeed, every association, from churches to bird watching groups, came under the supervision of the party and the state to make certain that the proper attitudes and orientations were spread among the population.

To guarantee Germany's racial purity, "undesirable" individuals were sterilized or killed; these included the feebleminded, the elderly and infirm, the incurably ill, as well as defective infants and homosexuals. The purity program finally came to include geno-

cide; all gypsies and millions of Jews were slaughtered, as were large numbers of Poles (especially Slavic Poles) and Russians. Hitler also tried to develop a "racially pure" leadership for the future. This elite would, Hitler felt, guarantee a thousand-year empire, greater than the Holy Roman Empire —which had been the First Reich. But Germany also needed living space (*Lebennsraum*), Hitler claimed; and he sought to obtain it primarily at the expense of the "racially inferior" peoples to the east. This ambition eventually led him to invade the Soviet Union.

CONTEMPORARY GERMANY: [5] At the conclusion of World War II, Germany was in ruins. Having defeated Hitler, the Allies prepared to prevent the German people from ever again becoming a threat to world peace. Numerous plans were made for trying war criminals, for lengthy occupation, and for permanently splitting Germany into a number of fragments and limiting her industrial capacity. A three-power European Advisory Commission was established to make recommendations on what to do with a defeated Germany.

The commission made a detailed plan for postwar zones of occupation and presented its proposals two years later (February 1945) to the Big Three at Yalta. The plan was accepted with some modifications, the most important of which involved carving an occupation zone for France out of the British and American zones.

Yalta marked the high point of Allied unity. When the Potsdam Conference met later in 1945—with Harry Truman replacing Franklin D. Roosevelt and Clement Attlee taking over from Winston Churchill— relations were still cordial, but increasing disagreement foreshadowed the conflict that was to come. Unable to agree upon what Germany's boundaries should be, the Allies decided to leave final determination of the

---

[5] For reasons of space, the discussions of postwar Germany will deal only with the Federal Republic of Germany. Unless otherwise specified, the word "Germany" will usually refer to West Germany.

new borders to a future peace conference. And in fact it was not until 1970 that Chancellor Willy Brandt signed peace treaties with both the U.S.S.R. and Poland settling Germany's postwar boundaries.

The Potsdam Conference also completed the agreements on the occupation of Germany, providing for an Allied Control Council with ultimate authority. Berlin was to remain an enclave in the Soviet zone, governed jointly by the Allies and split into four sectors. After Potsdam, however, the Soviet Union and the Western Allies found it more and more difficult to reach any kind of agreement on common policies. Within a short time, this friction became part and parcel of the cold war. Divergent programs were instituted in the different zones of occupation, the Soviets deciding the fate of what was to become the German Democratic Republic, while France, England, and the United States eventually worked out common policies for the western zone.

One upshot of the East-West split was the merger of the three western zones, and then, in 1949, the formation of the German Federal Republic from these three zones. The political structure of the German Federal Republic was determined by a "Basic Law" drafted largely by the Germans themselves in a Constituent Assembly that met during 1948 and 1949. The Basic Law, however, was subject to the approval of the Allies, who did exercise significant influence over the deliberations at several points. The Basic Law was and is considered to be a temporary expedient to be replaced by a constitution whenever a formal peace treaty reuniting the two Germanies is signed. Although specifically a transitional document, it presumes to represent not only West Germans but those Germans "to whom participation was denied," namely, those living in East Germany and, at that time (1949), the Saar.

The Basic Law was ratified by the Allies and the German people in 1949, and shortly thereafter the first general elections were held. The creation of the Federal Republic did not mean, however, that West Germany had been granted full sovereignty. The Allied High Commissioners kept the reins of power in many areas and retained the right to withdraw all privileges in case of emergency. But because of the intensification of the Cold War and the desire to enlist the cooperation of West Germany in the defense of Europe, the re-entry of Germany into the family of nations proceeded apace. In 1955 Germany was admitted to the North Atlantic Treaty Organization and at the same time granted full sovereignty.

From 1949 to 1963, Germany was led by Chancellor Konrad Adenauer, of the Christian Democratic Party. His shrewdness, toughness, and ability—particularly in the use of power—enabled him to dominate the political scene. Under his leadership German politics was relatively quiescent. Radical groups, both of the right and the left, more or less disappeared from the political scene, and the new generation of Germans seemed committed to moderate policies and political parties. In Germany, as in other countries, sociologists spoke and wrote of the end of ideology, and deplored the relative lack of political concern or enthusiasm.

With Adenauer's departure from the scene, German politics began to change. In the mid-1960's a right-wing neo-nationalist political party, the National Democratic Party, scored significant electoral victories and even gained some national strength, only to see its support quickly erode. Soon thereafter, German university students, following the lead of their American counterparts, moved to the left and began to engage in the same kind of confrontation politics with which Americans had become familiar. By the early 1970's, despite reduced student activism, German political life was showing signs of strain, and at least some observers were wondering if a repetition of the failure of the Weimar Republic might be in the offing.

However, the possibilities of such a repetition seem extremely slight. Although German society clearly contains authoritarian elements and political strains a generation after Hitler, Germany in the 1970's is very

TABLE 2.3 GROWTH RATES OF GROSS NATIONAL PRODUCT:
EUROPE AND THE UNITED STATES [1]

Selected Periods, 1913–1973

	United States		France		West Germany [2]		United Kingdom	
	total	per capita	total	per capita	total	per capita	total	per capita
1913–1929	3.1%	1.7%	1.7%	1.8%	0.4%	—	0.8%	0.3%
1929–1950	2.9	1.7	—	—	1.9	0.7%	1.6	1.2
1950–1960	3.2	1.5	4.6	3.7	8.5	6.9	2.7	2.3
1960–1969	4.5	3.2	5.8	4.7	4.7	3.7	2.8	2.1
1969–1973	3.5	2.6	6.1	5.2	5.0	4.2	2.8	2.5

[1] Rates represent annual compounded changes in real output.

[2] Beginning in 1960, includes Saar and West Berlin.

Adapted from *Statistical Abstract of the United States, 1969*, p. 313; *Statistical Abstract, 1973*, p. 814; *Statistical Abstract, 1974*, p. 824.

different from the Germany of forty years ago.

As one author put it, *Bonn ist nicht Weimar*.[6] Germany in the twenties was a nation of anguishing contradictions, facing forward, looking backward, fragmented, bitter, desperate—a nation of weak and rapidly changing governments. Germany in the seventies, although unsettled and even anxious about dissension, uncertain of its direction and of its place in the world, has, nevertheless, the experience of a generation of relative stability and success with institutions established under the Bonn government. The nation has become integrated into Western alliances and is at peace with neighbors to the East. From the perspective of its own past and in the view of several other nearby governments that are in alliance with Germany, German institutions seem relatively effective and stable.

A sign of the changes which have taken place in Germany was the formation in 1969, of the first government led by the Social Democratic party. Aside from a number of domestic reforms the years which followed produced a series of agreements designed to regularize relations between the German Federal Republic, and the Soviet Union, East Germany, and Poland.

Postwar developments have continued the process of weakening traditional values which the Nazis, despite their propaganda, quickened. Many German Protestants who fled from East Germany into West Germany settled in predominantly Catholic areas, reducing religious separateness. The economic growth common to all European nations after the war (Table 2.3) produced still further changes. The ubiquitous automobile and new highways have greatly enhanced geographic mobility; television and radio have helped to create an ever more homogeneous culture, drawing Germans closer together even as they introduce ideas and values typical of other European nations. And the continued rise in power of non-European countries not only has added to the Germans' feeling that they are an integral part of Europe, but also has led most of them to accept the fact that Germany is only a "small country" that cannot hope to be more than a second-rank power. A series of economic and political shocks could conceiveably pose a threat to German democracy. But whatever Germany's future, the combination

[6] Fritz René Alleman, *Bonn ist nicht Weimar* (Cologne: Kiepenheuer and Witsch, 1956).

of disparate forces that brought the triumph of National Socialism is no longer present.

4. SOME PRELIMINARY CONCLUSIONS

During the past several years, Britain, France, and Germany have confronted essentially the same problems, problems generated by the changes that have taken place in European society. Each has been involved in a process of national integration as the nation-state became the predominant form of European social organization, and within that framework each has been concerned with the problem of the relationship between secular and religious authority. All three societies have also had to cope with the problems engendered by the Industrial Revolution and the erosion of traditional forms of behavior and political authority.

The manner in which the three nations met these problems depended upon a number of factors, principally the religious and class structures of their traditional societies, their geographic positions, and the time sequence in which the problems themselves arose. The political patterns and political institutions that have come to characterize these societies, while clearly European, reflect the unique historical development of each, as we shall see in more detail in succeeding chapters.

Of the three, Britain was the most successful in dealing relatively peacefully with its problems. The British had created a national state and an adaptable national community based on mutual class rights and responsibilities before the onset of industrialization. The forces that led to industrializa-tion were indigenous and could be incorporated into traditional structures even as they modified them. The result was a unique fusion of traditional feudal and modern institutions.

All three Western European countries are conventionally labeled constitutional democracies. While the appellation is not incorrect, it is less than fully useful as a description of the political process in any of them. They are more accurately described, in Robert Dahl's term, as "polyarchies," inasmuch as political decisions result from competition among a plurality of elites of varying power and influence that freely vie for the support of the larger public.[7] They can also be described as pluralistic, reconciliation regimes because politics in all of them is conceived as a process whereby various interests in the community freely compete for a share of the community's values according to certain rules; the political system is conceived as a mechanism by which the goals sought by these interests can somehow be integrated into overall policies that will command the assent of most of the people.

All three nations are now modern as the term is generally used, and developments during the past twenty years have considerably reduced differences among them. As the European student movement indicates, events in any one of the three nations have an almost instantaneous impact upon the other nations, and the problems now faced by all of them, as Europe approaches a postindustrial age, are of much the same order.

[7] See Robert A. Dahl and Charles E. Lindblom, *Politics, Economics and Welfare* (New York: Harper & Row, 1953).

Above: Workers' councils. Courtesy German Information Center. *Right:* Spraying fruit trees. Courtesy French Embassy Press & Information Division.

Steel plants in Lorraine, France. Courtesy French Embassy Press & Information Division. *Opposite page:* Free University, West Berlin. Courtesy German Information Center.

PART TWO
Social and Cultural Bases of European Politics

Left: Game of Boules. Courtesy French Embassy Press & Information Division. *Below:* "Open Door," a live weekly BBC program. BBC Copyright Photograph.

3

Industrialization
and
Change

1. SOURCES OF COHESION AND CONFLICT

To Marxists, the political system of any society is part of its superstructure; while political decisions are not without importance they are, for the most part, dependent upon more basic economic factors. The analysis of any society's politics, however, is necessarily more complex if one rejects a purely Marxist interpretation or other monistic theories. The structure of political institutions, the emergence of a charismatic political figure, even ill-chosen public policies—all can have a significant impact upon the society and affect its future development. Theorizing becomes even more complicated if one is willing to entertain the possibility that such factors as the environment of the society and the cultural values of its population must all be taken into account in attempting to understand the problems it faces and the structure of its politics. It is the argument of this volume that such is the case—that to understand the politics of any society, one must examine the interrelationships of these and other variables.

Certainly the manner in which societies have organized their system of productive relationships has greatly influenced their social and political life; broadly conceived, the economic system is one of the more important determinants of social and political consciousness. An individual's relation to a given mode of production does influence his life-style: the peasant's frame of reference is quite different from that of the industrial worker and that of both differs from the perspective of the lord of the manor or the capitalist entrepreneur. Structurally, then, the transition from various primitive or peasant societies to modern industrial ones has been the most significant social change of the past two hundred years.

Historically, too, the question of how to distribute material goods, power, and prestige among various strata of the society has been among the most important sources of social conflict. The next section of this chapter offers a brief summary of how the evolution of an industrial society had its impact upon all facets of European life; Chapter 4 will deal primarily with the class structure of various European countries as it has influenced political attitudes and actions.

The economic system of any social order, however, does not emerge naturally as the result of an inner dialectical movement, as Marx thought. Rather, the manner in which a society—be it traditional or modern —mobilizes and distributes its resources is determined by its cultural heritage, particularly by the values and beliefs in each society relevant to power and politics. Some of these values and beliefs are shared by the society as a whole, and some characterize particular segments of the population. This value segmentation may derive from social class position, but it may also be linked to religious and ethnic differences. Indeed, there is much to be said for the view that the religious variable has, in the past, been of key importance in determining the general culture of most societies and that religious and ethnic antagonism and conflict have presented more serious problems to the political system than has class conflict. Religious and ethnic factors will be discussed in Chapter 5. Finally, Chapter 6 will examine another source of societal tension in connection with the mobilization and distribution of resources: intergenerational conflicts; this chapter will also seek to determine whether the student movement that began in the late 1960's was a radical break with student movements of earlier generations.

Thus far the general sources of conflict have been noted. Yet all societies must develop sources of cohesion, mechanisms by which their members are motivated to accept the more important norms of the society and to perform those tasks that the society defines as productive. The family is still important in this respect, although both the mass media and education have brought the influence of the larger community to bear as well. How the process of socialization is organized depends upon a variety of factors, one being the society's economic structure and general culture. But the structure of the family itself, the system of formal education which has been developed, and the organization of the media of communication may also serve as agents of social change— or, equally, may inhibit social change. Educational systems also determine what kind of training will be received by social and political elites. All these topics are treated in Chapter 7.

Discussion of them will, it is hoped, not only help us understand the political conflicts within European political systems, insofar as these are reflections of group antagonisms; it will also clarify the values and beliefs that help to determine what goals each of the societies deems most important, and the means by which each tries to attain them. The relationship is by no means unilateral, however: political decisions made in the past have significantly affected the political culture and group structures of the societies with which we are concerned; such decisions have also affected the institutions within them that are responsible for socialization or the communication of information. The role of education in European societies cannot be understood apart from public policy decisions in the field of education. The sectional divisions of this volume, then, are in a sense arbitrary. Every social system consists of an intricate web of relationships; it would be foolish to insist upon too sharp a differentiation between what is properly considered political and other aspects of the life of the society.

2. THE POLITICS OF EUROPEAN INDUSTRIAL SOCIETIES

Britain, France, and Germany are highly developed industrial societies experiencing rather rapid technological and social change. Thus they have come increasingly to resemble one another in some very significant ways. In every case, industrialization has involved a more or less radical break with traditional social and cultural patterns, although these patterns have not entirely disappeared. All three have become highly urbanized. In each, the population is almost entirely literate, and both geographic and social mobility are high compared with earlier periods. Moreover, the structure of social life has become highly differentiated, and the world of the machine has partially replaced the natural environment.

It is not always easy to determine causal relationships. Yet, increased mobility and literacy have obviously involved wider contacts with the world and have tended both to broaden perspectives and, more importantly, to weaken the hold of traditional authority. The extended family, with its complex net of kinship relations, has broken down in favor of the conjugal family (husband, wife, and children); at the same time, the authority of the husband over the wife and the authority of the parents over their children have been reduced. These changes, coupled with the instrumental view of the world fostered by modern science and technology, have resulted in a decline of religious sensibility and a growing urgency to satisfy personal, and for the most part material, needs.

Further, the emphasis on production and on the skills required in both science and industry has raised the status of the professional, including the scientist and the manager; these groups have come increasingly to serve as models for legitimate authority, with skill rather than birth providing the criterion for differential rewards. Greater specialization has led to the multiplication of impersonal, functionally specific relationships, while urban life has produced a deterioration in the communal patterns associated with the village and the small city. These transformations, all leading to the replacement of traditional authority by functionally based authority, have had immense implications for the political process in every country with which we are concerned.

In general, the class patterns of each of these societies have grown more complex; a plurality of "strategic elites" within a given society has replaced the relatively simple class divisions that seemed to characterize Europe, at least during an earlier period. This means that it is far more difficult to determine with any precision where power really lies and how political decisions are actually made.

TABLE 3.1   PER CAPITA NATIONAL INCOME, 1960, 1968, and 1972
In U. S. dollars

	1960	1968	1972
Germany	1,188	2,005	3,739
France	1,202	2,292	3,403
Britain	1,276	1,716	2,523
United States	2,559	3,898	4,943

Source: United Nations, *Statistical Yearbook, 1973*, pp. 592–593.

Although wealth and power continue to be unevenly distributed in all European countries, today a new Europe is emerging, one whose social structure is different even from that of the period immediately preceding World War II. The real wages of industrial workers in most European countries have more than doubled since the war and, while large segments of the working class and the peasantry are by no means affluent there can be no gainsaying the general trend by which more and more Europeans are brought into the orbit of the consumer society. Social mobility, too, is on the increase; positions at the top are being opened to children of middle-class and lower-middle-class backgrounds who are taking advantage of expanded educational opportunities. The size of the elite stratum is itself growing rapidly in proportion with the continued growth of professional services. Even within industry, "managers" are replacing "entrepreneurs," and control is being separated from ownership. Then, too, the complexion of the work force is changing: the number of white-collar jobs is rising much more rapidly than the demand for industrial workers.

The newly developed self-consciousness of the working classes and their more active participation in social and political life have significantly altered the whole power structure of these societies. As late as 1913 no more than 25 percent of the population of many European countries was eligible to vote; today the norm in Western Europe is universal suffrage. Seventy-five years ago trade unions were still operating on the border of illegality; today, with the possible exception of France, they command considerable economic and political power.

The political impact of increased affluence and social mobility is not yet clear. During the 1950's these variables seemed related to the diminished intensity of political conflict. On the other hand, advanced industrial society is generating new structural bases for conflict; new values that feed political tension, and new issues that reflect a questioning of many of the assumptions as to the benefits of material abundance. Thus advanced industrial society has required a growing group of white-collar workers who have demonstrated a tendency towards discontent and militancy. Much of this discontent is related to changing work values. Higher salaries and more benefits are no

longer sufficient for work satisfaction, and more young workers, both in factories and in offices, expect their work to be rewarding in itself. Furthermore, it now appears that many of the products of advanced industrial society may be threatening the quality of life, and even survival itself. Along with an abundance of consumer products and increased affluence, modernity has created in Europe dangerously polluted rivers and seas, ugly and alienating housing developments, and a rising rate of violent crime, especially among young people. Finally, the oil crisis and the short supply of other raw materials now threaten to curtail industrial expansion at a time when mass expectations and political stability have become linked to a rising standard of living.

TABLE 3.2   PORTION OF TOTAL INCOME RECEIVED BY TOP TEN PERCENT OF FAMILIES BEFORE TAXES

	1938	1954 [1]	1964 [2]
Britain	38.0%	30.4%	29.3%
France	—	34.1	36.8 [3]
West Germany	39.0 [4]	44.0	41.4
United States	36.0	30.0	28.0

[1] French data for 1956; German, for 1955.

[2] Figures applicable, in a comparative sense, for the early 1970's.

[3] Data for 1962.

[4] Data for all Germany in 1936.

Sources: United Nations, Department of Economic and Social Affairs, *Economic Survey of Europe in 1956* (Geneva: United Nations Publication, 1957), chap. 9, p. 6; United Nations, *Incomes in Postwar Europe* (Geneva: United Nations Publication, 1967), chap. 6, p. 15; *Statistical Abstract of the United States, 1939*, p. 313; *Statistical Abstract, 1968*, p. 323.

TABLE 3.3   SAMPLING OF COMPARATIVE NET SALARIES, 1972

In multiples of a factory worker's pay

	Corpora-tion head	Factory manager	Upper adminis-tration	Engineer	Factory foreman	Worker
Britain	12.0	7.8	4.5	3.7	2.3	1
Germany	10.4	6.6	3.7	3.0	1.8	1
France	10.7	7.2	4.6	3.9	2.3	1
United States	7.8	5.2	3.3	2.8	2.2	1

Source: Centre d'études des revenues et des coûts; reprinted in *Le Monde,* March 10, 1972.

4

Sources and Organization
of Political Conflict:
Social Class

1. GENTRY, PEASANTS, AND FARMERS

INTRODUCTION: Today, the European landed aristocracy has all but disappeared, the peasant is being replaced by the farmer, and the proportion of those who till the soil is declining rapidly. In none of the three Western European nations we are discussing do those employed in agriculture make up more than 14 percent of the working force. In each country the distinctive "peasant mentality" is becoming part of the past, and the commercial farmer is integrating into the developing industrial society. Nevertheless, in some parts of France and Germany traditional attitudes are still fairly strong. In both countries, moreover, many farm holdings are too small to provide an adequate standard of living for their owners, and efforts by the two governments to encourage marginal farmers to leave the land have met with resistance.

THE BRITISH PATTERN: By the end of the eighteenth century, independent peasants were no longer a significant social force in Britain. The enclosure movement, which began in the later Middle Ages, had resulted in the concentration of land in the hands of a comparatively small number of families, and the large-scale commercial agriculture of the eighteenth century completed the process. The absence of a highly traditional landowning peasantry enabled the British to avoid some of the tension between urban and rural life that was present in both France and

TABLE 4.1 THE DECLINE OF FARMING AS AN OCCUPATION

Percentage of work force engaged in agriculture

	1850–60	1900	1930	1950	1960	1970
Britain	18	8	8	6	6	3
France	60–65	42	34	28	21	14
Germany [1]	—	40	30	22	11	9
United States	59	36	19	11	7	4

[1] Post–World War II percentages apply only to West Germany.

Sources: European data from Folke Dovring, *Land and Labor in Europe* (The Hague: M. Nijhoff, 1965); from *Agriculture in Western Europe* by Michael Tracy. © 1964 by Michael Tracy. Reprinted by permission of Praeger Publishers, Inc., New York, and Jonathan Cape, Ltd. United States data to 1900 from *Statistical Abstract of the United States, 1937,* sec. 23; from 1930, *National Income and Product Accounts of the U.S., 1965,* pp. 90–94; Office of European Cooperation and Development, *Labor Force Statistics, 1959–1970* (Paris, 1972), pp. 70, 186, 198, 384.

Germany. Furthermore, the Industrial Revolution, in conjunction with free trade, resulted in the abrupt decline of agriculture as the major source of national wealth, and for all but a few, as a way of life. By 1900 less than 9 percent of the British working force was employed in agriculture as against 40 to 45 percent for other European countries.

In the meantime, the nature of the landed interest itself was undergoing change. Much of the landed aristocracy gave way to a new class of farmers. The movement in this direction accelerated in the years between the two world wars when, by some estimates, at least one-fourth of British land holdings changed hands. It took the new ownership patterns to bring about effective farmers' associations. In 1908, after a number of unsuccessful efforts at organization, the National Farmer's Union (NFU), representing both farmers (owner-occupiers) and farm tenants, came into existence. Since that year it has grown until today its membership includes the great bulk of the full-time farmers in England and Wales.

Despite the small size of the British agricultural population, the NFU has been fairly successful in obtaining government policies it considers favorable to its interests. The union's ability to do so stems from both the continuing British idealization of rural life (shared by America, Germany, and France) and the desire of every British government to make sure that the nation can produce a reasonable portion of its food supply. That farmers are concentrated in a number of marginal election districts also helps. In the 1930's the NFU was more or less associated with the Conservative Party. Then as now, however, its politics were officially neutral.

In summary, a small agricultural population, the absence of a legacy of urban-rural tension, and an effective interest group able to articulate farmers' demands have meant that agricultural issues have not been salient in British politics at the party and electoral level.

THE FRENCH PATTERN: By the time of the Revolution, France already possessed a substantial "free" peasant population. Following the Revolution the population was augmented by the redistribution of property that had belonged to the Catholic Church and the aristocracy. This redistribution not only increased the number of small peasant holdings, but also helped to make a sizeable number of peasants loyal to the Revolution and to alienate them from the church.

The common (although not universal) practice in bequeathing land in France differed from the British pattern in that land was divided equally among all sons. This practice, which was formalized in Napoleon's Civil Code, insured the continued fragmentation of peasant holdings and thereby inhibited the introduction of more rational agricultural methods. As a result, well into the middle of the nineteenth century peasants in France remained largely untouched by agricultural technology. Peasants in surrounding countries were increasingly producing for commercial markets and being transformed into farmers; those in France were not. Some large-scale commercial farming did develop in the north of France and in certain areas dedicated primarily to winemaking. These were the exceptions, however. With the richest soil in Western Europe, France never came close to producing up to her capacity.

The relatively small size of individual holdings, however, was not the only problem. In other countries, such as Germany, the Netherlands, and Denmark, where the average size of many farms was comparable with those of France, or even smaller, size was not a barrier to the application of mechanization and scientific techniques through cooperative efforts. In France, however, such cooperation was made more difficult by the suspicion and individual isolation that long characterized French social life. As one author described a fairly typical French village in the early 1950's: "As we came to know . . . families . . . it seemed to us . . . that all . . . were suspicious of each other. 'Of course you can trust me and my family and a few other people . . . *mais les autres.* . . .'"[1] Likewise, after studying one community, a prominent French rural sociologist concluded that, with some exceptions among young people, the inhabitants had neighbors but no friends.[2]

The suspicion among individuals also defined attitudes toward the state. To the peasant, the state was traditionally an instrument that one manipulated, if possible, to secure special privileges such as subsidies; but it was not to be trusted, especially if it were in the hands of "les autres"—a generalized and hostile *them*. If therefore, the state attempted to implement policies that seemed to run counter to immediate interests, it was quite legitimate to use any technique, including violence, to defeat its efforts. The history of France is replete with minor and major peasant upheavals ranging from the tarring and feathering of tax collectors to the destruction of competitors' crops. Beyond all this, the continued predominance of traditional Catholic attitudes toward life and work hampered the development of more rational agricultural organization.

After World War II, peasant attitudes underwent important changes—and, as a consequence, so, too, did the structure of French agriculture. Modernization programs were initiated by the Fourth Republic and continued under the Fifth. Combined with important shifts in peasant attitudes, they are changing the contours of rural life. The state has been attempting to facilitate the consolidation of scattered holdings and to remove marginal farms from production; consequently, the number of small holdings has declined, and the size of the average holdings has increased (see Tables 2.2 and 4.1, pp. 34 and 57). An intensive effort has also been made to provide peasants with modern agricultural tools—the number of farm tractors in France tripled between 1955 and 1964—and to break traditional peasant resistance toward the use of machinery. The younger generation is increasingly enthusiastic about technical training, once universally regarded as useless. In Catholic areas, a Catholic Agricultural Youth movement (*Jeunesse agricole chrétienne*—JAC) sprang up and is working actively and effectively to encourage consolidation and modernization. And, in every part of France, peasants have begun to join cooperatives of various kinds.

[1] Lawrence Wylie, *Village in the Vaucluse* (Cambridge, Mass.: Harvard Unversity Press, 1957), p. 194.

[2] Henri Mendras, *Études de Sociologie Rurale* (Paris: Armand Colin, 1953), p. 75.

Yet problems persist. The older generation continues to balk at making changes; given the problems of overproduction, increased efficiency has been a mixed blessing. Modernization and the common agricultural policy of the European Economic Community have generally tended to benefit the more efficient commercial farms of the northwest and the Paris region, whereas tradition, distance from commercial centers, and the quality of the soil have held back many of the smaller, less efficient farmers of the south and Brittany. Often the policies of the Fifth Republic seemed oriented toward preserving the more efficient agricultural enterprises and driving the marginal farmers from the land. Certainly, the gap between the income of the latter group and that of the rest of the country has widened, with the consequence that the government has been plagued by farm strikes and outbreaks of violence.

Like all Frenchmen, the peasants have been sharply divided ideologically; these divisions were, and are, related in a complex way to religious practice, size of holdings, and type of crops. During a substantial part of the nineteenth century, peasants in those areas where the church was strong tended to be anti-republican; anticlerical areas tended toward a politically radical but in some ways socially conservative type of Jacobinism, distrusting not only the church, but also business, the city, and radical social ideas. The votes of these latter peasants went to the Radical Socialist Party, which, during most of the Third Republic, was divided by an attempt to reconcile its peasant base with the revolutionary catchwords that gained the vote of the urban working class, when these two groups had in common only Jacobin slogans and hostility to the church. In fact, it is not surprising that, as in Germany, the same peasants who usually voted for Radical Socialist deputies sometimes supported Fascist or quasi-Fascist movements, including that of Pierre Poujade, during the last years of the Fourth Republic.

Ideological division and the characteristic suspiciousness of French peasants have hampered the organization of groups to articulate their interests. The best organized and the most politically successful have been those representing the minority of commercial and semicommercial farmers. For example, groups like the *Fédération des associations viticoles*—the "alcohol" lobby—have succeeded in obtaining special subsidies and protective tariffs.

The most broadly based agricultural organization today is the *Fédération nationale des syndicats d'exploitants agricoles*—FNSEA (National Federation of Farmers' Unions), although its membership includes only a small percentage of French farmers. Until the mid-sixties the federation was in the hands of moderately conservative farm groups that were primarily concerned with the maintenance of farm prices rather than a structural reform of agriculture.

Beginning in 1959 the FNSEA's youth sections, which had come under the domination of the JAC (*Jeunesse agricole chrétienne*), gained control of the parent federation on the basis of a program of cooperative agriculture. The take-over was aided by the upsurge of peasant violence in western and southern France during the 1960's. In May, 1961, the most extensive and violent jacquerie in modern French history broke out, and peasant agitation continued throughout the remainder of the decade. By 1971, however, the new "establishment" of the FNSEA was itself being challenged by a left wing favorable to the encouragement of direct action and agitation.

Throughout the Fourth Republic the French Communist Party exercised important minority influence within the FNSEA, controlling several departmental federations. The Communists were particularly reluctant to form a minority peasant organization that would be isolated from the mainstream of the peasant movement. However, the loss of peasant votes in the early elections of the Fifth Republic, and the success of JAC convinced the Communists to sponsor a semi-independent organization that would draw its support from the growing protest of small family farmers. Thus the *Mouvement de défense de l'exploitation familiale*—MODEF (Movement for the Defense of Family

Farms) came into existence in 1959. It united Communist elements that had continued to operate within FNSEA with departmental federations which had been excluded from the national federation in the early fifties. MODEF has spoken out strongly for the defense of the family farm, and since the mid-sixties it has tended to favor the development of cooperative efforts among small farmers. Yet with its ideal remaining essentially a defense of the swiftly changing present, MODEF had less success than the youth section of FNSEA in attracting young farmers seeking innovative ways of reorganizing French peasant life. Nevertheless, the Communist group now holds close to one-third of the seats in the semi-official advisory bodies known as the Chambers of Agriculture.

The upsurge of political activism among French peasants in some ways mirrors the past. Peasant organization is still weak, and much of the activism behind the rejuvenated organizations consists of periodic, violent outbursts. Nevertheless, even as the number of French peasants continues to decline each year, a new generation of them has accepted technology and cooperation as a basis for survival.

THE GERMAN PATTERN: Regional variations in German agriculture were at least as great as those in France. In the west and south, feudal patterns gradually gave way to individual peasant holdings. Although some reasonably large-scale commercial farming developed, the standard was the independent peasant proprietor who worked his farm with the aid of his family and a few farm workers. In the east, the pattern differed considerably. The Prussian aristocracy had acquired its estates by the conquest of Slavic peoples, and aristocratic domination continued long after feudal patterns had broken down elsewhere. Then, the end of feudalism was accompanied by large-scale enclosures that produced a sharp two-class division between aristocrat and landless agricultural workers. At the end of the nineteenth century a handful of Junkers still owned more than 40 percent of the available agricultural land, and until after World War II the agricultural workers on these estates were still almost totally dependent upon their employers, who often joined a benevolent paternalism with authoritarian control of their workers' activities.

During the 1920's, the peasant's natural animosity toward a central government and a social atmosphere that seemed to be undermining traditional patterns brought more and more of them into, or at least into sympathy with, the Nazi Party. With its emphasis on the moral superiority of those who were close to the soil, its assertion of the racial equality of all Germans, its half-concealed anti-Junkerism, and its anti-Semitism, the party appealed to the peasant's resentment of aristocratic authority even as it promised concrete measures to alleviate his economic distress. Many villages voted very early and solidly for the Nazis.

After World War II, the bifurcation of Germany and the Soviet domination of most of what was formerly Prussia brought an end to the hegemony of the aristocracy. Since the truncated Federal Republic incorporated only areas in which smaller holdings predominated, the nature of Germany's agricultural problem changed. To begin with, less than 10 percent of the total work force is today employed in agriculture; and, given the relatively small size of holdings, farm workers have practically disappeared as a group. The Federal Republic is now actively encouraging the consolidation of holdings and the development of cooperatives in order to make the most effective use of modern technology. Furthermore, the peasant is no longer isolated from urban life. What evidence we have indicates that the peasant is still more authoritarian than the urban dweller, but the cultural differences between city and country are disappearing. That many German villages today contain a substantial number of persons of urban background who commute to work in the city has contributed to the erosion of traditional values.

TABLE 4.2   EVOLUTION OF FEDERAL GERMAN AGRARIAN
STRUCTURE, 1949–1964

Type	Size (acres)	Numbers (in 1,000s)		Percentage of holdings		Percentage of agricultural land	
		1949	1964	1949	1964	1949	1964
Capitalist	125 +	15.8	16.8	0.8	1.1	10.3	10.5
Large peasant	50–125	112.7	126.4	5.8	8.7	24.0	28.5
Middle peasant	25–50	256.9	295.8	13.2	19.7	26.2	31.8
Small peasant and part-time	12.5–25	404.5	308.1	20.8	20.6	21.1	17.2
	5–12.5	555.1	343.2	28.5	22.9	13.6	8.7
Part-time	1.25–5	602.6	403.8	30.9	27.0	4.8	3.3
		1,947.6	1,494.1	100.0	100.0	100.0	100.0

Adapted from S. H. Franklin, *The European Peasantry* (London: Methuen Co., 1969), p. 23, reprinted by permission of the publisher.

The first national agricultural interest group in Germany was the Junker-dominated Farmers' League, which was founded in 1897 to press for higher agricultural tariffs. After World War I the organization reformed as the *Landbund* and took a particularly conservative line, associating itself closely with the Nationalist Party. The other agricultural groups formed during the 1920's all claimed to speak directly for the independent peasant, though their religious, ideological, and local differences kept them from achieving any national significance until the years immediately preceding the rise of Hitler. At that time peasant unrest increased, and regional peasant organizations, most of which took a strong anti-urban line, expanded quickly. Utlimately, however, the peasant expressed his discontent by voting for the Nazi Party.

In 1949 various farm organizations joined on the national level, this time to form the German Farmers' League (*Deutscher Bauernverband*), whose membership now comprises more than 75 percent of all independent farmers. The relative homogeneity of the farm population has enabled farmers to speak with a common voice, and the changing nature of peasant attitudes, to-gether with the changing politics of the Federal Republic, has prompted the organization to take a moderate line. In some cases, it has even worked with the trade unions to achieve common ends. The League is generally considered to be one of the most powerful pressure groups in West Germany, having been extremely effective in securing subsidies and other forms of state assistance.

2.   ENTREPRENEURS AND MANAGERS

INTRODUCTION: The Industrial Revolution in Britain was initiated by an entrepreneurial elite drawn from diverse backgrounds. Some were gentry who had either invested in industry capital derived from their land or else had used their political position to take advantage of economic opportunities; but most of the innovators came from varying segments of a constantly expanding urban middle class. France's pattern of industrialization, though less marked, resembled that of the British; so, too, did the German, except that a vital role in industrialization was played by the state, which remained under the control of the Prussian aristocracy.

In all Western European nations the recent evolution of the entrepreneurial role reveals certain common trends: the increasing separation of ownership and management; the development of a new managerial class, recruited more and more from the universities; and the decline of the economic power of the business community in general both because of the state's greater participation in economic activity and the emergence of other powerful interests within the community. In Western Europe the business firm has become increasingly bureaucratized, and the ratio of administrative to production personnel has grown.

One of the major influences on the changing pattern of European business has been the example set by the United States. Since the mid-fifties, Europeans have come to realize more frequently that American research techniques and innovations have far outpaced their own; consequently, certain segments of the European market have been dominated by American products, and American multinational corporations have played a larger and larger role in Europe. During the decade of the sixties, foreign companies, including American, deeply penetrated the European market, and many more companies were established in Europe by foreigners than by European investors. In the late sixties and early seventies, however, European transnational corporations have been among the fastest growing in the world, and have outstripped the growth of American corporations in the European market.[3]

THE BRITISH PATTERN: An unusually large portion of those responsible for Britain's industrial growth were from Calvinist lower-middle-class or artisan backgrounds, men who managed to amass fortunes through a combination of luck, shrewdness, and hard work. These newly prosperous businessmen tended to be less concerned about the welfare of those they employed than were entrepreneurs of gentry background. Nonetheless, their Protestant and utilitarian values, so beautifully caricatured by Dickens, never dominated British society as they did American. In fact, they were quickly fused with an older tradition that maintained that social success—the acceptance as gentlemen—depended on certain behavior patterns. Even if the newly rich businessman did not harbor these ambitions, certainly his sons did, especially after having attended the "right" schools.

The resultant pattern of business behavior emphasized a sense of civic responsibility, a reasonably high code of business ethics, and, as with other elite groups, the notion that the ideal man of business was a gentleman of broad humanist background, not a trained technician. The tradition of the amateur and the gentleman, whatever its virtues, is partially responsible for some of the shortcomings of British entrepreneurship in the second half of the twentieth century. The British themselves have slowly come to recognize this fact, and today an education in engineering and economics is more readily accepted as useful background for business activity.

Compared with their French and German counterparts, British businessmen as a political group accepted with good grace democratic institutions, the organization of trade unions by workers, and the social-service state. They also developed some fairly cohesive organizations for dealing with economic and political problems. The most important of these was the Federation of British Industries (FBI), which in 1965 joined with two other business associations to form the Confederation of British Industries. In the period between the two world wars, the Federation was closely, if informally associated with the Conservative Party, although there is little evidence that it systematically

3 See J. J. Servan-Schreiber, *The American Challenge*, trans. Ronald Steel (New York: Atheneum, 1968): Louis Armand and Michel Drancourt, *The European Challenge* (London: Weidenfeld and Nicholson, 1970): and Stephen Hymer and Robert Rowthorn, "Multinational Corporations and International Oligarchy: The Non-American Challenge," in *The International Corporation: A Symposium*, ed. Charles Kindleberger (Cambridge, Mass.: MIT Press, 1971), p. 65.

attempted to exert pressure on the government; indeed, its leadership seems always to have deferred to government officials.

Its caution increased after World War II. Federation leadership preferred to heighten the image of business by presenting "reasonable" arguments, rather than by using pressure, and concentrated on demonstrating how cooperative it would be if the programs of either party were "reasonable." As successive British governments moved in the direction of national planning in the 1960's, the relations between industry and government grew closer, under both the Conservatives and Labor. There is no question, however, that British businessmen see their interests as being fostered and represented by the Conservative and not the Labor Party; hence businessmen have been an influential component on one side of the nation's social-class dichotomy that has been the foundation of British politics. In the 1970's, as the Labor Party showed signs of pressing further its aim of government nationalization of major industries, businessmen were being reminded once again that their historic alliance with the Conservative Party was both natural and, in their eyes, justified.

THE FRENCH PATTERN: It is far more difficult to generalize about the French business community than it is about those in Britain or America, where the attitudes of entrepreneurs and managers toward business and politics are related to such matters as the size, nature and regional location of the business enterprise. In France the diversity of types of enterprise is much greater, ranging from the large, highly rationalized firm that makes effective use of technological innovation (such as the gas industry, oil, electricity, and some automobile firms) to thousands of traditional family firms that refuse even to use decent methods of accounting, the better to evade the tax collector.

A substantial number of large French enterprises, employing hundreds of workers have been established since the nineteenth century; even so French industry has been dominated by the values and the interests of the small family firm. In general, the French businessman has preferred security and small profits to risk. His aim was simply to make enough to enjoy a life of culture and to pass on the family business, his patrimony, to his heirs. He was wary of the corporate form, uninterested in expanding markets, and suspicious of his more aggressive competitors. Thus, the French businessman has assimilated some traditional upper-class values and behavior patterns. Finally, French entrepreneurs, large and small, in the past have been for the most part violently opposed to workers' efforts to organize for the purpose of winning economic concessions; throughout the nineteenth century, the forceful intervention of the state was used to repress attempts at such organization. The businessman considered his relationship to the worker to be that of father to child. Workers were thought to be stupid and rather primitive, easily stirred to violence by agitators but just as easily controlled if one stood firm. Any concessions would only spoil them and lead to even greater demands. These attitudes were only rarely associated with the sense of noblesse oblige that characterized businessmen in Britain and Germany.

Politically, French businessmen grew increasingly conservative as they became better established and more defensive about their own interests. During the first part of the nineteenth century, there were liberal and anticlerical elements within the French bourgeoisie, but by the 1870's they had become conservative and had returned to the fold of the church, because they associated religious skepticism with radical democracy, mob rule, and socialism. Under the Third and Fourth Republics, businessmen protected themselves from the controls that might have been exercised through Parliament by using contacts with the upper echelons of the bureaucracy—men of a similar class background, many of whom hoped to move to the business community at some future time in their lives.

These beliefs and values of the French bourgeoisie were a natural outgrowth of French social patterns—they were the values of a stagnant society, one in which the rate of population growth was sluggish and the market laggard. To the French businessman, moreover, liberalism *did* seem to have radical consequences, and the working class *was* hostile and prone to violence. Preoccupied with security and stability, he has in the past exhibited entrepreneurial timidity, he has tried to avoid competition and technical innovation, and he has opposed union organization as a threat to his authority and to his way of life. The result has been, until recently, a slackness in French economic development and a plethora of small, marginal, family-owned firms, employing only thirty to forty workers, catering to specialized demands, and resisting expansion.

These traditional business attitudes have been undergoing rapid modification since the early fifties.[4] Concern for security has given way to concern for growth and modernization. Though the behavior of all French entrepreneurs has not always reflected this change, the old values of the family firm are in the process of disappearing. Since 1945, industry has become more concentrated, the number of small firms has declined, and most importantly, the dominant firms of French industry have moved away from the production of select high-priced goods and, under growing pressure from the Common Market, have begun manufacturing for a mass market. This expansion of the mass market has encouraged the growth of mass-consumption outlets, including a network of supermarkets. In the last decade these outlets have increased their share of the market tenfold, and Frenchmen have doubled the amount of money spent on personal goods.

While the French businessman's attitudes toward economic expansion and modernization have altered, his attitudes toward workers and unions have not. French entrepreneurs remain distrustful of unions and sensitive about what they regard as challenges to their authority at the plant. Many of the larger firms have made an effort to stabilize their relations with trade-union organizations; nevertheless, most employers in France have indicated little inclination to share the fruits of economic expansion with their workers.[5] If the French businessman is now less violent in his opposition to union organization, no stable pattern of union-management relations has as yet materialized.

Despite the myths created by leftist critics, French business was poorly organized before World War II. A national business organization, the *Confédération générale de la production française* (CGPF), was formed in 1920, but the association spoke for only a small segment of French industry. Distrust among French businessmen prevented the formation of strong business organizations like those in Britain and Germany, even for technical cooperation; the French family firm jealously guarded its "business secrets." Nonetheless, in at least one respect business cooperation was sufficient: trade associations usually had the authority needed to enforce price levels high enough to enable even inefficient companies to survive.

With the liberation, the CGPF was reorganized as the *Conseil national du patronat français—CNPF (the National Council of French Employers)*. Again its structure was federal, with membership open to regional and industrial organizations. Like the CGPF during the Third Republic, the CNPF relied on informal contacts rather than formal pressures. Its influence increased during the last years of the Fourth Republic, as the prestige and importance of large business began to grow; in the early years of the Fifth Republic it increased still further. Both the relatively pro-business attitude of de Gaulle and his associates and the Parliament's limited power as compared to

[4] Nathanial David Milder, "The Political Culture of the French Business Community" (Ph.D. diss., Cornell University, 1970).

[5] Ibid., p. 87.

that of the bureaucracy were important factors here.

Since the 1960's the CNPF has become the exponent of neo-liberalism in France. The association, dominated by big business, has supported economic expansion and modernization, often at the expense of marginal firms, and has bitterly denounced government controls over the economy. In 1965 it issued an ideological declaration of these views, and in 1969 it once again declared its support for accelerated industrialization and modernization. Though the association remains adamant about the "essential prerogatives of management within the plant," it has negotiated important agreements covering unemployment compensation and retirement benefits with the national trade-union organizations—including the Communist-dominated General Confederation of Labor. Thus the CNPF has reflected more and more the growing confidence and dynamism of those French entrepreneurs who are no longer afraid to take risks and compete, and who have become less apprehensive about trade-union radicalism. This confidence is also indicated by mounting pressure within the CNPF to develop a stronger, more disciplined, more coordinated strategy for the advancement of French business. The most important progressive group within the confederation, however, the Young Managers (*Jeunes Patrons*), has withdrawn from the organization.

The values and interests of small companies in France have continued to be represented by the *Confédération générale des petites et moyennes entreprises*—CGPME (General Confederation of Small and Medium Enterprises), which is affiliated with the CNPF but has followed an independent line, emphasizing the cult of the little man and simultaneously opposing modernization, labor unions, taxes, trusts, European cooperation, and the "malefactors" of wealth.

Periodically, the CGPME has been outflanked on the Jacobin right, first by the Poujadist movement of the early fifties, and again by a neo-Poujadist movement that burst onto the scene in 1969. Pierre Pou-

jade's *Union des commerçants et artisans*, later the *Union et fraternité français*, started among small shopkeepers and peasants in 1953 and quickly developed into a national crusade against the government's efforts to collect taxes. After a major electoral success in 1956 in which the Poujadists received 2.6 million votes, the movement began to wane, and Poujade himself was defeated in elections in 1958 and 1962. By 1967 Poujade was a supporter of the Gaullist regime.

In 1969 a "neo-Poujadist" movement suddenly emerged, as young artisans and shopkeepers protested against a compulsory medical plan that had been developed by the CGPME in cooperation with the government. Spreading rapidly throughout the country, the movement challenged the authority of the CGPME and Poujadist groups by organizing large, often violent demonstrations. By 1973 the militant artisans and shopkeepers had formed their own national organization, *Comité interprofessionel de défense de l'Union national des travailleurs indépendents*—CID–UNATI (The Interprofessional Committee for the Defense of the National Union of Independent Workers), and had succeeded in their campaign for protective legislation. In October, 1973, the National Assembly passed (without a single dissenting vote) legislation establishing commercial commissions in each department with the power to veto the opening of large stores and supermarkets. Thus, small business and commerce have continued to demonstrate impressive strength.

THE GERMAN PATTERN: A large commercial bourgeoisie developed in some of Germany's free cities in the late Middle Ages. Yet German society remained primarily agricultural until the middle of the nineteenth century. With government encouragement the nation then entered upon a period of rapid industrialization. The state subsidized and protected industry; it initiated programs in transportation and other fields that facilitated economic development; and it encouraged rational reorganization and combination (cartels) as a means for ordering the market. From the very beginning, then, German industry came under state influence and was highly concentrated.

German businessmen tended to be orderly, disciplined, and technologically efficient. More than other European countries, Germany encouraged the managerial elite to receive the equivalent of a college education. One comprehensive study estimates that in 1959 some 31 percent of the top level of German management, compared with 19 percent in the United States, had received advanced degrees.[6] In their employee relations, German businessmen emulated the aristocracy whose values they had made their own; their authoritarian paternalism outdid even that of the British. Individual plants established insurance programs before the state did; and, in contrast with France, every effort was made to provide satisfactory working conditions. Partly as a consequence of this paternalism, the German businessman believed that attempts by trade unions to assert independent bargaining power were an unwarranted challenge to his authority, and he vigorously resisted them.

Most businessmen were also hostile in varying degrees to the Weimar Republic. Though few supported the Nazi Party initially, by 1932, when support was slipping from the nationalist parties and the Communist Party was growing, many businessmen had turned to Hitler. Even then they expected to be able to control him by surrounding him with more "responsible" figures. In the end, of course, Hitler completely dominated them, and German business found itself forced to organize its economic activities within the framework set by the Nazi leadership, though profits were, in general, untouched by the regime. Like most other groups within German society, businessmen found some of the more extremist policies of the regime distasteful, but only a few dared to resist them.

At the end of World War II, the condition of German business was chaotic. The Allies held that many business leaders had been to some extent responsible for the Nazi regime and believed that the high degree of cartelization had contributed to the rise of National Socialism. Some German businessmen were tried for and found guilty of complicity in Nazi war crimes, and the most prominent industrial empires were broken up. This took place largely under the impetus of the Americans, for British officials, have never looked with dread upon business mergers.

Several of the industrial leaders, including perhaps the most famous of them all, Alfred Krupp of the armaments family, lost no time in regaining and integrating their holdings after their release from prison. And the tendency toward greater concentration has continued apace in Germany as it has in industrial countries throughout the world. During the economic crunch of the 1960's, for example, thirty German steel companies, facing a glut in the steel market and possibly ruinous competition, entered into an agreement setting up four organizations through which the price of steel would be stabilized and steel products marketed. During the business slump of 1971 and 1972, there was another push toward rationalization and consolidation in German firms. Of the hundred thousand businesses in the Federal Republic today, 1 percent produces 40 percent of the total output.

In reaction to the tight controls of the Nazi period, businessmen turned with alacrity to the "free market" policies of the Christian Democratic Union, even cautiously accepting Germany's first antitrust law (which was strengthened by the Socialist-Liberal Coalition in 1973). German business in the postwar years has also demonstrated more willingness to share its power with German trade unions. German labor and industry were brought together in the first postwar years in opposing the Allied dismantling of German industry. Since then both sides have generally seen the necessity for compromise and for arriving at decisions which are mutually beneficial. The relative industrial peace which German industry has enjoyed has obviously been

6 From Heinz Hartmann, *Authority and Organization in German Industry* (Princeton, N.J.: Princeton University Press, 1959), p. 165.

very beneficial to it in its difficult postwar adjustment and in meeting increasing foreign competition (see Table 4.5, p. 77).

Traditional authoritarian attitudes are still in evidence, especially among the older or senior German executives, and despite the remarkable economic performance of many German firms, German executives tend to be somewhat inbred and hidebound. Many of them were slow to react to the business slump in the early seventies, for which they seemed ill-prepared, perhaps because German companies had been able to expand sales and profits so fast for two decades. The lack of mobility among senior executives, who like many civil servants cling to the same firm throughout their business lives, also militates against innovation. But as in other sectors of German life, the new generation of executives are more sophisticated and open-minded.

The first German business association, the Central Association of German Industrialists, was founded in 1876. The League of Industrialists was formed in 1895, and until World War I the two organizations were rivals. After the war the two merged to form the *Reichsverband der Deutschen Industrie* —RDI (National Association of German Industry), and the new organization became highly centralized. It was dominated by large businesses to a greater extent than were comparable organizations in either France or Britain. It offered the conservative political parties financial aid in return for the promise of favorable policies, and it achieved considerable influence within the upper levels of the federal bureaucracy.

With the coming of the Nazi regime, business and trade associations were incorporated into the state structure and were brought under the control of both the state and the Nazi Party; they were not permitted to reconstitute themselves until some years after World War II. The successor to the RDI is the *Bundesverband der Deutschen Industrie* —BDI (Federation of German Industry), an organization whose membership is limited to federally structured associations representing different branches of industry. Ap-

proximately ninety-four thousand employers —about 98 percent of those eligible—are members of the federation through their associations.

The BDI and other business groups continue to maintain direct ("quasi-official") contacts with both individual deputies and the government. They contribute to all non-Socialist parties, especially the Christian Democratic Union and the FDP (Free Democratic Party). The industrial federation has been dominated by a pro-CDU faction and has generally supported European economic integration. However, a small vociferous group has continually called for a more "nationalistic" economic policy.

Two other national business associations are of some, but certainly less, importance on the German political scene. The first, *Deutscher Industrie und Handelstag*—DIHT (German Chamber of Commerce and Industry), closely resembles the United States Chamber of Commerce. Membership in the DIHT is now compulsory for all enterprises, thus giving it a quasi-official status. The second group, *Bundesvereinung der Deutschen Arbeitgeberverbände*—BDA (Federation of German Employers' Association), serves primarily as a coordinating and advisory center to employers in matters relating to labor and social policies. It recommends basic wage policies to its members and participates with the government in certain aspects of social security and the labor market.

3. THE EUROPEAN WORKER

INTRODUCTION: The European Industrial Revolution of the eighteenth and nineteenth centuries transformed both peasant and artisan into industrial workers tied to the rhythm of the machine in an urban factory system. It is undoubtedly true that much of the inspiration for early anarchist and Socialist movements came as a reaction to the change in life-style demanded by industrialization. Yet the machine promised to improve the material conditions of life and re-

TABLE 4.3   WEEKLY WORKING HOURS, SELECTED COUNTRIES

	1870	1913	1929	1938	1950	1960	1967	1971
Britain	63.0	53.8	46.9	46.5	45.9	46.1	43.3	42.2
France	63.0	53.8	48.0	38.7	45.0	45.9	46.1	45.1
Germany	63.0	53.8	46.0	48.5	48.2	45.6	42.3	43.2
United States	63.0	53.8	44.2	35.6	40.5	39.7	40.0	37.0

Adapted from Angus Maddison, *Economic Growth in the West* (New York: Twentieth Century Fund, 1964), p. 228, and International Labour Office, *Yearbook of Labour Statistics 1956–1967* (Paris, 1969), p. 163, and *Yearbook of Labour Statistics, 1972* (Paris, 1972), p. 475.

duce the effort required for achieving a satisfactory level of existence. This promise has slowly been fulfilled. In every European country, hours of work have gradually been reduced.

At least as important, the standard of living of the average worker has risen sharply since World War II (see Table 4.4, p. 69). In some cases, his style of life is no longer qualitatively different from that of other social groups; moreover, the expansion of state and social services has given him more and more protection against unemployment and illness, as well as the opportunity to obtain the skills necessary for moving a step or two up in the class system.

Working conditions, too, have improved. Though the average factory worker still performs rather simple, relatively meaningless tasks, industrial plants often provide reasonably congenial surroundings; also, in recent years, more attention has been paid to creating patterns of social relations in the plant that reduce the tedium of the work situation. There is also evidence that opportunities for in-plant promotion have expanded.

Finally, workers as a class are no longer merely acted upon. As a group, they play a much more active role in making social policy than it did a hundred or even fifty years ago. In every Western country, trade unions are now a legitimate part of the power structure, however much their strength and roles may vary. In every Western country, too, the worker is fully enfranchised and has access to information that enables him to participate at least to some extent in political life.

All these changes are the result of an increasing affluence, of the transformation of social attitudes over the past hundred years, and of workers' having developed mechanisms for protecting and advancing their own interests. Primary among these mechanisms are the trade unions, in part the direct descendants of the old artisan guilds and in part new creations.

It is little wonder, then, that some significant changes have occurred in working-class consciousness, and in the distinctive qualities of working-class culture. The European worker's life has become increasingly private; more workers seem to be spending evenings at home watching television and weekends and vacations on the road in their new cars. Many workers who once thought primarily of rising with their class are increasingly concerned with making more money as individuals. More and more skilled and even semiskilled workers now have the earning power, the fringe benefits, and the employment security of middle-class white-collar workers, and their life-styles have become similar as well. In outlook and orientation, the working class is closer to other strata today than it was twenty years ago, if only because almost all segments of the population have come to share elements of a common mass culture.

Class and class differences have not disappeared, however. The evidence that we have indicates a diminished intensity of conflict

TABLE 4.4 OWNERSHIP OF CONSUMER DURABLES BY WHITE– AND BLUE–COLLAR WORKERS IN FRANCE, 1963 AND 1971

Percentage of families owning at least one

	All families		White-collar		Blue-collar	
	1963	1971	1963	1971	1963	1971
Washing machine	31%	60%	34%	65%	37%	68%
Refrigerator	41	83	53	90	43	86
Television set	27	74	30	79	31	79
Automobile	39	58	40	62	36	67

Source: Institut National de la Statistique et des Études Économiques, *Annuaire Statistique de la France, 1973* (Paris: INSEE, 1973), p. 575.

among classes, rather than a decline in awareness of class as such. Industrial conflicts have been institutionalized, and working-class organizations have developed an established pattern of relations with employers' groups and the state for resolving most industrial conflicts. Nevertheless, much of the anger of class consciousness remains and explodes in numerous violent strikes in France, and a large number of "unofficial" strikes in Britain. Under pressure from their followers, union leaders have increasingly demanded a greater portion of the economic pie. More recently there have been growing demands for greater authority by workers and their representatives over decisions taken at the factory level. Thus, despite the relative affluence of European workers, and despite the changes in working-class life-style, a new militancy and new issues continue to nurture class differences.

Among the most important developments in all European societies during the past fifty years has been the increase in the number of white-collar workers and professional people. The emergence of a stratum of white-collar workers was a result of the increasing size and differentiation of economic enterprises and the consequent devolution and bureaucratization of managerial authority. In France, white-collar workers constituted about 2.3 percent of the nonagricultural work force in 1851, 18.2 percent in 1921, 23.3 percent in 1946, and more than 30 percent today, including government employees.

The present figure for Germany and Britain is also more than 30 percent.

The increase in the number of white-collar workers and the decline in status differentiation between white-collar and blue-collar workers have undoubtedly contributed to a convergence in their political orientations. White-collar workers have never been quite so attached to the status quo as was the old "independent" middle class, and have usually tended to support, or at least accept, political action regulating private property. The reasons for this are fairly clear. In smaller, more traditional factories, white-collar workers can identify with management. They are salaried whereas blue-collar workers are not, and their relationships with employers are likely to be nformal. In larger enterprises this relationship does not hold, nor does it exist where work becomes routinized and impersonal—that is, where it increasingly resembles that of industrial workers. German studies, for example, have shown that white-collar workers in large modern factories are more inclined to express dissatisfaction with their jobs and to vote Socialist than their counterparts in smaller, more traditional business enterprises.[7] Studies in France indicate considerable dissatisfaction and collective consciousness among the growing number of

[7] Juan Linz, "The Social Basis of German Politics" (unpublished doctoral dissertation, Columbia University, 1958), p. 538.

white-collar workers. In a survey published early in 1968, more white-collar workers than any other socioeconomic category reported that they belong to a class and that they felt class conflict to still be a reality. Furthermore, almost three quarters of those surveyed, once again more than any other socioeconomic category, felt that France's increased wealth is being distributed inequitably.[8]

THE BRITISH PATTERN: By the first quarter of the nineteenth century, a substantial modern working class had developed in Britain. It included those in traditional crafts such as the building trades, but it was increasingly augmented by unskilled ex-farmers working at jobs created by the machine—jobs that involved simple operations within the framework of a factory system. In trades not eliminated by the machine, modern trade unions were created, or evolved out of the old guilds. By the middle of the nineteenth century a number of strong craft unions had been established, and by the end of the century the unskilled and semiskilled were also moving quickly into trade-union organizations. In 1894 the total number of British workers in trade unions was about 1,530,000. By 1914 the figure had risen to more than 4,000,000, or well over one-third of the working force.[9] Except for short periods, this percentage has never been equaled in France. It was not achieved until the 1930's in the United States, where the number of workers in trade unions has dropped back to about 30 percent.

In America a lack of class consciousness and the acceptance of economic individualism by the workers hampered the development of an effective trade-union movement. In France, the sharp cleavages that ran through the working class, the violent hostility of the peasantry and the business elites,

and the rather slow pace of industrialization inhibited the growth of trade unions. In Britain, on the other hand, there was the workers' sense of class solidarity and discipline, an intense class consciousness and pride that, for many workers, was combined with a sense of deference toward "betters." The attitudes of British businessmen were also important. In contrast with American businessmen, who saw trade unions as violating the sacred doctrine of laissez-faire, or with French businessmen, who tended to equate unions with revolution, British businessmen, reflecting the carry-over of traditional values, saw trade unions as merely one of the corporate organizations, "estates," of which society is composed.

Working-class solidarity plus the relatively favorable attitude of British elite groups resulted in the passage of legislation facilitating trade-union growth. The Combination Acts, which had prohibited organizations of either working men or employers, were repealed in 1824–25, and although unions were inhibited by various restrictions until 1867 (and to a certain extent even until the Trades Disputes Act of 1906), their legality and that of peacefully conducted strikes were acknowledged by the middle of the nineteenth century. The National Insurance Act of 1911, which provided medical and other benefits for workers, included a provision that such funds be administered in part by the trade unions. Thus, in effect, the state was encouraging workers to join trade unions, and within two years after passage of the bill union membership rose by more than a million.

Britain differed from France in that the development of working-class self-consciousness did not result in an upsurge of violence. This was partly because of the influence of Methodism upon the working-class elite (a good many trade-union organizers began as Methodist lay preachers), and partly because the British working class—in a society in which important elites had demonstrated a sense of social responsibility—did not feel as alienated as the French.

8 *Sondages*, no. 1 (1968), p. 45. Also see Seymour Martin Lipset, *Political Man* (Garden City, N.Y.: Doubleday & Co., 1963) p. 254.

9 B. C. Roberts, *Trade Union Government and Administration in Great Britain* (Cambridge, Mass.: Harvard University Press, 1956), pp. 472, 474.

Violence did threaten to flare up between 1900 and 1914 as the unions of the unskilled developed, and a newly self-conscious generation of trade-union organizers found themselves attracted to Marxist and syndicalist doctrines. However, the very success of the trade-union movement served to weaken such impulses. The trade unions provided a career for the ambitious and transformed young radicals into "responsible leaders" who had large union treasuries to worry about. Moreover, trade-union leaders who negotiated as equals with businessmen found it increasingly difficult to think of the business community as an undifferentiated, totally wicked "them"; workers with powerful unions to protect them and advance their interests felt that they now had a stake in the existing system. In the next generation, in fact, the early militants were to be replaced by men who had worked up slowly in the union hierarchy and were emotionally more attuned to the boardroom than to the picket line. There were exceptions to this mode of accommodation on the part of union leaders in industries with a long record of bad labor-management relations, such as mining. But in general, the success of British trade unionism encouraged moderation.

In 1868 the major British trade unions joined to form the Trades Union Congress (TUC), whose function it was not only to shape common policy but also to enable the unions to bring their total strength to bear in lobbying for desired legislation. Over the years, the authority of the TUC has slowly grown. Individual unions still retain a good deal of independence, but compared with the United States, where trade unions gained only a precarious and short-lived unity on the national level after World War II, and with France, where such unity has never been achieved, British ability to subordinate the interests of individual unions to a larger whole is rather impressive. Here again the class consciousness of British workers had considerable impact, as did the tradition by which society is seen as made up of estates rather than merely individuals. The British trade-union movement also differed from the French and American movements in that it was instrumental in founding a Socialist party, the Labor Party, to which it is still closely tied.

Today membership in unions is well over ten million, almost 43 percent of the total labor force, but it varies widely from industry to industry. Something like 90 percent of those who work in coal mines are union members, compared with some 15 percent in distributive trades. The movement is dominated by a few large "general" and industrial unions, such as the Transport and General Workers Union (T&GWU); the eight largest unions contain almost 50 percent of the total membership. The T&GWU alone has a membership of almost 1.5 million. By the beginning of the 1970's the question being asked was whether these unions, increasingly dominated by left-wing leadership, might not be opening a new chapter in Britain's industrial relations and, through their influence on the Labor Party, upon its political history. With the country facing unprecedented economic difficulties—including soaring inflation—worker militancy seemed to be increasing; the word "moderate" was becoming anathema, and the slogans of class conflict were as conspicuous in union oratory as they had ever been.

Even earlier, the nature of trade-union organization in England had begun to raise new problems. Originally, British unions were organized on the basis of individual crafts; as with so many other aspects of British life, the traditional pattern has continued to exert a good deal of influence. Thus, even the so-called general or industrial unions like the huge Transport and General Workers Union, are basically amalgamations of various craft groups. Since negotiations are conducted by craft or job on a national level, the national leadership is unequipped to handle problems in any given plant; such matters are left to the shop stewards of the various unions represented there. Further, most unions tend to have something of a "craft" mentality, and are greatly concerned with preserving the particular jobs, however obsolete or unskilled, of their members. Unions then have been quite conservative about automation and other attempts to rationalize the organization of work.

The result has been a substantial growth of "flash" (unofficial) strikes—strikes led by shop stewards at the plant level—which even when not endorsed by the national leadership, have had cripping effects upon productivity. The pattern is such that a settlement with one group of workers at a plant can be followed by walkouts by others as each attempts to improve its position. Thus, although the actual number of working days lost per year because of strikes has often been less than either in France or the United States, the relative damage to the British economy has been greater.

As important as the economic impact of strikes has been, their visibility to the British public has been equally important; they intrude conspicuously upon the everyday life of the British citizen as he finds that his train to work has been canceled, that his mail is not delivered, or that the power supply to his home or place of work is threatened. Prime Minister Heath attempted, unsuccessfully, to capitalize upon public resentment against work stoppages when he prematurely called for a general election in early 1974. In the midst of an economic emergency, precipitated by the Arab oil embargo but exacerbated by a slowdown and later a strike by coal miners demanding higher pay, and with the entire country forced to work only a three-day week, Heath ran on the platform of "Who Runs Britain?" Although the electorate did not respond in the way Heath had hoped, and indeed seemed to have sympathy for the miners, the fact that the small parties, rather than the Labor Party, benefited most from the swing away from the Conservative government suggested that the prime minister was not entirely inaccurate in his assessment of the public's view of such trade-union tactics. Indeed, polls have shown that large numbers of working-class voters believe that British trade unions are too powerful and that they

have injured the nation's economy by unwarranted strikes.

Popular sentiment made it possible for the Labor government in 1968 to introduce an industrial-relations bill that, *inter alia,* would have allowed the government to invoke a twenty-eight-day "conciliation pause" when a strike was threatened. Vehement opposition from the Trades Union Council and from the left wing of the Labor Party, however, forced the Labor government to withdraw its own bill, an occurrence virtually unprecedented in modern parliamentary history. A Conservative government, more resistant to these pressures, enacted its own industrial-relations bill amidst even greater parliamentary turmoil in 1971. Industrial relations clearly worsened under the new act, however, so that even the business community came to call for its repeal. The new Labor government elected in 1974 placed top priority upon drawing up a new measure.

THE FRENCH PATTERN: Until 1884, to be a French worker was, in effect, to live in a police state. Trade unions were still illegal (although partly tolerated); workers were forced to carry a passbook (livret) which they presented to local police authorities upon assuming a new job. They could not change jobs unless their previous employer signified that they had fulfilled all their legal obligations to him.

Both the *livret* and the restrictions upon associations of workers had their origins in the Revolution and its aftermath. The legal prohibition of trade unions was partly based on the belief that no group should interfere with the free contractual relationship between employer and employee; but bourgeois antagonism to working-class organization, sustained by the class antagonism that permeated French life, was also relevant.

Trade unions were finally legalized in 1884, twenty years after Napoleon III had given French workers the right to strike. Their growth, however, was inhibited by the same factors as before: the slowness of French industrialization, the small size of the French firm, and the French business-man's deep hostility toward unions. But there were internal causes as well: like other classes, French workers showed a persistent resistance to disciplined organization, and union organizations themselves thwarted political affiliation with the Socialist parties that claimed to speak for the working class. Instead, the unions advocated a syndicalist ideology which maintained that no bourgeois politicians, whatever their party, could be trusted and that any improvement in the workingman's lot must come through the direct action of the working class itself, through its own organizations.

Thus, before World War I, French industrial relations were characterized by violent strikes, often just as violently repressed, and by the failure of French workers to establish a mass trade-union organization. Moreover, union organizations were unable to control the strike and to use it as a weapon for bargaining. More often than not strikes tended to be angry outbursts at particular plants rather than a considered part of union strategy. Just after the war, the *Confédération générale du travail*—CGT (General Confederation of Labor), which had united in 1895, developed a reformist "minimum program." With a massive influx of new members, the CGT leadership was confident it could bring about meaningful changes. It overestimated its ability to control and direct strikes, however, and the years between 1918 and 1922 were marked by a series of disastrous, uncontrolled massive strike movements that overwhelmed and frustrated the confederation leaders. In addition, the reformist program and the impact of the Russian Revolution badly divided the leaders and militants, and in 1921 the CGT split, with the radical faction forming its own organization, the *Confédération générale du travail unifié* (CGTU) By the late twenties, the CGTU had come under the aegis of the French Communist Party. Trade-union membership, which had jumped into the millions at the end of the war, declined precipitously.

The pattern recurred again and again. In 1936, after the election of the Popular Front government, trade-union membership grew quickly, and the CGT and CGTU merged; as before, the decline was just as swift, and the Communists were forced out of the CGT. The end of World War II brought yet another influx of workers, and trade-union membership rose to more than six million; again, Communist and reformist trade unions merged, and again with the onset of the cold war, the organization split. This time the Communist-dominated faction retained control over the CGT, and the reformist elements were forced to build their own organization, the *Confédération générale du travail/Force ouvrière*—CGT/FO (General Confederation of Labor—Workers' Force). By 1952, total trade-union membership was well below three million.

The CGT has remained the most important national trade-union organization, despite the fact that its membership is probably less than two million.[10] After a period of isolation during the fifties, the CGT began to collaborate in the sixties with other union organizations and to plan an active role in collective negotiations with employers and the state. The *Force ouvrière*, on the contrary, has stagnated; except for a few manufacturing areas, its membership consists largely of white-collar workers.

The strongest of the non-Communist national union organizations today is the former French Confederation of Christian Workers (*Confédération française des travailleurs chrétiens*—CFTC). Founded as a specifically Catholic trade union that hoped to bring workers back to the Catholic Church, it originally attracted white-collar employees and was relatively conservative. After World War II, however, the CFTC came under the dominance of young militants who had emerged from the *Jeunesse ouvrière chrétienne*—JOC (Young Christian Workers) and the Resistance. At the same time, the CFTC broadened its industrial base.

[10] Characteristically, it is difficult to obtain accurate figures on trade-union membership in France. Unions regularly offer inflated estimates.

Though it worked actively with the Popular Republican Movement, serving as a liberalizing influence, it also made less and less of its religious origins, and, in 1964, it changed its name to the *Confédération française démocratique du travail*—CFDT (French Democratic Confederation of Labor). A few of the more conservative unions have since split with the new organization in order to retain their traditional Christian orientation, even as the CFDT has become more militant. In 1968, the CFDT was the only major trade-union organization that unabashedly supported the student upheaval. In many ways, the CFDT has become considerably more radical than the CGT, and for the first time the CGT is being challenged from the left.

Thus the French trade union movement remains highly fragmented; anarchist unions and a substantial number of unaffiliated unions continue to exist. Furthermore, more than 75 percent of French workers do not belong to any union organization whatsoever. Probably no more than 20 percent of the industrial blue-collar workers belong to a union. White-collar workers in private industry are also poorly organized, but probably a majority of those in the public services belong either to a union associated with one of the national confederations, or to *la Fédération de l'education nationale*—FEN (Federation of National Education), the independent union of public school teachers.

Nevertheless, the strike level and participation of non-affiliated workers in strikes remain high. As in the past, the central union organizations make little attempt to control the initiation of strike action. Strikes that are initiated by union organizations are often called for only a few hours or for a day, the purpose being to "test the climate," or to demonstrate the influence and representativeness of the union that calls them. Indeed, with small memberships, French union organizations depend for their bargaining power on the expansion of strike movements among unorganized workers.

By 1968, the condition of French workers had improved far less than that of their British and German counterparts. Skilled workers, especially, were beginning to share in the consumer revolution, but many of the less skilled were earning wages not much higher than in the 1920's. Whereas the distribution of income among various strata of the British and German populations had become more nearly equal, the opposite was true in France.[11] Charles de Gaulle had preferred to concentrate on economic growth and on "grandeur" in the form of nuclear weapons rather than on social-welfare measures. Whatever advances the working class had made in the postwar period owed little to collective bargaining; rather, they came from a fairly tight labor market; political decisions establishing minimum wages, vacations, and social benefits; the extension by administrative fiat of some private agreements to whole categories of workers; and the unilateral action of a few enlightened employers.

The spontaneous strikes of 1968 paralyzed the nation. The exact number of strikers is not certain, but perhaps as many as ten million, half the working population, were idle by the end of May. It is clear that the rapid spread of the strikes was related to the modernization of France during the postwar period. Transistor radios and television helped spread the news of each successive strike and of factory occupations throughout the country, and the largest plants became focal points for the expanding strike movement. Although there were some demands for "worker control," the demands by strikers remained relatively moderate. Workers in some areas were reluctant to end their occupation of factories, but most French workers were less interested in overturning the system than in gaining a greater share of its profits. The strikes were settled only after the government and employers' representatives promised sizable, across-the-board wage increases, the expansion of profit-sharing schemes, and plans for the establishment of "union presence" within the factory walls. (Plant unions had no legal standing in France before 1968.)

[11] Stephen R. Graubard, ed., *A New Europe?* (Boston: Houghton Mifflin Co., 1964), p. 350.

Continuing inflation, prompted partly by the strikes and by price rises permitted by the government, has eaten away some of the workers' gains; it has also faced the government with continuing unrest. Violent strikes, plant seizures, and clashes with the police have not ceased. Certainly the most dramatic plant seizure occurred in 1973 at the watch factory of the bankrupt Lip organization in eastern France. When the management of Lip decided to close the factory, the workers took over the plant and continued to produce and sell the watches themselves. After nine months of difficult negotiations, Lip was resuscitated and reopened in January, 1974.

Collective negotiations and administrative extensions have brought some important gains including a 1970 national agreement improving the blue-collar worker's security by requiring that by 1975 he be paid a monthly salary rather than an hourly wage. Nevertheless, a sense of collective deprivation remains strong among blue-collar workers and among the growing number of white collar workers as well.

The events of 1968 marked the emergence of a younger generation of militant workers who seem to expect a great deal more than their fathers did. They are less content with the old revolutionary slogans and are less satisfied by symbolic gains. Much of the violence and the anger of strikes since 1968 (and even before) has been an expression of this discontent. Union organizations have remained weak, however, and have found it difficult to channel expressions of mass unrest into political action.

THE GERMAN PATTERN: As in Britain, German workers began to organize early in the process of industrialization. In fact, given Germany's late start and the laws (in effect from 1878 to 1890), against trade unions, they grew at a remarkable pace; by 1913 about three million workers were union members.

Socialist intellectuals provided the major impetus for trade-union organization in Germany. Though a few unions were avowedly nonpolitical and nonideological, most were closely tied to the German Social Democratic Party and, from the beginning, accepted as their ultimate aim the creation of a Socialist society. The Socialist, or "free," unions quickly developed a national organization, the General Commission of Trade Unions, which after World War I, became the *Allgemeine Deutsche Gewerkschaftsbund* (General German Federation of Labor).

Both the ideological orientation and the effective organization of German trade unions are to be explained partly by the same variables that affected almost every European country. To these, however, must be added the rapidity with which Germany industrialized, the high concentration of German industry, and the characteristic German capacity for organization and discipline.

Like their British counterparts, the leaders of the German trade-union movement became more moderate as trade unions grew in size; they also became essentially reformist even as they retained revolutionary slogans —despite a temporary upsurge of Communist strength just after World War I. The unions' deference to both tradition and constituted authority may have served to reduce their economic and political effectiveness; but it should also be remembered that the Socialist trade unions were among the few important groups that were fully committed to democracy throughout the Weimar period.

Immediately after Germany's defeat in World War II, the trade-union movement began to reorganize with strong encouragement from the Allies, who regarded trade-union leaders as among the most responsible democratic individuals within the country. Initially the unions adopted a traditional Socialist program; but the cold war, the success of the Christian Democrats' "free market policy," the change in Socialist Party leadership, and the general erosion of ideological divisions prompted a turn to other policies. Most trade-union leaders came to see their primary task to be the creation of a fully unified trade-union movement. Thus the *Deutscher Gewerkschaftsbund*—DGB (German Federation of Trade Unions), created in 1949, specifically disassociated itself from the Socialist Party and maintained that officially, at least, it would remain politically neutral and would concern itself only with pressing for the universal well being of the working class. It thus adopted the American model of "nonpolitical" trade unionism. As a result, it was able to attract the Christian unions and several others that had once refused to affiliate with the DGB for ideological reasons.

The DGB today has a membership of some seven million—about 30 percent of the total working force. Its growth rate has declined in recent years; even the ratio of union members to the total working force has dropped. Varying widely, the proportion of union members is highest among miners, metal workers, and railroad workers and lowest, as might be expected, among agricultural and trade workers. The organization's federal structure is probably somewhat stronger than its British counterpart, but the individual unions that compose it still have considerable leeway.

Traditionally, German unions organized according to craft or occupation, with white-collar workers, manual workers, and civil servants all belonging to separate unions. The sharpness of status differences in Germany intensified these divisions. After 1945, however, the number of unions was deliberately reduced, and they were regrouped along industrial lines. Thus, today, the DGB consists of sixteen vertical unions, of which the metal workers, miners, and public-service unions are the most important. The DGB is not, however, the only German federation. The *Deutscher Beamtenbund* (German Federation of Civil Servants) had some seven hundred thousand members primarily in the civil service, and the *Deutsche Angestelltengewerkschaft* (German Union of White-Collar Workers) has approximately five hundred thousand members.

Even though the DGB has formally maintained political neutrality, its sympathies are clearly with the Social Democrats, and it still works closely with them. Some of the unions—the Metal Workers, for example,

which is the most powerful component of the DGB, and the largest labor union in Europe —are even more closely connected to the party. Conflict over political leanings did lead to one split within the DGB in 1953, when many Catholic unionists left the parent organization in protest over an election manifesto that they regarded as too pro-Socialist. With strong support from some members of the Catholic clergy and some encouragement from Chancellor Konrad Adenauer, they organized a German Christian Trade Union Movement; but its total membership has never exceeded two hundred thousand.

German trade unions have no formal status at the plant level. Instead, workers at each factory are represented by an elected "works council," which has certain rights to "co-determination" and consultation on various matters affecting working conditions and personnel policy. These councils were first conceived during the Weimar period by moderate Socialists who hoped thus to insure workers' participation in plant management.

German trade unions pressed hard for the principle of co-determination after World War II, and in 1951 the government passed a law establishing co-determination in the coal-mining, iron, and steel industries. This principle was extended to several other sectors in 1952. In effect, it guarantees worker participation in managerial decisions on questions such as changes in the nature of the enterprise, mergers, and shutdowns. It was hoped that such participation would help to democratize the economic system, but although labor representatives have had some influence, they are still not equal partners in managerial decision-making.

As part of their election promise to continue the growth of the German economy as well as to make its fruits more equitably available, the Social Democrats substantially amended the co-determination act in 1971. The most recent act sets up a company-wide works council in every enterprise with more than twenty employees. Today with some 14,200 union works councils operating in factories, stores, and offices and another

TABLE 4.5 COMPARISON OF DAYS LOST THROUGH INDUSTRIAL DISPUTES
Per thousand persons employed

	Average for 5 years (1953–1957)	Average for 5 years (1958–1962)	Average for 10 years (1953–1962)	Average for 5 years (1962–1966)	Average for 5 years' (1967–1971)	Average for 10 years (1962–1971)
France	550	238	394	322	312 [1]	318 [2]
Britain	282	318	300	228	596	412
West Germany	122	16	69	34	78	56

[1] Average for 1967 and 1969–1971 only.

[2] Average for 1961–1967 and 1969–1971 only.

Sources: Adapted from *Ministry of Labour Gazette* 71 (October, 1963): 400, and *Department of Employment Gazette* 80 (October, 1972): 899.

38,000 works councils operating in companies where labor is not organized by unions, a very large part of the nonagricultural sector of the country is working to some degree under the principle of co-determination, and proposals have been made to grant workers parity representation on corporate boards as well as to appoint persons to represent their interests in day-to-day management decisions.

Unquestionably, the average worker is still more concerned with wages than in policy making, and it was his (or her) acceptance of the need to increase production in order to increase wages that helped bring about the German economic miracle. Given this orientation German workers have been relatively quiescent in the postwar period as against their French or British counterparts.

However, there is at least some evidence that this may change in the future, especially if the Federal Republic loses some of its competitive edge in the world market and if unemployment—which has been increasing since 1973—continues to rise. As is the case with workers in other European countries, full employment and constantly rising real wages have been assumed to be the natural order of things. Anything which threatened these aspirations to affluence could have significant political results.

In Germany, as in other industrial nations, status differences among various social strata have continued to decline since World War II, even as opportunities for social mobility have increased for the working class. Indeed, it is more and more difficult to speak of a ruling elite. Rather, what we find is a number of functional elites which are more or less separate from each other and which hold sway over different power centers within the nation. Thus, political sociologists speak of political, economic, communications, and bureaucratic elites. Among the various hierarchies it is probably the political which is most open.[12]

Beyond this, continued economic prosperity and various welfare measures have considerably improved the condition of the working class and contributed to the relative decline of class antagonism as compared to the Weimar period. Inequalities, of course, persist. Indeed, income is probably less equally distributed today than it was immediately after World War II, with those Germans who are "self-employed" (everyone from peddlers to owners of industrial

[12] See Klaus von Beyme, *Die Politische Elite in der Bundesrepublik Deutschland* (Munich: Piper, 1971), p. 205.

TABLE 4.6   SOCIAL STRATA IN WEST GERMANY, 1970

Social Strata	Present generation	Father's generation	Paternal grandfather's generation
Self-employed professionals	2.0%	1.8%	1.6%
Civil servants	10.8	11.3	8.5
Salaried professionals, managers, clerical and sales persons	24.0	11.5	5.4
Entrepreneurs, businessmen, independent artisans	10.5	15.8	21.2
Farmers	5.5	13.8	24.1
Skilled workers and salaried artisans	35.4	30.5	21.4
Other workers	11.8	15.3	17.8
Number of cases	(11,418)	(11,467)	(6,562)

Adapted from Gerhard Kleining, "Struktur- und Prestigemobilitaet in der Bundesrepublik Deutschland," *Koelner Zeitschrift fuer Soziologie und Sozialpsychologie* 23 (1971): 9, reprinted by permission of the author.

plants) earning on the average twice as much as salaried workers. Further, while educational opportunities are expanding, only 12 percent of university students come from working-class backgrounds even though the working class constitutes approximately 53 percent of the population.

These continued inequalities have been one of the strongest sources of student criticism of the political order. Nevertheless, Germany today is more socially homogeneous than at any time in its modern history, and the trend seems to be toward decreasing status and class differences.

5

Sources and Organization of Political Conflict: Religious, Ethnic, and Regional Differences

1. THE CHURCH: BELIEF AND POWER

Almost all major civilizations have developed a distinction between the world of the spirit and the world of the flesh. The contrast between Christianity and Eastern religions lay not in that distinction, but rather in the fact that the Christian Church counseled secular action as the road to salvation, assumed that both sacred and profane experience could be understood through the application of human reason, distinguished sharply between religious institutions and political ones, and placed great emphasis upon the individual's personal relations to a transcendent deity.

These Christian values profoundly affected European development. They were relat-

ed to the emergence of the scientific world view. They supported activities that required the inhibition of individual desires in the interest of the larger community. They sanctified existing authority relations and the system of social stratification. Most importantly, religious institutions insured that members were socialized into the community —that they were provided with those standards and beliefs necessary for performing the tasks that would enable the society to adapt effectively to its environment.

The secularization of political authority, which occurred first in the West, produced a tension between secular and religious institutions that has continued into our time. It resulted in greatly diminished authority for the organized church within the larger framework of the nation-state, and it placed religious institutions in competition with other powerful groups for political privilege and influence. In the European countries that we are discussing, the simultaneous existence of numerous religious communities, as well as communities whose avowed intention has been the elimination of religion, has made this competition intense. Thus both Catholic and Protestant churches have often been active contestants in European political conflicts about policy, and in conflicts about the nature of the regime.

2. THE DEVELOPMENT OF CHRISTIANITY IN WESTERN EUROPE

THE ROMAN CATHOLIC CHURCH: By the thirteenth century, the Roman Catholic Church in the West had been transformed from a loosely organized sect of "religious enthusiasts" into a highly institutionalized bureaucratic structure of authority, a complex hierarchy of religious officials whose apex was the pope. The authority of the papacy, by no means absolute, continued to be challenged by those who claimed that ultimate legitimacy lay with general councils of church bishops; yet it was clear, even by that time, that the logic of the structure favored centralization. By that time, too, the church possessed the highly structured body of religious thought that it has retained, with relatively minor modification, to the present.

To the medieval church the universe was the creation of God. Both its structure and its ultimate purpose were determined by His will, and only by accepting the fact of this determination could one understand the world. Life itself was considered both a testing and a preparation for salvation, which could be achieved only through the Catholic Church (or, at least, was very unlikely to be achieved outside this church). A few men could come to God through knowledge, but for the vast majority the truths of the Catholic Church had to be con-

veyed through allegory and a symbolism that appealed to the soul; thus the church's role was that of a teacher. Its goal was to control education in the widest sense, including the prohibition of books and other materials that might be harmful to faith.

According to the church, the individual, in this life, was to follow his calling—to take his natural place in a community governed by secular leaders whose authority, ultimately derived from God, was justified only if they fulfilled their proper function: the organization of human activity so as to achieve the general welfare, and full cooperation with the church to insure a Christian (that is, Catholic) community.

In the sight of God, all men were equal—in fact, a poor man might have an edge on salvation; still, the church taught that inequality in this world was natural and justified, a reflection of man's fall from grace. This justification entailed support of private property, but it did not follow that such property could be used willfully and irresponsibly; the rich were responsible for the poor, and their wealth had to be used in accordance with certain ethical precepts. Thus, employers were required to provide a just wage, and money was not to be lent at interest; the community, in fact, had the right to regulate economic activities in close detail so as to insure that these contributed to its overall welfare.

Within the community, man's natural state was monogamous marriage (except for those who remained celibate in response to a higher calling). Because the institution of marriage was sanctified, neither divorce nor extramarital sexual activity was permitted. The purpose of marriage was procreation; it followed that the artificial limiting of the family violated both divine and natural law.

From the sixteenth century onward, the Catholic Church suffered a series of upheavals. Its secular power as well as its religious authority were weakened by the consolidation of the national state, the Protestant Reformation, and an increasingly scientific and secular culture.

THE REFORMATION: The Protestant Reformation in Europe took many forms, determined by accidental factors as well as the national tradition within which it developed. In Prussia and other German principalities, Lutheranism became the dominant religion and state church, exalting established hierarchical authority. Its authoritarian characteristics were as much German as Lutheran, as is indicated by its development in the Scandinavian countries, where Lutheranism was rather less authoritarian. In France, where Protestants were reduced to a small minority, Calvinism predominated. In England, the Anglican Church became the state church—a peculiarly English institution that after some evolution represented an uneasy compromise between a national Catholicism and the more radical Protestant churches. Among the latter, the Calvinist orientation quickly became uppermost, although just as quickly it fragmented into such sects as the Presbyterian, Congregationalist, Baptist, and Quaker.

The growth of a secular culture, the spread of liberalism, and the development of an industrial society in the eighteenth century—with its emphasis on free thought, free economic activity, and generally acquisitive economic values—represented an even more devastating attack on basic Catholic assumptions. Nor was this attack limited to the economic and political spheres: the newer concern with the satisfaction of individual wants and needs had its effect upon marriage, divorce, and general sexual morality.

On the whole the Protestant sects managed to adjust to these patterns with reasonable ease. Radical Calvinism had, in fact, been partially responsible for the newer outlook, and the radical separation of faith and science, which fairly early came to characterize the viewpoint of many Protestants, permitted the ready acceptance of scientific doctrines. The lack of a centrally organized authoritarian pattern of control and the frequent fragmentation of Protestantism also permitted, and even encouraged, prompt adjustment to newer trends in opinion. The same fragmentation contributed, as well, to an insistence on toleration within Protestant communities and the quick acceptance of, or even pressure for, a separation of secular and religious authority. All these circumstances were far less true of Lutheran Germany, of course, for reasons that will be dealt with later.

The slower adjustment of the Catholic Church to the patterns of an industrial society stemmed from a completely contrary set of factors. On the whole, the church clung to traditional doctrine and gave support to the traditional social order. This traditionalism caused liberals in Catholic countries (as opposed, for example, to Britain and the United States) to be strongly anticlerical, and to identify the Catholic Church with the medieval social order and the encouragement of fantastic superstition. It was, they believed, one of the major obstacles to the true human happiness that could be achieved through science, free trade, and a constitutionally tolerant political order.

The violent anticlericalism of the French Revolution was the result of all these factors and did not, as is often proposed, merely represent resentment of the large landholdings of the church; a similar anticlericalism spread, with the ideas of the Revolution, to other Catholic European countries.

The Catholic Church's reaction was to pronounce anathema on liberalism and all that was associated with it, although republican governments were considered legitimate provided they respected the right of the church to exercise authority over education and family life—hence the ready recognition of the new American republic in the eighteenth century. Still, through most of the nineteenth century the Catholic Church identified liberal democracy with "license" and militant atheism, and in almost every European country ranged itself with traditionalist elements. The mutual antagonism between liberal reformers and the church maintained itself as each group's actions confirmed the suspicions of the other. The most famous statement of the church's position in this regard was the encyclical *Quanta*

Cura and its attached Syllabus of Errors (1864), which leveled a violent attack upon popular sovereignty, toleration, and the whole liberal conception of freedom of thought.

The church's reaction to liberalism even caused it to forget some traditional doctrine. During the nineteenth century, for example, the church condemned trade unionism and social reform almost indiscriminately, associating these movements with anticlericalism and with ideas hostile to Catholicism. In such attitudes, of course, the church was rejecting its own traditional social message, or burying the more positive aspects of that message in a barrage of negative and purely defensive criticism.

Leo XIII, whose pontificate followed that of Pius IX in 1878, permitted some adjustments in church doctrine, even as he condemned "modernist" tendencies within the church. He was also prepared to accept democracy as a legitimate form of government under certain circumstances; moreover, he condoned religious toleration under conditions in which its denial would result in significant social evils. Leo's policies coincided with the beginnings of a decline in anticlericalism among European liberals. In most cases, church and state had become separated, and the real political power of the church effectively reduced; therefore, newer generations of liberals found themselves less and less antagonistic to the Catholic Church, and identified anticlericalism with socialism and later with communism.

This pattern continued and developed through the first part of the twentieth century, abetted by an increasingly social outlook in the church, as manifested in the encyclicals *Rerum novarum* (1891), *Quadragesimo anno* (1931), and *Mater et Magistra* (1961). In each of these the church lent its support to the legitimacy of working-class organization and pressed for social-reform legislation of varying kinds. By the beginning of the twentieth century, the Catholic Church had therefore reluctantly accepted the idea of a secular republic, and had freed its supporters to defend the interests of the church within such a political order. The conflict between church and state was changing from a conflict about the regime to a context over policy.

FERMENT: During the 1920's and 1930's, the Catholic Church flirted with Fascist and quasi-Fascist movements in several countries, hoping to reach a *modus vivendi* with them as a defense against communism. Since World War II, however, the papacy has tended increasingly to identify legitimate government with representative government, although it has refrained from criticizing church leadership in those countries where the church has continued to support authoritarian regimes.

Two other postwar developments have had their effect on the Catholic Church. The first has been the mounting pressure within it, especially in France, Germany, the United States, and in parts of Latin America, for a formal restatement of its attitude toward liberty and toleration, and a fuller acceptance of these values as good in themselves. The second has been the ecumenical movement. Christians became much more aware of the fact that what they have in common is at least as important as the differences among them.

The ferment within the church came to the surface during the short pontificate of John XXIII and has continued under his successor, Paul VI. The calling of a second Vatican Council (1962–65) not only revealed the power of more modern currents of thought and brought about pronouncements liberalizing the views of the church and increasing the power of the bishops, priests, and laity; it also provided psychological support for those within the church who held even more radical views. The Catholic Church today has fully accepted religious freedom; it is accepting, if not encouraging, a more active and questioning role on the part of the laity. Further, it has become open to varieties of modern biblical criticism that accept the method and findings of science and see much of traditional religious doctrine as metaphorically, not literally, true. Indeed, the Council implicitly accepted a very non-Thomistic view of theology, one that held that religious truth, rather than being fixed, might well evolve as mankind itself evolved. And finally, the church is attempting to identify itself with reform programs for the reduction of economic inequality and the promotion of social welfare.

Strong conservative elements remain within the church, however, as indicated by Paul VI's 1968 encyclical on birth control, which, to the disappointment of many, reaffirmed in even stronger terms the traditional Catholic stand on that issue. Aside from purely doctrinal considerations, the Vatican obviously was becoming more and more concerned with what it considered the precipitous decline of papal authority, as manifested in the formation of "underground" churches in many countries and in the increasing attacks upon the authority of bishops and the doctrines of clerical celibacy. If, indeed, the encyclical was designed to dampen desires for change, it failed dismally. Negative reactions among both the laity and the clergy were expressed with a stridency scarcely conceivable twenty years earlier, and many bishops, now openly critical of the Curia for what they consider its refusal to permit free discussion of basic issues in the church, are demanding a larger voice in its government.

Within Protestantism, too, searching analyses and criticisms of the Bible, and of revealed religion in general, proceeded apace. By the mid-twentieth century, traditional Protestant positions, including the belief in a personal deity standing apart from nature, were giving way to a conception of religion as one among many ways by which man tries to answer the ultimate personal and moral questions about his existence. The line between Protestantism and secular humanism is becoming increasingly blurred.

3. ETHNIC AND REGIONAL STRIFE

Ethnic and racial contact, conflict, and amalgamation, along with regional conflicts,

have been among the basic themes of human history. Western Europe itself is a fusion of many ethnic groups: Celts, Normans, Picts, Goths, Saxons, Vandals, whose identity and locale were gradually submerged in the larger territorial units that became nation-states. In general, the history of civilization is the development of ever larger social units, the members of which share a common identity.

Regional conflicts within European countries were a product of the consolidation of the European nation-state. They have been most intense, and remain important, where regional divisions are reinforced by religious or ethnic divisions. However, because of the migrations of various ethnic groups, ethnic conflict is not necessarily related to regional divisions.

Historically, cultural as well as physical differences among population groups have been the result of particular adaptations to diverse environments. These differences begin to erode as various people form a community. The pace of erosion is now growing because technology is producing a world culture—a culture sharing more and more common features imparted through the tremendous growth of communications and transportation networks, and through the imperatives of creating and maintaining an industrial society.

Initial contacts between ethnic groups have often been marked by considerable violence; the history of the world is a record of mass enslavement and murder. People—especially the militarily more efficient—competing for scarce resources have always found it psychologically easier to kill, exploit, or enslave than to reach a peaceful accommodation with those whose language and culture differed from their own. Even when groups have finally become part of a unified community, tensions have persisted; on occasion, they have been exacerbated by the very processes of change directed toward amalgamation. In highly traditional multi-ethnic societies, different groups could exist in relatively close proximity without even being aware of each other. But as economic and political development, growing economic interdependence, and competition broaden contact, recognition of ethnic differences begins to appear.

The problem of ethnic tension would be far simpler if, indeed, its sources were only economic; unfortunately, its roots lie much deeper. Every major society has been built on the repression of sexual and other instinctual drives. The success of repressive mechanisms has required that particular styles of life be reinforced with strong moral sanctions. There is no greater threat to an individual's equanimity than the discovery that those things that he holds sacred—and that involve repression—are not accepted by others. His equilibrium requires that sexual and other mores different from his own be condemned, and that those adhering to other standards be labeled savages, or barbarians. It is a short step from this attitude to the justification of exploitation or carnage. Thus, Europeans slaughtered Africans and American Indians without serious qualms; Christians slaughtered Muslims, Jews, and even fellow Christians. Jews, when they had the power, killed other peoples and seized their lands; Arabs enslaved or killed black Africans and Hindus; and Chinese slaughtered "barbarians." In southern Africa, the Bushmen were hunted down first by the Hottentots and then by the Boers.

In the twentieth century, ethnic conflict contributed to the outbreak of World War I, and the Nazi attempt to unite ethnic Germans into the Reich was the major factor behind the German expansionist impulse that set off World War II. Of course, the Nazi attempt to exterminate Jews marked the high point of ethnic hatred in Europe. Since World War II, more than eight million migrants have arrived in France, Germany, and Britain in search of employment opportunities, a search facilitated by the development of the European Community. The immigration has had certain common features. All three countries have needed unskilled workers, and it is these jobs that the immigrants have filled. Most of them have been young men, arriving either unmarried or without their families. Although the majority of them probably planned to return home, many have settled permanently in the host nation. In all three countries the migration has resulted in serious problems of accommodation, and conflicts between ethnic groups have sometimes led to outbursts of violence. At the same time events in both France and the United Kingdom have rekindled older ethnic conflicts which, until the 1960's, had been thought to be on their way to final resolution.

4. THE BRITISH PATTERN

RELIGIOUS CONFLICT: After a period of repression of Protestant sects during the Restoration, the Glorious Revolution of 1689 ushered in a settlement that paved the way for a religiously pluralistic society marked by relative toleration and, eventually, religious neutrality on the part of the state. Today the Church of England is still the officially established church, but in actuality it is little more than the largest. The monarch is its head, its representatives sit in the House of Lords, the highest members of the clergy are appointed by the queen (on the advice of her prime minister), and the creed of the church can be changed only by Parliament. In fact, however, the church is self-governing and self-supporting.

Until the mid-nineteenth century, the Catholic Church in Britain remained very small. Most Catholics were from old aristocratic families that had retained the faith. The great Irish migration changed all that. The Catholic population swelled, and tightly knit communities of Irish Catholic workers were established. But whether because their numbers were relatively small or because of the peculiarities of the British environment, such groups never proliferated as they did in Germany.

Surveys have shown that 69 percent of the English population regard themselves as members of the Church of England, 11 percent as Nonconformists (for example, Methodists, Baptists), and 10 percent as Catho-

TABLE 5.1   RELIGIOUS BELIEF: A FOUR–NATION SURVEY

	Percent of respondents believing in:			Percent of respondents attending church within last 4 weeks
	God	Life after death	The Devil	
Britain	77	38	21	21
France	73	35	17	47
West Germany	81	41	25	54
United States	98	73	60	64

Sources: Gallup International, as reported in *Gallup Political Index* (London), August, 1968; fieldwork, May, 1968. The responses on church attendance have been extrapolated from the reported data. The question asked British respondents was not identical with that asked respondents in the other three countries.

lics. (The proportion of Church of England members is much lower in Wales, Scotland, and Northern Ireland.)   Despite this indication of nominal identification, Britain today is largely a secular society, much more so than the United States. Whereas 21 percent of the British population attend church at least once a month, the figure in the United States is 64 percent; and whereas 98 percent of Americans when polled affirm a belief in God, and 73 percent in life after death, the comparable figures for Britain are only 77 percent and 38 percent (Table 5.1). The decline in Anglican church membership and attendance has been noticed since the turn of the century, and today many parish churches have been closed.

These secular trends notwithstanding, the state continues to grant heavy financial subsidies to church-run schools, mainly Anglican and Catholic, and since 1944 pupils in the state-run schools have been required to take a nondenominational course in religion. Reflective of the low salience of religion in contemporary British society, these practices have not been the subject of serious political debate. Nor have the subjects of abortion and birth control aroused controversy within the electorate, even though the National

Health Service subsidizes both practices. On none of these matters do the parties take stands, and voting behavior in Britain is only marginally influenced by religious identification.

ETHNIC AND REGIONAL CONFLICT: The United Kingdom is a conglomeration of four nations: England, Scotland, Wales, and Northern Ireland. The four have been united in a single kingdom only since 1801, though the union between England and Wales dates back to 1535 and that between England and Scotland to 1707. The loss of most of Ireland in 1922 reduced the Irish part of the kingdom to only the six northern counties. Each nation has its own history and cultural traditions, and one quarter of the population in both Wales and Northern Ireland each speaks its own language. Surveys have shown that majorities in each of the three Celtic nations do not regard themselves as Britishers or Englishmen, but rather as nationals of their own countries.

The three outer, ethnically defined regions within the United Kingdom have not usually been seen as presenting a serious political problem for the London-centered regime. Indeed, accounts of the political system of the United Kingdom have often either ignored their existence or have mistakenly spoken of the kingdom's population as being homogeneous. No doubt partly accounting for this perspective is the fact that the regions have comparatively small populations; Scotland comprises about 9 percent of the kingdom's population, Wales about 5 percent, and Northern Ireland 3 percent. Much more important, however, in explaining the absence of a serious political challenge from these regions are the steps which have been taken to institutionalize certain degrees of autonomous status.

These steps have been most conspicuous with respect to Ireland. The largest part of the Irish problem was "solved" in 1922 simply by granting complete independence to most of that island, which became the Irish Republic, and by granting to the remaining six northern counties semi-autonomous status, including their own constitution and parliament. While Scotland lacks its own parliament, a secretary of state for Scotland sits in the cabinet at Westminster and presides over the Scottish Office, the major component of which is located in Saint Andrew's House in Edinburgh. Scotland also has its own legal system, its own currency, and a distinctive system of local government. In the House of Commons Scotland can boast of more seats than its population would normally warrant (currently seventy-one seats rather than fifty-seven), and there is a standing committee on Scottish affairs. Provisions for Wales have been much less extensive, although a separate ministry for Wales was established in 1962. Wales also enjoys over-representation in the House of Commons.

These steps to prevent the intrusion of ethnic-regional politics into the national political arena have not been entirely successful. Since 1968 violence in Northern Ireland between the Protestant majority and Catholic minority has brought the "Irish question" back again into Parliament at Westminister, and in 1972 and again in 1974 the Constitution was suspended and direct rule from London imposed. At the political level, regional parties are beginning to play a significant role. Welsh and Scottish nationalist parties, founded in the 1960's, both won seats in the 1974 general elections, and Northern Ireland Protestants, who traditionally have worked within the Conservative

TABLE 5.2   NATIONAL IDENTITY IN SCOTLAND, WALES, AND NORTHERN IRELAND

Respondent thinks of self as	Scotland [1]	Wales	Northern Ireland
British	29%	15%	29%
English	—	13	—
Scottish	67	1	—
Welsh	1	69	—
Ulster	*	*	21
Irish	*	1	43
Other mixed, don't know	4	—	7

[1] Glasgow only.

* Alternative not offered.

Source: Separate surveys as compiled and reported in Richard Rose, *The United Kingdom as a Multi-National State* (Glasgow: University of Strathclyde, 1970), p. 10.

Party, broke away in 1974 to elect their own independent delegation to the House of Commons.

In an effort to appease nationalist sentiment, a Labor Government in 1969 appointed a Commission on the Constitution to examine the relations of the three Celtic nations, as well as regions within England, with the central government. The commission reported in 1973, urging a general devolution of political authority from London. However, because the members of the commission were not unanimous in their views and because some of the recommendations, such as the call for elected regional assemblies, could be expected to have far-reaching political implications, it was doubtful that the report would spur quick action.

To the kingdom's historic ethnic divisions has been added since the 1950's an ethnic problem within England. As the need for unskilled labor increased and the prospect of immigration quotas, in Britain and elsewhere, became more real, immigrants from Pakistan, India, and Jamaica increased rapidly, so that by 1970 this so-called "coloured" population had reached close to 3 percent of the total British population. In some urban centers, the proportion reached 10 percent. The Englishman's attitudes toward the "coloured" are a consequence of a general hostility toward "foreigners," compounded by the "color question" and cultural differences. As in the United States, the main difficulty has been housing. In 1965 Parliament prohibited discrimination in the rental or sale of apartments or houses, and three years later, the prohibition was extended to employment and trade-union membership.

Nevertheless, conflicts—including race riots—have erupted. The Conservative government, in response to public pressure, finally sponsored restrictive legislation, the Commonwealth Immigration Act of 1962, which clearly discriminated against "coloured" immigrants even though the bill made no mention of race or color. The Labor government continued these restrictions and, in 1965, reduced from 20,000 to 8,500 a year the number of West Indians and Asians that could enter the country. Immigration permits were restricted to those who had either specialized skills or jobs awaiting them in Britain. In 1968, faced with the fairly substantial immigration of Indians and Pakistanis from Kenya, the Labor government introduced, and Parliament quickly passed, legislation to exclude most of them. The public debates made it obvious that color was the principal factor involved. Anti-"coloured" sentiment ran high again in 1972 as 20,000 Asians ejected from Uganda were admitted into Britain. Obviously, the "color question" has become an issue in British politics, though the immigrants have not yet themselves formed a cohesive group within the political system.

5. THE FRENCH PATTERN

RELIGIOUS CONFLICT: For some time before the French Revolution, the Catholic Church in France had become identified with the worst aspects of the old regime. Its substantial landholdings were free from taxation, its clergy was not subject to regular courts of law, and its drive against heretical doctrines was enthusiastically supported by the state. Yet these close ties worked in both directions. The French monarchy, in turn, exercised considerable authority in determining who would fill various ecclesiastical offices, and it significantly influenced church policy in many respects. This mutually advantageous association helps explain why the enmity toward the monarchy on the part of those who led the French Revolution was extended to the church.

In general, the Catholic Church in France was hostile to the Third Republic, though the movement of many of the French clergy toward support of the republic was encouraged by Leo XIII, whose encyclical letter of 1892, *Au Milieu des Sollicitudes*, stated for the first time that the church was neutral with respect to forms of government, provided its own rights were protected. With the establishment of a strong republican majority in the French National Assembly in 1877, successive governments had been circumscribing the prerogatives of the church, particularly in education. The pope's letter, therefore, was received with extreme reservation, and as "foreign intervention," by some church leaders who opposed the secular policies of the Third Republic. Moreover, shortly after the issuance of the letter, the Dreyfus Affair erupted.

Captain Alfred Dreyfus, a French army officer of Jewish descent, was convicted in 1894 of treason and sent to Devil's Island. The conviction was based on forged evidence and was later rescinded, but in the meantime the affair polarized the French community, and the church once again identified itself with anti-republican France.

The aftermath of the Dreyfus affair was the full separation of church and state, and the end of state support for any church activities whatever. The decrees effecting this separation confiscated substantial amounts of church property, but this impoverishment was counteracted by the fact that the church now became a private organization, with no further governmental regulation of its activities.

The church's reluctant acceptance of the separation and the unity engendered by World War I served to diminish gradually the intensity of conflict between the state and the church hierarchy. Nevertheless, despite the *modus vivendi* between the organized church and the state, a wide gulf remained for a time between Catholic and secular France. To a great extent the "Catholic ghetto" was geographically separate from secular France, had a separate education system, separate career patterns, and different values. This separation was reinforced by the social and economic stagnation in France between the two world wars, and was manifested in extreme mutual distrust.

Since World War II, the social and economic development of France and the growing social commitment of church leadership have gradually reduced the gap between Catholic and secular France. To be sure,

practicing Catholics have continued to vote for parties of the right in large numbers, Catholics have continued to press for aid to Catholic schools, (which they received after 1951) and members of the hierarchy have sometimes urged support for the MRP (Popular Republican Movement) or the Gaullists to achieve this goal. On other issues, too, serious conflict has developed. In the fall of 1974, for example, the church strongly opposed government-supported legislation which eased France's prewar abortion law.

On the other hand the hierarchy no longer identifies its interests as closely with the political right as it once did, and bishops have frequently criticized the French business community. Beyond this, individual priests have taken active social reformist roles, and the Catholic youth movement has spawned some of the most active and "radical" trade union and peasant leaders in recent years. (See Chapter 4.) Indeed, liberal pressures for reform within the hierarchy are increasing.

In recent years the political attitudes of Catholic elites has often been far to the left of the political attitudes of the mass of observant Catholics, especially those most active in church affairs (see Table 5.3.) Nevertheless, the Catholic left has facilitated the reduction of distrust between Catholic and secular France that has existed since the revolution. Thus, in a survey taken in 1966, almost half the practicing Catholics declared that they would not be opposed to common action with the Communists, and fewer than 7 percent of the respondents (whether practicing Catholics or not) regarded aid to church schools as an important issue.[1]

The Protestant community in France is relatively small and has been so since the revocation of the Edict of Nantes in 1685 led large numbers of Protestants either to migrate or abjure their faith. While French Calvinism had obtained considerable support among the rural population, it had also

[1] *Le Nouvel Observeteur*, October 26, 1966, pp. 33–35.

TABLE 5.3   THE POLITICAL PREFERENCES OF FRENCH CATHOLICS
AND NON–BELIEVERS, 1973

Political preference	Practice		Non-prac-ticing	Consider self a Catholic	Belong or belonged to organization close to Catholicism
	Regularly	Sometimes			
Communist	1%	14%	32%	14%	18%
Socialist	10	22	31	22	24
Reform	16	13	11	14	12
Majority	70	47	20	46	43
Other	3	4	6	4	3

Adapted from *Sondages*, no. 1, 1973, p. 39.

drawn to it a significant proportion of the urban aristocracy and bourgeoisie. It was this group that suffered most and emigrated in the largest numbers, depriving France of many individuals who had contributed to its economic growth and scientific achievement. By the time persecution eased, the remnants of the French Protestant community consisted largely of peasants and the rural petite bourgeoisie.

Throughout the nineteenth century, legal discrimination against Protestants gradually diminished, and by 1905, when church and state were separated, French Protestants were free to worship as they chose. In the meantime, Protestants began to leave the countryside with greater frequency to enter industry, the professions, and politics; in all three fields, they came to exercise an influence beyond their numbers. Today Protestants tend to be concentrated in Alsace, the Paris region, and some wine-growing areas of south-central France. Of the approximately 800,000 Protestants—1.6 percent of the French population—more than 500,000 are urban dwellers. In rural areas, their class position does not differ markedly from that of their neighbors; in urban areas, however, their status is mostly middle class.[1]

[1] See A. Coutrot and F. Dreyfus, *Les Forces religieuses dans la société française* (Paris: Librairie Armand Colin, 1965), p. 114.

Throughout most of the nineteenth century, Protestants as a whole identified with the left, partly because they believed that a "*laïc*" republic would be more inclined to protect their interests than one dominated or supported by the Catholic Church. This pattern has continued to the present. The exceptions are the Lutherans of Alsace, who have remained more conservative.

Perhaps more significant, Protestants are represented far out of proportion to their numbers in important economic and political positions. Roughly two-thirds of them occupy positions in business, banking, and the civil service, and a large number of the leaders of the Socialist Party are well-known Protestants, a fact that perhaps contributes to the complaint by left-wing Catholics that they do not feel "at ease" with the Socialists.

ETHNIC AND REGIONAL CONFLICT: For more than two hundred years, the French monarchy, the French Empire, and the French republics have attempted to undermine the regional parochialism of the ancient French provinces, as well as much of the cultural uniqueness that supported that independence. By the end of the Napoleonic period, the provinces were under the firm administrative control of Paris, and the lines of communication came to correspond with the lines of political authority. It is not surprising, therefore, that organized regional political movements and interregional conflicts have been rare in modern France. Nevertheless, until recently many aspects of regional culture remained untouched by the central administration and were supported by a regional cultural revival during the Third Republic. In literature and film, regional differences were extolled as a protest against the political and cultural domination of Paris.

Since the end of World War II, however, the cultural uniqueness of even the most remote regions of France has been touched by the impact of spreading urbanization and industrialization. Frenchmen have begun to move about the country in growing numbers, diluting the old regional cultures with ideas and values of other regions—along with the values of urban-industrial society. Most of this constant movement has been into the cities, and today more than 70 percent of Frenchmen live in urban areas. Between 1962 and 1968 almost a third of the French population moved from the communes they had inhabited.

This economic and social change has not obliterated regional commitments and loyalties. In the past decade a revival of interest in regional culture and diversity, as an antedote to the rootlessness of modern industrial society, has once again occurred in many parts of France—an interest that has paralleled increasing political agitation for economic and political decentralization. The growing support for some kind of regional government has been related less to the cultural diversity of the country, however, than to a concern with the economic hegemony of the Paris region and, more recently, to political revitalization in the post–de Gaulle period. The concern with regional development led to administrative reorganization in the early 1960's and brought about in 1974 the establishment of regional assemblies, members of which are selected by the elected officials of the region.

Support for regional government has been fueled by the emergence of direct-action movements for regional autonomy in southern France, Corsica, and Brittany. The Bre-

ton Liberation Front engaged in a series of violent actions in 1968 and 1969 that evoked considerable sympathy from more moderate groups in the province. The region had been in economic decline for many years, and since the early 1950's it had experienced intense and often violent strikes by workers, fishermen and farmers. Without much question, the renewed regional consciousness has been accompanied by a sense of economic deprivation. Thus, at the very time that the old regions have lost many of their traditional supports because of political centralization, urbanization, and industrialization, they have gained new support from a revived interest in regional culture and a concern with uneven economic development.[2]

In the past, ethnic divisions have not been an important source of political conflict in France, despite the presence during the last century of large numbers of foreign residents. That so many non-French residents never became French citizens meant that they could not participate in the political life of the nation without risking deportation. Those foreigners who were able to assimilate French culture were generally accepted into French society; those who could not remained a community apart and made few demands upon the political system.

The French have done relatively little for the large postwar influx of migrant workers. Algerian immigrants, for example, are concentrated in the worst slums in France and are subject to many of the same prejudices experienced by black Americans. As a result, periodic outbursts of ethnic violence have occurred. In the fall of 1973, for example, an outbreak of violence and murder against Algerians took place in France after a bus driver in Marseille was killed by an Algerian worker. This was followed by strikes and demonstrations of immigrant workers, and by considerable soul searching in the intellectual and political communities.

The French National Assembly has passed legislation providing for civil and criminal

2 See Cynthia H. Enloe, *Ethnic Conflict and Development* (Boston: Little, Brown & Co., 1973).

penalties against employers who discriminate because of racial, ethnic, or national origins. Enforcement of the law has been lax, however, and large companies have been able to violate it with impunity.

6. THE GERMAN PATTERN

RELIGIOUS CONFLICT: German Catholicism developed along lines conditioned both by the general features of German culture and by the fact that until World War II Catholics were a distinct, though sizable, minority in a country dominated by a fairly conservative Protestant establishment.

As a self-conscious minority suffering from considerable discrimination, German Catholics early on sought to protect Catholic interests by developing a specifically Catholic political party, the Center Party. In addition, they created an extensive network of other organizations—trade unions, youth groups, newspapers, and agricultural associations—that aimed to insulate the Catholic community against the blandishments of Protestants and, if possible, to expand its influence.

The domination of Germany by Protestant Prussia (and, in general, of both Prussia and Germany by orientations that were centralizing, Lutheran Protestant, and autocratic) meant that Catholics found themselves taking a more liberal position than, they might have otherwise. Before World War I they supported constitutional limitations upon the monarch (after all, the monarchy was Protestant), federalism rather than centralism (a federal regime and local autonomy favored minority interests), and freedom of group activity rather than state-imposed restrictions. (Freedom for all groups meant, for example, that Catholics could establish and maintain their own schools.) German Catholics also were much more aware than Protestants of the necessity for social reform, since they tended to come from the less advantaged sectors of the population.

Except for certain groups in Bavaria, most Catholics supported the Weimar Republic; and support for the Catholic Center Party, a mainstay of the Republic, was as constant and sustained as for any other party in the Weimar Republic. With some notable exceptions, both the Catholic Church and the Catholic Center Party were hostile to nazism—even though Hitler was nominally a Catholic—believing that its racism and totalitarianism marked it as an essentially anti-Catholic force. Yet the Catholic Church quickly (some say too quickly) accepted the Nazi regime, and attempted to reach an accommodation with it: the concordat with the Vatican promised Catholic acquiescence in return for permission for the church to continue its own activities.

German Protestantism was a conservative political force well into the twentieth century. To the orthodox, the belief in original sin meant that while it might be possible for the individual, through grace, to live according to the ethics of love, the world would continue to be ruled by force. It was impossible to establish the kingdom of God in this world, and order—constantly threatened by chaos and anarchy—could be imposed only by a strong government. Consequently, obedience to established authority must be enjoined, even if the government should abuse its power and become a tyranny. Further, since life on earth was a way station, the true Christian concerned himself with spiritual rather than worldly matters.

The support these views gave to a traditionalist, authoritarian regime is obvious. In Brandenburg-Prussia, where Lutheranism was the state religion, the church became a cog in the state bureaucracy. By the end of the eighteenth century, Lutheran ministers had been made responsible for vital statistics, schools, and poor relief, and the pulpit was used by the state for all announcements concerning taxes, public health, and roads. All ecclesiastical—and, incidentally, academic—appointments were closely regulated by state authorities.

Under the Weimar Republic, the Lutheran Church was partially disestablished. Full

MAP 5.1 ROMAN CATHOLIC POPULATION OF WEST GERMANY

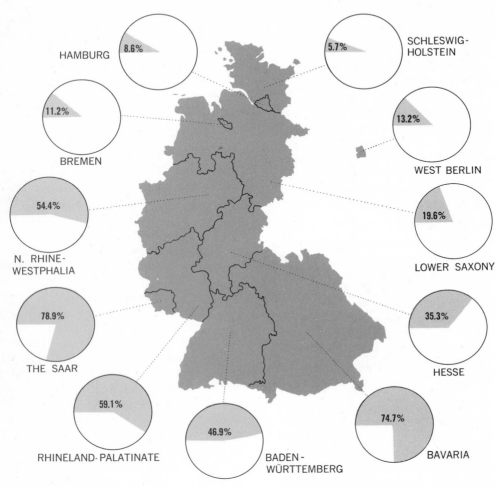

Adapted from *The German Tribune*, April 29, 1967,
p. 4, reprinted by permission of the publisher.

religious freedom was declared, and the state was deprived of the right to name ecclesiastical officers. The Weimar period was also marked by increased liberal ferment within the Lutheran Church. Nonetheless, many of the clergy remained hostile to the republic, and many came to support the Nazi movement. Indeed most Protestant ministers either remained silent or supported the Nazi regime, especially during the war years.

After the war, the German religious picture changed fundamentally. The Nazi regime's repression of Catholics and Protestants alike had brought the two groups closer together, and the growing secularization of postwar German society, as well as changes in the outlook of both Catholics and Protestants, served to reduce their mutual suspiciousness. Furthermore, while Catholics had constituted only about one-third of the population of prewar Germany, they made up approximately 49 percent of the population of the German Federal Republic because of the loss of lands in the east and the influx of refugees. It should be added,

TABLE 5.4   RELIGIOUS AFFILIATION OF GERMAN ELITES
Figures in rounded-out percentages

	Politics	Public administration	Business	Non-business associations	Mass media	University professors	All elites
Protestant	45	47	58	33	60	68	50
Roman Catholic	42	27	19	30	21	14	28
Other and none	6	0	14	23	9	14	10
No answer	8	27	8	15	10	5	13

Source: From Lewis J. Edinger, *Politics in Germany: Attitudes and Processes*, p. 181   Copyright © 1968 by Little, Brown and Company (Inc.).   Adapted by permission.

however, that social mobility is still somewhat lower among Catholics than among Protestants, so that the latter make up a larger segment of the urban elite.

Perhaps the most significant sign of the increasing accommodation between Catholics and Protestants was the replacement of the old Catholic Center Party by the Christian Democratic Union and its Bavarian affiliate, the (*Christlich Demokratische Union/Christlich Soziale Union*—CDU/CSU (Christian Social Union), one of whose specific aims is to transcend denominational lines and unite Christians of all persuasions. Since 1955 the political partisanship of the Catholic Church has declined considerably because of changes both within the church and within the opposition Social Democratic Party. Even in Bavaria, the German Catholic establishment has moved haltingly in the direction of greater liberalism. Thus, in 1973 the Catholic bishops formally forbade priests from publicly professing party preferences, working within a political party, or working for the election of party candidates. As for Protestantism, leading Protestant dignitaries meeting at Treysa in 1945 concluded that the church had erred fundamentally in teaching that the only duty owed the state was obedience. In the future, it was maintained, the churches should foster among the faithful a sense of civic responsibility and

an awareness of the realities of political and social life. Meanwhile, the long-term trend toward secularization of German life is continuing. Attendance at Protestant churches has declined dramatically, and the Catholic church reported a 71 percent drop in the number of priests ordained from 1962–1972 as against the previous decade. We may well wonder with one author whether, when all is said and done, "a *Katholikentag* or a *Kirchentag* has as much effect on the future of the Federal Republic as do a few numbers of *Der Spiegel*, or a few television programs."[3]

ETHNIC AND REGIONAL CONFLICT: The Germans of Hitler's former Reich, now numbering some 80 million, constitute the largest ethnic group in Europe outside the Soviet Union. Their present division into West and East German states is a continuation of the persistent difficulty Germans have had in creating a united nation-state. At the beginning of the nineteenth century, Germany was divided into nearly eighteen hundred different political units; only in 1871 did Germany achieve statehood—centuries later than Britain and France. Although the postwar division of the Germans has been stabilized, that division is not necessarily a permanent condition; indeed, part of the ra-

[3] Alfred Grosser, *Germany in Our Time*, trans. Paul Stephenson (New York: Praeger, 1971), p. 241.

tionale for the West German government's action in recognizing East Germany in 1972 was that recognition seemed perhaps the best possible way of working toward eventual reunion. But whatever the chances for reunification, today as in earlier eras, there are many people both to the east and the west of the Germans who do not relish such a prospect.

The major territorial divisions of Germany prior to unification were along broadly tribal lines—Prussians, Bavarians, Swabians, Hessians, Saxons—and the constitution of the German Empire recognized those divisions. The German historian Heinrich von Treitschke's characterization of the Reich as a union of "a lion, a half-dozen foxes, and a score of mice" neatly emphasizes the power disparity in the Reich; but, despite their size, the non-Prussian German states were insistent upon maintaining their separate identities.

Since the creation of the Reich, the trend toward lessening the differences among the Germanic groups and regions has been continuous if not steady. The forces making for greater homogeneity seem ineluctable— the most decisive among them being industrialization and urbanization. Today less than 10 percent of the people are engaged in agricultural pursuits, which occupied more than 60 percent of the population one hundred years ago. Moreover, 65 percent of the people now live in urban areas—20 percent in the eleven cities with a population of 500,000 or more—whereas less than half that many did a century ago. This flight from the land and the growth of urban areas, as well as the creation of modern communications and transportation networks, have all been factors in decreasing cultural differences among the Germans and diminishing the importance of regional variations. Another factor was the centralization of political authority, which World War I had necessitated. Moreover, while the framers of the Weimar Constitution were intent upon weakening Prussia's importance in the political life of the nation, they were also anxious to increase the authority of the

central government at the expense of the member states, and they did so.

Despite their glorification of the peasant and his way of life, the Nazis added impetus to the forces making for greater cultural homogeneity and political unity. They also added forces of their own by emphasizing the unity and oneness of all German people, by their dictatorial policies, and by their attempts at the "coordination" of all aspects of German life.

World War II brought about the most massive migration of peoples in modern times; and as a major part of this movement, 12 million persons of Germanic background resettled in what is today West Germany. They included refugees from East Germany and from what had formerly been German territory—East Prussia, Silesia, Pomerania—as well as from other countries, including Czechoslovakia, Hungary, Poland, and Russia. It is one of the ironies of history that the absorption of these people (one of every five persons in the republic is a refugee) and the integration of them into the West German society and economy (they have been an important part of the German work force) has taken place on less than two-thirds of the territory which, Hitler proclaimed, made the Germans a "people without territory" (*Volk ohne Raum*). Some refugees continue to harbor thoughts of one day returning to the homeland (*Heimat*) east of the Oder-Neisse, but West Germany's recent recognition of the borders drawn after World War II makes such hopes fanciful.

During the late 1960's and early 1970's dramatic changes took place in German foreign policy regarding its eastern neighbors and the land that had formerly belonged to Germany. These developments could be attributed to the successful integration of the refugees and to a change in public attitudes toward the areas from which the refugees had fled. Perhaps the most important regional difference today is still that between the north and the south—despite the network of superhighways and the expansion of the mass media. Among the Germans it is still the Bavarians who insist most strongly upon their differences with other areas in Germany. One indicator of this insistence is the steadfast refusal of the Christian Social Union (CSU) to merge into the Christian Democratic Union (CDU), though other differences, including religion, also exist. Most of Bavaria is heavily Catholic, and many parts of Bavaria are still predominantly agricultural.

That the Germans continue to cultivate their regional political differences is evident in the structure and operation of their government—its federal character reflects both the policies of the occupying powers and the wishes of the Germans themselves. But Germans also cherish their cultural decentralization. Even when Berlin was at its height as the political and cultural capital of the nation, it did not dominate German life and letters to the extent that Paris and London dominate France and England; and certainly this cultural federalism is even more pronounced now with Bonn as the capital. The question in the Federal Republic is not so much whether there should be some decentralization, but rather whether the existing divisions are the most viable ones. Germany, like other industrial nations, is groping toward some compromise between historical and traditional divisions and the exi-

gencies of a modern, highly interdependent urban society.

Like France and England, Germany has also experienced a massive influx of immigrants from southern Europe and the Middle East since the middle 1950's. The government has made some efforts to accommodate these migrants, who are officially termed "guest workers" rather than foreign workers. Some employers have made an effort to provide for their needs, for example, a number of factories employing Muslims have built mosques and organized special canteens, and Spanish priests have been brought in to help with the needs of Spanish Catholic workers. In addition, special cultural centers have been built and some special housing at reasonable prices has been provided. Other employers however, have behaved in a rather more exploitive fashion, paying quite low wages. In many cases migrants have been forced to pay exorbitantly high rents for barrack-type accommodations.

Very few of the guest workers have been absorbed into the larger community. During the mild recession of 1966–67 almost half had to return to their own countries, and demands for deportation were again raised in the recession of 1974–75.

Sources and Organization
of Political Conflict:
Youth

1. YOUTH AND CHANGE IN WESTERN EUROPE

Ever since the Enlightenment, a tradition of rebelliousness has existed among middle-class European youth. Often it has involved the adoption by young people of radical ideologies designed *really* to achieve goals their parents merely talked about; sometimes it has been simply a matter of rejecting parental and societal values and becoming "bohemians" extolling the value of self-expression. Partially free of parental control, and largely free of adult responsibilities and commitments, European college-age youth, especially, have at times been a motor force for change; indeed, their rebelliousness has been partly responsible for the continued dynamism of Western society.

The relative conservatism of most primitive societies was maintained because the socialization process blocked the development of new orientations. The decline of the family's role in socialization and the exposure of young people to milieus in which they learn new orientations and have the opportunity to modify or even reject parental values have been among the major factors contributing to the institutionalization of social change in Europe and the United States.

Bohemianism and radicalism as forms of rebellion have, in the past, been options open only to upper-class and middle-class youth. Until recently the young person of working-class background was initiated into adult responsibilities at a much earlier age; his radicalism, at least in Western Europe, was directly related to his class position and did not involve deviation from parental norms. More and more frequently, however, rebellion among working-class youth is now expressed as a rejection of existing working-class organizations and as a movement toward more radical action. In nations where the great majority of working-class children leave school at fifteen and can look forward to a life of routine manual labor, delinquency is also a form of working-class protest. The problem has become more acute with the decline of parental authority, a decline that has been accentuated by the fact that young men can earn enough to support themselves almost from the moment they leave school. Television and other mass media, of course, have aggravated the malaise by making these youngsters aware of life-styles that are denied them.

The proportion of young people who rebel against parental or societal control has always been small, though the impact of this rebelliousness has on occasion been significant. It is likely to be much greater when the society is undergoing rapid changes—when traditional values are being severely attacked. It is under these circumstances that the generation gap is widest.

2. REBELLIOUSNESS AND YOUTH ORGANIZATIONS

The clash in the late 1960's between university students and the larger community was not exactly a new phenomenon. In the Middle Ages, young scholars frequently invaded surrounding towns, raping women and engaging in other forms of mayhem. On occasion the community retaliated vigorously; for example, Oxford became the scene of a violent clash in 1354:

All night the citizens from surrounding towns and villages poured into Oxford . . . They caught certain scholars walking after dinner . . . killing one and wound-

ing others. Then on into the University quarter itself, where the scholars defended themselves desperately. . . . But the army of townsmen was not to be denied. The students were overwhelmed . . . . For two days the mob rioted and pillaged and slew . . . . When the pillage was over, the University had vanished, seemingly never to return.[1]

European universities during the nineteenth and early twentieth centuries were hotbeds of radical activity, and students figured significantly in many of the revolutions that occurred. Marx himself pointed to the role of students in the German upheaval of 1848. It was, of course, the radical parties of the left that were the first to take advantage of youthful enthusiasm and to establish youth auxiliaries. In Germany a Socialist youth movement was initiated as early as 1904, although it was not given official status until 1909. Both the French and the British Socialist parties set up youth affiliates somewhat later. In all three countries youth groups were more militant than the parent party and were supported by the left within the party. As a consequence, the parent organization often found itself at odds with its youth groups. In France, the youth section of the Communist Party was heavily Trotskyite during most of the 1920's, and in Germany Socialist youth groups frequently clashed with the Social Democratic Party because of what they considered its timidity.

Where more than one major party of the left existed, youth was generally drawn to the more radical. In France the Socialist youth groups were eclipsed by the Communists, as they were in Germany. Liberal and conservative parties in Europe attempted to create their own youth affiliates—but without much success. In fact, the only parties that could compete with the left were Catholic political parties, like the German Center Party, or parties of the radical right, such

[1] Quoted in A. H. Halsey and Stephen Marks, "British Student Politics," in *Daedalus*, 97 (Winter, 1968), p. 116.

as the National Socialists. Youth forces and counterforces varied substantially from country to country, and they were related in each case to the nation's culture and its political and social structure.

In France the very fragmentation of French society and politics not only offered the university student an opportunity to choose among many ideologies, but provided the rationale for that bohemian nihilism that became the hallmark of Paris's Left Bank. During most of the nineteenth and twentieth centuries it was for the most part left-wing causes that inspired the majority of student activists. Socialist and, later, Communist parties were not only associated in the minds of these students with freedom from all "bourgeois" restraints, but they also allowed the activists to identify with the working class. In addition, the lack of employment opportunities for lower-middle-class university graduates—to whom only a few posts in traditional occupations were available—contributed to the genesis of an "intellectual proletariat" in the late nineteenth century and up to the beginning of World War II.

Though the general movement of French university students was to the left, radical right-wing movements were not without support. At the time of the Dreyfus Affair, for instance, right-wing students fought with leftist groups at the Sorbonne, often attacking more liberal professors:

During the winter of 1908–1909 a series of public lectures was announced at the Sorbonne, to be given by a Lycée professor by the name of Thalamas, who was said to have "insulted" Joan of Arc. At the first lecture a group of newly formed Camelots du Roi (street vendors of the king) appeared, led by Maurice Pujo; they drowned out the professor with catcalls and bombarded him with various objects; finally one of the group jumped onto the rostrum and brutally slapped the defenseless professor. For the next few weeks the course had to be given under police protection. . . . On the next-to-last day of the course, using a strategy requiring military precision, they man-aged to enter the auditorium, in spite of the heavy police guard, and beat up the lecturer on the rostrum. Both state and university actually yielded: the course was not completed.[2]

In Germany youthful militancy was concentrated less among university students and was channeled more easily to the radical right. It was the sons of peasants, white-collar workers, and army officers who embraced National Socialism with the most fervor and with the most genuine idealism. The Social Democrats and Communists did manage to maintain some support among the younger population throughout the 1920's, but in the last years of the decade they lost out to the National Socialists. For example, in 1931 only 19.1 percent of the Social Democratic Party membership was between the ages of eighteen and thirty; for the Nazi Party, the corresponding figure was 37.6 percent. The Nazi movement attracted many of the national youth groups that had been organized at the turn of the century for traditional and folk dancing and for direct contact with nature through long hikes. Many of these groups sought the restoration of traditional German society—as they understood it—and they made much of the purity of the German *Volk*. In general, the youth who joined these groups believed they were reacting against the centralization and mechanization of bourgeois, industrial society.

The precepts of these organized youth movements were not without support at the university level, even though the movements themselves were never extended to the campus. Infatuation with the idea of the German *Volk* and the romantic glorification of German society and the German nation were vital aspects of life within the dueling fraternities that were so important at the universities. Here again there were many divisions, but the general movement of university students was to the right—and to the

[2] Ernest Nolte, *Three Faces of Fascism*, trans. Leila Vannewitz (New York: Holt, Rinehart and Winston, Inc., 1966), p. 69.

TABLE 6.1   THE EXPANSION OF THE UNIVERSITY POPULATION
IN BRITAIN, FRANCE AND GERMANY, 1950–1971

	Percentage of 20–24 year-olds in Higher Education			Number of Students in Higher Education (thousands)		
	1950	1965	1970–71	1965	1969	1970–71
Britain	4	4.4	6.5	192.2	251.6	266.1
France	4.1	11.7	18.9	413.8	616 [1]	752 [1]
Germany	3.4	6.9	9.3	253.2	299.9	343.5

[1] Does not include private universities and institutes.

Sources: Data derived from *faits et Chiffres 1973* (Paris: Le Nouvel Observatur, 1973), p. 50; *Annual Abstract of Statistics 1975* (London: Central Statistical Office, 1973), pp. 14, 125–128; *Handbook of Statistics for the Federal Republic of Germany* (Stuttgart: W. Kohlhammer GMBH, 1970), p. 18; *UNESCO Statistical Yearbook, 1972* (New York: United Nations, 1973), pp. 356–361; Anthony Sampson, *Anatomy of Europe* (New York: Harper and Row, 1968), p. 402.

anti-Semitic right at that. By the late 1920's, the National Socialist Party had captured the leadership of rightist groups at many institutions, where at first pressures and then riots sometimes resulted in the dismissal of liberal and jewish professors. Once in power The Naxis dissolved the various independent youth organizations throughout Germany, and the party's youth affiliate was designated as the sole coordinator of all youth activity.

In Britain the pattern was quite different. Young people, and especially middle-class students, did flock to the Labor Party, especially in the 1930's, but the whole tradition of British life worked against a massive commitment of the type which characterized both France and Germany.

3.   STUDENT ACTIVISM SINCE WORLD WAR II

In the years following World War II, especially in the 1950's, student political activity in Europe significantly declined.

The situation differed, of course, from country to country. British students had never developed a reputation for real political activism; thus the decline there was only relative. In Germany the decline in political activity by students was so pronounced that they became known as the "skeptical generation." Their concern with postwar reconstruction and their reaction against any ideological commitments were in striking contrast with student activism during the Weimar period. In France student activism continued during the late 1940's and declined in the 1950's, only to re-emerge with the later phases of the Algerian War.

In these years of political torpor, however, forces were at work that would provide the setting for renewed—and occasionally explosive—student activism. Student populations were burgeoning throughout Europe. For example, during the decade of the 1960's the number of university students in France more than tripled. More importantly, by the latter part of the decade, the overcrowding of university facilities on the Continent especially was becoming a critical problem. In Germany, in 1968, there were thirty-two students for every faculty member, while in France the ratio was twenty-four to one. In Britain, on the other hand, there were eight students for every faculty member. Moreover, the erosion of traditional patterns of authority in the society and the greater independence of young people were beginning to have implications for the structure of authority within the university. And, as the United States and Soviet Union moved toward a policy of "detente" and new generations entered universities, ideological disillusionment was becoming a matter of history rather than a personal experience. Finally, the growth of mass communications, particularly television, was creating the possibility of mobilizing students to an extent not conceivable in previous decades.

Interestingly enough, what undoubtedly crystallized all these factors into a sudden wave of student activism in the late 1960's was the appearance of a radical student movement in the United States. The traumas associated with the racial crisis, American policy in Vietnam, the draft for military service, and, indeed, the relationship of the United States (and Western Europe as a whole) to the developing nations of the world had caused widespread repercussions on the American campus. The civil-rights movement provided a new set of tactics for American students, tactics that were further refined as student opposition to the war in Vietnam grew. By way of television, United States civil-rights demonstrations and demonstrations against the war became part of a common European experience, and student activists capitalized on this experience by traveling from one country to another to foster a rebellious mood on the European campus.

Developments in the United States influenced Europe in an even more profound manner. To Europeans, as indeed to the rest of the world, the United States had come to symbolize Western political and economic institutions. Thus the failures of American foreign policy and of American social justice as evidenced by the racial conflict in the United States served to direct the attention of many European students to what they considered the social injustices of their own societies.

The way was suddenly opened for the revival of utopian radicalism—for fresh assaults upon society and upon the structure of the universities themselves, considered now as pawns of the larger, corrupt community. Identifying themselves with revolutions and revolutionaries in the underdeveloped countries, some students began to think in terms of direct confrontation not only against the university and governmental authorities, but against the established European left as well, including the Communist Party.

The extent of student rebelliousness, in the extreme form at least, should not be exaggerated. Revolutionary student groups tend to be relatively small, drawing upon broader student support only on certain issues. Moreover, ideas often expressed by certain students, particularly the priority given to freer expression and participation, seem to be far more appealing to middle-class youth than to young people from lower-class backgrounds.

However small the movement that began in 1966–67 was, it has had considerable impact, particularly in connection with university reform. Its more general impact has probably been greatest in France and smallest in Britain, and the most important result of its general impact is that it reactivated the politics of the left. Unlike student movements of the past, the main thrust of the present student movement has stimulated, rather than reflected, conflict in the larger political arena, and as a consequence European communism, for the first time in its history, is being confronted by a serious challenge from the left.

Unquestionably, some of the problems that troubled the students reflect changes in Europe's culture and social structure. There is now a demand for greater equality, a shift of emphasis and concern from economic growth and personal affluence to the overall "quality" of the society. Insofar as this is true, students may well represent the advance guard in responding to the developments of the last twenty years and a portent of things to come.

THE BRITISH PATTERN: All major British parties have youth affiliates. They emphasize political discussion and education as well as canvassing, and they seek to influence party policy through the publication of pamphlets. As in other European countries, however, the most politically active youth organizations during the past several years have been student groups. The chief British student organization is the National Union of Students (NUS). There are other student groups loosely associated with the political parties, and more recently an array of *ad hoc* "revolutionary" left-wing groups has formed. *The New Left Review* was originally sponsored partly by students.

Student activism reached something of a high in 1960 and 1961 with the formation of the Committee for Nuclear Disarmament (CND), which sponsored demonstrations and marches urging Britain's unilateral rejection of nuclear weapons. But after a year or two, the CND's membership dropped off, and the next spurt in student activity did not come until 1966 and 1967. In the meantime, more radical student organizations were founded whose aim was to reshape British education by giving students more power in university decisions. Their membership remained small, but their militant activism resulted in pushing the NUS to the left.

By 1967 British students were ripe for a new brand of activism—"confrontation" politics. The most dramatic exercise of confrontation occurred at the London School of Economics over issues that combined elements of student syndicalism with attempts to influence the larger society on "racism" and the Vietnam War. At this point, with British students clearly influenced by events in the United States and beginning to establish contact with other European student groups, their activism escalated quickly, though it did not reach the level of violence that took place in other nations.

Sporadic student demonstrations continued into the 1970's. However, their focus shifted away from London to the provincial universities, and the demonstrations were uncoordinated efforts involving relatively small numbers of students. The NUS continued to discuss ideological objectives, but

it began to concentrate on specific policy demands. Having in 1968 reached agreement with the Committee of Vice Chancellors of the Universities regarding a student voice in university governance, the union then entered into negotiations with the government over the size of maintenance grants for university students. Its success in reaching agreement on this matter suggests that the NUS has taken its proper place in the galaxy of legitimate interest groups with which every government must deal. What is more, the Representation of the People Act of 1969 giving the vote to eighteen-year-olds, combined with a court decision declaring that students could exercise their franchise in the parliamentary constituency in which their university is located, suggests that student demands might be acquiring a new strategic importance in British politics.

THE FRENCH PATTERN: French university students, organized in the *Union nationale des étudiants de France*—UNEF (The National Council of French Students), played a leading roll in the movement against the Algerian War. Before 1958 and after 1963, however, the general pattern of political activity among French students was one of relative calm. Membership in student affiliates of political parties declined, and student initiative in politics was insignificant.

However, though the universities were relatively calm, nonstudent youth movements particularly Catholic youth movements, had considerable influence throughout the fifties and sixties in the trade-union and peasant sectors of French society. In the 1960's these movements of nonstudent youth came to represent a new radicalism that helped to effect social and economic change in France. (See Chapter 4.)

In 1967 signs of student radicalism re-emerged in the universities. Influenced by the growing student movement in the United States, but perhaps more by the radical German students, nuclei of student radicals formed at French universities on the fringes of UNEF. By 1968, UNEF, whose strength had been greatly reduced by government harassment after the Algerian War, was once again an important spokesman for an expanding student movement which, however, it did not control.[3] Radical groups clashed with the educational authorities, as well as with the "established" left. Then, in May, 1968, with a sizable portion of the French student body supporting them, the radicals faced the Gaullist regime in a massive confrontation in the streets. The events of May and June—rioting, police bludgeoning, street fighting, mass arrests—touched off the largest general strike in French history, and for nearly eight weeks, normal life throughout most of France came to a virtual halt.

The upshot of the clash was a new national election in which the left as a whole felt the sting of a popular backlash and slipped, at least, temporarily, into disarray. Nevertheless, the riots and strikes were not devoid of success. They compelled the de Gaulle government to initiate some reforms in industry, and to outline new university programs that would permit greater decentralization of the university system and more participation in decisions by both faculty and students. The disturbances also precipitated a balance-of-payments crisis that, in turn, raised questions about the regime's general economic policies.

The reforms, initiated by de Gaulle's Minister of Education Edgar Faure and supported by the president himself, involved more than just greater participation by the students in certain aspects of university de-

cision-making. They were designed to decentralize the university system by giving individual universities greater autonomy. Their objective also was to reduce the size of individual universities, to replace faculties by American-style departments, and to curb the authority of senior professors. The events of 1968 also resulted in a reordering of governmental budgetary priorities, and large amounts of public funds were redirected to the development of the university system.

The violent student movement of 1968 lost its momentum only gradually. Throughout 1968–69 education came to a standstill in many university centers, and in numerous secondary schools as well. Since then, the momentum of violence has gradually declined, as student support has waned and government suppression has become more intense. In June, 1970, the Gaullist majority adopted what became known as the "anti-wrecker" law, which made it possible to hold a participant in a demonstration legally responsible for violence committed, even if he committed no act of violence himself. During the early 1970's, large numbers of often heavily armed police regularly patrolled the Latin Quarter of Paris. From January, 1970, to June, 1971, more than 15,000 persons were picked up for questioning.[4]

During the three years after UNEF played such an important role in the events of 1968, the organization was rendered impotent by protracted internal strife. As the organization lost members and influence, Communists and groups further to the left fought for control. In opposition to the leftist groups, the Communist faction supported participation in joint councils established as a result of the university reorganization in 1968, and devoted its energies toward fighting for immediate student demands rather than toward using the university as a base for broader revolutionary activity.

In 1971 UNEF split into two organizations, one controlled by the Communist fac-

[3] In 1961 UNEF was officially banned by the government, and its official subsidy was cut off. The ban resulted from UNEF meetings with Algerian students in Switzerland, and from calls for demonstrations in favor of a cease fire. At the same time Gaullist agents established La Fédération nationale des étudiants de France—FNEF (the National Federation of French Students), which still exists. The ban was removed at the end of the war, but official harassment continued. Subsidies were not restored until 1967. During the long years of protracted conflict with UNEF, the Gaullist regime had effectively destroyed its own links with the most representative student organization. See Philip Williams and Martin Harrison, Politics and Society in De Gaulle's Republic (Garden City, N.Y.: Doubleday & Co., Anchor Books, 1973), pp. 376–79, for a detailed case study of these events.

[4] Le Monde, June 13–14, 1971.

tion (UNEF—Renouveau), the other by a Trotskyist group (UNEF—Unité Syndicale). By 1975, the Communist-controlled UNEF had become the largest and best organized group within the student movement, while the Trotskyist UNEF had declined in membership and influence. The Communist-controlled organization held almost a third of the student seats on the university councils and had begun to rebuild UNEF as a student service organization and pressure group. With only 27,000 members, however, they possessed hardly a third of the UNEF membership of 1960.

Some student groups, particularly, Trotskyist and Maoist groups, have centered their attention on young workers. Members of these groups have taken factory jobs and have aided and abetted a continuing mood of revolt among young workers, a mood that has been expressed in violent strikes and the seizure of factories. The influence of students among workers, nonetheless, has been limited by the class distrust that has always marked relations between workers and middle-class radicals.

The turbulance of UNEF politics has also been characteristic of the student and youth affiliates of the major political parties. The Communists, for example, have been moved to purge their student organization several times since the mid-sixties, while the Gaullist youth actually severed their affiliation with the party after the presidential election of 1974.

The political weight of French youth, a force that has been felt so frequently in the streets, will now be felt in the electoral process, as a result of the lowering of the voting age from twenty-one to eighteen in 1974. Not surprisingly, surveys indicate that the lowering of the voting age will favor the parties of the left.

THE GERMAN PATTERN: For German youth, the collapse of the Third Reich brought several years of intense disillusionment and passivity. The German sociologist, Helmut Schelsky, referred to the youth of Germany in the first decade after the war

as *Die Skeptische Generation*.[5] Yet German youth also came to demonstrate many characteristics common to young people all over Europe—traits that disapproving elders frequently considered reflections of "Americanization." Furthermore, some Protestant and Catholic youths were organizing the Federal Youth Council (*Bundesjugendring*). While dueling fraternities were reappearing at some universities in the 1950's, many other adolescents seemed to content themselves with the latest American dances, hot rods, and sexual adventures.

Party youth affiliates became active again in the early 1960's, and, as might be expected, took lines to the left of parent bodies. As it had during the Weimar Republic, the Social Democratic Party found itself forced to disaffiliate its youth organization, the German Socialist Student Alliance (*Sozialistischer Deutscher Studentenbund*—SDS) and to form a new one—the *Jusos*. The SDS continued to exert an influence on students, however, and, between 1967 and 1969, to grow in strength, even as its successor moved somewhat to the left.

Under the leadership of such radicals as Fritz Teufel and "Red" Rudi Dutschke, the SDS had mobilized students to press for the complete revamping of the university structure. The students, joined by junior faculty members who also felt themselves discriminated against, demanded not only full student participation in university decision-making, but also—going beyond the university issue—demanded the "democratization" of German society. German student confrontations came to involve more continuous violence, including the burning of periodicals and books, over a longer period of time than did student activism in other nations. But the youth protests in Germany have also resulted in steps toward reforming the university structure.

The basic structure of the German university was laid down at the beginning of the nineteenth century, and as enrollments grew

[5] Helmut Schelsky, *Die Skeptische Generation* (Düsseldorf: Diederich, 1957).

through the years, increasing numbers of students became subjected to authoritarian administrative hierarchies, aloof professors, overcrowded classrooms, and outdated curricula. German universities were also open to criticism because the student population was disproportionately represented by upper-middle-class and middle-class youths. After World War II many institutions and social practices in Germany were changed, but German universities and German schools in general remained bound by nineteenth-century strictures until the late 1960's. One authority even wrote of "the German educational catastrophe."[6] Radical students, therefore, were not alone in talking about the crisis in German education. Much of the student protest was an upshot of the conflict between the students' changing social mores and attitudes, on the one hand, and the anachronistic and authoritarian educational system, on the other. One form that this protest still takes is criticism of the elders for the Nazi past and their failure to establish more thoroughgoing democratic patterns in the Federal Republic.

Despite its relative geographical isolation, West Berlin has been at the center of the student-protest movement in Germany. In June of 1967, on the occasion of the Shah of Iran's visit to West Berlin, a policeman shot and killed a German student protester; his death provoked riots and demonstrations throughout Germany and helped to make Dutschke, a brilliant Marxist orator, a popular figure. The following spring, Dutschke himself was seriously wounded in an attempt to assassinate him, and again street fighting and massive demonstrations broke out in Berlin, Frankfurt, Munich, and other large cities. By the early seventies, however, student unrest in Germany had passed its peak; one symptom of its decline was that in March, 1970, the SDS announced its own dissolution.

Unlike their counterparts in France, German students have evoked little sympathy from the trade unions, whose membership has grown more hostile to them as events have unfolded. In fact, the Federation of German Labor Unions has staged processions to counter the demonstrations of radical students and to show its support for the authorities. German student protesters, moreover, have never had the support of as large a proportion of intellectuals as have students in other European nations—or even of the left within the intellectual community. Indeed, one principal weakness of the German student-protest movement is that it did not have and has not developed support in the broader nonacademic world. On the contrary, the students seem to have awakened very deep distrust and even anxiety in part of the German population.

Student protesters in Germany have been instrumental, nevertheless, in raising the level of public awareness of serious failings within Germany's educational system—and thus in pointing up the disparities that presently exist between the ideals upon which the republic was founded and social reality. One possible offshoot of the student protests is the very widespread movement in the Federal Republic today among parents calling for a greater say in their children's schooling.

Parents throughout the land are organizing themselves in parent-teacher associations and demanding more control in such matters as the composition of classes, the introduction of new teaching and learning materials, the alteration of lesson times, types of school experiments. They have even taken to the Constitutional Court in Karlsruhe the issue of their right to share in decision-making on matters relating to their children's education and have received the backing of the Court under Article 6 of the Constitution, which states in part that the "care and education of children is the natural right of parents and the duty first and foremost incumbent upon them." Although this movement is only part of a much broader wave of citizen-initiated movements (Bürgerinitiativen) in the Federal Republic today, it is all the more remarkable because German citizens

---

[6] George Picht, "Die deutsche Bildungskatastrope," in *Christ und Welt*, February, 1964.

have been very disinclined historically to take an initiative on social and political matters.

Most state governments have now given students and junior faculty a voice, along with professors, in university affairs. Some state governments have also been building new universities and expanding existing facilities in an attempt to accommodate the growing number of students. Formidable problems, however, still exist within the universities and between the universities and German society.

In the wake of the unrest in the early seventies, politicians from Munich to Berlin, fearful that some of the students and professors in the newly reformed universities were getting out of hand, threatened to curtail the traditional autonomy of the German universities. Indeed, many of the less radical professors charged that they were continually harassed, that there had been serious interference with their academic freedom, and that new appointments to academic positions were being made on purely political grounds —that left-wing students and faculty supporters were willing to appoint left-wing teachers whatever their qualifications.

During the height of student unrest in the late 1960's many German students expressed their contempt for parties and electoral politics altogether by organizing themselves into an "extra-parliamentary opposition" (*Ausserparlamentarische Opposition*—APO). Because it was easy for the Social Democratic Party to dissociate itself from such groups, the emergence of the APO was perhaps fortunate for both the internal cohesion and the electoral image of the Social Democrats. By contrast, in the early seventies, while there were numerous splinter groups and factions on the left, including at least three different Communist organizations, the Jusos (youth affiliate of the Social Dem-

ocratic Party) are now trying to work within the party and the established political order. The Jusos, who have become quite strong SPD in numerous local organizations and who are represented by more than thirty Bundestag deputies, have become increasingly outspoken in their criticism of the "bourgeois" and compromising position of the parent organization—much to the dismay and embarrassment of party leaders. They are trying to draw the SDP back to its original ideological professions. But for leaders whose rise to power has been facilitated by a dampening of the party's ideological program, this move on the part of the Jusos is tantamount to relegating the party to a permanent role of opposition. That there is no easy answer either for the party or its radical elements seems clear, for in one form or another the dissident left seems to be here to stay.

While much, if not most, student protest in Germany has come historically from the right, almost all of it in Bonn has been coming from the left. There are other significant differences between the present situation and German student movements of the past. Unlike many of the youth groups of the imperial and Weimar periods, there is a pronounced political motif in much of the student activity of the last decade. Moreover, although even at its height the student movement has taken in only a small percentage of young people and the school population, it does seem to be indicative of a broader disposition in Germany to let people have more to say in decisions affecting their lives. While some of the unrest and movement for change in Germany is unquestionably rooted in authoritarianism, the participants present a very different picture from what is often taken to be the typically apolitical and passively obedient German of the past.

7

Agents of Political Socialization: The Family, the Schools, and the Mass Media

1. INTRODUCTION

Whatever instincts man possesses, most of his reactions to his external environment are learned. It is the infant's plasticity and helplessness that necessitate a long period of care and teaching before he can deal effectively with the world around him. In these early years he begins to learn forms of behavior that are appropriate to the society of which he is part—and the skills required for a useful place in that society.

In most traditional societies, behavioral patterns and skills are transmitted largely through the family, whatever the family structure may be. In advanced and constantly changing societies, the role of the family, although still crucial, has gradually declined, and specialized institutions—for instance, schools—have become more and more vital in the socialization process.

Socialization, of course, does not end with adulthood. In contemporary societies, the mass media have an important effect in the progressive restructuring of attitudes and beliefs; they also provide a continuing source of knowledge. Because most twentieth-century societies are highly differentiated, individuals develop separate perceptions of reality, depending upon their functions and associates in society. Almost every activity in which the individual participates, even vicariously, affects his insight, values, and motivations. Even an election campaign is part of the general process of socialization.

This chapter will concentrate on three institutions crucial to the socialization process —the family, the schools, and the mass media—underscoring aspects of each that are most directly related to the formation and change of political attitudes. The institutions cited are not the only ones involved in the socialization process. Indeed, most community institutions take part in the socialization of the citizen. And most of the institutions considered here have functions in addition to that of socialization. Educational institutions, for instance, provide citizens with the skills necessary to adapt to their environments; the mass media not only offer information but provide entertainment. Though the socializing role of these institutions will be emphasized, some of their other functions will also be treated.

2. THE FAMILY

For the past thousand years, Western family systems have differed considerably from those in the Far and Middle East and in Africa. The West lacked the clan systems of the Middle and Far East; young people have always had more to say about whom they would—or would not—marry; and polygamy and regularized concubinage have not been integral parts of Western culture.

For centuries the father dominated the Western family and the rights of mother and child were minimal. The force largely responsible for upsetting this pattern was Calvinism, and the domination of the United States by a Calvinist ethic has resulted in continuing differences between American and European family structures. A substantially higher portion of Americans, for example, remember having had the opportunity to participate in family decisions as children than do Germans (Table 7.1). Far more than Europeans, Americans tend to regard husbands and wives as more or less equal companions in marriage; they are also far less strict than Europeans in disciplining their children. In recent decades the British have moved more quickly toward a "democratic" and "permissive" family structure than have the French, and the French faster than the Germans, although the differences between France and Germany are marginal.

The relationship between family structures and political attitudes is difficult to measure with any precision. During the 1940's and 1950's, many authors argued that there was an obvious parallel between the authoritarian nature of the German family and the growth of National Socialism.[1]

[1] See, for example, Bertram Schaffner, *Father Land. A Study of Authoritarianism in the German Family* (New York: Columbia University Press, 1948) and David Rodnick, *Post-War Germans* (New Haven, Conn.: Yale University Press, 1958).

TABLE 7.1 PARTICIPATION BY YOUTH IN FAMILY DECISION–MAKING

Extent of remembered participation	United States	Britain	Germany
Had some influence	73%	69%	54%
Had no influence	22	26	37
Don't know	5	5	9

Selections adapted from Gabriel A. Almond and Sidney Verba, *The Civic Culture: Political Attitudes and Democracy in Five Nations* (copyright © 1963 by Princeton University Press), p. 331. Reprinted by permission of Princeton University Press.

TABLE 7.2   FAMILIAL AUTHORITY RELATIONS IN THE PARENTAL
AND CONTEMPORARY GENERATIONS, 1959–1960

In percentages

Predominant authority figure(s) identified by respondents	Germany		Britain		United States	
	Generation		Generation		Generation	
	Parental	Present	Parental	Present	Parental	Present
Father	30	17	23	12	22	8
Mother	13	8	18	7	14	7
Father-Mother together	39	63	45	76	46	81
Other	18	12	14	5	18	4

Adapted from Friedheim Neidhardt, "Die Familie in Deutschland," in Karl M. Bolte, Friedheim Neidhardt, and Horst Holzer, *Deutsche Gesellschaft im Wandel* (Opladen: Leske, 1970), p. 57, reprinted by permission of the publisher.

There is indeed some evidence that youngsters who grow up within a family framework of rigid discipline feel less competent to participate in political activity.   Other studies indicate that an authoritarian family structure is correlated with a strict insistence upon the rightness of traditional norms and a lack of flexibility toward or empathy with those who hold different values.   There is also a good deal of evidence to show that young people reared in an authoritarian manner tend to expect hostility from those outside the immediate family—and are less likely to take on personal responsibility for actions in which they transgress authority.

The pattern of internal family organization, then, and the manner in which children are raised would seem to be related in some way to the type of political action that characterizes a society.   Yet the relationship is by no means simple or incontrovertible; a number of societies in which fairly authoritarian families are the general rule are also noted for their democratic institutions.   Nor can this factor alone explain the rise of National Socialism in twentieth-century Germany, for family patterns throughout Europe were all far more authoritarian in the eighteenth and nineteenth centuries than in the twentieth.

Interestingly enough, there has been a marked decline in the authority of the father in the German family since World War II. Indeed, one German social psychologist has described Germany as being on the path toward a "fatherless society." [2]   The result has been a shift toward more cooperative patterns between the father and mother. According to one estimate, partnerlike relations between the parents exist today in approximately two-thirds of all families the Federal Republic [3] (Table 7.2).   In addition, and partially as a consequence, children now have more say in family matters. Thus the recent generations of German students, who grew up in more egalitarian families, have become increasingly reluctant merely to accept existing conditions.

The family also tends to pass on its political and social values to the next generation. Here, too, however, the influence of the fam-

[2] Alexander Mitscherlich, *Auf dem Weg zur vaterlosen Gesellschaft* (Munich: Piper, 1963).

[3] Friedhelm Neidhardt, "Die Familie in Deutschland," in Karl M. Bolte, Friedhelm Neidhardt, and Horst Holzer, *Deutsche Gesellschaft im Wandel* (Opladen: Leske, 1970).

TABLE 7.3 INFLUENCE OF FAMILY: PARENT–CHILD AGREEMENT
ON PARTY IDENTIFICATION, 1969

Percentage of children in agreement with parents

| | Age | |
	15–17	18–21
Britain	36	42
Germany	41	50
France	29	19

This table from "Preadult Development of Political Party Identification in Western Democracies," by Jack Dennis and Donald J. McCrone is reprinted from *Comparative Political Studies* Vol. 3, No. 2 (July 1970) p. 257 by permission of the Publisher, Sage Publications, Inc.

ily, as distinct from other agencies of socialization, is complex and sometimes unclear. We have evidence, for example, that children in Britain and Germany currently tend more and more to share the party identification of their parents as they approach adulthood. Yet a far smaller percentage of French youth share the party identification of their parents, and as they get older the percentage declines (Table 7.3).

The social values and aspirations that families pass on to their children also seem to be important in determining their success. Only a small proportion of Europe's working-class children, for example, are able to gain the credentials for university entrance; for them, it is often necessary to escape from family influence in order to rise socially and economically. For middle-class students, family influence ecourages social and economic success. A 1968 study of *lycée* students in France revealed that few of the lower-class students who had attained the secondary-school level believed that their families had had any influence on their lives, whereas the vast majority of their upper-middle-class schoolmates felt that the influence of their families was most important. Moreover, though only those lower-class students who had been successful in school had aspirations to high-status positions, the upper-middle-class students tended to aspire to high-status positions, regardless of how well

they did in school.[4] Without much question, then, the family has been an important institution for transmitting and perpetuating political and social values—although the extent and nature of family influence has not been identical in all countries.

There are now indications, however, that the structure and influence of the European family are undergoing important changes, and that these changes are related both to changing attitudes in general and to the changing attitudes of women in particular. When a cross section of French youth between the ages of fifteen and twenty-nine were asked in 1957 if their generation would be different from that of their parents, only 16 percent thought it would be; when the same question was posed to the same age group in 1969, 92 percent thought their generation would be "very different." In 1957, young people were concerned as much about their family life as they were about their careers; twelve years later, more French young people were concerned about their careers than anything else. While fewer than 40 percent felt that marriage was important for a good life, (more than half felt that it was not) twice that number indicated that to be happy in one's work, to continue to learn, to travel and to have a nice apartment were

[4] Raymond Boudon, "Sources of Student Protest in France," *Annals of the American Academy of Political and Social Science* (May, 1971), p. 145.

more important necessities for happiness; and the difference between men and women was not significant. Above all, 89 percent of the women and 79 percent of the men attached importance to having children only if and when one wants.[5]

The changing attitudes of European women are becoming manifest as new opportunities for them open in the labor market. Since World War II, women have been entering the labor market in increasing numbers. In England, France, and Germany almost half the adult women are now employed outside the home. Just as important, the kind of work they are doing has been changing. Before World War II most women worked on farms, in artisan shops, and in factories, particularly clothing and textile factories. Today, however, the majority of women work in offices, primarily in the service sector of the economy. Furthermore, ever larger numbers of them are involved in career-oriented managerial positions and in the professions.[6]

This new career orientation among European women can also be seen in the greater proportion of women graduating from universities and other institutions of higher education. Discrimination against women workers still persists, especially with regard to salaries; even so, more European women than ever are concerned with work and careers outside the home—a trend that is bound to loosen kinship networks further and to continue the decline in influence of family values upon children. For young people, the norms of their "peer culture" will compete more and more with those set by their families, and the educational system will become an even more critical factor in the socialization process.

[5] Franciose Giroux, "La Nouvelle Vogue," *L'Express*, Feb. 17–23, 1969, pp. 39–46.

[6] See the study by Evelyne Sullerot for the Commission of the European Communities, *The Employment of Women and the Problems It Raises in the Member States of the European Community* (Luxembourg, 1972), p. 28. See also her *Histoire et sociologie du travail féminin* (Paris: Éditions Gonthier, 1968).

3. THE SCHOOLS

In most traditional societies, formal education was reserved for the few. But today, if a society is to mobilize its resources to the fullest and create an industrial culture, education must be extended to the many. Not only is widespread literacy essential, but the number of required specialized skills that cannot be taught in the home or through apprenticeship is rising geometrically. Technological growth has reached the point where only those who are professionally dedicated to mastering fairly limited aspects of the new sciences can provide the requisite training for a new generation. And as competence in technical fields becomes necessary to the society, education becomes a prime source of social mobility.

THE DEVELOPMENT OF EDUCATION IN WESTERN EUROPE: With the collapse of the Roman Empire, the Catholic Church took over most of the schools that survived and used them primarily for the propagation of Christian doctrine. Church schools were, in fact, about the only ones to outlast the triumph of the "barbarians" in the West. Education was directed to preparing young men for the priesthood; it was primarily moral and disciplinary rather than intellectual.

Not until the eleventh and twelfth centuries did education, in the classical sense, begin once again to take form. The first universities were founded in Bologna in 1158 and in Paris in 1180. By 1600, Western Europe boasted 108 universities. At about the same time, various guilds opened "professional" schools, and private, secular institutions were established for more general educational purposes. Education to equip the lower classes with basic skills was also begun. Unlike the *Gymnasium* in Germany or the British grammar school, both of which prepared future members of the elite for university training, all these schools were regarded as terminal.

During the Renaissance, religious authorities began to lose control over education.

TABLE 7.4   WOMEN IN EUROPE

	Britain	Germany	France
Percentage of labor force composed of women, 1969	36	37	37
Percentage of women (aged 14–65) in labor force, 1968–1969	49	41	47
Percentage of married women in labor force, 1968–1969	37	34	38
Percentage of women (aged 18–24) in higher education			
1960	3.5	2.7	6.2
1969	7.4	6.4	12.9
Percentage of university students who are women, 1968–1969	28	25	44
Percentage of university graduates who are women	25	31	37
Women's salaries as a percentage of men's salaries, 1969			
Low-qualified jobs [1]	50	75	67 [3]
High-qualified jobs [2]	41	79	64 [3]
Women as a percentage of			
Doctors	25	18	18
Lawyers	5	3	10
Judges	—	2	10
Engineers	—	—	3.6
University professors	2 [4]	1 [5]	23 [6]

[1] By low-qualified, we mean: Britain and France—manual workers; Germany—lowest of four categories. These percentages have been stable for ten years.

[2] By high-qualified, we mean: Britain—administrative/clerical/technical; Germany—highest of four categories; France—higher management. These percentages have been stable for ten years.

[3] Figures are for 1967.

[4] Seventeen percent of teaching staff.

[5] Eight percent of teaching staff.

[6] Thirty percent of teaching staff.

Sources: Data derived from Statistical Yearbook, 1971 (Paris: UNESCO, 1972), pp. 114–117, 238–240, 311–313, 341–343, 446–447; Annual Abtract of Statistics, 1970 (London: H.M.S.O., 1970), pp. 11, 18, 113, 118, 119, 122, 148–149; Britain, 1972, An Official Handbook (London: H.M. S.O., 1970), p. 391; Handbook of Statistics, 1970 (Stuttgart, 1970), pp. 32, 52–53, 167; Tableaux de l'économie française, 1970 (Paris: INSEE, 1970), pp. 143, 163–166; Le Monde, June 11–12, 1967; Commission of the European Communities, The Employment of Women and the Problem it Raises in the Member States of the European Community (Luxembourg, 1972), passim; Evelyne Sullerot, Histoire et sociologie du travail féminin (Paris: Éditions Gonthier, 1968), pp. 225–228, 256–264.

The trend was reversed during the Reformation and Counter-Reformation, but by the nineteenth century the nation-state, seeing the connection between literacy and economic power, had come to take jurisdiction over the education of its citizens. By the end of that century most of the countries in Western Europe were providing compulsory schooling for all children between the ages of six or seven and thirteen or fourteen.

In all countries, however, including the three we are discussing, denominational schools continued to flourish within the educational system. Many times intense conflicts occurred between those who believed that the church had a role to play in the educational process and those who maintained that education should remain under the exclusive control of secular authorities. This dispute was more bitter in Catholic countries because partisans of the church and the secular state both came to regard control of the education system as the key to control of the next generation; it has continued, although in muted form, to this day. Thus in France the supporters of aid to private schools and those opposed to all subventions engaged in acrimonious debate throughout the early years of the Fourth Republic. Each side organized rallies and petitions, and some of the clergy counseled their parishioners to refuse to pay taxes unless aid was forthcoming. It was a major election issue in 1951 and, shortly afterward, the *Loi Barange*, authorizing some aid to Catholic schools, was passed by the National Assembly. The de Gaulle government also sponsored, successfully, legislation assisting the parochial schools, and again the proposals sparked a serious political conflict. In Germany today, with large majorities of both Catholics and Protestants preferring to send their children to nondenominational schools, the issue of aid to Catholic schools no longer stirs the controversy it did as recently as the 1950's.

EDUCATION AND CLASS: Until the mid-twentieth century, education in most European countries remained segregated by so-cial class. The mass of the population received an elementary education and then some vocational training until they were fifteen or sixteen. Relatively few went from elementary school to the privately run "public" schools or "grammar" schools in Britain,[6] to the state-run *lycées* in France, or to the state-run *Gymnasia* in Germany. Rather, these secondary schools were the training grounds for elites in each of the three countries, available mainly to those in the middle class, and their graduates went on to dominate the political and social life of these nations. In Britain, for example, although the "public" schools educated a mere fraction of the population, their graduates made up 56 percent of the members of Commons and filled the bulk of positions in the upper levels of government, especially the foreign service, during the 1920's and 1930's. Foreign-service personnel are still predominantly public-school graduates. Harold Wilson was only the second twentieth-century prime minister not to be a public-school alumnus. Edward Heath was the third, and the first of his Conservative Party.

In all three countries narrow recruitment patterns have been breaking down as the effects of broadened educational opportunities have begun to be felt. Since World War II the movement toward the comprehensive secondary schools, so characteristic of the United States, has been gaining ground, and more and more young people are entering university-preparatory programs. In France especially the new flexibility has had a profound effect on the educational filtering process. Nonetheless, all European systems still retain a larger element of tradition than the American, and relatively fewer

---

[6] The public school derives its name from the fact that it is directed by a board of governors who, unlike those managing many other private schools, have no financial stake in the institution. The oldest public schools are Winchester (1382) and Eton (1440). The designation "grammar" schools was originally given to privately run secondary schools which were nonboarding and which originally concentrated on Latin grammar. Today the term also applies to state-run secondary schools which stress academic subjects, i. e., which are not comprehensive.

lower-class children are able to advance through the system. For example, even by 1973 less than half of the secondary-school population in Britain were in comprehensive high schools; privately run secondary schools, as well as the state-run grammar schools into which only students of demonstrated ability are placed, were still strong. In Germany also the two-track system of education was still in operation, with only about 10 percent of the students entering the academic *Gymnasia*. In France, 60 percent of the secondary-school students were in comprehensive schools by 1973. However, less than a third of the children of working-class parents remained in school beyond the age of fifteen and less than a third of all secondary-school children continued in academic programs. As late as 1970 only 6.5 percent of the relevant age group was enrolled in institutions of higher learning in Britain, only 9.3 percent in Germany, and 18.9 percent in France. The comparable figure for the United States was 31 percent.

In part because of scholarships offered to them, children of working-class background in Britain have always had more educational opportunities relative to middle class youth than have young people of comparable background in France or Germany. In this sense Britain has always been a less stratified society than either France or Germany. The pattern has continued to this day. In the 1970's the ratio of university students from working-class backgrounds in the United States was approximately 1:2, whereas in Britain it was 1:3; in France, 1:8; and in West Germany, 1:15.

EDUCATION AND CULTURE: Schools perpetuate the values and attitudes of a nation's culture, and often the distinctive characteristics of that culture can be traced to these agents of socialization. Both Britain and Germany offer particularly clear illustrations.

In Britain, the aim of the Victorian public school was to turn out young men of good character who could adapt themselves to any situation. Students were expected to learn how to give and take orders, with younger students being placed under the authority of older ones. The public-school graduate was ideally an individual of broad general culture, knowing some, but not too much, Latin and Greek. He would be a gentleman, combining the best features of aristocratic bearing and taste; he would be sexually and emotionally restrained, fairly good at sports, and not too materialistic.

All of these values and characteristics, which were perpetuated also by the privately run grammar schools, came to prevail in the major institutions of British society, and perpetuated themselves well into the twentieth century. After World War II, however, they came under increasing attack and, indeed, the public schools have gradually adapted to a more egalitarian and technological milieu even as they have attempted to retain "the best of the past."

Nevertheless, attacks upon them, especially by the left, have, if anything, grown in intensity. The basic charge is that the privately run schools continue to cultivate elitist attitudes in their students, even as the public persists in exhibiting what critics would describe as an unhealthy deference to the public-school product. Added to this judgment is the argument that the kind of training offered is out of tune with the modern trends, that it encourages the cult of the amateur that is responsible for Britain's remaining a "fuddy-duddy" society, while America and even France and Germany place more emphasis on the natural and social sciences.

Critics of German education have charged that the German school has traditionally been even more responsible than the German family for instilling attitudes toward authority which were not supportive of democratic government. Not only have students been taught unquestioning submission to authority, but their curriculum has dwelt on private and personal values at the expense of public and political values. Albert Speer, chief architect of the Third Reich and one of Hitler's most trusted advisers, describes his schooling in his memoirs:

*Our German teacher, an enthusiastic dem-
ocrat, often read aloud to us from the liberal
Frankfurter Zeitung. But for this teacher I
would have remained altogether nonpolitical
in school. For we were being educated in
terms of a conservative bourgeois view of
the world. In spite of the Revolution which
had brought in the Weimar Republic, it was
still impressed upon us that the distribution
of power in society and the traditional authorities were part of the God-given order of
things. We remained largely untouched by
the currents stirring everywhere during the
early twenties. In school, there could be no
criticism of courses or subject matter, let
alone of the ruling powers in the state. Un-
conditional faith in the authority of the
school was required. It never even occurred
to us to doubt the order of things, for as students we were subjected to the dictates of a
virtually absolutist system. Moreover, there
were no subjects such as sociology which
might have sharpened out political
judgments.*[7]

The postwar period witnessed a gradual
erosion of traditional authoritarian patterns
in German schools although they remained,
relatively, bastions of conservativism until
the middle and late 1960's. Nor did the proportion of children entering universities increase very rapidly. The Social Democratic
Liberal coalition which came to power in the
late 1960's, however, set a goal of reforming
curriculum; increasing university enrollments to roughly 23 percent of the relevant
age group and to halving the student teacher
ratio in primary and secondary schools by
1980. However, these plans have been limited by the fact that education is, primarily,
the responsibility of the states, and by
budget cuts resulting from the post-1973
economic crisis. In 1975, a student who
wanted to study medicine or dentistry had a
projected wait of ten years for a university
place. Perhaps the most important indica-

tion of change in German education is the
emergence, for the first time, of groups actively and continuously pressuring authorities for changes at all educational levels.
Nevertheless, aspirations for higher education are growing more rapidly than opportunities. In 1975–76, 60 thousand eligible
secondary school graduates could not be admitted to universities because of a shortage
of places. If present trends continue, the
surplus of students over places may reach
200,000 by 1985.

4.   THE MASS MEDIA: THE PRESS

DEVELOPMENT: The origins of the European mass media can be traced back to the
Roman Empire, where their primary function was dissemination of information by
the government to officials and to the population. The *Acta diurna* of the Empire was
an official publication in bulletin-board
form; in addition to communicating official
government decrees, it served many other
functions that characterize mass media today, reporting, for example, news of crime,
sports, and "sensational" events.

With the invention of the printing press
in the fifteenth century, communications
technology began to grow at a spectacular
rate. The result was not only the mass output of books, but the evolution of media spe-
cializing in providing "news" to a widening
audience. The printing press thus permitted the expansion of cultural horizons, as
well as the amalgamation of peoples into
ever larger units. The idea that the press
might serve another function—provide a
source of news and opinion free from government censorship, and hence act both as a
check upon government and as a means by
which the community could refine its attitudes on public policy—began to appear only
with the development of liberalism and the
democratic state. It is not surprising, then,
that the concept of a "free press" was first
propounded in Britain and first realized in
the United States, nor any accident that a
mass-circulation press appeared first in the

[7] Albert Speer, *Inside the Third Reich*, trans.
Richard and Clara Winston (New York: Macmillan
Co., 1970), pp. 7–8.

United States and then in Britain. The latter phenomenon was accompanied by mass literacy, which, of course, it required in order to prosper. The success of the mass-circulation press was also contingent upon technological innovations that permitted the printing of large numbers of newspapers quickly and cheaply, and the speedy transmission of news to and from all parts of the world.

In both France and Germany the growth of the press took a quite different form. Aside from the fact that newspapers regarded themselves as quasi-literary journals, many of them were sponsored during the late nineteenth and early twentieth centuries by religious and political groups. Both the Catholic church and political parties, especially the mass parties of the left and the right, looked upon newspapers as a crucial part of their effort to create a total environment for their constituents—either to protect them from a hostile (secular or radical) world in the case of Catholics, or, in the case of Socialists, Communists, or National Socialists, to prepare them for tomorrow's new world. Every major party and some minor parties published their own newspapers. In all of them, articles were highly personal, usually signed, and primarily expressions of opinion rather than attempts to relate the news. As late as 1930 Germany newspapers included 444 published by the various nationalist parties, 312 published by the Catholic Center Party and the church, 169 published by the Socialists, and 8 published by the National Socialist Party.

Another feature common to France and Germany was the existence of newspapers which received subsidies from the government, or from special-interest groups, or which were owned by the government and served as "official" papers. The result was a continued succession of news stories of dubious accuracy in which fact and propaganda were mixed, or even from which fact was conspicuously absent.

In the aftermath of World War I, popular, "commercial" newspapers in France and Germany began to replace the party or church press, at least in terms of circulation. The end of World War II did nothing to change the general pattern: the commercial press increased in circulation, the special press declined. In 1946, for example, the daily organ of the French Communist Party, *L'Humanité*, had a total circulation of five hundred thousand; by 1950 its circulation had dropped to fewer than two hundred thousand, where it has since remained. The same has been true of the newspapers of other political parties. In the 1930's there were 34 daily newspapers in Paris, 15 of them the organs of political groups. Today there are only 10, and most of them lack party affiliation. In Germany, even where a party newspaper has continued to exist, its orientation has become more and more commercial. In 1930 about half the German newspapers represented some political party: today less than 20 percent do, and in terms of circulation, no more than 4 or 5 percent.

The growth of the press as a commercial venture requiring large outlays of capital and heavy reliance upon advertising revenue has had a significant effect on the number of newspapers published. As both competition and operating costs have increased, the number has been declining even as overall circulation has risen. In several countries, most particularly Britain, which early developed the tradition of a national press centered in London, newspaper ownership has fallen into fewer and fewer hands. By the 1960's more than 65 percent of the circulation of the British press was controlled by three organizations. In Germany, the roughly 1,150 daily newspapers published today compares with 4,700 published during the Weimar Republic.

In Britain the concentration of newspaper ownership is paralleled by a geographical concentration in London. The French press is less concentrated in this respect. Today, the press in the provinces accounts for more than two-thirds of newspaper circulation—almost exactly the reverse of the prewar situation. Such papers as *La Dépêche de Toulouse* have sound reputations. Geographical concentration is least apparent in Germany. The divorce of Berlin from Western Germany and the emphasis on a federal governmental structure have made the local and regional press far more important than it was during the Weimar years.

THE BRITISH PATTERN: Reflecting the cultural differences between the classes in Britain, a particularly sharp dichotomy can be seen between the "quality" press and the "popular" press. The former, limited to the *Times*, the *Guardian*, the *Observer* (published on Sundays only), and, to a certain extent, the *Daily Telegraph*, concentrates on the presentation of serious news. The "popular" press emphasizes entertainment and life's gaudier aspects to an extent that even Americans brought up on the *Daily News* or the Hearst newspapers might find rather shocking. Augmenting the field of serious newspapers are several high-quality weeklies such as the *New Statesman*, the *Spectator*, and the *Economist*.

One of the basic differences between Britain and the United States is that despite changes that have occurred since World War II, the British press, like the population at large, still tends to defer to government authority. The reluctance of the press to "take out after" government leaders contrasts sharply with American practice (illustrated by the Watergate exposé); this reluctance reflects both the greater sense of traditional community in Britain and the fact that most newspapermen in Britain have come from lower-class backgrounds and have less education than the political leaders. Most journalists are not college or university graduates, and it is no accident that most of them who serve as members of Parliament still sit on the Labor benches.

There are four other important points of difference. First, while the United States and Britain both have libel laws, these laws are far more severe and far more strictly enforced in Britain. Indeed United States Supreme Court decisions in the 1960's have made it all but impossible for any public official to win a libel suit against a newspaper

for comments on his public activities. Second, the British press is prohibited by law from commenting on cases that are being litigated in the courts, and, as with libel laws, this prohibition is enforced. Third, party discipline inhibits leaks of a kind that are quite commonplace in the United States. Finally, the British Official Secrets Act, which provides very severe penalties for the divulging or publication of "classified" information, makes it very unlikely that the press would have access to or be willing to print the kind of documents (such as the "Pentagon papers") that have been published in the United States during the past several years.

THE FRENCH PATTERN: In France, many of the older newspapers went out of existence following World War II as a result of their collaboration with the Nazis. Today the most influential papers include the daily *Le Monde* and the weekly *L'Express*. Both are independent and honest according to their own lights and, in contrast with American newspapers, offer far more in-depth reporting in a more concise form. French weeklies, both serious and popular, have gained wide acceptance since the war. They range from the moderate-left *L'Express* through the brilliantly satirical *Le Canard Enchainé*, which frequently receives leaks from disgruntled officials, to the entertainment-oriented *Paris Match*, which has a circulation of 1.2 million. The three most important trends in the French press since the second world war have been the decline of the party newspapers, the general decline in the number of daily newspapers, and the increasing importance of the regional and local press in terms of circulation.

On the whole, French newspapers are better written and more accurate than before the war. However, there is still little real division between news reporting and editorial comment, and at times the latter dominates the former. This is perhaps, related to the fact that national newspapers in particular tend to have a well-defined, often partisan readership. *Le Monde*, for example, has a virtual monopoly of the moderate-lift, intellectual readers. Nevertheless, the French press lacks a "muckraking" tradition, and reporters rarely dig behind the government handouts. In 1973, "everyone in Paris" seemed to know that President Pompidou was dying, but the press continued to report government-inspired stories that the president's health was fine.

Government subsidies of the press are still used from time to time to cull effective support, though much less so than during the Fourth Republic, and individual reporters are regularly subject to police violence when covering riots. The government also continues to seize individual issues of newspapers containing stories it regards as a "threat to national security." Between 1955 and 1962, for example, 269 issues were confiscated, most of them for their reporting of the Algerian War. In many cases, the seizures were illegal, but even so, it was almost impossible for the newspapers to obtain compensation. One of the first announcements made by newly elected President Giscard d'Estaing in the spring of 1974 was that his government would discontinue the practice of confiscating newspapers.

THE GERMAN PATTERN: The quality of German newspapers since World War II is generally better than it was before the Naxi regime even though no German paper has quite the international status that a few attained during the Weimar period. There are now several journalism schools, journalists are getting better training on the job, and while there is still more subjective reporting than in the best British or United States papers, the good papers make strenuous efforts at objective news coverage. Surveys show that the Germans rely more heavily upon newspapers for information on public affairs than do the British, the French, or the Americans; and such newspapers as *Die Zeit* and *Die Welt*, both of Hamburg, the *Suddeutsche Zeitung* of Munich, and the *Frankfurter Allgemeine* and *Frankfurter Rundschau* are on a par with the best in Europe. However, Germany lacks prestigious national newspapers.

In *Der Spiegel,* whose circulation has risen rapidly to over a million, Germany has a weekly news magazine patterned after *Time.* In addition to news items, publisher Rudolf Augstein has encouraged the writing of long, unsigned articles, casual in style but slanted in viewpoint, which have sometimes seemed irresponsible. The journal is exceptionally well informed, however, and has refused to kowtow to government authority. Indeed, in 1962, as the result of its publication of certain hitherto classified information on the German army, Augstein was arrested, and the offices of his journal were sealed. *Der Spiegel* had engaged for many years in a bitter feud with Franz Joseph Strauss, a leading Christian Democrat and at one time Germany's defense minister. The government's action, carried out in the clumsiest and most authoritarian fashion, resulted in the reshuffling of the Adenauer cabinet and, after long and acrimonious debate, in the dismissal of Strauss from his post. *Der Spiegel* soon resumed publishing, and charges against all those arrested were either dropped or dismissed; the West German Constitutional Court, however, refused to declare the seizures unconstitutional; half the judges argued that the state had not been unreasonable in assuming that *Der Spiegel* unlawfully possessed secret military documents.

Both the issues of consolidation and the role of the press in German life came to a head in 1967–68 with the mounting of verbal and physical assaults upon the Springer organization by left-wing students. The latter argued that the large circulation of Springer's newspapers (Springer controls about 38 percent of the daily and 84 percent of the Sunday newspaper market) was part and parcel of Germany's continued authoritarianism. But the attacks against Springer stemmed not only from the size of his newspapers' circulation, but also from his political opinions, which are bourgeois, conservative, and fairly nationalistic, although by no means right-wing. A committee set up by

**FIGURE 7.1   SHARE OF THE SPRINGER PUBLISHING HOUSE IN THE
NEWSPAPER MARKET OF THE FEDERAL REPUBLIC OF
GERMANY, 1966**

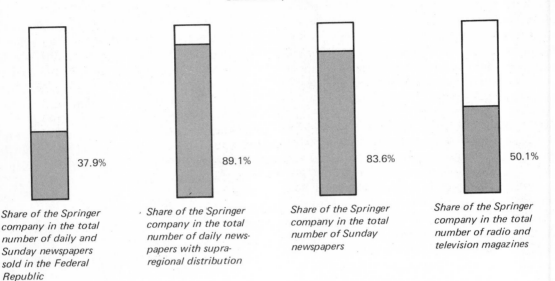

37.9%

*Share of the Springer
company in the total
number of daily and
Sunday newspapers
sold in the Federal
Republic*

89.1%

*Share of the Springer
company in the total
number of daily news-
papers with supra-
regional distribution*

83.6%

*Share of the Springer
company in the total
number of Sunday
newspapers*

50.1%

*Share of the Springer
company in the total
number of radio and
television magazines*

Adapted from Horst Holzer, "Massenkommunikation
und Demokratie in der Bundesrepublik Deutschland,"
in Karl M. Bolte, Friedhelm Neidhardt, and Horst
Holzer, *Deutsche Gesellschaft im Wahdel* (Opladen:
Leske, 1970), p. 270, reprinted by permission of the
publisher.

parliament to investigate the issues involved suggested that no one organization should be permitted to control more than 30 percent of daily newspaper circulation. The proposal, however, has not yet become law; the only immediate tangible result of the student demonstrations was Springer's decision to liquidate some of his magazine holdings in order to concentrate on his newspaper empire.

In general, German newspapers, including those that are pro-government, have been quite willing to criticize the nation's leaders. Many have also consistently fought and exposed neo-Nazi elements. If the press is relatively moderate politically, it is far more independent today than it has ever been in the past. Nevertheless, in contrast to the weekly *Der Spiegel*, the daily press rarely, engages in investigative reporting and "muckraking" criticism.

During the later years of the Weimar Republic, and in contrast to the early years, re-

pression against newspapers became commonplace. During the chancellorship of Heinrich Brüning, for example, 284 newspaper issues were suspended, primarily those of the Communist and National Socialist press. The Nazis, of course, abolished all freedom of the press. Today, freedom of the press is guaranteed by the Basic Law. The only limits upon this freedom are those prohibiting publication of items that might corrupt young people or violate an individual's honor. Article 80 also provides that whoever abuses the freedom of expression to attack free democratic institutions forfeits his basic rights.

5.   THE MASS MEDIA: RADIO AND TELEVISION

Radio, the telephone and telegraph, and especially television, have produced a second revolution in communications. Today, a vast

TABLE 7.5   NEWSPAPER CIRCULATION AND TELEVISION
RECEIVERS, 1965–1970

per 1000 population

| | Newspaper circulation | | Television receivers | |
	1965	1970–72	1965	1972
Britain	479	528	255	304
Germany	326	319	207	291
France	245	237	114	236

Adapted from *Statistical Abstract of the United States,*
1974, pp. 839–840; and Anthony Sampson, *Anatomy of
Europe* (New York: Harper & Row, 1968), p. 275.

proportion of the population in all modern states obtains much of its impression of events from television broadcasts.

Television is a factor in broadening the outlook of masses of people—even as it contributes to cultural homogenization within all European nations. Television has also become a prime instrument of social mobilization. Events that might have had only local significance thirty years ago now take on national, and sometimes international, dimensions. The spread of student "confrontations" from America to Europe was caused at least in part by television. Group demands—with attendant disorder a possibility—have been escalated far more quickly since television has widely publicized them and has been able to reveal more sharply to different groups where and how their interests actually conflict. As for political leaders, their constant exposure to a mass audience places them under tremendous strains in spite of the obvious advantages they can derive from extensive publicity.

The impact of television can be overstated, of course. Research indicates that newspapers, and more significantly, face-to-face discussions are still extremely important in structuring social and political attitudes. The message of the media, in other words, is altered through existing orientations, and through primary associations and personal influence before its impact is felt.

THE BRITISH PATTERN: The British Broadcasting Company was licensed in 1923 as a private corporation. Sir John Reith, its first manager, quickly developed strong convictions about the proper role of broadcasting as a public service, and he proceeded to put them into effect without hindrance from either station managers or the government. The implementation of Reith's policies was followed by a government commission of inquiry which concluded that the BBC should not permit advertising and that radio broadcasting should be financed by a license fee for each radio set—a method that still provides BBC radio and television with its only significant source of income. In 1926 the BBC was converted into a public corporation, independent in matters of day-to-day administration, but ultimately answerable to the cabinet and to Parliament on general policy.

In 1954 a Conservative government, after a rather nasty fight over the principle of introducing commercialism to the airwaves, sponsored legislation creating a commercial television service. A new corporation, the Independent Television Authority (ITA), was created with the responsibility for appointing commercial broadcasting companies in more than a dozen regions and for supervision of their performance. These companies were to sell time spots of controlled length and frequency to advertisers who would have no say in program content. The

BBC retained control of all broadcasting facilities. The result of the duel system of
television broadcasting has been the introduction of more "popular" entertainment, as
well as the adoption by the BBC of experi-
mentation and social boldness that have gone
beyond anything on American or Continental television. Encouraged by what was
seen as the success of commercial television,
a new Conservative government in 1971 announced proposals to establish a series of
sixty local commercial radio stations; these
would supplement the twenty BBC-run local
radio stations that a Labor government had
set up beginning in 1966. The ITA, renamed the Independent Broadcasting Authority, would control the operation of the
new stations under the Conservatives' plan.

The BBC has long maintained a reputation for studied impartiality in dealing with
political news, and at first television retained this "balanced" quality. But by the
1960's political commentary became slightly
acerbic; political figures appearing on television were giving and receiving some fairly
cutting barbs—and arousing the hostility of
some political leaders. The BBC, however,
has yet to develop a pattern of political commentary on television comparable with that
of stations in the United States. Concern
with objectivity—whatever its virtues—has
all too frequently had an inhibiting effect
upon the lively presentation of political
news.

THE FRENCH PATTERN: In Third Republic
France private, regulated networks were allowed to broadcast along with an official government station. Under the Fourth Republic, both radio and television were brought
completely under government control, and
though they were supposedly given quasi-independent status, they were frequently used
as a propaganda device, especially in times of
crisis. In its first years the de Gaulle regime
was even more efficient in using television
for its own ends. Thus, legislation that theoretically transferred the control of television
to a quasi-independent body—the *Office
de Radiodiffusion Télévision Française*

(ORTF), modeled after the BBC—made
little difference; the leading personnel remained Gaullist.

After 1964, the regime loosened its restrictions to permit the presentation of opposition viewpoints. However, when ORTF
personnel rebelled against government attempts to manage the news in 1968 by going
on strike, the size of the television staff was
"reduced," and strike leaders were fired.
Once again in 1969, the prime minister announced an experiment in the "liberalization" of television news. But in July, 1972,
the "independent" news units were dissolved
and the director fired.

Governmental interference was not the
only problem faced by French television.
While cultural standards were originally
rather high, little appeared on French television to appeal to working-class audiences; in
northeastern France, viewers were turning
to telecasts from Luxembourg and the Saar.
Moreover, the financing of television by fees
was not producing needed funds. The government responded by catering somewhat
more to popular tastes, by authorizing commercials in 1968, and by reorganizing and
decentralizing the ORTF in 1972 to encourage better and more diverse programming.
However, the reality and the threat of persistent government interference have hampered all efforts to reform the ORTF. In
the fall of 1973, the director of the newly organized office was dismissed by the President of the Republic when he refused to
obey an order of the Minister of the Interior
to dismiss two leftist producers in the cultural section of French radio. In August,
1974, ORTF officially ceased to exist, and
French radio and each of the three television networks were reestablished, each with
its own director and staff. The production
of programs, however, remained in a single,
separate unit. The result has been some
productive programming competition among
the television networks. Each of the new
units is supposed to be independent of government control, but this defies a well-es-
tablished tradition that has survived numerous administrative reforms.

THE GERMAN PATTERN: In Weimar Germany radio was organized under an independent public corporation, and it was conducted with commendable impartiality. The National Socialist regime, of course, centralized control of broadcasting, and radio became an instrument of state propaganda pure and simple. After 1945 both radio and television were decentralized among the *Länder,* and are supervised by part-time boards of parliamentarians and representatives of numerous interest groups. However, the nine regional stations are banded together in a loose network, *Arbeitsgemeinschaft Rundfunkanstalten Deutschland* (RDF) and meet regularly to discuss mutual problems.

In the late 1950's demand grew for a national channel, and after complicated court battles, the *Zeites Deutsches Fernsehen* (ZDF) was created on the UHF band. The ZDF operates under a board of directors consisting of representatives from the Federal Government, the *Länder,* and various occupational groups. The ZDF is required to coordinate its activities with the RDF in order to insure that citizens always have a choice of programming. Financing is by a combination of license fees and advertising, with the latter gradually providing an increasing share of revenue. However, advertisers have no say in program content, and there are no television commercials after 8 p.m.

From the beginning German television has actively involved itself in political commentary of various sorts and has tended to take a strongly reformist posture, reminding viewers of the horrors of the Nazi regime and "exposing" the activities of right-wing groups. Politicians have been interviewed regularly and handled rather roughly. In fact, one of the longest-running programs on German television is *"Internationaler Frühschoppen"* ("International Morning Drink"), in which the German moderator invites journalists from five countries to a glass of wine and discussion of current issues. There is also an equivalent to "Meet the Press" in a program called *"Zur Person,"* ("In Person"), in which German political figures appear for questions and discussion. And perhaps in line with the findings that the average German does have a relatively high level of political information among the peoples of the West, Germany's television channels devote more time proportionally to political topics than does any other major Western European network.

But certainly the biggest success and the most talked about program on German television is one that began on local television in Cologne and that because of its popularity is now being broadcast nationally—*"Ein Herz und eine Seele."* "One Heart and one Soul" is a German version of the BBC's "Til Death Do Us Part" and of the American "All in the Family" show. Its protagonist is one Alfred Tetzlaff, whose rightist, racist, and authoritarian views have provoked a stir among Germans and people in other countries as well—some of whom see in it a propaganda vehicle for the radical right. Even though the author himself leans to the left and declares that he intends it as satire, issues of authoritarianism and extremist political views are still so ambivalent in Germany as to leave the impact of this program upon the millions of viewers open to question.

nous sommes Communistes,

DES FEMMES ET DES HOMMES COMME VOUS

NOUS VOULONS CONSTRUIRE UNE VIE HUMAINE ET LIBRE
LE SOCIALISME
AVEC NOUS, FAITES CE CHEMIN

DEVENEZ MEMBRE
DU PARTI COMMUNISTE FRANÇAIS

Left: French Communist Party poster. *Below:* General Election in Britain, 1974. Courtesy British Information Services. *Opposite page:* Harold Wilson, Gerald Ford, Valéry Giscard d'Estaing, Helmut Schmidt. Courtesy German Information Center.

PART THREE
Political Parties

Political Parties:

The
European
Pattern

1. INTRODUCTION

Democratic theory assumes that individuals and groups within the society will be given relatively free play in urging the adoption of their demands as public policy. The contest is justified by the belief that it will produce results that represent a creative response to the needs of most citizens. The major limitation placed upon the expression of demands is that those who make them not resort to violence.

Political parties have emerged as the instrument for waging this competitive struggle of freely expressed demands. Because the number of demands that can be made upon the political system by its members is theoretically infinite, one function of political parties is to aggregate them into a smaller number of alternatives. If the democratic system is working well, political parties will also serve other functions: they will enable members of the society to make more rational policy choices by spelling out actual or possible consequences to different alternatives, and they will provide expressive satisfactions in the form of rhetorical combat. The political elites who staff the parties—mostly elected public officeholders or aspiring candidates—will be rewarded by seeing their demands translated into programs, by the satisfaction that comes with exercising authority, and by the material rewards that are often a by-product of the exercise of authority.

It should be emphasized that the functions fulfilled by political parties in a democratic political order can be handled by other structures, as indeed they have been through most of recorded history. It may well be true that a politics of parties will turn out to have been a transitory type of political order, limited in time to the nineteenth and twentieth centuries.

2. PARTIES AND ELECTORAL SYSTEMS

All democratic societies characterized by competitive party systems face the problem of creating machinery for reflecting the expressed preferences of voters. Ideally, representation on decision-making bodies should accurately reflect all the opinions that exist within the society itself. It is not too difficult to demonstrate, however, the logical impossibility of achieving this goal or even of creating an electoral system that mirrors the will of the majority, when all the various positions on all issues, as well as the intensity of feeling about particular issues, are taken into account.[1] The best any electoral system can hope for is to provide a rough approximation of the feelings of different groups on the issues that are most important to them. Historically, two systems of representation, each with a number of modifications, have been most commonly used: single-member electoral districts with election by plurality or majority, and multimember districts with election by proportional representation.[2] Because many political scientists have believed that the type of system chosen influences the number and character of political parties in important ways, with significant consequences for the political system, it is worth outlining in some detail the structure of these two systems of representation. The

possible impact of electoral arrangements will be discussed after they have been described.[3]

SINGLE-MEMBER DISTRICTS: Britain and the United States have used a system of single-member election districts, with a *plurality* of the votes cast necessary for election. Both nations are divided into districts from which only one candidate can be elected. In each election the candidate with the largest number of votes is declared the winner, even if he receives fewer than a majority of the ballots. Assume a field of four candidates receiving the following portion of the votes cast:

Candidate A   35 percent
Candidate B   25 percent
Candidate C   20 percent
Candidate D   20 percent

In this example, Candidate *A* would be the victor.

In France during the Fifth Republic, as during most of the Third Republic, a system of single-member districts is combined with the requirement that a candidate receive a majority of the vote to be elected. If no candidate does so on the first ballot, a second election is held and only a plurality is necessary. Thus, in the example cited above, a second ballot would be required.[4]

A system of single-member districts with election by plurality tends to discriminate heavily against smaller political parties, to distort the result of voting, and to reduce the range of opinions represented in legislative bodies. Assume, for instance, a nation

[1] See Robert A. Dahl, *A Preface to Democratic Theory* (Chicago: University of Chicago Press, 1956).

[2] There are still other variations, such as two-member districts with preferential ballots, but these have not been used widely enough to merit consideration here.

[3] The classic exposition is that of F. A. Hermens, *Democracy or Anarchy?* (Notre Dame, Ind.: University of Notre Dame Press, 1941). See also Maurice Duverger, *Political Parties*, 2nd trans. rev. ed., Barbara and Robert North (London: Methven & Co., 1959); and Douglas W. Rae, *The Political Consequences of Electoral Laws*, rev. ed. (New Haven, Conn.: Yale University Press, 1971).

[4] Any candidate may compete a second time provided (since 1967) he has received at least 10 percent of the vote. More usually, however, an agreement is reached whereby some parties withdraw their candidates in return for the promise of political favors.

with 100 single-member electoral districts and four political parties, whose total vote is distributed more or less in the proportions listed in the example just given. Assuming further that the vote of each party is spread uniformly throughout the country, the largest party (Party A) would elect all its candidates, receiving 100 percent of the seats in the legislature—on the basis of 35 percent of the popular vote. The smaller the party, of course, the greater the discrimination. With 19.3 percent of the vote in the February, 1974, election, for instance, the British Liberal Party obtained only 14 seats, 109 fewer than it would have received under a system of proportional representation. Labor, on the other hand, got 301 seats, 192 more than it would have on a proportional basis; indeed, Labor polled fewer votes than the Conservative Party which it replaced as the governing party.

Provisions for a second ballot are fundamentally an attempt at "minimax." Those voters whose own candidate has no chance of being elected can vote for their second preference in the runoff election. In France, for example, a Radical voter might support a Gaullist candidate rather than chance the election of a Communist. Further, parties with little hope of winning on the second ballot can negotiate between elections; one party may withdraw its candidate in return for promises that the other will do the same in another electoral district, or in return for policy or other concessions. This system can, and does, distort electoral results. The French Communists in 1958 received only 2.2 percent of the parliamentary seats even though they won some 20.7 percent of the popular vote on the second ballot, because other parties would not enter into electoral alliance with them. In 1967, however, they entered into an arrangement with other left-wing parties in which each agreed to support the strongest candidate on the second ballot. As a result, they captured 15.3 percent of the seats in the Assembly, although their popular vote had increased by only 1 percent.

MULTIMEMBER DISTRICTS: Any system of proportional representation (PR) is designed to insure the "fair" representation of every possible political tendency. Basically, proportional representation involves multimember election districts and a process by which votes are divided among the candidates participating in the election.[5] In most European countries the list system of proportional representation is used. Under this system each major party enters a list of candidates equal in length to the number of seats to be filled. For example, let us assume that four political parties are competing in a district with five seats at stake, and that the votes are distributed as follows:

List A   13,500 votes
List B   4,500 votes
List C   4,500 votes
List D   1,500 votes

In this example it would be easy to divide the seats among the parties. List A would receive three seats and B and C one seat each. List D would receive no seats. As it is, List D has been discriminated against and the votes of its supporters wasted.

Discrimination is likely to be greater, as will the difficulty of distributing seats, if the votes received are not in neat proportion. For example, let us assume that the following distribution of votes had occurred:

List A   8,700 votes
List B   6,800 votes
List C   5,200 votes
List D   3,300 votes

If 5 seats are again at stake, the party lists are entitled to seats as follows: List A, 1.813 seats; List B, 1.416; List C, 1.083, and List D, 0.687 seats. No matter how the seats are divided, some votes are going to be lost. One way to minimize this waste is to reduce the number and increase the size of

[5] The description of systems of proportional representation is largely derived from W. H. M. McKenzie, *Free Elections* (New York: Rinehart and Company, 1958).

TABLE 8.1   DISTRIBUTION OF SEATS BY HIGHEST AVERAGE

List	Calculation of first seat	Calculation of second seat	Calculation of third seat	Calculation of fourth seat	Calculation of final seat	Total seats
A	8,700	4,350	4,350	4,350	2,900	2
B	6,800	6,800	3,400	3,400	3,400	2
C	5,200	5,200	5,200	2,600	2,600	1
D	3,300	3,300	3,300	3,300	3,300	0

electoral districts.   Another way is to employ techniques that have been developed to insure the fairest possible distribution. Two techniques, or variations of them, are most commonly used: the *highest average* and the *greatest remainder.*

In distributing seats in terms of the *highest average*, the votes of each list are first divided by one; the list with the highest average (which, of course, is equal to its vote) receives the first seat.   Thus, List A, with a highest average vote of 8,700, receives the first seat.   Its total is then divided by two (one plus the seat that it has obtained); the resulting quotient, 4,350, is noted in column 3 ("Calculation of second seat") of Table 8.1.   As will be seen from this table, List B (in the same column) has the highest average (6,800 divided by one) and therefore receives the second seat.   The average for List B is then divided by two (one plus the seat that it has received), and the resulting quotient, 3,400, appears in column 4 ("Calculation of third seat").   Here (fourth column of the table) List C has the

highest average, 5,200, and therefore receives the third seat.   The process is repeated in the calculation of the fourth seat, which goes to List A, with a highest average (after division by two) of 4,350.   The final seat is received by List B, with a highest average (after division by two) of 3,400, and List D receives none.

In the method of the *greatest remainder,* the total number of votes cast is divided by the number of seats available.   The seats received by any list are the result of dividing its votes by the quotient thus obtained.   The remaining seats are distributed among competing lists in terms of the remainders available after the initial distribution has taken place.   In this case the quotient is 4,800, and each of the three largest parties receives one seat.   The largest remainder is that of List A, which gets a second seat.   List D now has the largest remainder and, thus, receives the final seat (Table 8.2).

In general, the method of the highest average tends to favor larger parties, while that of the greatest remainder favors small-

TABLE 8.2   DISTRIBUTION OF SEATS BY GREATEST REMAINER

List	Votes	Seats won by quotient	Remainder	Total seats
A	8,700	1	3,900	2
B	6,800	1	2,000	1
C	5,200	1	400	1
D	3,300	0	3,300	1

er ones. Thus, the method of the highest average would allot two seats each to Lists A and B, one seat to List C, and none to List D. If the greatest remainder were used, however, List A would receive two seats and each of the other lists would obtain one.

The French under the Fourth Republic used the highest average, except, after 1950, in the Department of the Seine (the Paris region). The Germans used the method of the greatest remainder during the Weimar period. In fact, the electoral law went still further to insure accurate representation; a national constituency was established that allowed "wasted" remainders to be collected and used for the election of candidates from national party lists to the Reichstag.

Under a rigid list system of proportional representation, voters choose among party lists rather than individuals, and candidates from the list are declared elected in the order of their appearance on it. Thus, if Party D presented a list of five candidates and were entitled to two seats, the first two candidates on its list would normally be returned to the parliament. The arrangement minimizes the role of the individual candidate, underscores the importance of party voting, and places a good deal of power in the hands of party leaders, who usually determine the order in which names will appear. Understandably, individual candidates who might have a large following but who are, for some reason, not destined for first place consider this procedure unfair.

A flexible list system is one which permits the voter to change the order of the names on the list, to distribute his vote among a number of lists, or even to compose his own list (panachage). During periods of its history France has experimented with some of these procedures, but the problems have proved overly complex.

PROPORTIONAL REPRESENTATION, PROS AND CONS: Proportional representation has always been supported on the ground that it allows for a more equitable delineation of voters' preferences. Since the collapse of the Weimar Republic, however, PR has fall-en into some disrepute. As for plurality elections in single-member election districts, most of the proponents argue that the apparent unfairness of this method is actually a virtue. First, the plurality method tends to reduce to two the number of parties competing for office; it fails to award legislative seats to small parties, and consequently, it also encourages the potential supporters of small parties to vote for larger parties rather than waste their vote. Second, the plurality method encourages the major parties to broaden their appeal so as to attract the votes of potential small-party supporters; in so doing they become moderate in their program or philosophy. Finally, by reducing the parties to two, the method virtually assures a legislative majority for one of them—a situation which makes stable parliamentary government more likely and which enables voters more easily to determine the quality of their representatives' performance in office.

It is argued that proportional representation has the opposite effects. First, it encourages the creation and maintenance of many parties because it guarantees legislative rewards to all of them, or at least to most of them; it may encourage fragmentation into still smaller groups, some of them of the narrowest and most radical kind. Second, in a parlimaentary system where there is a multiplicity of parties, the likely result is coalition cabinets. Coalitions can be stable and provide effective government, as the example of the Scandinavian countries illustrates. But they are often composed of men who find it difficult to compromise, lest they lose their political identity. The result may be either rapid changes of government, or one government remaining in office by doing nothing. During the twelve years of the Fourth Republic, France was governed by twenty-five different cabinets, and though a change in government often meant only a slight shifting of personnel, the development of any consistent, long-range policies was difficult if not impossible. Such a situation is likely to produce still further polarization of politics. In a coalition government, furthermore, a very small party may be placed in a politically strategic position. In France under the Fourth Republic the Radical Socialist Party supplied more prime ministers than any other party even though it was one of the smaller political factions.

Finally, it is argued that under proportional representation citizens do not have an effective choice because there is no rational course of action by which responsibility for public policy can be assigned to a particular party. Unable to cast a ballot for a party that he can hold accountable for its performance in office, a citizen's voting choice is more likely to be inspired primarily by ideological rhetoric.

Elections by single-member district and a double ballot may yield many of the same results as proportional representation. Thus, the possibility of a second election creates a multiplicity of smaller parties that hope to benefit through "deals," even if their candidates are not successful.

While the foregoing arguments make a certain amount of sense, some important qualifications are required. Single-member plurality elections do discourage third and fourth parties; yet these parties will develop and be supported regardless of electoral mechanisms if they represent an ideological or ethnic minority ignored by the larger parties. This is particularly true if the minority group is geographically segregated and has its own strongholds. The British Liberals have retained a few seats in Parliament thanks mainly to some positions of strength in Wales and Scotland. Similarly, empirical evidence demonstrates that the seeming logic of proportional representation, or of the double-ballot system, does not always hold. Sweden, Norway, and Denmark have all used proportional representation, yet rather than experiencing a progressive fragmentation of the party system, no more than four large parties have been maintained; and each of these nations has a relatively stable political system. Primary elections in many states of the American South, such as Georgia and Alabama, are conducted under a double-ballot system, but the factions that emerge as a result have no lasting power because they have no permanent geographic base of operation.

The case for the moderating effects of single-member districts with plurality elections is not especially convincing, either. One can argue that in a country marked by sharp political divisions single-member districts are most likely to result in polarization of the electorate around the extreme parties. Certainly the rise of the British Labor Party as a replacement for the British Liberals was not the victory of a more moderate party over a more extreme one. One can also argue that if a radical minority finds itself unrepresented in the political system, it is more likely to turn to violence than it would if it were so represented. Further, if we examine the historical development of the electoral systems in Britain and France, we arrive at the conclusion that the reasons for the adoption of one system over another may well have been partially related to the societal differences between the two nations. The British saw little need to concern themselves with the representation of a whole host of political groups. In France, on the other hand, the very multiplicity of factions has led to the adoption of more complicated electoral mechanisms, and political groups have taken turns trying to bend the electoral system to secure political advantage.

In sum, then, the relationship among electoral systems, party systems, and the functioning of political systems is not easy to unravel. The election system is an important factor among several that determine political outcomes. It is difficult to believe that the politics of the United States or Great Britain would have developed very differently if elections had been proportional representation, or that in the Weimar Republic another electoral system would have been enough to yield a stable polity. Moreover, the time at which PR or other systems are introduced may be crucial. In an effectively functioning two-party system, the introduction of PR may not make much difference; then again, once a multiplicity of reasonably well-organized parties has materialized, replacing PR by single-member districts may not affect the political scene.

3. THE DEVELOPMENT OF EUROPEAN PARTIES

European political parties, in the modern sense, began to take form only in the nineteenth century, with the beginnings of industrialization, the emergence of liberalism as a political ideology, the gradual extension of the suffrage, and the creation of parliamentary regimes. To be sure, factions or "connexions" had existed earlier in Britain. In the eighteenth century, one could speak of Whigs and Tories and trace their antecedents back to the English Civil War. The lines between them, however, were blurred, and, with limited suffrage and a Parliament consisting almost entirely of gentlemen, "connexions" formed and reformed, based on individual, family, regional, or religious factors.

The American and French revolutions had an enormous impact upon the development of political parties. In the United States, commitment to a government based on the participation of the people resulted in a fairly rapid extension of voting rights and the early emergence of modern political parties. By 1840, American Whigs and Democrats were using most of the techniques associated with contemporary electoral campaigns. In Britain and on the Continent, the evolution of modern parties was much slower. In most of Europe, the first attempt to form enduring factions came from liberals who wished to change the existing social order.

In Germany, liberal political groups started to organize in 1848, and in France, the Jacobins of the revolutionary period were followed by numerous groups that formed throughout the nineteenth century, although political parties as such did not appear until the turn of the century. The formation of "liberal" parties caused, in response, the founding of a series of "conservative" organizations dedicated to preserving the patterns of the traditional society. In Britain, on the other hand, conservative gentlemen saw the need for organization at about the same time as liberal reformers. Thus the founding of the Carlton Club in 1832 preceded by four years that of the liberals' Reform Club.

4. TYPES OF PARTY ORGANIZATION

On the whole, conservative and liberal parties in Europe were *parties of notables* —men of substance who organized in order to achieve common ends or serve particular interests. And although they appealed to the electorate, their organizational efforts were always limited (especially in the case of conservatives) by a distaste, bred of their traditional values, for developing a truly mass party. Initially this inhibition was not too important; the electorate was still small, and the practice of public voting permitted not only bribery but intimidation. By the 1880's, however, most European countries had established the secret ballot, and most were well on the way to universal manhood suffrage. Traditional political methods no longer sufficed. The legislators who had been elected more or less as individuals now found it necessary to form national organizations for the purposes of picking suitable candidates and conducting election campaigns. These organizations, for the most part, remained under the control of the parliamentary leaders or local notables.

The first European *mass parties* were the Socialist parties. Founded by trade unions or reformers, and with the working class as their source of strength, they differed from the older parties in five important respects. First, they were initially organized outside the parliamentary structure rather than within it. Second, they were part of ideological "movements" based on a *Weltanschauung* that demanded the total transformation of society. Third, their organization was composed of and dependent upon dues-paying members who were expected to work continuously for the party on a voluntary basis. Fourth, mass parties usually established affiliated organizations, such as youth groups and women's sections, designed to create a subculture in which members reinforced one another's loyalties and were protected from the corrupting influences of the larger society. Finally, they imposed on their elected members in parliament a discipline that contrasted sharply with the independence tolerated by the older parties.

The impact of the Socialists and the growing need to organize a larger electorate compelled other parties to look again to their structure. The effort to organize more conservative parties varied with national circumstances. In Britain, the existence of a two-party system and the acceptance of a democratic polity by the Conservatives led them to adopt a mass-membership structure of their own. In France, political fragmentation and the conservatives' persistent distaste for appealing to the masses handicapped such organization. The same factors operated even more strongly in Germany, and the collapse of German conservatism in the post-World War I period was due partly to its inability to come to terms with the new mass society.

Although European liberal parties were among the first to develop a modern structure, they, too, did not succeed in creating a mass base. Some of the same factors operated here that inhibited the conservatives. Their ideology notwithstanding, liberal parties were led by a class-conscious middle class that to a certain extent remained suspicious of the industrial proletariat and shied away from "demagoguery." Liberal ideology itself was an impediment, particularly its individualistic emphasis and its conception of the state as a broker whose function it was to facilitate negotiations among competing regional, individual, and group interests.

The only other mass parties that sprang up in the nineteenth century were those that catered to minority ethnic or religious groups. The Irish Nationalists and the German Center (Catholic) Party, both created as mass organizations, were based on an appeal to a particular group. In a society where the reins of power were held by a hostile establishment, this was the only manner in which minorities could protect their interests.

After World War I, two other types of mass parties, which were to have a prodigious effect upon the remainder of the twentieth century, burst forth in Europe: the Fascist and the Communist. Both were highly ideological, demanding the immediate and total transformation of their society; the mass base of Fascist parties made it clear that they were not merely "conservative" parties; both the Communist and Fascist parties can be seen as part of a broad reaction to the tensions produced by social change.

In the post–World War II period, Christian Democratic parties appeared in Western Europe with the aim of both uniting Catholicism—or more vaguely Christianity—with democracy and of breaking away from the traditional image of Catholic conservatism. Within a few years, however, most of them had lost their original élan and, while retaining something of a mass base, had become primarily pragmatic parties of the center or center left.

Indeed, the trend in Europe after World War II through the 1950's and the first part of the 1960's was away from mass parties and toward the cadre parties led by professional politicians. This political trend also involved the increasing bureaucratization of party structure, greater use of new publicity techniques, and the closer identification of parties, on the national level at least, with political leaders who were able to register a favorable television image. The trend toward bureaucratization and professionalism seemed to be taking place even in the Communist parties, a phenomenon interpreted by some as implying that the problems faced by technologically advanced nations are, in fact, "technical" rather than "ideological." It was against this trend that students (and many intellectuals) claimed to be rebelling during the 1960's. And by the 1970's the trend had, in fact, been slowed if not reversed, as all parties attempted to respond, more or less, to demands for greater participation. The late 1960's and 1970's also witnessed a small renaissance of ideological concerns, although, as compared to pre–World War II Europe it was still the "catch all" or "pragmatic quality of political parties that was noticeable.

5. THE BASES OF PARTY SUPPORT

By far the most significant source of political cleavage in Western Europe since the nineteenth century has been that of social class. Class division is most clearly apparent in Britain. There, anywhere from 60 to 70 percent of the working class support the Labor Party, as contrasted with 10 to 16 percent of the upper middle class who do so. About 45 percent of German workers support the German Social Democratic Party or other Socialist groups; the comparable percentage for professional men and businessmen is about 12. In France, class cleavage in voting is somewhat less marked; about 60 percent of the working-class supported the Communist or Socialist parties in 1973; both parties, however, received 32 percent of the vote of French businessmen and professionals in 1973.

There are, of course, differences in working-class voting patterns. Most workers in difficult occupations, occupations subject to marked economic fluctuations, or occupations like mining, where the workers live and work in fairly isolated communities, tend more to the left. Also, workers in larger factories usually vote in larger proportions for left-wing parties than do those in smaller factories, where the relation between employer and employee is often closer.

Europe's farmers are more conservative than the urban working class. In Britain, the small agricultural population favors the Conservative Party. In France's 1973 elections, only about 27 percent of the peasant and farmer populations voted for left-wing parties, whereas some 49 percent voted for the Gaullists. Earlier, many peasants and farmers had supported Pierre Poujade's semi-Fascist political organization. In Germany, only 12 percent of the farmers support the Socialist Party, whereas about 50 percent or more support the Christian Democratic Union.

While social class is the factor most closely related to voting differences, other variables are still significant. In Germany the religious issue, with its historical and in some cases regional roots, continues to have an impact, and in France religious commitment has been more important than class as a determinant of voting. Practicing Catholics in Germany and France vote heavily for center and conservative parties—including the Catholic parties. Protestants are more inclined to vote for left-wing parties, a pattern than in France is partly due to their minority status, and in Germany is associated with the fact that the more conservative party is the Christian Democratic Union. Jews, as a third religious group in Europe, also tend to vote for parties of the left, again partly because of their minority status. Agnostics and atheists are most likely to vote radically left.

Another variable of consequence is that women are more likely to be conservative voters than men. In the British election of 1970, only 42.2 percent of the men voted for the Conservative Party, nearly eight percentage points less than the women's Conservative vote. In France and until 1972 in Germany also, women voted either for more conservative or more religiously oriented parties in larger numbers than men. In 1973 only 42 percent of those who voted for the Communist Party in France were women, whereas 57 percent of the supporters of the Gaullist URP were women. Whether the "Women's Liberation Movement" that emerged in the late 1960's will produce a change in this pattern remains to be seen.

A general indication of voter alignment is given in Table 8.3.

TABLE 8.3   GENERAL PATTERN OF LEFT–WING VOTING

Higher leftist vote	*Lower leftist vote*
Larger cities	Smaller towns, country
Larger plants	Smaller plants
Groups with high unemployment rates	Groups with low unemployment rates
Minority ethnic or religious groups	Majority ethnic or religious groups
Men	Women
Economically advanced regions	Economically backward regions
Manual workers	White-collar workers
Specific occupations: Miners, fishermen, commercial farmers, sailors, longshoremen, forestry workers	Specific occupations: Servants, service workers, peasants, subsistence farmers
Less skilled workers	More skilled workers

Adapted from Seymour Martin Lipset, *Political Man* (New York: Doubleday, 1960), p. 244. Copyright © 1959, 1960 by the author, reprinted by permission of the publisher.

6.   CONCLUSIONS

Thus far we have discussed the general development of European parties, as well as types of voting arrangements, party structures, and the bases of party support. The contrasts between European and American patterns are apparent. The Republican and Democratic parties are basically liberal parties. In Europe, however, liberal parties became identified with a particular ideology. Their identification with laissez-faire capitalism lost them the support of the workers, while their victory in matters such as the mass franchise and the separation of church and state left them with little more to say. In the United States, on the contrary, the relative absence of class consciousness, together with the fact that the culture was incompatible with specifically ethnic or religious parties, meant that nothing comparable to the mass-membership, highly organized European parties of the left ever developed to challenge the two parties that shared a common liberal wellspring. Indeed the almost total dominance of a "liberal" political culture led leaders of both parties to assume that they were essentially pragmatic "non-ideological" political organizations.

The next several chapters will concentrate on how European party systems evolved, why they evolved in different ways, and the consequences of the differences. These chapters will introduce each party in the order of its historical appearance, describe its development, and focus on the interplay of those forces that have resulted in the contemporary—and still changing—political scene.

The
British
Party System

1. THE DEVELOPMENT OF POLITICAL PARTIES

Traditionally, the origin of modern British parties goes back to the conflict between Cavaliers and Roundheads—between those who supported Charles I during the Civil War (1642–48) and stood for a high church (with leanings toward Catholicism), and those who represented the Presbyterian and dissenting sects as well as English commerce. One can, in any event, identify two reasonably coherent—albeit temporary—factions in the parliament of 1679. One group, again tending to represent the interests of Presbyterians and Dissenters, sought passage of an Act of Exclusion to prevent the duke of York (later James II) from ascend-

ing the throne upon the death of his brother Charles. By their opponents, members of this group who were opposed to the succession of the duke were called "Whigs"—a Scots-Gaelic term meaning "cattle thieves." The second faction supported noninterference and its members were labeled "Tories," a term meaning "Irish papist outlaw." The typical Tory was described as a "monster with an English face, a French heart, and an Irish conscience. A creature of a large forehead, prodigious mouth, supple hams, and no brains."

During the next century, the names continued to refer to two loosely defined groups. The term "party" had as yet little significance; real power and real differences of opinion were distributed among a multiplicity of factions and determined by a great many personal, regional, and family loyalties. A good number of parliamentary seats were controlled by the king or the landed aristocracy, and many were bought and sold quite openly.

The formation of modern political parties began only after the Reform Bill of 1832 and other laws regarding suffrage had so enlarged the electorate that party organization became more and more necessary. Between 1830 and 1880, the Whigs became Liberals and the Tories Conservatives, and both parties established political machines. The transformation was slow. Even after 1832, the choice of candidates lay in the hands of notables—gentlemen who reached informal agreements as to which constituencies they would represent—and local concerns still affected these choices. In time, both parties created a more formal organization.

In general, the social basis of Liberal leadership was still Nonconformist—that is, non-Anglican, or relating to such Protestant sects as the Congregationalist, Methodist, or Baptist—and the Conservatives represented the establishment. Liberals were drawn increasingly from the newer commercial strata, Conservatives from the traditional landholding class. Nonetheless, party organization and party identification were still weak during the middle of the nineteenth century. The existence of Irish Nationalists further complicated matters so that one found a variety of factions—Whigs, Conservatives, Peelites (Conservatives who accepted free trade), Radicals (those who took a more liberal line on the suffrage and tended to be anti-monarchical), and the Irish—all forming an assortment of loose and changing alliances.

The Reform Acts of 1867 and 1884, and the Ballot Act of 1872, which provided for secret voting, contributed to the modernization of party structure. The Reform Acts also more than quadrupled the electorate—to almost five million—and the Ballot Act all but eliminated the practice of buying parliamentary seats and the use of social or economic pressure by the gentry or businessmen to insure that their tenants or workers voted the "right" way. Political parties became internally more homogeneous and more sharply differentiated from one another. And as the parties worked to enlist the voters' support, party organization became tighter and party discipline stricter. Both the Conservatives and the Liberals created national organizations outside Parliament (the National Union of Conservative and Unionist Associations in 1867 and the National Liberal Federation in 1877). Control over both parties remained firmly in the hands of the parliamentarians, however, despite attempts by some political figures to change the party hierarchy.

The Labor Party, established in 1901, represented a unique departure in British politics. Here was a party founded outside Parliament and specifically designed as a mass party of the working class. Self-consciously ideological and considering itself a "movement," it created a whole host of subsidiary organizations for the sole purpose of making the party an integral part of the lives of those who supported it. It quickly attained a high degree of discipline, and its sense of unity, identity, and direction, its hostility toward the opposition, and the fact that working-class and lower-middle-class candidates had to rely heavily upon party financial support made this discipline effective.

With the decline of the Liberal Party in the 1920's, Conservatives and Laborites came face to face across the aisle in the House of Commons. Thus, after a short period in which three major parties competed for power, the British again entered a period of two-party competition.

2. THE NATURE AND EXPLANATION OF THE PARTY SYSTEM

British politics since 1931 has been marked by electoral rivalry between two parties and the periodic alternation in office between them (Table 9.1). Each party, moreover, has adopted its own ideological stance, has campaigned on the basis of reasonably well-defined programs, and, once in office, has proceeded, by and large, to carry them out. Both parties have also been supported by a fairly large core of dues-paying members—militants and enthusiasts—to whom party work is something of a mission. Because of these several characteristics, many commentators have spoken of British government in these years as fulfilling the model of responsible party government.

To be sure, these generalized characteristics must be qualified. A number of smaller parties, most notably the Liberals, and, since the 1960's, nationalist parties from Scotland and Wales, continue to participate in electoral compaigns and always manage to win a few seats. Indeed, in the first of two elections held in 1974, their total was so large that for the first time since the 1920's neither of the major parties won a parliamentary majority. Also, though it is legitimate to emphasize the ideological differences between the Labor and Conservative parties, neither has ever been known for the kind of doctrinal rigidity that has been a common feature of so many Continental parties. Just as important, the Conservative Party has been far less self-consciously ideological than the Labor Party. The two have moved closer to each other in outlook since the end of World War II, especially as the realities of international economics and world politics have narrowed the options open to any government. Further, the opinions expressed by the partisan supporters of each have been shown to be only imperfectly related to the positions taken by the respective parties. Indeed, a survey has shown that even the ideological code words "left" and "right" are meaningful to only about one-fifth of the entire electorate. Nevertheless, despite these several departures from the responsible party model, the British party system remains unique. It differs from the American in that it features disciplined, mass parties, and it differs from Continental systems in that it features only two major parties, each

normally capable of winning a majority in the parliament.

What explains this unique party system? As stated in the previous chapter, at least one component of the explanation for a two-party system can be found in the plurality method of election that is based on a single-member district. Then, too, unlike the United States, Britain is not composed of a multiplicity of states around which separate party systems can form. Nor does it hold separate elections for a president and a congress. Yet the most satisfactory answers to our question are to be found elsewhere than in electoral laws, legal centralization, or formal institutional structures.

One explanation pertains to the fact that a disciplined mass-party system emerged in response to the founding of the Labor Party; the Labor Party was united by its own Socialist vision of the world, and it organized a mass base to achieve its ideological goals. The Conservative Party, long used to a tradition of member independence, founded its own organization base and imposed similar parliamentary discipline as a way to prevent the victory of its ideological foe. Even today more than 90 percent of Labor Party supporters report that they perceive the party battle as being one of competing class interests, while only 35 percent of Conservative supporters see the party struggle in this light. A second and related explanation is that given a two-party system, the logic of the parliamentary system forces members of Parliament to remain loyal to their party lest their ideological opponents gain or retain control of the government. For a British MP to break discipline is to open the way for the opposition to come to power—as well as to alienate his party colleagues. In the Labor Party a vote contrary to party directive may result in expulsion from the party, and in both parties constituency party officers and members expect loyalty to the party leaders in Parliament. Unlike the American pattern, where voters traditionally have been more concerned with local issues and personality, the loss of the party label in

TABLE 9.1   SEATS WON IN BRITISH GENERAL ELECTIONS SINCE 1931

Year	Total	Conservative	Labor	Liberal	Other	Overall majority
1931	615	521	52	37	5	Con. 427
1935	615	431	154	21	9	Con. 247
1945	640	213	393	12	22	Lab. 146
1950	625	298	315	9	3	Lab. 5
1951	625	321	295	6	3	Con. 17
1955	630	345	277	6	2	Con. 60
1959	630	365	258	6	1	Con. 100
1964	630	303	317	9	1	Lab. 4
1966	630	253	363	12	2	Lab. 96
1970	630	330	287	6	7	Con. 30
1974 (Feb.)	635	296	301	14	24 [1]	Lab. plurality of 5
1974 (Oct.)	635	276	319	13	27 [2]	Lab. 3

[1] Including 11 Loyalists from Northern Ireland, 7 Scottish Nationalists, and 2 Plaid Cymru (Wales).

[2] Including 10 Loyalists from Northern Ireland, 11 Scottish Nationalists, and 3 Plaid Cymru (Wales).

Sources: Peter G. J. Pulzer, *Political Representation and Elections in Britain*, 3rd ed. (London: George Allen & Unwin, 1975), p. 99, reprinted by permission. Data for 1931 and 1935 from Herman Finer, *Governments of Greater European Powers* (New York: Henry Holt & Co., 1956.)

Britain has usually meant political extinction.

A third explanation for the uniqueness of the British two-party system was offered in Part II: the absence of the number and types of cleavages—religious, among others —that have characterized Continental societies. Finally, as argued in Chapter 2, the pattern of British historical development resulted in a set of cultural values that maximize attachment to the community and minimize social conflict. Thus, despite the cleavage of conflicting party loyalties, nearly half of the British voters believe the opposition party would, for the most part, govern just as well as their own. Other studies have shown that both Labor and Conservative party supporters pick almost the same traits as important in a party leader: strong leadership, the willingness to make unpopular decisions, honesty, and sincerity; just as noteworthy, they chose these qualities in the same order. In short, Britons appear to agree that it is as important to have effective government as it is to have one's own party in power.

3.   SOURCES OF PARTY SUPPORT

To win a general election in Britain, a party must recieve the most votes in half plus one of the 635 (formerly 630) constituencies into which Britain is divided. Until 1974 a single party had won such a parliamentary majority in every postwar election (Table 9.1). Moreover, with the exceptions of the 1951 and February, 1974, elections (Table 9.2), the arithmetic in recent elections has worked out so that the winning party has also received at least the plurality (but not the majority) of the popular vote cast. It would be a mistake, however, to view each general election as a contest for the support of the total electorate. The hard facts are that 95 percent of the elector-

TABLE 9.2   VOTE CAST IN BRITISH GENERAL ELECTIONS SINCE 1945

Year	Electorate	Conserv-ative	Labor	Liberal	Other	Turnout
1945 [1]	32,836,419	39.8%	48.3%	9.1%	2.8%	73.3%
1950	34,269,770	43.5	46.1	9.1	1.3	84.0
1951	34,645,573	48.0	48.8	2.5	0.7	82.5
1955	34,858,263	49.7	46.4	2.7	0.2	76.8
1959	35,397,080	49.4	43.8	5.9	1.0	78.8
1964	35,892,572	43.4	44.1	11.2	1.3	77.0
1966	35,966,975	41.9	47.9	8.5	1.7	75.8
1970	39,384,364	46.4	42.9	7.5	3.2	72.0
1974 (Feb.)	39,798,899	38.1	37.2	19.3	5.4	78.7
1974 (Oct.)	40,074,780	35.9	39.5	18.3	6.2	72.8

[1] Voting figures adjusted to allow for double-member constituencies in which electors had two votes each, and to omit university seats.

Adapted from Pulzer, *Political Representation*, p. 99, reprinted by permission.

ate identify with one of the parties, that 80 percent claim they always remain faithful to their party, and that about 70 percent of the constituencies, because of uneven distribution of party support, are considered safe for one party or the other. In short, the British party system has rested on stable foundations.

The structure of this partisan attachment can be most easily described in terms of so-cial class.[1] A comparative study of four "Anglo-Saxon" democracies has shown that Britain ranks highest in the correlation between a person's social class and his partisan preference. What this means in Britain is that the large majority of those engaged

[1] The most comprehensive account of British voting behavior, on which much of the following account is based, is to be found in David Butler and Donald Stokes, *Political Change in Britain*, college ed. (New York: St. Martin's Press, 1971).

TABLE 9.3   PARTY PREFERENCES OF SELECTED GROUPS, 1970

	All	Men	Women	18–24	65 +	Middle class AB	Middle class C1	Working class C2	Working class DE
Conservative	46.2%	42.2%	49.9%	42.3%	56.2%	79.1%	59.2%	34.6%	33.2%
Labor	43.8	47.3	40.6	47.2	37.1	10.4	30.5	55.4	57.3
Liberal	7.6	7.3	7.8	8.4	5.1	9.5	8.8	7.0	6.4
Other	2.4	3.2	1.7	2.1	1.6	1.0	1.5	3.0	3.1

Adapted from David Butler and Michael Pinto-Duschinsky, *The British General Election of 1970* (New York: St. Martin's Press, 1971), p. 342, reprinted by permission. For the purposes of this table the terms "middle class" and "working class" have been superimposed upon the National Opinion Poll's classifications of AB (managerial, professional), C1 (supervisory, clerical), C2 (skilled manual workers), and DE (semi-skilled, unskilled, pensioners).

TABLE 9.4 PARTY IDENTIFICATION AND SOCIAL CLASS, 1963

Percent of total

	Conservative Party Identifiers	Labor Party Identifiers	Middle class	Working class
Middle class	48	10		
Working class	52	90		
Conservative identifiers			80	32
Labor identifiers			20	68

Adapted from David Butler and Donald Stokes, *Political Change in Britain*, college ed. (New York: St. Martin's Press, 1971), pp. 121–122, reprinted by permission of the publishers. The class definitions (based on occupation) used for this table differ slightly from those used in Table 9.3.

in manual occupations—most of whom describe themselves as "working-class"—identify with and vote for the Labor Party, and that the large majority of nonmanual workers—most of whom describe themselves as "middle-class"—identify with and vote for the Conservative Party (Tables 9.3 and 9.4). Yet the fact that the Conservatives have governed far more often than Labor, in a nation where nearly 70 percent of the electorate describes itself as working-class, shows that though the correlation between class and voting behavior may be high, it is by no means perfect. About one-third of the self-described working class is loyal to the Conservative Party, and so large is this total in terms of the number of votes that fully

half of the Conservative Party's electoral support usually comes from members of the working class. Of course, some middle-class voters also "cross over" to vote Labor; but both proportionately and, more importantly, in absolute numbers of voters the total is much smaller. The various explanations for the phenomenon of "working-class Conservatism" include traditional attitudes of deference toward one's "betters"; the identification of the Conservative Party with the dominant religious, educational, and economic institutions of the society; the belief by some workers that Conservatives are more likely to allow advancement on the basis of ability; and, simple, partisan loyalty inherited from parents who lived at a period in his-

TABLE 9.5 PARTY AND RELIGIOUS IDENTIFICATION
BY SOCIAL CLASS, 1963

	Middle Class		Working Class	
	Church of England	Noncon- formist	Church of England	Noncon- formist
Conservative	72%	41%	30%	22%
Labor	10	22	55	62
Liberal	18	37	15	16

Adapted from Butler and Stokes, *Political Change in Britain*, p. 99, reprinted by permission of the publisher.

tory when the Labor Party was yet to be born or was in its infancy.

Factors other than class have also been shown to be associated with partisan preference. The Conservative Party is favored by women, by persons in the older age brackets, and by those who identify with the Angelican Church (Table 9.5). To some extent the association of Anglicanism and Conservatism reflects no more than the fact that the established church has drawn its support disproportionately from the middle class. Yet even within the middle class and within the working class, Anglicanism has been associated with Conservative preference; thus religious identification is seen as still another factor helping to explain working-class conservatism. A lesser factor affecting voting behavior is regionalism; members of the working class in the north of England for example, are more likely to vote Labor than are their fellow class members in the southeast (Map 9.1).

The Liberal Party draws its vote from all strata of the population. It still retains a regional base in the "Celtic Fringe"—Wales, Scotland, and parts of southwest England—and, in general, its supporters are those with a Nonconformist religious background. Today, the Liberals are a party of transients

MAP 9.1 LABOR PARTY'S SHARE OF MAJOR PARTY VOTE, 1970, BY REGION

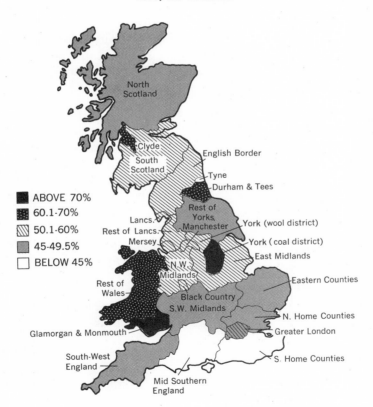

Adapted from P. G. J. Pulzer, *Political Representation and Elections in Britain*, rev. ed. (London: George Allen & Unwin, 1972), p. 126, reprinted by permission of the publisher.

—voters who have left either the Conservative or the Labor Party and are trying to decide what to do next. No more than one-third of the Liberal Party vote is stable.

If party allegiance is analyzed not in terms of a voter's own sociological characteristics, but rather in terms of family background, the most powerful predictor of a voter's behavior in Britain is the party preference of his parents (Table 9.6). It is this strong influence of family socialization that

TABLE 9.6 PARTY PREFERENCE ACCORDING TO PARENTS' PARTY PREFERENCE

Respondent's own present preference	Parents' partisanship		
	Both parents Conservative	Parents divided	Both parents Labor
Conservative	75%	37%	10%
Labor	14	49	81
Liberal	8	10	6
Other	—	—	—
None	3	4	3

Source: Butler and Stokes, *Political Change in Britain*, p. 36, reprinted by permission of the publisher.

has led the authors of the impressive study reporting these findings to speculate that the Labor Party may fare much better during the last quarter of the twentieth century than it has during the first three quarters. Only as the century progresses will those who cannot recall being raised in a Labor Party family gradually disappear from the electorate. It is for this reason, as well as the declining influence of religious identifications, that the phenomenon of working-class conservatism is much less apparent in the younger generation of voters than it is among the older generation. The pattern of greater Conservative support among all older voters can be similarly explained.

4. THE LIBERAL PARTY

DEVELOPMENT AND CHARACTER: The term "liberal" was first applied to the "advanced" segments of the Whigs in Parliament in the early nineteenth century by their Tory opponents, who wished to identify them with the detested "radical" ideas of the French *libéraux*. It was not, however, until the Gladstone ministry of 1868–74 that the term came into common currency. Gladstone, who was prime minister on four different occasions, dominated the party until his death and represented, in his own person, the transition from eighteenth-century Whiggery to nineteenth-century Liberalism. Gradually, he had been converted both to full extension of the suffrage and free trade —major Liberal policies. While Gladstone generally supported a laissez-faire economic policy, he was not averse to measures of social reform designed to aid the "less fortunate"; he was also strongly anti-imperialist, and eventually came around to supporting Irish Home Rule.

It was, in fact, the question of Home Rule for Ireland that caused the first of many party splits, for it was on this issue that Joseph Chamberlain led his followers out of the Liberal camp and eventually into the Conservative. Chamberlain's critique became a broader one as he tried, albeit unsuccessfully, to tie the issue of social reform to support for the empire, attacking the hallowed doctrine of free trade.

The split consigned the Liberals to the wilderness until 1905, when they returned to power under the leadership of Herbert Asquith and Lloyd George. In the years from 1905 to 1914 the Liberal Party moved decisively, if moderately, to the left. Income taxes were raised to finance new programs of social reform, and the secondary position of the House of Lords was formalized by the Parliament Act of 1911. The party, however, remained committed to both free trade and liberal capitalism.

A personal rivalry between Lloyd George and Herbert Asquith again split the party during World War I—a split that continued after the war and helped speed the final eclipse of the Liberal Party. In 1922 the Liberal Party vote dropped to 30 percent of the total; in the election of 1924, it fell still further: the party received only 17.6 percent of the votes cast and, because of the operation of single-member-district plurality elections, an even smaller proportion of parliamentary seats. After that, the party's decline continued apace amid still further divisions, and in the election of 1945 the Liberals received only 9.1 percent of the votes cast. Their share was to drop to 2.6 percent in 1951.

The reasons for the decline of the Liberal Party are fairly obvious. Its purely political program had been more or less achieved by the end of World War I and had come to be fully accepted by all political parties. The remainder of its program (free enterprise and free trade) was not such as to continue to attract widespread enthusiasm. Larger portions of its working-class support slipped away into the Labor Party; the working class preferred either a party that represented the working class, or, in the case of the more tradition-minded, one that inspired deference and defended tradition. Some of the Liberal Party's more radical middle-class support turned to socialism and the Labor Party as constituting the heirs of the reform tradition, but the bulk of the middle class preferred the Conservatives. In an era of tougher competition from other industrial nations, free trade no longer held the same magic appeal it once did. Moreover, the balance of political power had shifted, and the commercial strata were now part of the establishment. They identified with a national tradition that had become their own and distrusted Liberal rhetoric as contributing not only to an erosion of social hierarchy, but to the threat of working-class radicalism.

In the late 1950's and early 1960's the Liberal Party experienced something of a revival. Its percentage of the popular vote rose to 5.9 in 1959 and to 11.2 in 1964. To many younger voters, both the Labor and Conservative parties seemed to be "conservative" —each wedded in its own way to outmoded doctrines that no longer corresponded to the real world. But the revival was soon seen to be as temporary as it was modest; in the

1966 elections, the Liberals' vote fell once again, to 8.5 percent of the total, and in 1970 to 7.5 percent.

In the early 1970's, as public disenchantment with the two major parties became increasingly apparent, opinion polls began to register spectacular Liberal gains. Once again the Liberals seemed about to assume a powerful place in British politics, this time by offering the voters an alternative to the "old" parties, now locked in combat over trade-union and other economic questions. The results of the February, 1974, election both confirmed and denied this prophecy. Led by popular Jeremy Thorpe, the Liberals polled nearly 20 percent of the total vote, by far the party's most impressive performance in modern political history. Yet once again the election system took its toll; the Liberals won fourteen seats, only a few more than they had won in 1970. The major difference turned out to be that in the new Parliament those fourteen seats were now crucial; no party had a majority. Thorpe entered into discussions with Heath about the possibility of a Conservative-Liberal Coalition government, but when no agreement could be reached, Thorpe resumed his place as head of an opposition party. When the October election again produced a razor-thin margin for the governing party, it was clear that the Liberals would continue to occupy a strategic opposition role.

THE PATTERN OF DECISION-MAKING: Like the Conservative Party, the Liberal Party began as a parliamentary party, and until the 1920's the key decisions were made by those party members who were in Parliament. In 1877 the party had created a mass organization, the National Liberal Federation, which its organizers hoped would become the effective center of policy-making. While the federation was not without influence, it remained for about fifty years under the control of parliamentary leadership.

The Liberal Party never developed the degree of discipline that the Labor Party was to achieve. This was true partly because of ideological premises that rejected a mass party of the Labor type; but added to this factor was a purely structural cause: the Liberal Party declined in power and size before its institutional mechanisms for party discipline could be established. As an organization with no hope of serving as a government—and hence devoid of those expedient pressures for coherence—the Liberal Party today is characterized by semi-anarchy. Its parliamentary party, its mass party, and its party leader all tend to move in several directions at the same time—and to wrangle interminably over very minor doctrinal points. Further, the constituency or local organizations of the party go more or less their own way, subject only to advice from the central office. Their independence extends to the nomination of candidates. In the Conservative and Labor parties, the central offices have at least the theoretical right to exercise a veto; in any event, candidate choices by local organizations must be cleared with them. In the Liberal Party, many candidates are nominated without any notification of the national organs.

The basic unit of the Liberal Party is the annual Assembly, consisting of about one thousand delegates drawn from the constituency parties and the Liberal Parliamentary Party (LPP). The policies adopted at the assembly are theoretically those of the party outside Parliament, and not necessarily those of the LPP. The assembly elects a smaller body, the council, which meets quarterly, and an executive committee, which meets at least once a month to look after routine affairs. The onus of fund raising and propaganda rests with the council, which is also responsible for the party's paid professional staff.

The leader of the Liberal Parliamentary Party is the leader of the Liberal Party as a whole. For many years he was subject to annual re-elections, but today, because of the small size of the party, this practice has been dropped. The parliamentary leader's authority over his colleagues and over the mass party is extremely limited, however, and the mass party has been able to force

his resignation when it believed him to be no longer useful.

The LPP meets regularly to formulate politics on various issues, but there is little or no attempt to enforce party discipline; members are free to vote in Parliament as they please. Though the party outside Parliament has, on occasion, attempted to press its own claims as the chief policy-making body, it has had slight success. And to make the policy impasse complete, the parliamentary party has been unable to impose its views upon the mass party. All of these weaknesses will assume added significance if the strategic vote of the Liberals in the party system increases.

5. THE CONSERVATIVE PARTY

DEVELOPMENT AND CHARACTER: After experiencing a long decline in the first part of the eighteenth century, the Tory Party entered upon a period of predominance in British politics under the leadership of William Pitt the Younger. This ascendancy lasted until 1830; after that, the party split repeatedly, and a number of its followers, including Gladstone, moved over to the Whigs. From 1830 to 1874, the Tories were seldom in office and only once in power. It was during these years that the name of the party was changed to Conservative in an effort to mold a better public image.

The modern Conservative Party was born with the leadership of Benjamin Disraeli, who during his first and second ministries was responsible for important measures of social legislation and the Electoral Reform Act of 1867. It was during Disraeli's leadership, too, that the Conservative Party created the National Union—the beginnings of a mass party designed to serve as handmaiden to the parliamentary party and the party leader in the organization and financing of electoral campaigns. From the beginning, the national party organization, in contrast with that of the Labor Party, was expected to remain subordinate to the parliamentary party and the party leader. And it has. The national group, however, has not been without influence on the formation of party policy and in the determination of the choice of leadership.

Disraeli's hope that the Conservative Party would appeal to the mass public as a political instrument dedicated both to a hierarchical social order and to social reform was not realized. After his death, the leadership was dominated by business interests, which accepted the party as their natural habitat, and the record of the party in the late nineteenth and early twentieth centuries was essentially one of opposing social change.

Not until Neville Chamberlain rose to prominence in the party in the 1930's did the Conservative government, in response to the Depression and to Britain's changing world position, take the lead in using the power of the state to effect social change. It was the Chamberlain government of the late 1930's that laid the foundations of the postwar welfare state and took many measures toward the nationalization of important sectors of the British economy.

The defeat of the Conservative Party in 1945 by the Laborites prompted some self-examination. The Conservatives not only reorganized and democratized their party structure, but, under the leadership of such men as R. A. Butler and Harold Macmillan, fully committed themselves to accepting the reforms that the Labor Party was then initiating. The Conservatives also endorsed the idea of an economy in which the government would not only guarantee more job opportunities but would use fiscal and monetary controls to insure full employment.

Once in power after 1951, the Conservatives put into practice all these accepted commitments. Fiscal and monetary controls were used extensively, direct taxes remained high, and welfare expenditures increased in proportion to the growth of the economy. Near the end of their tenure in office, the Conservatives moved even more directly toward the idea of a managed economy by creating, in 1962, the National Economic Development Council ("Neddy") to provide for the systematic national planning of economic growth.

By 1964, there was a general conviction that the Conservative Party, after three successive terms of office, would be defeated in the election of that year. A sex scandal involving high government officials had tarnished its reputation, and while the country was prosperous, there were signs of a growing intellectual malaise. Britain's rate of economic growth had fallen behind that of the Continental countries, and the per capita income of both France and Germany was threatening to exceed Britain's. There seemed to be the distinct feeling that Conservative Party leaders had failed to modernize the country or to bring it back to the center of the world stage. The resignation of Harold Macmillan as prime minister and leader of the party had not helped Conservative fortunes; his successor, Alex Douglas-Home, was chosen—after considerable acrimony—because he had fewer enemies than any other candidate.

Nevertheless, on election day in 1964, Labor squeaked by with only a bare plurality. With the imminence of new elections, the Conservatives re-examined their structure and image once again. Home stepped down, after instituting a new policy of electing the party leader, and was replaced by Edward Heath, formerly Lord Privy Seal. During the campaign preceding the elections in March, 1966, the Conservatives, now led by newer faces, attempted to present themselves as the party that would "modernize" Britain. Despite their efforts, however, or rather because of Harold Wilson's rather solid performance as prime minister, their message did not get across, and Labor substantially increased its parliamentary majority. In 1970, however, Heath surprised the pollsters, as well as many members of his own party who doubted the effectiveness of his leadership, and led the Conservative Party back into office. But by 1974 Heath's effectiveness was again being questioned. As prime minister, he had clearly mishandled the coal miners' grievances, he had made major retreats from his once-heralded "free enterprise" stance, his pro-Common Market policy had alienated many Conservatives, and, most seriously, he had badly miscalculated when he called prematurely, for a new election in February, 1974. The Conservative Party was again in opposition. Still led by Heath, the party suffered a more decisive defeat in the October election of that year.

Traditionally, the Conservative Party has spent less time than Labor on considering, or at least arguing about, broad ideological issues. The party is flexible on policy issues, because, far more than the Labor Party, Conservatives are an organization dedicated to governing the nation—that is, far more than the Labor Party, they are attuned to giving the public what it feels it needs. This is not to say that the Conservatives no longer have an ideological position. Notwithstanding the fact that they increasingly represent the new professional business technocracy committed to a managed economy, many in the party, including Heath and his successor Margaret Thatcher, want to minimize government intervention in the economy to allow individual enterprise to flourish. The inauguration by Conservative governments of commercial television and radio reflects this bias, as does the Heath government's restoring to private ownership certain profitable portions of the nationalized industries. Heath's unsuccessful attempt to resist the imposition of wage and price controls illustrates the same viewpoint. The Conservatives have pledged themselves to extensive welfare programs, but they argue that some of them, such as public housing, should be formulated only for the poor, the elderly, and the infirm. They remain steadfast believers in social hierarchy and in the need for leadership by a responsible political and social elite. More than among the Laborites, there is in the Tory Party a nostalgia for the traditional elements of the British past, including the monarchy and the House of Lords.

There was a period during the 1950's in which powerful Conservatives, resisting the pace of decolonization, seemed on the verge of causing a serious division within the party. Bitterly opposed to the rapidity with which Britain was relinquishing the façade of being a world power, the most extreme members of this group labeled themselves the "Empire Loyalists." Today the right wing of the party articulates the ideals of "law and order" and strict immigration controls and, along with the left wing of the Labor Party, considers the Common Market anathema. The Monday Club, a group with its own headquarters and publications, is the organizational focus for Conservatives sharing these viewpoints. Another party unit, the Bow Group, was formed in 1951 and represents the more modern or "technocratic" wing of the party; it schedules study discussions and publishes pamphlets on Conservative policy issues. The ideological divisions within the Conservative Parliamentary Party can be seen in the "free" votes that are cast on private member bills. On five such votes taken during 1966–69—concerning abortion, reform of laws pertaining to homosexuality, divorce, Sunday entertainment, and capital punishment—the aggregate totals showed 69 percent of the Conservatives on the anti-liberal, anti-reform side to 31 percent on the liberal side. The comparable figures for Labor were 10 percent and 90 percent.

One additional latent division within the Conservative Party became manifest in 1974. As its official title indicates, the Conservative Party contains within its ranks supporters in Northern Ireland who style themselves Unionists and whose allegiance can be traced back to the last century, when Conservatives opposed home rule for Ireland. With Northern Ireland's government and status again in doubt in 1974, eleven members of Parliament elected in February of that year from Northern Ireland formed a separate "loyalist" parliamentary group, instead of following the usual practice of accepting the Conservative whip. Had they remained within the party, the Heath government would have continued in office. The October election again yielded a separate "loyalist" party.

STRUCTURE AND DYNAMICS: The Conservative Party began as a party of notables in Parliament clustered about a leader, or leaders. In response to the gradual enlargement of the electorate and the rise of nationally organized parties, it created its own mass organization; in response to the greater democratization of British society, it has democratized parts of its own structure. Even so, the party's organization still reflects its parliamentary origins and its ties to more traditional concepts of political life. Power is lodged within the parliamentary party, and especially in the party leader who is personally responsible for the party's program—which is *his* program— and, moreover, is directly in charge of the party's bureaucratic apparatus.

Until 1964, Conservative leaders materialized from within the party without any formal election upon the retirement or death of the incumbent. What happened, in effect, was that when the party was in power, the more powerful figures would take soundings in the party and suggest to the king (or queen) the person who, they believed, could command the loyalty of both the parliamentary party and the mass party. The monarch, relying upon his ancient prerogative, would call to the palace the person suggested and name him prime minister. He would then be elected unanimously by the Conservative Parliamentary Party (CPP) as leader of the party. If the leader departed while the party was in opposition, the post was usually left vacant until the next general election, when a new leader would "emerge."

Most often in the past the choice of party leader has been rather clear-cut because one party member has fairly well established himself as heir apparent; Anthony Eden's succeeding to the post of prime minister after Winston Churchill's retirement in 1955 is such an example. On other occasions, as with the selection of Lord Home in 1963, an attempt was made to choose from among several contenders a leader who had offended the fewest people. Home himself came to share the view that the method of selecting the party leader had to be changed, and a

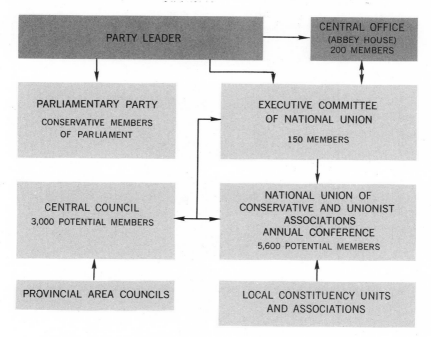

FIGURE 9.1 THE STRUCTURE OF THE CONSERVATIVE PARTY

procedure for a formal election by the parliamentary party was adopted in 1965. In 1974 that procedure was modified, so that now the leader must be re-elected annually. Though the manner in which the Conservative Party leader is selected has changed, his powers remain undiminished. He is still free to choose his own "shadow cabinet" when the party is in opposition.[2] He appoints the other party spokesmen in the Parliament and exercises those controls over the national organization that were noted previously. Further, although he appears from

[2] The term "shadow cabinet" is applied to that group of opposition party leaders who would theoretically form the ministry if their party were in power. Each member is responsible for criticizing the government in a specific area. Thus, the shadow secretary of state for foreign affairs would have primary responsibility for attacking the government's foreign policy.

time to time before his parliamentary colleagues to explain and discuss his policy, such appearances are not mandatory, nor are they required at the yearly conference of the mass party.

The National Union of Conservative and Unionist Associations is the mass organization of the Conservative Party. Its functions include the promotion of Conservative and Unionist Associations in every constituency. Membership in the National Union is open to all who share the principles of the Conservative Party, upon the payment of a small fee; total membership in 1970 was estimated at about 1.5 million, four times as great as Labor's constituency party membership.

Each year the National Union holds an Annual Conference for approximately two and a half days. Attended by elected dele-

FIGURE 9.2   THE SOCIOECONOMIC BACKGROUND OF BRITISH
PARTY OFFICERS, MEMBERS, AND SUPPORTERS

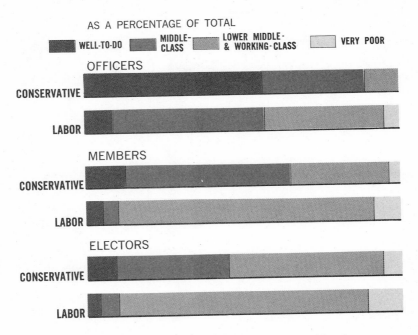

Adapted from Jean Blondel, *Voters, Parties and Leaders* (Harmondsworth, Middlesex, Eng.: Penguin Books, Ltd., 1963), p. 98, reprinted by permission of the publisher.

gates from the constituency organizations as well as by members of the party's central council, the conference is essentially an occasion for rhetoric and expressions of party unity. It hears the reports of the central council and of its executive committee, but not of the party leader, who addresses a mass rally only after the conference has formally adjourned.

The more than 3,600 delegates who attend the annual conferences do not view their role as policy-makers, and any policy motions adopted by the conference are seen as advisory only. Nevertheless, debate does take place, votes are taken—nearly always by voice—and divisions in the party can clearly be discerned on touchy issues. Recent controversy has revolved around policy on comprehensive schools, capital punishment, and immigration controls. The widening left-right split within the party is evidenced by the fact that although not a single ballot vote was demanded between 1951 and 1966, at least one has been demanded at the majority of annual meetings held since then.

The central council is theoretically the governing body of the National Union. It consists of the party leader and other party officials as well as Conservative MP's and representatives from provincial area councils and from each constituency. However, its large size (about 1,200) and the infrequency of its meetings—only one a year—limit its effectiveness and its capacity as a decision-making body.

The executive committee of the National Union consists of approximately 150 members, including the party leader and principal party officials as well as representatives from provincial area councils. It ordinarily meets every other month and is empowered to act for the central council between council meetings. Functions of the committee include ruling on the acceptance or removal of National Union constituency representatives, and the election of representatives to the different advisory committees that serve the national organization. From time to time, the executive committee initiates studies on public issues and makes policy recommenda-

tions to the party leader. As is true of other party groups, however, its opinions are merely advisory.

In addition to the executive committee, there are national advisory committees on which the party leader relies. Some of these committees—among them the Advisory Committee on Policy, the Consultative Committee on Party Finance, and the Standing Advisory Committee on Party Finance—are the most influential organizations in the party, but like the party's bureaucratic apparatus, they are responsible to the party leader rather than to the National Union. The principal officers of the Advisory Committee on Policy—for example, the chairman and vice chairman—are appointees of the party leader, whereas the fifteen other members are selected by the CPP and the executive committee of the National Union. Yet the entire committee is responsible solely to the party leader. It has at its disposal the resources of the Conservative Research Department, and has, on many occasions, been responsible for formulating Conservative Party policy.

On the local level, the constituency organization is the basic unit of the Conservative Party. Relatively autonomous, it is concerned essentially with spreading Conservative principles, raising money, generating enthusiasm to elect Conservatives to Parliament, and nominating those candidates. For many members, the organization serves an important social function—and often is as well the opening wedge for a political career. The effective head of the constituency is an elected chairman aided by a central office representative who is a paid constituency agent. Candidates for constituency chairman are selected from a list either prepared by the central office or submitted to the central office for approval. Although manual workers constitute roughly half of the voters who support the Conservative Party, they make up only a small proportion of the membership in the party's constituency organizations, which tend to have a distinctly middle-class atmosphere. An even smaller proportion of manual workers exists among party activists—that is, members who take an active part in running the affairs of the local organization.[3] There is some evidence that activists in the local organization are more rigidly ideological in their stance than is the rank-and-file membership, and certainly more so than the electoral supporters; however, their militancy does not reach the extremes of their Labor Party equivalents.

The Conservative Party's central office—Abbey House—was created in 1870 as part of its effort to reach voters enfranchised by the Reform Act of 1867.[4] Over the years the central office has grown in size, until today it consists of approximately two hundred administrative and clerical personnel, about one-third of whom are full-time paid bureaucrats. Like the National Union, the central office is the instrument of the parliamentary party—or more particularly of its leader. The head of the office, whose title is chairman of party organization, is appointed by the party leader, as are the vice chairmen and the treasurer. Because of its administrative functions, the chairmanship is an office of considerable importance, although it has little public authority over policy.

The central office organizes local party groups, prepares propaganda, draws up lists of recommended candidates, and oversees the general efficiency of the party structure. It works closely with area and constituency organizations, and attempts to guide them in the direction desired by the leadership.

Especially since World War II, the central office has greatly expanded its propaganda and research efforts. The Conservative Political Center concentrates on preparing special publications for activists, and the Conservative Research Department investi-

gates and analyzes the general problems of party policy. During periods when the Conservative Party is in opposition, and, therefore, without the services of the government bureaucracy, party leadership is particularly reliant upon the central office's services.

POWER AND POLICY: The closest observers of the Conservative Party have always had difficulty tracing its dynamics of power: in the Conservative Party, even more than in the Labor Party, many decisions are made informally and in private. On paper at least, the position of the party leader is extremely strong and that of the mass organization quite weak when compared with the Labor Party. Yet the reality is not that simple. It is certainly true that the Conservative party leader enjoys far more power on paper than the Labor party leader, and that, until 1965 at least, he was more often than not the choice of party notables. However, the choice usually reflected an attempt to meet the wishes of the Conservative Parliamentary Party.

The power of the party in Parliament is indicated by the fact that, since 1922, six of the eight men who have served as leaders of the Conservative Party have left office under conditions that suggest the exercise of pressure by Conservative MP's. Austen Chamberlain, for instance, resigned after the parliamentary party passed a motion, in 1922 (over his opposition), urging that the party not join an election coalition with the Liberals. Neville Chamberlain quit as prime minister in 1940, after he had lost the confidence of many Conservatives in Parliament. Anthony Eden resigned the prime ministership after the Suez fiasco of 1956, while Macmillan resigned shortly before and Home shortly after the election campaign of 1964; in all these cases there is evidence not only that support among members of the parliamentary party had declined, but that Conservatives throughout the country were restive because they believed the party leader was no longer an asset. By far the most dramatic example of leadership change, however, occurred in early 1975, when, operat-

[3] The proportion of party activists to total membership is small. In a constituency organization of five thousand, probably no more than two or three hundred attend meetings regularly and do other party work.

[4] The central offices of both parties are popularly referred to by the names of the buildings in which they are located—Abbey House and Transport House.

ing under its new rules, the parliamentary party for the first time was given the opportunity of renewing or terminating the services of its leader. In a dramatic election contest, the leader Edward Heath was deposed by Margaret Thatcher.

The Conservative Party, both in Parliament and throughout the nation, has always been rather more attuned to office than has the Labor Party. To be sure, no Conservative leader could move too far ahead of his party. But in office or out, he is permitted a good deal of political leeway. In consultation with his cabinet—real or shadow—and various advisers, the Conservative leader formulates policies as reactions to what are thought to be the needs of the nation. There is very little direct participation in policy decisions by either the parliamentary party or the mass party. A particular policy may on occasion raise the hackles of some in the party, and their response may extend to active opposition, as, for example, the anger of those opposed to the Heath government's Common Market policy, or its immigration policy. But on the whole, provided the party leader limits himself to initiating reforms within the broad and ever-evolving social and economic system that the Conservatives seek to preserve, he will be given his head. The leader, after all, is supposed to lead. Thus, the party continues to accept the oligarchic pattern of decision-making that has been the one major characteristic of its ideological orientation. For Conservatives, the real test of leadership is whether or not policies are pragmatic, whether they preserve and enhance the national inheritance within the framework of the existing system—and, of course, whether they insure that the Conservative Party will be the party in power.

6. THE LABOR PARTY

DEVELOPMENT AND CHARACTER: The British Labor Party is the product of a number of disparate groups. The first were the Socialist organizations, most importantly the Fabian Society and the Social Democratic Federation. The federation was formed in 1881 by an English disciple of Marx, H. M. Hyndman, as a political party. It constantly split into factions, and its influence had all but disappeared by World War I. But at the turn of the century, it served to introduce a whole generation of trade-union and Labor Party leaders, including such figures as Ernest Bevin, to the intricacies of Socialist theory.

The Fabian Society was and is of much more lasting importance. Founded in 1883–84 as a small discussion group of intellectuals, the Fabian Society soon turned to socialism. The famous *Fabian Essays*, first published in 1889 and including contributions by such noted writers as Sidney and Beatrice Webb and George Bernard Shaw, had a tremendous impact upon a whole generation of British intellectuals. The socialism preached by the society was, of course, a peculiarly British kind, rejecting class conflict as a leading principle and emphasizing rational administrative reform.

For many years the Fabian Society served as the most important research arm of the Labor Party, and through it have passed most of the party's important leaders. Subsequently, with the development of a research organization that functioned strictly within the Labor Party, the society's functions have declined.

The second major group that helped shape the Labor Party was the Independent Labor Party (ILP), founded by James Keir Hardy, a Scots miner and former Methodist lay preacher. The ILP was again ostensibly Socialist but, at its founding, not Marxist; aspects of it were reminiscent of a peculiarly Scottish Protestant type of religious revivalism. Alone, the ILP could never have obtained enough votes to be counted as a potent political force. But after the Labor Party was finally formed, the ILP served for many years as its constituency organization, drawing to it middle-class radicals who could not become active in the practical politics of the Labor Party in any other way. (Until 1918, individuals could join the Labor

Party only as members of one of the organizations of which the party was composed.) Most of the important early leaders of the Labor Party, including Ramsay MacDonald, Philip Snowden, and Clement Attlee, were at one time or another members of the ILP.

The third major group contributing to the formation of the Labor Party was the Trades Union Congress, the loosely organized association of British trade unions. Within the congress, sentiment had been growing during the last decade of the nineteenth century for an organization dedicated to electing working-class men to Parliament and the achievement of social reform. Younger union leaders and those from the newer unskilled unions wished to go further and establish a Socialist Party, but they represented a distinct minority.

In 1900 representatives of all these groups —the Fabians, the Social Democratic Federation, the ILP, and the trade unions—converged to form the Labor Representation Committee. Spurred by the Taff Vale Decision of 1901, which seemed to imply that unions could be sued for financial losses incurred during strikes, the support of the trade unions for the new group grew rapidly. It took the name of the Labor Party in 1906, but until World War I it remained a minor party serving primarily as the left wing of the Liberals.

After World War I, partly as the result of the radicalism induced by the war, the Labor Party suddenly became one of the major contenders for political power in what was now virtually a three-party system. It adopted a new and avowedly Socialist program—still its fundamental statement of aims—and a new formal constitution that provided for a constituency organization and attempted to coordinate the other segments of the party.

The Labor Party, during the 1920's, continued to grow at a rather phenomenal pace and, in fact, formed two short-lived minority governments in 1924 and 1929. The second of these was in office when the Great Depression hit, and the decision of the prime minister and party leader, Ramsay Mac-

Donald, to form a national government with the Conservatives and the Liberals shook the party to its core. In the election of 1931, Labor lost some two million votes, although its organization remained intact with only a few of the more prominent members joining the new government. To many in the party, MacDonald had been an unsatisfactory "moderate," and this fact plus the ravages of the Depression and the rise of National Socialism in Germany pushed the party further to the left during the 1930's, a direction fervidly endorsed by the more articulate middle-class intellectuals who flocked to its standards.

The radicals within the Labor Party, however, remained a relatively small minority, and the party that came to office under Attlee in 1945 took a moderate stance. It fulfilled its immediate nationalization promises, instituted a National Health Service, and found itself siding with the United States against the Soviet Union (albeit with some reservations) on foreign affairs.

By 1950 the Labor Party was facing a crisis; its leadership—and, indeed, the party itself—seemed to have lost its way. The social measures it introduced had not created an ideal society; on the contrary, as many new problems had been raised as had been solved. The problem of establishing a new program was debated by the party throughout the 1950's—while it lost three elections in a row. Since that period the party has been divided into two major ideological factions, usually described by the labels left and right, or militant and moderate.

In the late 1950's and early 1960's the more moderate faction of the party was dominant. Composed largely of middle-class intellectuals and with strong parliamentary support, this group, under the initial leadership of Hugh Gaitskell, argued that the party should drop its Socialist ideology and become a party of radical reform, because capitalism had fundamentally bettered its character. Socialism might remain as a distant goal, but Britain would be a "mixed" economy for a long time to come; to harp on class themes and employ Socialist bombast would only lose votes. Some within this moderate wing have also emphasized that Britain must modernize its economy and society, that it must apply the techniques of science and the findings of social science to restructure British social and economic life.

Those in the left wing of the party are still committed to socialism and still proclaim that the Labor Party is a class party. For some within this camp—primarily trade unionists—the commitment is largely rhetorical and emotional; their major goal continues to be the traditional one of obtaining more wage and pension benefits for the working class. To a more articulate minority, however—which styles itself the "new left"—British society is as inegalitarian as ever, and, even more important, the whole structure of capitalist society alienates man from himself by accentuating competitive values. If cultural and social life is to reach new heights and produce a genuinely humane democratic society in which each man fulfills himself, new sets of community purposes, defined by the community, must be developed; for this to occur, the capitalist ethos of British society must be drastically altered. The new left draws the greater part of its strength from the academic community and especially from the literary intelligentsia, and it has achieved some notable victories within the party. At the 1960 Annual Conference it was able to engineer the adoption of defense and foreign-policy resolutions that were opposed by both Gaitskell and the parliamentary party. It was also able to quash attempts to remove the objective of a socialist economy from the party constitution.

When Gaitskell died in 1963 and was replaced as party leader by Harold Wilson, many thought the left wing of the Labor Party now had one of its own to head it. Once in power, however, Wilson turned out to be primarily a moderate, stressing the need to modernize Britain) in order to provide her with the economic muscle required to meet current and future challenges. To the dismay and anger of his erstwhile supporters, he refused to attack American poli-

cy in Vietnam. Equally serious, he tried to introduce effective wage restraints and to outlaw wildcat strikes, and he spoke favorably of Britain's possible entry into the Common Market. These three policies were not only anathema to the ideologues on the left, they were abhorrent to most trade-union leaders—and at a time when the leaders of the two largest trade unions were showing themselves to be militantly left-wing in outlook. The combination proved too powerful for Wilson. He abandoned his anti-strike proposals, he was unable to enforce an effective policy of wage and price controls, and after his party's defeat in 1970 he did an about-face on his Common Market position. As might be expected, the price of these concessions to the left was the alienation of many within the party's moderate wing, most dramatically revealed with the resignation of Deputy Leader Roy Jenkins. The strength of the left wing was again demonstrated at the 1971 Annual Conference when, over the objections of the leadership, the conference called for a sweeping program of nationalization, including banks and insurance companies. The strength of the left continued to be felt in subsequent conferences, culminating in the passage of resolutions against Britain's Common Market membership, even as Harold Wilson was urging British entry.

STRUCTURE AND DYNAMICS: Like Socialist parties throughout Europe, the British Labor Party began its life as a mass organization outside Parliament. Its ideology stressed both equality and popular participation, and it tried from the very beginning to create an institutional structure that would serve, in some sense, as a model for the kind of society it eventually hoped to create. Key decisions on party policy were to be made by a democratically elected Annual Conference; the party was to have a chairman rather than a leader,[5] party members were to ad-

[5] The term "leader of the Labor Party" replaced the term "chairman" in the 1920's. The party leader is elected by the Parliamentary Labor Party (PLP). The term "chairman of the Labor Party" is now

dress each other by their first names and as "comrade." Furthermore, those elected to Parliament under Labor Party support were to derive their policies from the mass party, which represented the most advanced segments of the working class and its allies. Even before the party had taken an official Socialist position, it was far more self-consciously ideological than the Conservative Party. Whatever may have been the pragmatic and limited aims of many of the trade unionists who supported the Labor Party, the intellectuals who joined and came to lead it were motivated much more by principle.

The structure of the Labor Party still reflects the fact that it was founded as an association of many groups. However, the various Socialist societies, with the possible exception of the Fabian Society, have little influence on political decisions. The influence of members of the Cooperative societies is also slight. Thus the three key groups within the Labor Party are the trade unions, the constituency parties, and the Labor members of Parliament. The key structural elements are the Annual Conference, the national executive committee (NEC), and the Parliamentary Labor Party.

The trade unions provide the party with most of its members and most of its money. Not all British trade unions, of course, are affiliated with the party, and not all those affiliated do so in terms of full membership. Unless a union member objects, however, he contributes to a political levy that can be used by trade-union officials for political purposes. It can be used to pay a union's membership dues to the Labor Party, thereby increasing the number of votes the union can command at the Annual Conference. It can also be used to cover direct contributions to the NEC or to local parties, both of which allow the unions a greater degree of influence on the nomination of local-party candi-

used for the chairman of the national executive committee of the mass party. Until 1972, the parliamentary party elected a chairman only when the party had taken office and the leader had become prime minister; at that time a separate post of chairman of the PLP was created.

dates. Many Labor Party candidates are union-sponsored, generally from heavily trade-union districts—and hence safe for the Labor Party—a circumstance that in the past has given the party more of a trade-union cast in defeat than in victory.

Most trade-union members are not overly concerned with day-to-day political decisions; consequently they have permitted trade-union officials considerable freedom. The trade-union leadership, in turn, has shared this attitude and delegated a good deal of authority to the political leadership of the party with the proviso that it must not contravene traditional working-class attitudes and feelings—a peculiar and hard-to-summarize combination of class consciousness, Socialist slogans, distrust of employers, and bread-and-butter concerns, added to a general conservatism toward the traditional values of British society. However, since the political passivity of trade-union members automatically places power in the hands of union officers, especially the general secretary of a union, it is the attitudes and feelings of these leaders that are of essential importance.

The constituency organizations of the Labor Party are its basic operating units. As in the Conservative Party, local organizations are responsible for the general spreading of the word, as well as the nomination of parliamentary candidates. Membership is open to all who subscribe to party principles and are willing to pay nominal dues. Individuals can also affiliate with the local Labor Party through their local trade-union branch, or through the local Cooperative Society or Socialist Society. The governing body of the constituency party is the General Management Committee (GMC), which consists of representatives from ward committees and affiliated organizations; the GMC in turn delegates its authority to a smaller executive committee. The principal officer is the secretary of the local party, especially if he is at the same time a paid election agent.

Altogether, constituency party membership in 1970 stood at an estimated 385,000.

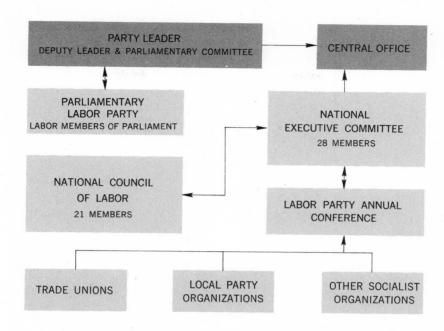

FIGURE 9.3   THE STRUCTURE OF THE LABOR PARTY

This figure was only about one-fourth as large as the Conservative's constituency membership, an ironical contrast considering the fact that it was Labor that transformed Britain from a cadre-party system to a mass-party system. It should be noted, however, that if Labor membership is interpreted to include all union members whose political levy is used to pay membership dues, the Labor figure—more than six million in 1970—exceeds the Conservative figure by about six to one. There is another important contrast as well. Far more so than in the Conservative Party, efforts of the party activists, that is, those party members who work diligently for the party, are part of an emotional commitment to party goals. It is not surprising, therefore, that these volunteers, spurred by a sense of mission, tend to stand to the left of the ordinary Labor Party member or supporter on election day. Nor is it surprising that their fervor has had its effect within the constituency parties, which have often supported left-wing resolutions at Annual Conferences in greater proportions than have trade unions. Even further, members of the national executive committee who are elected by the constituency parties have usually been more to the left than those elected by the trade unions. There are, however, factors that limit the leftward movement of constituency parties. The national executive committee can expel—and has expelled—branches that have strayed too far from official Labor Party policy. Also, as far as nominations are concerned, a search for candidates who can command the support of the more conservative trade unions often exerts a moderating influence.

The functions of the three-day Annual Conference include the election of the national executive committee, consideration of the outgoing NEC's annual report and the reports of other committees, and voting upon resolutions submitted by the membership. The party leader is expected to appear before the conference to express and defend his views, which can be subject to a conference vote.

Votes at the three-day Annual Conference are distributed in proportion to affiliated membership, so that the six largest national trade unions can dominate the sessions. Together these unions account for about half the total votes at the conference. Trade-union members have traditionally cast their votes as a bloc; that is, the representatives of the union at the conference decide by a majority vote what position they will take, and then present a united front on the conference floor. Because trade-union leaders at the conference are without a mandate on many issues, a very few individuals have a very large number of votes in their pockets. It was for this reason that the constituency parties fought so hard in the 1930's to change the method of electing the national executive committee. Originally the entire conference had voted on each section. Today, the seven NEC members allocated to the constituency parties are voted upon by the constituency section alone.

The NEC is responsible for the day-to-day operation of the party and controls its growing bureaucracy. It consists of the party treasurer, elected by the whole conference; twelve trade-union delegates; seven delegates elected by the constituency parties; one delegate each from the Socialist and Cooperative societies; five women elected by the conference; and the leader and deputy leader of the party serving *ex officio*. The NEC prepares the party program and issues general policy statements; it also keeps a list of prospective candidates, and its approval is required for candidates nominated by constituency organizations. Although this power has been used sparingly, the executive committee has, from time to time, rejected nominees, especially members of the Communist Party or Trotskyites. It can also disaffiliate constituency organizations that refuse to comply with the party rules, and (though this is rarely done) it can expel members from the party.

The NEC of the Labor Party is more diverse in membership than its Conservative counterpart. The election of twelve trade-union representatives assures the presence of a sizable number of people who began life as ordinary workers. Constituency and women's representatives, on the other hand, invariably have a middle-class background. Between 1952 and 1963, only three of the

nineteen persons who served as NEC representatives of the women's or constituency sections were of working-class background. The remainder represented the professions, with teachers and journalists predominating. Almost all the constituency and women's representatives are MP's, as are four or five of the trade-union representatives. This is natural: delegates are likely to vote for candidates who have some sort of reputation, and within the party MP's are likely to have a distinct advantage.

Turnover on the NEC is rather slow. Although elections are held annually, the average term of service is about five years. In the constituency sections at least, large-scale shifts occur only when there are overall shifts in the strengths of factions within the party. During the 1950's, for example, the more conservative representatives from the constituency section were gradually replaced by supporters of Aneurin Bevan.

The central office (Transport House) of the Labor Party, under the direction of the executive committee, is responsible for maintaining contact with and guiding local organizations. It provides speakers, arranges conferences, carries on research, edits party publications and propaganda, and examines and trains the agents who direct local campaigns. It also manages the party's funds.

The Parliamentary Labor Party consists of all Labor members of the House of Commons plus some Labor peers from the House of Lords. It elects the party leader (annually when in opposition), as well as the deputy leader, and the chief whip. Historically, not one Labor party leader has been forced from office once elected, although George Lansbury resigned in 1935 after the Annual Conference had supported policies with which he disagreed. There have, nonetheless, been a number of attempts to replace the party leader, although on only one occasion has this led to a vote—Wilson's unsuccessful move in 1961 to unseat Gaitskell.

POWER AND POLICY: The Labor Party's ideology and its structure give the decision-making process within the party a far more open quality than that which prevails in the Conservative Party. Invariably the Labor Party's squabbles are fought out in public. Whether the mass party actually plays a larger decision-making part in the Labor Party than it does in the Conservative Party is, nevertheless, a question to which differing interpretive answers can be given. A persuasive argument can be made that it does, that the actions of the Parliamentary Labor Party (PLP), both in and out of office, are significantly influenced by conference resolutions. On the other hand, the parliamentary party and the leader do not accept conference resolutions with which they disagree. When the 1960 conference disregarded the pleas of the parliamentary leadership and adopted pacifist resolutions on national-defense policies, Gaitskell stated quite explicitly that the party in Parliament would continue to follow the policies it considered correct. He admitted, however, that failure to change conference policy might lead to disastrous consequences for the party in the long run, and at the following year's conference, after the leadership had modified its own stand, a compromise was reached which received conference support. Wilson took an even stronger stand against conference policy resolutions in the late 1960's, particularly on resolutions attacking his government's programs to control prices and wages; he made it clear he would not feel bound by any conference decisions on this issue.

Regardless of how one interprets the extent of influence exerted by conference resolutions, what is not open to dispute is that the Annual Conference provides an opportunity for the ideological militants, especially those from the constituency parties, to try to exert their influence on party policy. Whereas the Conservative conferences went for sixteen years without the need for a card vote on a policy resolution, several written ballots are common features of every Labor conference. The direction of the attempts to influence the Labor conference is always leftward. Responsible to a wider constituency and also used to the give-and-take of

the parliamentary experience, the parliamentary party has usually been more "moderate"—that is, more pragmatic—than the conference delegates. Whether the left-directed resolutions are adopted is largely dependent upon whether the leaders of the big unions cast their bloc votes for or against the position taken by the parliamentary leadership.

The composition of the NEC helps to assure that the parliamentary leadership will prevail. As already indicated, the prestige of national office has meant that PLP members dominate the national committee. Their primacy has minimized NEC adoption of positions at variance with what the parliamentary party believes to be possible or wise. Furthermore, the executive committee, through its disciplinary powers, its hold on the party bureaucracy, and its control over the agenda of the Annual Conference, commands considerable power. Given the size and the short duration of Annual Conferences, the relative lack of information available to delegates, and a general unwillingness to upset the applecart, successful full-scale rebellions are rather rare.

To set the parliamentary party and the NEC apart from the Annual Conference is, however, misleading. When policy differences occur within the party, as they did over entrance into the Common Market in the 1970's, they are likely to take place simultaneously within all three structural units of the party. Thus when he was campaigning for a "yes" vote in the Common Market referendum in 1975, Prime Minister Wilson found himself opposed by a majority of the Annual Conference, a majority of the NEC, a majority of the PLP, and a substantial minority of his own cabinet. Prolonged conflict among the units of the party, moreover, cannot be tolerated; the militants see the "cause" as being damaged, while members of the more moderate leadership see the chances of electoral success impaired. Wilson's vacillation on the question of Common Market membership can best be understood as an attempt by him to hold the party together in the face of vigorous anti-Market sentiment both in the unions and in the left wing of the parliamentary and constituency parties. His apparent inconsistencies can be compared with the switch made by the Annual Conference on defense policy in 1961; in both instances, protracted disagreement was viewed as resulting in incalculable long-term damage to the party.

7. ON THE HUSTINGS [6]

LEGAL REQUIREMENTS: The Parliament Act of 1911 limits the life of a parliament to five years, though the party in office usually calls for an election before that time expires. To vote in Britain, one must be over eighteen, a British subject, and have one's name inscribed on the voting register. Aliens, hereditary peers, felons, and persons convicted of past election offenses are excluded from the franchise. Voting lists are made up once a year; a form is sent to every house in the nation and householders must state the name, age, and citizenship of those living at the residence. After the rolls are compiled, an announcement appears that the register is being prepared, and everyone is invited to check to see if his name is on it.

Election campaigns are comparatively short affairs. The first step is an announcement by the prime minister that on a certain date—usually in about ten days' time —the queen will dissolve Parliament. As soon as Parliament is dissolved, a royal proclamation is published summoning a new one, and the election must be held within three weeks.

Writs are issued to all the constituencies commanding them to return a representative to Parliament.[7] The very next day, the local returning officer must put up an announcement that there is to be an election; and within eight days of the summons to the new parliament, the nominations of the candidates must be complete. Parliamentary candidates require nominations by two voters and support by another eight. The candidate must also put down a £150 deposit, which is returned if the candidate polls more than one-eighth of the total votes cast; otherwise it goes to the state to help pay election expenses.

THE CANDIDATES: The national organs in both the Conservative and Labor parties theoretically retain ultimate control over the nomination of candidates. In fact, however, the constituency parties are relatively autonomous.

In the Conservative Party, the preliminary work in securing a candidate is done by a local election committee appointed by the chairman of the local party in consultation with the National Union's Advisory Committee on Candidates. Local Conservative Party leaders interested in running for Parliament may make their desires known (unobtrusively, of course) to the Selection Committee, or they may try to get placed on the list of possible candidates at the central office. Because there is no residence requirement for national office in Britain, the local party has a far wider choice than in the United States. Other things being equal, however, Conservatives prefer local people, or at least candidates who will agree to settle in the constituency and promise to give it their full attention. All names gathered by the Conservative Party's Selection Committee must be approved by its Advisory Committee on Candidates, but in only one case since 1945 has the Advisory Committee refused to allow a potential candidate to be considered.

The Advisory Committee has had some success in placing Conservative luminaries who have lost their seats, though it has by no means found the constituency parties overwhelmingly enthusiastic about accepting its suggestions. The committee has had even less success in persuading local parties to consider candidates who would give the party a more representative character in

---

[6] The term is Norse in origin and refers to open-air meetings. In modern times it has been used to describe election campaigns.

[7] A politically impartial Boundary Commission redraws constituency boundaries as population shifts warrant.

Parliament. The majority of Conservative Party candidates tend to be professional men (in law, public relations, and the armed forces) or businessmen—in any event, distinctly middle class. Despite the urging of the central office, local organizations have been extremely loath to adopt Jews, workers, or women as candidates. In the election of 1970, however, 9 Jews (an all-time high) were elected Conservative MP's, but this compared with 31 in the smaller Labor Parliamentary Party. More important, in that election only 2 Conservative MP's out of the 330 elected were manual workers, though about half of the Conservative Party vote comes from manual workers. Even this token representation disappeared in the elections of 1974.

The Selection Committee generally recommends a list of three or four names to the executive council of the local party, which then invites those nominated to a special meeting. The candidates are asked to speak, usually for about twenty minutes, and to answer questions, after which a vote is taken. The council's choice is then submitted to a general meeting of the local party, where it is almost always approved.

The task of prospective candidates is not always terribly pleasant. As one MP described it:

It is a gala occasion for the selectors; slow torture for the candidates. So great is the strain of maintaining an amicable conversation with his rivals and their wives, that it is a relief for the applicant to leave the anteroom . . . for the ten or twenty-minute interview which may alter the entire direction of his life. . . . They do not want a speech about party policy. They want to discover what sort of person he is, or is capable of pretending to be. . . .[8]

In fact, Conservatives are rarely concerned about ideology.

What most associations want is a man of solid character. Not necessarily a brilliant man. . . . in fact they may distrust a chap who seems too brilliant or flashy or glib. They want someone who looks good and sounds right. They want someone they can count on to do the right thing. . . .[9]

Very few incumbent MP's are denied renomination by the party. A number of Conservative MP's have on occasion abstained or voted against the party on important votes since World War II, but the national agencies have *never* challenged their readoption. During the same period, however, a number of constituency parties failed to readopt incumbent MP's. Some of these refusals involved objections relating to "personal" deficiencies; others were related to policy splits in the Conservative Party.

The process of selecting Labor Party candidates resembles that of the Conservatives in many ways, but here again, central control and ideological questions are more important than in the Conservative Party. Prospective Labor candidates are not permitted to raise their own names publicly before a local party; only through private channels can they make their political ambitions known. They must be nominated by one of three groups: the national executive committee, a ward committee, or an affiliated organization such as a trade union. The names of proposed candidates are submitted to the NEC, which may also take the initiative in suggesting names. In the latter case special care is taken, for local parties are sensitive about pressure from above. Labor Party militants, of course, have a tendency to regard all authority as arbitrary.

The NEC maintains two lists, one of possible candidates who have trade-union sponsorship, and one of those who do not. Sponsorship is usually an important consideration, inasmuch as trade unions may pay up to 80 percent of the campaign expendi-

[8] Quoted in Austin Ranney, *Pathways to Parliament: Candidate Selection in Great Britain* (Madison: University of Wisconsin Press, 1965), p. 60.

[9] A central office official quoted in Ranney, *Pathways to Parliament*, pp. 60–61.

tures. Constituency parties with their dominant left-wing, usually middle-class, majorities are, therefore, often torn between their desire to find a candidate who mirrors their views and their need to accept a superannuated trade unionist.

Prospective Labor candidates also appear before a selection conference that, in spite of differences, is as forbidding as its Conservative counterpart.

Constituency parties want people who are forceful speakers and who will campaign hard. They are also favorably disposed toward the person who has already indicated his devotion through service in the party or a trade union. All this considered, a local man will be given preference over an outsider. As in the Conservative Party, women seem to have less of a chance for nomination than men. There seems also to be some prejudice against Catholics, although as we have seen, hardly any against Jews.

The Labor Party elects a good many manual workers to Parliament; their proportion of the total number of elected Labor candidates depends, however, upon the party's fortune. With a considerably larger number of trade-union MP's than non-trade-union MP's coming from safe Labor districts, the proportion of the party's representation held by the former varies inversely with the number of seats won by the party. In 1959, when the Conservatives won a substantial electoral victory, 35 percent of the Labor candidates elected to Parliament came from working-class backgrounds; in 1966 it was only 30 percent. Whatever the percentage variance of manual workers, the proportion of trade-union officials nominated for Parliament is gradually dropping. Moreover, even for seats sponsored by trade unions, middle-class aspirants with a university education are becoming more attractive as party candidates. They are usually professional men, predominantly lawyers, teachers, or journalists.

Control by the national executive over nominations is stronger than in the Conservative Party, although, again, the NEC has not been notoriously successful in securing

good seats for favorites. Labor's central office, nevertheless, has exercised more authority than the Conservatives' Abbey House in preventing the adoption of candidates it did not like, or in preventing local associations from turning down candidates it found congenial.

THE CAMPAIGN: The foundation of the parliamentary campaign is the canvass. It is the aim of each party to call on every voter in the district and to learn, if possible, how he will vote. Very little effort is expended on those who uphold the other party, but supporters and marginals are flooded with campaign literature. Candidates appear at street rallies—and endure a considerable amount of rough heckling; national party figures concentrate their political efforts on crucial districts, and both parties make arrangements to get their supporters to the polls. Both are also making greater use of public-relations firms and techniques. Laborites were slower than the Conservatives in picking up this maneuver, believing it to be un-Socialist, but they have overcome their earlier qualms. Since 1959, the parties have used television broadcasts, which are allocated among the parties in proportion to their votes at the preceding election.

Both parties have come to rely more and more on paid professional agents, whose job it is to know the intricacies of the election law, to direct the work of fighting a campaign, and, between campaigns, to maintain and build the party organization. Successful agents may be promoted to better paying constituencies, or to the party's central office. The Conservative Party's agents are generally better paid, better trained, and about twice as numerous as the Labor Party's. Labor, however, can draw upon a somewhat larger pool of dedicated militants.

British law sets fairly low limits upon campaign expenditures and fairly tight restrictions upon the manner in which these funds may be used. For example, the services of bands may be accepted only as a free gift; even a cup of tea at campaign headquarters must be paid for to avoid the charge of "treating." There are, however, no limits on the amount of money that can be spent between campaigns (the Conservatives spend far more); nor are there restrictions upon expenditures by private groups such as trade unions or individual firms whose advertising, though not directly favoring a particular political party, may create a disposition to favor one against the other. Most talk about party financial advantage bogs down in disagreement as to how such expenditures can be effectively regulated.

In the nineteenth century most political campaigns were financed out of the pockets of the candidates, a practice that continued in the Conservative Party until after its defeat in 1945. As the national organization of the party grew, the Conservatives turned to industry for contributions, and evidence exists that a few hundred large-scale donations met most of the party's needs in the interwar period.

After World War II, the Conservatives stressed the need for local parties to meet their own expenses by broadening their fund-raising base. The party also ·initiated public appeals to raise money. Direct contributions from a few large backers are far less crucial to party finances today than they used to be. The exact distribution of financial contributions is difficult to measure because there is no legal requirement that they be published and the Conservative Party is quite secretive. However, the party's annual income probably runs close to £3 million a year.

From the beginning, the Labor Party has relied heavily upon the contributions of trade unions, supplemented by individual affiliation dues and assistance from a few angels. The total income of the party today is probably about £1 million a year, of which the trade-union contribution is more than £400,000.

8. CHANGE AND TRANSITION

Modern British political parties took form at a time when social-class issues of a certain type were the most significant determinants of political attitudes. The structure of the party system and the orientation of both the Conservative and Labor parties was the result of a complex interaction of cultural, socioeconomic, and political factors, some of which the British shared with other European nations, others of which were typically British. All these variables contributed to the evolution of a disciplined mass two-party system in which rather moderate political parties alternated in office with, however, the Conservatives representing the normal majority.

In recent years some of the major features of this sytem have begun to change. Class issues have become less significant. The electorate perceives less and less difference between the parties and the class composition of the two parliamentary parties becomes more and more alike, and as both parties become catch-all parties trying to outbid each other in promising services to the voters. Labor supporters now join Conservative supporters in condemning trade unions for their disruptive tactics and the harm inflicted on the economy. The leadership cadres of both parties include larger numbers of professionally trained young men and women who are impatient with established political traditions. Both parties now have massive bureaucratic organizations, and both have experienced a dramatic decrease in the number and functional significance of their mass memberships. The mass media have placed increasing emphasis upon individual personalities, especially the party leader's, although the importance of personality has not become nearly as great as it is in the United States. Finally, the composition of the electorate continues to change; as in all democracies, each general election presents a new mix of generations and life experiences.

New issues are also emerging in British life—issues involving racial, ethnic, and regional conflicts. The migration of Pakistanis, Indians, and West Indians to Britain has exposed racial antipathies, and though the issue has not yet become a source of intense interparty disagreement, it might well become one. As crime rates have risen, "law and order" as an issue has become more politically salient. At least as significant has been the emergence of Welsh and Scottish nationalist parties representing a combination of regional and cultural aspirations— sometimes fused with radical politics, sometimes with conservative ideas. The Common Market has also been a controversial issue, one that has united, oddly enough, right- wing Conservatives with left-wing Laborites. All these developments, coupled with the growing demand for a more open style of politics and wider public participation, indicate that the British party system may be undergoing long-term change. The failure of any party to win a parliamentary majority in the February, 1974 election, along with an unprecedented referendum (on the Common Market) in June, 1975, may come to be seen as a landmark in the transition to a new type of party politics.

The
French
Party System

1. THE NATURE OF THE FRENCH PARTY SYSTEM

MULTIPLICITY: The French political system has always differed from the British and American in the often paralyzing multiplicity of its political parties and in its continuing retention of powerful factions that are committed, at least rhetorically, to changing the system in fundamental ways —by force if necessary. Every possible ideological current that has caused a ripple of any political significance whatsoever in Europe—from the most unreconstructed conservatism, through communism, Trotskyism, anarchism, and a half dozen shades of socialism—seems, at one time or another, to have developed its own political party in France.

During the Fourth Republic, ten to twenty parties competed for office at each national election. In France, moreover, there have long been antagonism and suspicion—even between political groups whose ideological positions have differed only marginally.

These multiple, often shifting party cleavages have prevented the party system from aggregating diverse group interests and have seriously reduced the possibilities for creating a government that could govern; that could evolve and effect a coherent set of public policies, and that could develop the necessary leadership for coping with immediate and long-range problems. Except for relatively short historical periods, no other institution or combination of institutions has been able to fill the vacuum created by the failure of the French party system. What may be said for the system, however, is that as it operated under the Third and Fourth Republic it kept the political conflicts from exploding into civil war.

ORGANIZATION: French parties run the whole gamut of types described in Chapter 8. The Communist Party is organizationally still a good example of a mass-disciplined ideological party, reflecting its origins as a mass movement outside the Parliament. In contrast, the traditional conservative and liberal parties have been decentralized cadre parties, similar to American parties.

Unlike the British, French parties of the right and center, operating within the multi-party system, have not been able to create disciplined organizations. They have persisted on the basis of strong regional and local loyalties. Even the more disciplined So-

cialists have had more difficulty maintaining party cohesion as they acquired deeper and more extensive local roots. Historically, there has always been in France an organizational gap between grass-roots party organization and the organization of parliamentary groups, and with the exception of the Communist Party, no French party has ever achieved the coherence and the discipline of British parties.

At the local level, even the Communist Party may be fragmented. Lawrence Wylie has described the problems in one village:

In view of the passion which politics arouses . . . one might expect the political parties to be well organized and active. This is not the case. Even the Communist Party is loosely held together. In the winter of 1950–1951, it was split with such dissension that some people thought it would not be in a position to support its candidates in

TABLE 10.1   FIRST BALLOT RESULTS IN FRENCH PARLIAMENTARY
ELECTIONS, 1945–1973

Voting in Metropolitan France

	1945	(Nov. 10) 1946	1951	1956	1958	1962	1967	1968	1973
Communists	26.0%	28.6%	25.9%	25.7%	18.9%	21.8%	22.5%	20.0%	21.1%
Socialists	23.8	17.9	14.9	14.8	15.5	12.7	18.8 [1]	16.5	20.4 [5]
Radicals	11.1	12.4	11.2	13.4	8.3	7.6			
Gaullists	0.0	1.6	20.4	4.4	20.4	31.9	37.8 [2]	43.6	34.5 [6]
MRP	24.9	26.4	12.8	11.1	11.2	8.9	12.8 [4]	10.3	12.4 [7]
Conservatives	13.3	12.8	12.3	14.4	22.9	13.9 [3]			
Extreme right				13.3	3.0	0.9	0.9	0.1	2.8

[1] Allied in the Federation of the Left.
[2] Gaullists and Independent Republicans allied.
[3] Both pro- and anti-Gaullist conservatives.
[4] MRP and anti-Gaullist conservatives allied in Centre Démocrate.
[5] Includes Socialists and allied Radicals.
[6] Gaullists, Independent Republicans, and Pro-Gaullist Centrists.
[7] Reform movement includes Radicals, CD, and anti-Gaullist conservatives.
Source: *Le Monde*, various editions, reprinted by permission.

TABLE 10.2   SEATS WON IN METROPOLITAN FRANCE NATIONAL
ASSEMBLY ELECTIONS, 1945–1973

Number of seats won

	1945	(Nov.) 1946	1951	1956	1958	1962	1967	1968	1973
Communists	148	166	97	145	10	41	73	34	73
Socialists	134	90	94	92	42	65	116 [1]	57 [1]	101 [4]
Radicals	23	55	77	77	34	41			
MRP and Center	141	158	82	72	54	36	41 [2]	33 [2]	31 [5]
Conservatives	62	70	80	96	111	48			
Gaullists	—	5	107	16	194	225	244 [3]	354 [3]	261 [6]
Extreme right				42					

[1] Federation of the Democratic and Socialist Left.
[2] Democratic Center.
[3] Includes both UDR and RI.
[4] Includes both PS and Radicals of the left.
[5] Reform movement, includes Radical Party and Democratic Center.
[6] Includes UDR, RI, and pro-Gaullist centrists.

Adapted from Roy Pierce, *French Political Institutions*, 2nd ed. (New York: Harper & Row, 1973), p. 160, and various issues of *Le Monde*.

the next elections.   The trouble was that some members of the party like to hunt rabbits with ferrets, and others like to hunt them with a gun.   Since the ferret is more effective than the gun . . .   the gun men accused the ferret men of ruining the sport . . ." [1]

VOTING: Studies of French voting patterns have also revealed vivid contrasts with British and American patterns.   Whereas class divisions are perhaps more intense than in Britain, and although parties of the left speak in terms of social classes, no single French party comes anywhere near mobilizing the support of any class in French society.   In the 1973 elections an estimated 33 percent of the working class voted for the Communist Party; but 22 percent backed the Gaullists, while 27 percent supported the Socialists (see Table 10.3).   Survey analyses of the working-class vote throughout the entire period of the Fifth Republic confirm this pattern of fragmentation.   Other social strata are likewise fragmented in their support of political parties.

Further, the voting behavior of Frenchmen—depending, of course, on the point of view—has been a rather peculiar combination of erraticism and stability, quite unlike the British or American pattern.   Both the Third and the Fourth Republics were marked by the sudden rise and almost equally sudden collapse of "flash" parties appealing to particular groups, or of organizations claiming to transcend ideological divisions and calling themselves "movements," "rallies," or "unions."   Quite often they were dominated by "heroic" leaders who relied upon personal charisma as a substitute for political programs.   On the other hand, an examination of the French electoral map reveals that areas that voted left in 1849 were still

[1] *Village in the Vaucluse* (Cambridge, Mass.: Harvard University Press, 1958), p. 212.

voting for left-wing candidates in the 1960's, and that areas that leaned to the right were also expressing roughly the same preferences a century later. Some of France's departments with left-wing majorities are in regions that became "dechristianized" at about the time of the French Revolution, although the sources of dechristianization

TABLE 10.3   SUPPORT FOR POLITICAL PARTIES IN FRANCE

I.   How Different Social Groups Voted in French Legislative Elections in 1967, 1968, and 1973 (percentage of each group that voted for each party).[1]

	Communists			Socialists			Center			Gaullists			Diverse Groups		
	1967	1968	1973	1967	1968	1973	1967	1968	1973	1967	1968	1973	1967	1968	1973
Farmers	13	12	8	14	20	19	19	12	16	45	48	49	18	8	9
Businessmen	12	10	12	12	13	22	18	15	22	44	53	36	14	9	8
Executives, professionals		9	11		10	22		23	20		48	39		10	8
White-collar workers	18	21	17	22	15	29	15	12	19	35	40	23	10	12	12
Blue-collar workers	31	33	33	18	18	27	11	8	14	30	31	22	10	10	4

[1] In 1967 and 1968 the Socialists included the parties in the Federation of the Democratic and Socialist Left and, in 1973, those Radicals who did not join the Reform Movement. In 1973, the Center included the groups in the Reform Movement. The Gaullists included the parties of the Gaullist majority for all three elections. The percentages should be read across. Thus, in 1967, 31 percent of blue-collar workers voted for the Communists, 18 percent for the Socialists, 11 percent for the center parties, 30 percent for the Gaullist parties, and 10 percent for other parties.

Sources: *Sondages* no. 3, 1967, p. 55; no. 2, 1968, p. 102; and Jean Charlot, *Quand la gauche peut gagner* (Paris: Editions Alain Moreau, 1973), p. 59.

II.   The Composition of the Electorates of French Political Parties in 1973 (percentage of those who voted for party in each category).

	Communists	Socialists	Reform Movement	Gaullists
Men	58	49	57	43
Women	42	51	43	57
Age				
21–34	34	29	30	25
35–49	26	32	32	28
50–64	24	26	21	23
65+	16	13	17	24
Social groups				
Farmers	2	11	18	17
Businessmen	5	6	11	10
Executive/professionals	2	9	9	7
White-collar workers	15	20	22	15
Blue-collar workers	52	35	20	24
Retired	24	19	20	27

TABLE 10.3   SUPPORT FOR POLITICAL PARTIES IN FRANCE —Continued·

II.   The Composition of the Electorates of French Political Parties in 1973
(percentage of those who voted for party in each category).

	Communists	Socialists	Reform Movement	Gaullists
Residence				
Rural communes	14	23	35	37
Cities less than 20 thousand population	14	12	12	17
Cities 20–100 thousand population	18	14	14	12
Cities 100+ thousand population	28	31	21	22
Paris region	26	20	18	12
Religious Orientation				
Practicing Catholics	1	7	23	28
Attend Church occasionally	28	43	43	50
Non-practicing Catholics	47	37	25	17
No Religion or other	24	13	9	5

Source: Polls taken by I.F.O.P. December 16–21, 1972, reported in *Les Forces politiques et les élections de mars 1973* (Paris Imprimerie du Monde, 1973), pp. 5–19. The percentages should be read down. Thus, in 1973, 58 percent of the Communist electorate were men, 42 percent women.

have earlier historical roots. The old county of Toulouse, part of the "Red Belt" of the Midi today, was noted for its radicalism as far back as the Albigensian wars of the thirteenth century. Other dechristianized areas were Jansenist in the seventeenth century, whereas some regions, for example, the Vendée in western France, have been supporting the clerical right since the Revolution. Even today religion, more than any other variable, accounts for differences in party voting.

LOCALISM: Ideological rhetoric, as already indicated, has always characterized French politics. It seems paradoxical, therefore, that local interests have also been crucial. During the Third Republic some two-thirds of the deputies elected to national office started out as local officials, and a good many hung on to their local offices while serving in Parliament. Just which political banner they carried made little difference; they all emphasized to voters their ability to obtain subsidies—and defend their localities—from the national government, if and when elected. Promises like this were bound

to have local appeal, for almost all local funds had to come from national coffers. Party strength was further dependent upon the ability of the national organizations to find local notables willing to serve as their candidates.

French politics, then, from the end of the Franco-Prussian War to the fall of France in 1940, reflected the durability of local attachments in largely rural and small-town areas. Moreover, localism was reinforced by the fragmentation of French politics. Since no single party was going to govern and enact its program, rhetoric and real politics were two different worlds. Under the Fourth Republic, politics came to be more national in focus; nevertheless, when that republic fell in 1958 three quarters of the members of the National Assembly were also serving on local councils, most of them as mayors.

LOW INVOLVEMENT: Despite the fact that many French parties can boast a core of active militants, a distinctive feature of the French party system has been that the identification of the average citizen with political

**MAP 10.1   CONTINUITY IN FRENCH VOTING PATTERNS:
TRADITIONAL VOTING IN FRANCE**

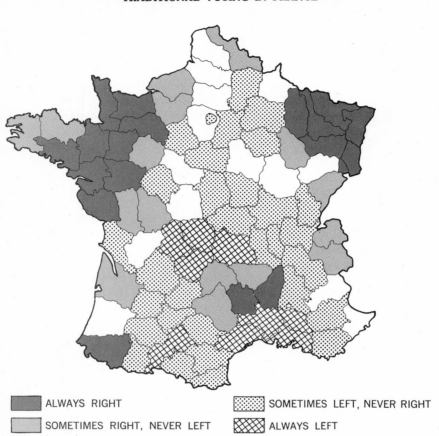

■ ALWAYS RIGHT   ▨ SOMETIMES LEFT, NEVER RIGHT

▨ SOMETIMES RIGHT, NEVER LEFT   ▩ ALWAYS LEFT

□ INTERMEDIATE OR INCONSISTENT

Adapted from **Gordon Wright,** *France in Modern
Times* (Chicago: Rand McNally, 1960), p. 478. Reprinted by permission of the publisher.

parties has been far more tenuous than has
that of the average Briton, German, or
American, although electoral turnouts have
generally been high. The Frenchman's lack
of involvement with parties partially explains the recurrent emergence of the "flash"
movements described earlier. Party identification has been stronger among the more
stable parties of the left than among the less
stable and less well-organized parties of the
right. Recent studies show that the strong
Gaullist conservative party that emerged
after 1962 has attracted many of the older

nonidentifiers and converted them into party
loyalists, while many of the younger nonidentifiers have been converted into loyalists
of parties of the left. This alignment of
party support was directly related to support for or opposition to de Gaulle himself;
just how long it will continue under his successors is difficult to predict.[2]

[2] See Ronald Inglehart and Avram Hochstein,
"Alignment of the Electorate in France and the
United States," *Comparative Political Studies 5*, no. 3
(October, 1972); pp. 343–372.

MAP 10.2 CONTINUITY IN FRENCH VOTING PATTERNS:
THE DE GAULLE VOTE, 1965

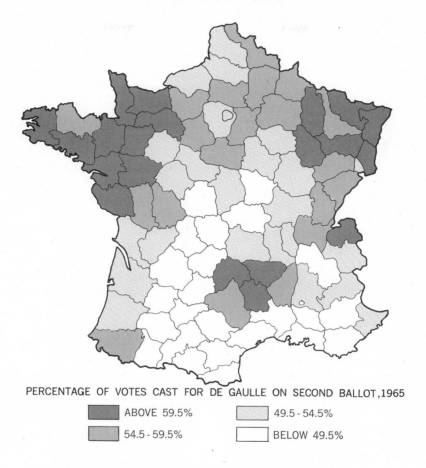

PERCENTAGE OF VOTES CAST FOR DE GAULLE ON SECOND BALLOT,1965

ABOVE 59.5%   49.5 - 54.5%

54.5 - 59.5%   BELOW 49.5%

Adapted from Wright, *France in Modern Times*, p.
479. Reprinted by permission.

2. EXPLANATION OF THE FRENCH PARTY SYSTEM

Explanations of the French party system have been legion. As indicated in Chapter 8, some political scientists, in discussing the fragmentation of the system, have stressed the effect of proportional representation during the Fourth Republic, or the use of single-member districts and ballotage (a second ballot) during the Third and Fifth. (Thirteen of the sixteen elections held in the Third Republic used single-member districts and a double ballot; all elections under the Fifth Republic have used this method.) Others have stressed aspects of the French national character, and still others have argued that the nature of the party system reflects certain basic conflicts in French society that are a heritage of its historical development.

Electoral mechanisms *have* played an important role in determining both the relative strength of French parties in Parliament, and the nature of political coalitions and electoral strategies adopted by the parties. During the Third and Fifth Republics, with the single-member district, double-ballot system in use, the number of seats received by a party has depended heavily on its ability to forge alliances, hence to moderate and broaden its appeal, between the first and second ballot. It can be argued that this system has encouraged party moderation also in the sense that at the second round the candidate nearest the center attracts voters fearful of victory by one of the "more dangerous" candidates. Electoral mechanisms have not, however, had much effect on the existence of a multitude of parties. Many of the smaller, more sectarian parties have not been put out of business simply by electoral mechanisms biased against them. As part of the same phenomenon, French voters have always been willing to vote for a party even though it obviously had no chance of achieving governmental power.

More important than electoral mechanisms in affecting the number of parties has probably been the fact that until recently France has been a parliamentary, not a presidential, regime—the parliamentary system being fully compatible with multiparty coalitions. Until the Fifth Republic there was no single independent executive that could be awarded to the party able to attract the largest number of voters.

Yet more fundamental than structural arrangements in explaining the French party system has been the fragmentation of French social and political life. As was stressed in Chapter 2, this fragmentation has been woven into the whole tapestry of French history; it is the product of the trauma of the Revolution and modernization. Like comparable events in many other European Catholic nations, the French Revolution produced a schism that to this day has divided French society into two hostile subcultures: the one traditional and Catholic; the other, at least on the surface, dedicated to the ideas of liberty, the Enlightenment, secularization, and science. But the Revolution and modernization led to additional subcultural cleavages as well, ones based on class, region, and locality. From all these cultural divisions, a plethora of political ideologies emerged that froze positions already

taken in organized political life, so that new problems always surfaced before old conflicts were resolved.

This situation was partly related to the rather slow rate of economic growth that contributed to the perpetuation of traditional patterns of social organization. At least as important were certain cultural attitudes. The Frenchman's so-called individualism has made it difficult to develop common conceptions of national purpose and authority in France. Often willing to see authority imposed from the top because he recognizes that it is necessary if the society is to cohere at all, the Frenchman also tries to keep it at arm's length in order to protect himself. To him, those in authority are almost never to be trusted; he has believed that, except for his immediate family or some limited group, he is surrounded by *les autres*, who seek to exploit his weaknesses for their own benefit.

The distrust in which political parties have been held by the French public is also partly the result of the political situation in which the parties have historically found themselves. Because no party was able to form a government by itself during the Third and Fourth Republics, all parties (except the Communists) were forced to compromise their programs seriously, and, in Parliament, deputies found themselves spending more time entering into deals in order to secure meager advantages than in facing the political problems that could not (in the circumstances) be resolved. And because little could really be changed or accomplished under this kind of political system, those who participated in politics were corrupted. It is not surprising, therefore, that the identification of the average French citizen with political parties has been tenuous, and that he has placed only limited trust in them as expressions of solidarity and instruments of change. To a large extent, the political party is still seen as one of a variety of institutions (and not necessarily the most effective) for defending one's interests.

Accordingly, although the French political community has been divided into a multitude

TABLE 10.4   FRENCHMEN'S REASONS FOR SUPPORTING A POLITICAL PARTY

	PCF	SFIO	Radicals	MRP	Independents	Gaullists
Defense of one's interests	28%	24%	27%	22%	30%	11%
Desire to work for progress	7	6	11	2	9	5
Association with those who have the same ideas	1	2	3	6	3	5
Loyalty to class	2	1	4	3	2	1
To shape the future of France and of the world	4	7	11	13	24	33
To work for the country	32	28	18	27	17	23
To build a new society	19	17	13	20	9	14
No response	7	15	13	7	6	8

Adapted from Pierre Fougeyrollas, *La conscience politique dans la France contemporaine* (Paris: Editions Denoël, 1963), p. 100, reprinted by permission of the publisher.

of mutually hostile camps, the organization of these camps has been surprisingly weak. This weakness of organizational authority, which derives from a distrust of leadership, has made it more difficult for political parties to find a *modus vivendi* among themselves in France than in Britain and Germany. The frequent volitility of French politics has been less related to the existence of a multitude of political camps, than to the difficulty that party leaders have had in organizing and leading these camps.

In an effort to provide a systematic and yet dynamic picture of the development of the French party system, the sections that follow will discuss French national parties in the order of their *historical appearance* on the political scene. Limitations of space do not permit as full a discussion of each party as that given to the three parties of Britain, and some of the smaller parties will receive rather short shrift (see Figure 10.1).

3.   THE JACOBIN LEFT

DEVELOPMENT: The radical tradition in France traces its origins to the Jacobins of the French Revolution. The Jacobin clubs represented in embryo form the beginnings of an organized political party. Throughout the nineteenth century, however, like every other political tendency in France, radicalism also remained merely that—a tendency. From time to time groups such as Masonic lodges developed the rudiments of a political organization, but, for the most part, the politics of radicalism revolved about personalities and parliamentary cliques.

The term "radical" did not become an actual part of the French political vocabulary until about 1830, when it was used to describe opponents of the monarchy who were unwilling to compromise with their republican ideals. These "radicals" combined a faith in universal suffrage with violent anticlericalism, a fervent belief in education and science, civil liberties, and, somewhat later, strong opposition to imperialism. In essence their program was liberal; but whereas in Britain, Whigs and radicals remained in the same political camp and eventually transformed themselves into the Liberal Party, French liberalism split into two irreconcilable political entities. The right wing—*Orléanistes* and, later, moderate republicans—was willing to compromise with the monarchy and the church. These "whigs" saw radicalism as opening the way to mob violence and mob rule, and the radicals saw French whiggery as essentially a reactionary force.

FIGURE 10.1 MAJOR FRENCH POLITICAL PARTIES, 1902–1975

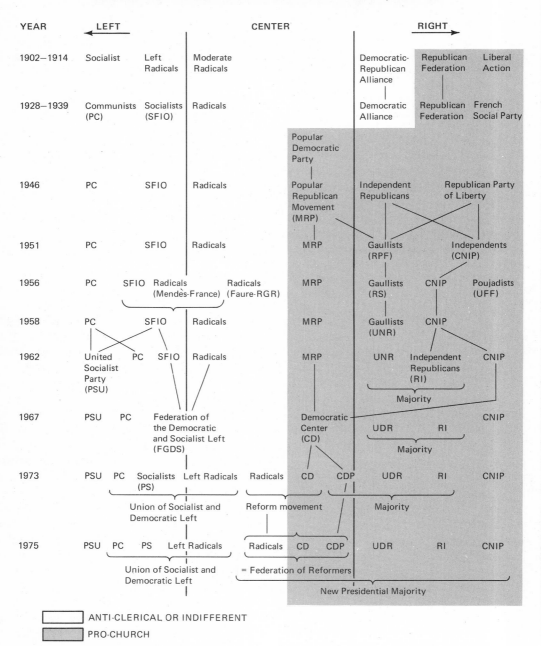

Sources: Thomas T. Mackie and Richard Rose, *The International Almanac of Electoral History* (New York: Free Press, 1974), pp. 128–139; Philip M. Williams, *Crisis and Compromise* (London: Longmans Green & Co., 1964), pt. II; Peter Campbell, *French Electoral Systems and Elections Since 1789* (Hamden, Conn.: Shoe String Press, 1965).

From the fall of the empire in 1870 to the beginning of the twentieth century, radicals were returned to Parliament in increasing numbers. In 1901 the two major radical groups, the Republican Radicals and the Socialist Radicals, fused to form the *Parti républicain radical et radical socialiste* (Radical Republican and Radical Socialist Party), thus becoming the largest political party in the Chamber of Deputies.[3] In 1910 the Radicals received 38 percent of the popular vote, the largest they were ever to attain, but by that time they had seen most of their program enacted into law: all forms of government censorship had been abolished, church and state separated, compulsory primary education laws passed, and a mildly progressive income tax adopted.

By World War I the bases of Radical electoral strength had begun to shift. Initially, the various radical tendencies had derived considerable support from urban workers. However, the rise of Socialist parties sapped the strength of Radicals in these areas. Further, the middle classes of the large cities began to move to the right, even as workers moved to the left. Increasingly, the center of Radical power was to be found among the middle class of small towns and villages —schoolteachers, shopkeepers, country doctors, and lawyers who acted as the spokesmen for the inarticulate peasantry. Hostile to the new industrial society, they also feared and distrusted the "socialism" of the rapidly growing cities.

Thus, the Radical Party was drawn in two directions at once. Its anticlericalism, and its rhetoric of egalitarianism, led the party into coalitions with the Socialists and later the Communists. On the other hand, its commitment to private property (to the economic interests of the small-town middle class) and its fear of the urban working class, consistently drew the party into alliances with the economic right. During the period between the two world wars, it vacillated between these positions. After the

World War I, when the danger from the left seemed paramount, they allied themselves with the right. Then, in 1924, they formed an electoral alliance with the Socialists. In 1934, when the Republic was in danger, they joined a popular front with the Socialists and Communists, only to bring the government down over its social policies. Committed to appeasement, the Radicals supported the Munich agreement and the establishment of the government at Vichy.

It is, of course difficult to speak of the Radicals as a unit, for they remained throughout this period a loosely organized cadre organization. Local notables dominated the regional organizations, and parliamentarians accepted no party discipline. In 1924, when the Radical Party in the Chamber of Deputies was allied with the Socialists, the Radicals in the Senate supported the right. They were an authentic part of the liberal tradition, but their peasant and small-town base inhibited even a partial adjustment to changing problems. Nevertheless, because they were politically flexible, radical politicians continued to dominate Third Republic governments, even though popular support for the Radical Party continued to fall during the interwar period.

Because of the close identification of the Radical Party with the Third Republic and Vichy, the Radicals received only 11 percent of the popular vote in the 1945 election. Their role in the Fourth Republic nevertheless, was very similar to that in the Third. Of the nineteen premiers who served from 1946 to 1958, eleven came from the Radical Party or closely allied groups. And during the entire twelve-year period, Radical politicians moved back and forth among the parties, collaborating first with the Communist and Socialist parties and later with the Gaullists and the conservatives. In the first elections under the Fifth Republic, their percentage dropped to less than 8 and in 1962 it fell to 7.

For a short time, between 1955 and 1957, the party was led by Pierre Mendès-France, who attempted to remake it into a more modern, disciplined organization that would

---

[3] Most commentators on the French political scene use the terms "Radical Party" and "Radical-Socialist Party" interchangeably.

have a broader popular appeal. He also attempted to create an image of a party dedicated to economic modernization and social reform—in short, a pragmatic party of the left. The attempt collapsed, however, soon after Mendès-France resigned his ministry in May, 1956, and the Radical Party never recovered from this effort.

The Radical Party supported de Gaulle until 1962, and then came out strongly in opposition to the regime. In 1965, the party entered into an alliance with the Socialists to form the *Fédération de la gauche démocrate et socialiste*—FGDS (Federation of the Democratic and Socialist Left) behind the presidential candidacy of François Mitterrand, the leader of one of those small splinter parties between the left wing of the Radical Party and the Socialist Party. The Federation continued its activities through the 1967 and 1968 elections, entering into an electoral alliance with the Communist Party. In the 1967 elections the number of parliamentary seats won by the parties composing the Federation increased from 105 to 116. The 1968 elections, however, were a debacle for the Federation, which lost 61 seats.

In the aftermath of the 1968 election, the Federation collapsed under the impact of mutual recriminations. Then in October, 1969, Maurice Faure, president of the Radical Party, invited Jean-Jacques Servan-Schreiber to become general secretary of the party. Servan-Schreiber, well-known editor of the left-of-center weekly newsmagazine *L'Express*, had an international reputation and a "Kennedy" style; he seemed to be the ideal person to resuscitate the fortunes of the sinking party. His plan, reminiscent of the Mendès-France operation, was to form a broad center-left, non-Communist coalition based on a bold new reform program. In 1970 a special congress of the Radical Party did adopt a new program entitled "Heaven and Earth."

The party's attempts to form an alliance with the Socialists, however, were not successful, and in 1971 it joined with other groups of the center, and the former Popu-

lar Republican Movement (MRP), to form the Reform Movement (*Mouvement Réformateur*). The result of this drift to the right was yet another split in the party. Servan-Schreiber installed his own followers in key party posts, he defeated Faure for the party presidency, and the dissidents—including Faure, all the Radicals in the Assembly, and half the Radical senators—were expelled from the party. The dissidents joined with the reorganized Socialist Party in preparation for the 1973 election. The first round of this election was a catastrophe for the Reform Movement; it received only 12.5 percent of the vote. Its poor showing was compounded by disagreement about strategy for the second round among the parties that constitute the movement. With thirty-one representatives in the New Assembly, the influence of the divided Reform Movement appeared to be slight. However, after supporting M. Giscard d'Estaing in the presidential elections in May, 1974, the leaders of the movement were rewarded with ministerial posts in the new cabinet. Although M. Servan-Schreiber resigned within two weeks, in protest against a government decision to conduct nuclear tests, the importance of the Reform representatives has been increased by the President's need for support among nonGaullists in the National Assembly. Under considerable pressure from the president, in March, 1975, the Radicals joined with virtually all of the small parties of the center, as well as their partners in the Reform Movement, to form the *Fédération des Réformateurs* (the Federation of Reformers). The new federation, together with the Gaullists and the Independents, became part of the developing "presidential majority." Thus, once again, the influence of the Radicals appears to be linked to the importance of the party in coalition formation.

STRUCTURE, SUPPORT AND POLICY: The Radicals have been a loosely organized cadre party. Coordination between parliamentarians and the party outside Parliament has always been minimal. So, too, has coordination among parliamentarians and among local party federations. To the Radicals' natural distrust of discipline have been added the pressures and opportunities of a fragmented multiparty system, and the temptations and opportunities for acquiring office through political maneuvering.

The primary local unit of the party is the base committee in each constituency. Under new statutes, adopted in 1970, the base committees choose legislative candidates, who must be approved by the departmental federation, and invested by the executive committee of the party. The departmental federations decide on election tactics, but these tactics will now be coordinated with those of the other parties in the Federation of Reformers. Membership is open to individuals that support the party's program. The federations send delegates—on the basis of one per fifty members—to the National Congress, which meets each year. Other voting delegates to the congress include the members of the executive committee, the departmental councillors, the mayors, and some of the municipal councillors of the Radical Party, all of the candidates invested by the party in the last elections, and the newspaper editors affiliated with the party. The congress approves the party program along with reports placed before it by the executive committee, and elects the party president, but the day-to-day running of the party is in the hands of the executive committee and the bureau, which is selected by the committee.

The executive committee is dominated by party bureaucrats. Thus, about a third of its members are also members of the bureau, the heads of study commissions (named by the committee), and former officers. The other two-thirds are drawn from the parliamentary group and the federations. The largest federations from the most populous regions are entitled to the largest representation. The executive committee meets once a month to make major policy decisions for the party, but the bureau meets more frequently and in fact seems to make the important decisions. Thus, on May 14, 1974,

M. Servan-Schreiber, the president of the party, announced that he would support Giscard d'Estaing in the second round of the presidential elections; only then did the executive committee "ratify" the decision.

These party statutes, adopted in 1970, give considerably more power to those elements within the party from larger cities and more populated areas. They also create a stronger, more centralized organization under the leadership of Servan-Schreiber. In the past, Radical members of Parliament have voted on all sides of every issue; they have also been responsible (during the Fourth Republic) for overthrowing Radical prime ministers, and they have joined parliamentary intergroups with other parties, such as the Gaullists, without fear of being disciplined. While party discipline in voting has not improved much, the reorganized party has been able to set limits. Thus, in 1973, those Radicals in the Assembly that continued to support the alliance with the Socialists were expelled from the party and opposed in the elections.

The party had a nominal membership of some 80,000 to 100,000 before World War II. By 1959, however, party membership had fallen to 20,000 and, once again, the Radicals were the representatives of small-town, nineteenth-century France. By the time of the party congress of June, 1972, however, Servan-Schreiber had once again attracted young people into the party ranks; their presence, together with their desire for a truly Radical alternative to the Communists, gave a lift to party-membership rolls, and in 1973 the Radicals claimed 30,000 members. By 1974, however, membership in the party had begun to fall off again as a result both of internal conflicts and lack of electoral success.

4. THE TRADITIONAL RIGHT

BACKGROUND: The right in France has historically included a potpourri of political beliefs—the "ultras" of the Restoration, the quasi-Fascist leagues of the 1930's, the

Orléanistes of the 1850's, and the "moderates" of the turn of the century. As late as the 1930's there was a right wing, with a significant following, that still lamented the fall of the monarchy and that had aspirations of restoring at least some elements of "traditional" France. It was this group, whose social base lay with old aristocratic families, elements of the military, traditional commerce, and some of the religious peasantry, that held a majority during the first years of the Third Republic; that was discredited by the Dreyfus Affair; and that re-emerged to provide much of the impetus for the Vichy experiment.

There was also a right that was republican, albeit not enthusiastically so, committed to economic laissez-faire, to low taxes on business, but also to modernization and to support for the army. What the multitude of right-wing groups held in common was support for the church, religious schools and religious values. However, for some supporters of the right, the church merely provided protection against radicalism, "Bolshevism," and rule by the masses. Particularly after World War I, anti-Communism was a strong unifying force for the groups of the political right.

Although numerous governments were formed by the right during the Third Republic, and although the forces of the right joined in an electoral alliance and parliamentary group—the *Bloc National*—in 1919, there was, properly speaking, no conservative party in France until after World War II. One reason for this was that conservative factions tended to distrust mass organization as smacking of mob rule. Also, most members of Parliament who conceived of themselves as being on the right could and did depend largely upon their contacts with the bureaucracy to preserve their established interests, and to secure favors for themselves and their constituents. Thus, the French conservatives did not organize a party because (for one thing) they did not have to; so long as the nation remained politically fragmented, they could achieve their goals by other means. While the right did form

blocs from time to time in defense of conservative interests, it was only during the Fourth Republic that circumstances prompted some real attempts to establish an organized conservative party. The effort was a failure, partly because the potential constituency of the conservatives was pre-empted by de Gaulle.

Most right-wing politicians were discredited at the time of the Liberation because of their general association with Vichy. Those remaining set about organizing what they hoped would be the great conservative party of the Fourth Republic, the *Parti républicain de Liberté*—PRL (Republican Party of Liberty). However, the PRL neither built up an effective organization nor acquired a popular following. Along with a number of other conservative groupings, a loose holding company was formed in 1948, the *Centre national des indépendants et paysans*—CNIP (National Center of Independents and Peasants). In 1951 the CNIP received 12.3 percent of the vote, and shortly thereafter Antoine Pinay, a conservative, was elected premier.

In the 1956 election, a new combination of Independents and dissident Gaullists led by Pinay received 14.4 percent of the popular vote, and formed a single conservative group in the National Assembly. Two years later the Independents reached the peak of their growth. Supporting the new regime and, thus, riding on de Gaulle's coattails, the CNIP obtained nearly 20 percent of the vote on the first ballot and almost 24 percent on the second. With 132 seats in the assembly, they ranked second only to de Gaulle's *Union pour la nouvelle république*—UNR. Moreover, Pinay returned to power as finance minister in de Gaulle's cabinet.

The internal unity of the CNIP and its delight with de Gaulle were not to last long. Members of the CNIP split with him on four crucial issues: Algeria, which they favored retaining; economic policies, which led to Pinay's resignation; the power of the National Assembly, which they did not wish to see curbed; and France's ties to the Atlantic Alliance, which they wanted maintained.

By 1962 the CNIP had split into three factions, and in the parliamentary elections of that year, its percentage of the popular vote dropped to 13.9. Only forty-eight Independents were returned to Parliament, largely because of Gaullist support. Most of these formed a parliamentary group called the *Républicans indépendents*—RI (Independent Republicans) under the leadership of Valéry Giscard d'Estaing, supported de Gaulle on crucial issues, yet tried to retain a degree of independence.

The power and the influence of the Independent Republicans, and their most important leader, Giscard d'Estaing, continued to vary with the strength of the Gaullist party. When the Gaullists needed the RI to maintain their parliamentary majority after the 1967 legislative elections, the influence of the party increased; it declined with the solid Gaullist victory in 1968. As a result of the 1973 legislative elections, the Independent Republicans, with fifty-four seats in the Assembly, once again held the margin of the majority—and, as a consequence, their influence and Giscard d'Estaing's increased. The new cabinet, appointed after Giscard d'Estaing's victory in the presidential elections in 1974, is dominated by the leaders of the party. The RI has now formed both a common parliamentary group and an electoral alliance with the remnant of the CNIP. However, as in the past, both parties remain collections of notables; 90 percent of the RI deputies are also mayors who rely upon local contacts for their election.

STRUCTURE, SUPPORT AND POLICY: Despite the efforts of Roger Duchet, founder of the CNIP and its general secretary during most of the Fourth Republic, the Independents remained, and remain still, the least organized of the major parties. After 1954 they began to hold national congresses for the purpose of formulating some sort of common program. Control of the CNIP, however, was retained by its parliamentary leadership, which was composed primarily of local figures whose ties with constituents were direct. Thus, while the party label did

prove of some assistance in the 1956 elections, it was never sufficient to make or break a candidate. The Independent Republicans maintained the same organizational pattern.

Before 1939 the strongholds of conservatism had been in the Catholic west, the eastern frontier departments, and the Massif Central. In the Fifth Republic, however, the MRP and even the UNR drew off many voters whose support of the Independents had been based primarily on religious conviction. In comparison with the Gaullists, the Independents have received a much larger proportion of their vote from less industrialized areas. Their leadership has also come principally from rural and small-town France, and their parliamentary representation has always included more peasants than any other parliamentary group. Traditional conservatism had never been averse to extensive government intervention in the economy; in fact, as already indicated, the social policies of the Vichy regime helped pave the way for greater participation by the state in the Fourth and Fifth Republics. However, dominated by rural and traditional bourgeois elements, the outlook of the Independents has tended to be Malthusian and defensive, conceiving the state as primarily designed to protect their vested interests; the major objective of the Independents has been to hold on to what they have. Here they have been in contrast with many of the Gaullists, who, in terms of national policy, have been influenced by technocrats dedicated to the principle of authority but also to policies that have as their purpose the modernization of France and the creation of a social-welfare state.

The Independent Republicans and their leader, M. Giscard d'Estaing, have emerged as a classical liberal group. Committed to business, deflationary economic policy, and more recently to a united Europe, the party has opposed the participation schemes of the left-wing Gaullists, and some of the more anti-American manifestations of Gaullist foreign policy.

Traditional anti-republicanism of the Vichy stripe all but expired with the Liberation, and only two really right-wing political groupings have emerged in France since World War II. Both have proved ephemeral. In 1956 the *Union et fraternité française* (UFF)—the Poujadists—received almost 12 percent of the vote; two years later the UFF had all but disappeared. In 1965 Jean-Louis Tixier-Vignancour, a prominent right-wing lawyer, received some 5 percent of the vote on the first presidential ballot, but he was unable to create a political organization.

5.   THE SOCIALIST LEFT

EVOLUTION: Socialist ideas and even a Socialist political faction in France can be traced to the French Revolution. An organized Socialist Party did not really begin to surface, however, until the 1870's and 1880's, when an atmosphere of relative freedom and the pace of industrialization opened the way for the political organization of the working class. In France, unlike Britain, revolutionary Marxism was an integral part of Socialist thinking from the very beginning, although non-Marxist elements—anarchist and syndicalist—also developed revolutionary theories. Again, unlike their British counterparts, none of these left-wing movements was able to establish a close organizational relationship with the trade-union movement. French trade-union leaders distrusted "bourgeois" politicians and preferred to concentrate on their own programs of direct action.

In 1905 several Socialist groups merged to form a unified Socialist Party, the French Section of the Workers' International (*Section française de l'internationale ouvrière*— SFIO). It was the first mass party to form in France.

From the beginning the Socialists were divided between a revolutionary and a reformist faction. At the eve of World War I, the reformists seemed to be winning out even as the SFIO was becoming a major political organization. The War and its aftermath, however, radicalized large sections of the party and in 1920 it split. The majority of the party's militants, including some of its most brilliant younger members, voted to join Lenin's Third International and formed the French Communist Party. They took with them part of the party's treasury as well as the party newspaper, *L'Humanité*.

Under the leadership of Léon Blum, however, the SFIO gradually rebuilt itself, and its proportion of the popular vote rose from 8 to 18 percent between 1924 and 1928. The success of Blum's endeavors had much to do with the change in the party's appeal—and clientele. Increasingly, its strength was coming from anticlerical white-collar workers and teachers, as well as peasants, who now considered the Socialists to be more advanced than the Radicals and yet reasonably safe. Simultaneously, the party was losing much of its working-class support to the better organized and more actively militant Communist Party, particularly in the newer industrial areas.

The shift in supporters was closely associated with the continuing reformist orientation within the Socialist Party, despite the rhetorical militancy that characterized it during the period of the Popular Front of the 1930's. The Popular Front was a political alliance of Socialists, Communists, and Radicals united to save the republic from what they considered to be a Fascist threat. The victory of the Popular Front in the 1936 elections led to the formation of the first Socialist-led government in French history, headed by Léon Blum as premier.

Cooperation between the Socialists and the Communists was reestablished during the period immediately following World War II. Given the record of the Communists in the Resistance and the prestige of the Soviet Union at that time, Blum and others were unable to get the SFIO to reconsider its Marxist slogans in terms of contemporary realities, and the more militant cadres won control of the party's machinery. As the Cold War grew in intensity, however, the Communist and Socialist alliance again fell apart, and the Communists were driven from the government by a Socialist premier. By this time, however, the Communists had come to dominate the trade-union movement, forcing many workers of a Socialist but non-Communist bent to set up a rival organization.

By 1949 it was evident that, except for certain areas of Northern France, the Socialists could no longer claim to speak for the working class. Participation by the party in a number of coalition governments with the Radicals, the MRP, and other "bourgeois" parties had impaired its reputation as a working-class party. By 1954 the party had lost two-thirds of its dues-paying members, even though by then the party had decided to remain in opposition in order to be in a position to criticize safely the government's "reactionary," "clerical" policies. In 1956 the Socialists joined with the resuscitated Radicals, led by Mendès-France, in an electoral alliance—the Republican Front —a strategy that proved partially successful. Guy Mollet, the head of the SFIO became premier, a post he held until May, 1957. Finally, after bitter internal wrangling, the party, under Mollet's leadership, supported de Gaulle's coming to power in 1958.

By 1961, however, the SFIO had moved into opposition to the de Gaulle government. In preparation for the legislative elections of 1962, the Socialists agreed with the Communists that the candidate from one party would withdraw on the second round in favor of a better-placed candidate of the other. In this way, the SFIO was able to increase its seats by a third over 1958, although its electoral support actually declined, and to become the largest opposition party in the Assembly.

For the next three years the party searched for some basis for a new party alignment preparatory to the presidential elections of 1965. After unsuccessfully trying to form a centrist alliance with the Radicals and the MRP behind the candidacy of Gaston Defferre, mayor of Marseilles and leader of the party's anti-Communist group, they finally settled for a "small" federation with the Radicals, the *Féderation de la gauche démocrate et socialiste*—FGDS (The Federation of the Democratic and Socialist Left). The Federation, along with the Communists, supported the candidacy of François Mitterrand (see below p. 185). The Federation continued to function through the elections of 1968, when it was shattered by disagreements about the "events" of that year.

With the collapse of the Federation in 1968, the party reorganized and was renamed the *Parti socialiste*—PS. Despite the new name, however, the Socialist candidate in the presidential election of 1969, Gaston Defferre, received only 5 percent of the vote. After the debacle of 1969, the Socialists once again began to make a concerted effort to form a credible opposition on the left in anticipation of the legislative elections of 1973. The party consolidated with Mitterrand's followers, and with numerous groups of the Catholic left. By a narrow majority, the 1971 party congress elected Mitterrand national secretary and voted to negotiate a detailed governmental program with the Communists and other leftist parties. The reorganization injected new dynamism into the party, and in 1972 the Socialist Party was able, after many years, to report an increase in its membership.

During the pre-election discussions of 1972, Mitterrand pursued a strategy he hoped would unite the Socialists in a broad left coalition that would include both Servan-Schreiber's Radicals and the Communists; the plan finally failed, however, because the Radicals, pressured by their allies in the Reform Movement, were unable to agree to it. Nevertheless, in July, 1972, Socialists, Communists and dissident Radicals did reach an agreement on strategy and common goals; thus for the first time since the Socialist-Communist split in 1920 France's two major socialist parties were united on strategy and common goals, and were committed to governing together.

The renovated Socialist Party did not, in fact, do as well in the elections of 1973 as it had hoped. Even so, with 4.5 million votes in the first round, the Socialists approached their highest total (reached in 1946) and more than doubled their seats in the Assembly. In 1967 the party had attracted only 18 percent of the working-class vote; in 1973 its percentage jumped to 27. Clearly, the reorganization and attractive leadership had brought new life to the old party. The rising Socialist strength was confirmed in by-elections and local elections after 1973. Moreover, the campaign of François Mitterrand for the presidency in 1974 firmly and finally established the Socialists as a party capable of governing and Mitterrand as a strong leader of the opposition.

The very success of the Socialists, however, has brought into question their alliance with the Communists. Stung by the increase of working class support that the Socialists were attracting, the Communists began a systematic campaign against the leadership of the PS during the winter of 1974–75. Both parties continue to maintain allegiance to the main lines of their common program, but major aspects of the program are now being renegotiated.

STRUCTURE, SUPPORT AND POLICY: Like all European Socialist parties, the Socialists were organized as a mass party. Their basic operating unit was and is the section, which may be regarded as the equivalent of the constituency organization of British parties. However, whereas France is now divided into about 470 electoral districts, the party section is based on the commune—communes, as well as departments, being the fundamental administrative units in France. Theoretically, every commune has one section, but in fact there are only about 8,000 sections in France as against 38,000 communes. A section has no fixed membership, varying from as few as twenty to more than a thousand. Membership is determined by the purchase of a permanent card, an annual voucher, and monthly stamps. The *Parti Socialiste* now claims 120,000 members.

A large city may be divided into several sections, which are then coordinated by a city committee. Most sections, however, are organized directly into departmental federations that hold an annual congress at which the sections are represented in proportion to their membership. The Federation Congress is responsible for selecting delegates to the National Congress, which must meet every two years, but which in fact has met more frequently since 1971. The number of delegates and votes at the National Congress are determined by the number of members in each departmental federation. The party is directed by an executive committee, consisting of eighty-one members elected by the National Congress; the executive committee then appoints a bureau from among its members, headed by a first secretary, and a secretariat responsible for running the day-to-day affairs of the party. At every level, from the section to the national bureau, all major factions of the party are assured of representation in governing bodies by a system of proportional representation. This was the condition upon which the various Socialist factions united in 1971. Aside from the National Congress, the party has established a national convention to keep in touch with grass-roots militants. The convention, composed of one delegate from each federation, meets at least twice a year, and is joined by the parliamentary group and the executive committee.

Historically, as with the British Labor Party, conflicts have often developed between the party organization and the Parliamentary Group. Time and time again, the executive committee, prodded by militants, has threatened to discipline its representatives in Parliament for supporting governments or legislation that it opposed. Members of the Assembly have on occasion been expelled from the party and departmental federations disbanded. Even so, the ability of the executive committee, or even the parliamentary party, to punish rebels has been limited both by a political system that encourages the formation of new factions and by a localism that has often granted individual deputies and federations support even when they were disowned by the national organization. Thus, for the most part the Socialists have maintained the facade of organizational unity by temporizing on important issues and by being extremely lenient with party deviants. In short, though party discipline has been strong enough to prevent minorities from moving in new ideological directions, the party has been unable to hold people in line when there were major disagreements over tactics.

Under the new rules formulated in 1971, the executive committee and the Parliamentary Group meet together to decide major issues of policy. In case of disagreement between the two, the issue must be decided by a national convention. This mechanism of control over the Parliamentary Group has not yet been tested.

Like so many other French political parties, the Socialists have long been burdened by the battle cries of the past. Their anticlerical dogma, their membership in Masonic lodges, and their continued attachment to nineteenth-century catchwords have until recently given them an archaic air that failed to attract new voters or militants. Furthermore, the fact that the party had continually compromised its own revolutionary rhetoric for the sake of day-to-day political advantage had caused many to believe that as an organization it is completely opportunistic. Its divorce from the trade-union movement and its general composition had meant that it lacked even the Communists' advantage of a reasonably effective bureaucratic machine actively doing something about working-class needs.

In the past few years, the party has attempted to address some of these basic problems. The reorganization has reduced the influence of some of the more traditional elements within the party, and it has attracted some dynamic new leaders. The integration of left-wing Catholic groups, and numerous "new left" elements, into the party, has brought the party new and important influence in the trade union movement. The renovated party organization, and the party program, imply a strong desire by the *Parti socialiste* to connect political principle with

a detailed program and to relate both to political action.

6. THE COMMUNIST PARTY

AFTER WORLD WAR I: The (French Communist Party) *Parti communiste français* —PCF was organized by militants who took control of the Tours Conference of the Socialist Party in 1920. Theoretically, those who joined accepted the rules laid down by the Third International and were amenable to the kind of discipline Lenin considered the *sine qua non* for successful revolutionary activity.

Actually, the party contained many left-wing anarchists, as well as many militants, who considered themselves disciplined left-wing Marxists but who were unwilling to take orders from any party leadership, much less an international one centered in a "backward" country like Russia. The lack of discipline of party cadres, in fact, was among the most pressing problems faced by the infant organization, a problem compounded by Moscow's demand that the party "bolshevize" itself by setting up Communist cells in factories. Since such cells exposed workers to the danger of punitive action by employers, the suggestion was not enthusiastically received. Problems of the newly formed party were further complicated by the conflict between Stalin and Trotsky and by Trotsky's eventual expulsion from Soviet leadership.

As a consequence, the PCF split and resplit, purged and repurged itself, during the 1920's—and the number of militants dropped precipitously. Given its own unwillingness to enter into alliances with other parties on the second ballot, and the unwillingness of other parties to ally themselves with the Communists, its parliamentary influence during the decade was also quite limited. While the party received more than 11 percent of the total vote cast in 1928, it controlled less than 2 percent of the seats in the Chamber of Deputies.

Despite these difficulties, the French Communist Party did survive, and strengthened both its electoral and factory organization. Because of its organizational capacity it was able to take full advantage of the movement to the left among voters during the period of the Popular Front; in the elections of 1936, in fact, the PCF received 15 percent of the popular vote. But the ultimate failure of the Popular Front, the Munich crisis, and finally the Nazi-Soviet nonaggression pact resulted in considerable diminution of Communist strength—as did the party's attempted collaboration with the Nazis in the first days after the fall of France.

After the German attack on the Soviet Union, the Communist Party played a leading role in the Resistance. The efficiency of its underground apparatus and the dedication of its militants gave it a tremendous advantage over other Resistance groups. Although its efforts have often been exaggerated, the reputation it acquired during the war and the members it recruited while fighting the Germans enhanced both the party's postwar prestige and its strength. The party also put to use the chaotic days immediately after the Liberation, eliminating a number of its enemies who were charged with being collaborators.

The Communists emerged as the largest party in France in the first postwar elections, with 26 percent of the vote. Collaboration with Vichy had tainted almost all of the traditional parties, as it had, indeed, compromised large segments of the middle class. Consequently, despite its short period of flirtation with the Nazis, the Communist Party represented for a great many all that was noble in the French revolutionary tradition. The number of party militants soared, and the circulation of the party paper, *L'Humanité*, rose to a record 450,000.

For the first time in French history the Communist Party participated, together with the Socialists and the MRP, in the operation of the government. The general secretary of the party, Maurice Thorez, returned from exile in Moscow, at the invitation of General de Gaulle, to become vice premier in 1944, and Communist leaders occupied key ministries responsible for reconstruction and the management of nationalized industries. The new Communist slogan was "production," and the party used its influence with the trade unions and the working class to suppress strike movements. By 1947, however, the pressures of the emerging Cold War on one hand and an expanding strike movement on the other had made Communist participation in the tri-partite government untenable. In May, 1947, after the Communists had voted no confidence against the government in which they were participating (the motion failed to carry), the five Communist ministers were dismissed from the cabinet. The Communists have not participated in a French government since that date.

The party maintained its strength through the late 1940's. The inability of the Fourth Republic to muster effective policies, and the continuance of prickly class differences within French society contributed to the ability of the Communists to survive the pressures of the Cold War. Also the party developed a strong base outside of national government. Where the party came to dominate municipal governments, its militants proved themselves to be hard workers, dedicated to civic improvement; within the trade-union movement they became effective organizers.

By the early fifties, however, there were signs of a spreading organizational malaise within the party. The number of militants declined; it became more difficult to organize mass demonstrations; newspaper circulation began to slip; and the party revealed the kind of creakiness that comes from domination by static bureaucracy. Most of the party's leaders, including Thorez, had been in power for a long time —tied to traditional slogans and outmoded ways of doing things.

By 1956 the party had decided to abandon its total opposition to the Fourth Republic. The Communist deputies in the National Assembly supported the Republican Front of

Socialists and Mendès-France Radicals, as well as the social reform measures proposed by the new government. As part of the party strategy to build up support for a new "popular front" government, the Communist deputies also voted for special governmental decree powers—which included the power to set aside civil liberties—in Algeria.

The Gaullist surge in 1958 made inroads into Communist vote-getting power. From a percentage in 1956 of just under 26, party electoral support fell to 18.9 percent on the first ballot in 1958; and although it rose to nearly 22 percent in 1962, it remained almost a million and a half votes shy of its earlier peak strength.

With the 1962 election, the Communist Party showed signs of regaining its strength —partly because of a resurgent desire by other parties of the left to form a common front against de Gaulle, and partly because of the PCF's own changing image. Although it did not move as far or as quickly as the Italian Communist Party in establishing its independence from Moscow, the French party did come to assert itself on a number of minor issues. It also began, self-consciously, to revise parts of its doctrine in order to assure other political parties that it was no longer committed to the suppression of all non-Communist groups during the transition to communism.

The burnishing of a new image was aided by the general Communist process of "de-Stalinization," a process furthered by the death in 1964 of Maurice Thorez and the subsequent increase in the power of the party's new general secretary, Waldeck Rochet.

In the year following the death of Thorez, the party did not put up its own presidential candidate but supported Mitterrand, and through 1966 and 1967 it worked actively to reach agreements with the Federation of the Democratic and Socialist Left on supporting the strongest left-wing candidate on the second ballot in the legislative elections.

In the elections of 1967, the Communist Party benefited tremendously from its new alliance. Although its percentage of the to-tal vote increased only slightly, the party almost doubled its parliamentary representation. Of more importance, the party's image was improving. Public-opinion polls indicated an increasing willingness on the part of members of other parties, especially the Socialists, to see Communists in a new government.

Although the PCF split with the Socialists and Radicals over its support of the Arabs—echoing Moscow's position during the Arab-Israeli conflict of 1967—this did not prevent continued cooperation with the FGDS (Federation of the Socialist and Democratic Left) and the publication of a number of joint statements revealing substantial agreement on domestic economic reforms.

The events of May and June, 1968, were as much a surprise to the Communists as they were to other political parties. After some hesitation, the PCF attacked the leaders of the student uprisings with a special vehemence reserved for enemies on the left; to the Communists the student attempt to ally with the striking workers was a challenge to their own domain, and therefore a most dangerous threat. Moreover, the students were posing a revolutionary challenge at the very moment when the PCF was attempting to transform itself into an acceptable electoral party. In cooperation with the CGT, the party was instrumental in getting the workers to end their strike once immediate economic demands had been met.

Yet the party's moderation during the 1968 crisis was of little immediate political value, as the election that followed demonstrated. Its percentage of the national vote dropped by two points, and it lost more than half its parliamentary seats. The Gaullist campaign blamed the Communists for the chaos of May and June, and large numbers of Federation supporters who in years past were willing to vote for a Communist on the second ballot refused to do so (see Figure 10.2). The students, meanwhile, attacked the PCF for having become an established party of order.

The results of the election of 1968, and the Soviet invasion of Czechoslovakia a month

nous sommes communistes,

DES FEMMES ET DES HOMMES COMME VOUS

NOUS VOULONS CONSTRUIRE UNE VIE HUMAINE ET LIBRE
LE SOCIALISME
AVEC NOUS, FAITES CE CHEMIN

**DEVENEZ MEMBRE
DU PARTI COMMUNISTE FRANÇAIS**

We are communists, men and women like you.
We want to build a free and humane life: socialism.

Take this road with us.
Become a member of the French Communist Party.

later (the PCF opposed the invasion but agreed with the Soviet criticism of Czech attempts to reform its Communist regime), broke apart the emerging alliance of the left. In the 1969 presidential election, the left could not agree on a single candidate, and the Communists ran Jacques Duclos, a wartime Resistance leader, who did surprisingly well (see Table 10.5).

For most of 1969 and 1970, the party was internally divided by the events of 1968 and the Czechoslovakian crisis. By late 1970, however, under the leadership of Georges Marchais, the party was attracting thousands of Frenchmen to hundreds of open debates at the grass-roots level, where party representatives were prepared to deal with even sensitive questions with a new frankness. At the same time, the Socialists were renewing the contacts that eventually led to the signing of a Common Program in July, 1972. Thus, slowly, the PCF began to repair the damage of 1968 (see Figure 10.2). In the elections of 1973, the Communists regained their 1967 level and succeeded in doubling the number of seats they had held in

TABLE 10.5 THE FRENCH PRESIDENTIAL
ELECTIONS OF 1965, 1969, AND 1974

1965 Candidate	First ballot December 5, 1965	Second ballot December 19, 1965
deGaulle	43.7%	54.5%
Mitterand	32.2	45.5
Lecanuet	15.9	
Tixier-Vignancour	5.3	
Others	2.9	

1969 Candidate	First ballot June 1, 1969	Second ballot June 15, 1969
Pompidou	44.0%	57.6%
Poher	23.4	42.4
Duclos	21.5	
Defferre	5.1	
Rocard	3.7	
Ducatel	1.3	
Krivine	1.0	

1974 Candidate	First ballot May 5, 1974	Second ballot May 19, 1974
Mitterand	43.2%	49.2%
Giscard d'Estaing	32.6	50.8
Chaban-Delmas	15.1	
Royer	13.2	
Laguiller	2.3	
Dumont	1.3	
Le Pen	.7	
Muller	1.7	
Krivine	.4	
Renouvin	.2	
Heraud	.1	

Sources: *Le Monde*, December 30, 1965; June 17, 1969; and *Le Monde*, May 21, 1974, reprinted by permission of the publisher.

1968. Although they expressed reservations about the impressive showing of the Socialists in 1973, the Communists supported Mitterand's candidacy in 1974 on the basis of the commitments of the Common Program. The PCF was even willing to accept in the proposed Mitterand cabinet such old adversaries as Gaston Defferre and Pierre Mendès-France, as long as the commitment to the Common Program was assured.

The reaction of the PCF to Mitterand's near-win was mixed. On one hand, nearly half the country had voted for the united left and the Common Program; on the other hand, many of the older militants believed that the party had conceded too much in the campaign, and that much of the new support for the left would ultimately go to the Socialists. Thus, immediately after the 1974 election, pressure began to grow among some middle level militants for the party to reassert its initiative within the left, and to check the rapidly increasing influence of the Socialists. While, for the moment, the alliance of the left does not appear to be in danger of collapsing, the PCF in 1975 seemed to be internally divided and most preoccupied with its rivalry with the Socialists. Nevertheless, the Common Program alliance remains the strongest and best organized political force in France.

STRUCTURE, SUPPORT, AND POLICY: The structure of the French Communist Party is in the Soviet mold. With certain national modifications, the French organization generally operates under the Leninist principle of "democratic centralism"—that is, full discussion of all decisions, *and* full obedience to a central authority by all elements within the party once a decision is made. The organization is essentially military in form, with control emanating from the top and the key position filled by co-optation.

The basic unit of the party is the cell, which consists of at least three members, but ideally of about twenty-five. Theoretically, a cell should function at a place of work; but the party does permit the organization of basic units at places of residence. The latter are strongly preferred by members, and indeed only about one-fourth of the twenty thousand cells function at places of work. Directing each cell is a bureau com-

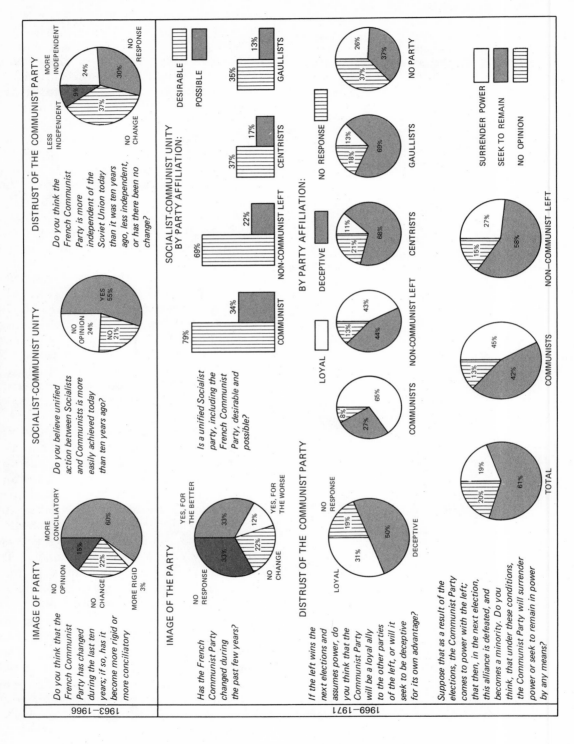

FIGURE 10.2   ATTITUDES TOWARD THE FRENCH COMMUNIST PARTY
BEFORE AND AFTER 1968

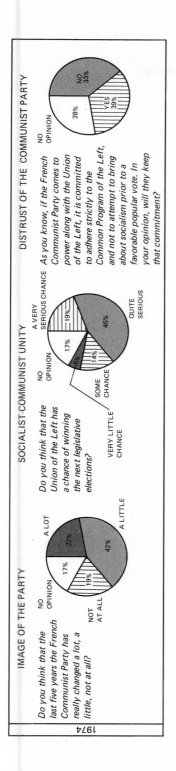

IMAGE OF THE PARTY

Do you think that the last five years the French Communist Party has really changed a lot, a little, not at all?

NO OPINION 17%
A LOT 22%
A LITTLE 42%
NOT AT ALL 19%

SOCIALIST-COMMUNIST UNITY

Do you think that the Union of the Left has a chance of winning the next legislative elections?

A VERY SERIOUS CHANCE 19%
NO OPINION 17%
QUITE SERIOUS 45%
SOME CHANCE 14%
VERY LITTLE CHANCE 5%

DISTRUST OF THE COMMUNIST PARTY

As you know, if the French Communist Party comes to power along with the Union of the Left, it is committed to adhere strictly to the Common Program of the Left, and not to attempt to bring about socialism prior to a favorable popular vote. In your opinion, will they keep that commitment?

NO OPINION 28%
NO 33%
YES 39%

1974

posed of a secretary and a treasurer; the secretary is the chief official, selected by membership of the cell. Cells are grouped in the section—a grouping of cells with "a common direction and a common activity." Again, the key section officer is known as the secretary; he is "ratified" by yet higher-level officials and is assisted by specialized party workers, such as agents for propaganda and for women's work, who share responsibility for the activities of the section.

Elected from each of the sections in a given department are federation members. These federations—one for each of France's ninety-five departments—are ultimately responsible for the party's activities on the departmental level and are dominated by a secretariat composed of full-time salaried bureaucrats who have made a career of party work. The party tries to recruit persons of working-class background for these posts; in order to prevent departmental sclerosis, it rotates staff members among federations.

The National Congress of the Communist Party, which usually meets every three years, is composed of delegates from the membership, usually section and federation officers. Early congresses were often characterized by bitter debate, but from 1928 until recently the party's leadership has transformed them into paradigms of dullness. The congress "elects" a central committee, which in turn selects from its own members a politburo and a secretariat. The actual direction of the PCF is in the hands of the secretariat, and more particularly the general secretary—despite some recent tendencies toward liberalization.

Lines of communication in the party are hierarchical. At the top level, the rate of turnover has been extremely slow, and generally has resulted from the purging of members who for some reason have broken with party discipline. Manuel Thorez, for example, remained general secretary from 1936 until just before his death in 1964. Direction from the top is maintained primarily by a process of co-option. Thus only the cell is more or less free to choose its officers; at every other level, the selection of

officers (including delegates to federation or national congresses) must be ratified by commissions at the next highest level. The uniform flow of authority is also maintained by a high degree of compartmentalization: direct contact between sections or federations, except as directed by the Central Committee or the Political Bureau (politburo) is discouraged. Although there is often a good deal of debate and discussion at party meetings, particularly at the lower levels, this is usually initiated and defined from above. Unlike the Socialist Party, the Communist emphasis upon "ideological and political cohesion" forbids factions and organized opposition to decisions that have already been reached.

The politburo completely dominates Communist candidates elected to the National Assembly. It approves the parliamentary party's choice of officers, has a veto over all decisions made by the parliamentary party, and gives instructions in advance on all important matters. Every Communist candidate for election to the National Assembly must agree in advance to resign if called upon to do so by the party. He also turns his full salary over to the party and receives in return the equivalent of a skilled worker's wage. Party leaders and officials have usually found seats in Parliament, but because of the secondary importance assigned parliamentary activity, Communist parliamentarians have not been among the most dynamic individuals in the organization, a circumstance that has contributed to the party's ability to control its parliamentary delegation.

In addition to the General Confederation of Labor (see above p. 73), the party controls a variety of other mass organizations. One of the most vocal is the Union of French Women, which replicates the party in structure and which publishes both a weekly and a monthly journal. The Communists have, in fact, been extremely successful in recruiting female militants. In the mid-seventies, one out of three members of the party was a woman. Communist youth groups include Young Farmers,

Young Communists, Girls of France, and Communist Students. The party also controls a Workers' Sports and Gymnastics Federation, a National Union of Aged Workers, a Federation of Tenants, and various organizations for the "defense of peace." "Progressive" non-Communists are welcomed into all of these groups, and many of the organizations are regarded as mechanisms for party recruitment.

Communist newspapers and periodicals bring a special Communist perspective to a variety of subjects from politics and economics to the arts and sports. The newspaper *l'Humanité* with a circulation at present of about 185,000 is published daily; there is also a special Sunday edition that reaches perhaps half-a-million people. Periodicals include *Économie et Politique* and *La Nouvelle Revue Internationale*.

Finally, the party maintains a number of commercial organizations, including numerous import-export firms, that either earn money for the party or perform necessary services. One of these is La Banque Commerciale Pour l'Europe du Nord; since the majority of its personnel are party members, secrecy with respect to the party's financial transactions is assured. The PCF also runs a dozen publishing houses for its literature, among them Éditions Sociales, Le Cercle d'Art, and Le Chant du Monde, a music-printing and recording company. In addition to a publicity office and a printing press for posters and political tracts, the PCF operates many bookstores and a distribution center for its books and magazines.

One indication of the effectiveness of the party communications system is the annual turnout of more than half a million people at the *Fête Humanité*, a party fair and fundraising event in the Paris region, publicized only through party channels.

The Communist Party has, in the past, exhibited a great capacity for attracting a solid core of dedicated militants among both the working class and among intellectuals of middle-class background. The PCF runs its own system of schools for educating its militants. In the late sixties, one out of every

five or six new members entered the education system, and among the delegates to the party congress in 1970, 750 of the 960 delegates were then registered in party schools. Those who have entered the party have done so for a variety of reasons, not the least of which, in the case of workers, has been the sense of comradeship offered by work in the local organization.

Very often, new members of working-class background who enter the party have very little real comprehension of Marxist theory. Once they have entered, however, they gradually find themselves surrounded only by party members. They are encouraged to bring their families to party meetings, to read party publications, and to associate primarily with party members. In a real sense, they become part of a community, so that fairly soon, especially if they have become part of the paid bureaucracy and have entered the class of white-collar workers, a break with the party would involve a psychological wrench of considerable magnitude. Once this stage has been reached, it is possible for the leadership to take all sorts of steps without fear that a member will react negatively or question its authority, for the psychological strain of doing so would be too great. As a consequence of all these circumstances, it becomes possible for the working-class party member to retain a highly distorted picture of the society around him, to continue to insist, for example, that the living standards of his class are falling when, in fact, the objective evidence points quite the other way.

The very size and organization of the PCF have given it other advantages. Because it controls France's strongest trade union, the CGT (*Confédération générale du travail*), anyone interested in a successful trade-union career is well advised to become a party member. The party's intellectual cadres have played important roles in the movie industry, many of the scientific research centers, and, during the 1940's, branches of the government bureaucracy. Moreover, Communist control over middle-size municipalities has slowly but steadily increased. In 1975 the PCF controlled 45 of the 193 French cities with a population of more than thirty thousand—a local-government power at this level greater than that of any other single party. It is perfectly logical, therefore, for a young worker interested in rising in any one of these institutions to enhance his chances by becoming a Communist militant.

By the 1960's, the party and its affiliated organizations, such as the trade unions, had become an integral part of the established political system; and it had a vested interest in making sure that no revolutionary turmoil caused a situation in which the party might be destroyed or driven underground. By the time of its Eighteenth Congress in 1967, the PCF had begun to move in the direction of coalition with other parties of the left. The party was being challenged, however, by small groups of young Trotskyists and Maoists, who thought that what was really needed was a restoration of revolutionary (non-bureaucratic) élan. The party was also faced with the difficulty of reconciling a traditional Marxist ideology with a world in which such an ideology no longer seemed relevant even to those intellectuals who opposed the system, many of whom were turning to the young Marx in a search for what might appropriatey be labeled "existentialist socialism."

The events of 1968 and 1969 brought some of these issues to a climax. The response of the party was to continue to develop its new line. It advocated a broad coalition of all working people against "monopoly capitalism" as the basis for reform, and the eventual movement towards socialism. This line served as a basis for the Common Program of Government with the Socialists in 1972. During the election campaigns of 1973 and 1974 the party continued to assure a still distrustful electorate, as well as its Socialist partners, of its reformist intentions. Party leaders replied to questions at mass meetings with frankness, and vowed, as part of the joint program with the Socialists, to surrender governmental power once they no longer commanded a majority—something the PCF

had never before pledged. On the basis of the new line, the party has recruited large numbers of militants, many of whom are still being integrated into the PCF organization.

The majority of those who vote Communist seem to do so out of a feeling that the PCF is truly the party of the working class, even though many distrust it. The bulk of its supporters today are not revolutionaries, and are not interested in importing Soviet institutions into France. They are attracted to the party because it has been, in their eyes, less compromised by the system, and because of the effectiveness of the party's militants. A study completed in 1966 found that only 1 percent of Communist voters considered the PCF as "that party that wants revolution."

Although the PCF vote is unlikely to increase much beyond its present level of about 5 million, the party continues to expand in other ways. The membership of the party, currently over 300,000 is slowly growing; at the same time, the number of cells has also been increasing. The PCF has also been steadily increasing its control over municipalities and has gained votes in the elections of departmental councilors.

Numerous parties to the left of the Communists have also been growing since 1958. The most important of these is the *Parti socialiste unifié*—PSU (Unified Socialist Party), which has united, tenuously, factions reflecting the range of tendencies on the far left. Some fifteen other parties, including those that are Maoist, Trotskyist, and anarchist in persuasion, are also making their appeals, each with some organization and some following, but none with enough appeal to attract any substantial electoral support.

7.   THE RISE AND DECLINE OF THE CATHOLIC LEFT

DEVELOPMENT: The Popular Republican Movement (MRP) was formed within the Resistance in 1944 as an attempt to transcend the divisions of French political and social life by forging a political movement that was both Catholic and leftist. It referred to itself as a movement rather than a party because it hoped to rise above the traditional party system and provide France with a new basis for political consensus. In 1945 and 1946 it was one of the nation's three major parties, claiming 100,000 members and commanding about 25 percent of the vote.

The domestic program of the MRP was clearly of the left, calling for nationalization where necessary, the extension of social services, a publicly supported housing program, increases in family allowances, and extended social-security benfits. The party militants saw the party as a movement for social reform, willing to work with the SFIO and the PCF. As it turned out, however, its electoral support came from large numbers of conservative voters, who saw the MRP as the least dangerous of the left-wing parties at a time when conservatism was out of style. Many of their votes soon went to de Gaulle's RPF (Rally of the French People).

After 1947, the party moved to the economic right as it gave first priority to aid to Catholic schools and sought allies among the more conservative groups in the Assembly. Because of its conservative constituency, and because the school issue divided it from the SFIO (French Section of the Workers' International), the MRP's original enthusiasm for social reform quickly faded away. During the early 1950's, although its electoral support dwindled to 11 percent of the vote, MRP ministers held key posts in many of the more conservative governments. Two MRP leaders, Robert Schumann and Georges Bidault, were ministers of foreign affairs for most of the first ten years of the Fourth Republic and created the structure of European unity along with their Christian Democratic counterparts in Germany and Italy.

Between 1955 and 1958, however, the strength of the MRP declined further as some militants turned to the left, out of disgust with the party's increasing conservativism, while others moved to the right, because of its policy on Algeria. In 1958, the party supported de Gaulle and participated in the first government of the Fifth Republic. In May, 1962, the MRP ministers resigned from the government, in protest against de Gaulle's policy on European unity. Nevertheless a large number of the increased Gaullist vote in the 1962 elections came from the MRP.

After 1966 the MRP transformed itself first into the *Centre démocrate* and then into the Party of Progress and Modern Democracy (*Progrès et démocratie moderne*—PDM). The new group (formed after Jean Lecanuet, head of the MRP, received about 16 percent of the 1965 presidential vote) was based largely on the old MRP, though it also attracted some former Independents who did not wish to support de Gaulle, and some Radicals who were unhappy with the Federation of the Left. Billing itself as a moderate alternative to de Gaulle, the PDM hoped to lure a sizable portion of the French electorate. In this it failed dismally. Many of its potential supporters, as well as some of its best leaders and militants, moved into the Gaullist majority or into the renovated Socialist Party.

The presidential candidacy in 1969 of a member of the PDM political bureau, Alain Poher, split the party. Jacques Duhamel, leader of the PDM group in the Assembly, supported Georges Pompidou, and he and two of his PDM colleagues were rewarded with ministries; they formed their own group, the *CDP* (*Centre démocrate et progrès*), and remained part of the Gaullist majority. The opposition, led by Lecanuet, reverted to the name Centre démocrate (CD). In 1971 the CD became part of the Reform Movement with the Radicals. With the clerical and anticlerical center united, Christian Democracy of the MRP stamp seemed to have died out as a distinctly political movement in France.

Although the legislative elections of 1973 did little to boost the fortunes of the CD, Giscard d'Estaing's victory in 1974 was important for the party leadership. In the new government, Jean Lecanuet, president of the CD, became Minister of Justice, and Pierre

Abelin, General Secretary, was named Minister of Cooperation.

In March, 1975, the leaders of the *Centre démocrate* and the *Centre démocrate et progrès* joined with the Radicals and several smaller parties to form *Fédération des réformateurs* (Federation of Reformers). The Federation now forms part of the presidential majority.

STRUCTURE, SUPPORT, AND POLICY: At its founding the MRP regarded itself as a democratic mass party, and it created a fairly complex organization with sections, federations, a national congress, and various smaller executive bodies. In actuality, the real decision-making power in the party slipped gradually into the hands of its parliamentary delegation, which, beginning with youthful enthusiasm, stayed in power so long that its age and the parliamentary system itself eventually transformed it into a more conservative bloc. In the late 1940's and early 1950's the most effective recruiting grounds for the party and for the spread of MRP propaganda were the Catholic action groups, particularly those with a younger membership. By the late 1950's, however, the dedication of these groups to the party had waned.

Among French voters the MRP received considerable support from white-collar workers and from traditionally Catholic rural areas such as the Vendée. In fact, except for its very first years, it was never really a national party in terms of electoral support. Although the party no longer exists as an entity, the former MRP organization provides most of the activists for the CD. The groups making up the CD, however, are divided between the more conservative and more liberal elements. The future of the party is linked to the centrist coalition that President Giscard d'Estaing is attempting to construct. If the CD was an unimportant and marginal part of the opposition before 1974, it is now a more significant (though still marginal) part of a presidential majority "in-formation." The CD now claims about 25,000 members.

8. GAULLISM: THE UNION OF DEMOCRATS FOR THE REPUBLIC

DEVELOPMENTS: The Union of Democrats for the Republic (*Union des démocrates pour la république*—UDR) is the most recent name adopted by the political movement that emerged in 1947 as the Rally of the French People (*Rassemblement du peuple français*—RPF).

The central figure in both, until 1969, was Charles de Gaulle.[4] In the early days of the movement, left-wing intellectuals tended to identify Gaullism with the traditional right, and the antiparliamentary right at that. This was and is a mistaken view, for like all parties of its type, the UDR did not fit neatly into the political spectrum. De Gaulle himself seemed to believe in a vague corporatism, derived from traditional Catholic ideology and involving worker representation on boards of management; he also endorsed national planning and community control of economic activity. His economic ideas, however, remained relatively sketchy; economics never interested him very much, and he always placed primary emphasis upon political reforms. He was convinced that a parliamentary system after the British model was not suited to the French temperament, which, in his view, required institutions to counteract the centrifugal tendencies always present in France. Such institutions, he argued, might legitimately include a strong president with the power to dissolve Parliament and even to bypass it through a national referendum. The president should represent a force powerful enough to act in the name of the nation as a whole; he should be, in a sense, above partisan politics—an arbiter.

[4] The Gaullist party retained the name "Rally of the French People" until 1953, when de Gaulle withdrew from politics. In 1958, de Gaulle supporters created the *Union pour la nouvelle république*—UNR; in 1967 the UNR became the *Union pour la nouvelle république/Union démocratique du travail*—UNR/UDT. Just before the 1968 election, the party changed its name once again, to *Union pour la défense de la cinquième république*—UDR. In 1973 the UDR and its allies ran under the name Union of Republicans of Progress for the Support of the President of the

DeGaulle's appeal met with an astonishing response. Thousands of Frenchmen joined the RPF (Rally of the French People), providing a cadre of young and vigorous militants; and members of many of the other parties, especially the MRP and the Radicals, joined a Gaullist parliamentary intergroup that permitted them to retain their traditional attachments. In the municipal elections of 1947, the RPF and its allies received some 40 percent of the votes cast. De Gaulle hoped that the mandate would force Parliament to dissolve itself and that new elections would bring him to power. Parliament, however, refused to accommodate him. The center and center-left parties saw in de Gaulle a pattern of Caesarism whose tradition went back to Napoleon I; the MRP and the Socialists both forbade members of their parliamentary parties to join the Gaullist intergroup, and though almost one-half of the MRP's electoral strength went to de Gaulle, the party's militants held firm.

What de Gaulle did receive as a result of the 1947 elections was the support of moderate and right-wing deputies in his parliamentary intergroup. These were men who considered him and his party the most respectable, or least dangerous, of the new political forces. For a while he hoped to use his intergroup to paralyze the work of Parliament in the hope that its inability to function would result in his being called to office. He insisted that those considering themselves Gaullists should not participate in or support any non-Gaullist government. However, the tactic did not work; the Socialists, the MRP, and the Radicals drew together to preserve the Fourth Republic and, while divergencies among them did, in fact, prevent really effective government action, the result was a modicum of stability. As conservatism regained respectability, those drawn to de Gaulle found it difficult to resist the rewards of office and refused to accept a discipline that would prevent them from partaking of these rewards.

Republic (*Union des Républicains de Progrès pour le soutien au Président de la République*—URP).

In late 1949 de Gaulle took another step. The RPF, though still calling itself a rally, actively entered the political scene, forming the cadres of a mass party to participate in the 1951 elections; the party received 22.5 percent of the vote and thereby became the second largest in the country. Only a change in the electoral system pushed through in 1950 by the center parties prevented the Communists and Gaullists together from having enough deputies to paralyze the work of the Assembly completely.

Once again, de Gaulle's following failed to hold together. Technocrats and modernizers found themselves at odds with more traditional elements; clericals and anticlericals revived their differences; the left and the right within the RPF felt themselves equally uncomfortable in each other's embrace. The result was a breakdown of party discipline. The splintering of the party in Parliament weakened it among the electorate. De Gaulle came to represent less and less the figure of a powerful leader who could solve the problems of France. In the Paris municipal elections of 1953, the vote of the RPF showed a marked decline. Two days later de Gaulle, having decided that for the moment further political action would only weaken his position, dissolved the RPF and retired once more.

The last word, however, had not been spoken. In the Algerian crisis of 1958, de Gaulle's followers pushed the general forward once again, and once again the ambiguity of his position, and his prestige, made him the least unacceptable alternative, this time in a deteriorating situation that brought France to the brink of civil war.

The results were the return to power of Charles de Gaulle and the formation of the constitution of the Fifth Republic. A new "nonparty" designed to unite all Frenchmen of good will, the *Union pour la nouvelle république*—UNR (Union for the New Republic) was created; and in the 1958 elections, the UNR received 20.4 percent of the vote on the first ballot and 26.4 percent on the second. The Gaullists in fact won fewer votes but more seats—because of the change in the election system from proportional representation to single-member districts—than did the RPF in 1951. The UNR elected 198 deputies to the 465 seats available, and although it did not have a majority, the expressions of support for de Gaulle as the newly elected president of the republic led to the expectation that there would be little difficulty in establishing a cabinet that could command the support of a substantial part of the National Assembly. Such in fact was the case: the cabinet of Michel Debré—who had been handpicked as premier by de Gaulle—was invested by a vote of 453 to 56. In the elections of November, 1962, the Gaullists and their allies gained a majority in the National Assembly, largely at the expense of the center and the right; of the 77 new seats they won, 75 were taken over from center and right-wing parties.[5] In some ways, the results of the election of 1958 marked a significant watershed in French politics. More than 70 percent of the new deputies from metropolitan France had never sat in the Assembly before, and in the election of 1962 even more new faces arrived on the national scene.

De Gaulle's popularity, however, like that of all politicians, was not impervious to changes in the public mood, and by 1965 it was slipping; by 1965, also, the left was making progress in unifying itself—at least for electoral purposes.

De Gaulle won the presidential election of 1965—the first popular presidential election of the Fifth Republic—but he was unable to win on the first round. The candidate of the united left, Mitterrand, and that of the center, Lecanuet, made surprisingly good showings, and a run-off election between de Gaulle and Mitterrand was required. In the Assembly elections of 1967, the Gaullist group (The UNR and its allies) was reduced by forty seats. Seventy-three Gaullist deputies lost their seats, sixty-five of them to the left. The result was that the Union for the New Republic was forced to depend upon the support of the Independent Republicans. Nonetheless, the loyalty of the party held—even through the trying events of 1968. And in the elections of June, 1968, the electorate gave its overwhelming support to the party of order; almost 50 percent of the votes cast went to the Gaullist majority. The majority won 354 of the 487 seats in the National Assembly.

The voters' verdict, however, was primarily a reaction to fears of disorder rather than a new increase in support for de Gaulle. This assessment was clearly confirmed by the failure of these same voters a year later to endorse his plans for reorganizing the French senate and for creating new regional political organizations. De Gaulle, placing his presidency on the line, was defeated. He resigned, and a new phase opened in the development of the UDR (Union of Democrats for the Republic) as Pompidou, who won the 1969 presidential election, took over as de Gaulle's successor.

As the 1973 Assembly elections approached, the Gaullists began voicing many of the same slogans they had used in the 1968 campaign. "The French need security and tranquility," argued President Pompidou, "and with us they have had it and will have it." With opinion polls showing the public only mildly receptive to this re-election strategy, the Gaullists abandoned these tactics and published a detailed program that could compete with the programs of the left and the reformist center. The change in strategy, though averting defeat, was not a resounding success; the Gaullists lost eighty-nine seats and were able to retain control of the government only through a coalition arrangement with the Independent Republicans and the Center for Democracy and Progress. The majority coalition received fewer votes than the Communist-Socialist coalition in the first found and about as many in the second. Paradoxically, the success of the left in the elections of 1973 increased the influence of the traditional conservatives within the reduced majority coalition.

[5] Much of this material is taken from Jean Charlot's *The Gaullist Phenomenon* (New York: Praeger, 1971).

The weakened UDR became increasingly divided against itself during the year after the 1973 elections. As President Pompidou's illness became progressively worse, his leadership of the party began to slip, and there was no strong leader to replace him. Party discipline broke down on major legislative proposals during the Assembly session of 1973, and there was open competition for the leadership mantle of the dying president. The division within the party became even sharper during the presidential campaign in May, 1974, after Pompidou's death. Although the central committee and the parliamentary group of the UDR endorsed the candidacy of its former prime minister, Jacques Chaban-Delmas, "without condition," two other UDR aspirants stayed in the race. (They dropped out, however, before the first round.) In addition, Valéry Giscard d'Estaing—the leader of the Independent Republicans (RI), minister of finance, and a member of the Majority coalition—was not deterred from challenging the official UDR candidate. As the polls indicated the growing strength of Giscard d'Estaing, he was openly supported by a group of UDR deputies led by Jacques Chirac, the Minister of the Interior. Chaban-Delmas was eliminated in the first round of the election with a mere 15 percent of the vote, and Giscard d'Estaing defeated Mitterrand two weeks later (with UDR support) by a narrow margin of 1.4 percent. When Chirac was named premier by the new president, he became the unofficial leader of the badly divided Gaullist party, and gradually wrested control of the party machinery from the old party "barons." Within a year, Chirac had succeeded in bringing a surprising degree of unity to the UDR. Nevertheless, the UDR is no longer *the* governing party, or even the most important of the governing parties. Although the Gaullists are the "majority within the presidential majority" in terms of seats in the National Assembly, they hold a minority of the cabinet posts. In 1975, a sharp contest developed between M. Chirac, the leader of the UDR and M. Poniatowski, the leader of the Independent Republicans, over the designation of official "majority candidates" in the next legislative elections. At stake was the relative strength of the two conservative parties, and the control of the presidential majority.

The UDR developed as an instrument of government, committed to the president of the Republic. Although the party has lost the presidency, it is still united by a commitment to the perquisites of power, channelled through the premier. In addition, centrifugal tendencies have been checked by the emergence of the powerful alliance of the left.

STRUCTURE, SUPPORT AND POLICY. The Rally of the French People was created as a "movement" above parties, and de Gaulle was inclined to oppose the formation of organized cadres. As indicated earlier, however, he was stymied in this inclination by his inability to obtain commitments and loyalty from individuals elected by the other parties. By the time the RPF was dissolved, therefore, it had developed a reasonably tight-knit organization under the aegis of Jacques Soutstelle and others. Both workshop organizations, modeled after Communist cells and designed to counteract them, and local units based on French administrative divisions—communes, cantons, and arrondissements—had been formed.

The RPF also built up a political structure on the regional and national level, culminating in a national congress and a national council. The congress, ostensibly the fount of the party's national policy, elected the president of the party and the national council, which met several times a year to deal with specific party problems that the congress, because of its size, could not handle. The most important organization within the RPF was the executive committee, a policy group controlled by de Gaulle himself: he picked its members, convoked its weekly meetings, and even dismissed those whose attitudes displeased him.

All in all the fundamentals of policy were decided by de Gaulle and those around him whom he trusted; disagreement with national policy could lead only to submission or resignation. Even so, there were gaps in the authoritarian nature of the party. In a good many areas it had never defined its position clearly, and departmental and local organizations as well as members of Parliament were left with considerable flexibility on particular policy matters. Nor was de Gaulle completely isolated from pressures. On a number of occasions he retreated or compromised. The organizational problems of the RPF were to some extent a result of the tensions between the ideological Gaullists, on the one hand, who saw their objectives in terms of building a disciplined mass conservative party that would draw support from all groups in the population, and, on the other, many of the constituency-oriented Gaullists, who were more interested in maintaining their independence in a conservative cadre party modeled after the Radicals. De Gaulle ultimately dissolved the RPF because of this tension.

When the UNR (Union for the New Republic) was formed in 1958, it could draw upon the talents of many of the same men who had been responsible for organizing the RPF. At first de Gaulle was opposed to recreating a political party, for he believed that his job was to bring about a political transistion and that the UNR had no future. It was on this issue, as well as that of Algeria, that he split with the party's right wing, which was ejected from the organization. By the mid-sixties, however, some of de Gaulle's animus toward party organization had been overcome.

The parliamentary party began to take form after the 1962 elections. Unlike the parliamentary groups of the center and the right during the Fourth Republic, the Gaullist group became tightly organized and disciplined, and its leaders have been able to direct their energies toward facilitating the work of the government, as do parliamentary leaders in Britain. The members of the parliamentary party executive committee are elected by regional subgroups of Gaullist deputies, and it is through this committee that the cabinet has coordinated its program in the National Assembly. The president of the parliamentary group, who is chairman of the executive committee, and the heads of the permanent committees of the Assembly have been generally chosen by the premier and the president of the Republic, but other party positions have been sharply contested.

The Gaullist deputies have also served on various specialized study groups that parallel the committees of the Assembly. Those few study groups that have been able to develop their own networks of communications with secondary and professional organizations have had some say on policy. Most of these groups, however, have been ineffective, and, outside the executive committee, the party has developed no mechanism for exerting real influence over government policy.

Until 1967 the Gaullists maintained merely a skeletal organization outside Parliament, active only at election time. After the election losses of 1967, however, Georges Pompidou, then premier, was convinced that it was necessary to prepare the party for the post–de Gaulle period. The reorganization that emerged out of the Congress was supposed to give greater weight within the national organization to both the parliamentary party and the representatives of the militants. The Executive Bureau of the party, which replaced a political bureau dominated by a group of ministers and former ministers, was broadened to include a majority elected by the party Central Committee. In fact, the Bureau has included a mixture of cabinet members, federation secretaries, and backbenchers. The Central Committee, elected by the annual Congress in such a way as to give representation to the parliamentary group, the constituency organizations, and prominent party personalities, also elects the general secretary of the party.

Also, as a result of the reorganization in 1967, the electoral district rather than the department became the basic unit of organization of the party. However, the general secretary names the secretaries of department federations, who in turn name the secretaries for each of the constituency unions in the department. Although some officials are also elected by militants at each level, clearly the organization is dominated by a hierarchical bureaucracy. Nevertheless, since 1967, when the party began a membership campaign, it has almost doubled its membership to about 150,000 in 1973. Until now, the party organization has served as a set of conveyor belts to support its leadership in power. Under the leadership of M. Chirac, this has continued to be true, with Chirac serving as the "animator" for the president. At the same time there has been an attempt to rejuvenate the local cadres, and to develop a program for change around which the UDR can mobilize. Clearly, however, the future unity of the UDR will depend upon its success as an electoral machine linked to power and patronage.

The Gaullists have attracted diverse mass support. The RPF, while it had great appeal for traditional conservative voters, also attracted a following unlike that of older conservative parties. During its early years especially, it was supported by a higher proportion of younger voters than any party except the Communist, and it also drew a sizable vote from the working class. In fact, its center of gravity was in the newer industrial areas, not in those rural areas that had theretofore provided the main support for conservatism. In essence it was a "catchall" party. Like the American parties it drew upon many groups for support, but its solid power base was among those elements of the middle class anxious for both reform and order and not deeply committed to other political organizations.

On the other hand, the constituency of the UDR has become increasingly traditional-conservative over the years. In 1973, compared to other parties, the UDR drew a larger percentage of its support from the oldest sectors of the population, rural communes, and practicing Catholics. (See Table 10.3). Moreover, the strongest party constituency unions in 1972 were in traditionally conservative, "static" France, and its members tended to be over forty (80 percent of

them), wealthy, and practicing Catholics (87 percent).[6]

Although the party's deputies have been moderately conservative, the present divisions within the party emphasize the fact that they have never been a monolithic group. There have always been local notables who resented the discipline imposed from the top; social reformers, who believed in the Gaullist commitment to "participation"; and étatiste modernists, who were committed to industrial development. This diverse group has been held together by an organization that was built on electoral success and the perquisites of power; discipline has paid off. It is not clear, however, whether the united party will survive the major electoral setbacks of 1973 and 1974, and the passing away of its leadership.

9.   ELECTORAL POLITICS IN FRANCE

Prospective candidates for the National Assembly must send a formal application to local government authorities at least twenty-one days before the first ballot. Those eligible to vote are registered on permanent electoral rolls. Registration is completed by the municipal authorities on the basis of their lists of residents. Each year the rolls are open for a limited period of time to enable anyone concerned to check the accuracy of the voting lists. The law strictly regulates written as well as radio and television propaganda. All candidates of national parties (those presenting candidates in at least 75 of about 480 districts) are permitted a limited amount of broadcast time, the expense of which is borne by the state. Candidates must pay for the distribution of their own campaign material, but if they poll more than 5 percent of the vote on the first ballot, such expenses are refunded.

Electoral expenses in France have been far less than in Britain or the United States. Estimates for presidential candidates in

6 *Les forces politiques et les élections de mars, 1973* (Paris: S.A.R.L. Le Monde, 1973), p. 7.

1965 and 1969 range from sixty thousand to 3 million dollars. While the finances of most parties are a well-kept secret, they are all relatively poor. Right-wing and center parties generally get most of their money from special-interest groups—and from the pockets of individual candidates. On the left, a greater effort is made to raise money through dues, raffles, and social affairs. Communists and Socialists also obtain money from elected deputies, and the Communists have used funds accruing to the party from its commercial ventures. The MRP (Popular Republican Movement) probably received some financial assistance from Christian Democratic parties in other countries, and the Socialists have been aided by the American and British trade unionists. Undoubtedly, the Communist Party has received financial support from the Soviet Union.

ELECTORAL SYSTEM: When the Fourth Republic came into existence, every party but the Radical preferred some form of proportional representation. New parties such as the MRP believed that proportional representation would orient the voters to ideas rather than men, and thus weaken the power of local notables—a view also held by the Socialists and Communists. All three parties thought that a list system of PR, in which party leaders would control the position of the candidate on the list, would strengthen party discipline. But the MRP and the Socialists also calculated that only PR could prevent the Communists from completely dominating the national legislature. Out of the complicated party negotiations on voting methods a new election law was passed that provided for a rigid list system of PR based on comparatively small constituencies; the law did not allow for the national pooling of votes. The fact that the constituencies were small permitted local reputation to remain of some importance in campaigns, even though there is no local residence requirement for candidates in France.

Fear that the system as it stood would give a negative majority to the Communists and to de Gaulle's RPF led the center parties to change the electoral law. Just before the 1951 elections, a new law was promulgated that allowed a preferential vote and permitted parties to form pre-election alliances in any constituency except the Paris area. If the combined list won a majority of the votes in the constituency, the list would receive all the votes; if it failed to win a majority, the seats would be divided proportionally. The law had its intended effect: in 1951 the Communists won seventy-one fewer seats and the RPF twenty-one fewer seats than they would have under the 1946 law. The old law allowed the Communists one seat for every 26,000 votes, and the Radicals one for every 59,000. The new law gave the Radicals one seat for every 28,000 and the Communists one for every 52,000.

When de Gaulle swept into power in 1958, the UNR was split on the question of how to elect members to the National Assembly. Some party members believed that PR had distinct advantages for them; the view of the majority, however, was that a return to single-member districts with a double ballot would be more advantageous, and this was the method finally adopted. Under the new constitution, too, any deputy who joined the government had to resign his parliamentary seat. To obviate the necessity of frequent by-elections, then, each deputy was required to campaign with a substitute (*suppléant*) who would replace him if he entered the government.

10. CHANGE AND TRANSITION

Perhaps the most outstanding political feature of Fifth Republic France has been the reduction in the number of parties. The most dramatic aspect of this change has been the rise of the Gaullist UDR as a potential majority party capable of drawing votes from all sectors of the populace. Understandably, the rise of the UDR has in turn stimulated attempts by the anti-Gaullist parties of the center and the left to consolidate their strength, to renovate their programs, and to develop new issues around which to build their organizations. In the process, many of the old issues that have divided the traditional parties have been negotiated or put aside. The Communists have been directing their energies toward developing a reformist electoral strategy with other parties of the left, and the old religious issue has ceased to prevent joint efforts in the center. The increased unity of the left, on the other hand, has reinforced the unity of the UDR, and stimulated the consolidation of the center parties.

At the same time, election campaigns for national office are taking on a national tone, despite the return to single-member districts. Within the limits imposed by the government, all political parties have been relying more and more on television, public-relations campaigns, and public-opinion polls in determining their strategy. The effects of the UDR and of de Gaulle as a leader of national and international stature cannot be underestimated. De Gaulle's was a government that governed; hence it became identified with concrete policies for which it assumed responsibility. Voters, consequently, have come to examine opposition parties in terms of concrete alternatives on national and international policy. This is a lesson the Gaullists themselves learned in 1973, when they were forced to conclude that a detailed electoral program would be more effective than an anti-Communist fear campaign.

Beyond this, the establishment of a popularly elected president has served to offer the voters clear alternatives. The turnout in the 1965 and 1974 elections was extremely high, and while it was much lower in 1969, studies of voter opinion have revealed a sense of tremendous satisfaction on the part of citizens who felt their vote would actually count for something in fairly straightforward terms.

None of these changes should be exaggerated, of course. Local interests and local prejudices are still important. The majority of deputies elected in 1958 held local offices, and de Gaulle went so far as to encourage

members of the cabinet to establish local political roots and to seek local office. Protestants still expect representation in Alsace, veterinarians are at a premium as candidates in the countryside, and doctors are in political demand everywhere. Furthermore, all candidates—including Communists—tailor their messages to the constituency. Nevertheless, the differences between today's political trends and the pre–World War II pattern are sufficient to warrant comment and explanation.

The most fundamental explanation for these changes has undoubtedly been economic and social modernization, which has taken the edge off traditional political divisions. France is becoming increasingly urbanized and suburbanized. Problems of industrialization and urbanization are national, not regional, in their impact. With the growth of mass communications and the spread of available consumer goods, class and regional divisions are marked less and less by strikingly different life-styles. Traditional rural and regional allegiances are breaking down, and the mass media are making people aware of national issues. Some studies have also indicated that values of class solidarity among young workers and working-class children are giving way to values of individual achievement. Finally, most Frenchmen seem to accept a mixed economy in which the state plays a major role in planning and fostering economic growth.

Political parties evolved at a time when France was sharply divided by class, religion, and region, and at a time when the values of smallness dominated French life. Parties both reflected and helped to perpetuate these divisions and these values. Since the end of World War II, socio-economic divisions have grown less intense. France is increasingly dominated by the values of urban, industrial society; and under the pressure of a strong national executive, a consensus on the nation's political institutions seems to be emerging among the major parties.

On the other hand, if the struggle among the organized parties over institutions seems to have grown less intense, the intensity of the struggle for the output of industrial society—a larger piece of the pie—seems to have increased. This struggle will certainly grow more intense with the increasing constraints on consumption and employment imposed unequally by the energy crisis. Thus, modernization, the strong presidency, and the development of an institutional consensus have not necessarily provided a sufficient basis for the consolidation and stabilization of the party system.

11

The
German
Party System

1. THE NATURE AND EXPLANATION OF THE PARTY SYSTEM

BEFORE 1945: The Revolution of 1848 not only brought Prussia its first constitution and parliament, it also sparked the founding of the nation's first political parties. Organized by coalitions of notables, various liberal and conservative groupings began to appear at this time in both Parliament and the nation.

Under the empire formed in 1871, political organizing proceeded apace. Political horizons soon broadened with the emergence of Socialist groups and a specifically Catholic party, the German Center Party (*Deutsche Zentrums Partei*), organized to defend Catholic minority interests in the Second Reich. The ethnic diversity of the new German nation-state and the enduring importance of regional ties prompted the founding of parties representing Bavarians, Danes, Hanoverians, Poles, and Alsatians. Also making their appearance were small, pre-Fascist, anti-Semitic organizations.

The large number of political parties bidding for office in the late nineteenth century relfected more than the diversity of the national community. Also contributing to the splintering of the party system was the use of the double-ballot method of election. An even more important factor was the impotence of the Reichstag. Because the popularly elected national legislative body had little power over public policy or over the composition of an executive branch that served

201

at the emperor's pleasure, political parties did not conceive of themselves as representing potential majorities that might form a government. Party leaders, therefore, felt free to play up the particular world view (*Weltanschauung*) that their organizations claimed to represent.

The disintegration of the German Empire in 1918 and the formation of the Weimar Republic failed to effect any decline in the number of political parties. On the contrary, during the 1920's, under a system of proportional representation, as many as forty-one parties put up candidates for seats in the Reichstag. Election lists included such parties as the People's Coalition of the Victims of Inflation, the Party of House and Landowners, and the Nonpolitical List of War Victims, Work Invalids, and Welfare Recipients. (Table 11.1).

These organizations put up candidates at election after election—even though many of them could not hope to be represented in the parliament because of the requirement that a party receive at least sixty thousand votes nationally to attain a seat. Several of the parties did, of course, manage to form coalitions on the national level. But their ideological rigidity, mutual suspicion, and limited definition of self-interest made these coalitions unworkable at their worst and unstable at their best. The result was that thirteen governments followed one another in quick succession during the fourteen years of the Weimar Republic.

The fragmentation of the party system was caused partly by the system of proportional representation established by the republic. But more important was the fact that although some of the older regional and ethnic differences had lost their immediacy,

TABLE 11.1   REICHSTAG ELECTIONS 1919–1933

	National Assembly Jan. 19, 1919	June 6, 1920	May 4, 1924	Dec. 7, 1924	May 20, 1928	Sept. 14, 1930	July 31, 1932	Nov. 6, 1932	March 5, 1933	Nov. 12, 1933
Majority Socialists	37.9%	21.6%	20.5%	26.0%	29.8%	24.5%	21.6%	20.4%	18.3%	
Independent Socialists	7.6	17.9								
Communist Party		2.1	12.6	9.0	10.6	13.1	14.6	16.9	12.3	
Center Party	19.7	13.6	13.4	13.6	12.1	11.8	12.5	11.9	11.7	
Bavarian People's Party		4.4	3.2	3.7	3.0	3.0	3.2	3.1	2.7	
Democratic Party	18.6	8.3	5.7	6.3	4.9	3.8	1.0	1.0	0.8	
People's Party	4.4	13.9	9.2	10.1	8.7	4.5	1.2	1.9	1.1	
Wirtschaftspartei	0.9	0.8	2.4	3.3	4.5	3.9	6.4	0.3		
National People's Party	10.3	14.9	19.5	20.5	14.2	7.0	5.9	8.8	8.0	
Christlich-soz. Volksdienst						2.5	1.1	1.2	1.0	
Landbund			1.9	1.6	0.6	0.5	0.2	0.3	0.2	
Christlich-natl. Bauern und Landvolk					1.8	3.0	0.2	0.1		
Deutsch Hannover Partei	0.2	0.9	1.0	0.8	0.5	0.4	0.1	0.2	0.1	
Deutsch Bauern Partei					1.5	1.0	0.3	0.4	0.3	
National Socialists			6.5	3.0	2.6	18.3	37.4	33.1	43.9	92.2
Other parties	0.4	1.6	4.0	2.0	4.8	3.1	0.9	2.2	0.3	

German social life had, if anything, become more variegated. Rather than seeking a basis for bringing new voters under their rubric, parties increased the ideological fervor of their pronouncements. The Social Democrats for example, even after the loss of their extreme left wing to the Communist Party, continued to espouse a Marxist program, thereby eliminating the possibility of attracting substantial middle-class support.

Most parties also stepped up their efforts to foster special little societies of their own in an attempt to isolate their members from the larger community. The Social Democrats had been the first to do so under the empire, through the establishment of newspapers, youth groups, women's auxiliaries, and housing projects in which their members might live as a community. The efforts of the Catholic-supported Center Party were bent in the same direction. During the Weimar years, the conservatives and the liberals likewise created bureaucratic machines, as well as satellite organizations designed to separate the party member from the society around him. By the mid-1920's, many of the parties had also created para-military organizations, though none of these developed the street-fighting capacities of the National Socialists.

One of the major reasons for the collapse of the Weimar Republic, then, was that the party system failed to aggregate the multiple interests of the German people into a reasonably coherent set of pragmatic political alternatives. Indeed, the parties drove additional wedges into the disparate elements of German society and reinforced the mutual hostility with which each regarded the others. The decay of social and political life fed on itself.

German political culture had always emphasized the importance of developing systematic ideological positions that defined what was morally and politically right, and then taking action. Given this perspective, it was difficult for Germans to conceive of politics as representing, in part at least, a pragmatic competition for power to govern; to engage in political bargaining was to act immorally. Consequently, even under the best circumstances, German politicians found it hard to compromise on principle. And the intensive group self-isolation, suspi-

TABLE 11.2   CONSOLIDATION OF THE GERMAN PARTY SYSTEM

	1928	1949	1953	1957	1961	1965	1969	1972
Number of parties presenting candidates	41	14	15	14	8	10	13	8
Number of parties gaining parliamentary seats	15	11	6	4	3	3	3	3
Percentage of votes won by three largest parties	56.1	72.1	83.5	89.7	94.3	96.4	94.6	99.1
Percentage of seats won by three largest parties	58.7	80.1	91.0	96.6	100.0	100.0	100.0	100.0
Index of overrepresentation of three largest parties (ratio of percentage of seats to percentage of votes)	1.05	1.11	1.09	1.08	1.06	1.04	1.06	1.01

Sources: Gerhard Loewenberg, "The Remaking of the German Party System," *Polity* I (1968): 103, reprinted by permission of the publisher; figures for 1972 from *The Bulletin* (Bonn, West Germany), December 5, 1972, p. 325.

TABLE 11.3 GERMAN ELECTORAL RESULTS 1949–1972

	1949	1953	1957	1961	1965	1969	1972
% of electorate voting	78.5%	86.0%	87.8%	87.7%	86.8%	86.7%	91.1%
SPD	29.2	28.8	31.8	36.2	39.3	42.7	45.8
CDU	25.2	36.4	39.7	35.8	38.0	36.6	35.2
CSU	5.8	8.8	10.5	9.6	9.6	9.5	9.7
FDP	11.9	9.5	7.7	12.8	9.5	5.8	8.4
Others	27.8	16.5	10.3	5.7	3.6	5.4	0.9
(including the NPD)					2.0	4.3	0.6

Sources: Statistisches Bundesamt, *Statistisches Jahrbuch fuer die Bundesrepublik Deutschland* (Stuttgart: Kohlhammer, 1971), p. 115; and *The Bulletin* (Bonn, West Germany), December 5, 1972, p. 325.

cion, and self-righteousness of the 1920's only lessened the likelihood of compromise. Thus was government in Weimar immobilized.

The failure of republican governments to respond to the people's needs was one important reason for the rise of the National Socialist Party and, ultimately, the destruction of the Weimar Republic. The Nazis had built up a huge infrastructure around their party; once in power, they imposed it upon the state apparatus, and ruthlessly proceeded to eliminate all other political organizations.

SINCE 1945: With the end of World War II, political activity slowly revived in West Germany. Although at first there were a number of political parties in Bonn, they gradually thinned out; between 1949 and 1969 Germany became, essentially, a two party, or better a two and one-half, party system.

In 1949, fourteen parties put up candidates for public office. The two major parties, the *Christlich Demokratische Union/Christlich Soziale Union*—CDU/CSU (Christian Democratic Union/Christian Social Union) and the *Sozialdemokratische Partei Deutschlands*—SPD (Social Democratic Party) received more than 60 percent

of the vote in the Bundestag election.[1] Six other parties each managed to obtain more than 3 percent and eleven parties altogether were represented in the lower house. In 1957, the two major parties received 82 percent of the vote between them; for the first time in German history, one party, the Christian Democrats, won a majority of legislative seats in a free election. In the election of 1965, the two major parties together polled an even larger majority—87 percent of the vote—and only one other political group, the *Freie Demokratische Partei*—FDP (Free Democratic Party), was represented in the Bundestag. That pattern continued in 1969 and 1972. (See Tables 11.2 and 11.3.)

The surge of votes for West Germany's two major parties was at the expense of special-interest factions and extremist parties. The Communist Party, after a reasonably respectable showing in the first postwar elections, sank in strength; and the appeal of the different radical right-wing parties was of little real national consequence until 1967. At that time, the *National Demokratische Partei Deutschlands*—NPD (National

---

[1] The CDU and the CSU, the Bavarian branch, are in fact two distinct parties, and the CSU is eager to maintain its separate identity, but the two parties are affiliated organizationally and usually act together. Following common usage, therefore, when CDU is used in this text, CDU/CSU is meant, unless otherwise indicated.

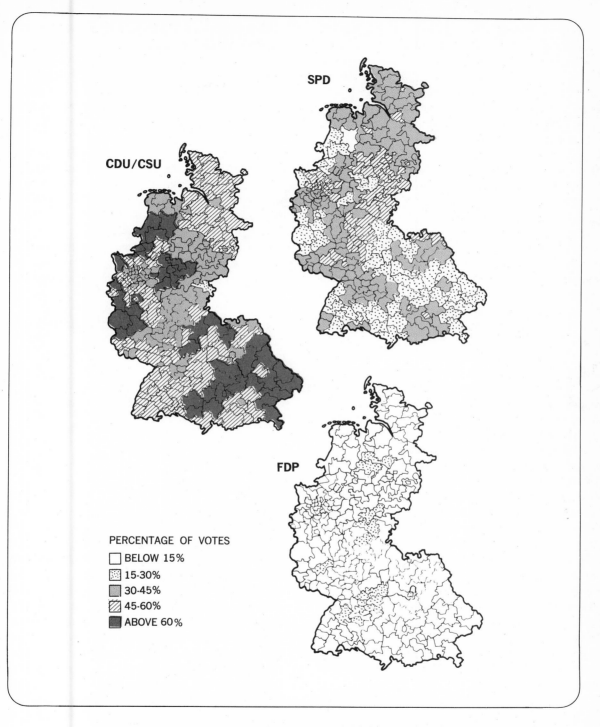

CDU/CSU

SPD

FDP

PERCENTAGE OF VOTES
☐ BELOW 15%
▨ 15-30%
▨ 30-45%
▨ 45-60%
▨ ABOVE 60%

MAP 11.1   GEOGRAPHY OF THE 1965 BUNDESTAG ELECTION

Adapted from *Frankfurter Allgemeine Zeitung*, October 1, 1965, p. 4.

Democratic Party) was able to capitalize on a resurgence of right-wing nationalism. Between 1966 and 1968, the NPD managed to obtain as much as 12 percent of the vote in some state (*Land*) elections although it has never received enough votes to be represented in Parliament. Despite rumblings on the left and right, however, it is the comparative decline of "extremist" political views that is still the most significant fact about post–World War II German politics.

Both of West Germany's major parties have tended increasingly to soften the edges of strict ideology and to make broader, more inclusive appeals to the electorate, although this tendency was partly reversed by an upsurge on the left of the Social Democratic Party in the late 1960's and early 1970's. Though the Christian Democrats and the Social Democrats lean for support on somewhat different social groups, and though they still have significant differences on important policy questions, both foreign and domestic, they have unquestionably moved closer together in recent years. Indeed, there are those in Germany, primarily intellectuals and university students, who believe the two parties have moved so close together as to be almost ideologically indistinguishable. To them, a lack of meaningful alternative policies has resulted. They argue that many important issues—including a re-examination of the authoritarianism that, they maintain, continues to pervade much of German life—have been evaded. Their feelings were partly confirmed by the 1966–69 coalition government of the CDU and SPD. Certainly, the formation of the Grand Coalition contributed to the development of a radical "extraparliamentary" opposition among university students who believed that the German party system no longer offered the nation meaningful alternatives.

Nor has "extraparliamentary" political activity been confined to students in recent years. Inspired by such activity a number of direct action, issue-specific movements have developed. These have included the almost yearly demonstrations by farmers against the pricing policies worked out by the Ministers of Agriculture at the level of the European Community's Council of Ministers. More importantly, over a thousand direct action citizen initiatives (Bürger Initiativen) have occurred since 1969, involving such issues as proposed transit fare increases, building projects, street planning, railroad service and airport locations. By and large such actions have been far more moderate than much of the student activity, but given the traditional German penchant for obeying "legitimate" institutional authority, they may augur some far reaching changes in the nation's politcal culture.

The postwar alterations in the German party system for the most part reflect certain fundamental changes in German social life brought about by both the Nazi experience and World War II. As pointed out in Chapter 2, many of the particularly traumatic conflicts associated with Germany's transition from a traditional society to a modern one have been resolved. Both the Nazi revolution and the war succeeded in effectively eliminating traditional German conservatism by undermining the old class structure of German society. Postwar economic and social developments have furthered the process. The decline of regional, ethnic, and religious variations has also blunted the edge of old political conflicts. There is evidence that the attitudes of German voters have also changed, that they no longer feel their political differences as intensely as they once did. Most of them seem to take a more detached and practical view of politics, explaining their voting preference in terms of economic self-interest. They seem to believe that both major parties are now *regierungsfaehig*, that is, capable of governing. By the early 1960's "socialism" no longer seemed to be a scare word for many middle-class Germans, and, after twenty years of rule by the Christian Democrats—fourteen of them under Konrad Adenauer—the first postwar Socialist government was formed by Willy Brandt in 1969.

Although the German voters returned Brandt's government to power in 1972 with a much large majority, the Socialists have

FIGURE 11.1   THE BUNDESTAG, 1949–1972

THE BUNDESTAG

(FIGURES INDICATE NUMBER OF REPRESENTATIVES)

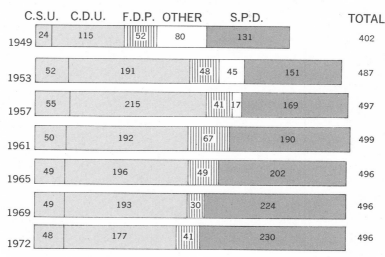

	C.S.U.	C.D.U.	F.D.P.	OTHER	S.P.D.	TOTAL
1949	24	115	52	80	131	402
1953	52	191	48	45	151	487
1957	55	215	41	17	169	497
1961	50	192	67		190	499
1965	49	196	49		202	496
1969	49	193	30		224	496
1972	48	177	41		230	496

Adapted from *Die Zeit*, November 28, 1972, p. 3.

been hurt both by events (continuing inflation, strikes, and rising unemployment), and by divisions within the party. In May, 1974, Brandt was forced to resign as chancellor in the wake of a spy scandal involving one of his closest collaborators. The new chancellor, Helmut Schmidt, is far less flamboyant and rather more conservative than Brandt. Nevertheless, public opinion polls indicate that the Socialists approach the 1976 election with the image of a party that has drifted to the left.

2.   SOURCES OF PARTY SUPPORT

The Christian Democratic Union was the Federal Republic's largest party between 1949 and 1972, when it was overtaken by the Social Democratic Party. Officially committed to a broadly "Christian" approach to politics, it has supported policies designed, in its view, to combine a free-market economy with social responsibility, and to encourage natural associations such as the family. Aside from a few splinter groups, the CDU is the nearest thing to a conservative party in Germany today. Its major competitor is the SPD, originally a Marxist party, but now committed to pragmatic reform. The remnants of traditional German liberalism are represented by the Free Democratic Party, which owes its survival in part to Germany's postwar electoral system. As a party, the FDP remains both vaguely anticlerical and Protestant. Committed to a free-market economy, its economic program for many years was difficult to distinguish from the CDU's. In the past decade, however, it has become more liberal and has tried to establish itself as a democratic reformist party of the center-left. Like other liberal parties, it is marked by considerable factionalism.

Social class continues to be the single most important determinant of voting behavior in Germany. The electoral support of the Social Democrats, for example, comes largely from industrial workers, even though the party in more recent elections has been successfully wooing middle-class voters. The best estimates are that: of German industri-

TABLE 11.4   PARTY PREFERENCES OF SELECTED GROUPS OF GERMAN VOTERS, GENERAL ELECTIONS OF 1965, 1969, AND 1972

In percentages [1]

	SPD			CDU/CSU			FDP		
	1965	1969	1972	1965	1969	1972	1965	1969	1972
Union membership									
Union member	52	52	63	27	20	22	2	3	9
Nonmember	27	29	46	37	30	35	5	3	9
Sex									
Male	36	39	50	34	28	33	6	4	10
Female	28	29	48	36	28	33	2	2	8
Religion									
Catholic	20	25	38	47	40	45	3	2	6
Non-Catholic	42	42	60	25	19	21	5	4	12
Church attendance									
One a week	6	11	16	65	58	65	2	0	5
Once a month	28	32	35	37	23	52	5	3	7
Several times a year	} 34	} 36	51	} 30	} 21	30	} 3	} 3	12
Once a year			63			22			10
Less than once a year	45	42	63	23	21	21	7	5	11
Never	57	59	68	13	12	19	5	4	9
Formal education									
Elementary only	32	28	48	38	30	33	1	1	5
Elementary plus occupational	44	46	56	28	24	29	2	2	7
Some high school	21	26	40	41	32	40	7	7	13
High school graduate	19	39	27	38	26	53	27	7	16
University	26	35	26	40	22	47	15	8	21
Age									
Under 19	—	—	63	—	—	26	—	—	11
20–29	—	29	58	—	27	27	—	4	9
30–39	—	38	48	—	31	34	—	3	12
40–49	—	38	51	—	26	31	—	4	11
50–59	—	41	45	—	24	33	—	3	11
60–69	—	26	48	—	27	29	—	1	4
70–79	—	30	39	—	37	39	—	2	6
Over 80	—	0	34	—	42	39	—	8	0
Occupation									
Farmer	9	0	12	55	46	61	1	0	13
Civil service—low	13	33	46	50	32	34	7	7	14
Civil service—high	20	25	6	54	27	75	7	7	13
White collar—low	36	36	50	29	30	35	3	3	9
White collar—high	23	35	25	49	20	41	20	7	21
Unskilled worker	43	41	58	33	29	25	1	0	6
Skilled worker	48	47	64	21	20	21	1	7	7

[1] The percentages, which are rounded off and which are based on post-election surveys, should be read across.   Thus in 1965, 52 percent of union members voted SPD, 27 percent voted CDU/CSU, and 2 percent voted FDP, while the remainder did not vote or for other reasons did not answer the survey questions.

Source: Data derived from Max Kaase, "Die Bundestagswahl 1972: Probleme and Analysen," *Politische Vierteljahresschrift* (May, 1973): 189.

al and rural workers who indicated a party preference in 1972, about 67 percent supported the SPD; about 25 percent backed the CDU; and about 7 percent supported the FDP. As one might expect, trade-union members and workers in large modern plants in the major urban centers vote in greater proportions for the SPD.

The major factor preventing the SPD from obtaining a larger portion of the working-class vote seems to be the religious one. In the early years of the new republic, the church actively supported the CDU, and the clergy urged Catholics to vote for Christian candidates—instead of Socialist candidates, whom it considered materialistic and atheistic. Even so, some 30 percent of the Catholic voters (usually the less religious) supported the Social Democratic Party and in 1969, the SPD won a large percentage of its new support in Catholic urban districts. Since 1955 the political partisanship of the Catholic Church has declined considerably. Indeed, in 1973 the Catholic Bishop's Conference passed a resolution expressly forbidding priests from publicly professing party affiliations and from working for the election of a party. Nevertheless, polls today indicate that some 14 percent more Catholic workers than Protestant workers vote for the Christian Democrats and that the proportion of Catholic workers supporting the CDU over the Social Democrats rises with the worker's religiosity as measured by church attendance. Primarily because of the religious question, the Christian Democrats receive more support from unskilled workers than semi-skilled ones.

The German upper middle class—including professionals, businessmen, civil servants, and white-collar employees—gives its support primarily to the CDU and the FDP. Farmers and peasants, too, vote somewhat more heavily for the CDU and the FDP than for the Social Democrats, and again the question of which of the former two parties they support seems to be determined primarily by religious affiliation. Finally, the self-employed craftsmen usually give the Christian Democrats a rather lopsided endorsement, with the Socialists receiving only a tiny fraction of their vote.

3. THE LIBERAL TRADITION: THE FREE DEMOCRATIC PARTY

DEVELOPMENT: The Free Democratic Party of Germany is the heir of the German liberal tradition that came to the fore in 1848. Like the British Liberal Party and the French Radicals, it is but a remnant of a once powerful political force; like them, it looks both to the right and to the left in search of a position that can be publicly differentiated from those of the political giants against whom it competes. And, also like its French and British cousins, its makeup is sufficiently heterogeneous and transitory that its self-definition seems to change from year to year.

In the 1860's, German liberalism split into two factions. The National Liberals, who represented industrial interests and were on good terms with the Junkers, were at times among Bismarck's strongest supporters. The other faction, the Progressives, favored parliamentary democracy and showed much more concern for individual liberties. Committed to the need for social reform, the Progressives won considerable support from the commercial interests who believed in free trade, as well as from intellectuals and peasants.

With the end of the empire, in 1918, the two parties re-formed. Most National Liberals transferred their allegiance to the German People's Party, which, under the leadership of Gustav Stresemann, was extremely influential in Weimar politics during the middle 1920's. (After 1928, most of its support was captured by the National Socialists.) The German Democratic Party, the Weimar successor to the Progressives, was dedicated both to social reform and to the republic; one of its leaders, Hugo Preuss, was influential in drafting the Weimar constitution. During the first years of the republic, it cooperated with the Social Democrats and the Center Party to form the governing coalition, but in doing so the German Democratic Party lost most of its traditional base of support. The Democrats received 19 percent of the popular vote in the elections of 1919, the year the Weimar Republic was founded; the next year their vote dropped to less than 9 percent. In the last years of the republic, the party tried to develop a more nationalistic program—but it was too late: it garnered only 5 percent of the vote in 1928 and 1 percent in 1932.

POSTWAR SUPPORT AND STRATEGY: The Free Democratic Party, founded in 1948, represented an effort to recombine the old National Liberal and Progressive traditions. From the beginning, the more liberal wing of the party was based in southern Germany, while its more conservative candidates drew support from anticlerical, business, and professional interests in northern and western Germany. In the 1949 elections to the first Bundestag, the Free Democrats received only 11.9 percent of the vote. It quickly became evident that the party had little chance of developing into a major political force, and it was not long before many of its potential leaders defected to the Christian Democrats and the Social Democrats.

For the next decade, the Free Democrats continued to appeal primarily to anticlerical Protestants who could not bring themselves to support the Socialists or the CDU. In 1953 its percentage of the vote slipped to 9.-5; in 1957 it declined still further to 7.7. After that, the FDP engaged in a major effort to build up its organization and create a new image with broader appeal. Like liberal parties all over Europe, however, it had small success; the electorate had no interest in nineteenth-century liberalism, and the political distance between the two major parties was getting too narrow to allow room for a moderate third to maneuver. Actually, the FDP followed several strategies. In the Bundestag, it allied itself until 1966 with the Christian Democrats, joining the government as the minor partner of a coalition.

At the same time, it joined with the Social Democrats to form coalition governments in a number of *Länder*. Since 1969, however, the FDP has been in a coalition government with the Social Democrats on the national level.

When the party was established, its leadership came from its more progressive wing. By the late 1950's, however, its more conservative and nationalistic elements had come to predominate, a trend confirmed with the 1960 election of Erich Mende as party chairman. In both 1961 and 1965 the Free Democrats argued the dangers of CDU clericalism and the advantages of their own economic planning; they offered themselves as a group that would support the CDU but prevent it from following the wrong policies under the wrong leadership. In 1961 the strategy seemed to work; the popular vote of the FDP rose to 12.7 percent. Four years later, however, the party's vote dropped back to less than 10 percent—where it has since remained.

In 1966 the formation of a coalition government of the Christian Democratic Union and the Social Democrats left the FDP as the only opposition party in the country at the national level. The Grand Coalition, and the emergence of the NDP (National Democratic Party) and student activism, led the Free Democrats to adopt a new strategy. Thus, in 1967 and 1968 the party moved from a center-right to a center-left political position. Under Walter Scheel, the new party chairman, the CDU and SPD were both attacked as symptomatic of the staid, bureaucratic mentality that has typified German politics. Domestically, the Free Democrats urged the further democratization of German society; in foreign policy, they adopted an increasingly neutralist policy. In short, the party was cautiously trying on a new liberal image—radical but not Socialist, accepting the welfare state but desiring to humanize and "debureaucratize" it, and, above all, concerned with eliminating the authoritarian elements that have persistently appeared within the German community.

The strategy both succeeded and failed. The Free Democrats' share of the national vote in 1969 fell to 5.8 percent. Still, it was enough to permit the party to join the SPD for the first time in a national coalition and to secure for Scheel the post of foreign minister.

This official embrace of the Social Democrats was, even so, something of a risk. Party leaders had to ask themselves whether a moderate and successful regime led by the SPD might not capture those Free Democratic voters who in the past were anti-CDU, but unwilling to vote for a "radical" Socialist party or whether, on the other hand, the success of the new coalition might not drive the more conservative FDP members into the CDU. Indeed, the desertion of several FDP deputies to the CDU in 1972 helped to precipitate the fall elections. Many FDP sympathizers were concerned that, caught as it was, the party would drop below the 5 percent electoral minimum needed to remain in parliament. It came up with 8.4 percent of the vote in 1972, however, and with 41 seats in the Bundestag. In the spring of 1974, Walter Scheel, the leader of the FDP, was elected president of the republic. Thus it continues as an important third force in German politics and, one might add, a force disproportionate to its size.

As with the British Liberal Party the FDP now serves as a "swing" party, becoming the temporary home of SPD or CDU voters who wish to protest the policies of their normal party without going over completely to the opposition. Thus, there is evidence that the very good showing of the FDP in various *Land* elections from 1973 to 1975 was based on the desire of many normally Socialist voters to express dissatisfaction with the more radical elements in the SPD which had come to dominate some local party organizations.

4. THE DECLINE OF THE GERMAN RIGHT

Like the liberals, conservative political groupings made their appearance at the time of the 1848 Revolution and the Frankfurt Assembly, the first German parliament. Merging into a loosely organized Conservative Party, they drew their major support during the German Empire from the Junker aristocracy, owners of large businesses, and portions of the peasantry. The Conservatives were pro-Prussian, and hostile to both industrialism and capitalism, which they saw as opening the way to radicalism. They also served as the first political receptacle for anti-Semitism, which later, of course, became far more rabid. Though the Conservatives disliked Bismarck's endorsement of industrialization, universal suffrage, and social reform, they continued, for lack of an alternative, to back the government.

Eventually the conservatives saw the necessity of becoming a mass party, and in the 1880's they allied themselves with the Christian Social movement of Adolph Stöcker as a way of reaching the people. Their embrace of Stöcker, even though they disapproved of some of his rabble-rousing, was an important ingredient in making anti-Semitism more respectable.

After World War I, conservatives grouped themselves around the *Deutschnationale Volkspartei* (German National People's Party), which urged the restoration of the monarchy and the empire. Recognizing the need for developing a popular political base, the leadership tried to emulate the parties of the left by creating a mass organization—the use of the world *Volk* in the party's name is indicative of its concern for developing a mass base. And in an attempt to broaden its appeal during the late years of the Weimar Republic, it became stridently anti-Semitic. These efforts were of little avail, however, for the Nazi Party took away most of its support. Between 1928 and 1930, its percentage of the popular vote dropped from more than 14 to 7.

By 1921 Adolph Hitler had established himself as the leader of the *Nationale-sozialistische Deutsche Arbeiter Partei*—NSDAP (National Socialist German Worker's Party). The Nazi Party did not gain momentum until the final years of the twenties; it spent the decade, however, building up its organization—modeled very closely upon that of the Communists'. Aside from its nationalism and its anti-Semitism, the party program was vague and contradictory, promising all things to all groups. It would, for example, nationalize industry, but only the industry of those capitalists, who, like the Jews, were exploiting the German people. Relying upon violence and intimidation, the Nazis promised to end the civil disorder they had helped create, and they offered themselves as the only viable alternative to communism.

The Nazis were not really a conservative party; much of their rhetoric was characterized by anti-Prussian populism. In fact by drawing off the only groups that might have constructed a mass base for a genuinely conservative party, they seriously undermined traditional German conservatism. Their policies, World War II, and the division of Germany after the war effectively completed the job.

When political parties formed again in West Germany, most of the more conservative Germans and most ex-Nazis gravitated either to the Free Democratic Party or the Christian Democrats. A number of right-wing parties did crop up, including the conservative German Party (*Deutsche Partei*—DP) and the neo-Nazi Socialist Reich Party (*Sozialistische Reichspartei*—SRP), but except in a few local elections, their vote was never large. For a time, a move was also made to organize a party around the demands of the refugees from the East. The new group took on a glaringly nationalist coloration. By 1961, whoever, its vote and that of the DP, which it had joined to form the All-German Party, was down to 2.8 percent; in 1965, all the right-wing parties together polled only slightly more than 2 percent of the national vote.

Interestingly, the poor showing of right-wing parties in postwar elections was not precisely duplicated in a number of public-opinion polls taken during the 1950's and early 1960's, which demonstrated the continued existence of a good number of voters—from 10 to 15 percent—who could conceivably be mobilized by a nationalized populist party of the right. In 1966 just such a party—the National Democratic Party—was catapulted to national prominence because of its success in local elections in Hesse, where it received some 8 percent of the vote. In 1967 and 1968 the NPD won from 6 to 12 percent of the vote in *Land* and local elections throughout Germany.

The NPD was founded in 1964 by Adolf von Thadden, a right-wing politician who had been active in rightist splinter groups during the 1950's. Studies of its leadership and sympathizers indicate that it has a great attraction for supporters of earlier right-wing factions. The party is more popular among Protestants than among Catholics; its largest constituency consists of self-employed artisans and white-collar workers, though it also includes a sizable sampling of industrial workers and independent farmers. It appeals as well to professional soldiers and veterans. In fact, it draws upon a relatively representative cross-section of the German population.

Without much doubt, the success of the NPD (National Democratic Party) was fostered by the weaknesses in the government of Adenauer's successor, Ludwig Erhard, and the mild German recession of 1966 and 1967. The formation of the Grand Coalition also pushed some disaffected CDU members into its ranks; and, no doubt, the softening of Germany's international position during the 1960's and the rampages of leftist students drove still more voters to the right.

In some respects, the NPD may be classified as neo-Nazi despite disavowals by its leaders of any racist bias or anti-Semitism. But it is not much more than a pale imitation of the National Socialists if for no other reason than the lack of dynamic leadership. It is unquestionably authoritarian, though in 1968 the government was forced to drop plans for declaring it illegal for lack of evidence of undemocratic intent. Furthermore, few observers believed that, barring an economic catastrophe, it has any hope of becoming a major political force; and the fact that it is rent by internal conflicts and may well fragment into other parties does not enhance its future prospects for national success. Indeed, in the 1969 elections it polled only 4.3 percent of the vote and failed to elect a single representative to the Bundestag. But even though in 1972 its share of the vote dropped to a mere 0.6 percent, there still are authoritarian strains in German political culture which, particularly in times of crisis and conflict, groups like the NPD will be able to draw upon.

5. GERMAN SOCIALISM: THE SOCIAL DEMOCRATIC PARTY

HISTORY AND TRANSFORMATION: The Social Democratic Party of Germany was born in 1875, the official offspring of two parent Socialist organizations created in the 1860's. At its inaugural congress, the Socialists adopted a program that was strongly influenced in many ways by Marx but that also owed a good deal to the writings and rhetoric of Ferdinand Lassalle.[2] The program was, in fact, attacked by Marx for its lack of theoretical sophistication; his main criticisms were directed against its reformist emphases and its assumption that the state would continue to have an important function in a Socialist society.

Even though many of the earlier leaders of the Social Democrats were imbued with the tenets of Marx, the SPD did not become officially Marxist until the adoption of the Erfurt Program in 1891. By that time, a combination of factors, including the partial repression of the party by Bismarck, had given Marxist intellectuals, under the leadership of Karl Kautsky, a dominant role in defining the organization's political stance. The program was officially revolutionary, but the party did not eschew parliamentary activity designed to provide a platform for educating the proletariat and attaining social reforms.

[2] Lassalle had been the founder of the older of the two parent groups, the General Association of German Workers.

The SPD grew with amazing rapidity despite Bismarck's efforts at repression from 1879 to 1890. In 1877 it received nearly 9 percent of the vote cast; by 1890 its share was 20 percent; in 1903 it soared to roughly 32 percent and became the largest party in the nation, although not yet in the Reichstag.

By 1907, it had more than five hundred thousand dues-paying members. From the beginning, the Social Democratic Party was a mass party committed to creating a new society within Germany. It spawned a wide variety of groups to insulate Socialists from the larger community and re-educate them. It owned and published its own newspapers; it formed its own insurance company; it organized factories to be run by the workers; it even built its own apartment houses. The SPD also developed a close working relationship with the trade-union movement—which, to an extent, was its own creation—and trade-union leaders came to assume a significant part in its councils.

Within the party, reformist and non-Marxist voices continued to carry considerable weight, contrary to the party's official adoption of a Marxist and revolutionary program. Trade-union leaders especially, though they might use revolutionary rhetoric, were more concerned with immediate gains. And their rhetoric notwithstanding, most of the party's leaders were not about to lead the masses in a revolution. Eventually, a movement did develop among party intellectuals seeking to revamp the SPD's program. Led by Eduard Bernstein, the group wanted the party to emphasize its reformist character and enhance its appeal to other social groups by reconsidering its Marxist commitment. Nothing came of this effort, however; not only did the party remain officially attached to doctrines that alienated many Germans, but the doctrines were the very ones that the party was not prepared to implement. This rigidity prevented the Social Democrats from formulating programs that would have allowed them to cooperate with German liberals for the urgent purpose of attaining more limited goals.

During the World War I, the German Social Democrats, like most European Socialist
parties, supported their government. As the
war continued, however, the SPD began to
break apart, especially after the Russian
Revolution. Many of the radical Marxists
within the party supported the Bolshevik effort and eventually formed the German
Communist Party; others, including many
reformists, left the party because of their
opposition to the SPD's continued support of
the war, and formed the Independent Social
Democratic Party.

After World War I, the majority of the
Socialists joined with the army to suppress
an abortive leftist revolution and later collaborated with the Catholic Center Party
and two liberal parties to draw up a constitution for a new German republic. The Social Democrats were part of this governing
coalition in the first years of the republic;
by the mid-twenties, however, they were
back in opposition. One reason for their
change in political roles lay in the creation
and growth of the Communist Party, which,
in dividing the working-class vote, weakened
the overall influence of the left and placed
the reins of government in the hands of center and center-right political groups.

The contribution of the Socialists in
founding the republic and their acceptance
of the Versailles Treaty also saddled them
with the stigma of being anti-national and
dominated by Jewish intellectuals. This
stigma, together with their continued anticlericalism and a rhetoric that belied their
moderate actions, limited their appeal to
middle-class voters; yet to surrender their
rhetoric would have left them open to the
possibility of being even further outflanked
on the left by the Communists. The party
was also handicapped by an aged bureaucracy in which, during the 1920's, there was
very little turnover in personnel.

Shortly after World War II, the Social
Democratic Party began to reorganize itself.
At its first postwar organization meeting in
1945, a number of delegates urged association with the Communists; others, including
party leaders Erich Ollenhauer and Kurt

Schumacher, managed to forestall such an
option and secured a postponement of the
decision until a full conference could be
called the following year. By then, however,
the European situation had changed considerably. Western-Soviet amity was cooling,
and the compulsory merger of Communist
and Socialist groups in the Soviet zone of
Germany had disillusioned many Socialists
who had believed in the possibility of a democratic fusion. The proposal of marriage
with the Communists was, as a consequence,
decisively defeated.

With the reactivation of its formal organization, the SPD quickly grew in strength—
all traditional loyalties not having been
destroyed by the Nazis. By 1948 dues-
paying membership had reached 840,000,
and the party was winning roughly 35
percent of the popular vote in local elections. In the first postwar elections to the
Bundestag in 1949, the SPD received a little
more than 29 percent of the popular vote,
compared with 31 percent for the CDU. At
this time, however, antagonism between Adenauer and Schumacher, who now led the
Social Democrats, prevented the formation
of a coalition between the two parties in the
Bundestag. The Christian Democrats then
formed a government in coalition with some
of the minor parties, and the Social Democrats came to serve as the main source of opposition.

The Social Democratic Party no longer
considered itself bound by Marxist orthodox-
ies. Nevertheless, its rhetoric during the
early 1950's was still somewhat Marxist, and
its program called for the establishment of a
Socialist Germany. With the CDU, under
the leadership of Adenauer and Erhard,
moving away from both planning and the
nationalization of industry, differences between the parties in the economic area became increasingly obvious. To the economic
differences were added those over foreign
policy. Schumacher strongly opposed German rearmament and the formation of excessively close ties between Germany and the
United States, fearing that such actions
would reduce the possibility of German uni-

fication. He was particularly opposed to programs like the European Defense Community and the European coal and steel agreements, which he believed would align Germany with predominantly Catholic nations dominated by conservative parties.

Schumacher's policies, however, were notoriously unsuccessful. Though the Socialists continued to make a good showing in *Land* elections (the SPD in general has done better in state and local elections than in federal elections), their percentage of the popular vote in the 1953 elections slipped to 28.8, while that of the Christian Democrats rose from 31 to 45.2. Four years later, the election results were not much more satisfactory. The SPD's share of the total vote increased to 31.8 percent, but the CDU jumped its percentage to more than 50 and obtained a majority of the seats in the Bundestag.

Throughout this postwar era, of course, many changes had taken place in both the Socialist Party and German society. The economic policies of the Adenauer government had proved eminently successful, and the Federal Republic was recovering from the war at a fantastically rapid rate. In the party itself, a new generation of political figures, men who had little attachment to the more traditional slogans of power, was taking the reins. Led by people like Fritz Erler and Willy Brandt, who became mayor of Berlin in 1957, and supported by local and regional party leaders who had been elected to *Land* and municipal governments, they looked to a fundamental reorientation of the party. They were joined in their efforts by older leaders impressed with developments in Britain, and by many former Communists who had radically altered their views, including Herbert Wehner, who was to become vice-chairman of the party.

Like Bernstein before them, these men argued that the fallacies of Marxist economic and social analysis had been amply demonstrated. Capitalism was capable of continued development, and the job of a Socialist party should be to urge amendments and reforms as new problems emerged—and not to champion a new economic system based upon doctrinaire goals. To the SPD's new leaders, the Soviet experience showed convincingly that socialism did not automatically usher in utopia. They also maintained that the party's devotion to and concern with democratic procedures must be at least as strong as its concern with economic reform; their aim was to transform the SPD into a "people's" party rather than solely a working-class party. Finally, they argued that the party should accommodate itself to the Catholic Church by emphasizing that it was not hostile to organized religion, that it was prepared to compromise on the issue of denominational schools (accepting the existence of communal schools where the parents desired them), and that it would work with Catholics of the left to achieve concrete social reforms, reforms of the kind supported by Pope John XXIII's *Mater et Magistra*.

It was Schumacher who had started the party on the road to a re-examination of its doctrines and attitudes; and, as the efforts of leftists within the party were overcome, the process of developing a new program continued under Ollenhauer, his successor as party chairman. By the 1957 election, the party's action program was conspicuously moderate. "We Social Democrats," it stated in part, "demand free competition and private property conscious of its responsibilities to the general good."[3]

The new program (it has come to be known as the Godesberg program after the town where it was adopted) was formally adopted in 1959, and it was used as the basis of the 1961 and 1965 election campaigns as well as the two later ones. Brandt, one of the new generation of political leaders to whom rhetoric was no substitute for the careful analysis of social problems, was designated the party's new candidate for chancellor before the 1961 elections, and in 1963 he became the party's national chairman. Brandt had left Germany in 1933 and emi-

[3] Quoted in Peter H. Merkl, *Germany, Yesterday and Tomorrow* (New York: Oxford University Press, 1965), p. 316.

grated to Norway; after the Nazi occupation of that country, he fled to Sweden, returning to Germany after the war. Selecting two of the most important of the revisionists, Fritz Erler and especially Herbert Wehner, Brandt conducted an American-style campaign modeled after that of John F. Kennedy. His efforts did not go unrewarded; in 1961, the party's share of the vote rose to 36.3 percent, and in 1965 to 39.3 percent.

To many Social Democrats, however, the 1965 results were a disappointment. Though the SPD's image had improved, many Germans obviously still could not bring themselves to vote for the "red" antireligious party. The SPD was also handicapped by the natural reluctance of voters to switch during what was still an era of prosperity—and by the cutting attacks leveled against Brandt because of his illegitimate birth and his "unpatriotic" behavior.[4]

Party leaders, nevertheless, persisted in their new course and, in 1966, agreed to join a coalition government with the Christian Democrats in which the SPD would be a slightly junior partner. The move had mixed results. Many intellectuals, as well as university students, considered the coalition a sellout, and, in fact, agitation on the campus and rumblings within the party itself slightly shifted the SPD back toward the left between 1966 and 1969. The party assumed a somewhat more neutralist position in foreign affairs and urged a more conciliatory attitude with respect to East Germany. The moderate stance on public issues adopted by the Social Democratic leadership and its "responsible" participation in the Grand Coalition of the CDU and SPD enhanced its popularity; and after the 1969 parliamentary elections, the SDP was able to form a coalition government itself, this time with the Free Democratic Party a very junior partner. The Social Democratic Party had finally succeeded in reaching the goal toward

which it had been struggling since the inception of the Federal Republic: it was now a governing party with support in widely varying sectors and strata of German society.

While domestically its chief concern was the problem of inflation in a society bent on maintaining full employment, this first German Socialist government in more than thirty years was to make its most distinctive mark in foreign affairs. Basically, Willy Brandt as chancellor continued the policies he had enunciated as foreign minister of the Grand Coalition—policies of détente and reconciliation with the Soviet Union and Germany's eastern neighbors. While continuing to cooperate closely in Western alliances, Brandt signed a peace treaty with Moscow, opened diplomatic relations with the People's Republic of China, signed a peace treaty with Poland recognizing the Oder-Neisse line, and, most controversially, negotiated a treaty normalizing relations with the German Democratic Republic.

The mini-coalition (SPD and FDP) forged by Brandt with himself as chancellor held together despite initial scepticism. After three years and with the disaffection of several FDP members of Parliament, however, Brandt's already narrow parliamentary margin became intolerable. In a move unprecedented in the years of the Bonn Republic, Brandt provoked the premature dissolution of the Bundestag in 1972 by calling for a vote of confidence when he knew that he had no chance of getting one. In the new elections that followed, the SPD-FDP coalition was returned with a large majority.

In becoming Germany's largest party with 45.8 percent of the popular vote (the CDU-CSU won 44.9 percent), the SPD showed that it was a party with a broad national appeal and that it was not condemned to be the perpetual opposition as some had come to fear. The SPD has been building toward a position of power since the early fifties, increasing its popular vote by approximately 3 percent in every Bundestag election. One of the most interesting reasons for this, and

---

[4] For a short time he posed as a Norwegian soldier to escape the attention of the Gestapo. This has led to the spreading of rumors that he fought against Germany.

one that is indicative of longer-term changes in the party and nation, is the party's increasing support among women and young adults. With the reduction in 1972 of the voting age to eighteen, approximately four million young people became eligible to vote. Of those, it is estimated that nearly 63 percent voted Socialist in the 1972 elections, while only 26 percent voted CDU. Furthermore, while in 1965 only 28 percent of the women voted SPD, in 1972 the figure was 48 percent.

Unquestionably the SPD faces critical years ahead because of divisions within its own ranks as well as growing anxieties among German voters about strikes, unemployment, inflation and, especially relevant to the Socialists, the revival of Marxism. The voters of the middle who have swung to the Socialists can swing back to the CDU, as state and local elections after 1972 clearly demonstrate. But the Social Democratic leadership seems to be sensitive to voter sentiment, and although the immediate catalyst for Brandt's resignation from the chancellorship in 1974 was the discovery of an East German spy in his immediate circle of aides, the declining political fortunes of the SPD also played a role. Helmut Schmidt, Socialist politician from Hamburg, and former finance and defense minister who was elected by the Socialists and Free Democrats to succeed Brandt, pledged to continue the program with which the party went to the electorate. Supported by Brandt (who has remained SPD chairman) and by the unions, Schmidt has taken a harsher line toward the left-wing Young Socialists (Jusos), who, under his predecessor, had gained considerable influence in some party branches as well as at the Party Convention. Indeed, Juso influence had been instrumental in securing the adoption of a number of far-reaching social reform proposals at the 1973 Convention. By 1975, however, the political situation had changed. University ferment had declined and party leaders had concluded that the party's left was frightening away potential electoral support.

STRUCTURE AND DYNAMICS: The Social Democratic Party began as a democratically organized mass party. Local and regional branches gradually expanded throughout the entire nation; these groups elected delegates to the party's convention, its ultimate source of policy. Between party meetings, authority rested in an elected National Executive Committee, to which the parliamentary party was supposedly subordinate. Unlike the British Labor Party, the SPD maintained only an informal relationship with the trade unions, although the unions supported the party financially and worked closely with it.

As the SPD evolved, it began to exhibit many of the customary characteristics of large-scale organizations. Increasingly, the power to make decisions was taken over by the party bureaucracy—the national executive, parliamentary representatives, and the trade-union leadership. It was, in fact, this development that led Robert Michels to formulate his "iron law of oligarchy" after a study of the SPD just before World War I. If even the most democratically organized party, in theory, became highly stratified in terms of power, what hope was there for any political organization? [5] In the Weimar decade, the National Executive Committee and the parliamentary party were usually dominated by both party and trade-union bureaucrats who had slowly worked their way up through the SPD's apparatus. While the Social Democrats ossified, younger radicals migrated to the Communist Party.

When the SPD reorganized after World War II, it retained its basic structure and revived many of the groups and activities that had, under the Weimar Republic and earlier, practically made it a state within a state. But the SPD did not return to its initial ideal of a mass democratic party; rather, after 1945 the party evolved along lines already prefigured in the Weimar period— toward a pragmatic cadre party run by professional politicians. Authority fell to polit-

[5] See Robert Michels, *Political Parties* (New York: Crowell-Collier, 1962). His study has become a classic.

ical figures who could gain popular support, in either *Land* or national affairs, and to individuals who could combine party loyalty with expertise. The party bureaucracy is still very important, but it is certainly less so than it was in previous years.

With some 780,000 members whose dues provide most of its funds, the Social Democratic Party has by far the largest membership of any German party. The basic organizational unit is the local *Ortsverein*, which elects its own officers and is the agency through which dues are collected. The local branches enable members to maintain contact with each other, serve as agencies for recruiting, and have a limited voice in the conduct of elections and in some cases the nomination of candidates. The level of activity in most branches, while respectable, has dropped off in recent years.

The principal territorial units are the regional and subregional branches (*Bezirke* and *Unterbezirke*). These effectively determine who the party's national candidates will be and are largely responsible for organizing election campaigns. The regional groups hold regular congresses to which delegates are sent from local organizations. The congresses are dominated by an executive committee and council elected by the delegates with the approval of the party's national executive. Committees of specialists and closely affiliated groups of Socialist business and professional men assist regional executives in planning campaigns and in dealing with local and state political problems.

According to its statutes, the Social Democratic Party Convention, which meets every two years, is the party's "highest organ." It is composed of the members of the National Executive Committee, the Control Commission, which supervises party finances, and three hundred delegates elected from the *Bezirke*, a good portion of whom are paid party officials. The prime function of the convention is to listen to reports from the party executive, the parliamentary party organization (*Bundestagfraktion*), and the party's Control Commission. The conventions are

not without influence, and they elect the national party chairman as well as the National Executive Committee. Yet their significance in determining the direction of policy is even less than that of British party conventions, their function being primarily ritualistic.

The most important organs for declaring policy are the parliamentary *Fraktionen* (see below p. 306) and the National Executive Committee. The former consists of all SPD members in the Bundestag; it elects its own executive committee and chairman. The National Executive Committee is composed of thirty-three members. Since 1958 the NEC's work has fallen increasingly to a smaller group of nine members called the Presidium, which is elected by the executive committee. This second body is made up entirely of paid national officials and members of the Bundestag, and it meets almost every week. Since both the larger body and the smaller one are dominated by Bundestag members, the parliamentary party has more and more become the policy-making center for the Social Democrats.

Traditionally, the Social Democrats have not placed great stress on parliamentary ability. The office of parliamentary party chairman often went to the party's national chairman, a man who had risen as an organizer through the party bureaucracy. With the death of Ollenhauer in 1963, however, a trend which had been gathering force finally became dominant, and Fritz Erler, a leading parliamentary figure, was elected chairman of the parliamentary party. Since that time the post has been occupied by someone other than the national party chairman and by a person who has become prominent in the Bundestag. Nevertheless, unlike the situation in Britain, leadership of the parliamentary party does not automatically carry with it the role of candidate for the chancellorship when a general election is held. Thus when the National Executive Committee designated Willie Brandt to lead the party in the 1961 election (Ollenhauer had done so previously), it selected a popular mayor rather than a national parliamentary figure.

The selection of Helmut Schmidt to replace Brandt as chancellor in 1974 did, however, represent the elevation of a leader who had served both as chairman of the parliamentary party and later as a minister in Brandt's cabinet.

6. THE COMMUNIST PARTY

The German Communist Party (*Kommunistische Partei Deutschlands*—KPD) grew out of the Spartakus League, founded during World War I by group of radical Socialists under the leadership of Rosa Luxemburg and Karl Liebknecht. Luxemburg believed that the Communist revolution in Germany would occur if and only if the masses were ready for revolution. She also thought of it as being a democratic revolution from the very beginning, and in this regard she had early made known her opposition to Lenin's tactics and approach. After her death in 1919 and the defeat of her supporters, the KPD quickly took on the Bolshevik pattern of organization, losing the allegiance of many of the Jewish intellectuals who had so actively helped in its formation.

The party was rent by factional disputes throughout the 1920's, especially between those who wished to pursue a quasi-independent policy and those who, regarding the Soviet Union as the first "fatherland of all workers," considered their primary objective the protection of the Russian Revolution. Nevertheless, the KPD managed to attract some 10 percent of the vote, and despite (or perhaps because of) the military quality of its organization, it drew to itself thousands of young people who considered the Social Democrats far too tame. With the beginning of the Great Depression in 1928, its proportion of the popular vote, primarily from unemployed and unskilled workers, rose to 16 percent and its membership doubled.

During most of the Weimar years, the Communist Party actively preferred the victory of conservative or even reactionary forces over candidates of the SPD and the center. The Communists' argument was that the parties of reform merely helped to conceal the true evils of capitalism and that a victory for the right would reveal its exploitation of people and goals—its naked ugliness—and thus lead more quickly to a proletarian revolution. For this reason, their most violent hatred was reserved not for the conservatives or even the Nazis, but for the Social Democrats, whom they called "Social Fascists." In 1925, for example, the Communist Party refused to withdraw its candidate from the presidential election and join the Socialists and other republican parties in supporting the centrist candidate; they thereby assured the election of General Paul von Hindenburg—an event that later contributed to Hitler's ultimate victory. They followed the same tactics from 1930 to 1933, even joining the Nazis to bring down moderate governments.

The German Communist Party was convinced that Hitler's victory would be followed almost immediately by a Communist triumph. It was rudely disabused of its optimism after Hitler's takeover. Thousands of Communists were slaughtered or were sent to concentration camps, and the KPD was destroyed. Some of its leaders, however, did find their way to the Soviet Union.

In the first *Land* elections after the fall of the Third Reich, the KPD won 8 to 9 percent of the popular vote in West Germany. But its vote in the Bundestag elections of 1949 was 5.7 percent (in the last free election before Hitler's takeover, it had received 12.3 percent of the vote); in 1953 it skidded to 2.2 percent, and three years later it was outlawed by the German Constitutional Court, which cited Article 21 of the Constitution, under which parties that "seek to impair or abolish the free and democratic basic order" are unconstitutional.

Nevertheless, at the height of the student movement in 1968, a new German Communist Party (*Deutsche Kommunistische Partei*—DKP) was formed, pledging itself to follow a democratic road to communism. In alliance with the German Peace Union and other left-wing groups, the DKP ran candidates in the 1969 elections and again in 1972—without success. It has two Communist rivals on the party scene: the Communist Party of Germany (KPD) which uses the initials of the outlawed party and is Maoist in orientation, and the Communist Party of Germany/Marxist-Leninist (KPD/ML), which is calling for an armed uprising of the proletariat. It is unlikely that any one of them or all of them together will become a significant political force in Germany in the near future, given the strong and consistent antipathy to communism of the West German population.

7. THE CHRISTIAN DEMOCRATIC PARTY

EARLY HISTORY: At the 1848 Constituent Assembly in Prussia, a number of Catholic deputies met informally to discuss issues of common concern, and a Catholic *Fraktion* was later formed in the Prussian Diet. The impetus to create a specifically Catholic party, however, came as a result of the Austro-Prussian War, in which Catholic Austria, which had been defeated, was excluded from the empire. Once it was clear that Catholics would be a perpetual minority in the new Reich, the pressure to form a political organization intensified, and in 1870 the *Zentrumspartei* (Center Party) was officially created. Its first platform, the Soest Program, called for (1) preservation of the independence and the rights of the Catholic Church; (2) parity for all religious organizations; (3) the creation of a federal state (*Bundesstaat*) with autonomy provided for all the separate states of the Reich; (4) decentralization of administration; and (5) social reforms recognizing the legitimate demands of all groups.

The formation of the Center Party coincided with the beginnings of Bismarck's *Kulturkampf*. The proclamation of the doctrine of papal infallibility provided Bismarck with his excuse for a campaign to weaken German Catholicism, a campaign in which he was supported by the National Lib-

erals and the Progressives. The Jesuit order was dissolved and extensive anti-Catholic legislation was passed. Clerics who failed to obey the new laws were jailed.

The struggle continued until 1878, when the death of Pope Pius IX and the election of Leo XIII offered the opportunity for a reconciliation. Bismarck was becoming increasingly agitated over the gains of the Socialists, and both he and the conservatives feared that to continue the violent attack against Catholicism might weaken Christianity in general. The church's strength had not flagged in the struggle, however, nor had that of the Center Party, whose vote had risen from about 18 percent of the total in 1871 to almost 27 percent in 1877. In addition, the party had begun to establish a mass organization with its own newspapers and, supported by the Catholic Church, to create the kind of integrated community that has traditionally characterized mass ideological parties.

The Center Party was never a politically homogeneous unit, however. Its left came to favor constitutional reforms that would democratize state and governmental programs providing for more extensive social legislation; its right wing moved closer to the conservatives in orientation. Yet in spite of these differences, the party managed to obtain the votes of most Catholics, regardless of their class. For no matter how divided they might be on social and political issues, the crucial question for Catholics was protection of the church. Toward the end of the empire, many leaders on the left argued that the party should be more broadly based—a Christian party of social reform—but not much came of their argument.

In Weimar the Center Party again became an integral part of Reichstag maneuvers. In fact, it participated in every government of the republic. It was able to do this in part because it was itself divided on most social issues. While in the early years of the republic, the leftist group within the party predominated, by 1928 the right had gained the upperhand. And it was a member of this wing, Franz von Papen, who helped pave the way for Hitler's chancellorship by contending that the responsibility of office would moderate Nazi demands. In exchange for promises by Hitler that church rights would be protected, the Center Party joined with the other parties in voting him into power.

POSTWAR DEVELOPMENT: With the fall of Nazi Germany, a series of groups sprang up in the occupation zones advocating a political party that would draw its inspiration from an interdenominational Christian orientation. The leading proponents of the new party included Konrad Adenauer and Andreas Hermes, both of whom had been active in the old Center Party, and others who had been influential in the Christian trade-union movement. The proposal of an interdenominational party was not new; its origin can be traced to the empire. But the postwar era seemed a most propitious time for bridging the gap between Protestants and Catholics: old ideologies appeared to be discredited, and the churches drawn together by the common experience of persecution, were among the few viable forces remaining in German life. An interzonal meeting of the different groups involved was held at Bad Godesberg in the winter of 1945, and out of it emerged the beginnings of a new national organization. By 1947 its development was well under way, and in 1950 the Christian Democratic Party held its first federal congress and adopted a constitutional outlining its structure.

From its inception, the CDU was composed of dissimilar elements, from left-wing Catholics to conservative Protestants. But in its first flush of enthusiasm, it seemed to be dedicating itself to a genuine social revolution. Under the aegis of Karl Arnold and Jacob Kaiser, the party in the British zone adopted a program in 1947 that was essentially Christian Socialist. It sought such reforms as the nationalization of basic industries and participation by labor in management. As the party began to organize throughout West Germany, however, its leaders quickly realized that it was drawing its major support from the more conservative sectors of the population, and its political center of gravity shifted to the right. The shift was signaled by the consolidation of Adenauer's position as leader of the party in the late 1940's and early 1950's.

In 1949 the CDU adopted a new economic program on which it fought its first parliamentary elections—the "social market" policy of Ludwig Erhard, later Adenauer's minister of economics. Originally drawn to the FDP, Erhard, a Protestant, was also to become for a short time Adenauer's successor as chancellor and the leader of the CDU. In essence, Erhard's policies emphasized a freely competitive market economy, guided by government monetary policies. He pressed for the return of industries owned by the state to private ownership, as well as for legislation to reduce the power of cartels. At the same time, however, he encouraged the extension of social legislation.[6] The success of his program, after a brief period of inflation and heavy unemployment, was reflected in Germany's march to prosperity— and in the party's election victories in 1953 and 1957.

Although the Christian Democratic Union remained a coalition of groups in which the role of the left was important, prosperity and popular endorsement of its liberal-to-conservative policies encouraged the party to stand pat on its successes. Its economic policy continued to be neoliberal; its social policy, conservative. It did not, in other words, attempt to lead Germany in any new directions.

Adenauer's leadership, confirmed by his installation as chancellor, stamped the identity of party for the 1950's. The CDU was indeed an amalgamation of regional and economic interests, united primarily by antisocialism. But it was held together by a desire to remain in office and by the personality and prestige of Adenauer. His chief passion, aside from being chancellor, was foreign affairs: he worked tirelessly to estab-

[6] A fuller delineation of Erhard's policies is given in Chapter 17, pages 365–366.

lish a close relation with France and to encourage European integration. A native of the Rhineland, he had always been pro-French and anti-Prussian, and he was convinced that the reconciliation of France and Germany was as important as the attainment of German unity, if not more so. He strongly believed that only by tying his nation more closely to France could he insure the future stability of German democracy. Although Adenauer had brought Germany into the Atlantic Alliance, his attitude toward the United States cooled during the Kennedy administration; he became increasingly anxious that a Soviet-American détente might leave the Germans out on a limb. Nor was he especially unhappy to see the British, whom he regarded as basically anti-German, excluded from the Common Market.

By the late 1950's, Adenauer's popularity began to dwindle, and pressures mounted for him to retire. The slip in CDU fortunes in the 1961 elections was interpreted by the party as a sign that the eighty-five-year-old chancellor, whom the Germans referred to as *Der Alte*," had lost his appeal; defeats in *Land* elections in 1962 and 1963 seem to provide further evidence of this. Adenauer finally but reluctantly stepped down as chancellor in 1963, to be replaced by Erhard. However, he retained the post of party chairman (and considerable power) until March, 1966.

From the beginning, Adenauer's strong reservations about Erhard's ability to govern turned out to be almost totally correct. Factionalism arose within the CDU, and the "Rubber Lion," as many of his less charitable critics called him, came under attack for being incapable of controlling either his party or the operation of the government. In the vanguard of the attackers were a number of aspirants for chancellor, including Franz Joseph Strauss, the leader of the Bavarian Christian Social Union (CSU) and a former defense minister.

The CDU's victory in the 1965 elections did little to stem the criticism, and the mild recession that followed, along with Germa-ny's increasing difficulties in the international arena, only made it more caustic. Erhard was forced from the chancellorship in 1966, but the party factions responsible for his fall could agree on little except that they were glad he was gone. In the end, Kurt Georg Kiesinger, a former minister-president of the state of Baden-Württemberg and a man not closely identified with any particular group, was chosen as a compromise candidate. Kiesinger led the CDU into the Grand Coalition, the first of its kind, with the Social Democrats after his negotiations with the Free Democrats, the CDU's long-standing partners, fell through. The new coalition, however, failed to restore genuine party cohesion.

The CDU lost only three seats in the Bundestag in the 1969 parliamentary elections —its share of the popular vote declined from 47.6 percent to 46.1—but it was the Social Democratic Party and not the Christian Democratic Party that was now to be the chief party in a new coalition government. The CDU and the Free Democratic Party had failed in their negotiations for a coalition in 1966, and there had since that time been a further parting of the ways. Moreover, the Grand Coalition had brought the Social Democratic Party into the government and had given the SPD a taste of power. Given the increase in SPD representation in Parliament (224 seats versus 202 in 1965), Brandt perceived an opportunity to remain in power and made an offer to the FDP. The Free Democrats accepted and together the two parties formed a government with a bare majority in the Bundestag.

The identity of the CDU was inextricably bound up with the development of the Federal Republic—after all, it had been the principal governing party ever since 1949— and it was caught off guard by Brandt's bid for the chancellorship. Suddenly and unexpectedly, *it* was the opposition. Having always been a loose union of quite disparate groups and forces, the strains within the party following its removal from power became more pronounced.

The party continued to support Kiesinger by electing him party chairman for a two-year term in 1969. Even so, it was soon clear that he could not unite the disparate forces behind him for another bid at the chancellorship. Rainer Barzel, a North German Catholic who had fled from the East and who had headed the CDU parliamentary *Fraktion* since 1964, finally emerged as the man who would lead the Christian Democrats. The party's 1972 campaign was based upon sharp attacks on Brandt's *Ostpolitik*—his policy of détente with Russia and the countries of Eastern Europe—and charges that the prosperity and well-being that had been built up under twenty years of CDU rule were threatened. Even more emphatically than in 1969, the Christian Democrats were playing upon voter fears—of socialism, of a sell-out in diplomatic negotiations, and of economic catastrophe. The party, however, suffered a sharp setback; its percentage of the vote dropped to 44.8, its lowest since 1949.

The Christian Democratic Party is on the defensive today in many areas. While it is ineradicably associated with the basic framework and posture of the Federal Republic, Germany has been changing, and the CDU seems to be fighting a rearguard action. Thousands of people (perhaps as many as one million over the next decade) are continuing to leave the rural areas; yet the CDU has always been stronger there. Secularizing forces continue to undermine the hold of the church over its congregations; but the CDU has traditionally received its strongest support in the more heavily Catholic areas of the country. And the fact that, while the CDU gets a majority of the votes of people over sixty, it is apparently getting only about a third of the votes of the young voters does not augur well.

As its search for leadership indicates, the party has been going through a difficult period of adjustment. (Although many Germans may want another Adenauer, it is doubtful that any leader will replace him or come to dominate an entire era as he did.) From one point of view, the party today is a victim of its own success. For whereas it started with reformist intentions to build a new Germany purged of its Nazi past and of the forces that made Nazism possible, its early success and the indomitable leadership of Adenauer led it into an increasingly staid and hidebound image of itself and the German nation.

STRUCTURE AND DYNAMICS: Organizationally, the CDU stands somewhere between the Social Democratic Party and the Free Democrats. It has a membership of some four-hundred thousand, yet it relies upon local notables and professional politicians as the nucleus of its strength. It is essentially a "catchall" party, united by a vague adherence to "Christian doctrine" and antisocialism. The relative autonomy of many of the CDU groups was obscured by Adenauer's stature and his control over the party. Since his departure, these divisions have come out into the open, and as a result in the middle of the 1960's the party turned seriously to questions of internal organization.

Basically, the national organization of the Christian Democrats consists of nineteen *Land* parties, in addition to a twentieth that "represents" party members in Eastern Germany. (The CDU's state organizations do not coincide with the boundaries of the integrated *Lander*—in North Rhine-Westphalia, for example, there are CDU organizations for the North Rhine area and for Westphalia.) Bavaria's CSU maintains a separate organization but cooperates with the CDU in national elections and in the Bundestag. Under the leadership of Franz Joseph Strauss, the relatively cohesive CSU has been able to maintain an effective veto over broad aspects of CDU policy. Members of the four thousand CDU local organizations elect their own leadership and take on responsibility for nominating candidates, campaigning on the local level, and collecting dues. The party, however, secures most of its funds from business organizations, so that dues-collecting is not so important as it is in the SPD.

The party's governing body is a Federal Convention to which the *Land* parties send representatives. As is usually the case with such a conference, it functions mainly as a sounding board and device for rousing party enthusiasm. It does elect the party chairman and four deputy chairmen, and in that sense it is not without significance. But it is not a grass-roots convention. Its membership consists almost entirely of chairmen —chairmen of the state parties and chairmen of factions in the state legislatures— and other party officials; its votes, therefore, reflect the opinion of party chiefs, not necessarily the wishes of the party's rank and file.

The two executive organs of the party are the Federal Executive Committee (*Vorstand*) and the Federal Committee (*Ausschuss*). The *Vorstand* contains most of the importand *Land* and national party leaders and is dominated by the *Land* leadership. As part of the executive machinery, the party has created the post of general secretary to cope with organizational affairs.

The CDU also contains special organizations representing such interests as trade unions, youth, local government officials, Protestants, women, and civil servants; and a Committee for Economic Policy consults with business groups to obtain their opinions on policy matters, and about a third of the CDU deputies are associated with the Social Committees that speak for the left wing of the party, and that organize CDU working-class support. But none of these organizations, with the possible exception of the business committee, has much to say about party policy decisions. In addition to these special organizations, there are the lay groups affiliated with the Catholic Church; though these have no direct influence on party decisions, they do try to preserve an environment favorable to the CDU.

The two principal power groups within the Christian Democratic Party are the Executive Committee and the parliamentary party caucus, or *Fraktion*. Both, of course, include representatives from the states, and because the *Land* organizations exercise a powerful influence over party nominations, divisions tend to occur within each group

rather than between them. More than ever, policy decisions of the Christian Democrats are reached through an intricate series of touchy negotiations and under the omnipresent threat that party conflict will break out into the open.

As is the case with the SPD, the chairman of the CDU national party organization, the chairman of the CDU parliamentary party, and the CDU's candidate for chancellor are not necessarily the same. Nor are they necessarily chosen from the national parliamentary arena. Adenauer's successor was chosen by the National Executive Committee from among the cabinet ministers. However, when Erhard resigned in 1966, the committee presented the parliamentary party with a list of four candidates from which to choose; the winner on the third ballot (Kiesinger) was the minister-president of the state of Baden-Württemberg. Following the party's defeat under Kiesinger in the 1969 election, the party's choice for candidate for chancellor was Rainer Barzel, who had served as chairman of the parliamentary party since 1964. Barzel resigned his two chairmanships in 1973 (he had been made national party chairman in 1971), and for some time it remained unclear whether his successor as parliamentary party chairman (Karl Carstens) or his successor as national party chairman, the minister-president of the state of Rhineland-Palatinate (Helmut Kohl), would become the party's candidate for chancellor at the next election. After overcoming a challenge by Franz Joseph Strauss, Kohl was finally nominated as candidate for the chancellorship in May, 1975. The growing problems of the Socialists and the expectation of victory in 1976 have enabled Kohl to bring a temporary (and fragile) unity to the CDU.

The party's problem is only partly related to its leadership. Much of it pertains to events occurring inside and outside the Bonn Republic. The assumptions that guided the CDU through the 1950's are now in question, especially West Germany's relations with the German Democratic Republic and the United States. German domestic politics

FIGURE 11.2 A GERMAN BALLOT, 1969

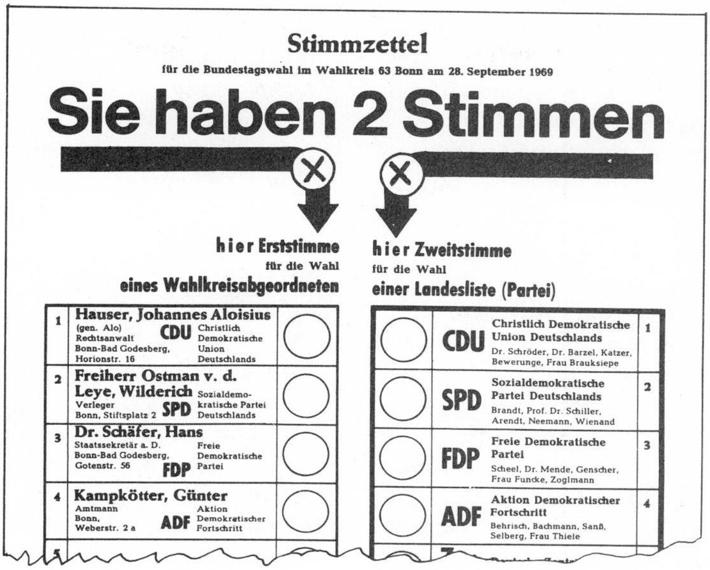

Stimmzettel

für die Bundestagswahl im Wahlkreis 63 Bonn am 28. September 1969

Sie haben 2 Stimmen

hier Erststimme für die Wahl **eines Wahlkreisabgeordneten**

hier Zweitstimme für die Wahl **einer Landesliste (Partei)**

1	**Hauser, Johannes Aloisius** (gen. Alo) Rechtsanwalt Bonn-Bad Godesberg, Horionstr. 16 — **CDU** Christlich Demokratische Union Deutschlands	○
2	**Freiherr Ostman v. d. Leye, Wilderich** Verleger Bonn, Stiftsplatz 2 — **SPD** Sozialdemokratische Partei Deutschlands	○
3	**Dr. Schäfer, Hans** Staatssekretär a. D. Bonn-Bad Godesberg, Gotenstr. 56 — **FDP** Freie Demokratische Partei	○
4	**Kampkötter, Günter** Amtmann Bonn, Weberstr. 2 a — **ADF** Aktion Demokratischer Fortschritt	○

○	**CDU** Christlich Demokratische Union Deutschlands — Dr. Schröder, Dr. Barzel, Katzer, Bewerunge, Frau Brauksiepe	1
○	**SPD** Sozialdemokratische Partei Deutschlands — Brandt, Prof. Dr. Schiller, Arendt, Neemann, Wienand	2
○	**FDP** Freie Demokratische Partei — Scheel, Dr. Mende, Genscher, Frau Funcke, Zoglmann	3
○	**ADF** Aktion Demokratischer Fortschritt — Behrisch, Bachmann, Sanß, Selberg, Frau Thiele	4

is entering a new phase. The very heterogeneity of the CDU makes it extremely difficult for the party to confront the new era with decisiveness. Its past victories stemmed partially from the fear that the Social Democrats would not be able to govern effectively. (Adenauer's declaration in Bamberg in 1957 that a victory for the SPD would mean the end of Germany is a rather famous example of that.) And as recent polls show, this fear persists among many Germans. But opposition to socialism, especially when the Social Democrats themselves are shying away from it, can hardly bring the necessary long term cohesion.

8. ELECTORAL POLITICS IN GERMANY

One of the major arguments against the list system of proportional representation in the Weimar Republic was that it not only splintered the party system, but that it also gave excessive power to party bureaucrats who chose the order in which candidates appeared on the voting lists. In addition, it was argued that the large size of electoral districts accented ideological considerations rather than the personality or record of individual candidates.

In an effort to correct these "faults," the Bonn Republic has adopted a two-ballot system. The nation is divided into 248 electoral districts, each of which elects one member to the Bundestag; here election is by plurality. In addition, another 248 candidates are elected from *Land* party lists; the number of seats available to each state is proportional to its share of the total number of citizens eligible to vote. In effect, each citizen votes twice. On the first ballot (*Erststimme*), he chooses between two or more candidates in his electoral district. On the second ballot (*Zweitstimme*), he votes for the party lists of candidates for his *Land*. (Figure 11.2.)

Seats in the Bundestag are distributed according to the percentage of the vote that a party receives on the *Land* list. The number of seats obtained in the single-member election districts is then subtracted from the total number of seats to which the party is entitled, and the remainder of the elected candidates are chosen from the state list itself. In the 1965 elections, for example, the

Free Democratic Party received 9.5 percent of the vote on its second (*Land* list) ballots. However, the FDP did not elect any candidates from the single-member districts. Thus, the forty-nine FDP candidates seated in the Bundestag—just over 9 percent of the total—were all drawn from *Land* lists.

Election results under the German system are much as they would be under a purely proportional system of representation, with two exceptions. First, if any political party elects more candidates in single-member districts than it is proportionally entitled to, it is allowed to retain the seats it has won and the size of the Bundestag is enlarged accordingly. Since passage of the electoral law in its present form, the size of the Bundestag has varied from 496 to 499. Second, no party is entitled to seats from the *Land* lists unless it either receives more than 5 percent of the total national vote or elects at least three candidates from the single-member constituencies.

The 5 percent minimum, by discouraging the growth of minor parties, or at least making it difficult for them, has helped to save Bonn from the political fragmentation that characterized the Weimar Republic. There is no proof that a minimum percentage discourages attempts to form new parties, but it obviously presents a hurdle—one that the National Democratic Party, for example, has failed to clear.

Whether the present system has achieved its other objective, that of creating a closer liaison between voters and candidates, is problematical. Local organizations do have considerable power in the nominations of candidates, especially of those for safe seats, for here candidates do not need the insurance of also appearing on the *Land* list. But the local parties tend to be the preserve of a small group of militants or of special-interest groups; there is not much evidence that the great mass of party supporters is involved in nomination decisions.

The *Land* lists are drawn up by regional party organizations. Theoretically, those chosen for the state lists take the high political road, emphasizing ideological or general policy issues, while constituency candidates concentrate on local needs. In fact, of course, there is a good deal of oratorical overlap, primarily because many, if not most, candidates seek—and get—a place on *Land* party lists in addition to a constituency nomination. *Land* party lists also present an opportunity to balance tickets. The CDU, as an example, carefully allocates places for Protestants and Catholics; it also makes sure that representatives of various interest groups are on the slate. Each party tries to have some women and some younger people on its ticket, and for a long time, certain *Länder* saw the advantage of a candidate or two who were members of the local refugee organization.

For the Social Democratic Party, the major source of funds in the post–World War II period has been membership dues. Additional money has been raised through special programs and through minor commercial ventures controlled by the party. Both Christian Democrats and Free Democrats, on the other hand, have relied upon a few sizable donations from business firms and trade associations for financial succor. In 1958, however, the Federal Constitutional Court declared that individual and business donations to political parties were not tax deductible, and these sources of income began immediately to dry up. The Free Democrats suffered most severely, but the Christian Democratic Union, because its campaign expenditures were usually higher than those of all other parties combined, also found itself in straits.

The Bundestag reacted to this situation by partially financing the parliamentary work of the three major parties—and the money allotted increased year by year. In 1966 the NPD which was not included in the government's largesse, finally brought the issue to the Federal Constitutional Court, which ruled that general payments of party expenses by the government were unconstitutional but implied that some money might be granted to defray campaign expenses if all political parties of a reasonable size received assistance.

By 1968 a compromise had been worked out to meet the court's implicit requirement. As amended by still another court decision, the law now states that all political parties will receive two and a half marks, the equivalent of about one U.S. dollar, for each vote obtained in a federal election, provided the party wins more than .5 percent of the total national vote. The amount advanced to each party is to be based on the results of the previous Bundestag election. The legislation also provides for publication of large party contributions from individuals or corporations. Similar legislation applying to state elections has been adopted by many *Land* governments.

9.   CONCLUSIONS

The party system of postwar Germany bears little resemblance to that of Weimar Germany. Instead of a multiplicity of parties defined in terms of either narrow interests or rigid ideologies, the Bonn Republic has sustained two political organizations whose differences, particularly in recent years, have become increasingly marginal. Thus the Socialists' finance and economics minister, Professor Karl Schiller, could move from the SPD to the CDU a few weeks before the 1972 election and campaign with another former economics minister, Professor Ludwig Erhard, on the CDU's platform. The Christian Democratic Union is in fact a basically conservative party run by professional politicians whose aims are to consolidate the gains made in the postwar years. The Social Democratic Party, though retaining elements of its traditional working-class background and ideology, has been edging toward the political center to become the majority party of moderate reform, despite renewed pressure from its left wing. Both now address their appeals to the widest possible spectrum of German voters.

This changed party system has been a key factor in the stability that has characterized the Bonn regime. That the Social Democratic Party was able to emerge from its role as opposition and become the chief party is a sign of strength not only, nor even chiefly, of the party itself, but also, and more importantly, of the party system as a whole. It seems questionable that any two-party system could long endure with one of the parties permanently in opposition. Thus, even though the policy gap between the CDU and the SPD has grown narrower over the years, the admission of the Social Democrats into the ranks of governing parties effectively offers the German voter more choice and more control.

Above: West German Bundestag. Courtesy
German Information Center. *Below:* French
National Assembly. Courtesy French Embassy
Press & Information Division. *Opposite page:*
British Houses of Parliament. Courtesy British
Information Services.

The Process of Government

12

Parliaments,
Executives,
Interest Groups:
The European Pattern

1. INSTITUTIONAL DEVELOPMENT

Modern parliamentary government, including the American presidential variant, is the great achievement of Western Europe, and more particularly of Britain. That it has been so widely adopted or proposed as an eventual goal by political societies around the world is an indication that it appeals to a fundamental sense of equity. And, indeed, it is difficult to conceive of any other arrangement compatible with the idea of self-government. This is not to say that the parliamentary regime represents humanity's highest achievement; it is certainly possible that its present forms will become obsolete and will eventually be replaced by others. For as we shall see, the variations upon a

common theme have been immense; parliamentarianism, even in Europe, has been constantly changing over the past century.

Parliaments sprang from a type of feudal society. Throughout Europe, with England as a partial exception, their authority declined during the age of absolute monarchy. Their revival and enhanced power were related to the emergence of new ideas and social classes. From the fifteenth through the nineteenth centuries, parliaments gradually came to the fore as political structures endowed with the authority to determine both the nation's goals and the means by which those goals should be implemented; they devised the rules by which the community would govern itself. Whether through relatively peaceful change or violent revolution,

231

monarchs were stripped of their power. The alternative to parliamentarianism was hereditary monarchy; today the alternative is the dictatorship of one man or party.

Modern parliaments differ greatly from their feudal predecessors. In feudal society, the king and parliament "discovered" the true law. Modern parliaments *make* the law; they are the ultimate source of legislative authority. Moreover, feudal parliaments were designed to represent the great estates of the realm; modern parliaments ostensibly represent individuals as individuals. The last difference is more apparent in America than in Europe. In most European nations the direct representation of social and economic groups has continued to be regarded as at least partially legitimate. Indeed, the Catholic Church has always maintained, as did Fascist regimes and certain brands of socialism (all harking back to an earlier tradition), that individual representation should be replaced by the representation of functional interests, such as agriculture, industry, and labor.

As European monarchs were divested of their power, some of their authority was transferred to an executive, or to executive bodies, responsible to the legislature itself. Though the parliament could legislate, it was thought, an executive body was needed to speak for the nation as a whole, to prepare general programs of action, to oversee administration, and to handle such matters as foreign policy. Under these premises, the executive evolved into the dominant branch of government. For a time during the nineteenth century, parliaments actually legislated—that is, they were the source of most laws. Today, in all the countries under discussion, the executive—whether cabinet, chancellor, or president—is the primary source of important new legislative proposals; parliaments have come to assume the role, primarily, of critical watchdogs, even as they legitimize political decisions and serve as public forums for the discussion of these decisions.

In Britain, the transition from parliamentary to cabinet government was a natural one, based, in some measure, on the development of a disciplined two-party system. In Germany and France, such an evolution did not occur. The fragmentation of the party system during the Weimar regime in Germany and during the Third and Fourth Republics in France inhibited the development of a stable and powerful yet responsible executive. Because Parliament could not itself legislate effectively in these two nations, either very little was done, or, in emergencies, the executive was given—or seized—the power to act by decree. In both France and the German Federal Republic attempts have been made to assure executive dominance over the legislature—in Germany, by requiring a "positive" vote of no-confidence; in France, by creating a popularly elected president with considerable authority.

The separation of the executive and the legislature, each directly responsible to the people and each with its own sphere of authority, was, to a large extent, an American invention, generated partly by a reading of Montesquieu and partly by American perceptions of the existing pattern of English government. Whatever its values in practice, and there are many, the belief that executive and legislative functions can be neatly separated has never made any sense from a theoretical point of view. In the United States, the president does not merely execute programs legislated by Congress; he is party leader, chief executive, and, increasingly, chief initiator of legislation, all rolled into one. In the same way, Congress legislates, oversees the execution of legislation, and figures crucially in such areas as foreign policy. Yet, the myth of separation has allowed the American Congress in the twentieth century to exercise more authority than its British counterpart, especially as a check upon the executive. For some time the American pattern was considered obsolete by many Europeans; today, however, at least some analysts believe that, in an age of specialization, parliaments, if they are to fulfill more than a rhetorical function, might do worse than to take a look at some of the devices that have preserved the power of the American Congress, including the committee system.

2. PARLIAMENTS

While parliaments are an almost universal phenomenon in the modern world, many of them, as in the Soviet Union and other one-party states, have little or no power. Even in true parliamentary regimes, legislative power is shared with other organs of government. As already indicated, the executive's control over the order in which proposed legislation is to be discussed, over the amount of time to be spent on particular bills and the initiation of legislation has seriously compromised the legislative function of parliaments. Judicial interpretation of laws in some nations has also limited parliamentary authority, and both the executive and the bureaucracy make policy in the process of putting general statutes into effect. Moreover, legislators themselves are, on the whole, generalists rather than experts in many areas and are, therefore, incapable of wielding the influence they had in the less confusing times of the nineteenth century.

The contention that parliaments have completely lost legislative authority is, of course, not correct. The Congress of the United States still has very considerable authority over the making of public policy, and though the authority of the legislature as a body is far less significant in Germany, France, and Britain, it is still important. In all three nations, although to different degrees, the power of the executive is founded on the discipline of party majorities in the parliament itself, and these majorities are not entirely passive. Prospective executive actions are always examined with an eye to the reaction of legislatures or at least to the reactions of those deputies who compose the parliamentary majority.

Parliaments perform other key functions. In cabinet and chancellor political systems like those of Britain and Germany, the government is responsible to the legislature, and even though the overturn of any regime re-

quires a split within the governing party, the possibility of such a political calamity affects decisions made by the executive. Similarly, in a "mixed" system such as France has, where there is a popularly elected president as well as a cabinet that is responsible to the legislature, the view of Parliament can never be completely ignored.

Despite the fact that bureaucrats are formally responsible only to the executive, their activity is not above the influence of most European legislatures, which review administrative decrees, intervene in the administrative process on behalf of constituents, and question ministers on the activities of civil servants under their jurisdiction. Where a committee system exists, legislatures may also conduct investigations of administrative activities. The investigatory functions of legislative committees, especially of important ones, are becoming increasingly vital in the twentieth century. Committees are quite powerful in the United States Congress; they are, however, less so in Germany, and still less so in France and, with some exceptions, they are of relatively little importance in Britain.

The bulk of the legislative work of most parliaments does not take place in plenary (full) sessions. Usually parliamentary chambers are fairly empty, with members delivering speeches to a few bored colleagues as others file in and out paying only a modicum of attention. To be sure, during a major debate the atmosphere can become exciting as exchanges grow keener. In fact, there have been times in the past, in Britain and the United States, when the exchange became so bitter that members punched, caned, or shot one another. Sessions in both legislatures have been somewhat calmer during the past century. Parliamentary bodies in other nations, however—in Germany during the Weimar Republic and in France under the Third and Fourth Republics—have witnessed considerable violence.

No matter how persuasive parliamentary speeches may sound, most members know long before the final tally is taken how they are going to vote on a piece of legislation.

The issue has already been determined by the party, or as the result of either committee work or pressure from constituents. Speeches, when not made for the purpose of delaying the proceedings, are directed primarily at the press. The real work of the parliament, then, takes place elsewhere.

Parliamentary rules set forth the procedures for introducing and considering proposed legislation. These bills may be drawn up outside the legislature, but usually they must be introduced by a member. In the United States, for example, many important pieces of legislation come from the executive, but the president must find a congressional sponsor. In a cabinet system, the government may introduce bills directly. In some cases, individual members of legislatures are not permitted to introduce legislation at all. In Germany, for example, all members must join a *Fraktion* consisting of at least fifteen deputies; only a *Fraktion* can introduce a bill and exercise certain other rights.

Once introduced, bills proceed through a series of steps, customarily referred to as "readings," a term derived from British practice. Traditionally, clerks read proposals three times in Parliament to insure that representatives have understood their contents. Today this is no longer necessary because bills are printed and distributed to all members; nonetheless, the terminology has been retained.

The methods of considering bills differ greatly. In the United States, Germany, and France, bills are sent to committees for study either immediately or shortly after being introduced. The power of these committees also varies. In the United States, they are still quite important; in Germany and France, where they exercised considerable authority during the Weimar period and the Third and Fourth Republics, their influence has diminished. In the House of Commons, legislative committees are of minor importance; bills are sent to committee only after they have been approved in general terms by Parliament, and committee discussions rarely result in significant changes in legislation. Where committees are powerful and political parties weak, committee chairmen and rapporteurs have considerable influence. When political parties are strong, especially in a two-party system, the committees, and hence committee chairmanships are not usually foci of legislative power.

Compensation for legislators also differs from nation to nation, although there is an increasing tendency to raise salaries and improve facilities. Members of the United States Congress are probably the best-paid legislators in the world; they also have the widest range of available services, including extensive office space, and the most liberal expense allowances. American politics, at least on the national level, has long been regarded as a profession like any other, and members are expected to receive commensurate salaries. Until recently, service in the British Parliament was looked upon as a duty of the political and social elite, something that should not be remunerated. With the rise of the Labor Party, sentiment shifted, albeit slowly; in fact many MP's supplement their salaries by part-time work by other occupations, or, in the case of trade-union MP's, by being partially subsidized.

Whether paid or unpaid, legislators are not necessarily the image of the population they represent. For a long time, Continental legislatures were the domain primarily of gentlemen. With the rise of Socialist parties, contingents of working-class members and middle-class and lower-middle-class radicals were added. Working-class strength in most pariaments is usually in direct proportion to the size of the Socialist or Communist vote, although not always. The French Communists, for instance, are much more concerned about having working men in Parliament than either the British Labor Party or the German Social Democrats. In both of the latter parties, many trade-union officials have been replaced by middle-class schoolteachers and journalists.

Most legislatures contain large contingents of lawyers—not only because of the nature of the profession, but also because it can more easily be resumed if a legislative career is interrupted. Lawyers are particularly prominent in the United States Congress. Americans have generally tended to think of politics as a process of regulating social intercourse by legal rules rather than as, say, in France, an area of ideological confrontation. British and French parliaments, on the other hand, contain substantial contingents of journalists and academics —a reflection in part, of the greater prestige of professional intellectuals in both societies. Further, all European legislatures contain a much larger representation of business executives than does the United States Congress. This can be explained by the fact that in Europe (contrary to the attitude in the United States) it is considered legitimate for business interests to be represented directly by businessmen; and, of course, European parliamentary schedules are often such as to permit executives to continue their professional activity while serving.[1]

The behavior of members of parliament is strongly influenced by the nation's political culture, as well as by the character of the legislative body of which they are a part. In Britain such has been the prestige of Parliament, at least until recently, that a distinct sense of community exists in being a member of an institution having its own style, tradition, and rules of the game. At the same time, the strict discipline of the two-party system in the House of Commons makes party reputation more important for political advancement than reputation. In the United States, on the other hand, party ties are much weaker; reputation, indeed even power, in the legislature depends much more upon personal qualities and how these relate to the general atmosphere of the House or the Senate. In France during the politically chaotic Third and Fourth Repub-

lics, there was much less sense of community, although most deputies did develop a kind of mutual understanding that enabled them to work together. The Communists, of course, were the major exception: they remained aloof, existing in a world dominated by party discipline.

All European legislatures consist of two houses. Originally, the differentiation was between a legislative body in which the aristocracy sat (the upper house) and one that, in some sense, represented the people (the lower house). In federal regimes, such as the German Empire, the upper house tended to represent not only the aristocracy but the various *Länder* as well. In the United States, the Senate, whose members were intially elected by the lower houses of the state legislatures, represented both the states and, theoretically, the elite of the community. Britain retained an upper house, based on modified aristocratic representation, longer than any other European country, although the power of the House of Lords was almost nil by the end of World War II. Under the French Third Republic, the Senate served as the "conservative" upper house and had somewhat less authority than the Chamber of Deputies. The constitution of the Fourth Republic provided for a very weak upper chamber; that of the Fifth slightly increased its power. In Germany the Weimar regime stripped the upper house of most of its power; under the Bonn constitution, the Bundesrat—representing federal but no longer aristocratic or conservative interests —has regained some of its traditional prerogatives. In the United States, the Senate was democratized by providing for the direct election of its members, and over the years it has retained, and perhaps even increased, its power.

3. THE EXECUTIVE

The particular division of functions between the legislature and the executive that has manifested itself in Europe is a direct outgrowth of European historical experi-

---

[1] In 1964 about 60 percent of the members of the American Congress were lawyers. In 1966 between 15 and 20 percent of British MP's were lawyers. The French parliament elected in 1967 contained 71 teachers and only 34 lawyers, in a total membership of 487.

ence. The development of European political institutions may be seen as a long process in which political power was taken away from the monarchy only to be returned to an executive responsible either to a popularly elected legislature or to the electorate itself.

In parliamentary regimes in which the executive is elected by the legislature, his power depends very much upon the party system. In France under the Third and Fourth Republics, for instance, and in Weimar Germany, the premier and chancellor were ineffective simply because the coalition governments they headed were usually based upon flimsy, transitory majorities composed of parties and politicians with widely divergent views. In Britain on the other hand, the existence of a system of two parties, each tautly controlled and each taking its turn in office, has conferred considerable power upon the executive. The cabinet is, to be sure, collectively the government, but the prime minister is far more than *primus inter pares*. The mere fact of his selection as party leader and prime minister yields him a national prominence that enhances his role far beyond that of any of his colleagues.

In systems like the American, in which a popularly elected president is entrusted with executive authority, his power rests to a great extent upon the fact that he is elected by the people as a whole. Inasmuch as his government cannot be overturned by a congressional vote, he is less dependent upon the legislature than is either the British prime minister or the German chancellor. Nevertheless, the political independence of American congressmen does place limitations upon presidential power. In the United States a substantial segment of party members in the legislature can defy a president of their own party without serious repercussions; in Britain such defiance could mean the fall of the government and new elections in which the dissident members might suffer defeat. Thus, whereas the American president, like the British prime minister, has become the chief legislator, he cannot be nearly so certain that programs emanating from the government will receive the kind of consideration he wishes. Moreover, because his road to office and his requirements for getting elected are often quite different from those for congressmen, he rarely has the working arrangement with legislators that a British prime minister does. The French pattern of "mixed" governments adds further complications to the interrelationship between the executive and the legislature. Since 1962 the president has been elected nationally and has held wide powers; yet executive authority is shared with a premier responsible to the legislature.

4. INTEREST GROUPS AND GOVERNMENTAL PROCESSES

Individuals who are linked together by common concerns, and who have an awareness of these concerns, constitute an interest group. As was seen in Part II, one of the major characteristics of modern societies has been the proliferation of interest groups formed on the basis of the members' functional position within the society. Workers, managers, teachers—all have formed interest groups.

The political style of interest groups, their degree of influence, their powers and techniques of persuasion depend upon the kind of society in which they operate. Where sharp social divisions exist, the demands of these groups are likely to be highly ideological and diffuse—that is, involving a total transformation of the society rather than the attainment of limited ends. Under such circumstances, compromise between authority and interest groups is almost impossible, and there is a greater likelihood of physical violence—as there is, also, when a group believes that its more limited legitimate demands cannot be met within the society's existing institutional structure. On the other hand, a society in which most of the people accept the community's basic norms is usually characterized by interest groups whose goal is limited simply to obtaining a somewhat larger share of the assets. Politics in such a society is more likely to be characterized by give-and-take relationships. Under such circumstances, coherent public policies are more easily formulated, and compromises with and between special-interest groups are more readily facilitated. In general, the politics of the United States and Britain has been one of accommodation. This is not to imply that both countries have not witnessed grave intergroup conflicts from time to time. In Britain the Irish question proved intractable and could be settled only by granting independence, after a good deal of bloodshed. Troubles have, of course, recently exploded once again, and in the United States, the race problem has periodically taken similar dimensions.

Quite naturally, almost all interest groups want access to those elites in the topmost decision-making positions and gravitate to the centers of power. In the France of the Fourth Republic, interests concentrated their efforts upon Parliament and its specialized committees; in the Fifth, their efforts have been directed at the executive. In Britain groups turn primarily to the cabinet and the bureaucracy. In all three nations that we are studying, some interest groups have supported one of the competing political parties. The activities of labor groups have been most conspicuous.

Techniques for obtaining the support of strategic political elites differ. What used to win the decision-makers' favor may be merely the presentation of "objective" information; it may also be the threat of a loss of votes, or even violence. French peasants in the 1960's, for instance, used violence with some success to prevent the government from reducing agricultural subsidies; some civil-rights groups in the United States, too, have used force. The tactic can be effective for a relatively small number that is unable to achieve its goals in other ways—provided it does not get out of hand and too deeply antagonize those against whom it is directed.

An important factor in determining the influence of interest groups on public policy is whether the political institutions and party system permit the presentation of systematic policy alternatives to the electorate— that is, whether there is responsible party government. In the United States, the lack of congressional party discipline and the consequent ability of congressional committees and even committee chairmen either to block or further legislation in the interests of relatively small organizations contribute to the immensely powerful role of interest groups in the American congress. And because they can be politically injured by the activities of a particular interest group, congressmen often place the demands of special interests above party loyalties. In Britain, on the other hand, with its disciplined parties and their capacity to form strong, responsible governments, interest groups have been forced to operate upon the government as a whole. Small, well-heeled groups, consequently, have been unable to establish strategic relations that can be used to block policy decision. And while group demands are always considered by the party in power, they are more likely to be considered only within the framework of overall policy.

Interestingly enough, while in some ways organized interest groups have had a greater influence on American politics than on British, the British, as well as the French and Germans, have been far more willing to recognize the existence of special interest groups and to provide for consultation with them as one legitimate aspect of political decision-making. Europeans still tend to think of the community as composed of estates, whereas Americans, under the influence of liberalism, believe more strongly that the legislature represents "the people," and that the relationship between "the people" and the government should not be impeded by the machinations of "interests."

5. INSTITUTIONS AND CONSTITUTIONS

In all but the simplest, more homogeneous societies, the authority to develop general rules—that is, a public policy—to bind the community as a whole is centered in governmental institutions. If these institutions are to exercise power for any length of time, they must be seen as legitimate. Legitimacy results when the institutions that exercise power are supported by the values that are inherent in the culture. In most modern states—Britain is the conspicuous exception—legitimation is also provided by formal constitutions that outline the functions that various governmental structures are to pursue in the role-making process. The fit between the formal constitutional rules and the actual structure of decision-making, however, is never perfect because informal procedures and authority relationships develop that circumvent or modify the formal mechanisms. The difference between a "written" and an "unwritten" constitution, therefore, is not as great as one might at first believe.

Another way of saying the same thing is that constitutional engineering—the deliberate redesigning of institutional structures with the purpose of achieving a particular goal, such as effective and stable government—yields the desired results only within rather broad limits. Other factors, like social cleavages, cultural values, and the party and interest-group system, can easily combine to frustrate the hopes of the constitution makers. These generalizations should become clear in the following three chapters. They examine the legislative and executive institutions of Britain, France, and West Germany.

13

Cabinet
Government
In Britain

1. THE NATURE AND EXPLANATION OF THE BRITISH SYSTEM

⌐The British cabinet—headed as it is by a powerful yet responsible executive—has historically provided the nation with relatively stable and effective government.⌐ In Weimar Germany and the Third and Fourth Republics of France, cabinets were usually shaky coalitions that unraveled fairly quickly; in Britain, cabinets have not only been cohesive, they have generally retained power between regular elections.

In both Germany and France, attempts by the executive to devise and effect comprehensive programs of public policy were frustrated at every turn by parliamentary factionalism or powerful committees—legislative roadblocks not uncommon in the United States. The British government's legislative program, by contrast, has usually advanced majestically through Parliament and been enacted into law without much modification. During Charles de Gaulle's presidency, the French executive dominated the legislature and managed to get its programs safely translated into law; the price of this achievement was the emasculation of Parliament. For a dozen years in postwar Germany, the linchpin of the Bonn governmental system was also a rather authoritarian, charismatic executive: Konrad Adenauer; his retirement in 1963 led to a crisis in the political system.

In trying to account for the differences between Britain and France, or between

Britain and Germany, many commentators have emphasized the British prime minister's power to dissolve Parliament. Yet this power was also vested in the French and German executive. Moreover, there is little evidence that the power of the British prime minister rests on his right to dissolve Parliament. Those chosen to form a government represent a common ideological outlook, and they are the leading members of a political party. A back-bench member is not likely to rebel against the decisions of the government, especially in view of the fact that a new election fought by a divided party would probably result in the party's defeat and, perhaps, his own as well. For the same reasons, no prime minister is likely to precipitate a situation that might set off this chain of events. A further explanation of the close relationship between the government and the back bench—closer than in either the German or French systems—has been the increasing number of MP's who have been taken into the government, currently about one hundred. For these reasons, then, no prime minister in the twentieth century has even tried to use the threat of dissolution as a means of insuring party discipline. The main advantage derived from his authority to dissolve Parliament lies in the government's ability to call for new elections at the time it considers most propitious to do so.

Other commentators, in trying to account for the stability of British government, have stressed that the British parliament was never, by tradition, expected to govern the nation; rather, except for a short period in the nineteenth century, its role has always been that of acting as a critic of the executive. Yet in France and Germany parliaments were also initially critics of the executive. Explanations of the British system that highlight the continuity of this tradition are, therefore, unsatisfactory. What must be explained are the reasons why tradition has continued to be viable in Britain and why it was broken in France and Germany.

If one wished to underscore a single factor to explain the British system of government, one would have to point to the emergence of a disciplined two-party system.[1] It is only because any cabinet taking office has been assured of the support of a cohesive majority that the British executive has been able to assert its dominance over the parliament. In France and Germany, at least until the Fifth Republic and the Bonn government, fragmented, multiparty systems inhibited the emergence of stable and effective government.

Nonetheless, any discussion of the sources of political stability in Britain would be misleading and incomplete were no mention made of the nation's political culture in which party and governmental institutions are embedded. The outstanding feature of that culture, the product of the pattern of historical development that was traced in Chapter 2, has been the continued intermingling of the old and new, and hence the continuity of traditional forms and values. One important consequence of this feature has been a sense of being part of an evolving organic community, a sense that has served to moderate social conflict and to produce consensus on the need for a government able to govern.

Traditional values still permeate British life. They encourage the maintenance of a class sytem associated on the positive side with a sense of noblesse oblige and community service and on the negative side with both snobbery and deference. They are tied in with the whole apparatus of the monarchy and the court, with the public schools, with Oxford and Cambridge, and with the "old boy" network that enables a British elite—by American standards comparatively small—to communicate freely and easily with one another, whether they are businessmen, civil servants, or top-level professionals. Traditional values are also reflected in the attitudes of those workers who still vote for Tory candidates because they prefer to be governed by their "betters." They are

[1] See chapter 9.

seen, too, in the ideal of the "amateur" whose broad interests in the classics, general deportment, and competence in socially approved sports supposedly fit him for an elite position in business, politics, or the professions.

These values have also contributed to a relatively high level of trust in the good intentions of the state and its officials, as well as to a sense of moderation that prevents any group from pushing its claims too far against what is considered to be the "objective" interest of the community as a whole. They are seen in the notion that the public interest is not merely the sum of expressed individual or group interests, but rather the interest of an evolving community, and in the assumption by any government that organized groups—making up the community as did the estates of the feudal realm—should be consulted before new policies are initiated.

One important component of Britain's traditional values merits special emphasis: the notion that public affairs should be run by the governors and not the governed, that the identity and protection of the public interest are best left to the governing elite. The role of the citizenry is to choose the governors; referenda, constituent pressure on MP's, or governments slavishly following mass opinions are all regarded as somehow "un-British." Thus, despite opinion polls showing substantial majorities of the public favoring contrary policies, Parliament has abolished the death penalty, has lifted the penalties on homosexuality, and has legalized abortions. Referring to these and other instances, the left-wing *New Statesman* expressed the traditional British attitude when it editorialized: "Better the liberal elitism of the statute book than the reactionary populism of the marketplace." The Conservative leadership acted on the same premise when it led Britain into the Common Market in the face of impressive evidence that majority opinion was at that time opposed to the move.

There is evidence that many of these traditions are eroding fairly rapidly. The con-

sequences of this erosion for the political system will be discussed at the end of the chapter.

2. THE DEVELOPMENT OF CABINET GOVERNMENT

FEUDAL ORIGINS: Anglo-Saxon England was not yet fully feudal at the time of the Norman invasion, and, indeed, the monarchy was weaker in many respects than in less highly developed political communities. After the Norman invasion, the monarch's authority spread very quickly. The Conqueror, having divided the land among his followers, made them all swear personal oaths of allegiance to him, thereby bringing into existence a single feudal community. Subsequently, monarchs periodically summoned "royal courts" at which they sought advice on matters of common interest.

This court of advisers became the *Curia Regis* or King's Court, which was, in effect, both a legislative and a judicial body. Out of that emerged the *Magnum Concilium* or Great Council—and, ultimately, the parliament. The king also had in attendance a smaller group of officials known as the Privy (private) Council, which eventually gave rise to the cabinet, a still smaller body, so called because of the palace room in which it met during the reign of Charles II. Such is the pervasiveness of tradition that the Privy Council still exists, and it is as a committee of the Privy Council that the cabinet today derives its legal authority.

Initially, the Great Council was composed entirely of the upper nobility and higher clergy. It insisted upon the right to be convened before granting the king money to meet his needs. In the thirteenth century, these councils came to be called parliaments, the term being derived from the French word *parlement*, i. e., "conversation." In the thirteenth century, too, knights and burgesses of the shires and boroughs, as well as the lower clergy, began to be invited to the parliament, one reason being that the monarchy needed additional sources of revenue.

The king's writs summoning the knights and burgesses required that local communities (communes or commons) also send a specified number of representatives. The role of the communes in the parliament was at first minimal, and many displayed a marked reluctance to be represented, recognizing that their attendance might well mean additional taxes. The lower clergy withdrew from the Great Council in the Fourteenth century, and the knights and burgesses began to deliberate separately—in the "Commons House," later the House of Commons. The House of Lords did not receive its official title until the reign of Henry VIII.

Parliament was originally regarded as a body that only "discovered" the true law, through a process of adjudication. Yet in fact, legislation was continuously being enacted. The first step in the passage of laws took the form of a petition addressed to the king from the barons, or to the barons and the king from the Commons. The primary weapon used by the Commons to have its petitions heeded was a refusal to grant the king supply (money) until its grievances were heard. Not surprisingly, it became customary for the consideration of grievances to precede the granting of supply. Because most of the king's funds came from the constituencies represented by the Commons, it also became customary to consider such grants—that is, financial legislation—in the lower house before they were reviewed by the barons.

During the fifteenth and sixteenth centuries forces were at work preparing the way for a shift in power from the House of Lords to the House of Commons, and a general increase in the power of Parliament. One of these forces was the new commercial class that began to demand a say in the nation's affairs. The implication of these changes became apparent during the reign of the Stuarts, when the English removed two kings, beheaded one of them, and established a short-lived republic. These conflicts were partly economic, partly religious, and partly constitutional, but it was the constitu-

tional aspect—whether sovereignty would reside in the king or in Parliament—that determined for all time the balance of power in British government. The results were the Bill of Rights of 1689, which laid down the requirement that Parliament must consent to all laws involving taxation and must meet regularly; and the Act of Settlement of 1701, which changed the order of succession and limited the monarchy to Protestants—requirements that clearly established parliamentary supremacy.

PARLIAMENTARY GOVERNMENT: The king was never more to exercise his ancient prerogative of rejecting legislation passed by both houses of Parliament. He did, nevertheless, retain a broad executive authority, mainly by virtue of his relationship with the Privy Council and its inner cabinet group of ministers. By this time the Privy Council had effectively become the executive arm of government, and the cabinet invariably included men who were members of Parliament and hence able to manage parliamentary affairs.

During the eighteenth century the cabinet continued to serve at the pleasure of the king, and only slowly did the practice develop of retaining in office cabinets that were supported by a parliamentary majority. In the early nineteenth century, for example, George III removed the so-called Ministry of All Talents with only a feeble protest on the part of Parliament, and as late as 1834 William IV, on his own initiative, dismissed Melbourne and called in Peel to form a new cabinet. By then, however, such arbitrary actions lacked legitimacy, and after Peel's repeated defeats in Parliament had forced the king to relent, there was no longer any question about the cabinet's dependency upon the will of Parliament.[2]

By the first quarter of the nineteenth century the practice had also developed of choosing the more important cabinet ministers from the Commons rather than the Lords.

[2] However, the notion of collective cabinet responsibility as an operative ideal did not develop fully until later in the century.

This was especially true of the king's first minister, the prime minister, a title that had originally been applied to Walpole and then to others who were asked to form governments. Paralleling these trends, cabinet responsibility devolved to the Commons only. After William's threat to pack the House of Lords with enough new peers to assure passage of the Reform Act of 1832, it was clear that the Lords could no longer reject bills ardently desired by the Commons.

The Reform Act of 1832 marked another turning point in the development of Parliament. Until then suffrage was limited, and many seats simply went to the highest bidder.[3] Now, the Commons became a more representative body, and, with the power of the monarchy and the House of Lords clearly in decline, there began what has been called the "golden age" of Parliament. Parliament and the voice of the individual MP seemed supreme, the sources alike of legislative decisions and decisions on the tenure and composition of cabinets. Because of the multiplicity of loosely organized factions within the Commons, the fall of a cabinet did not necessarily result in a new election; rather, as often as not cabinet defeats were followed by intraparliamentary negotiation, in the fashion of the French Fourth Republic and Weimar Germany. Nor did a defeat by the cabinet mean its automatic resignation. Melbourne and Peel, defeated a number of times on particular issues, continued to serve after accepting the determination of the House of Commons.

CABINET GOVERNMENT: Even during Parliament's "golden age," however, forces were at work that would shift the balance of power once again—this time from parliamentary government to cabinet government. Probably the most important factor contributing to the rising strength of the cabinet was the establishment of a disciplined two-party system, which meant that the cabinet was to be chosen from the majority party and that the cabinet's defeat really meant the defeat of the party. Beyond this, however, the increasing role being taken by the state in economic life insured that legislative proposals introduced by the cabinet would take an even larger share of the Common's time. National instead of local issues usurped the political scene, and the traditional role of the MP as sponsor of private bills affecting the local area began to recede. Most of the bills introduced were government bills, and most of Parliament's time was spent discussing government measures. Furthermore, little need was felt for specialized committees, which might serve as threats to party discipline and party leadership. Committees, then, all but disappeared, and the MP came to rely more and more upon the government itself for technical information. Opportunity to obtain other perspectives became restricted. By the end of the nineteenth century, what was once parliamentary government had been transformed into party government and cabinet government.

As the power of government as a whole increased, and the power of the cabinet increased, so too did the power of the prime minister. Slowly, ineluctably, he expanded his authority within the party and over the other members of the cabinet. All the king's old authority to choose ministers came to rest in the hands of the prime minister, who by the very nature of his position became identified with the party, even as the party became identified with him. Some would say that since 1945 British government has become a quasi-presidential regime, dominated by the prime minister and a rather anonymous government bureaucracy. There is some evidence to support this contention. Yet to call British government "quasi-presidential" rather than "cabinet" is to exaggerate the prime minister's role and

---

[3] The term "pocket borough" applies to constituencies that before the Reform Bill of 1832, were "owned" by the gentry or the crown in that they contained small populations whose voting behavior could be guaranteed through bribery or coercion. Bright young men of impecunious background often sought—and were sought out by members of the aristocracy—to serve as MP's from these constituencies. Naturally, they often served the interests of their benefactors.

to blur certain important distinctions that should become clear in this chapter.

THE CONSTITUTION: From monarchy to Parliament, from the whole Parliament to an increasingly democratically elected Commons, from Commons to cabinet, and from cabinet to prime minister—such has been the historical evolution of power in Britain's parliamentary institutions. The changes occurred gradually and imperceptibly, and there was never the belief that it was necessary to transform the institutions radically according to some abstract model. Hence, Britain is the only nation we are studying that lacks a formal constitution.

This is not to say, however, that it lacks a constitution, as the British understand the term. The constitution is said to be composed in part of certain key documents and legislative enactments. The first is the Magna Carta. Historical interpretation has transformed the charter from what it actually was—an attempt by a feudal barony to retain some of its rights—into one of the founts of British liberty. The charter's primary function, therefore, is symbolic, and as a symbol it illustrates the essential continuity of Britih institutions. It did, nevertheless, contain a number of points that enabled it to serve a symbolic function. Among these was the famous provision in Article 39 that no free man might be arrested, imprisoned, dispossessed, outlawed, exiled, or harassed in any way save by the lawful judgment of his peers or the law of the land.

Other British constitutional documents include the Petition of Right, drawn up in 1628 to "reassert" the "traditional" rights of Englishmen against Charles I, the Bill of Rights of 1689, and the Act of Settlement in 1701, the last two mentioned earlier in the chapter. To these must be added the Reform Bill of 1832, later acts that by degrees extended the suffrage, and the Parliament Act of 1911, which curtailed the powers of the House of Lords.

In the last analysis, however, the *conventions* of the constitution are still the most significant elements of its character. It is difficult to summarize these because they are constantly changing, but among the more important are the following:

1. Where Parliament has not legislated, the common law as interpreted by the judiciary is supreme, and the individual Briton is free to do anything not prohibited by law.

2. In matters of legislation, Parliament is absolutely sovereign; no authority, not even the courts, can override it. It can legislate on any matter it chooses.

3. The executive, in the form of the cabinet, is chosen from a popularly elected Parliament and is responsible to it. This means that if it loses majority support in Parliament on issues of major importance, it must resign to allow the opposition to form a government, or it must call for a new election.

4. Finally, although Britain is a constitutional monarchy, most of the duties performed by the monarch are ritualistic; power resides in Parliament and its cabinet.

The foregoing represents only the barest outline of what the British constitution is. In some sense, any attempt at a brief summary of its elements is a distortion. Our description of it will be reasonably complete only when we have concluded an examination of the complex interrelationship of British political institutions. In summary, these institutions exhibit that peculiar combination of the traditional and the modern so characteristic of British life. Only in Britain can a direct line be traced from feudal patterns to the twentieth century, adding to British institutions a sense of mystery and agelessness unequaled by those of any other nation. It is something of a paradox that the nation which has been the fount of modern representative government, and the model most copied by nations wishing to break with tradition, preserves so much of the old.

3. CABINET GOVERNMENT

British government is, as by now should be clear, dominated by the executive—the cabinet and the prime minister. It is appropriate, therefore, that we begin our account of the British governmental process with an analysis of the executive.

THE FORMATION OF THE CABINET: A government, or ministry, may today consist of 100 or more MP's. These include 20 or so members of the cabinet and approximately another 30 senior ministers who are not cabinet members. There are also some 50 junior ministers (called parliamentary secretaries), parliamentary private secretaries, and parliamentary whips.

There are far too many ministries (i. e. departments) for all of them to be included in a cohesive working body; hence most cabinets contain no more than 15 to 20 members. Traditional ministries, because of their great importance, are almost always included in the cabinet. Thus Treasury (the chancellor of the exchequer), Foreign Affairs (the secretary of state for foreign affairs), and the Home Department (secretary of state) are invariably represented. The lord chancellor, who administers the court system and who presides over the House of Lords, is also always a member. Other ministers may be included if their departments happen to be at the center of public attention. The 1945 Labor government included the minister of fuel and power and the minister of health; they were natural choices because of Labor's decision to nationalize the coal and gas industries and to sponsor a new health program. In 1972, with the Northern Ireland crisis before him, Edward Heath created the cabinet post of secretary for Northern Ireland affairs.

The prime minister can also bring into the cabinet ministers without portfolio—men he wants to include in the government but to whom he does not wish, for one reason or another, to assign departmental responsibilities. Other appointments that do not entail ministerial duties are made to fill posts on the Privy Council, posts that once had important functions but are now little more than sinecures. The chancellor of the Duchy of Lancaster, for example, is in charge of administering certain lands that have been owned by the crown since the thirteenth century; these holdings are now much reduced and the work of administration is done by a small board, leaving the chancellor free for other tasks. The same is true of the Lord Privy Seal, who was at one time a crown officer with certain important duties, especially related to the payment of money; today he has few functions. Nevertheless, the position has been held as a cabinet post by such men as Labor leader Clement Attlee and Conservative leader Heath.

The prime minister's power to appoint the government is obviously a crucial source of his own strength. Bringing a man to the center of power, or retaining him in a cabinet position of some importance, can give a prime minister an important call on the loyalties of the person whom he selects, since a position in government is one that few men desire to relinquish. Patrick Gordon Walker described it after having been Secretary of State for Commonwealth Relations in the Labor government from 1949 to 1951:

From being at the very heart of affairs and among the few dozen best-informed men in the world, faithfully served day and night, he suddenly reverts to obscurity. The invitations which a short time before had seemed to flow in embarrassing numbers, thin to a trickle. Workmen arrive to remove the direct line which linked him to his Private Office and by which he could control a great Department of State.[4]

The large number of ministerial posts now available to be filled goes a long way toward explaining the power that a prime minister today exerts over his own party. Indeed, the growth in the number of posts, double that of 1900, has been an important factor contributing to the increase of his power in the twentieth century.

The choices open to a Labor prime minister in cabinet selection are perhaps not as wide as those open to a Conservative prime minister—because the expectation has grown that the Labor leader will select from among those who have been elected to the

[4] Anthony Sampson, *Anatomy of Britain Today* (New York: Harper & Row, 1965), p. 129. One other means used by the prime minister to exact loyalty lies in his consignment of honors. Attlee distributed 23 peerages and knighthoods between 1945 and 1951: between 1951 and 1957, Conservative prime ministers distributed 104.

twelve-member parliamentary committee (see below). In practice, however, both leaders must take into account the same kind of variables if their government is to be politically and administratively successful.

Although personal connections are not unimportant in a successful parliamentary career, parliamentary performance is the key. The qualities required are an ability to comport oneself well on the floor and a willingness to subordinate personal wishes to party demands. Mavericks are, from time to time, successful, but they are few and far between. The usual ascent up the ladder is from ordinary MP to parliamentary secretary, to a noncabinet department, and from there to the cabinet itself. In general, those who sit in the cabinet are men who have been in the party for many years and gradually have established reputations. This hierarchical system has the advantage that the men finally achieving ministerial office know each other's strengths and weaknesses; on the other hand, the fact that those favored for cabinet posts are too often men who have made few enemies usually indicates that they also formed few original ideas. Some British commentators have argued that American presidents have a wider range of fresh talent to choose from in organizing administrations, and that the presidential system has, in the past fifty years, tapped a greater number of really dynamic leaders than has the British.

THE CABINET AS A TEAM: The cabinet is a body whose members share collective responsibility for all decisions taken by the government. Meetings are officially secret, and members are not normally supposed to reveal disagreements or, should they resign, to disclose the details of intracabinet maneuvers and conflicts; any criticism of official policy by a cabinet member is expected to be couched in fairly mild terms, lest he be accused of injuring the party. This code of conduct has been the general tradition since the middle of the nineteenth century, and prime ministers have enforced it, in many instances, by dismissing members who have openly expressed their disagreements over the government's policy. Nevertheless, in recent years the lid of secrecy attendant upon cabinet decisions has occasionally blown off. In 1969 Home Secretary James Callaghan actively opposed, both in the Commons and in the press, a cabinet decision to push for legislation against wildcat strikes; in 1975 seven cabinet ministers actively campaigned for a no vote in the Common Market referendum while Wilson and the cabinet majority were urging a "yes" vote.

Ordinarily, however, the cabinet functions well as a team, largely because its members have known each other for a very long time. They have worked together in Parliament, they have dined together, and they have drunk together, developing friendships and antagonisms—both of which bind them together—that can come only after long and intimate association. Here they differ considerably from the American cabinet, which is usually composed of appointees who scarcely know each other or, for that matter, the president. One other reason why the British cabinet functions well as a team is that its members have roughly equal political status.

It has always been evident that the prime minister is more than first among equals. He represents both his party and the government in the view of the electorate. In the last analysis it is he who must decide who will and who will not be in the government, and (by setting the agenda) what will and what will not be discussed at cabinet meetings. Moreover, in some areas, such as foreign policy, where rapid decisions may be necessary, the prime minister can act almost alone; many of Anthony Eden's decisions at the time of the 1956 Suez crisis were made without consulting more than a few colleagues. Then, too, cabinet members will usually support the prime minister, despite sharp disagreements, on issues he considers crucial to his administration; Harold Wilson, for example, has received the acquiescence of his colleagues time and time again, whatever their reservations.

Nevertheless, many cabinet members are men of power within the party. The prime minister can override them only with difficulty, especially on issues that do not require immediate action; and if he can dismiss some colleagues with equanimity, there are others whom he cannot, without seriously endangering himself politically. Macmillan fired seven cabinet members in 1962 in an attempt to refurbish the government's image; the result was such that he damaged both himself and his party. While Macmillan's action is often cited as an example of the degree of power a prime minister can wield, there were some in his cabinet, R. A. Butler for one, whom he simply could not touch because of their own individual base of political support. It is not true, then, as some have tried to argue, that Britain has developed a quasi-presidential system; there are too many effective limitations on the prime minister's power.

When Parliament is in session, the cabinet meets about once or twice a week at 10 Downing Street, under the chairmanship of the prime minister. It may be called more frequently on special occasions, and often, depending upon the prime minister, a smaller number of cabinet cronies will gather together for a particular purpose. Winston Churchill liked to meet with his cabinet intimates in the small hours of the morning, for he tended to work most of the night and sleep until late in the day.

In general, the cabinet's agenda has been prepared some days in advance and circulated to other members by the cabinet secretariat. Until 1916 the cabinet lacked a staff for this purpose, nor were minutes of its meetings kept. In many cases, it was difficult for members to agree on precisely what had happened. As Lord Curzon recalled it:

No record whatever was kept of our proceedings, except the private and personal letter written by the Prime Minister to the Sovereign, the contents of which, of course, are never seen by anybody else. The Cabinet often had the very haziest notion as to what its decisions were. . . . Cases frequently arose when the matter was left so much in doubt that a Minister went away and acted upon what he thought was a decision which subsequently turned out to be no decision at all, or was repudiated by his colleagues.[5]

Today the cabinet is served by a knowledgeable group of civil servants. This secretariat not only helps the prime minister to draw up the agenda, it also insures that memoranda on specific items of cabinet business are circulated and that ministers who are not cabinet members will be available if issues affecting thier ministry are to be discussed. The secretariat occasionally serves as a fact-finding body as well.

The nature and content of cabinet meetings are never constant. They depend largely upon the issues at stake and the personal style of the ministers. In earlier days meetings could be very casual, and even today, when the pace of activity is far more hectic, cabinet meetings can be discursive. Churchill, for instance, liked to try ideas on his colleagues, thinking out loud before arriving at any conclusions; sometimes only the first point on the agenda was reached. Attlee followed the agenda carefully, cutting off ministers who took too much time. Macmillan seems to have run fairly tight cabinet meetings; he would introduce a subject and then let senior ministers have their say, indicating his own position only when summarizing their views. Wilson, on the other hand, generally opens the discussion by stating his views and then, after the members have voiced their own opinions, polls the ministers in order to obtain something like a formal vote. Of course, on most issues the cabinet rarely makes policy at its full sessions. Rather, its primary concern is to ratify, at the highest levels, proposals developed either by the departments, under the aegis of individual ministers, or the cabinet committees, which consist of three or four ministers and a small staff.

It is difficult to determine with any precision the origins of much parliamentary leg-

[5] Cited in Sydney D. Bailey, *British Parliamentary Democracy*, 2nd ed. (Boston: Houghton Mifflin Co., 1962), p. 177.

islation. One study of the major sources of policy concluded that of fifty-nine bills passed by Parliament, during its 1936–37 session, only nine were initiated by the cabinet. Twenty-seven were proposed by administrative departments or interdepartmental committees; nine resulted largely from the demands of pressure groups; three could be attributed to government policy significantly doctored by outside pressure; seven had their basis in departmental policy, similarly modified; two were derived from local-government associations and two originated with MP's. A review of pending legislation in *The Times of London* in October, 1962, listed only one measure derived from the Conservative party's 1959 election manifesto, and a later review of pending legislation for the 1963–64 session estimated that sixteen of the twenty-two bills being considered had been initiated by various departments.[6] It is not true, however, as some have argued, that cabinet government in Britain is being replaced by bureaucratic government, for the decisions that come through departments are, naturally enough, in line with the overall policy of the government. Should a minister, for example, initiate, or permit his department to initiate, a policy that runs counter to the government's general position, he will have to satisfy his cabinet colleagues on the viability of the new policy. The use of expert administrators has removed some legislative initiative from both the cabinet and Parliament, but the ultimate political controls still operate. To be sure, the amount of cabinet activity in the area of legislation depends upon the government in power—as well as upon how long the government has been in power. During the first majority Labor government (1945–50), which had committed itself to a program of nationalization, the cabinet was more significant as an instigator of legislation than were the Conservative cabinets that preceded or followed it. The studies for the early 1960's cited above reflect the fact that the govern-

ment in office was a Conservative government and that it had held office for more than a decade. The study for 1936–37 was also made during the tenure of Conservatives who, effectively, had held the reins of power for almost five years.

THE INDIVIDUAL MINISTER: The individual minister as a member of the cabinet has three major responsibilities. He must join with his colleagues in collective action, participate in Parliament as a member of the front bench, and—a full-time task in itself—supervise and take full responsibility for the activity of his ministry. The minister coming to a major department is faced with a vast bureaucratic apparatus run by civil servants who over a period of time have developed considerable competence. They cannot help but try to suggest what the "facts" are to a minister who wishes to make substantial changes; but provided he is strong-minded, he is by no means helpless in the face of the "facts." It was widely argued by the left wing of the Labor Party that just after World War II Ernest Bevin had become a victim of the Foreign Office bureaucracy when he was attacked for his "pro-Arab" attitude during the 1948 Israeli-Arab conflict; as we now know, however, the Foreign Office was divided, and Bevin's policies, right or wrong, were his own. For one "fact" is, of course, that government departments consist of individuals with different opinions, and a good civil servant will bring this diversity to the attention of the minister.[7]

Furthermore, the minister has probably specialized in the area of the department he is now administering, and is, in general terms, familiar with its work. If the party has been in power before, he may have had some experience in the department as a junior minister; moreover, the relative stability of British governments gives him time to acquire a deeper understanding of the prob-

---

[6] S. A. Walkland, *The Legislative Process in Great Britain* (London: George Allen and Unwin, 1968), pp. 22–23.

[7] The role of the British bureaucracy will be discussed again in Chapter 16; it should be noted here, however, that to an astonishing degree it has, on the whole, served various masters impartially.

lems of direct concern to him. And, finally, he has several outside sources of assistance. He chooses a principal private secretary from among the younger civil servants in the department, and the personal relationship between the two permits the latter to become wholly cognizant of his chief's attitudes and to provide extremely valuable assistance. Further, the minister brings with him a number of ambitious young MP's as parliamentary secretaries (who are considered junior ministers) and parliamentary private secretaries. These men aid him in his contacts with back-benchers, the public, and pressure groups; they take care of the paper work and also serve, quite tellingly, as an additional source of information.

The minister's parliamentary and departmental secretaries also brief him for his parliamentary work, and his parliamentary private secretary is with him at question time on the floor of Parliament. The cabinet minister's performance in Parliament is crucial. However good an administrator he may be, his reputation in the party is to a certain extent based upon his reputation in the house—and careers can be made and unmade on the floor.

One further onus a minister carries is the total responsibility for his department, its flaws as well as its perfections. Major blunders committed by the department have been committed by him. Though he may have been unaware of them, more than one minister has been forced out of the government because of the actions of his departmental civil servants.

4. HOUSE OF COMMONS: COMPOSITION

For most of the nineteenth century, parliamentary representatives were almost entirely men of property who had gone to the same schools and mixed with the same groups before entering Westminster. In a very important sense, Parliament was a club in which the members, in terms of immediate status and background, had more in common with each other than with the vast majority of their constituents.

Today, the Commons is a far more representative body (Table 13.1). In terms of occupation, businessmen are most heavily represented, followed by lawyers, teachers, and journalists. Workers and union officials account for about 10 percent of the membership. The total range of educational attainment is also represented. The Commons is thus much more representative of the nation than is the legislature of many nations, including that of the United States.[8] Nevertheless, these aggregate statistics conceal significant differences between the two major parties. Businessmen are more than three times as plentiful in the Conservative as in the Labor Parliamentary Party, while workers and teachers are almost absent from the Conservative benches. The higher social class background of Conservative MP's is also reflected in the fact that more than three quarters of them attended a public school; the figure for Labor MP's is roughly one-fifth. These occupational and class statistics mirror the types of supporters each party attracts, with one conspicuous exception: the Parliamentary Conservative Party gives no evidence of having derived about half its electoral support from the working class.

One of the persistent components of the British political culture is that members of Parliament are not professional politicians, but amateurs who are engaging in politics out of a sense of civic duty. Thus, members theoretically should not spend all of their time in Parliament, but are encouraged to cultivate outside interests, including those that pay money.

It is for this reason that after the Middle Ages the practice of communities paying members small salaries disappeared; agitation for official salaries, primarily as a

---

[8] The dominance of middle-class lawyers in the American Congress can be explained by the absence of a Socialist party, by the fact that politics has not been regarded as a particularly estimable career, and by the fact that business has been its own justification and source of prestige.

TABLE 13.1   BACKGROUNDS OF
MP'S, 1974

Occupation	Labor	Conservative	Liberal	Other
Barristers, solicitors	43	59	3	3
Journalists	27	22	1	1
Teachers	76	8	2	6
Doctors	6	3	–	–
Farmers, landowners	–	21	2	3
Company Directors	3	72	3	2
Managers, executives	29	20	1	2
Other businesses	31	50	1	6
Clerical, technical	17	1	–	–
Engineers	29	3	1	–
Manual workers	28	–	–	–
Trade union officials	19	–	–	–
Party officials	3	4	–	–
Schools				
Oxford	60	80	3	1
Cambridge	24	73	2	3
Other universities	106	56	2	13
Eton	1	48	2	–
Harrow	–	10	–	–
Other public schools	24	116	3	2
Grammar	161	58	6	11
Secondary or technical	27	4	–	1

Source: *The Times Guide to the House of Commons*, October, 1974 (London, 1974), p. 281.

means of encouraging working-class representation in Parliament, did not develop again until the nineteenth century. Regular salaries were not paid until 1910, when members were given £400 a year; as late as 1964, they received a salary of only £1,750 ($4,900) annually, although the leader of the opposition was allowed an additional £1,250 per year. In that year, however, salaries of the rank-and-file MP's were raised to £3,250 ($9,100) a year, and those of cabinet-rank ministers from £5,000 ($14,000) to £8,500 ($23,800). In 1971 MP salaries were raised to £4,500 ($13,500), and ministerial salaries were increased proportionately. Another modest raise was scheduled for 1975. Nevertheless, parliamentary salaries are still far from adequate; compare, for example, the legislative salaries of members of the U.S. House of Representatives, who receive $42,500 a year and substantial staff and travel allowances. Consequently, many people in Britain who might be drawn into politics are not, and a number of MP's have declined to stand for re-election or refused ministerial posts for the simple reason that they could not afford them.

Parliament is organized, therefore, to permit "gentlemen" to engage in other occupations. It convenes at 2:30 in the afternoon, and sessions, while getting longer, are still well under two hundred days a year. What this effectively means is that the nation's business is not receiving the attention that more and more people believe it should get. Even though parliamentarians can theoretically hold other jobs, increasing numbers are finding it difficult to do so and at the same time to represent their constituents conscientiously. As a consequence, pressure is mounting for increases in both salaries and services.

Because of governmental control over legislature, the importance of party labels, and the national focus of British politics, British MP's probably spend less time receiving delegations from interest groups or visits from constituents than do American, French, or German legislators. Yet most of them do hold "surgeries" in their constituencies during which they serve as combination social worker and legal adviser. MP's can and do intercede for constituents in cases where they feel that legal rights have been ignored or abrogated by administrative bodies. And parliamentarians can and do use the Commons to raise questions brought to their attention by the public.

Compared with the services and accommodations available to an American congressman, those for an ordinary MP are spartan: MP's do not have private offices or secretaries, or, in many cases, desks or phones. It is still difficult for them to get adequate typing or clerical assistance; many do hire secretary-typists, but they do so on their own salaries or by using funds supplied by outside groups such as trade unions. There is nothing comparable to the Legislative Reference Service of the Library of Congress, and the House of Commons library itself is quite inadequate. Members of the Commons are forced to talk to their constituents in the halls of the House, and a good many must handle their own correspondence. An American congressman is said to have collapsed with shock some years back on being shown the writing rooms and the Library of Commons full of men writing letters in longhand. Even the new government office building, planned to closely adjoin Westminster, is not expected to meet satisfactorily all the needs of the British MP.

5. THE HOUSE OF COMMONS: THE PARTIES

All members of the Commons belong to a political party, and, on the whole, their votes are party votes. Occasionally a maverick or two finds his way into Westminster, but the vast majority of MP's are there because the party helped them get there, and the party never allows a member to forget his debt of allegiance. Continual violation of party discipline can lead to sanctions of one kind or another, the ultimate one being withdrawal of the whip—expulsion from the parliamentary party.[9]

It would be wrong, however, to think that party cohesion in the House of Commons stems simply from pressure exerted by the party whips, or from expectations of the constituency party, or from fear that dissension will accrue to the benefit of the other party. Cohesion is also generated by ideological ties. This can be seen when "free" votes are taken, as in the case of private members' bills (i. e., public bills introduced by back-benchers); large majorities within both parties gravitate "naturally" to the position expected of persons with liberal or conservative persuasions.

THE CONSERVATIVE PARTY: In Parliament, as in the nation, the Conservative Party revolves about the party leader. He or she appoints the chief party whip and can have the whip withdrawn from recalcitrant party members. The leader also appoints his shadow cabinet, a group of MP's who theoretically will take office in his government should he be called upon to form one.

The key organization of the Conservative Parliamentary Party (CPP)—known as the "1922 Committee," from the year in which it was first organized—meets once a week for

[9] The whips in each party are MP's who serve many functions, the most important of which is securing membership attendance for crucial votes. The term comes from fox-hunting parlance of the eighteenth century, where the whipper-in kept the hounds from straying by using a small whip. The most pressing duties fall upon the chief whips, who are important party officials.

an hour or so to obtain a general sense of what Conservative MP's think about the issues before Parliament. The meetings are informal, and the committee operates without standing rules. When the party is in opposition, all members are eligible to attend, and the whips and members of the shadow cabinet do so, reporting results of the deliberations to the party leader, who attends only if he has a message to deliver. When the party is in power, neither ministers nor junior ministers attend. Either the whips or the committee chairman, usually a prominent MP, reports to the prime minister.

The leader is also advised on policy matters by a business committee, which consists of the principal officers of the parliamentary party's main functional committees. There are about twenty of these functional committees, each dealing with a major field of government policy—such as foreign affairs, defense, trade and industry, finance —and their purpose is to help members develop expertise in special areas. These committees also often try to influence ministers directly, and when disagreement occurs, the matter at issue may be referred to the 1922 Committee.

The ultimate disciplinary sanction of withdrawing the whip has been used only rarely by the Conservative Party leadership, although more independent-minded Conservative members have occasionally resigned from the party—refused the whip—in protest over particular policies. Thus, while the sanction is theoretically important, it is also one that the party leadership is chary about using. A somewhat larger number of MP's have not been readopted as candidates by their constituents as the result of their policy stands; yet even here there is a reluctance to act and it is usually only after repeated disagreements that the constituency party will finally withdraw its support from the party maverick. When the maverick's position appears to be in accord with "true" Conservative principles, the constituency party is more likely to praise than to punish him. In the early 1970's, for example, Conservative MP's who objected to their govern-

ment's policy on immigration as being too liberal had nothing to fear from their constituency supporters.

On the whole, the CPP is prepared to give a Conservative prime minister a good deal of leeway on the formulation of policy, provided, of course, it does not feel he is stepping too far out of line with its sense of what Conservative voters want and expect. Occasionally, back-benchers will bridle over an issue on ideological grounds, although this happens far less frequently than in the Labor Party. Occasionally, too, the Conservative Parliamentary Party will register displeasure when it believes it has not been brought fully into policy discussions on crucial issues. Nevertheless, Conservative MP's regard it as the function of the leader to lead, and their definition of good leadership is primarily a pragmatic one: good leadership can be estimated by the party's standing among the voters. That thirty-nine Conservative MP's broke ranks in 1971 and voted against the Heath government's bill for entry into the Common Market—a highly unusual event—can be partly explained by the fact that this policy was clearly not popular with the British public.

THE LABOR PARTY: The organization of the Labor Party in Parliament differs somewhat from that of the Conservative. The differences are primarily attributable to the origin of the two parties: the Labor Party began its life outside Parliament as a mass, ideological party committed to "democratic" procedures, whereas the Conservatives started out as an aristocratic faction with close ties to traditional conceptions of hierarchy and the establishment.

The Parliamentary Labor Party (PLP) consists of all Labor members of the House of Commons and the House of Lords, although the latter do not vote on questions of special concern to the lower house. At the beginning of each session, the PLP elects a party leader, deputy party leader, and, since 1972, a PLP chairman. It also elects the chief party whip and a parliamentary committee of twelve members. Since 1955 the party leader has had the authority to appoint additional MP's, up to a total of thirty-nine, to act as a shadow cabinet and to sit on the front bench. Finally, the Labor Party has established numerous committees for back-benchers to encourage specialized knowledge in a particular area of government.

The PLP operates according to a set of standing orders, among them provisions for disciplining members who violate parliamentary party decisions. These measures, which include withdrawal of the whip, have been suspended from time to time to encourage voluntary agreement, but the continued existence of factionalism has always led to their reimposition in one form or another. As in the Conservative Party, members can abstain on certain issues that involve a "matter of conscience."

The PLP as a unit usually meets several times a month, and the parliamentary committee, when the party is in opposition, on the average of once a week to discuss the program of the coming week. Important issues are decided by a formal vote. The party leader and members of the shadow cabinet attend meetings of the parliamentary party, although they do so less frequently when Labor is in office than when it is in opposition. When in office, the PLP establishes a small consultative committee to serve as liaison between the cabinet and the party in Parliament.

The Labor Party's specialized committees have always offered party members the opportunity to become fairly expert on particular subjects, but their most important contributions have been made when the party is in office, and a complicated though informal relationship of mutual assistance develops between ministers and the respective committees.

To a far greater extent than among the Conservatives, informal groupings tend to proliferate in the party. Trade unionists, for example, often meet together to discuss common problems. In a more controversial vein, MP's to the left of the leadership have a tendency to form groups to push programs they like: the Keep Left group of the late 1940's, the Bevanite group of the early and middle 1950's, and the Victory for Socialism group of the late 1950's and early 1960's. Since 1964 the Tribune Group has been the organizational axis for the left wing of the party. Time and again the leadership has demanded the dissolution of such groups, believing them to hamper party unity; however, they always manage to surface again, under another name, a few years later.

In theory, the Labor prime minister takes his parliamentary party completely within his confidence; in practice, relations between the two have always been rather uncertain. The ideological commitment of many PLP members automatically limits the Labor prime minister's room for maneuver more than that of his Conservative counterpart. Also, many Labor MP's are more inclined than their Conservative colleagues to offer at least verbal resistance to the prime minister, even on issues on which they know he commands the support of the voters, simply because they believe his policies are wrong. While in the last analysis they may toe the line because they know a constantly divided party is likely to fare less well at the polls, the principle of harmony has never stayed the PLP's rather fractious tendencies.

The problems facing the prime minister have become more troublesome as the party has moved away from its traditional ideological moorings, and as the economic problems facing all governments have become more intractable. This situation also results from the increase in the numbers of Labor MP's who come from middle-class backgrounds and have had university training. Nearly 60 percent of the Labor MP's elected in the fall of 1974 were university graduates; workers accounted for only 9 percent, a decline of 28 percentage points since 1951. The older workingman, who "retired" to political office, is being replaced by a younger man who intends to pursue a political career and who consequently desires to participate in party decision-making. In 1968 twenty-three Labor MP's voted with Conservatives against Wilson's bill to control wages and prices; in 1969 the Wilson government was

forced to drop its fairly mild legislative proposals to curb wildcat strikes; and in 1971,
sixty-nine MP's, including Deputy Leader
Hugh Jenkins, defied party policy by voting
in favor of Britain's entry into the Common
Market.

6. THE HOUSE OF COMMONS:
TRADITIONS

As it is with the whole pattern of British
parliamentary government, much of the
Commons' procedure is still governed by hallowed tradition. When a new parliament
opens, it is the monarch and not the government of the day that presents the policy of
the government. This tradition finds its
source in the original raison d'être of Parliament—a body called together by the king to
consider his proposals. Members of the
Commons are summoned to hear the speech
from the throne, delivered in the chamber of
the House of Lords, by the Gentleman Usher
of the Black Rod, an office that dates back
to Henry VIII. Upon returning to their
own chamber, members of Commons give
the first reading to a Bill for the Better
Suppressing of Clandestine Outlawries, a
symbolic means of asserting once again the
right of Parliament to discuss grievances—
that is, legislation—before considering the
king's recommendations. The historical tradition of which the Commons is a part per-
vades Westminster Palace itself. For five
centuries the palace was the chief residence
of the king, and it has continued to serve as
a meeting place for both houses of Parliament even though this original justification
has long since vanished. When evening falls
and light in the Parliament is needed, the request is still: "Mr. Speaker, I call for can-
dles."

The great fire of 1834 destroyed most of
the palace buildings, and the Commons itself
was severely damaged during World War II.
When it was rebuilt, the original structure
of the Commons chamber—an oblong room,
small for its purpose, in which members sat
facing each other in two phalanxes of rising
benches—was retained despite many incon-
veniences. At the time, Winston Churchill
justified the retention on the ground that
the shape furthered a two-party system and
that both the size and the shape encouraged
easy exchange rather than harangue. While
there is something to be said for his argument, one suspects that the real motivation
lay in tradition for the sake of tradition.

In any event, today the House can seat
fewer than two-thirds of its members, even
providing them with neither desks nor
chairs. It measures 68 by 45 feet—less than
one-fourth the size of the U.S. House of
Representatives, which contains more than a
hundred fewer members. MP's face each
other on two sets of long benches, graded
upward, one on each side of the speaker.
This arrangement stands in marked contrast
to the semicircular shape of most legislative
chambers; members speak from their benches to each other, and the auditorium atmosphere that occurs in many chambers when
the speaker talks from a rostrum is absent.
To the right of the speaker sit the government and their supporters, ministers on the
front bench and rank-and-file members
trouped behind them. On the left side sit
the opposition, again with the leaders of the
party on the front benches and the same
grouping to the rear. When important
debates are held, the chamber is extremely
crowded because six hundred-odd persons
must then squeeze into a space designed to
hold 346. It may be true that a quality of
added excitement accrues, just as it is possible that the chamber's small size and shape
lend themselves to a more discursive exchange than might otherwise be the case.

The rules of debate in the Commons require that a member who wishes to speak
rise in his seat and, if male, have his head
uncovered. All members are required to address the chair, and to refer to other members not by their names but by a standard
circumlocution, such as "My right honorable
friend the Home Secretary." New members
are expected to remain fairly silent, though
each at some time does make a maiden
speech, theoretically on a noncontroversial

FIGURE 13.1   FLOOR PLAN OF THE HOUSE OF COMMONS

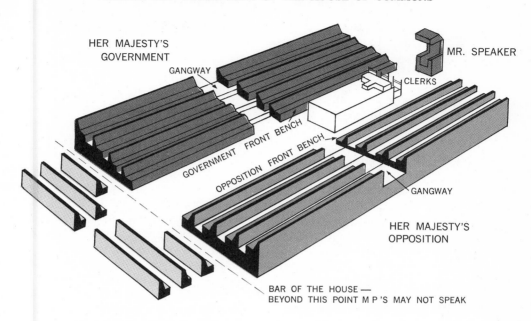

subject, which inevitably wins warm congratulations.

By long-established custom, too, members of Parliament are prohibited from using words calculated to incite a colleague, such as calling him "cowardly," "bloodthirsty," or "mendacious." Never should one MP say of another that he has not kept his word. These restrictions have taken some of the sting out of debates, but they have not prevented members from making caustic remarks about their fellow MP's. Harold Wilson, for instance, said of Harold Macmillan:

The right honourable gentleman is the only statesman of this century to claim . . . to embody all that is best in both Disraeli and Gladstone. In fact, of course, he is wrong. He has inherited the streak of charlatanry in Disraeli without his vision and the self-righteousness of Gladstone without his dedication to principle.[10]

Anthony Eden was described by one Labor MP during the Suez disaster as "an overripe banana, yellow outside, squishy in." Churchill once said of Attlee that he was "a

modest man with plenty to be modest about," and called Aneurin Bevan "a squalid nuisance." All in all, invective is kept within reasonable bounds, and the MP most respected is one who can insult cleverly, with a neat turn of phrase.

Tart tongues aside, the House does retain something of the quality of the aristocratic club it once was. This has many advantages: it can be argued that the continuance of tradition inspires a sense of history in MP's; that it smooths the cutting edges of their radicalism and blurs the lines of party conflict; and that the pageantry of Parliament and its emphasis on wit and behavior serve certain expressive needs for MP's, bolstering their feelings of importance and softening the hostilities that naturally materialize. On the other hand, radicals like Bevan have argued that this very blurring reinforces the establishment and inhibits that collision of political forces that produces necessary social changes. One disgruntled MP has declared that the rituals and rules in the Commons breed

a sense of anxiety and inferiority in people who don't know the rules. . . . It's

10 *Hansard Parliamentary Debates* 594 (Nov. 3, 1958): 628.

just like a public school: and that's why La-
bor MP's are overawed by it—because they
feel that only the Tory MP's know what a
public school is like.

7. THE HOUSE OF COMMONS AT WORK

The two-party system and cabinet government in Britain have made the organization of parliamentary business a comparatively simple matter—whatever current critics of Parliament may believe. That the issues dividing British society have not been, for the most part, extremely deep has allowed easy relationships to exist between members of the parties that many other political systems have not experienced, and the continued acceptance of certain cultural styles that are part of the national heritage has given the conduct of parliamentary business a uniquely British flavor.

THE STRUCTURE OF AUTHORITY: The organization of the Commons is the purview of two offices: the speaker of the House and the whips. The speaker, unlike speakers of most legislatures, is a man who has divested himself of party label when he assumes the post and who has, provided he discharges his duties acceptably, a lifetime tenure. Like speakers of most legislatures, he enforces the rules of debate, recognizes members who wish to speak from the floor, and, in general, is responsible for the conduct of parliamentary business. Both his responsibility and his authority are great, for his rulings and his ability to determine who should speak and when can have considerable effect upon the course of debate. Even so, the successful operation of the House as an ongoing body is contingent upon his ability to maintain a reputation for impartiality.

Once elected, the speaker in the Commons has a rather easy time of it. The agenda of parliamentary business is arranged in advance by the parties, and he has only to carry out their decisions. The parties themselves readily reach accord on the agenda because, given the discipline of the majority party, everyone knows it can set any legislative pace it wishes. The labors of the speak-er are further lightened because, whatever the disagreements of the two parties, both share a common belief in the importance of preserving certain rules of the game. It was not always thus, of course. When Charles I ordered his man, Speaker Charles Finch, to adjourn the House, Finch was held forcibly in place by some members, the doors were locked, and the House passed three resolutions the king had not wanted discussed. In 1929 several radical members of the Labor Party attempted to steal the speaker's mace so that the results of a vote suspending one of their group from Parliament for disobeying him could not be tabulated. During the Suez crisis, too, debate waxed so bitter that, at times, the speaker almost lost control and members came close to exchanging blows. The Common Market debate in 1971 featured similar riotous behavior.

The whips are party officials responsible for informing members about parliamentary business for the coming week, and for reminding them of their voting and attendance responsibilities. Among other duties, whips supply lists for committee memberships, and arrange for pairing of members. Each party has a chief whip and several assistant whips. The opposition whips are not paid, but governmental whips are given official titles, dating from some now forgotten time, that enable them to receive salaries. The government's chief whip is usually a member of the cabinet and serves as a source of communication between back-benchers and the prime minister. He and the chief whip of the opposition constitute the "usual channels" through which the organization of weekly business is decided, including the amount of time to be permitted for debate. The chores of assistant whips are much less significant.

Every Friday, the whips send all party members a written notice, also called a whip, outlining the program for the following week. The importance of a particular event is indicated by the wording: "Your attendance is requested" or "Your attendance is particularly requested," as well as by the underlining of the phrases. One line indicates that the matter is not of extreme urgency,

FIGURE 13.2 A TYPICAL WHIP IN THE HOUSE OF COMMONS

```
                    William Whiteley, M.P.
                      House of Commons

On Monday, 27 October, 1947, the House will meet
   at 2-30 p.m.

     Continuation of the General debate on the
     Address.
     Discussion of Germany until 8-30 p.m., then
     Opposition Amendment on Imperial Security.
     (Mr. J. P. L. Thomas).

     YOUR ATTENDANCE AT 3-30 p.m. AND THROUGHOUT THE
     SITTING IS REQUESTED.  A DIVISION WILL TAKE
     PLACE AT 11 p.m.

On Tuesday, 28th October, the House will meet at
   2-30 p.m.

     Debate on the Address.
     Opposition Amendment.

     YOUR ATTENDANCE AT 3-30 p.m. AND THROUGHOUT THE
     SITTING IS REQUESTED.

On Wednesday, 29th October, the House will meet at
   2-30 p.m.

     Conclusion of the debate on the Address.
     Opposition Amendment.

     YOUR ATTENDANCE AT 3-30 p.m. AND THROUGHOUT THE
     SITTING IS PARTICULARLY REQUESTED.  A MOST
     IMPORTANT DIVISION OR DIVISIONS WILL TAKE PLACE.

On Thursday, 30th October, the House will meet at
   2-30 p.m.

     Consideration of the Reports from the Committee
     of Privileges relating to the cases of the
     Hon. Members for Gravesend (Mr. Garry Allighan)
     and Doncaster (Mr. Evelyn Walkden).

     YOUR ATTENDANCE AT 3-30 p.m. AND THROUGHOUT THE
     SITTING IS REQUESTED.  THERE WILL BE A FREE
     VOTE OF THE HOUSE.

On Friday, 31st October, the House will meet at
   11 a.m.

     Expiring Laws Bill; Committee and remaining
     stages.
     Jersey and Guernsey (Financial and
     Provisions) Bill; 2nd Reading.
     Motions to approve the Fish Sales (Charges)
     Order and the 4 Purchase Tax Orders on the
     Paper.

     YOUR ATTENDANCE AT 11 a.m. AND THROUGHOUT THE
     SITTING IS REQUESTED.

Note.

During the week it is hoped to consider the Motion
relating to the Parliamentary Electors (War-Time
Registration) Act, 1944.
A Prayer has been tabled for consideration on
Tuesday.
```

Source: Herbert Morrison, *Government and Parliament* (Oxford: Oxford University Press, 1954), pp. 110–111. Reprinted by permission of the publisher.

two indicate a more important item of business, and three lines imply that the member had better be present unless he is able to offer an extremely good excuse.

THE ORDER OF BUSINESS: Today, the work of the Commons consists largely of discussing government measures, and it is the government, supported by the weight of its majority, that, in the last analysis, determines in what order these measures will be considered. Of course, the government is always careful to try to reach an equitable arrangement with the opposition, through the usual channels, on the order of parliamentary business. It remains extremely sensitive to any charge that it may have failed to allow the opposition sufficient time to discuss the major issues of public policy.

An average session of the Commons may witness the introduction of anywhere from seventy-five to a hundred major proposals for legislation. Of these, 90 to 100 percent will be introduced by the government itself, and 97 to 100 percent of them will be enacted into law, generally without notable changes. The extent to which the legislative program is planned by the government still hinges, to a large degree, upon circumstances, including which party is in power. For example, the first Labor government after World War II monopolized Parliament's time; during the years 1945 to 1948, not a single private member's bill was introduced.

Sessions of Parliament are usually organized in such a fashion as to permit ample discussion of the government's major policies. These policies become palpable not only in debate on particular bills, but also on such occasions as the Speech from the Throne, and during parliamentary consideration of appropriations. The amount of discussion time to be allotted is settled in advance by the party leaders who also, in the case of most policy issues, agree upon speakers. These agreements are not always completely satisfactory; the opposition occasionally believes that it has not been provided with adequate time to assess the government's proposal. Nevertheless, compared with other parliaments, the problems of getting legislation considered and enacted are handled with comparative dispatch—partly because the government, knowing it has the votes to push through its program, can afford to be generous; partly because it is acutely aware that riding roughshod over the opposition would injure it politically. The opposition, on the other hand, knows that attempts to inhibit legislative activity beyond a reasonable point will evoke public criticism. But perhaps the overriding reason is simply that both sides are convinced that the government should always be permitted to carry out its policies.

This would not be so, of course, if the community were split by fundamental conflicts, as it was in the latter part of the nineteenth century. At that time, Irish Nationalists in Parliament filibustered again and again in an attempt to block the normal operation of business. A little later, during the discussion of the Finance Bill of 1909, the Conservatives did exactly the same thing. These actions resulted in a number of standing orders, or rules of procedure, designed to limit debate: the kangaroo, by which a committee chairman selects certain amendments for discussion and leaps over others; the guillotine, by which the House of Commons sets a time limit on the discussion of certain sections of a bill; and simple cloture, by which debate is cut off after an MP calls for a vote. These rules were instituted because some members of Parliament did not accept the broad, established agreements on how Parliament should function; they were adopted because most members did. These standing orders are rarely used today, except in consultation with the opposition; for the most part, Parliament operates within a general consensus as to what kinds of behavior are legitimate.

LEGISLATING: About 75 percent of the time of the House of Commons is taken up with government-sponsored "public bills" and routine financial business. A public bill is a proposed law that affects the entire nation; as previously indicated, it may originate from several sources—the party, a royal commission report, an investigation or recommendation by a particular ministry, or an interest group such as the Trades Union Congress. In any event, before the public bill is presented to the Commons, it must pass through many hands. Even if the legislation does not originate in a ministry, the ministry concerned reviews its terms and makes recommendations, suggestions, and amendments.

The bill is also assessed by any interest group it is likely to affect. Every government engages in prior consultation with private organizations to secure their approval of a public bill, wherever possible; if the group withholds its complete endorsement, it is at least offered the opportunity to suggest any modifications that do not drastically change its substance. It is hoped that any opposition to the bill outside Parliament will, in this way, be reduced. Governments are also interested in obtaining whatever information the group has to offer on the subject of the law under consideration. On the whole, the British have never felt that distrust of "interests" so common to the American experience; in fact, almost every government since the turn of the century has encouraged the formation of nationally organized interest groups so that it can, when the occasion arises, readily consult with knowledgeable persons in the various sectors of the community.

After a proposed public bill wins cabinet approval, it is given to what is called the Parliamentary Counsel for drafting. The counsel office is in the Treasury, and is manned by highly expert civil servants with legal training, whose job is not only to make sure that the wording of the bill is precise, but also to check and recheck such matters as phraseology and all possible implications of the proposal's legal strictures; important pieces of legislation go through as many as twenty to twenty-five drafts before being submitted to the house.

All bills introduced into the house receive three readings; the first which is simply a formality, is by title only. Publication of the complete bill follows soon after. The bill is not actually read during the second and third "readings"; it is printed and distributed to members. The second reading is held about two weeks after the first, with debate lasting about a day or two. At this time the general principles of the bill are aired. If the bill is approved in principle by members of the Commons, it is sent to either a standing committee, a select committee, or, in matters of "constitutional importance," to a Committee of the Whole house. The third reading occurs after the bill returns from committee and all amendments to it have been debated and approved or rejected (report stage); it is, in short, a discussion of the bill in its final form before the house takes a vote on it. Both the discussion and the vote at this point are normally pro forma; the vote after debate on the second reading usually tells the story as to whether or not the bill will be approved by the Commons.

As noted earlier, the House of Commons lacks the specialized standing committees that have developed in the American, German, and French legislatures. Specialized select committees did spring up during the reign of Elizabeth I and continued to be created even during the nineteenth century, but they never attained permanent status because of the rise of disciplined parties and cabinet government. Today, there are standing committees consisting of from twenty to fifty members appointed to them in proportion to the party's strength in the Commons and on the basis of their interest in the subject matter of the legislation then under consideration by the committee. Decisions on committee membership are made by the speaker, assisted by his Committee on Selection, in consultation with party whips. Theoretically, a standing committee is permanent, while a select committee is appointed for a specific purpose and dissolved after its task has been accomplished. In practice, however, there is nothing permanent about a standing committee either, except possibly its name. The composition of all standing committees (with the exception of the two dealing with laws for Scotland and Wales) changes with the legislation under consideration.

A Committee of the Whole House is simply the House itself, operating as a committee under more flexible procedures and presided over by a chairman instead of the speaker. This committee dates from the seventeenth century, when it was used as a device to reduce royal influence during the discussion of crucial issues. At the time the speaker of the House served at the pleasure of the king; when a Committee of the Whole House was formed, the speaker simply left the chamber and thus could not report the content of debates to the monarch. In recent years the device has been used infrequently and, until 1967, primarily during the consideration of finance bills.

British standing committees operate quite differently from those in the United States and in various European legislatures. They never conduct hearings with outside witnesses, and they cannot suppress bills or hold them up in any way. Rather, their function is to take a bill after the Commons has approved it on second reading, and go over it line by line to consider amendments that can then be recommended to the Commons. When a bill leaves the committee, it enters the report stage; it is circulated to all members of the House and then debated on the floor. Debate and votes during the report stage deal entirely with proposed amendments to the legislation. The third reading is a final review of the amended legislation. The general principles of the amended bill are debated, and a vote of the MP's is taken. If it is approved, the bill is sent to the House of Lords and, when the Lords concur, to the monarch for royal assent.

In terms of the amount of time they consume, the most important public bills considered by the House each session are those relating to finance. The financial year begins April 1 with a budget statement by the chancellor of the exchequer outlining both estimated expenditure and the ways and means of meeting it. Financial bills are the result of several months' work, during which the Treasury and the cabinet, in consultation with the specialized agencies of the government, have collected the budget requests of all departments and related them to what they deem to be the general needs of the economy. Because it is obvious that the resolutions that comprise the financial program will pass into law almost as introduced, debate on the measures, which extends over several months, is primarily concerned with issues of public policy rather than with a detailed examination of specific debits and credits. As compared with the procedures in the American Congress, there are no specialized committees to scrutinize the financial proposals. Nor is there, on the other hand, the possibility of the outbreak of wild confusion over budgetary matters that so often, as in the United States, results in a hodge-podge of financial legislation only loosely related to the government's initial requests or needs. Traditionally, financial legislation was not even sent to a standing committee for detailed consideration. Rather, the committee stage was conducted by a Committee of the Whole House. In 1967, however, the Commons changed its procedures; finance bills are now considered by a standing committee of fifty whose sessions may be attended by the chancellor of the exchequer or other interested ministers. Here individual items can be examined more easily than they could before the house as a whole.

THE OPPOSITION AND THE POWER OF PARLIAMENT: Thus far, the emphasis of this chapter has been upon the predominant role of the government in the legislative process; and, indeed, compared with other parliamentary systems, it is the British executive—the cabinet and the prime minister—that is the most significant part of that process. Nevertheless, despite all the current talk about the decline of Parliament, the House of Commons continues to perform an important role.[11] It is the voice box for all varieties of opinion within the nation; it is also the arena in which the government and the opposi-

tion engage in continual debate, each striving to convince not only the other but the national electorate of the rightness of its position. When the opposition scores points in the debate, government leaders are anxious to deal with them. They may do so by stating their own case more effectively, by accepting opposition amendments to legislation, or by introducing amendments of their own that take opposition arguments into account. Whichever course it follows, the government's action is based partly on public opinion and partly on the degree of influence exercised by the opposition.

The Commonwealth Immigration Act of 1962, for example, was one of a series of legislative moves to curb immigration from the West Indies, India, and Pakistan. The Conservative government's rather mild bill was quite popular with the electorate, which most likely would have supported an even stronger measure. The Labor Party, however, was bitterly opposed at that time to any restrictions whatsoever, and their arguments persuaded the Conservatives to act more circumspectly than they might otherwise have done. (Ironically, the Labor Party, after it returned to power, passed far more stringent legislation on immigration.) Again, in 1963, the Conservatives reacted very quickly after the Labor opposition had used a series of rent scandals to attack earlier legislation freeing rents from control; almost immediately, the government appointed committees to investigate the situation and to consider modifications of the law. The Labor government in 1969 was forced to withdraw its reform plan for the House of Lords for fear that the plan would be defeated; opposition came from a segment of the Labor Party that believed the proposal did not go far enough and from Conservative Party members who either felt it went too far or were quite content to embarrass the government on a very touchy issue.

The influence of Parliament as an institution is also apparent from the importance of legislation introduced by back-benchers, that is, private members' bills; these bills are not

[11] The best treatment of parliamentary influence is to be found in Ronald Butt, *The Power of Parliament* (London: Constable & Co., 1967). For a contrary view see John P. Mackintosh, *The British Cabinet*, 2nd ed. (London; Stevens & Sons, 1968).

to be confused with private bills, which have a personal or local application only and originate mainly with local authorities.

Quite apart from its influence in the legislative process, the opposition party in the House of Commons is continually challenging the government to defend its policies. With the press observing from its place in the gallery above the speaker's chair, the challenges and the replies permit the public to become informed on the issues and to evaluate the government's performance. In addition to a question period, motions for adjournment at the end of the day's session provide the opposition—and government back-benchers as well—with purposefully designed opportunities to question and to challenge. On occasions of crisis, special sessions of Parliament may be called simply to debate government policy. In 1971, for example, a special session was held to debate the situation in Northern Ireland.

8. PARLIAMENT: INVESTIGATING AND CONTROLLING

The decline of parliamentary power in decision-making can, as we have just noted, be exaggerated. True, the House of Commons no longer legislates in the sense that it did for a short time in the late eighteenth and nineteenth centuries; nor does Parliament really overturn governments. And without question, the principal loci of power and authority are to be found in the majority party, the government, and the prime minister. Yet despite the ties of party and the power of the government, the Commons retains a sense of being a group that can and does transcend party lines and influence policy. It is this sense—of identity, of history, of importance—that today leads Parliament to fulfill, aside from its legitimizing function, the roles of critic, educator, and public spokesman. These roles are closely related. Parliamentary debates over legislation, the questioning of government policy by MP's, and the use of legislative devices for investigating government actions or social prob-

lems allow individuals and interest groups to express their views in the most important public forum in the nation. Further, they will allow Parliament the opportunity to keep tabs on government operations and to serve as part of the process by which the public is presented with alternative courses of action.

THE QUESTION PERIOD: Perhaps the most spectacular instrument used for these ends is the parliamentary question period, which lasts for about an hour at the beginning of proceedings in the Commons. The practice dates from the early nineteenth century, but it did not really develop until the twentieth, when the combination of disciplined parties and the government's monopoly of parliamentary time began to inhibit seriously the back-bencher's chances of participating in the initiation of policy. During this period, from Monday through Thursday, members receive oral answers to their questions on a wide range of matters that cannot effectively be handled in debate; usually these involve departmental policies in pursuance of a law and individual or group grievances. The questions either seek information or press for action, and supplementary questions arising out of the original answer may be allowed at the discretion of the speaker. The person to whom the question is addressed must be officially responsible for the subject matter; ministers, for instance, have refused to answer certain questions having to do with nationalized industries, which are operated as quasi-independent public corporations.

The questions and the supplementaries can provide some painful moments for ministers and their departments; but they can also provide the stimulus for important policy changes. A well-known case of the 1920's is described by Ivor Jennings as follows:

On 17 May 1928, Mr. T. Johnston, by private notice, asked the Home Secretary "whether he was aware that on Tuesday, the 15th of May, about 1:50 p. m., two police officers called at the place of business of Miss

Savidge, and without affording her any opportunity of communicating with her parents or legal advisers . . . conveyed her to Scotland Yard, and that there she was questioned by two police officers for a period exceeding five hours; and whether such action was authorized by the right hon. gentleman in connection with his inquiry into the Sir Leo Money Case?" The Home Secretary returned a soft answer, giving some information, and stating that he was making inquiries. Further questions followed, producing a telephoned message from Scotland Yard which, being read by the minister, was interrupted with cries of "Shame!" At the end of the questions Mr. Johnston moved the adjournment of the House. . . . A debate took place the same evening . . . (and) the Home Secretary . . . consented to a public inquiry. The inquiry resulted in some criticism of the police, and a Royal Commission then examined the whole question of police powers and practice.[12]

More recently charges by a daily newspaper in 1967 that private outgoing and incoming cables were being scrutinized by the British security services prompted a storm of questions to the prime minister. Wilson tried to fudge the issue, but after a series of supplementary questions he was forced to concede the need for an impartial inquiry into the allegations.

Most questions do not produce quite such dramatic results. In fact, most questions are handled through written answers, and most complaints through private negotiations. Nevertheless, questions can be telling; they can also serve as an opportunity for an ambitious—or resentful—MP to have his say and, if he is clever enough into the bargain, to score a point. Further, they mollify the back-bencher with a feeling of having some dialectic weapons at his disposal, thus bolstering both pride in the House and self-esteem.

COMMITTEES AND THE ADMINISTRATION: It is not quite accurate to say that the British Parliament has no specialized committees. The Commons has from time to time created select committees to investigate special matters of a factual nature, although for the most part these have lacked adequate staffs and the power to compel testimony. Again, governments have been loath to appoint committees because of their fear that party discipline might be subverted: there has been a preference for other methods of gathering information, chief among them the research and investigation conducted by the ministers. Even so, demands for alternate sources of parliamentary information have become more and more frequent, and in recent years three new select committees have been created. In 1956 the House of Commons created a quasi-permanent select committee on nationalized industries; pressure for creating the committee stemmed from the fact that nationalized industries are more or less independent, with the result that ministers can refuse to answer questions about their operations. Further, the problem of evaluating the efficiency of those operations is sufficiently complex to inhibit Parliament's effective control over them without professional assistance. The committee was given the power of subpoena and was authorized to employ a small staff. To date it has served a useful function, bringing to light and evaluating important information that might not otherwise have been available.

In January of 1967 the House established two more select committees: one to deal with the general problems of science and technology, the other to review agricultural problems. Both committees were also given the power to subpoena persons and records and to recruit small staffs. The creation of these two committees was regarded as an experiment that, if successful, would lead to the appointment of a number of other committees paralleling the government's departments. The purview of the science and technology committee crossed departmental lines, but it has continued to work without arousing much controversy; the agricultural committee, however, quickly came into direct conflict with the ministry it was to oversee.

---

[12] Ivor Jennings, *Parliament*, 2nd ed. (New York: Cambridge University Press, 1957), p. 105.

The upshot was that the agriculture minister and various civil servants complained about increased workloads and excessive interference, and after an extensive battle the committee was disbanded in 1969. At the same time, however, several other select committees were created, including one on race relations.

Other select committees that have been in existence for some time and oversee the expenditure of public funds are the public accounts and the estimates committees. Both are nonpartisan. The chairman of the accounts committee, which is concerned with insuring that money is spent for authorized purposes only, is usually a prominent member of the opposition. The estimates committee engages in constant spot checks on expenditures in an attempt to determine whether government economies can be made. Since both groups have the power of subpoena, they resemble in some ways the legislative committees of the American Congress and are respected by the bureaucracy.

The House of Commons and the House of Lords have each created a select committee on statutory instruments. Both were formed in response to Parliament's tendency to legislate in only the most general terms, thus granting to the government and bureaucracy the authority to make legal policy through the issuance of administrative decrees in the form of statutory instruments. The annual number of such decrees increased from 986 in 1906 to more than 2,000 a year in the 1960's, and it became obvious that the instruments are, in fact, a form of legislation. As of now, all decrees must lie before Parliament for forty days, during which time a member may move a "prayer" to annul the instrument. The function of the two committees is to draw the attention of their houses to an instrument if it believes that the Parliament as a whole may wish to consider its legality. Many critics, however, complain that only a small proportion of the decrees issued receive adequate attention.

THE PARLIAMENTARY COMMISSIONER: Though MP's used the Commons to raise questions brought to their attention by the public, the increasing influence of administrative agencies and tribunals in the day-to-day life of British citizens led to the creation in 1967 of a parliamentary commissioner to deal with citizens' complaints against administrators.

The commissioner is an officer of Parliament and can act only on complaints referred to him by MP's. He has no executive power, and his jurisdiction extends solely to central ministries; he has no authority to investigate local officials or the nationalized industries. He informs the MP who asked his intercession in the disposition of cases, and he is expected to submit annual and special reports to a parliamentary committee. Thus far the influence of the new post has been marginal; indeed, in one recent case the foreign office rejected a commissioner's report and refused to allow the parliamentary committee to investigate the matter further.

9. THOSE DIGNIFIED ASPECTS

THE HOUSE OF LORDS: Until 1911 the House of Lords and the House of Commons were theoretically coequal. In actuality, the fact that the prime minister was being chosen more and more often from the House of Commons, coupled with the fact that his authority depended upon that body, was concrete evidence of what little significant power the Lords had. Thus Bagehot, in his classic *The English Constitution*, first published in 1867, could refer to both the monarchy and, by implication, the House of Lords as well, as being those "dignified" aspects of British government, as opposed to the meaningful, "efficient" aspects.

When the Liberal government came to power in 1906, it embarked upon a broad program of social reform—and the Lords bridled. Their feeling was that some of the legislation threatened the foundations of the realm, and they vetoed some eighteen bills. That, as things turned out, was their last demonstration of any real power. The fight between the Liberals and the Lords, which was fundamentally a fight over how much power the Lords should have, came to a climax in 1909 and extended over a two-year period. Finally, the Lords, under threat by the king to produce a less conservative majority by creating new peers, acquiesced in their own burial. The Parliament Act of 1911 declared that henceforth the House of Lords would have only the power to delay legislation—and for no more than thirty days on financial legislation and no more than three years on other matters. In 1949 the Lords' power to delay on nonfinancial legislation was cut to one year by the Labor Party, which, during the 1930's, had threatened to abolish the House of Lords altogether.

The Conservative Party attempted in 1958 to bolster the prestige of the House of Lords. With the thought, perhaps, of eventually adding to the Lords' power, the Macmillan government initiated, and Parliament enacted, legislation for the creation of life peers—men and women who would be rewarded for public service by being given titles and seats in the house, but who could not pass their titles to their heirs. At about the same time, all peers were granted a small allowance for each day of attendance. The creation of life peers has not really changed the composition of the House of Lords; the fact is that most of them would probably have been granted hereditary peerages in any event. About half the Lords' membership consists of peers of the first creation, that is, persons granted peerages for outstanding service. In 1963, as the result of the desire of one labor MP to continue serving in the Commons, legislation was passed allowing individuals to renounce their titles; the most important effect of the law was to permit Lord Home to serve in the House of Commons as prime minister. A new landmark was passed in 1968 when the Labor government introduced legislation depriving hereditary peers of the right to vote in the House of Lords. The bill called for the House to consist essentially of life peers

chosen by the government in office. The proposal had to be withdrawn in 1969 because of the growing weakness of the Wilson government, but the fact that it was introduced is a clear indication that the days of the House of Lords in its present form are numbered. Neither Wilson nor Heath has appointed a single hereditary peer.

Today the real power of the House of Lords is almost entirely gone. Even its limited delaying prerogative has been used sparingly. Although there are approximately 950 persons eligible to sit in the Lords, those present usually average only about 100, and no more than 60 to 70 are regular attenders. To limit the possibility of the regulars being suddenly outflanked by "backwoodsmen" who might show up to vote on one or two issues, all peers must reply to a royal writ of summons at the beginning of each session, or be deemed to have taken a leave of absence.

All this is not to say that the Lords serve no useful function. The House of Lords has done some exceptionally good work examining private bills and amending hastily drawn public ones. It has also conducted intelligent, leisurely debates about important matters of public policy—debates that the Commons, caught up in its more rigid timetable, was unable to hold. There is, of course, some question as to whether anyone was really listening—and whether these same functions could not be performed more satisfactorily by a reformed House of Commons.

THE MONARCHY: As late as the first years of the twentieth century, the monarch might have had some say as to who was to become prime minister; today, this authority is practically nonexistent. Victoria did not want Gladstone, whom she vehemently disliked, but she had to accept him. George VI, after the resignation of Neville Chamberlain, preferred Lord Halifax to Winston Churchill in 1940, but the politicians made their own choice and the king could do little but accept the results. Elizabeth II has never even considered disputing the decision of party leaders, or the consensus of a formal party vote.

It is at least possible that Victoria, because of her personal popularity and because the mystique of monarchy was still strong, influenced the government of her day on some public issues. It is difficult, however, to find an instance in which the monarch can be said to have exercised any real authority in the twentieth century, although his advice may have been accepted on occasion. A cabinet decision was a cabinet decision, and that was that. For example, King George did stress his unwillingness to receive any ambassador from the Soviet regime which, after all, was responsible for the death of his cousins. But as Arthur Henderson, then foreign minister, reported, "I didn't argue or interrupt. I just let him run on, And then I said: 'Well your Majesty, that's the Cabinet decision . . . but perhaps the Prince of Wales could receive him for you?" [13] This was the solution adopted.

With the king relatively impotent, it was hard to become overwrought about the crown as an institution. There was some antimonarchial feeling in the left wing of the Labor Party in its early years, but it never amounted to much. The working class, though it might be self-conscious about its social position, was itself strongly attached to the institution of the monarchy. During the 1936 crisis over the desire of Edward VIII to marry an American divorcee, even the Communist *Daily Worker* joined with other newspapers in a self-imposed censorship, while American newspapers printed every detail of the "scandal."

The honor with which George VI invested the crown during the war years and the coronation of Elizabeth II brought an upsurge in the popularity of the monarchy, and the coronation itself was a vivid emotional experience for most Britons. Shortly thereafter, however, manifestations of disenchantment reappeared. Increasingly, the institution

has been satirized and criticized, and the royal family has found it can no longer rely upon the self-restraint of the fourth estate to protect its privacy. The court, with all its paraphernalia and tradition, remains; but ever larger numbers of Britons find it irrelevant.

The lasting power of the monarchy in the first "modern" state has long been the subject of comment and conjecture by foreign, and especially American, observers. They have explained its survival primarily in functional terms: it is a symbol not only of national unity but of the unity of the Commonwealth, albeit a vanishing Commonwealth, and it is a source of personal identification and pageantry in a dull, drab world. This may all be true. Yet the major explanation for the survival of the monarchy is that, like the American Constitution and Declaration of Independence, it represents continuity with the past—not ideological continuity, as is the case with the American documents, but the continuity of community. The monarchy represents the British community *qua* community, not only at the present moment but in its total development.

10. BRITISH INTEREST GROUPS AND POLITICS

Before the rise of the modern party system, parliamentary politics revolved largely about personal, regional, and economic interests. By modern standards, most of the legislation was private, local, and facultative. Even that which seemed to concern general national policies, such as canals or railways, had local implications, and MP's dealt with it as agents of local interests. In the twentieth century, however, and particularly with the rise of the Labor Party, the major economic interests came to coalesce and to cluster about one of the two major parties; the politics of interest groups gave way to the policies of parties. Business groups settled in the Conservative Party, while the trade unions were primarily the concern of the Labor Party. The impetus of the Labor

[13] Quoted in Hugh Dalton, *Call Back Yesterday* (London: F. Muller, 1953), p. 233.

Party, moreover, was ideological; rhetorically, at least, it was less interested in aggregating the interests of diverse groups than in implementing a particular program. Thus between the two world wars, and even immediately after World War II, the politics of groups was of far less significance in Britain than in France and the United States. Since the 1950's, the parties have modified their attitude toward interest groups. Ideological politics has not disappeared, nor have all groups turned equally to both major parties. Rather, most groups are concerned with and enter into negotiations with both political parties—and vice versa.

Today, with some exceptions, Parliament is not the central focus of interest-group activity. The relative lack of localism in British politics, the pervasive importance of party, and the dominance of the cabinet mean that groups cannot expect to accomplish very much by attempting to woo a bloc of back-benchers. The government, since it will be held responsible for the overall effects of all public policy, must evaluate the demands of any special group within a fairly broad frame of political reference. Hence, unlike the American scene, where lobbyists seek out individual congressmen, especially those on influential committees, the principal efforts of British groups are now directed at the administration and the bureaucracy. As for the government, at all stages in its administration of public affairs it seeks the advice and cooperation, if not the complete acquiescence, of the groups intimately involved with a particular law. Complex negotiations take place at all levels. Some of these contacts are informal, but even so, at least five hundred advisory committees attached to government ministries have been established for the purpose of bringing together civil servants and the representatives of interested associations to consult and bargain on a formal basis. Ministries often consult organizations well in advance of making legislative proposals or taking administrative action. Groups such as the Association of Municipal Corporations and the County Councils' Association have become closely involved with all decisions made by ministries that deal with problems of local government.

There are other variables, too, which make interest-group activity in Britain somewhat different in character from that of France or the United States. Britons have strongly believed that there exists a public interest that overrides group interests and that individual groups should not push too hard or too raucously to achieve their ends. Their belief is augmented by a continuing general commitment to civil behavior. Of course, this commitment does not always hold, as threatened strikes among doctors and wildcat industrial strikes indicate. Moreover, some of these attitudes are obviously eroding. But in a comparative perspective, the civility of British political behavior has been astonishing.

11. CHANGE AND TRANSITION

The signs of change in British values are omnipresent. All forms of traditional authority are under attack, and the old class values of deference and responsibility are disappearing. The traditional assumption that citizens are to be governed by their elected officials has been challenged, as citizen groups have been formed to press their demands on matters such as the disposition of highways and airports, immigration curbs, grammar schools, and public-housing rentals. In a reversal of policy, the Labor Party in 1972 called for the distinctly "un-British" technique of a public referendum to decide the question of Britain's remaining in the Common Market, and the issue was so decided in June, 1975.

As part of this trend, criticism by British intellectuals of their own political institutions has become more and more strident in recent years. It has been argued that the cabinet is being converted into presidential government, and that both Parliament and the cabinet have surrendered control over large areas of public policy to the bureaucracy. The studied amateurism and aristocratic tradition of the Commons has been attacked for preventing Parliament from adequately fulfilling its purpose, and the secrecy with which both cabinet and bureaucracy operate has been castigated as undemocratic. Within both parties, back-benchers are demanding a larger voice for Parliament in the process of making policy. In addition to specialized committees, they are asking for more office space, secretarial staffs, and improved library facilities. Other critics are calling for a devolution of power to local and regional governments.

Given the swift demise of the British Empire and the failure of her economy to grow apace with those of other European nations, it is not surprising that institutions once credited with being the source of Britain's greatness should now be fingered as the cause of her "decline," and that, in a world marked by increasing prestige for professional competence and greater demand for technical expertise, amateurism and ritual have come to seem not only outdated but a serious handicap. In a comparative perspective, however, the British Parliament remains one of the most effective political institutions in the world. Its capacity to arrive at fairly consistent general policies, to create an informed public, to safeguard the liberties of its citizens, and to maintain flexibility and a sense of national unity is still unequaled. The past success of British institutions is not, of course, an argument against change. Political institutions can become obsolete as the problems faced by a society alter, and there is little point in maintaining traditions that no longer serve a purpose or command respect. Yet every structural modification will inevitably be associated with a loss of some of the advantages of the present arrangements.

14

France:
From Parliamentary to
Presidential Government

1. INTRODUCTION

Throughout its history France has alternated between periods of fairly effective authoritarian leadership and periods of administrative and political chaos. The French have never developed that capacity to balance authority and participation in policymaking that has been the hallmark of the British political system. It has been our argument that this failure has reflected the fragmentation of the French political community and its inability to deal constructively with the vast problems created by France's transition from a traditional to a modern society. After 1870, the French attempted to create a parliamentary regime modeled on the British system. What resulted was an entirely different approach to the business of governing: the French were unable to duplicate the British parliamentary system simply because the institutions and attitudes that supported Britain's regime were absent in France. It was impossible in France both to develop a party system that could aggregate the interests of Frenchmen into a smaller number of coherent, alternative programs and to create governments that could govern. Such was the intensity of conflicts that beset French society that it was almost equally difficult to develop lasting agreement on the rules of the political game.

The advent of the Fifth Republic in 1958 provided France with ten years of relative political stability. Capitalizing on the social and economic changes that had taken place since World War II, and on the general disillusionment with the system of the Fourth Republic, Charles de Gaulle established a quasi-presidential regime. The main institution of the regime, a strong, popularly elected president has proven to be popular and durable. However, insofar as political stability was based largely upon support for the president and prime minister by a disciplined majority in the National Assembly, that stability is now endangered by the election of a non-Gaullist president in 1974 and by the divisions within the Gaullist majority.

This chapter will deal first with the govermental processes of the Third and Fourth Republics (1871–1940; 1946–58), focusing primarily upon the relation between those processes and the other aspects of the French political and social systems that have been discussed in earlier chapters. References will be made to the British pattern of government, for comparisons between the two nations can increase our understanding of both. Finally, we will examine the governmental institutions of the Fifth Republic in an effort to throw some light on the future of French politics.

2. PARLIAMENTARY GOVERNMENT

THE BEGINNINGS: The first meeting of the Estates-General of the Kingdom of France was held in Paris on April 10, 1302. As in England, the three estates of the realm—the nobility, the higher clergy, and the people—were represented, although from the beginning the third estate met separately. However, while the English Parliament commenced an existence that was to be almost uninterrupted until full sovereignty was placed in its hands, the Estates-General met only forty-two times in little more than three hundred years. Agents of the king disbanded it in 1615, and no further meetings were held until 1789. The failure of the Estates-General to increase its influence

and to transform itself into a genuine parliament was a direct reflection of the fragmentation of the French realm and the rise of absolutism.

At the meeting convened in 1789, the third estate demanded that all three estates meet in one assembly, and that the veto power held by the nobility and the higher clergy be abolished. Its point was quickly won, and the Estates-General was transformed into a National Assembly, which drew up France's first constitution; it was signed by the king on September 2, 1791. Since that time, the French have been governed under at least fourteen different constitutions and two provisional governments. The French experience is not unique. Rather, it accords with that of a large number of societies that have been so rent by fundamental social conflicts that they have been unable to reach lasting agreement even on the rules of the game.

Before the advent of the Third Republic, the constitutional form that lasted longest, though with substantial modifications along the way, was the Charter of 1814. The charter, which restored the monarchy, more or less followed the British constitutional model: the king was given wide executive authority in the field of foreign affairs; a legislature consisting of two houses, roughly equivalent to the House of Commons and the House of Lords, was formed; the king appointed his own cabinet from either chamber, and it was responsible to him. The king could also dissolve the parliament whenever he wished, and his assent was required before any proposal became law.

The charter was modified by the July Revolution of 1830, which brought Louis Philippe, of the House of Orléans, to the throne; it was destroyed by the February Revolution of 1848 and replaced by a republic. The constitution of the Second Republic, which lasted from 1848 to 1852, provided for a unicameral legislature and a popularly elected president. The republic was overthrown by Napoleon III, who established the Second Empire, which lasted until France's defeat by the Prussians.

THE THIRD REPUBLIC: From the French Revolution to the Franco-Prussian War, the French experience with parliamentary government was, therefore, checkered, to say the least. Only with the downfall of the Second Empire was a parliamentary regime exhibiting any real stability created.

The Third French Republic lacked a formal constitution. If the word is to be used at all, it can designate only a series of "temporary" organic laws. The Constituent Assembly had been dominated by monarchists and Bonapartists, and the only thing preventing the re-establishment of a monarchy was a split between those who favored the House of Orléans and those favoring the House of Bourbon; by the time that difference was resolved, the provisional regime had become institutionalized—and dominated by republicans.

The organic laws established a two-house legislature—a Chamber of Deputies and a Senate. The chamber was to be elected by universal manhood suffrage and the Senate elected indirectly by local notables. The terms of office for senators were longer than those of deputies and their age requirements higher. In general, it was expected that the senate would act as a conservative counterweight to the chamber.

Executive authority was divided between a president and a council of ministers headed by a vice president (premier). The president appointed all members of the council, or cabinet—including the vice president— but they were collectively responsible to the legislature. The president was elected at a joint meeting of the two chambers for a period of seven years, and he was given the authority to dissolve the legislature when he wished—part of the traditional prerogative of the monarchy.

Within a fairly short time the power of the president almost disappeared, and real authority became vested in the legislature and in the council of ministers and its vice president. Unlike the British system, however, both the cabinet and the premier remained extremely weak, and the legislature made and remade governments at will. Be-

tween 1871 and 1898, France was governed by thirty-nine cabinets, with an average life of eight months; between 1924 and 1940, by thirty-seven, with an average life of five months. Thus, an institutional pattern resembling Britain's, at least on the surface, actually functioned quite differently. The continued existence of a multiplicity of ideological factions and parties meant that cabinets were of necessity coalitions; to become a member of the French government, therefore—and especially to become premier—one had to obtain the support of a wide range of groups rather than of a single party. Furthermore, the fragility of any French government meant that maintaining oneself in office required considerable political dexterity; it also meant that cabinet members, each hoping to use a political crisis to advantage, could never constitute a body with a sense of collective responsibility. Secrets were invariably leaked, internal dissension constantly flared, and each member of the government was continually tempted to gently knife his colleagues in order to improve his own position.

Successful candidates for the premiership and other cabinet positions, therefore, tended to be nonideological brokers—men of balance, with sympathy and understanding for a variety of positions, but no strong commitment to any. They also tended to be men capable of satisfying the fairly narrow demands of particular interests. To be sure, in times of crisis, when crucial decisions could no longer be put off, dynamic leaders such as Clemenceau might be invested with tremendous power. But such men rarely lasted beyond the immediate crisis; their power was feared and distrusted, and their actions invariably alienated too many special interests.

With the French executive a constitutional weakling, the effective locus of power was the legislature. But its disunity, as well as the cumbersome size of both the Chamber of Deputies and the Senate, uniformly resulted in chaos. It was almost impossible to establish a reasonable timetable for considering legislation, and, in many cases, to set realistic limits on debate. Yet legislation had to receive some attention, if only so that deputies might engage in those minimal actions that permit the system to survive, and to satisfy—for their own survival—at least some of the demands of their constituents. Both houses, therefore, set up a complex series of committees that in many ways resembled the American pattern. Their function was to write, examine, and press for legislation—and to serve as a device for burying measures that deputies had to introduce in order to pacify special interests but were not anxious to have considered. The committees also served as watchdogs over the state bureaucracy, preventing it from stepping out of line—a task that was all the more important, since the weakness of the executive prevented it from exercising the kind of control over the bureaucracy that the British cabinet could.

Not surprisingly, the power of French legislative committees attracted men of considerable competence and ambition. The absence of effective, disciplined party organizations also enhanced the position of committees as a major source of expertise for members of the parliament, performing a function similar to that of legislative committees in the United States. Competition for committee assignments was fierce; only as a member of the right committee could one wield wide power or hope to secure passage of legislation in which one's interest was involved.

Government bills were first submitted to the relevant committee, which had the right to amend them or to introduce its own version of the proposed law. If the legislation was of paramount importance, its defeat could mean the resignation of the government. Since all members of important committees were anxious to become ministers, even if only for a short time, strong pressures developed to effect precisely such a collapse. The role of the committee's *rapporteur* was especially popular, since it was he who delivered the committee's report, and many promising politicians entered upon their first ministerial posts as the result of a telling attack upon a particular piece of government legislation. In essence the whole legislative situation was one that encouraged impassioned speeches and opposition for the sake of rhetoric and opposition.

The deficiencies of the system were, furthermore, self-generating. The manner in which governments were made and unmade, for example, also helped to undermine party discipline. Time after time, deputies broke party lines to bring down existing governments in the hope of entering a new one—or they supported a particular government with the same end in view. Only the Communists, and to a lesser extent the Socialists, were able to maintain a semblance of party cohesion.

Many attempts were made to strengthen the executive, but all of them failed. Proposals for a quasi-presidential form of government that might afford stability were opposed by the left because they were considered reactionary. Suggestions to strengthen the prime minister's office were persistently put forth by those parties that believed they could benefit from such a change, but they were opposed by others, especially on the left, who considered a strong premier a threat to liberty. This position was even truer of the Radicals than the Socialists; the former, aside from doctrinal considerations that caused them to be suspicious of all authority, believed that a more powerful executive would jeopardize their own position as a government broker.

Actually, the premier possessed far more potential power than he was able to exercise. The Third Republic's "constitution" had placed the authority to dissolve the Chamber of Deputies in the hands of the president, and, constitutionally, the premier could have assumed this authority as he had assumed other presidential prerogatives. This was exactly what had happened in Britain, where the power of the monarch to dissolve Parliament had been assumed by the prime minister. Many French commentators, misreading the British scene, thought that the British prime minister's power to dissolve Parliament explained the stability of British

governments, because, they argued, if deputies knew that bringing down a government
would precipitate a new election, they would
think twice before voting to do so.

France, however, was not Britain. The
tangled political system, the fixity of voting
patterns, and the lack of discipline in most
parties meant that single elections hardly
ever resulted in a basic shift in the legislative balance of power, as it usually did under a two-party system. Any premier who
dissolved Parliament would only have made
himself very unpopular with legislators for
having forced them to fight an election for
nothing. For him to dissolve Parliament,
then, would have been tantamount to committing political suicide.

French governments, consequently, rose
and fell without new elections being held.
One set of ministers was replaced by another set on the basis of intraparliamentary negotiations, much as had been the case in
Britain before the rise of the two-party system. And the governments did not, on the
whole, differ very much from one another.
After all, there were only a limited number
of politicians who could hope to secure the
backing of even a temporary majority, and
these "ministrables," as they were called,
were potential premiers or ministers only
because it was understood that they would
not rock the boat too boisterously.

In the last analysis, of course, the weaknesses of French government lay not in the
political institutions, but in the cleavages
that rent French society so deeply that no
one group was strong enough to resolve
them. France was, in the words of one author, a "stalemate" society;[1] its institutions
reflected that condition. It should be pointed out, nevertheless, that these institutions
did mold a viable republic, that they mobilized sufficient support to separate church
and state, and that they managed, through a
tenuous balance of political forces, to temper
conflicts that had previously burst into civil

[1] Stanley Hoffmann, "Paradoxes of the French
Political Community," in Hoffmann et al., *In Search
of France* (New York: Harper & Row, 1963), 94.

war. The Third Republic also preserved a
framework of order that permitted periods
of reasonably rapid economic development.
Before World War I, this was quite enough:
France was a rather prosperous country. In
the interwar period more was required, and
the essential impotence of French political
institutions contributed finally to the nation's inability to cope with its monumental
domestic and international problems.

THE FOURTH REPUBLIC: A Constituent
Assembly was elected in October, 1945, to
correct the faults in the governmental structure by creating what was eventually to become the constitution of the Fourth Republic. In the debates over the new constitution, Charles de Gaulle, the first head of the
postwar provisional government, called for a
strong executive in the form of a president.
This option, however, was rejected by the
political parties in control of the assembly,
and the proposed constitution placed government authority almost entirely in the hands
of a popularly elected National Assembly.
The constitution, however, was submitted to
a referendum and defeated. In 1946 a second assembly was elected to try again to
form a constitution; the new document
strengthened somewhat the executive power
of the premium and added a second, albeit
very weak, chamber: the Council of the Republic. The constitution also provided for a
president, but he was to be only a figure-
head, not unlike the president of the Third
Republic after 1877. Although almost one-
third of the eligible voters abstained, the
new constitution was approved in a referendum in October 1946.

Constitutional "tinkering", however, did
not result in increased stability. The fate of
attempts to strengthen the French executive
is an indication of just how unsuccessful
were such efforts. The premier's power
over the cabinet was supposedly enhanced by
changing the manner in which he was selected. Under the Third Republic, the president
had chosen the prime minister, who then
formed his cabinet and went to the Chamber
of Deputies for approval of himself and his

government. Only a relative majority—that is, a majority of those deputies present and voting—was required for election. The constitution of the Fourth Republic called for the prime minister to present himself and his program to the Assembly for a vote of confidence first; once granted, he would then select a cabinet and return to the Assembly for its approval. His investiture required an absolute majority—a majority of the total membership of the Assembly. The double investiture and the requirement of an absolute majority, it was expected, would add to the premier's prestige, and also prevent deputies from abstaining and thus avoiding responsibility for the government that was formed.

Other constitutional changes made for the ostensible purpose of strengthening the government included the prevention of snap votes of confidence, and the specific assignment to the premier of the power to dissolve the National Assembly. During the Third Republic, any government could be defeated on a snap vote of confidence called for during the equivalent of Britain's parliamentary question period. Under the provisions of the Fourth Republic's constitution, a government could be formally defeated only by a vote of censure or by a refusal to grant a vote of confidence, and a full day was required between the motion and the vote. Further, the government had to be defeated by an absolute majority. Of even greater importance was the provision that if after the first eighteen months of any parliament two governments were constitutionally defeated, the premier could dissolve the assembly.

The constitutional changes had little or no effect. The double investiture only complicated the forming of governments. On a number of occasions, the candidate proposed as prime minister would be approved after a long round of negotiations, only to see his proposed cabinet go down to defeat. The requirement for an absolute majority prompted the same stalemate. In 1953, for example, the cabinet fell in early May. The president consulted every party and canvassed all possible candidates for prime minister; several did obtain relative majorities, but none succeeded in obtaining an absolute one. After several weeks, prospective candidates refused to allow themselves to be considered for premier, and not until June 26 was an acceptable nominee found. Both constitutional provisions, incidentally, were repealed in 1954.

The power of dissolution was used only once. Despite the constitution, most governments considered defeat by a relative majority quite sufficient to close up shop, and others just fell apart. In a number of cases, potential candidates were approved only with the promise that they would not try to dissolve the Assembly even if the opportunity arose to do so.

The ability of any government to work out a systematic legislative program was similarly hampered. The political division within most governments made it virtually impossible to develop an adequate internal organization for the cabinet; the French finally created a general secretariat to prepare agendas, coordinate the work of the ministers, and serve on interdepartmental meetings. Yet no sense of collective responsibility manifested itself, nor was there ever any certainty that the bureaucracy serving the cabinet would be completely loyal. Secret information would be divulged if it contained any promise whatsoever of embarrassing those in power. French military plans even found their way to Ho Chi Minh, presumably with the connivance of French bureaucrats who opposed the war in Indochina.

Even if the premier seemed to have obtained widespread popular support, he could not effectively mobilize it in order to strengthen his position in the legislature and among his colleagues. The popularity of Pierre Mendès-France, for example, was not enough to maintain him in office. Deputies were quite aware of the fact that if they played their cards right they would not be held responsible for his inability to achieve ends that the public endorsed; they turned out to be correct. Other factors were involved in the downfall of Mendès-France, but in the end he, like so many before him, found that he could not press his programs through the National Assembly; with this failure, of course, his support eventually withered away. The public seemed cognizant of the problems faced by its premier, as indicated by the fact that most Frenchmen viewed government instability and ineffectiveness as among the most important of the country's problems. But the system's almost uncanny facility for resisting all attempts to reform itself infected the public with a sense of helplessness that only further contributed to its *incivism.*

Thus, as under the Third Republic, the locus of power came to be the National Assembly itself. And, once again, the legislature lacked the capacity or the willingness to organize itself for effective action. The Assembly's timetable was set by a conference of representatives of the political groups, and it included the presidents of the legislative committees. But securing agreement on the order of business was usually a lengthy ordeal that in itself became the subject of major clashes.

Nor could the speaker—the president of the Assembly—impose any real order. Unlike his American counterpart, the French speaker was not a party man; indeed, he never could have been elected if he had been. Although the center parties were careful to keep the post from falling to the Gaullists or the Communists, the person most often chosen was a man with influential connections within the Assembly; his authority, however, remained limited. The power of the British speaker depends on the acceptance by the vast majority of MP's of the rules of the game. But in France even the rules were at issue. Only occasionally could the assembly, or at least its majority, agree on procedure.

Also as under the Third Republic, standing committees again became not only the centers of power in the Assembly but the real agents in bringing down one government after another. The strategy of the government was to play one committee against the other—with, however, scant success, for in fact the committees were, once again, the captives of special interests. Half the members on the Committee for Reconstruction and War Damage, for instance, were from Normandy and Brittany, where the Allies had landed in World War II; all members of the Committee on Merchant Shipping and Fisheries had their home towns in coastal areas. Members were unanimous only in their desire to subsidize the particular interests they represented. In one week in 1951 the Labor Committee called for larger expenditures for family allowances; Interior sought more vigorous action on slums; the Press Committee announced its opposition to proposed economies in the National Film Center; and the Pensions Committee attempted to triple war pensions. Only the Finance Committee seemed to take an overall view—in this case conservative; its emphasis, an unpopular one, was on rejecting most proposals for the expenditure of money.

Its faults and inability to develop coherent programs notwithstanding, the legislature of the Fourth Republic did, after all, manage to support policies of relative austerity in order to promote economic growth immediately after World War II. It also legislated a considerable amount of social reform, mostly during the period just after the war, and during the early months of the ministry of Premier Guy Mollet in 1956. The first period was dominated by the three-party government that for a time provided a coherent basis for dealing with controversial decisions. When the tripartite system fell apart in 1947, and parties could no longer provide coherence for government policy, legislation was passed the following year permitting governments to resort to decree laws. These decrees enabled the government to take unpopular actions for which Parliament wished to avoid responsibility, though some of the decrees had to have final approval of Parliament. Between 1950 and 1953 nationalized industry in France was reorganized by decrees; in 1953 judicial, military, and civil-service promotion and retirement regulations were changed by decrees; in 1954 Pierre Mendès-France was granted special economic decree power through which he promised to shake up and reorganize the French economy (the decrees were later reversed); and in 1956–57 premiers were granted special decree powers to conduct the war in Algeria and to encroach upon civil liberties in Algeria and in France. Though usually limited in time, decree power and various kinds of limited special powers developed into an emergency motor force for the Fourth Republic that was later institutionalized in the constitution of the Fifth Republic.

In various ways, then, governments under the Fourth Republic were able to initiate and support some important changes.[2] Nevertheless, the political structure of the Fourth Republic was such as to reduce the possibilities of evolving and implementing effective national policies. The structure defied the efforts of France's most skillful politicians to overcome its limitations. It corrupted other deputies and prevented a meaningful approach to the fundamental problems of French society.

3. THE FIFTH REPUBLIC: THE CONSTITUTION

In June 1958, when the Fourth Republic collapsed and de Gaulle returned to power, he was granted special powers to draw up a new constitution, which was submitted to the people in September. It was approved by 79 percent of those voting.

The constitution of the Fifth Republic was an attempt to fuse presidential and parliamentary government, and at the same time to transform parliamentary government into cabinet government. It also created a second chamber with more power than had been assigned to the Fourth Republic's

Council of the Republic, but less than the amount delegated to the Third Republic's senate, whose name it adopted. For the first time in French history, a Constitutional Council was established for the purpose, among others, of ruling on the constitutionality of both legislation and any standing orders governing its operation that the legislature might adopt. Hitherto, the Assembly itself had been regarded as the arbiter of the constitutionality of its legislation and standing orders.

The French constitution can be amended easily; therefore the powers of the Constitutional Council cannot be equated with those of the United States Supreme Court. A constitutional amendment may be enacted either by a simple majority of both chambers plus confirmation by a national referendum, or by a three-fifths vote of the two chambers sitting jointly. Furthermore, until 1974 the Council could rule on the constitutionality of a law only if its opinion were sought by the president, the prime minister, or the president of either house of the legislature. Citizens could not appeal to it; neither could courts of law. Further, the jurisdiction awarded the Council was clearly such as to favor the executive; if the government believed that Parliament had legislated in a field reserved for executive regulation the issue could be referred to the Council for a definitive decision. However, if Parliament felt that the government had usurped its prerogative by issuing regulations on matters it believed to be legislative, deputies had no similar recourse. Further, the fact that the Council was stacked with Gaullist notables seemed to make it unlikely that it would decide issues in such a way as to embarrass the Gaullist majority. Indeed, during de Gaulle's tenure of office the Council was often referred to—with some legitimacy—as "the General's poodle."

Despite this, however, the Council did sometimes exercise independence of judgment. For one thing the Senate was never dominated by Gaullists, and the president of the Senate was one of those who could bring

---

[2] On the politics of the Fourth Republic, see Philip M. Williams, *Crisis and Compromise, Politics in the Fourth Republic* (London: Longmans, Green & Co., 1964).

cases to the Council. For another, some Gaullist notables, once taking on their new function, began to behave in surprising ways. Thus, in 1971, deciding a case brought by the president of the Senate, the Council ruled that a new law on associations, with which the government had obviously planned to harass left wing groups, was unconstitutional. Furthermore, in 1974, the Parliament passed a constitutional amendment which permits any sixty members of either the Assembly or the Senate to bring appeals to the Council. It is too early to judge the effect of this amendment, but it seems likely to enlarge both the Council's jurisdiction and role in French politics.

4. THE FIFTH REPUBLIC: THE PRESIDENCY

ELECTION: Six months after being granted special powers to draft a new constitution, de Gaulle swept into office as France's first elected president since Louis Napoleon with 77.5 percent of the vote, whipping his Communist opponent, Georges Maranne, and a retired school dean, Albert Chatelet. He was elected indirectly by an electoral college composed of members of Parliament and local notables, as specified in the original version of the constitution. The term of office was seven years. In 1962 de Gaulle submitted directly to the people an amendment providing for the popular election of the president. Despite the fact that he did not first submit his proposal to the legislature, thereby violating the spirit and the letter of the constitution—according to the Constitutional Council and the Council of State in advisory opinions —the amendment was approved. Under the provisions of that amendment, to be elected a candidate must receive an absolute majority of the votes. If no candidate is successful on the first ballot, a second election must be held within two weeks, in which, unless there is a withdrawal, the two candidates who received the largest number of votes compete for office. Somewhat ironically,

upon the expiration of de Gaulle's first term of office, he failed to achieve a majority in the first election to be held under these provisions; thus a run-off was precipitated between him and his principal opponent, François Mitterrand. Because there is no provision, as there is in the United States, for a vice-presidential succession, upon de Gaulle's resignation in 1969 another presidential election had to be held. Georges Pompidou was then the successful contestant, winning a second-ballot run-off (see Table 10.4) by a comfortable margin. Upon the death of Pompidou in 1974, another presidential election was held. This time the victor was Valery Giscard d'Estaing, who barely outpolled Mitterrand on the second-ballot run-off.

POWERS: The essential purpose of the constitution of the Fifth Republic was to strengthen the power of the executive at the expense of the legislature. Only in this way, in the opinion of de Gaulle and those who assisted him, could France achieve a stable, workable government. In a sense, the document was partially tailored to de Gaulle himself, and during his tenure as president he used it as an instrument rather than as a framework within which to act. Thus, the power balance between the premier and the president, incorporated into the constitution, shifted decisively to the president, and the role of the legislature was far smaller during his tenure of office than it has been under his successors.

The constitution bestows certain important executive powers specifically on the president, not the least of which is his right to appoint the premier. He had the authority to do so under both the Third and Fourth Republics, but this power is now more than a mere formality, given his electoral base and his power to dissolve the legislature and call for new elections. The only limitations upon his right to dissolve Parliament are the requirement that he consult with the premier and the presidents of both chambers, and that he cannot dissolve the legislature twice in the same year. In essence, this means that a refusal by the National Assembly to accept the premier designated by the popularly elected president could result in dissolution and new elections. On the other hand, if the president were confronted with a hostile majority in Parliament, it would perhaps be imprudent to call for new elections when the country had just voted that majority into office. In 1877 the president of the Third Republic dissolved Parliament because he was confronted with a hostile majority; an even more hostile majority was returned, and no Third Republic president ever dissolved Parliament again.

Another power given to the president is the right to refer government bills to the electorate in the form of a referendum. The procedure is not universally applicable; theoretically, the bill in question must concern either the organization of public powers or the relations between metropolitan France and other members of the French Community. Furthermore, according to the constitution, the president can call for a referendum only upon the request of the government, that is, the premier and the cabinet. De Gaulle, however, decided that it was up to him to make such decisions, and on two of the four occasions in which a referendum was held during his ten years as president he violated the relevant constitutional provisions. The first two referenda involved the Algerian question. In 1961 de Gaulle called

upon the French population to support a policy of self-determination for Algeria, and in April, 1962, the electorate was asked to approve agreements between the French government and the Algerian nationalist movement, establishing an independent Algeria. On both issues, it is fairly certain that the National Assembly would have supported de Gaulle; his appeal directly to the people can be understood only as a device used to demonstrate to both the military and the small group of fanatics still opposed to Algerian independence that he had the overwhelming support of the French people (Table 14.1).

In the use of the third referendum, again in 1962, de Gaulle, as noted above, appealed to the public over the head of a parliament that seemed bent on rejecting his proposal for a constitutional change providing for the direct election of the president. In so doing he violated the terms of his own constitution. He did the same thing in the 1969 referendum, which grouped together constitutional proposals for creating indirectly elected regional assemblies with limited powers of self-government; for supplanting the Senate with a new consultative chamber of representatives from the regional councils; and for changing the order of succession to the presidency. Essentially, these were plebiscites in which, by threatening to resign, de Gaulle gave the public the choice of accept-

TABLE 14.1   FRENCH REFERENDA, 1958–1972

Date	Registered voters (in millions)	Yes: % of votes cast	No: % of votes cast	Voter turnout	Spoiled ballots
9/28/58	26.61	79.25	20.74	84.94%	1.14%
1/ 8/61	27.18	75.26	24.73	76.49	2.18
4/ 8/62	26.99	90.70	9.29	75.59	4.06
10/28/62	27.58	61.75	38.25	77.25	2.02
4/27/69	28.02	46.82	53.17	81.58	2.21
4/23/72	29.82	68.31	31.68	60.24	6.99

Sources: *Le Monde*, September 30, 1958; January 10, 1961; April 10, 1962; October 30, 1962; April 29, 1969; April 30, 1972. Reprinted by permission of the publisher.

ing or rejecting his leadership. In all four referenda, however, the tactic was the same: he, de Gaulle, would establish once again his bond with the people and receive the pure expression of their will, thereby strengthening his hand.

In 1961 and 1962 the tactic worked: still fearful of the possibilities of disorder should anything happen to de Gaulle, the population supported him handsomely. In 1969 it failed. The anxieties that had swept de Gaulle's UDR (Union of Democrats for the Republic) to a massive victory in the 1968 elections had subsided, and Frenchmen no longer believe that de Gaulle was the only alternative to chaos.

In 1972 President Georges Pompidou also tried to use the referendum to boost his political fortunes and increase his prestige. When Britain decided to join the Common Market, he submitted the treaty to the French people for ratification; this was a vote he could not lose, while at the same time he could divide the opposition Communists and Socialists. When the results were in, however, it was clear that the president had suffered an important setback. The treaty was approved, but 40 percent of the electorate did not vote, and another 7 percent submitted spoiled ballots. Under the circumstances, everyone claimed victory.

Another special power given to the president by the constitution is the right to assume full powers in the case of certain emergencies. De Gaulle asserted at the time the constitution was adopted that this emergency power, as defined in Article 16, was to be used primarily in the event of a national disaster comparable with that of 1940. He invoked it only once, in April, 1961, in the wake of the revolt of the generals in Algeria, led by the *Secret Army Organization* (OAS), a group committed to France's retention of full control over its former colony. De Gaulle's action met with widespread approval. But a number of deputies pointed out that because the work of the "constitutional public authorities" had not been impaired, the use of the constitutional article went, strictly speaking, beyond its meaning.

Many commentators believe that protections against the use of Article 16 to establish a full dictatorship are not sufficient.

Notable among the other specific powers given to the president by the constitution of the Fifth Republic are those relating to foreign affairs. The president can take any measures necessary to preserve France's territorial integrity. He can negotiate treaties. And he has almost complete freedom of action with regard to problems arising from relations with both former dependencies still associated in some fashion with France and others within the so-called French Community whose status is still more or less colonial.

DEVELOPMENT OF THE OFFICE: de Gaulle's conception of the French presidency changed, at least publicly, during his tenure. Initially, he was in accord with Michel Debré, his choice as premier and the man who was largely responsible for the form of the constitution of the Fifth Republic. Debré had argued that the role of the president would be largely that of arbiter; he would mediate in the conflicting concerns of the various organs of government in order to insure national stability and direction. By the time of the 1962 referendum, however, it was obvious that de Gaulle conceived of himself as a figure whose function was to provide political leadership. As a consequence, the constitution was increasingly ignored or stretched to such a degree that major policy decisions, which should have been made by a government responsible to the legislature, were made personally by de Gaulle with the advice of the bureaucracy and a few trusted companions. Indeed, de Gaulle gathered about him his own special staff, composed largely of higher-echelon civil servants whose functions were similar to those of the White House office of the president of the United States, but who numbered about only thirty.

In the fields of foreign policy and defense, especially, de Gaulle's will was determinative. It was he who decided that Algeria should become independent and that France should have a nuclear-striking force. It was he who concluded that France's African colonies should determine for themselves their future association with the new French Community. It was he who vetoed Britain's admission into the European Common Market and who removed French forces from the command of the North Atlantic Treaty Organization. On the domestic front, many important questions were handled by presidential decree, leaving the legislature and the prime minister with rather routine tasks. It was de Gaulle who made the final decisions on educational reforms after the crisis of May, 1968; later in the same year, he determined that France would not devalue the franc. There were, of course, a number of important domestic issues with which de Gaulle did not directly concern himself— or on which he had no fixed opinion; on these, the premier, other cabinet members, and even the Assembly exercised considerable influence. For example, with de Gaulle's authorization it was Premier Pompidou who decided to force the members of the cabinet into electoral battle in March 1967 (with mixed results). Once again, it was Pompidou as premier who decided to ask the Assembly for decree powers to deal with economic and social questions later that same year.

It is not only what Charles de Gaulle did, however, but the manner in which he did it that has led many to describe him as a constitutional monarch. He stated again and again that he was France's steward, that he represented the will of France. He veiled his decisions in secrecy and effectively inhibited discussion of them before they were taken, thus leaving the public and many of his colleagues and staff uninformed as to his intentions. When he changed his mind, he often failed to inform even those closely associated with the issue, and they sometimes found themselves arguing a case that de Gaulle was shortly to repudiate.

The presidency reflected the personality and the prestige of de Gaulle to such an extent that it was difficult for most Frenchmen to separate the office from the man, and there was some question when de Gaulle left office in 1969 about how the institution would function in the future. One matter, however, seemed fairly certain—that the president would continue to be popularly elected, a constitutional right the public was not now likely to surrender.

As president, Pompidou only slowly developed his authority. For over a year, the president remained in the background as the premier, Jacques Chaban-Delmas, developed his plan for a "new society." Pompidou concentrated on a few important initiatives in foreign affairs, namely the easing of relations with the United States and the admission of Britain to the Common Market. By 1971, however, the major policy choices were being made by the president, though perhaps with more staff and ministerial consultation. Pompidou never gained the kind of control over the UDR that de Gaulle did. He controlled the party by balancing its internal forces rather than by dominating it. Far closer to the conservative center of gravity of the party than his predecessor, Pompidou was openly attacked by the Gaullist left on the charge that he had sold out the social-reform heart of Gaullism. Nevertheless, he was able to prevent Michel Debré from assuming the leadership of the UDR, and he saw to it that Chaban-Delmas did not resume his old post as president of the National Assembly when he was relieved of the premiership in 1972. Thus, with a style quite different from that of de Gaulle, Pompidou maintained the strong presidency.

The election of Valéry Giscard d'Estaing as the third president of the Fifth Republic raises many more questions and will probably bring about important changes in the development of the office. His style has been more open and intentionally less authoritarian than that of his predecessors. But the real questions about the future of the office are related to the fact that Giscard d'Estaing is the first president of the Fifth Republic who is attempting to govern without a disciplined majority. While the president has successfully organized a majority coalition of parties behind him, he has been forced to become a more skillful bargainer, and is more dependent upon his prime minister than either de Gaulle or Pompidou was.

5. THE FIFTH REPUBLIC: THE PREMIER AND THE GOVERNMENT

THE AGENT: The premier is, officially, the head of the French government. He chooses his ministers, whom the president appoints on his recommendation, and he can request their resignation. He is held constitutionally responsible for the work of the government—for guaranteeing that its laws are carried out and that the nation's defenses are adequate. The resignation of a premier automatically provokes the downfall of the government.

Despite these similarities with British parliamentary government, the premier under both de Gaulle and Pompidou was basically an agent of the president for organizing a parliamentary majority. Such was the general view of the premier's role as expressed in 1974 by Chirac, and this was essentially the role played by Debré (1958–62), Pompidou (1962–68), Maurice Couve de Murville (1968–69), Jacques Chaban-Delmas (1969–72), and Pierre Messmer (1972–74). In contrast with the British prime minister, only two of these first five premiers of the Fifth Republic were professional politicians before they assumed office: Debré and Chaban-Delmas. Pompidou had been a professor and banker, Couve de Murville a career diplomat, and Messmer a colonial administrator. Jacques Chirac, appointed by President Giscard d'Estaing in May, 1974, began his career as a high administrator, served on the staff of Premier and then President Pompidou, and was a cabinet minister from 1972 to 1974. After Pompidou's death, Chirac was the prime mover and organizer of the pro-Giscard forces within the UDR. Like his predecessors, his basic loyalty is to the president. No Fifth Republic premier has "emerged" from a party organization.

Unlike the constitution of the Fourth Republic, that of the Fifth does not require that a premier appointed by the president submit himself to the National Assembly for approval. If, however, he does present either his government or his program to the Assembly for approval, his government can be denied confidence by a majority vote and must resign. The first premier of the Fifth Republic, Debré, did engage the responsibility of his government, believing that the prime minister should serve at the pleasure of the parliament because he is, under the constitution, "responsible" to it. Debré's successor, Pompidou, did the same until 1966, when he emphasized the link between the government and the president by refusing to present his third government to the Assembly for confidence. Couve de Murville, Chaban-Delmas, and Messmer followed this example. Chirac, however, broke with this practice by successfully presenting his program before the National Assembly in June, 1974.

The National Assembly may force the premier's resignation through a vote of censure, or by refusing a request for confidence in his government or general program. Aside from these acts of the Assembly and by the resignation of the government before each new election, the constitution provides no other way in which a premier may be discharged from office. Nevertheless, Debré and Pompidou stepped down at the request of de Gaulle, and Pompidou similarly forced the resignation of Chaban-Delmas in the wake of scandals surrounding his government. Because the president has no constitutional authority to dismiss the premier, in each of the three cases the fiction was maintained that the premier had requested to be relieved of his duties.

Constitutionally, the policy-making group of the French government meets as the Council of Ministers when the president serves as chairman, and as the Council of the Cabinet when the premier is chairman. Under the Third Republic, the official policy-making body was the Council of Ministers, and the Council of the Cabinet was created to prepare the ministers' meetings. As power shifted from the presidency, the cabinet council became the real policy-making group; it remained so under the Fourth Republic, even though it was not mentioned in the constitution and its authority was officially derived from the Council of Ministers.

De Gaulle reversed the pattern. Key decisions were made at meetings of the Council of Ministers, for it was at these sessions, under his leadership, that policies were initiated that he felt should be the result of collective action. The premier and other ministers were not, however, completely passive; on many issues de Gaulle simply put into effect ideas that had been forwarded from various departments through the ministers, and he permitted fairly wide-ranging discussions of the issue at hand. Yet in the end, it was de Gaulle and de Gaulle alone who determined the outcome of matters he considered important. With somewhat less rigidity, Pompidou continued this style in his exercise of power until mid-1972, when his illness forced him to cede increasing power to advisors.

As president, Giscard d'Estaing has moderated presidential domination of the Council of Ministers by using a somewhat different style. Instead of working through a single minister, he has worked closely and directly with a number of key ministers, and has generally downgraded the role of the premier as the first among equals. In addition, he has reduced the role of the UDR (which has only twelve out of thirty-seven ministries), and has appointed a cabinet that is most distinguished by its loyalty to the president himself.

CONSTITUTIONAL REINFORCEMENT: Domination of policy-making by the president was not written into the constitution, which made every effort to strengthen the prime minister and the government in their own right. Among the constitutional provisions designed to achieve this purpose, five are of particular importance. The first, which made membership in the government incompatible with membership in Parliament, was intended to eliminate the game of musical chairs that had been played so frequently during the Third and Fourth Republics. De Gaulle's hope was that competition among the deputies for ministerial posts would be reduced, along with the tendency to overthrow governments for the sake of securing such posts. It was also believed that ministers free of parliamentary ties would not feel under as much pressure from both parties and constituents and thus would more readily consider the national rather than the partisan or local interest. By 1967, however, members of the government were running for Parliament even if they had never served in a political office before; as candidates they declared they would continue to look out for the interests of their constituents even though they could be expected to resign from their seats in Parliament in favor of their alternates once a new government was formed.[3]

The second constitutional provision requires an absolute majority in the Assembly for the overthrow of a government. A government may be brought down on a vote of censure or when the prime minister raises a question of confidence and loses, but since a motion of censure requires the signatures of one-tenth of the deputies, and since the same signatories cannot move another motion in the same session, government stability has been constitutionally enhanced. Even so, it is well to remember that most governments under the Fourth Republic fell apart despite the fact that the constitutional requirement for an absolute majority to unseat them had not been met.

The third important provision grants the government far wider authority to issue decrees that have the force of law. The provision extends beyond matters relating to the budget, where decrees can be issued if Parliament refuses to act. Because the Third Republic parliament was so often unable to agree on the details of legislation, it allowed

---

[3] The constitution states that each candidate for Parliament must run for office jointly with an alternate (*suppléant*), who replaces him if he takes a government post. Giscard d'Estaing has proposed a constitutional amendment that would permit former government members to return to their parliamentary seats six months after they leave the cabinet.

the government to take responsibility for filling in those details. The government was even granted authority to modify laws by decree in certain instances. Fourth Republic France relied upon the same expedients. The constitution of the Fifth Republic specifically delegates decree-issuing powers to the government, although, as under the Third and Fourth Republics, these powers are subject to eventual ratification by Parliament. The difference is basically one of viewpoint: it is now constitutionally acceptable for the assembly to delegate the responsibility for legislative details to the government. Still, there are restrictions upon this authority. Every government ordinance issued under decree-delegating legislation must be laid before Parliament in the form of a ratifying bill by a date specified in the enabling act. Unless Parliament then passes the bill, the ordinances issued by the government could be challenged as being *ultra vires*—beyond the legal scope of the government. There is a catch here, however: whereas the constitution provides that the ordinances must be laid before Parliament, it does not provide that they must be passed by Parliament or even debated, and on a number of occasions the government has complied with the letter of the law but blocked debate. A few of the ordinances that became effective in this manner have been successfully challenged in the courts; most, however, have not.

The fourth constitutional provision to reinforce the authority of the premier and the government designates the areas in which Parliament may legislate, and reserves all other matters for executive action—including the detailed application of general laws. To be sure, the powers granted the legislature are broad, but they are no longer unlimited. Unfortunately, it is not always easy to differentiate between the domain of "law," as defined by the constitution, and that of "regulations," under which the government can exercise its prerogative. Where the government and the parliament disagree, the premier or the president of either chamber of the National Assembly can bring the issue before the Constitutional Council; private citizens can also bring cases to the *Conseil d'État* on the ground that either the government or Parliament has exceeded its authority. Decisions have tended to extend the parliament's sphere of jurisdiction, although a good many issues have not been settled; the council's attitude seems to be that while Parliament can decide upon the objective of legislation, the government can decide the method of reaching the objective, except where the method determines or frustrates the objective. Thus, Parliament may pass a law setting up a new type of criminal court in Paris, Lyons, and Marseilles, but the extension of these courts to other towns would be a matter for governmental decision. One further reason for instituting this constitutional provision was to leave Parliament time to consider major legislative proposals by overcoming its tendency to preoccupy itself with a plethora of minor matters. In this connection the provision has been successful, and the number of minor bills introduced by private members has dropped from about eight hundred a year to two hundred.

Finally, the government has been given extensive control over the parliamentary timetable. Consideration of government bills takes priority, and the government now opens debate on its bills and has the right to propose amendments. Furthermore, it is the government's bill that is considered by the Assembly, not the bill as amended by committee. Committee amendments must now be submitted from the floor. The government can also object to amendments from the floor once debate on a bill has begun, and ministers can, if they wish, ask that the legislature decide on the bill as a whole without taking up each amendment seriatim (the "blocked" or "package" vote). Furthermore, the government can make the acceptance of a bill a matter of confidence; when that occurs, the bill becomes law unless the opposition puts down a censure motion with enough support to carry a majority of the whole house, not just those voting. These last two weapons have been frequently employed by the government to bring recalcitrant party members and allied groups into line and to put pressure on those who favored the legislation at hand but objected to particular amendments. By insisting on a package vote, the government has forced moderates to support it, lest the entire bill fail; and by making a bill a matter of confidence, it has forced deputies to reach a decision on a whole series of issues solely on the basis of their attitude toward the regime. Both weapons would not have been very effective under the Third and Fourth Republics, but they were used successfully to discipline the majority in the de Gaulle and Pompidou governments.

The government's control over the parliamentary timetable is clearly demonstrated by its new authority over financial legislation. During most of the Third Republic, deputies could introduce troublesome amendments or bills that had the effect of increasing appropriations or reducing taxes while the budget was being considered. The constitution of the Fourth Republic prohibited the introduction of measures involving a net increase in expenditure or a net reduction in public revenues during consideration of the budget; but that provision was easily evaded.

The constitution of the Fifth Republic asserts that no member of the French Parliament can introduce a legislative proposal that would either increase public expenditure or decrease public revenue. Such a provision might still be applied loosely. But the Constitutional Court has interpreted the restriction rather narrowly. It is still possible, however, to make proposals that would incur increased expenditures if they are *genuinely* compensated for in other areas, and the government has been forced to yield this point on numerous occasions.

The government's prime weapon in getting its way financially, aside from its authority to call for a package vote, is a constitutional provision that states that the executives budget becomes law automatically if Parliament fails to act within seventy days. This effectively prevents Parliament from delaying consideration of the budget until its

demands are met, a common practice during the Fourth Republic. The upshot has been the formulation of fairly rational budget procedures in comparison with any earlier period in French parliamentary history, although increasingly frequent complaints have been heard that the government sometimes steamrollers the budget through Parliament.

The strengthening of the executive under the Fifth Republic has, without question, increased the stability of the French government and promoted cohesion among governmental personnel. Moreover, during de Gaulle's presidency, the cabinet finally developed an effective secretariat, as did the office of the prime minister; and something like collective responsibility became a reality. The government's ministers were also able to achieve greater control over their departments, organizing personal staffs responsive to their views.

It must be emphasized, however, that virtually all of the devices that have strengthened the executive under the Fifth Republic are those pertaining to the premier rather than to the president. During the de Gaulle period the executive was granted special legislative powers on ten occasions, but on only two were these powers granted specifically to the president. All the controls over the legislative process that have been analyzed here are controls in the hands of the government and the premier. True, the premier is named by the president, but the premier has the right to choose his own cabinet, and the president has no constitutional right to remove him. Thus, although no Fifth Republic premier has thus far defied the president, considerable room exists for change in the effective power of the premier and the government, even if the present constitution should remain unchanged. We need not assume that the premier will continue to be the agent of the president, nor need we assume that the constitution condemns future parliaments to the control of an executive dominated by the president.

6. THE FIFTH REPUBLIC: THE LEGISLATURE

THE TWO CHAMBERS: As in the past, the parliament of Fifth Republic France is also made up of two houses, the National Assembly and the Senate. The lower chamber, the National Assembly, is composed of 487 deputies elected for five-year terms by universal suffrage; the upper chamber, the Senate, contains 274 deputies elected for nine-year terms by departmental electoral colleges. Every three years one-third of the Senate is renewed by the colleges, which consist of departmental deputies and councillors as well as delegates elected by the municipal councils of the department.

During the Fourth Republic, the Senate, or the Council of the Republic as it was then called, was extremely weak and largely ignored; de Gaulle, however, decided to increase its powers once again, primarily so that it could serve as a conservative check upon a National Assembly which he expected to be rather more radical in its political viewpoints. Besides, under the original constitution of the Fifth Republic, the Senate was elected by an electoral college that was basically the same as the one that elected the president; the Senate was viewed, therefore, as inherently more sympathetic to the perspective of the president.

Under the 1958 constitution, then, the two chambers were assigned equal powers except in three important respects: the Assembly's traditional power of being first to examine the budget was maintained; the cabinet was made responsible only to the National Assembly; and the Assembly was given the final word on legislation, if the government so desired. The constitution also provides that every bill be examined by both houses with a view to the adoption of an identical text; if, however, there is continuing disagreement on the text after two readings in each chamber, the premier can convene a joint conference committee, with an equal number of members from each chamber, and ask the committee to write a compromise text. The government then submits the compromise to both houses for their approval. If no agreement is reached, the premier can ask the National Assembly to rule "definitively" on the bill, but unless he does so, a Senate veto is final.

De Gaulle originally expected to use the Senate to block National Assembly proposals he disliked. The opposite occurred, however: the Assembly, with its Gaullist majorities, proved quite tractable; the Senate, with its over-representation of small-town France, and its under-representation of the Gaullist majority, turned out to be incorrigible so far as de Gaulle was concerned. As a result, the government was frequently forced to ask the Assembly to make the final decision on legislation, and the Senate's role in legislation was progressively diminished. In the end, of course, de Gaulle decided to eliminate the Senate—or, more accurately, to replace it with a much weaker chamber of a different kind—rather than deal with it any further. And it was this decision that precipitated the 1969 referendum that led to his resignation.

The moderate and moderate-left local notables over-represented in the Senate supported de Gaulle at the beginning of the Fifth Republic; later, however, they bitterly opposed the 1962 referendum amending the constitution and altering the constituency of the president. The UDR (Union of Democrats for the Republic) has never had more than 15 percent of the seats in the Senate, and throughout the Fifth Republic opposition parties continued to dominate the upper house even when they were reduced to a minority in the Assembly. The Senate still provides a forum for conservative criticism of Gaullist reforms, particularly agricultural reforms, but it has also been a place for the expression of ideas in defense of civil liberties often abused by arbitrary executive authority. Thus, it was the president of the Senate, Alain Poher, who requested that the Constitutional Council examine the Law on Associations passed in 1971 (see p. 276).

Two sessions of Parliament are held each year. The first, which is supposed to deal primarily with the budget, lasts eighty days;

the second, which is concerned with legislative programs, lasts ninety. although parliamentary committees can meet when Parliament is not sitting, Parliament itself is now in session a maximum of five and one-half months a year, as compared with a minimum of seven months during the Fourth Republic. In practice, between 1959 and 1974 the Assembly met an average of ninety-one days a year, and the Senate sixty-seven days. The decision to shorten the time was deliberately made to allow the government more breathing space between sessions, but by 1975 pressure was increasing to lengthen the time of parliamentary deliberations.

ORIENTATION AND PROCEDURE: The basic unit of political organization in both houses is the parliamentary group. The largest groups usually consist of members of a single political party, and bear their party's name. Members of loosely organized parties may be divided among two or more groups, and parties with less than thirty deputies—the minimum number for a group to be recognized as such—may join together to form a single group or may affiliate with one formed by a larger party. Group cohesion varies. The Communists, for instance, have acted with a good deal of unity; so have the Socialists. When de Gaulle was president, the UDR parliamentary group also maintained a high degree of discipline. During Pompidou's tenure as premier, the government kept in especially close contact with the group's elected political bureau and made a number of concessions in cases where individual deputies felt that proposed measures were contrary to the interests of their constituents; the government was also inclined to favor private members' bills introduced by UDR deputies as a reward for faithful service.

The official governing body of each house is known as the bureau, which in the National Assembly consists of the president and vice president of the chamber, various secretaries and several questeurs (officials responsible for certain administrative and financial matters). The function of the bureau as a collective body is to organize and supervise the different services in the Assembly and to advise the president on disciplinary matters and on the admissibility of bills or resolutions. With the exception of the president, who is elected for the duration of a parliamentary session by the whole Assembly, bureau officers are chosen at *Conférences des présidents,* special conferences held by the leaders of the parliamentary groups; these conferences are also responsible for drawing up the parliamentary timetable and allotting membership to committees. Voting at the conferences is usually proportional to party strength, although the Communist Party suffered from discrimination during most of the Gaullist period.

Nothing better illustrates the weakening of the French Parliament during de Gaulle's presidency than the fate of its standing committees. The power of such committees in controlling legislation and their stance as government watchdogs during the Third and Fourth Republics have already been described. The constitution of the Fifth Republic restricted the number of standing committees in each house to six, with the provision that ad hoc committees could be created for special purposes. The standing committees were expected to range in size from 30 to 125, and the purpose of the new constitutional criteria was to reduce their power by making them less specialized and hence less likely to be at the beck and call of particular interests. It was also believed that larger committees were less likely to develop troublesome cross-party views based on the acquired expertise of members.

As might be expected, deputies tried to get around the constitutional limitation by forming subcommittees. These were ruled unconstitutional by the Constitutional Court. Informal "working groups" then sprang up, although formal decisions had to be made by the committee as a whole. Nevertheless, for a while some of the working groups took on the characteristics of the smaller, specialized committees of the Third and Fourth Republics; they became dominated by the special-interest groups concerned with particular legislation, and some ministers considered them important enough to testify before them. In the end, however, UDR discipline and the broad political base of membership on the parent committees cut short the rising prestige of the working groups. During the Pompidou presidency even the standing committees were frequently bypassed by having key bills discussed in a special committee consisting of the leaders of parliamentary groups supporting the president. The committees and some special committees, nonetheless, have sometimes been surprisingly successful in effectively criticizing and changing government proposals—for example, the 1966 housing and defense budgets, and several agricultural bills in 1961 and 1962. More recently, in 1973, considerable support has developed both within the majority coalition and the opposition for a proposal that would give parliamentary *rapporteurs* who are investigating budget proposals access to now secret government documents. This proposal has been interpreted as an assertion of parliamentary power.

Still another "weapon" used by the French Parliament to maintain its pre-eminence over the government during the Third and Fourth Republics, but which has fallen into disuse under the Fifth, is the oral question period. In the Third Republic interpellations of ministers could lead to a snap vote of confidence and bring down the government immediately, and the disruptive device was employed with alarming frequency. During the Fourth Republic, a period of delay was instituted before a vote could be taken; far fewer governments were destroyed, but many were weakened.

Debré wanted to save the question period, which he regarded as a useful procedure, but the constitution of the Fifth Republic pointedly specified that no vote could be taken on any question posed. Thus, deputies could gain information and challenge the government as frequently as they liked, but they could not use questions for the purpose of overturning the government. The reform, however, went too far, or perhaps it was merely that Parliament lacked the kind of unwritten rules of the game to make the question periods valuable. Ministers often sent substitutes to answer questions, and the government unabashedly used its management of the legislative timetable to control which questions would be asked and when they would be debated. As a result, virtually all embarrassing questions from the opposition were generally stricken from the agenda of the one weekly session devoted to "free" questions.

During the first Assembly session under the presidency of Giscard d'Estaing, in 1974, there appeared to be some important changes in the use of the question period. The weekly sessions became more lively as did the important exchanges between government ministers and a more aggressive opposition. Even the Gaullist members were less reluctant to pose politically embarrassing questions.

The one other weapon that previous parliaments possessed, the censure motion, became almost equally difficult to use. Formerly, it could be introduced with comparative ease, but under the Fifth Republic's constitution, 10 percent of the Assembly must now propose a censure motion, and it cannot be voted upon until forty-eight hours after it is introduced. Only those voting for the motion are counted and a majority of the whole house is required to pass it, so that absentees and abstainers work to the advantage of the government. Further, the same signatories cannot propose another censure motion during the same session of Parliament. Only one censure motion has passed thus far in the Fifth Republic: after de Gaulle decided to submit his constitutional reform of the presidency directly to the people, a censure motion was passed that resulted in the election of November, 1962.

7. ON THE GAME OF POLITICS

The French National Assembly is housed in the Palais Bourbon on the left bank of the Pont de la Concorde, its home since 1798. The palace was declared national property at the beginning of the French Revolution, and after several other buildings had been tried, it was fitted out to quarter the National Assembly. The parliamentary chamber is shaped like an antique theater—a semicircular hall with rising rows of seats broken by radial passages. The front benches are reserved for the members of the government, and the deputies fan out behind them according to political affiliation, moving from right to left (Figure 14.1). There has, on occasion, been some squabbling among parties—for example, between the Radicals and the MRP (Popular Republican Movement) at the beginning of the Fourth Republic and between the UDR (Union of Democrats for

the Republic) and the Radicals during the Fifth—as to just where they should sit, but usually such matters are settled without too much fuss. Unlike the British Parliament and American Congress, where members usually speak from their seats, French deputies move to the rostrum to address their colleagues; the custom is also observed in the Senate, located in the Palais du Luxembourg, a short distance away, whose chamber is constructed along the same general lines.

A parliamentary career in France remains somewhat uncertain. During the seventy years of the Third Republic, 4,892 deputies

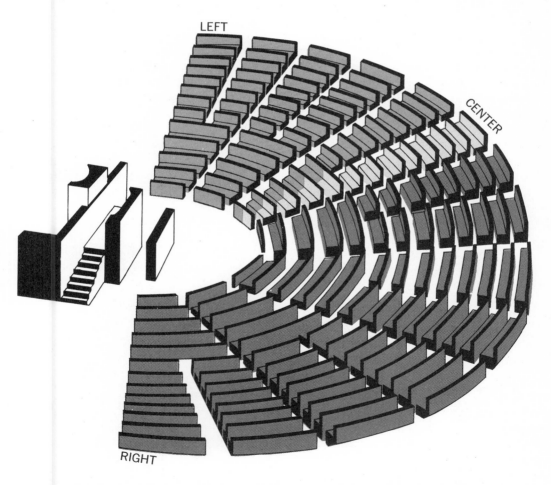

FIGURE 14.1 FLOOR PLAN OF THE FRENCH NATIONAL ASSEMBLY, 1974

were seated, and during the Fourth 1,112 were elected from metropolitan France. Of those elected during the Third Republic, 46 percent served but one term and another 21 percent only two. A mere 3 percent of the deputies were elected seven or more times, many of them having more or less inherited their seats in areas of rural France still loyal to the old aristocracy. In the Fifth Republic, the high turnover of deputies continues. Sixty-three percent of the deputies elected in 1958 were new to the Assembly; and by 1962, 80 percent of its members had never sat during the Fourth Republic. More than 25 percent of the deputies elected in 1967 were new arrivals.

During the Third Republic, approximately 20 percent of the parliamentarians were members of the legal profession, but more than 30 percent pursued other "intellectual" professions, including teaching and journalism (see Table 14.2). During the Fourth Republic, especially at sessions in which the Communist Party representation was quite large, a substantial working-class representation was also present—21 percent, if white-collar employees are included.

In general, members of the French Parliament in the years of the Third Republic came from humbler backgrounds than did their British contemporaries, for the hold of the aristocracy and upper bourgeoisie on the levers of governmental power was broken earlier in France than in Britain. Moreover, if we define the term "intellectual" broadly, and include professors, secondary-school teachers, journalists, and writers, the role of this group in Parliament was consid-

TABLE 14.2   OCCUPATIONS OF DEPUTIES IN THREE REPUBLICS

	Third Republic	Fourth Republic		Fifth Republic		
	1936	1956	1968	1962	1967	1973
Farmers	13.5%	10%	11.5%	9%	7%	5.3%
Workers	13.5	13	1.5	5	6.5	4.7
Clerks		9	5	8	6.5	3.0
Teachers	10.5	6.5	2	4	14	14.6
Professors		8.5	8	6		
Lawyers	20	13	16	11	10	9.5
Doctors	8	5	12	12	10	11.9
Journalists	9	4.5	5	4	4	3.2
High civil servants	3.5	4	8	9	9	5.3
Officers and priests	1	1.5	2.5	4	2	.6
Engineers	2	4.5	6	4	5	3.4
Managers	2	5	7	9	5.5	4.4
Businessmen	14	10	15.5	14.5	8	11.4
Shopkeepers	0	6	0	0	0	3.6
Others	3	0	0	0	12.5	19.1

Adapted from Philip M. Williams, *The French Parliament, 1958–1967* (London: George Allen & Unwin, 1968), p. 34, reprinted by permission of the publisher; 1973 data derived from *Le Monde*, March 14, 1973.

erably higher in France than in Britain. One writer in the 1920's called post-World War I France the "Republic of the Professors," a not inaccurate appellation.

Far more than in Britain, too, the road to Parliament lay through local government offices. During much of the Third Republic, more than two-thirds of the deputies had held a local office before being elected to Parliament. The figure for the post-World War II Fourth Republic was about 40 percent, and even the 1958 (Fifth Republic) election, which produced massive political changes in parliamentary personnel, failed to alter the fact that more than three-fourths of the deputies had held local office at one time or another. The percentage remained high during subsequent elections. As for those deputies who came to Parliament by way of other routes, many of them made haste to weld local ties as soon as they could. The composition of the Fifth Republic Parliament changed somewhat in other respects. The proportion of deputies with a working-class background dropped off initially, in part as a result of the decline in Communist Party strength; the number of lawyers also decreased, whereas the representation of other professions, especially teachers and high civil servants, rose sharply.

Most French deputies of the Third and Fourth Republics had to give up their occupations because Parliament took up so much of their time. Sessions normally lasted from eight months to a year, and deputies who came from areas outside Paris had to remain in the city for most of the week. The shortened sessions of the Fifth Republic have allowed more time for certain types of professional activity, but it is still difficult for most deputies to be anything but professional parliamentarians. Since 1910 the deputies' salaries have been reasonably adequate, and they were raised again during the Fifth Republic. In addition, they are allowed some funds for a small staff. While their remuneration is not comparable to American standards, it is fairly lavish when contrasted with the British.

Deputies in both the Third and Fourth Republics spent considerable time in contact with, and doing favors for, their constituents. If anything, the extreme centralization of France meant that every decision on local issues had to come from Paris, and this placed a greater burden on the deputy than either his British or American counterpart experienced. In the Fourth Republic, proportional representation tended to divorce deputies from constituents—but far less than those who wrote its constitution had expected, since so many deputies were also local mayors or councillors. Regardless of how a Frenchman voted nationally, he was far more concerned, however, with a new school or a new road or another subsidy; he knew his deputy was doing something if a school was built. The result, of course, was that deputies, already overburdened with the time-consuming schedule of parliamentary debates, found the rest of their hours taken up with efforts to satisfy the various groups that were pressing in upon them. While president of the Finance Committee, Mendés-France described the situation this way: "I open my mail at breakfast. There are at least two to three hundred letters every morning, three-fourths of which are requests for special favors." [4] One deputy noted recently that he had written forty thousand letters in 1971 requesting government favors for his constituents.

One of the parliamentary problems of the Fourth Republic was absenteeism—always a touchy issue in the game of politics. Deputies would take off for the provinces, leaving their mandate with friends, even friends in opposition parties. One or two Communist deputies could harass the entire government by proxy voting for sixty or seventy of their colleagues in an almost empty chamber. The Fifth Republic's "organic laws," drafted under Debré's guidance to supplement the constitution, attempted to do away with the evils of voting by proxy. No member could hold more than one proxy, and proxies were

[4] David Schoenbrun, *As France Goes* (New York: Harper & Co., 1957), pp. 147–148.

permitted for only a few specified reasons such as family illness; members who were absent too often would forfeit part of their salaries. Proxy voting was also made physically more difficult by the substitution of individual electronic voting devices for paper ballots at each deputy's bench; proxy voters would now have to leap over benches in order to do their colleagues a favor. Even so, the impediments to absenteeism proved of little avail: the deputies most in demand as proxy holders only became younger and younger and more and more agile. Cooperation on proxy voting continued to extend across party lines, and not a few Gaullists would gladly cast a Socialist vote against a government bill—in return, of course, for the same favor.

8. INTEREST-GROUP POLITICS IN FRANCE

THE ROLE OF INTEREST GROUPS: Part of the mythology of French politics during much of the Third Republic, for the left at least, was that organized interest groups were intrinsically evil: there should be no intermediate bodies, it was believed, between the individual and the state. The hostility of the French left to corporatism can be partially explained by the heritage of the French Revolution.

Despite the official ideology, however, interest groups proliferated during the late nineteenth and early twentieth centuries. In France as in Britain, the government turned to some of these groups for advice or assistance as state intervention in the economy became more and more important. The Vichy regime added considerably to the list of special-interest groups "represented" in the administration of public policy, and by the later years of the Fourth Republic, more than two thousand advisory groups of one kind or another were attached to government agencies.

Interest-group activity in France during the Third and Fourth Republics was considerably different from group activity in Britain. The formation of functionally specific associations is partly a product of modernization, and insofar as France was a more traditional nation in many ways, with a fairly large peasant and artisan base, this was reflected in interest-group activity. Organizations were relatively weak and ephemeral—forming, dissolving, and forming again. The fragmentation and mutual suspicion permeating much of French life also made organizational cooperation difficult. When organizations did form, they found it difficult to attract and sustain a large and disciplined membership. It was impossible to collect dues and to convince members that sustained activity was necessary for success. The left might talk of powerful business organizations that controlled France, and the conservatives might quake at the increasing power of the trade unions; but in fact, both sides exaggerated the strength of their opponents, for neither business nor labor was organized with nearly the strength, efficiency, and intensity of their counterparts in Germany and Britain.

Another aspect of organizational weakness has been the inability of leaders of mass interest groups to control the actions of those for whom they speak. Most of the largest, most bitter strikes in French history have not been initiated (and have sometimes been opposed) by trade-union organizations. Nor is this tradition of mass action limited to workers. In 1969 and 1970 French shopkeepers, angry over a social-insurance scheme that their representatives had negotiated and supported, rose up in violence— and their targets included their own leaders. Spontaneous peasant strikes and violence against the government's agricultural policies have been more common under the Fifth Republic than under the Fourth. On the other side, the government has often refused to take the leaders of these groups seriously unless and until they have "demonstrated" their ability to mobilize the masses for whom they claimed to speak.

For the simple reason that power was extremely disorganized in the French political system under the Third and Fourth Republics, members of the National Assembly and the executive, including the bureaucracy, were all targets of interest-group activity. In the Assembly, deputies sympathetic to a particular special interest would form a "study group," meeting from time to time to try to load legislative committees with deputies attuned to the concerns of their interest group. They would also try to colonize the bureaucracy with supporters of their interest group.

The result was not unlike the governmental pattern in the United States: not only did various ministries fight with one another, but constant friction also existed within the ministries and the parliamentary committees. Since most governments ruled with such tenuous majorities that even the defection of a few deputies could bring them down, many special-interest groups were able to veto a bill they considered detrimental by influencing a small number of deputies. (But for the same reasons, few groups were able to push through important legislation for their own benefit.) Also, because parties were poorly organized and most deputies depended for their political survival upon establishing good constituent relations on an individual basis, they felt far more at the mercy of particular interests than did their British counterparts. They would, therefore, introduce measure after measure totally unrelated to any overall conception of government policy, though many hoped their proposals would be buried in committee—as, indeed, most of them were. Thus, the policies that emerged from Parliament often reflected the hodgepodge of unrelated group demands. In all, then, interest groups in the Third and Fourth Republics contributed to the government instability which prevented the effective consideration and implementation of public policy.

CHANGE AND TRANSITION: In the later years of the Fourth Republic, the parliamentary and public activity of special-interest groups began to show signs of change. Not only were some groups developing a better organizational capacity, but, more impor-

tant, they were demonstrating an increasing sense of responsibility. As distinct from the initial, violent opposition to the formation of the European Coal and Steel Community by many businessmen, for example, substantial portions of French business, including some of its more reactionary spokesmen, took a far more positive attitude toward the Common Market.

During the Fifth Republic almost every major pressure group has manifested an interest in and a capacity for pragmatic bargaining both with their adversaries and with the state. In the process they have begun to develop training programs for their representatives and supporting services to maximize their influence at the bargaining table. This new strategy, however, has not meant that the leaders of mass organizations have gained greater control over the actions of those they represent—as the 1969 revolt of the small shopkeepers demonstrates. Indeed, notwithstanding the trend toward pragmatic bargaining among interest groups, many commentators have noted the high level of violence and street action during the Fifth Republic. Some of this activity has been initiated and utilized by unions and farmers' organizations in the process of bargaining, but generally the most violent protests have not been controlled by any organization.

In a sense, this anomic mass violence has been encouraged by and related to the restructuring of interest-group activity that has taken place under the Fifth Republic. The shift in governmental power from the legislature to the executive and administrative elites has meant that decision-making has become more remote and less immediately responsive. It became apparent to many during the early years of the Fifth Republic that violent, mass outbursts did pay off, that they augmented the bargaining power of interest organizations in direct confrontation with the administration. As political scientist Stanley Hoffman has observed, "Never before has the resort of violence been so widespread and treated so casually. The ungodly spectacle of party squabbles and cabinet crises has been eliminated, only to be replaced by an even ungodlier one." [5] Compared with the past, however, direct confrontation has been more specifically directed at policy rather than constitutional arrangements. Thus, the origin of many of the most important social reforms of the Fifth Republic can be traced to a crisis exploited by interest organizations. It is therefore impossible to understand the patterns of interest-group activity without understanding the destabilizing but invigorating role often played by spontaneous mass action. In this context we can also understand why journalists have referred to interest groups, particularly the unions, as the "real" opposition in the Fifth Republic.

9.   RETROSPECT AND PROSPECT: THE NATURE AND EXPLANATION OF FRENCH GOVERNMENTAL INSTITUTIONS

The governmental process in France from the end of the Franco-Prussian War to de Gaulle's Fifth Republic reflected the political divisions in French society and the lack of organizational cohesion among French political parties and interest groups. All governments were based on coalitions of parties—themselves coalitions of diverse groups —and none could act decisively lest it lose the shaky majority that had put it into office.   The result was a series of weak governments incapable of governing, governments that served mainly as brokers among various groups.

Because voters could not make judgments on the basis of policies actually carried out, they were encouraged to continue making them on the basis of an ideological rhetoric that never had to meet the crucial test of being translated into concrete public policies. The same ideological slogans were consequently repeated year after year and decade after decade, and since no one really expected either parties or governments to promulgate policies bearing any really close relation to ideological pronouncements, most

voters continued to assess their deputies on the basis of whether or not they had managed to obtain certain limited economic favors—a special subsidy, a paved road, a new school, a wage increase.

The governments most likely to remain in office for the longest time were the least ideological, and the most willing and able to act as clever brokers among the various groups. The whole process reduced the prestige of politics in the eyes of the voters and discredited the parliamentary system. It also postponed the day when France would at last have to tangle with the crucial problems that beset a modern nation.

The faults of the system should not be overstated. In times of crisis, France usually managed to establish reasonably strong governments. And the system did, on the whole, offer a framework within which political and social life remained fairly peaceful and democratic freedoms prevailed, no mean accomplishment. Charles de Gaulle is a case in point—a strong man put in office at a moment of crisis. His objective was to reform French political institutions even as he pushed through economic and social reforms to modernize and strengthen the nation.

Today, after more than fifteen years of relatively stable and effective government, the strong executive seems to be institutionalized in France. Important political groups in the nation continue to argue that the French political system has failed to deal adequately with many vital social problems. However, few advocate a return to the institutions of the Third or Fourth Republic. Without question, there is considerable room for change within the Fifth Republic's constitutional arrangements. Should the majority come apart, the dependence of the president upon the premier could increase. A premier who derives his authority from a parliamentary majority would be more likely to facilitate Parliament's integration into the decision-making process: much of the present docility of Parliament is due less to constitutional arrangements than to the un-

[5] Hoffmann, *op. cit.*, p. 94.

willingness of the majority to assert its prerogatives.

Yet even if the legislature were to reassert its powers, it is hard to envisage a National Assembly as powerful or as disorganized as the assemblies of the Fourth Republic. France in 1975 is not the France of 1958. Small-town, rural, isolated France is quickly disappearing, and the modern sector of French life is becoming increasingly significant. Many of the old cleavages have become less sharp, and much of the traditional ideology seems archaic. Further, voters have now experienced government that can govern. They have voted in elections in which they knew their decisions would make a difference; their appreciation of this opportunity has been such that they would obviously be extremely impatient with anything closely resembling a return to governmental paralysis.

Of course, France is not, nor has it ever been, politically somnolent. Irreconcilable cross-currents of political, and social theory still exist, and these may be seen in the often violent way in which interest groups now present and support their demands. The crises of the Fourth Republic were in Parliament; the crises of the Fifth have been in the streets.

15

Parliamentary Government in Germany

1. NATURE AND EXPLANATION OF GERMAN PARLIAMENTARY INSTITUTIONS

PRE—WORLD WAR I: The constitution of the Imperial Reich, which came into existence in 1871, placed power in the hands of the emperor, his chancellor, and the Federal Council (*Bundesrat*). The council, a body composed of representatives appointed by the state governments, shared with the emperor and the chancellor the tasks of making treaties, authorizing appointments, and declaring war. It also determined what bills were to be brought before the Reichstag, an assembly elected by universal manhood suffrage. As the supreme constitutional and administrative court of the empire, the Federal Council also rendered decisions in disputes among the different states.

Prussia, as the dominant power, enjoyed a privileged position in the empire. Not only did the Prussian king fill the role of emperor, but Prussians held the presidency and chairmanships of all standing committees in the Federal Council. Moreover, within this body, the Prussians had sufficient votes to defeat any constitutional amendment, as well as to veto all proposed changes affecting the army, the navy, and finances. In addition, the Prussian chancellor served simultaneously as the imperial chancellor.

Executive authority was placed with the emperor, who, as supreme commander of the army and navy, exercised almost complete control over foreign affairs. He had the right to convoke and dismiss both the Federal Council and the Reichstag, and the chancellor as well as other officials were directly responsible to him.

The Reichstag's powers were extremely circumscribed. Even its requests for information could be, and often were, ignored with impunity. Further, although the Reichstag's approval was required for the annual budget and other financial transactions, such as loans, it was unable to use this authority to wrest any real concessions, at least during Bismarck's chancellorship. Nor was its prestige very high. It became known in popular parlance as the *Quasselbude*, or, roughly, chatterbox. Despite this, and despite the fact that the electoral system was designed to insure the over-representation of rural claims, the Reichstag's debates were not without effect. It could serve as a national sounding board, and, indeed, parliamentary debates frequently so annoyed the emperor that he dissolved the Reichstag, requiring new electors.

After Bismarck's fall, the Reichstag became more assertive. On several occasions between 1906 and 1914, it forced the government to backtrack on policy; more important, after 1909 the government took into account parliamentary sentiment in appointing ministers. Moreover, for the first time (1909) in German history, a Reich chancellor, Prince von Bülow, was forced to resign when his program for financial reform failed to pass the Reichstag. Finally, in 1912 the newly elected Reichstag instituted a vote of no confidence against the government. The device, however, was used only once, in 1913—and to no effect: it was simply ignored. The coming of the war almost automatically eliminated the possibility of legislative reform within the framework of existing institutions.

On the whole, the governments of the German states were no less authoritarian than the central government. The system of representation in the elected assemblies assured control by conservative elements, as did the lack of executive responsibility to the legislature. Nevertheless, the empire was a *Rechtstaat*—a state ruled by law—and, except for certain periods, the civil rights of its citizens were protected, including the right to criticize the government both orally and in print.

The authoritarian nature of the national and state governments was only partially due to the constitutional assignment of power. More significant was the fact that the elites in German society preferred an authoritarian regime. German society in the late nineteenth century was dominated by an aristocracy that, far more than its French or British counterparts, emphasized the values of status, discipline, and "manliness." These virtues were defined largely in military terms. The road to social improvement for the petit-bourgeois young man was to attend a business college, join a dueling fraternity and acquire a scar, and then enter into those circles that might enable him to marry the daughter of his employer.

The emphasis upon self-control and status was related to a need for an ordered environment and strong sources of authority. The whole structure of German society was authoritarian, orderly, and disciplined; in mirroring these values, it also perpetuated them. Crime rates, for example, were relatively low; and business, scientific, and military life were characterized by a passion for order that undoubtedly played a role in the industrial, scientific, and military success that the empire achieved so quickly.

The "responsible" German would do his public duty by obeying the law. He tended to regard those who rejected traditional values, especially when such a rejection threatened the public order, as wicked men who should be punished by "right-thinking" people. By contrast, the American pattern has much more often regarded group deviation as a function of faults in the system that must be adjusted in order to re-establish a consensus.

The "responsible" German would also do his duty by voting, but he would leave other political affairs in the hands of those whose superior authority gave them the right to make political decisions. Students of German political culture have often noted the relative absence of feelings of civic obligation and competence; that is, in comparison with citizens of Britain and France, Germans have scored relatively low in the incidence of belief that one should participate in community affairs and that one is able to influence the course of political events by doing so.[1]

THE WEIMAR PERIOD: After the defeat of Germany in World War I, and the crushing of a "radical" Socialist move to create a Socialist state, a National Constituent Assembly was elected to write a new constitution. Following extensive discussions and revisions, the constitution was promulgated on August 11, 1919. A long, complicated document, it contained an elaborate bill of rights and other democratic provisions, including the referendum and the recall.

In its day, the constitution of Weimar was hailed as the most enlightened and democratic instrument of any major country. The intention of its writers was to make the Reichstag the center of power. The political system it called for was predicated on a belief in popular sovereignty, and the Reichstag, a popularly elected assembly, was to represent the sovereign will of the people directly. But while the Reichstag was at the center of power on paper, in practice it became immobilized by party divisions; and over the course of the Republic, power shifted more and more from the Reichstag to the executive.

The Reichstag had the power to overrule the upper house—the Federal Council—by a two-thirds vote, and both the chancellor and members of the cabinet were made responsible to it. The Reichstag was also given the power to establish committees of inquiry and to question members of the government on policy and programs. It is true that a popularly elected president had the power to dissolve the Reichstag—but only once on a given issue; a new lower house then had to be elected within sixty days and assembled within another thirty. It is also true that the Reichstag could pass enabling acts giving the chancellor the power to legislate by decree—but these acts required passage by a two-thirds vote, and the limits of the decree authority were set by the act itself. Furthermore, Article 48 of the constitution gave the president the right not only to rule by decree in order to maintain public order but also to suspend certain civil liberties in time of national emergency. This constitutional grant was not inordinate, however; it was to be invoked only with the approval of the cabinet, and only on condition that the Reichstag be kept fully informed of the actions taken by the government. But because the Reichstag became so fundamentally divided against itself, President Paul von Hindenburg began to use his powers under Article 48 extensively in the last years of Weimar. Between 1930 and 1932 Hindenburg was to make extensive use of this "emergency" power to appoint and dismiss chancellors. He could do so, however, only because the Reichstag was unable to agree on a candidate for the office. This was an experience that the framers of the Bonn constitution would not in later years treat lightly.

Elections to the Reichstag proceeded under a system of proportional representation that was intended to insure the full expression of every possible ideological viewpoint. The resulting multiplicity of political parties, all of them defining their interests in relatively ideological terms and displaying a general unwillingness to compromise and to bargain for the sake of agreement, made it almost impossible to process political demands. Coalitions formed and reformed; with an average life of eight months, cabinets rose and collapsed; and election after election was held without breaking the impasse in the legislature. In frustration and despair, the Reichstag voted enabling legislation to permit the cabinet to act by decree on those critical, public matters that the individual deputies were too timid or too divided to consider. Finally in 1933, after

[1] See, for example, Gabriel Almond and Sidney Verba, *The Civic Culture* (Princeton, N.J.: Princeton University Press, 1963).

four major elections in six months, with one government giving way to another, Chancellor Franz von Papen persuaded the eighty-three-year-old Hindenburg to ask Adolf Hitler, as leader of the National Socialists, to form a government. (Von Papen, of course, believed that as vice chancellor he could control Hitler.) Using force and cajolery, Hitler pushed through an enabling act in March, 1933, that allowed him to rule by decree and to establish the Nazi dictatorship. Combining the roles of party leader, chancellor, and, after 1934, president, Hitler transformed the Weimar Republic into a totalitarian state.

After the fall of the republic, the Weimar constitution came under heavy criticism. Both Article 48, which had been used under circumstances that amounted to presidential dictatorship, and the provision for enabling acts, which allowed Hitler to obtain almost unlimited authority, were blamed for the collapse of the Weimar Republic. So, too, was the system of proportional representation; this, critics argued, encouraged a multiplicity of parties and prevented effective policy decisions. The malaise that destroyed the republic, however, was social as well as political; the same instruments, under other circumstances, would not have been used in the same way. As we noted in Chapter 2, it was the fragmentation of German political and social life, not the weaknesses of the constitution, that destroyed the Weimar Republic. Torn apart by tensions induced by the rapid modernization of an extremely rigid traditional society, Germans were unable to construct institutions that would have permitted them to find a peaceful solution to their problems.

THE NAZI REGIME: The government created by Hitler was a totalitarian police state in which the fundamental decisions were made by him, often with the advice of small groups of trusted comrades. The Weimar constitution was not rescinded, the Reichstag continued to exist, and elections and even plebiscites were held. But in the Nazi elections, only one slate of candidates was permitted to campaign for office, and in the plebiscites, the "people" were allowed only to ratify decisions already taken.

Unlike the regime of the Soviets, that of the Nazis was not completely a party dictatorship. Hitler preferred to work through the traditional state machinery—after purging it of "unreliable" elements—and the party never completely permeated the armed forces. Also, a private sector of the economy remained in existence, albeit heavily controlled; but even this meant only that the Nazis were able to achieve their economic goals by exercising control rather than by wholesale nationalization.

We know now that behind the facade of unity and simple hierarchic command which the Hitler regime presented to the world, incredible confusion and overlapping of jurisdictions prevailed. Hitler's subordinates used their positions to increase their power and to curry favor with the Führer, and Hitler adroitly played off one subordinate against another to make sure that no one emerged as a possible competitor. Because of the highly personal nature of the regime, and the fact that it had not succeeded in institutionalizing the Nazi Party as the sole source of leadership recruitment or as a policy-making body, there is some question as to whether the apparatus would have survived Hitler's death. It seems likely that even if the Nazis had not been defeated, the Third Reich would eventually have been transformed into a bureaucratic dictatorship that would probably have eroded.

THE BONN REPUBLIC: Immediately after the conclusion of hostilities in 1945, the Western occupying powers began to revive local political institutions in their zones. As the Cold War developed, France, Britain, and the United States moved further along these lines, first integrating their zones economically and then encouraging the Germans to create a new set of national institutions. The machinery for drafting a constitution was put into motion by the Western military governors in the spring of 1948, and that summer the minister presidents of the German states (*Länder*) commissioned a group of constitutional and political experts to prepare a draft Basic Law for what was to become the Federal Republic of Germany. By fall, a Parliamentary Council elected by the *Länder* was meeting in Bonn to consider just what form the Basic Law should take.[2]

After lengthy negotiations among members of the Parliamentary Council representing the political parties (there were twenty-seven representatives from both the Christian Democratic Party and the Social Democratic Party, five from all other parties) and between the council members and the military governors, the Basic Law won final approval from the Parliamentary Council on May 8, 1949, and from the military governors on May 12. After consideration by the state legislatures, the Basic Law was officially promulgated on May 23, and the first general election under the new law was held three months later. At a special ceremony held at the Allied headquarters on September 21, the Federal Republic of Germany came formally into existence. The framework of government created by the Parliamentary Council consists of an executive (the president, the chancellor, and the cabinet), a bicameral legislature (the Bundestag, or lower house, and the Bundesrat, or senate), and a judiciary that includes the Federal Constitutional Court.[3]

[2] The Parliamentary Council resolved to retain the designation Basic Law (*Grundgestez*) until a reunited Germany could draft a constitution.

[3] The Constitutional Court was created in imitation of, and with the encouragement of, the Americans. Although one can find some antecedent precedents, the idea that a judicial body should have final word on the meaning of the constitution has not, historically, been part of the Continental or English tradition. The Court has the authority to review the compatibility of federal and *Land* legislation with the Basic Law, and cases may be brought to its attention by various governmental organs as well as individuals. Unlike the practice in the United States, issues may be brought to the Court for judgment for "abstract" review, i. e., without waiting for an actual controversy to arise from the application of a law.

While the Court has made a number of landmark decisions, its power thus far in no way compares with that of its American counterpart. For a fairly recent discussion, see Daniel P. Kommers, "The Fed-

2. THE BONN REPUBLIC: THE PRESIDENCY

The Weimar experience—with its potentially all-powerful, popularly elected president—aroused strong suspiciousness in postwar Germany concerning presidential government. Yet even in clearly parliamentary regimes, such as the French Fourth Republic, the need had been felt for a figure who would serve as an expression of the continuity of the state—perhaps an elected monarch, albeit a constitutional one, without power.

Basically, the office of the president in the Bonn Republic is just that. The constitution says that he will be elected at a federal convention—a special meeting of Bundestag members and an equal number of members elected, according to proportional representation, by the state assemblies. The president, whose term of office is five years, is responsible for such routine tasks as receiving ambassadors and issuing letters of appointment to officials, countersigned by a cabinet minister. He also proposes to the Bundestag candidates for chancellor, appoints ministers on the chancellor's recommendation, and can dissolve the Bundestag in certain special situations. Under all but the most extreme circumstances, he has no real power. The powers that are conferred are far less extensive than those available to most other European presidents.

The president was deprived of the authority granted under Article 48 of the Weimar constitution to suspend any of the long list of fundamental rights now guaranteed in a rather comprehensive bill of rights. After years of acrimonious debate, however, the Bundestag in 1968 did give the government extended powers in case of national emergency. Plagued by memories of the use of Article 48 during the Weimar Republic, the Bundestag was extremely careful to limit the use of such powers and provided for con-

eral Constitutional Courts in the West German Political System," in Joel B. Grossman and Joseph P. Tanenhaus, eds. *Frontiers of Judicial Research* (New York: John Wiley & Sons, 1968).

tinuous legislative supervision should they be exercised.

In the first election in 1949, the presidency went to Theodor Heuss, a leader of the Free Democratic Party, who institutionalized the office by playing the role of wise, nonpartisan elder statesman. Such was the affection he engendered that he was re-elected unanimously in 1954. When the question of Heuss's successor came up in 1959 (the president can be re-elected only once), Chancellor Adenauer, under increasing pressure to step aside and let a younger man take over the chancellorship, considered running himself. Adenauer let it be known that he considered the office one that could influence policy, especially in the area of foreign affairs. Adenauer insisted, however, that if he sought the presidency, he would have to be allowed by the Christian Democratic Party to choose his successor as chancellor. When his party refused to do this, Adenauer decided to remain as chancellor, and, at the last minute, the Christian Democratic Party found another candidate in Heinrich Luebke, the minister of agriculture.

Luebke, who at times seemed to feel ill at ease with the constraints of his office, took a more partisan stance as president—particularly, just before and during Erhard's term as chancellor. But he was, nevertheless, elected to a second term. Subsequently, in a change reflecting the evanescence of the political scene, Gustav Heinemann, a Socialist minister of justice, was narrowly elected president in 1969. He was the first Social Democrat to be elected president of Germany since Friedrich Ebert, the first president of the Weimar Republic. Heinemann tried to reduce the ceremonial aspects of the office and projected an image of himself as a citizen's president, apparently in recognition of the fact that as the powers of the president are very limited, the actual influence that he wields depends primarily upon his personality. Walter Scheel, who in 1974 became the fourth president of the Federal Republic, had been the head of the FDP and the foreign minister in Brandt's government. These credentials assured him a somewhat greater role in influencing the substance of policy than that which had been possessed by his predecessors. In the year after taking office President Scheel spoke out forcefully in favor of pending controversial legislation and became the first West German head of state since Theodor Heuss to make an official visit to the United States.

3. THE BONN REPUBLIC: THE CHANCELLOR AND THE CABINET

CHANCELLOR DEMOCRACY: In drafting the constitution, the Parliamentary Council was anxious to provide for the stability that was lacking during the Weimar period. Council delegates had become convinced that it was necessary to establish a constitutional system that would permit the government to act in terms of a relatively consistent set of programs. They also concluded that German government should no longer be subject to overthrow by extremists who could agree on little else except their opposition to the existing regime. Assuming the continuation of a multiparty system, they believed that most governments would be coalitions, and that it would be impossible to develop the kind of strong cabinet so typical of British politics. They therefore concentrated their efforts on strengthening the position of the chancellor; it was their purpose to provide his office with sufficient power to guarantee effective governance.

The chancellor, who is personally responsible for general government policy, is elected every four years at the beginning of a new Bundestag. The Bundestag votes on the president's nominee for chancellor without prior debate. If the nominee is not elected by a majority—an absolute majority —of the total membership, the Bundestag must vote on another nominee. Only after a two-week deadlock may the Bundestag, with the approval of the president, elect a chancellor by a majority of those present and voting—a plurality.

Once elected, the chancellor is not required to ask for a vote of confidence for his government's program or for approval of the list of ministers whom he appoints. He can be removed only by a motion of no confidence, at which time the Bundestag must elect his successor by an absolute majority. One of the rare times in which an attempt has been made to unseat the ruling chancellor was in 1972, when the CDU tried and failed to unseat Brandt and replace him with Rainer Brazel. This provision for the "constructive" vote of nonconfidence was intended to prevent a repetition of the Weimar experience in which the extreme left and the extreme right combined to overturn centrist governments but could not agree on any candidate to replace the officials they had unseated.

The fact that the chancellor does not have to resign or ask for a vote of confidence if one of the government's measures fails to receive a majority makes the German government more independent of the Bundestag than it was in Weimar, or more so that a British government, for example, is of the House of Commons. If the government, however, is more independent of the Bundestag, the Bundestag is also more independent, in one way, of the government. A German government has much less control over the legislative calendar and, more importantly, over legislation itself, than does a British government.

The chancellor can ask for a vote of confidence at any time he so chooses, and if defeated, he can request that the Bundestag be dissolved by the president and new elections held, as Brandt did for the first and only time in 1972. Nor is this the end of his authority. If the Bundestag refuses to pass legislation that the chancellor declares to be urgent, the president—with the consent of the Bundesrat—may declare a state of legislative emergency. The legislation is then resubmitted to the Bundestag. If it is again not passed, or passed in a form not satisfactory to the government, the bill becomes law upon passage by the Bundesrat.

The chancellor, together with the president of the republic and the cabinet of federal ministers, constitutes the German executive. Ministers are appointed by the chancellor after his election by the Bundestag, and they serve at his discretion. In "correcting" the mistakes of Weimar, the authors of the Bonn constitution downgraded the presidency and attempted to insure executive stability by creating a strong chancellor. In clearly defining the chancellorship as the leading position in the government, they hoped to establish a stable focus of authority.

These constitutional provisions clearly had their expected effect under Konrad Adenauer. The first chancellor of the new republic so effectively dominated the government that commentators spoke of West Germany's system of government as "chancellor democracy." Adenauer regarded his ministers primarily as technical experts subordinate to him, and he alone decided issues of general policy. Majority approval from the cabinet, as was required by the cabinet's standing orders, was usually automatic. On a number of occasions, he made personal decisions and only later informed the cabinet about them. Adenauer's chief concern, however, was foreign affairs. By and large he left the development of domestic policy to the cabinet and the ministries. The minister of finance and the economic minister, especially, had a great deal of leeway in making decisions.

Adenauer's successor, Ludwig Erhard, moved in the direction of genuine collegiality, cheerfully admitting to being overruled by the cabinet on a number of occasions. Neither his temperament nor the serious divisions within his party permitted him to repeat Adenauer's performance. A similar collegiality was manifested within the Grand Coalition cabinet. The exigencies of maintaining the coalition precluded Kurt Georg Kiesinger from asserting dominance. And neither Kiesinger as chancellor nor Willy Brandt as vice chancellor was in a position to dominate his party as had Adenauer. Moreover, the most important ministers were leading party figures in their own right. The cabinet, therefore, could rely upon the Bundestag's approval for only those policies upon which substantial agreement could be reached.

Brandt's relationship to his party after taking office in 1969 more closely resembled that of the British prime minister than that of any previous chancellor. He was clearly a party man, first of all, and his position depended on popular support for the SPD. Though not forgetting his status as *primus inter pares*, Brandt cultivated a collegial relationship among his cabinet members. In fact, some of his own cabinet colleagues, as well as countrymen, criticized him for keeping too loose a rein on the party leaders whom he brought into his cabinets.

Chancellor Helmut Schmidt, on the other hand, exercised rather more control over the cabinet after assuming office. Exploiting an adverse economic climate, he clamped down on those ministries associated with social welfare expenditures that tended to be dominated by the "left wing" of the SPD.

In the final years of Adenauer's tenure, both the legislature and the political parties began to reassert their authority. Adenauer tenaciously resisted these pressures, and his opposition to Erhard as chancellor was based on his lack of faith in Erhard's capacity to exercise authoritative leadership. As it is now turning out, however, Erhard's unwillingness and inability to dominate the

government to anywhere near the same degree that Adenauer did seems to have presaged longer-term changes in the workings of the Bonn Republic—changes toward a truly cabinet system of government. Thus, unlike the situation in Weimar, where an unbridgeable gap seemed to exist between the political institutions and the environment, in Bonn the institutions have been more supportive of and responsive to changes in the social and political climate.

THE CHANCELLERY: The constitution provides that the chancellor is responsible for the general direction of public policy, and the chancellor's office, the Federal Chancellery, was created to assist him in this task. Under Adenauer, the office was an extremely powerful one; its first director, Secretary of State Hans Globke, was for many years the second most powerful man in West Germany. Globke set up a staff of nearly one hundred high-level officials, organized to parallel the ministries of the federal government and to supervise the progress of legislation. In its coordinating capacity, the chancellery minimized the formulation of policies that were objectionable to Adenauer. Adenauer relied upon the office to keep tabs on his ministries in the years of his greatest authority, and Globke could effectively veto

TABLE 15.1 QUANTITATIVE MEASURES OF BUNDESTAG WORK, 1953–72

	BUNDESTAG SESSIONS OF				
Activity	*1953–57*	*1957–61*	*1961–65*	*1965–69*	*1969–72*
Plenary sessions	227	168	198	247	199
Party meetings	1,777	675	727	802	529
Committee meetings	4,389	2,493	2,986	2,692	1,449
Investigating committees	34	0	37	19	
Bills					
Introduced	877	613	635	654	546
Passed	507	424	427	463	334
Oral questions	1,069	1,375	4,786	10,480	11,073
Pages of printed parliamentary record (in thousands)	13.6	9.8	10.1	13.9	11.8

legislative proposals emanating from minis-tries by reporting his objections to the chan-cellor.

The power of the chancellor's office and the technical qualifications of its personnel were such that it questioned ministries con-cerning issues that might eventually become legislative projects and, in conjunction with the legislative committee of the cabinet, set priorities for the government's program. It prepared cabinet agendas, insured that bills submitted by one department had received the clearance of others, and supplied the chancellor with a summary of proposed laws and the issues they raised. It also served as the channel of communication between the government and Parliament, transmitting bills approved by the cabinet to the legisla-ture. Finally, it received all parliamentary inquiries for referral to the relevant minis-tries.

The authority of the chancellery declined somewhat during Erhard's administration and became less of a personal instrument. That decline continued under the Kiesinger-Brandt coalition. The staff was even larger and more professional than it once was, con-taining not only Christian Democrats but Social Democrats as well. But this pluralism prevented the chancellery from both for-mulating a consistent point of view and im-posing it upon governmental departments as it once did.

In a very important sense the strength of the Adenauer chancellery rested upon his ba-sically conservative (if pluralist) philoso-phy. As long as no significant social re-forms were contemplated, Adenauer could effectively play social forces and bureaucrat-ic factions off against one another. Hence, in domestic matters at least, Adenauer drew strength from his role as political broker. Once it became apparent that the regime had stabilized and new reformist issues be-gan to impose themselves upon the agenda, his power necessarily declined.

In line with the Social Democratic leader-ship's interest in rationalizing governmental procedures, Brandt appointed Horst Ehmke, one-time dean of the Freiburg law faculty,

to head the chancellery and converted the former secretariat into a ministry. Under Ehmke, a number of steps were taken to modernize that office and make it more effi-cient and responsive to the chancellor. How-ever, Ehmke's "interference" was resented by other ministers and Brandt's initiative ultimately came to naught.

One other agency used by Adenauer to good effect was the Federal Press and Infor-mation Bureau. Controlled directly by the chancellor, the bureau had at its disposal a special fund running to some three million dollars a year—which permitted the subsidi-zation of favored periodicals, newspapers, and journalists. The fund was particularly effective in rural areas and small towns, which had less access to different news sources. Though the bureau's influence di-minished considerably under the coalition government it was still large in comparison with government press offices in Britain and France. Under Brandt this bureau was also reorganized and modernized.

GOVERNMENT AND PARLIAMENT: Most ministers under the German Empire were key civil servants and were paid accordingly. Even as members of the government, they were considered first of all to be administra-tors of public policy and only secondarily po-litical figures. Most Weimar ministers were picked by Parliament, but they continued to be paid as civil-service scales allowed, and they received retirement benefits after four years of service.

Following these traditions, Adenauer drew a number of his ministers from the bu-reaucracy, and even those who were party and parliamentary leaders were treated as experts in their specific areas rather than as members of a political team. Despite the continued participation of ministers in par-liamentary debates and their extended pres-ence at committee meetings, their relations to Parliament more closely resembled the American pattern, or the French pattern un-der de Gaulle, than the British pattern. Ministers tended not only to approach the discussion of legislation as "experts," but to impose their "expert" knowledge upon Parliament. Parliament, for its part, through committees and specialized parliamentary groups, regarded itself as something of an independent force. Even members of the Christian Democratic Union did not look upon cabinet ministers as representatives or symbols of their own party. Although a high degree of party discipline was maintained in votes on legislation, such votes were always preceded by lengthy negotiations of a kind which made it clear that party members considered their interests and those of the government to be quite different in many areas.

With Erhard as chancellor, the CDU begain affirming its corporate will—and the government began negotiating more and more with the parliamentary party. As several strong party leaders emerged, relations between the government and the party moved closer to the British political pattern; party divisions were reflected in the cabinet, and the stability of the government became increasingly contingent upon the loyalty of the party in Parliament. It was Erhard's failure to command such loyalty that caused his downfall. Kiesinger, of course, was forced to bring into the cabinet Christian Democratic leaders representing a variety of factions, just as Brandt sought to include within the cabinet those Socialists who could command rank-and-file support. Not only is the German cabinet today much more of an organization of "coequals," but more than ever before it must weigh the reaction of the parliamentary party in making its decisions.

Indicative of the government's greater need and readiness to take parliamentary parties into consideration was the creation in 1967 of the post of parliamentary state secretary in six of the larger ministries. In the British tradition, these secretaries are drawn from Parliament and serve the same functions as their British counterparts: they aid the minister both in departmental coordination and in his work with Parliament. Most important, they strengthen the position of the government by bringing into it ambitious young parliamentarians who, it is hoped, will develop a vested interest in supporting cabinet decisions. The Brandt government in 1969 expanded this practice by providing state secretaries, with increased authority, for all its ministries.

One source of discontinuity between government and Parliament is that chancellors may be drawn from positions outside the national parliamentary arena. Thus during the period of the Grand Coalition neither Chancellor Kiesinger nor Deputy Chancellor Brandt was a member of the Bundestag, but rather assumed his post directly from his position in state or city government.

THE INDIVIDUAL MINISTER: As in other parliamentary countries, ministers in Germany function in three major capacities: as part of the collective decision-making machinery of the cabinet, as heads of their own ministries, and as explicators and defenders of their policies before Parliament. But because of Germany's federal structure, the administrative duties of most ministers are far less burdensome—and confer far less authority—than those of British and French ministers. Since federal programs are administered by state bureaucracies, German ministries are rather small, and ministerial decisions must always take into account the attitudes of state governments. In drawing up legislation, for example, ministers enter into negotiations with *Land* officials at an early stage.

Thus far, their parliamentary chores have also been less taxing than those of British ministers. Even though they are expected, as we shall see, to appear before committees, the Bundestag has yet to develop that British kind of parliamentary give-and-take that puts a minister on his mettle. The old status gap between government official and parliamentarian, which derived from a time when ministers were responsible only to the emperor, still has its effect—even if it is a diminished one.

4. THE BONN REPUBLIC: THE BUNDESTAG [4]

THE PARLIAMENTARY PROFESSION: The Reichstag building in Berlin, in which the German Parliament met from 1894 until the rise of Hitler, was constructed in the rectangular shape of the British Commons, but with the semicircular, rising rows of seats and radial passages of the French Chamber of Deputies and the American Congress. Since World War II, however, the status of Berlin has meant that the Reichstag cannot be used by the Federal Republic. The current legislative building in Bonn, the *Bundeshaus*, is located on the bank of the Rhine. Originally constructed as a teachers' training college, it was commandeered by the government in 1949 and remodeled. The semicircular design of the Reichstag has been retained, but most of the space is taken over by chairs and desks, and members wishing to speak from their seats cannot do so without turning their backs either on many deputies or on members of the cabinet. Originally, the government bench was on a dais several feet above the floor of the Bundestag so that ministers literally looked down on many of their colleagues. Symbolic of changes taking place in the Bonn Republic, however, an agreement was reached in 1969 to lower the bench to the floor. In the same year, a new parliamentary office building was completed that for the first time provides each member of the Bundestag with adequate accommodations.

Bundestag deputies represent a fairly wide cross-section of the population, although persons of middle-class background predominate. The largest single group in the postwar period, as was true during the Weimar decade, has been public employees; they compose about 20 percent of the deputies (see Table 15.2). Their representation is far more characteristic of Continental countries than of Britain or the United States,

for it is considered legitimate for members of the civil service to take a leave of absence to run for Parliament. It must be remembered that in both France and Germany national unity was created by monarchs assisted by a powerful state bureaucracy; in both nations, although to a greater extent in Germany, a strong centralized bureaucracy preceded the establishment of parliamentary institutions.

Professional politicians form another large and growing segment of the Bundestag —although they are more characteristic of the Social Democratic Party's representation than that of the Christian Democratic Union. And, of course, the professions, especially law, are heavily represented. The Bundestag also contains a good many deputies who are, at the same time, representative of trade unions and business or farm organizations. More than in Britain and France, and far more than in the United States, it is not considered unethical for a member of Parliament to retain his interest-group connections.

The percentage of blue- and white-collar workers who are deputies is rather small and has been declining even among the Social Democrats, despite the fact that the SPD has been self-consciously a working-class party and still gets the bulk of its support from working-class voters. Catholics, somewhat understandably, predominate among Christian Democratic deputies; over the years, only about 15 percent of the SPD deputies have been Catholic—the remainder have been either Protestant or without religious affiliation—and Protestants have tended to predominate in the cabinet.

Members of the Bundestag are well paid by European standards, and as of 1969 each deputy has been provided with a special assistant. Most deputies try to maintain other sources of income; some even hold another political post, serving as mayor or local councillor and commuting to Bonn when Parliament is in session. A number are salaried members of interest groups. Multiple job-holding is quite easy in the Bonn Republic: the Bundestag holds few plenary ses-

[4] Discussion of the Bundestag relies heavily on Gerhard Loewenberg, *Parliament in the German Political System* (Ithaca, N.Y.: Cornell University Press, 1967).

TABLE 15.2 OCCUPATIONAL BACKGROUND OF
GERMAN DEPUTIES [1]

	SPD	CDU	CSU	FDP	Total
Professional politicians, party functionaries	53	34	4	6	97
Labor-union officials	41	16	1	–	58
Other interest-group officials	12	27	9	4	52
Civil servants	57	33	14	2	106
Teachers and professors	27	17	3	2	49
Entrepreneurs, executives	7	16	3	2	28
Small businessmen	1	16	3	1	21
Farmers	1	22	5	5	33
Lawyers	7	6	3	4	20
Public accountants	2	2	1	1	6
Other professional categories: doctors, architects, engineers, etc.	7	–	–	1	8
Journalists	7	6	2	1	16
White-collar workers	7	2	1	1	11
Blue-collar workers	1	–	–	–	1
Housewives	3	3	–	–	6
Not identifiable	4	1	–	1	6
Total deputies	237	201	49	31	518

[1] Based on data for the 1969–1972 Bundestag, includes the 22 Berlin deputies.

Source: Heino Kaack, *Geschichte und Struktur des deutschen Parteie-systems* (Opladen: Westdeutscher Verlag, 1971), p. 659, reprinted by permission of the publisher.

sions, usually on just two days of the week. Still, the proportion of Bundestag members who are full-time professional politicians is increasing.

Friendships in the Bundestag will cross party lines only rarely, and speeches still have that dull ponderousness so typical of German parliamentary oratory. There is little of the witty give-and-take that occurs in the British Parliament. During the Weimar period parliamentary sessions were enlivened by considerable uproar and an occasional punch in the nose, and similar conduct marked the first years of the Bonn Republic. With the disappearance of extremist parties, however, proceedings have become more sedate.

One of the major aspects of the postwar generation of parliamentarians—indeed, of most of the German elite—is the high frequency of agreement on the political rules of the game and the strong sense of satisfaction with the operation of the new political system. This is even truer of the men now in secondary leadership positions who were children during the Nazi era. These men lack the sense of attachment to traditional subgroups in German life, including both class and church, and they share a reasonably flexible and unromantic outlook. Speaking the language of practicality, most of them are well-informed university graduates with managerial skills, and a style that tends to lack the fire of previous generations.

Some intellectuals see the emergence of this new style as a sign of the dehumanization of social life and a precursor of the faceless bureaucratic state. They are hostile to the "pragmatism" of the new men of power, who, they claim, are avoiding those fundamental human issues that require an existential commitment. The rise of an extra-parliamentary opposition in Germany was partly a reflection of displeasure with the new breed of politicians. Yet despite some turbulent currents running in the other direction, political developments in Germany accord with those taking place in most other Western countries; political leadership in all of them is becoming less rhetorical in a traditional sense and more oriented toward professional concern with the intricacies of managing modern industrial societies. Though the new breed may lack some of the flair of an earlier, more romantic age, one suspects that it will in the long run be associated with a more humane politics.

THE ROLE OF POLITICAL PARTIES: The parliamentary party (*Fraktion*) has had semi-official status in the German Parliament since the turn of the century. From 1871 to 1933, special meeting rooms were placed at the disposal of the *Fraktionen*, and members of the legislative committees were chosen by each *Fraktion* in proportion to its membership in Parliament. This important practice is in effect again in Bonn. Under the rules of the Bundestag, an officially recognized parliamentary group must consist of at least fifteen members of the same political party, unless an exception is specifically granted. If a member of the Bundestag belongs to a party that does not have sufficient strength to form a *Fraktion*, he may attend meetings of an existing *Fraktion* as an associate, though the likelihood of his obtaining a desirable committee assignment is not very great.

The *Fraktionen* are the primary organizations of the Bundestag. They guide the work of the MdB's (*Mitglied des Bundestages*—Member of the Bundestag) both in the lower house as a whole and in committee. It is only within a *Fraktion* that a legislator, if he is to make a name for himself

can do so. And because campaign funds come from party coffers, it is very difficult for the individual deputy not to go along with party policies as interpreted in the *Fraktion*. The *Fraktion* leaders, moreover, are especially vital links in the legislative process because the Bundestag can amend and even completely rewrite legislation submitted by the government.

Each *Fraktion* is governed by a charter spelling out the rights and duties of its members. The charters are similar in terms of formal structure, with each *Fraktion* coordinated by an executive committee (*Vorstand*) composed of a chairman, several vice-chairmen, and one or more parliamentary floor leaders who correspond to whips in the House of Commons. All *Fraktionen* have specialized working committees to handle substantive questions of policy. However, because of its small size, the Free Democratic Party has not carried the committee process quite as far as have the two major parties. Differences between the *Fraktionen* of the Christian Democratic Party and the Social Democrats are closely related to their general history.[5] The method of operation of the CDU/CSU (Christian Democratic Union/Christian Social Union) reflects its regional decentralization (especially the quasi-independence of the Bavarian Christian Social Union), and the fact that it is a holding company for various interests; conversely, the organization of the SPD (Social Democratic Party), reflects the homogeneity and sense of discipline that stem from its heritage as an ideological mass party.

THE CDU/CSU FRAKTION: The party *Fraktion* of the CDU/CSU is a conglomeration of many organized interests. Deputies of the Christian Social Union, for example, form a separate *Land* group, which has its own chairman and deputy chairman. In each Bundestag, the association of the two parties is the result of a specific agreement, usually involving assurances that members of the CSU will be allotted a certain number

[5] Discussion of the FDP is omitted.

of leadership and committee posts. The Christian Democratic *Fraktion* also contains representatives of different economic groups. The "labor group" is probably the best organized of these; it has its own executive and its own office, and meets fairly regularly. Expressing its views in regular conferences and in a monthly periodical, the labor group is a fairly cohesive force within the party. Other economic interest groups within the CDU *Fraktion* include the "discussion group on middle-class affairs," the "study group on food and agriculture," and a more informal group representing large industry. Still others speak for CDU supporters who fled East Germany or were expelled from other countries. Such groups are considered a legitimate expression of interests within the Christian Democratic Party, and they receive both official recognition and financial support from the parliamentary party. It should be noted, however, that the core of the parliamentary leadership consists of professional politicians who usually avoid too close identification with any particular interest, and who see their primary function as that of maintaining party unity.

The CDU *Fraktion* caucuses at least once a week when the Bundestag or its committees are in session. Because of its size and organization, the caucus is primarily a meeting in which policies are ratified and views expressed. Its success in presenting the public with a united political position, therefore, depends upon the care with which meetings are prepared. The development of an integrated party policy is one of the functions of the *Fraktion*'s six working subgroups. In addition to legal issues, these subgroups deal with economic questions, foreign and financial affairs, problems of defense and social policy, and, as well, with certain matters pertaining to science and publishing. The subgroups parallel the committee structure of Parliament, and their chairmen are recommended by the party's executive committee and elected by the caucus. Group chairmen within the *Fraktion* are experts in the fields with which they are concerned; chairmen of the relevant Bundestag committees are almost never chosen as chairmen of the working groups.

The intricate relationships among the groups that compose the parliamentary party are a ready-made source of internal rancor. The job of its executive committee, therefore, is to integrate conflicting pressures. The committee is elected at the beginning of the parliamentary year and is subject to re-election after one year. Every effort is made to secure a balanced representation of party interests. Within the committee, a smaller "council of eleven" provides day-to-day leadership, meeting privately prior to meetings of the entire committee in efforts to secure agreement on important points of the agenda.

In effect, the executive committee and its inner body are the seat of power in the final determination of party policy: 85 to 90 percent of the committee's recommendations are accepted by the caucus. Preceding debate is for the most part only desultory, with rarely more than two-thirds of the caucus members present. This is not to say that the executive committee dominates the party; its primary efforts are directed toward smoothing over differences, and almost any important group within the party can veto its policy proposals.

The job of the executive committee and its elected chairman, then, is that of mediator. It is extremely difficult to discipline members of the Christian Democratic Party, and, in fact, deputies have been expelled from the ranks only on rare occasions. Under these circumstances, the ability of the CDU *Fraktion* to retain its cohesion remains open to question.

THE SOCIAL DEMOCRATIC FRAKTION: The Social Democratic Party continues to be a more homogeneous group than the CDU. Its national organization is more highly centralized; and although diverse interests exist within the party, they have not developed an organizational base, at least in Parliament. The prime effort of the SPD has been directed not toward reconciling diverse interests within the party, but toward widening its appeal so as to bring in new groups. Like the CDU parliamentary party, the SPD *Fraktion* is divided into working groups that parallel the Bundestag committees. The chairman and deputy chairman of each working group are elected by the caucus and enjoy considerable security of tenure.

The parliamentary party is headed by an elected chairman and executive committee. The posts provide, as in the CDU, a strong base from which to influence the formation of party policy, and hence have often been hotly contested. Also as in the CDU, a smaller group within the executive committee meets weekly in advance of the larger one to determine the agenda and to seek to secure agreement on crucial issues.

Recommendations of the executive committee are generally accepted by the caucus, although the Socialist Party's caucus figures somewhat more importantly in the party's decision-making process than does that of the CDU. Attendance of deputies varies, from two-thirds to threequarters of the nominal membership, and deliberations are less public than those of the CDU caucus. Divisions of opinion are rarely between the executive and the caucus; more often, the disagreements are among the party's leaders. Members who disagree with decisions of the caucus are, however, expected not to speak in the Bundestag against the position of the party.

THE STRUCTURE OF AUTHORITY: The key officer of the Bundestag is the president, who is elected by secret ballot at the beginning of each session.[6] The president is assisted by three vice presidents, each chosen from a different party, and by a council of elders composed of officers and other representatives of the *Fraktionen*. The council is theoretically only advisory, but it is analogous to the British "usual channels"; it allocates the time for debate and chooses the chairmen of the Bundestag's standing committees. With the departure of the more extremist groups from the Bundestag, the council has been able to settle with considerable ease such matters as length of debate and the allocation of floor time to the political parties. Because party discipline is reasonably strong, thereby making the question of timetables of secondary importance, the Bundestag president does not have to be as partisan as the American Speaker of the House, though he is somewhat more so than his British counterpart. His role is, however, not quite so important as that of the British speaker because German deputies often appeal to the council of elders for rulings on points of order.

Each party has its parliamentary whips, who work closely with the party chairman. Although the whips of the governing party, having no access to the cabinet, lack the authority of British whips, they do perform many of the same functions, and they are important members of the council of elders.

After the *Fraktionen*, the most important groups in the Bundestag are the specialized standing committees. They have grown more and more powerful as the Bonn regime has evolved, although they do not compare in strength with congressional committees in the United States or with the standing committees that operated in France under the Third and Fourth Republics. During the early years of the Federal Republic, there were thirty-eight such committees; the number has now been trimmed to nineteen, paralleling, in general, the important ministries. Committee membership is proportional to party strength, and members are selected by the party *Fraktion*. Each committee chooses its own chairman, who has the service of a special assistant appointed from the Bundestag staff and that of several secretaries. Nevertheless, committee members are coming to feel that they need more professional help, and there have been suggestions that committee staffs be upgraded.

The question of which committee receives a bill can have some bearing on the final form it will take—inasmuch as each responds more readily to the demands of its particu-

---

6 For the first time in German history, the Bundestag in 1972 elected a woman, Annemarie Regner-Loncarevic, as its president.

lar interests. Decisions on bill assignments are worked out by negotiation among the committees themselves, with final referral being up to the council of elders and the parties. to avoid extended controversy or the necessity of a vote by the whole house, one committee has often been placed in charge of reporting a given bill while several others have been permitted to consider it and offer suggestions.

Officials of the ministry initiating a proposed law have privileged access to committee meetings and can be heard at any time. Under the Bonn constitution, committees, like the Bundestag itself, may compel the attendance of ministers. Committee deliberations are usually not open to the press or the public, on the theory that open hearings reduce the objectivity of the proceedings; but on the other hand, they are not secret. Any deputy is free to attend and is permitted to report proceedings to outsiders. Persons other than parliamentarians may attend with committee permission. Many committees keep stenographic reports of their discussions, and these, together with committee records, are available to the press.

On the whole committees are creatures of the Bundestag and the parties. Whereas a few have developed some autonomy, it would be difficult if not impossible for them to pigeonhole measures desired by the Bundestag as a whole. The committees have, of course, been used by the Bundestag to bury legislation, but only for those proposals that party leaders had decided were best forgotten.

The committee members of each party operate as a team. They are led by a "foreman," who assigns responsibility for each bill to a particular deputy, and they meet regularly as a subcommittee of one of the working groups of the parliamentary party. Committee meetings generally involve a painstaking, article-by-article scrutiny of proposed legislation; in these meetings the chairman, the experts in each party, representatives of both the government and the particular ministry responsible for the bill, and the committee reporter take over most of the discussion.

Committee chairmen exercise considerable power in the Bundestag. They will determine the schedule of committee meetings and the priority of items on the legislative agenda. Because committee meetings are limited to about nine days a month, chairmen can delay as well as facilitate deliberations. They cannot, however, block indefinitely the discussion of legislation, although they can effectively kill measures introduced late in a session by dragging their feet. Furthermore, chairmen also appoint the reporter for each bill—the person whose task it is to prepare a written report for the Bundestag on the committee's deliberations and an explanation of the changes that the committee recommends. The analyses prepared by individual reporters will naturally differ: even so, the emphasis is upon objective reporting. In this regard reporters have generally set a high standard, which is testimony to the relative lack of ideological heat that has characterized the work of the Bundestag in recent years.

Committees are beginning to develop a sense of corporate unity centered in a common command of subject matter and identification with particular interests. This feeling is aided by the privacy of committee meetings which permits voting across party lines. On many occasions committee members have agreed to rewrite bills and have brought their parties around to the committee's position.

Certain committees, including Defense, Foreign Affairs, Inter-German Relations, and Internal Affairs, have authority to initiate investigations not immediately related to legislation. The Bundestag itself possesses the power to investigate matters that may not, at least initially, be related to proposed legislation. Committees to handle such investigations can be established at any time on the motion of one-fourth of the membership. They may hold open or private investigations and recommend legislative action. The Bundestag may also instigate full-scale debate on the policies of ministers, either on a motion of interpolation introduced by thirty members, or when the budget is being considered. Thus far, the Bundestag has been loath to take advantage of these powers, partly because members feel they might open the way to the kind of demagoguery that characterized the Weimar Republic.

DEBATES AND QUESTIONS: The Bundestag's lack of ample time for full-dress debates and the emphasis on committee work mean that floor action is not nearly so important or so provocative as it is in Britain in the House of Commons. In 1952, to encourage participation by individual deputies, the Bundestag inaugurated a question period similar to that of the British Parliament. The rules of the Bundestag originally provided for one question hour a month, and deputies had to submit their questions— which could deal only with clarification of facts—well in advance. Since then, however, the rules have been relaxed. "Urgent" questions are now allowed to be introduced as late as noon of the day before they are to be answered, and deputies are permitted to ask supplementary questions from the floor.

At first, these innovations failed to enliven the floor proceedings, in large part because only a few deputies bothered to ask questions. About three hundred were submitted at each session, compared with twelve to fifteen thousand in the House of Commons. Also, the *Fraktion* dominated the question period, rather than allowing it to be used by individual deputies. Nor did Adenauer's refusal to answer questions establish an encouraging precedent. Perhaps most important, the questions tended to be long and dull, and the answers equally so. There has, however, been some improvement in recent years. Questions have become briefer and have acquired a certain verve, and deputies seem to be exercising some degree of independence. During the *Spiegel* affair (see p. 117 for instance, the question period was used by the opposition Social Democrats to embarrass Franz Joseph Strauss, then minister of defense; the uproar eventually led to his resignation. In 1965 questions directed against the government brought to light the fact that federal funds had been

used to pay for pro-Erhard newspaper advertisements shortly before the election. The formation of the Kiesinger-Brandt coalition government made the question period somewhat less pertinent, for the obvious reason that the two major parties were not eager to challenge the government publicly and the Free Democratic Party was unable to use the period effectively. During the period of the Brandt-Scheel government, (1969–1974), however, CDU/CSU delegates used the question period effectively to sustain their attack on the coalition's *Ostpolitik*, by bringing to light unpublished ancillary agreements worked out between Bonn and Moscow negotiators.

In 1965 still another innovation was introduced: on the application of fifteen members, a debate on a "definite subject of general current interest" could be placed on the agenda. The debates are limited to an hour; each speaker is required to talk extemporaneously, and for no more than five minutes. So far, the procedure has not been used too frequently because of the wariness with which the political parties look upon ill-prepared floor debates.

5. THE BONN REPUBLIC: THE BUNDESRAT

The upper chamber of the German legislature has far more historical continuity than the Bundestag. As we have pointed out, during the empire the Bundesrat was the repository of considerable power. Its approval was required for all Reich legislation, it could decide what legislative proposals were to be considered by the Reichstag, and it supervised the administration of all laws in the Reich. Essentially, the Bundesrat was an assembly of envoys from state governments. Its conservative bias, partly the result of its domination by Prussians, was perhaps less important than were its efforts on behalf of the *Länder* to win concessions from the federal government. German federalism was based less on separate spheres of authority than on a distinction between the formulation of policies at the national level, on the one hand, and their execution by the states, on the other; at the same time, the Bundesrat was ruled by bureaucrats from the states (*Länder*) who sought to enhance their administrative autonomy.

The Weimer constitution shifted the balance of federal power to the Reichstag; but the Reichsrat, as the upper house was then called, could still act as a brake on the Reichstag. The Reichsrat, however, had only a limited power of veto. If it objected to any piece of legislation, a public referendum could be ordered by the president or, alternatively, the Reichstag could overrule the Reichsrat by a two-thirds majority. It was not easy to obtain such a majority in the lower house, however, and because governments shied from the use of referenda, they were reluctant to press measures the Reichsrat would not accept. That the *Länder* were still responsible for the execution of laws was another factor abetting the continued authority of the Reichsrat.

After the defeat of Nazi Germany, the Allies and the major German political groups were divided on how the second house should be constituted and what power it should possess. Two major proposals were made regarding its form. The Christian Democratic Union, the most federalist of the parties, wanted a Bundesrat, in the German tradition, to represent and be responsible to the *Land* governments; the Socialists wanted a senate chamber elected by the people on the basis of proportional representation. The CDU also wanted a chamber that would be equal in power to the Bundestag, while the Socialists wanted the lower house to predominate. A compromise was reached that created a state-appointed Bundesrat, but placed it in a subordinate position to the Bundestag —though it was given considerably more power than its Weimar predecessor.

The Bundesrat consists of forty-one members of the state cabinets—five from each of the four *Länder* having more than six million residents, four from each of three *Länder* having between two and six million inhabitants, and three each from the three

small *Länder* having less than two million. Members are picked by their *Land* governments, which may at any time recall them. According to the constitution, the votes of each *Land* must be cast as a bloc, and each delegation votes in accordance with instructions from its state government.

Approval of the Bundesrat is required for all constitutional amendments and for all legislation affecting the administrative, tax, and territorial interests of the *Länder*. On "ordinary" legislation, however, the Bundesrat has only a limited veto power. If it rejects a given measure, the veto can be overruled by an equivalent majority in the Bundestag—that is, if it rejects a proposal by a majority of two-thirds, the bill can become law only if the Bundestag, with at least a majority of its members present, passes it by a two-thirds majority of those present and voting. It was thought initially that the great bulk of national legislation would fall into the "ordinary" category. But because most laws are administered by the *Länder* and thus affect *Länder* interests, almost all important laws (in fact, more than 50 percent of all laws passed) require Bundesrat approval.

This interpretation and the fact that federal ordinances require Bundesrat approval before they can take effect have considerably enhanced the power of the upper chamber. The federal government is careful to consult the *Länder* before introducing legislation, and the threat of a Bundesrat veto, although it has been used sparingly, has been sufficient to secure substantial modifications in government proposals. During the early years of the Adenauer administration, the chancellor's control of his party was such that he could usually have his own way in the upper house, too, on matters he considered essential. By the early 1960's, however, party loyalties were being superseded by *Land* interests. Moreover, the problems of administration and authority became more and more difficult to resolve as events forced the government to move into areas originally considered the domain of the states.

The importance of the Bundesrat and of politics at the state level becomes quite clear when, as has been the case since 1969, the party which is in opposition in the Bundestag has a majority of the votes in the Bundesrat. The Christian Democrats, who have controlled twenty-one of the forty-one votes in the upper chamber since 1969, have been able to amend as well as to impede legislation coming from the governing parties in the lower house. Moreover, because state elections are held at widely varying times, the composition of the Bundesrat can change at any time during a government's term in office.

Most of the work of the Bundesrat is done *in camera*; plenary sessions are devoted to general remarks and formal votes, and debate is rarely lively. Rather, an array of committees manned by bureaucratic experts from the *Länder* determines policy before any piece of proposed legislation reaches the floor. Consequently, the work of the Bundesrat has not attracted much public attention. Public-opinion polls indicate that few Germans have any real understanding of its functions.

6. LAW-MAKING

LEGISLATIVE INITIATIVE: According to the constitution, bills may be introduced by the government, the Bundesrat, or the Bundestag. In practice, the Bundesrat itself introduces very few bills; and the *Länder*, preoccupied with administration, have rarely been interested in advancing legislative proposals on the national level. Their main concern has been in amending or revising legislation to serve their own interests.

The Bundestag exercises its prerogative with far greater frequency. About 18 percent of the bills passed in the sixth session of the Bundestag (1969–1972) came from the lower house as against about 4 percent which originated in the Bundesrat. Some of these the work of individual deputies seeking to advance the cause of some interest group, and the bills were often introduced simply to pressure the government into sponsoring a

particular program or to influence the details of legislation under consideration. Most of the bills, however, were the work of the *Fraktionen*.

The balance of bills passed by the Bundestag—some 78 percent—came directly from the government, and were originally drawn up by the cabinet or a ministry.[7] The drafting of legislation involves consultations among ministries and the chancellor's office, and between the government and *Land* officials and interest groups. Government ministers regularly invite members of national groups to discuss legislative proposals in an effort to win their approval—or at least to reduce their opposition. As in Britain, such conferences are regarded as perfectly legitimate and are usually fairly frequent; the German government, also like the British, encourages the amalgamation of interest groups into more unified, national associations that can speak with one voice. The extent of rapport between the government and certain interest groups is indicated by the policy of the Federation of German Industries, which, during the Adenauer era, addressed most of its formal statements of opinion regarding legislation to the Ministry of Economics instead of to the Bundestag.

Consultations also take place between the government and the parliamentary party leaders who are not in the cabinet, especially on proposals likely to yield controversy. In some cases, these party leaders have even participated in cabinet meetings, although such procedures are the exception rather than the rule. Some ministries, such as the Ministry of Labor, have established working relationships with the relevant committee chairmen in the Bundestag. Again, the extent of contact often depends upon the personalities of those involved. The Ministry of Labor established good relations with the Committee on Social Policy during the Aden-

[7] Reflecting the importance of the Bundesrat in the eyes of the framers of the Basic Law, the constitution requires that the government submit a bill to the Bundesrat first. However, the government can, and frequently does, get around this stipulation by having a deputy or *Fraktion* introduce the measure in the Bundestag.

FIGURE 15.1 THE GERMAN LEGISLATIVE PROCESS

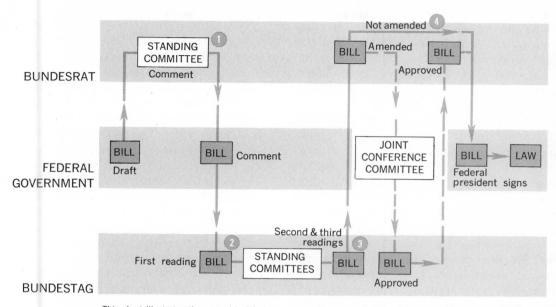

This chart illustrates the normal legislative process with respect to bills originated by the federal government; it does not depict the procedure for bills originating in the Bundesrat or Bundestag.

1. Transmits only amendatory proposals.

2. Introduced by the federal government, followed by general debate; if it is clear from the debate that the Bundestag either will approve or reject the proposal, it may not be sent to standing committee and may go directly into 2nd reading.

3. If amended in 2nd reading, 3rd reading usually is delayed 48 hours.

4. If the time period (2 weeks) elapses without the taking of amendatory action, the proposal also is sent to the federal government for promulgation. At this stage, the proposal also is sometimes sent to standing committee.

Adapted from Elmer Plischke, *Contemporary Governments of Germany*, 2nd ed. (Boston: Houghton Mifflin, 1969), p. 8, reprinted by permission of the publisher.

auer period, but those between the Ministry of Interior and the Committee on Interior Affairs were severely strained for a long time, to the detriment of the government's program.

When government bills are submitted to the Bundesrat for first passage, *Land* ministries are under great pressure to formulate their positions because the time allotted for them to do so is short. The Bundesrat has only three weeks to consider a bill on "first passage" before it automatically moves on to the Bundestag. Where consultation has occurred beforehand, the problem is eased, but final decisions must still be made. The bills

get most of their attention in committee session; once deliberations there have been completed, the *Land* cabinets decide how their Bundesrat representatives should vote. At this stage the Bundesrat concerns itself largely with detailed amendments to legislative proposals. The government transmits these, and its responses, to the Bundestag, along with the text of the bill.

BUNDESTAG CONSIDERATION: In the Bundestag, proposed legislation is first discussed by the parliamentary *Fraktionen* and their specialized subcommittees. By the time a bill receives its first reading, each party must already have determined whether or not it wishes to debate the proposed legislation, what views it will express, and who will do the speaking; it also must decide to which committee or committees the legislation should be referred, usually after working groups have expressed their recommendations at party caucuses and differences of opinion have been ironed out.

The question of which committee should receive a particular bill and which committee or committees should be allowed to comment on it has led to any number of controversies. The committees themselves, interest groups, the parties, and individual deputies all compete to obtain the committee assignment they consider most appropriate. For a while, the difficulties of reaching agreement caused a proliferation of committee assignments, such that some measures were under the simultaneous consideration of as many as eight or nine committees. More recently, efforts have been made to limit to two the number of committees considering a bill, although three or four is not unknown.

During the days or weeks preceding the floor debate, negotiations on the bill to secure support or revisions continue. Interest groups approach deputies, and members of the working parties seek out government ministers, representatives of special interests, and other deputies who might have special concern with the measure—either for or against it. At times it is informally agreed that the bill will be revised in committee.

The debate on the first reading is invariably a staid affair. If the bill is important, this is probably the first occasion that it will be brought to the public's attention through the press. With floor discussions arranged in advance, there is little chance of surprise developments. Even so, public reaction and newspaper pressure begin to be felt at this point, and they can affect the attitudes of the government and the various parties concerned with the proposed legislation.

When the committee has completed its deliberations and prepared its report, the polit-

ical parties make a final determination of the stand they will take during the second and the third readings. Members of each party on the committee in charge of the bill recommend a position to the parallel working group in their party; that group, in turn, makes a recommendation to the executive committee of the party.

In general, the position the parties take on a bill is that which has been recommended by their experts, a factor that seems more and more likely to erode party differences. To be sure, such has not always been the case. During the 1950's and into the 1960's, the Socialists were split over the question of German rearmament, and the party's defense experts were not consistently able to carry the day against those Socialists who viewed the creation and maintenance of a new German army with anxiety. Furthermore, complications quite naturally occur when several committees are considering a bill and the experts on each disagree, or when Bundestag members believe that a committee or committee member has become the mouthpiece of special interests.

The second reading in the Bundestag is devoted to discussion and debate on individual sections of the bill, and the consideration of each section is followed by a vote. Different viewpoints within the parties may be expressed on the floor. The third reading is another general discussion of the bill, this time as amended. Though amendments may be introduced on the floor at the third reading, such a procedure is unusual. With the showdown on the measure at hand, emphasis is now on party unity, and members are cajoled into accepting the final decision of the party—or, if they are opposed to it, at least abstaining from voting.

THE FINAL STAGES: Once a bill has passed the Bundestag, it goes to or is returned to the Bundesrat. In the case of bills introduced in the lower chamber, this may be, of course, the first opportunity the Bundesrat has had to examine them. Usually the Bundesrat is reluctant to reject measures passed by the lower house, even if its own recommendations have not been accepted. Such measures are ordinarily sent to the conference committee to iron out differences between the two houses. The committee is composed equally of members of both houses; Bundesrat members tend to be ministers of *Land* governments, those from the Bundestag party leaders or committee chairmen. Each *Land* is entitled to one member, and the Bundestag parties participate in proportion to their parliamentary representation.

Conference committee meetings are secret, although federal ministers and their assistants may attend. Often the committee will recruit special subcommittees of experts to deal with technical aspects of the bill on which it is attempting to effect a compromise. The committee addresses itself only to those matters about which the two houses differ.

The committee recommendation is first presented to the Bundestag, where it is voted without debate, and then sent to the Bundesrat. In its workings the committee has served as a joint committee of both houses. Rarely does it accept the Bundestag's point of view without some modifications, while approximately one-third of the committee's recommendations have involved full acceptance of the Bundesrat's version of the legislation.

Finally, once a bill has won Parliament's approval, it is forwarded to the government for its formal acceptance and promulgation by the president. The president can refuse to sign a bill only if he has doubts as to its constitutionality; this has occurred in only one case of any importance. The Federal Constitutional Court is the ultimate authority on the constitutionality of a measure.

7. INTEREST GROUPS

THEIR ROLE: The rapid industrialization of Germany in the late nineteenth century produced a pattern of group behavior in which modern and traditional elements were interwoven, not always smoothly. While many traditional elements in Germany's cul-

ture and social structure remained unchanged, an increasing number of functional interest groups, representing labor, industry, and agriculture, came into existence. They operated, however, in a context in which regional, ethnic, and religious factors were extremely important. Such provincialism often prevented effective cooperation among those whose economic interests actually coincided—Socialist trade unions, for instance, found it difficult to organize Catholic workers. The Reichstag and the *Land* legislative bodies were the focus of considerable interest-group activity. Yet those representing industrial and landholding interests relied more heavily upon, and paid more attention to, the Bundesrat and the federal bureaucracy. Here, after all, was where the real power lay; besides, these were men of their own social class, naturally sympathetic to industrial and landholding interests.

As sectional and economic differences became more complicated during the Weimar years, interest groups defined their aims in terms that became more and more exacting and inflexible. Interest-group behavior influenced the political party system as many groups became closely identified with rigidly doctrinaire minor parties, thus reducing the possibility of effective governance. Interest groups also affected the operation of the Reichstag, as on all too many occasions that body concentrated on meaningless ideological rhetoric or wrangled interminably over extremely minor issues while, by default, the most important decisions concerning the republic were made by the president and his intimate advisers or were not made at all.

With the advent of the Nazi regime, independent associational life was eliminated. Several groups, including both the army and the Catholic Church, did manage to retain a modicum of independence, but most others were able to act only within the confines of "fronts" organized by the Nazi Party. The business community got a good number of things it wanted by bribing party officials and using bureaucratic contacts; but on many occasions the party and the Nazi-organized Labor Front subjected the business community to demands that it considered very unreasonable—and about which it could do nothing. In fact, a not insignificant portion of the business community believed that the Hitler regime was far too pro-labor.

Under the Bonn Republic, the pattern of interest-group activity has shifted significantly. In Germany, as in other industrial nations, the trend has continued toward fewer and larger associations representing functional groups. Perhaps more important, the major parties, particularly the Christian Democrats, are tending more and more to be coalitions of interests whose demands have to be balanced off and aggregated into a larger political whole. The processing of group demands has become easier not only because they are now fairly specific and limited, but because the groups themselves are more willing to compromise. Political leaders and the leaders of interest groups have, by and large, come to accept the idea of politics as a bargaining process. More and more frequently, they speak the same language and understand their opponents' point of view. There is a much greater feeling today that group demands must be placed within the context of a broader general interest, and much more willingness on the part of specific interests to accept certain rules of the game as binding. The changes are, of course, partially the result of the spectacular growth of the German economy since World War II. But they also stem from memories of Weimar and the reasons for its failure. There is also an awareness that conflict would be counterproductive, given the role of West Germany in the world market.

In general, Germans have a mixed attitude toward the activity of interest groups. Many more of them speak of working through such groups to achieve political goals than do Britons or Americans. Nevertheless, considerable suspicion still exists about some aspects of interest-group political activity—as if, somehow, policies should simply be based on what is right and not necessarily on what interest groups want. Far fewer Germans than Americans or Brit-

ons—or, today, Frenchmen—join civic associations that cut across interest lines to obtain nonpolitical or even political objectives. In this sense, the strata in German society appear to be more segregated than in other European societies.

THEIR TACTICS: Interest-group activity is directed at the public, the legislature, and the executive. Until recently, the effort expended to influence the legislature has been greater in Germany than in either Britain or Fifth Republic France—primarily because the Christian Democratic Party is less disciplined than either of the British parties and because the German executive has been less powerful—even under a man like Adenauer—than the executive of Fifth Republic France under de Gaulle. Furthermore, because the *Länder* exercise considerable power, more time is spent trying to sway local officials than in either of the other nations, though most interests naturally regard the national scene as of crucial importance.

In their attempts to influence the legislature, most important trade and labor associations do not hesitate to use the front door: they encourage their members to seek parliamentary seats. Despite some concern that the interests might come to dominate the Bundestag, such a procedure is considered quite proper—an attitude that is a carry-over of a more traditional orientation toward functional representation. In addition to their efforts to gain their ends from within, interest groups also make sizable contributions to party coffers. This is most notable in business support of the Free Democrats and the CDU. During most of the postwar period, some 35 percent of the Christian Democratic deputies have been directly affiliated with interest associations, mostly business, and approximately one-fourth of the Social Democratic deputies have been trade-union representatives.

Members of the Bundesrat are rarely approached directly by representatives of interest groups. From time to time, groups may forward memoranda to Bundesrat committees when a bill is being discussed. But this action is generally pro forma, for Bundesrat members are essentially agents of state (*Land*) governments. Instead, groups concentrate on the appropriate *Land* ministries or the minister-president of a *Land*, and they try to win support in *Land* parliaments.

As in other European nations, there is in Germany considerable consultation between the bureaucracy and interest groups. Many government agencies in the *Länder* have advisory bodies, composed of interest-group representatives attached to them. On the federal level, the cabinet discusses legislation with interest groups; and, in fact, the administrative procedures of all the principal ministries stipulate that the appropriate spokesmen of associations must be consulted during consideration of legislation. Generally, these ministries are also provided with an advisory council of nongovernmental experts who are interest-group representatives.

There is no question, then, that interest-group influence over legislation is greater in Germany than it is in Britain. German legislators still defer to bureaucratic expertise and look for bureaucratic solutions to public issues. The community of interest and outlook between members of the bureaucracy and business groups is especially strong, even stronger than in France, where the working relationship is also close.

The organization of interests in the Federal Republic has, therefore, a distinctly conservative bias which, in the 1950's and 1960's, was only aggravated by the proclivity of the Germans to emphasize social harmony and to avoid conflict. It was relatively simple, given the role of Bundestag Committees, for large interest groups to veto innovations which affected them negatively. Aside from other changes, however, a new dimension in West German politics which has allowed political figures to circumvent some roadblocks has been the Federal Republics affiliation with various European transnational organizations. Given the growing interpenetration of OECD economies, differences in the pattern of interest group influence among various West European nations are becoming less and less significant.

8. FEDERALISM IN WEST GERMANY

THE GERMAN LÄNDER: Following both its own predilection and that of the Allied powers, especially the Americans, the Constituent Assembly divided authority (albeit not equally) between the federal government and the state governments. Unlike Britain and France, Germany is a federal state.

With the exception of Bavaria, the largest of the German *Länder* (North Rhine–Westphalia is the most populous), and the Hanseatic city-states of Hamburg and Bremen, the German *Länder* are new creations. Their borders were redrawn after World War II, and some *Länder*, including, most importantly, Prussia, were dissolved. The *Länder* today are more equal in size and resources than they once were (Table 15.3). They are now without historical identification, however, and in some cases, the states are regions for which logical economic and governmental plans cannot be made. It is not surprising that most Germans feel less and less attachment to these once proud, even defiant, and historically important entities.

Formally, there are three different kinds of political power in the federation: namely, exclusive, concurrent, and residual. The first are powers which the federal government holds exclusively; the second, those which the federal government and the states (*Länder*) share; and the third, those which remain with the states. But as in other federal systems, the powers of the federal government are growing rapidly at the expense of the states, and developments will almost certainly continue in that direction. The most important areas in which they still exercise some autonomy are education, police, and cultural activities (e. g., opera, theater, and orchestra). But even here, strong pressures exist for the federal government to establish uniform policies and to assume more and more of the costs of culture-related pro-

TABLE 15.3   THE LÄNDER OF THE GERMAN FEDERAL REPUBLIC
AND WEST BERLIN

	Area (in thousands of square miles)	Population, 1971 (in millions)	Population density (per square mile)	Cities with population over 100,000	1970 per capita taxable income (in dollars)	Seats in Bundes-rat
North Rhine-Westphalia	13.1	17.1	1,305	34	4,548	5
Bavaria	27.2	10.7	393	5	4,304	5
Baden-Wuerttemberg	13.8	9.1	653	5	4,564	5
Lower Saxony	18.2	7.2	396	6	3,813	5
Hesse	8.2	5.5	671	5	4,510	4
Rhineland-Palatinate	7.6	3.7	487	3	4,103	4
Schleswig-Holstein	6.1	2.5	410	2	3,579	4
Hamburg	0.27	1.8	9,259	1	7,347	3
Bremen	0.15	0.7	4,667	2	5,979	3
Saar	1.0	1.1	1,100	1	3,851	3
(West Berlin)	0.19	2.1	9,048	1	4,880	(4)[1]
Totals and averages	95.81	61.5	2,580	65	4,679	41

[1] Nonvoting members.
Adapted from Statistisches Bundesamt, *Statistisches Jahrbuch fuer die Bundesrepublik Deutschland, 1972* (Stuttgart: Kohlhammer, 1972), pp. 25, 519; and Lewis Edinger, *Politics in Germany* (Boston: Little, Brown, 1968), p. 14, copyright 1968, Little, Brown and Company, Inc.

grams.   If the legislative competence of the German states has become narrower and narrower, however, they are still a vital link in the political life of the nation—through administration.   Unlike the United States, for example, where the federal government also administers most of the programs it legislates, the German states are the administrative vehicles for most national legislation.

The governments of the *Länder* closely resemble that of the Federal Republic, even though, except for Bavaria, they are unicameral. (In this, as in other ways—the continued existence of the CSU, for example—one sees indications that local pride is most pronounced in Bavaria.)   Their electoral systems also coincide with that of Bonn. With the exception of Bremen and Ham-

burg, the state executive is composed of a minister-president and a cabinet.   The former can be removed only by a vote of no confidence; but his powers, by comparison with those of the chancellor of the republic, are not extensive. Since the primary function of the *Land* government is administration rather than policy-making, it is men with administrative experience who are most frequently nominated for cabinet posts.

Land elections have not been without impact on the national scene.   Because Germany does not have by-elections to replace Bundestag deputies who resign, die, or are removed—the deputy is simply replaced by the next candidate on that particular party's electoral list—state and local elections have become an important barometer of people's dispositions toward the federal government. For, while the candidates for the state diets do run on local and regional issues, they and the electorate know that what is also being registered is popular sentiment about the functioning of the government in Bonn. It was the unmistakable decline of CDU fortunes in several *Land* elections in 1963 that led the party to press for Adenauer's retirement; and it was an important factor in bringing about the CDU/SPD coalition after the fall of Erhard. Again, it was the weakness of the Social Democrats in state and local elections in 1973 and 1974 that contributed to the resignation of Willy Brandt.

The continued existence of the states in Germany has given a certain flexibility to German politics which it might otherwise have sorely missed. While the SPD, for example, was blocked from power at the national level for twenty years, it governed at the state level—in Hamburg, in Hesse, in Berlin, and in Bremen. Moreover, in a number of states, Christian Democratic and Social Democratic coalitions had been in existence prior to the Grand Coalition of these two parties, and in others the Socialists had joined with the Free Democrats to form a majority. Thus, not only have the German people been exposed to differing power constellations, but the parties themselves had continuous experience in and out of office prior to assuming power in Bonn. This statement, of course, applies to individual politicians as well as to party organizations. Adenauer, for instance, was mayor of Cologne during the Weimar Republic; and Willy Brandt made his reputation as mayor of Berlin before becoming the leader of the SPD and ultimately chancellor of his country. Former chancellor Kiesinger served most of his political career in Württemberg-Baden, where he was minister-president; and Helmut Kohl, CDU chairman and nominee for chancellor was head of the state of Rhineland-Palatinate.

On the other hand, Chancellor Helmut Schmidt's experience in SPD politics has been almost entirely national and parliamentary. Schmidt was first elected to the Bun-

destag in 1953 and served there with only a four-year absence (1961–65) as senator of the city-state, his native Hamburg, where he was responsible for the department of the interior. Resuming his parliamentary career in 1965, Schmidt was named Minister of Defense in 1969 and Minister of Economics and Finance (to take over from Karl Schiller) in June, 1972.

Many problems faced by Germany today require governmental structures that transcend *Land* boundaries. Yet moves by the national government to establish workable regional organizations are constantly thwarted by an unwillingness on the part of the *Länder* to relinquish any of their authority. The ambiguous nature of the Bundesrat's power in respect to legislation is such that *Land* governments are in a position to block almost any proposal which they feel will diminish their own prerogatives. Hence, in some ways, the division of authority between the federal and the *Land* governments is proving to be more and more dysfunctional. Although many people, including politicians, are becoming impatient about these entanglements, it is unlikely that any major change in the basic structure of the Federal Republic will occur.

One rationale for the formation of the Grand Coalition was the promise that it would carry out a reform program granting the federal government more authority to meet the nation's challenges; and the coalition did indeed manage to secure some moderate changes. The Financial Reform Act of 1969 was one important piece of legislation to come out of those discussions. Per-capita income among the German *Länder* varied in 1970 from a low of $3,579 in Schleswig-Holstein and $3,813 in Lower Saxony to a high of $7,347 in Hamburg. Thus, without some equalizing measures, the richer *Länder* would have had much more money than the poorer states to spend for education, which is the single biggest item in *Länder* budgets. Through the redistribution of revenues which this act makes possible, the per-capita expenditure of the poorest *Land* is brought to within 92 percent of that of the richest. In such ways is the Federal Republic today attempting to meet the exigencies of a modern democratic state while continuing to honor the structures and practices of bygone eras.

WEST BERLIN: Berlin's position in the Federal Republic (between the two Germanies and as well between the East and the West) is very anomalous. Occupied Germany, as we have seen, was divided into four zones, and so was Berlin. The city, which became the capital of Prussia in 1701 and later the capital of the Reich, has been, of course, one of the world's major cities and a vital center of culture and learning. Like the rest of Germany, Berlin was to be jointly ruled. From the beginning, however, the Allies were unable to agree upon common policies either for Berlin or for the rest of Germany. And as the Cold War intensified, cooperation between the Western nations and the Soviet Union became more and more difficult. Finally, in 1948, the Russians tried to detach Berlin from West Germany by halting all traffic through Communist East Germany into the city. The blockade failed and the city continued to be made up of the western sectors, which remained under the joint administration of the Allies, and East Berlin, which was later to become part of the German Democratic Republic. In 1950, a constitution was promulgated for West Berlin, and a political organization similar to that of a German state was established for the isolated city. Berliners now elect a House of Representatives (*Abgeordnetenhaus*) for four years, and the executive consists of a cabinet (*Senat*) and a governing mayor responsible to the house. Western Germans wanted to incorporate West Berlin into the Federal Republic, but the Allies vetoed the proposal, arguing that a change in Berlin's status might give the Russians an excuse to abrogate rights of free access to the city through East German territory. In a statement issued upon the formal granting of sovereignty to the Bonn Republic in 1955, the three Allied commanders continued to reserve certain ultimate rights in Berlin while granting complete freedom of administration to the city's elected officials.

West Berlin's ties with the Federal Republic are, today, extremely close. Officially Berliners cannot vote in national elections, but twenty-two members of the Bundestag are from Berlin; four Berliners sit in the Bundesrat. While deputies from Berlin cannot vote in plenary session, they do vote on committees. The federal government has passed laws applicable to Berlin, with the Berlin legislature merely enacting a "covering law" that incorporates the terms of the legislation. The Bonn government has also granted extensive subsidies to Berlin—one important means of survival on which the city continues to depend.

Despite the bifurcation of the city, the citizens of Berlin could move relatively freely between the Western and Communist zones until 1961. That freedom, however, resulted in the defection of many of East Germany's vitally needed technicians and skilled workers. Mounting desertions finally caused the Communists to erect a wall in August, 1961, between the two zones and eventually between the two Germanies; heavily patrolled and constantly reinforced, it has achieved its purpose—curtailing the desertions and furnishing the East German regime with a sense of stability. The barrier also served to demoralize those West Germans who had believed that the collapse of the German Democratic Republic and the reunion of the two Germanies were inevitable.

In the meantime, Communist harassment of West Berliners has continued to produce occasional crises, such as the one in 1969 over West Germany's decision to hold its presidential election in Berlin, a practice that had been in effect for fifteen years. (To prevent any unnecessary provocations, the Allies have since refused to permit the West Germans to hold their presidential elections in West Berlin, and Walter Scheel was elected in Bonn in 1974.) Official Soviet and East German protests were registered, and their nettling delays of traffic into West Berlin occurred, but the election

went off as scheduled. The 1972 treaty normalizing relations between the Federal Republic and the German Democratic Republic was intended in part to lessen just such sources of friction and to ease the access of West Berliners to East Berlin.

9. PROSPECTS FOR DEMOCRATIC STABILITY

Whatever its limitations, parliamentary government has proven far more successful in postwar Germany than it was during even the best of the Weimar years. This success is less the result of constitutional eingineering than the consequence of cultural and social changes that have occurred. The elimination of certain traditional and extremist sectors from the community (see Chapter 2) has made the Federal Republic a more homogeneous society, politically and socially, than its predecessor. Despite some countertrends, German political life today is characterized by a broad consensus, with the public as well as the elites of both major parties committed to democratic institutions. Mass attitudes are also changing. As elsewhere in Europe, formal status is less and less important among social strata; skill is replacing birth as the basis for social advancement; leisure is increasingly valued—perhaps somewhat frenetically—for its own sake; and the gap between the attitudes of the urban and rural populations is disappearing. So, too, the structure of the family is far less authoritarian, in both husband-wife and parent-child relationships. In Germany, as in other parts of Western Europe, traditional forms of authority are under siege and are yielding. Finally, in a nation where feelings of civic obligation and civic competence have been traditionally lacking, citizen-directed community groups have begun to spring up for such causes as environental protection or the protection of buildings which are of historical or architectural interest.

Some traditional patterns do, of course, continue to persist. Thus the appearance of the National Democratic Party on the right and the radical splinter groups on the left demonstrates the continued existence of authoritarian trends in a segment of the German population. Furthermore, many observers have noted that political life, including legislative life, retains a bureaucratic character that tries to muffle disorder lest it get too far out of hand. These features notwithstanding, after over twenty-five years of existence, the German Federal Republic would appear to be anchored in an increasingly supportive environment and culture.

16

Bureaucracy
and the
Political System

1. THE DEVELOPMENT OF CIVIL BUREAUCRACY

The administrative structures that are such an integral part of modern societies are fundamentally mechanisms for mobilizing resources to gain specific ends. Whether these structures are within governmental institutions, political parties, or in business organizations, they become more complex as contemporary social orders grow in breadth and intricacy. Historically, the most efficient administrative structures have been those that approximated the model of rational bureaucratic authority described by Max Weber; for Weber the following are essential characteristics of bureaucratic organization, either public or private: (1) Organiza-

tions function according to sets of standardized routines. (2) Administrative roles are highly specialized and differentiated, and inhere in offices, not individuals. (3) Service in the bureaucracy is a career for trained professionals who are paid salaries and are protected from arbitrary dismissal. (4) Recruitment for bureaucratic positions is based on achievement, as demonstrated competitively. (5) Coordination is facilitated by organizing offices or bureaus hierarchically, as the term "bureaucracy" suggests.

Although complex administrative structures developed within nations outside Europe, such as China, it was in Western Europe that modern bureaucracies first emerged, in both the private and public spheres. Indeed, the first modern bureau-

TABLE 16.1   THE FATHERS OF HIGHER CIVIL
SERVANTS IN BRITAIN, FRANCE, AND
THE UNITED STATES

	Britain 1949–1952	France 1945–1951	United States 1959
Shopkeepers, businessmen, etc.	17.8%	11.4%	20%
Governmental employees	27	50.2	?
Business employees	13.3	8.3	24
Professionals	30.4	23.1	20
Skilled workers	8.7	3.3	17
Total for middle classes	97.2%	96.4%	81%
Unskilled workers	1.5	—	4
Agricultural workers and farmers	1.3	3.6	15
Total for lower classes	2.8%	3.6%	19%

Adapted from V. Subramaniam, "Representative Bureaucracy: A Re-assessment," *American Political Science Review* 61, 4 (December, 1967): 1016.

cracy was created by the Roman Catholic Church; this later served as a model for monarchs who wanted to extend their power or mobilize more effectively the resources of the community. It was in the eighteenth and nineteenth centuries, however, that a general rationalizing of bureaucratic organization would be seen occurring throughout Europe. Perhaps the first notable attempts to create an organization approximating the Weberian model were those of the Prussian monarchy, culminating in the General Code of 1794. Under its provisions, the merit system was extended to every major administrative post. The Napoleonic period saw somewhat similar developments in France, where the entire French bureaucracy was recast along national—and extraordinarily rational—lines. In Britain, the comparative ease with which a relatively effective nation-state had been created inhibited changes in recruitment patterns until after the 1860's. The Northcote-Trevelyan Report of 1854 then gave impetus for bureaucratic reform.

Whatever the differences among individual European countries, in all of them the state came to be regarded as a creative instrument, and a career in the state service as a highly respectable one for the scions of upper-class families. In this respect Europe differed from the United States, where the sons of the "better" families went into business or the professions. Yet the attitudes displayed by civil servants (as well as the attitudes displayed toward them) differed in the three countries we are discussing. In Britain, service to the community, as defined by the community, was looked upon as transcending personal or class interests. This attitude certainly did not completely eliminate class biases, but British civil servants did exhibit a remarkable ability to subordinate their own views to those of elected political leaders, no matter how much they disagreed with them. Thus, despite the fact that the ideological conflicts that divided the British in the nineteenth century were profound, they could readily conceive of a bureaucracy composed of gentlemen who would serve a constantly changing national interest.

In these attitudes Britain differed from both France and Germany, where the bu-

FIGURE 16.1   CITIZENS' ATTITUDES TOWARD GOVERNMENT OFFICIALS: BRITAIN AND GERMANY

"How would you expect to be treated by government officials?"

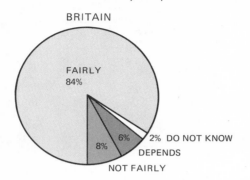

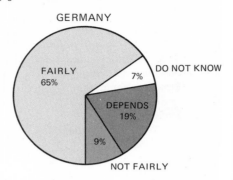

"What sort of consideration would you expect government officials to give to your point of view?"

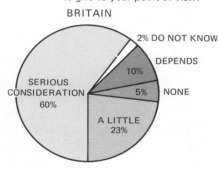

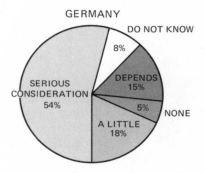

Selection adapted from Gabriel Almond and Sidney Verba, *The Civic Culture; Political Attitudes and Democracy in Five Nations* (copyright © 1963 by Princeton University Press), pp. 108, 109. Reprinted by permission of Princeton University Press.

reaucracy remained even more a closed caste, decidedly weighted in favor of the *haute bourgeoisie* and the aristocracy. French and German bureaucrats, like their British counterparts, came to view themselves as, in some sense, representing the best interests of the nation; unlike British bureaucrats, however, many regarded it as their job to define the best interests of the community, believing that their definition was superior to any possible results of the ballot box. Some bureaucrats of the Weimar Republic and the French Third Republic, for example, tried to sabotage policies they believed were destroying the national heritage. In the

postwar era, both nations have moved toward democratization of the bureaucracy, though their educational structure and cultural prejudices are such that they have a long way to go.

Although the primary purpose of European bureaucracies has been to implement government policies, they have also helped to make policy, to influence policy as they implemented it, to aggregate public and private interests, and to assist groups in the articulation of their special interests. The scope of bureaucratic discretion is suggested by the variety of roles that bureaucrats may fill, and this range of responsibilities has been greatly expanded in recent years because of a growing trend toward skeletal legislation which gives high-level bureaucrats the authority to make important policy decisions in the name of bureaucratic "rules." Thus the problem of bureaucratic attitudes as well as the problem of control and direction of the bureaucracy have become more pressing.

Today all European bureaucracies face similar problems. In an age in which the state has taken on a number of tasks requiring technical knowledge and careful planning, a new balance must be found between the need for expertise and innovation in the bureaucracy and the need to keep bureaucrats subject to the authority of political leaders. In an age in which the actions of the state directly influence every aspect of a citizen's life, a new balance must be found between community needs and individual rights. And in an age in which old forms of authority are eroding and demands are being registered for "open" politics with full community participation, legislators must find a new way of mediating between the requirements of effective governance and the desire of those governed to help make the decisions that affect them.

2. THE BRITISH PATTERN

ORIGINS AND DEVELOPMENT: The most striking circumstance surrounding the evolution of the British bureaucracy is the almost total lack of thought given to the subject until the end of the eighteenth century. While Continental monarchs were striving mightily to create a satisfactory bureaucratic apparatus, the British more or less ignored the problem. Laws passed by Parliament from the middle of the sixteenth century to the end of the eighteenth were carried out not by professional agents of the central authority but by local gentry. No qualifications were required, and central control was minimal. In fact, controls were handled largely by the courts; if local officials failed to deal with matters as required by law, they could

be charged before a court with malfeasance or misfeasance and fined. A kind of part-time local inspectorate materialized in the person of informers who received a portion of the fine if violations were proved in court.

Most of the principal departments of government—e. g., agriculture, education, labor —date from the nineteenth century as the central government, with the beginnings of the Industrial Revolution, assumed a more active part in the regulation of the life of the nation. It was only then that a national bureaucracy began to take shape, and with it the problems of reforming recruitment procedures. Before the 1860's the small national bureaucracy was filled in a variety of ways. Many departments used at least qualifying examinations, though not competitive ones, but a very large number of appointments were filled on the basis of patronage. Moreover, a good many offices were sinecures designed to provide an income in exchange for almost no work at all. The assertion that the British bureaucracy was filled with "the bastard and idiot sons of the aristocracy" might not have been entirely accurate, but it did contain elements of truth. (A noteworthy exception was John Stuart Mill, whose sinecure in the India Office gave him the opportunity to write many of his important books.)

Impelled by liberal ideas, the reforms recommended by the Northcote-Trevelyan Report were designed to create a rational bureaucratic organization on a nationwide basis. The report called for the creation of a merit civil service based on competitive examinations. However, unlike the French or German pattern, the report did not suggest the formation of a corps of technocrats trained in law or engineering. The general feeling was that the upper levels of the civil service should consist of intelligent young men of breeding—talented amateurs, in other words—who could handle many tasks well. All that was needed to have the nation operate smoothly was a corps of "superior" men to coordinate its efforts and, where necessary, to guide it. The national government was supposed to serve as a regulating mechanism which insured that the natural forces of the community came into play in a reasonable and reasonably harmonious way, at the same time that it extended aid to its less fortunate members. However, while both tasks were considered important, there was little sense of any necessity for bureaucrats, especially, to direct the nation toward any particular social or economic goals. Hence the job of the civil servant was to advise political leaders impartially and to enforce impartially the rules established for regulating British society. The civil service fulfilled its task remarkably well, and came to deserve its high reputation in Britain and abroad. Even after the Labor Party came into office in 1945, there was little serious criticism of the service, except with regard to its class structure.

Beginning about 1960, however, criticism of the civil service came to be more plentiful and incisive. The argument, fundamentally, was that the old conceptions were obsolete; the affairs of every modern society had become so vast that, of necessity, government itself must become a source of innovation, and this can happen only if it is organized and staffed with the kind of professional and technical talent that the twentieth century requires. These criticisms led to the appointment in 1966 of a committee to study the entire structure of the civil service. Popularly referred to as the Fulton Committee, after its chairman, John Scott Fulton, the committee's report was issued in 1968, and many of its recommendations have been implemented.

STRUCTURE AND TRADITIONS: The backbone of the British administrative structure is provided by the ministries. Each is organized hierarchically under a minister who assumes responsibility before the Parliament for both general policy and for all the actions of civil servants under his authority. Immediately below each minister and responsible for the management of the department is a senior civil servant, the permanent secretary. His purpose is to serve any gov-

ernment equally well, presumably in a nonpolitical way. The office is unique to the British: in most European nations and in the United States, those whose position is equivalent to the British permanent secretary are bureaucrats of known sympathy with the policies of the government of the day, even if they are not political appointees. The permanent secretary is normally assisted by one or more deputy secretaries, each in charge of several sections, and below them are the undersecretaries and assistant secretaries who head up the lower-echelon divisions of the department. Within these divisions, smaller units are administered by principals and assistant principals.

Attached to many ministries are one or more committees that provide expert advice or secure the representation of segments of the public. Some of these committees are established by statute; others have been created by ministers themselves. Thus, the minister of health is officially advised by the Central Health Services Council, whose members include, among others, the presidents of the Royal College of Surgeons and the Royal College of Physicians, together with representatives of the medical, dental, and nursing professions. He is also advised by a number of other committees on such subjects as hospital management and the services of general practitioners.

In Britain the power to reorganize executive departments is considered part of the prerogative of the crown—and, hence, the government. In addition, the existence of a tightly controlled party system guarantees that the government can push through almost any organizational structure it considers reasonable. Further, unlike the United States or France under the Third and Fourth Republics, the British government has complete authority over its civil servants. No civil servant can be pressured by a member of Parliament to follow a particular set of policies, nor can he turn to an MP in the hope of circumventing the government's general program. Again, the crucial factor here is two-party discipline within the parliamentary framework. In the United

States Congress, the power of legislative committees and of the legislature itself in relation to the executive is such as to encourage the establishment of associations among bureaucrats, congressmen, and interest groups. Civil servants can be pressured by threats to reduce or even cut off appropriations, and bureaucrats can turn to Congress if they wish, to circumvent the administration's efforts to reduce their appropriations, keep their activities within the perimeter of an overall program, or assign some of their functions to another bureau or department. French politics before the Fifth Republic was distinguished by much the same kind of interrelationships.

The British executive's control over his bureaucracy is reinforced in two ways: by the doctrine of a minister's personal responsibility for his department, and by a tacit agreement that bureaucrats must not only avoid public statements expressing personal opinions, but must also maintain complete secrecy on matters that do not have to be made public. By comparison, the business of government in Washington is conducted in a fishbowl, with administrators often baring their souls to the press and Congress alike. The British tradition of secrecy is rooted in part in the traditional attitude that citizen participation in public affairs should be limited to selection of the governors, and in part to the strength of the government in its dealings with Parliament. The tradition of secrecy has, nevertheless, come under increasing attack. Thus the Fulton Committee recommended that civil servants be permitted to explain the work of departments before Parliament and the public, and that the secrecy with which the government conducts its business be lifted. Strong pressure has also been exerted on the government to review the Official Secrets Act. The belief that civil servants should be less anonymous is shared by many permanent secretaries. Yet the government has been very cautious about taking the wraps off its operation. Though it is clear that, as in all European countries, a more "open" politics is becoming the order of the day, a shift in the relationship between top-level civil servants and governmental ministers would undoubtedly have a far-reaching impact on Parliament and the party system.

For domestic policy, the most important department in the British administrative structure has traditionally been the Treasury. The Treasury is accountable for all financial transactions of the government, but it has many other functions. Until 1968 it was responsible for the recruitment, training, promotion, and salary schedules of all civil-service employees. Its supervision of the staffing and finances of other departments permitted it to investigate both their policies and their organizational effectiveness. It still has much to say about both short- and long-range economic planning. The Treasury's greatest power, however, is its effective control of the budget—a power immeasurably enhanced by the unique position in British government of the chancellor of the exchequer. The Treasury can veto departmental budgetary estimates, and while ministers can appeal to the cabinet, the chancellor can be overridden only with considerable difficulty. Even after estimates are voted, ministries can draw money only through a requisition by the Treasury. Any increase in the number or salaries of officials in a department must receive Treasury approval, despite the fact that the particular ministry may have sufficient funds to pay them. Very rarely, however, does the Treasury command departments. Rather, it works closely with them on all phases of program development and implementation, seeking to increase efficiency and, in the case of interdepartmental disputes, helping to coordinate activities. Because of its prestige, the Treasury attracts the best minds in the civil service, a circumstance of considerable assistance to the department in carrying out its numerous functions.

The Treasury has often been reproached for what some regard as its excessive conservatism and its emphasis upon short-range manipulation instead of long-term policy considerations. When Labor came to power in 1945, the general prejudices against Treasury attitudes led to the creation of a Ministry of Economic Affairs charged with producing long-range economic plans. The ministry, however, was eventually absorbed by the Treasury. In 1964 Labor repeated its earlier effort to remove the responsibility for long-range planning from the Treasury by creating a Department of Economic Affairs, but in 1969, with the abolition of this department, the Treasury once again regained its supremacy in economic policy. About this time the Treasury did, however, lose one of its traditional roles. In accordance with the recommendation of the Fulton Committee, responsibility for personnel recruitment and management was taken from the Treasury and placed in a special Civil Service Department under the direct control of the prime minister.

THE CIVIL SERVICE: Until 1971 the civil service was divided into three major classes. Members of the clerical class were recruited usually between the ages of sixteen and eighteen, and they performed largely routine services. The executive class was recruited both through promotion from below and through open examination; they undertook preliminary investigations of governmental problems, collected data for parliamentary questions, and took on minor administrative responsibilities. Finally, members of the administrative class, recruited for the most part directly from among honor students graduating from universities, constituted the recognized elite group of the civil service.

Following the Fulton recommendations, the three classes of the civil service have now been merged into a new system of occupational groupings. Nevertheless, the most distinctive feature of the former system remains; though no longer called the administrative class, there is still a select group of civil servants identified as being responsible for managing departments and shouldering the responsibility for making and executing policy, and who are especially recruited for these all-important roles. Although only a few of this group can look forward to reaching the post of permanent secretary, of which there are only about thirty, or even the position of deputy secretary or under secretary, any member of this select group is seen as having five principal obligations:

1. Overseeing the day-to-day operation of his particular departmental branch.
2. Voicing his views on the advancement of his department's policy.
3. Helping prepare legislation. From time to time he will work out the details of a bill for his minister. He also helps draft cabinet memoranda and prepares departmental rules, orders, and regulations pertaining to legislation.
4. Briefing his minister for discussions in the House of Commons and in committee. He may actually attend the debate, to provide ready information for his minister.
5. Preparing parliamentary answers for his minister and supplying him with material for speeches.

Because of the important role played by top civil servants in Britain, the method of their recruitment has long been the subject of comment. Until the end of World War II, the traditional means of recruitment consisted of a series of competitive written examinations, plus a short interview, given to university honors graduates. The first three examinations tested the student's ability to express himself well in the English language, his grasp of contemporary affairs, and his facility in expounding on a topic that any intelligent young man should be able to discuss. The subject matter of the other five written tests could be chosen from a list of sixty or more, and a candidate's ability to read Sanskrit counted as heavily as one in an area more relevant to immediate national concerns. This method of recruitment was largely geared to the kind of student produced by Oxford and Cambridge.

At the end of World War II, Method II was introduced as an alternative approach to recruitment. Originally designed as a temporary expedient for civil-service applicants whose academic talents had become rusty while serving in the armed forces, it was retained and eventually became the more popular means of entering the administrative class. Candidates using Method II took the three examinations required of all Method I candidates, but the selection procedure was largely based on a series of individual and group interviews that tested leadership qualities.

By 1971 both methods of recruitment had been discarded in favor of a new system made up of administrative trainees. As before, the majority of those selected as trainees are university honors graduates. However, a greater portion than before are recruited from below, from persons with a minimum of two years' service. In either case the candidate is given a series of examinations and interviews similar to those devised for Method II. A probationary period then follows, lasting at least two years, during which the candidates serve as administrative trainees in their departments. They then enroll in a sixteen-week course at the Civil Service College, the founding of which further reflects the influence of the Fulton Report. For the next four years the candidates continue to be assessed, further trained, and "streamed" into ability groupings. Some will be designated for high-level posts, while others will be deemed more suitable for middle-management, an area in the service thought to be in particular need of strengthening.

The various changes that have been made in the recruitment of the administrative class, by whatever name it is called, are in large part a response to two types of criticisms leveled against it. The first was that the administrative class was very much a part of the British establishment, that it had social ties with Conservative Party politicians and with the business community. That this portrayal was once accurate there can be little doubt. For example, of the permanent secretaries who served between 1900 and 1919, 64 percent had been to a public school, and most of these to the most prestigious schools such as Eton and Harrow. Even more than half the permanent secretaries who served between 1945 and 1963 were public-school graduates, though the representation of the top schools had sharply declined (Table 16.2). After 1945, however, recruitment to the administrative class came to be from fairly varied middle-class backgrounds. This resulted partly from a greater emphasis upon promotion from the executive class into the administrative class, and partly from an increasing number of scholarships that made the public schools, as well as Oxford and Cambridge, less and less exclusive. The post-1970 recruitment innovations may be expected to add still further to the background diversification of those in the upper echelons of the service.

It is no longer true, then, that the administrative class constitutes a part of the establishment. Despite the anxieties of the Labor Party left, postwar Labor ministers have found that civil servants have been loyal to the goverment—many, in fact, throwing themselves wholeheartedly into carrying out the new ministerial policies. Indeed, Conservatives have often complained bitterly that the bureaucracy seems excessively committed to nationalization. A study for the Fulton Committee found that the majority of the administrative class recruited since 1945 voted for the Labor Party in the 1966 election, and that by and large they do not move in the same social circles as the business and political communities. If not part of an establishment, however, the top civil servants do share with each other a set of common orientations and connections based in part on their university background. This rapport certainly facilitates their work, even as it may limit their perspective. Permanent secretaries find it quite easy to work on the whole array of interdepartmental committees that try to iron out differences and devise common policies.

The second criticism made against the administrative class is that its members have been generalists, not specialists, although, in the view of many, this characteristic has been responsible for the high regard in which the administrative class has usually been held. Members of the class have been recruited on the basis of mind and charac-

TABLE 16.2   THE EDUCATIONAL BACKGROUND OF
BRITISH PERMANENT SECRETARIES

	1900–1919	*1920–1924*	*1945–1963*
Twenty of the best known public schools	51.0%	27.4%	26.5%
Other public schools	13.2	33.9	27.7
Private schools not classified as public schools	9.4	19.4	20.5
Schools administered by local authorities	0.0	8.1	15.7
Other schools	13.2	4.8	9.6
No attendance at secondary school	1.9	0.0	0.0
Information not available	11.3	6.4	0.0

Adapted from John S. Harris and Thomas V. Garcia, "The Permanent Secretaries: Britain's Top Administrators," *Public Administration Review,* 24:
(March, 1966), p. 33, reprinted by permission of the publisher.

ter, both of which they supposedly bring to bear upon the problems faced by the departments they serve. They have entered the service at an early age, and have received very little in-service training, either in management techniques or in skills pertaining to the functions performed by their departments. Such skills have traditionally been regarded as being completely unnecessary, because the ideal member of this class could and would simply take advice from the professionals and, on the basis of his mature evaluation of what the situation required, would translate this advice into cogent proposals. Technically trained professionals were considered to lack the breadth of viewpoint to determine policy; the expert was to be on tap but not on top, lest he push his own pet projects too hard. Indeed, permanent secretaries tended to be rotated regularly from department to department to prevent them from becoming too closely identified with one bureaucratic point of view. Management techniques, after all, were common-sense matters merely requiring sound judgment. As one commentator observed:

. . . *the British administrator travel-*
ing abroad is shocked to discover that many

countries are administered by men who read
books about public administration. . . .
Such people are committing the crime of
learning from books something that one just
does. It is rather like venturing into matri-
mony only after a course of Havelock Ellis,
which, for a healthy nature, should not
strictly be necessary.[1]

The Fulton Report contained a slashing attack on the "amateurism" of the administrative class. It urged that the dichotomy between "specialists" and "generalists" be ended and that professionals, such as engineers, be trained in management techniques and promoted to policy-making positions upon demonstrated competence. Another recommendation of the Fulton Committee was that greater stress be placed on recruiting candidates with training in "relevent" subjects, such as political science and economics. In making this recommendation, the committee was not without support from administrators themselves, many of whom believed that their traditional university courses had not been very useful. The es-

[1] C. H. Sisson, *The Spirit of British Administration*
(London: Faber & Faber, 1959), p. 28.

tablishment of a civil-service college to provide training in management techniques, as well as substantive course work such as economics and finance, was a third recommendation. Finally, though accepting the institution of the permanent secretary, the committee advocated that ministers also recruit special senior policy advisers from the bureaucracy, the universities, or even the business community—men who could make possible a constant interchange of ideas between the civil service and other segments of the community. In short, the entire emphasis of the Fulton report was on the need for increased specialization and expertise.

The effect of the Fulton Report will be to remold the British civil service somewhat in the American pattern, reducing both the gap between generalists and specialists and the distinctions among civil-service classes. As already indicated, the Civil Service College has now been established, the old classes have been eliminated, thereby paving the way for the entry of technical personnel into management positions, and the practice of bringing in outside technical experts for certain administrative posts—already begun before the Fulton Report—is continuing. The only major recommendation of the Fulton Committee explicitly rejected was that preference in recruitment be given to university graduates with "relevant" course work. These innovations notwithstanding, the general administrator has thus far shown no signs of being replaced as the dominant figure in the service. The selection, training, and streaming of the administrative trainees is still designed to produce a class of senior civil servants that can serve ministers by synthesizing the contributions of specialists, placing these in the context of political realities, and by formulating policy alternatives. If the new administrator turns out not quite to fit the old model of the "talented amateur," it is even less likely that he will fit the model of the narrow specialist.

CONTROL AND ACCOUNTABILITY: The British civil service has often been commended for its deep sense of responsibility to both the public and its political superiors. Corruption is practically nonexistent, and bureaucrats' dealings with the public have engendered an impressive reputation for their fairness and civility. Even so, Parliament has manifested a growing dissatisfaction with its ability to hold the bureaucracy accountable for its operation. Some critics believe that holding a minister accountable for the work of his entire department is anachronistic and that responsibility could be better assured by strengthening parliamentary committees. Already Parliament has established a select committee to oversee the operations of the nationalized industries.

The effectiveness of judicial controls upon bureaucratic action has also been a subject of discussion. For years the British felt little need to follow the Continent and create a body of administrative law applicable under a separate court system. The common-law courts, plus the efficacy of external political controls, were seen as sufficient bulwarks against the misuse of public authority. As a consequence, the only remedy to persons injured by an administrative act was to file suit for damages in the regular courts against the official or officials responsible. The British continued (as have the Americans) to adhere to the essentially feudal notion that the state as such could not be liable for the actions of its officers, and hence could not be sued. The advantages claimed for the British approach were that it placed all citizens, including public officials, on the same plane; by comparison, it was argued, the so-called administrative courts, composed as they were of bureaucrats, could never render the private citizen his due because they would tend to favor the bureaucracy.

By the 1920's, however, it had become evident that the British approach was not altogether satisfactory. The state was interfering more and more directly in the lives of its citizens—with a corresponding increase in the occasions on which citizens wished to seek legal redress. And, in a good many cases, no adequate remedy was available. A fire truck responding to an alarm might injure a citizen on the road, but unless the driver had been negligent, the citizen could not collect damages. A series of legal fictions created by the courts in the 1920's and 1930's to chip away at the doctrine of state immunity, together with several parliamentary acts, expanded the number of instances in which a citizen or his family could obtain redress from the government in case of injury, death, or loss of property. Finally, in 1947, the Crown Proceedings Act explicitly opened the door to suits against the crown, "as if the crown were a fellow citizen." Nevertheless, compared with the Continental practice, the opportunities for obtaining redress are still limited, and the absence of any administrative courts to handle such suits means that efforts to win redress are both time-consuming and expensive.

Administrative courts on the Continent also review allegations by citizens to the effect that officials have exceeded their authority. For a long time, both Englishmen and Americans preferred to rely upon the regular court system to handle these complaints, for the common-law courts were considered the ultimate repositories of liberty. But in actuality, it became decidedly more difficult to operate on this basis: court calendars were being overcrowded with technically complex matters, and judges were notoriously loath to interfere with actions whose rationale and implications they could understand only with difficulty. The end result was the growth of a large number of administrative tribunals; one such tribunal, for example, now has jurisdiction over workmen's compensation cases, and the procedures are far less time-consuming and much less expensive. Contrary to the classic separation-of-powers doctrine, there is every evidence that the rights of the plaintiff are fully protected, despite the fact that administrators are acting as judges. The function of the regular courts has been preserved by their being given authority to review decisions of the tribunals.

3. THE FRENCH PATTERN [2]

ORIGINS AND DEVELOPMENT: By the time of Louis XIV, the French state could boast of an extensive bureaucratic apparatus scattered throughout the nation and supervised by the king's *intendants.* The creation of a bureaucracy dependent upon the throne was part of the monarchy's effort to unify the realm and give it direction. Omnipresent though the bureaucracy was, it was hardly efficient. Many important offices were inherited or bought; because a good number of these had the power to confer titles, the ranks of officeholders burgeoned. Understandably, the methods of acquiring offices were scarcely conducive to the establishment of a well-run operation—or, usually, to the recruitment of real talent.

The French Revolution and Napoleon not only transformed the French state, they remodeled its entire administrative apparatus. The bureaucrat was no longer the servant of the crown, but of his nation. His office and powers were explicitly defined by law. Further, the structure of the government itself was more rationally organized and grouped into a coherent set of hierarchical ministries. Provincial autonomy was swept away, and the nation was reorganized into administrative departments controlled by prefects appointed in Paris.

Just as important was the effort to create a bureaucratic apparatus staffed with able men. Napoleon's conception of the effective bureaucrat was that of a person trained in the practical sciences, especially engineering, and the highest state posts were filled by young graduates of technical schools such as the *École Polytechnique.*

Although the system created by Napoleon set the guidelines for recruitment by the French administration, between 1815 and 1870 appointments and promotions were

[2] Much of the historical discussion is based on Alfred Diamant's essay "The French Administrative System: The Republic Passes but the Administration Remains," in William J. Siffin, ed., *Toward the Comparative Study of Public Administration* (Bloomington, Indiana University Press, 1957), pp. 182–218.

largely contingent upon personal connections, and the upper level of the system became the province of the *haute bourgeoisie* and the aristocracy. To a considerable extent, however, those in the higher echelons continued to be drawn from Napoleon's *Grandes Écoles,* and they possessed an essential degree of technical proficiency. Their capabilities notwithstanding, they shared, by and large, the views of their class on social and economic questions. They were not averse to the state interceding in economic affairs from a rather mercantilist point of view, but they lacked that faith held by the British middle class in the possibilities and advantages of economic expansion. the point, of course, can be overstressed. Many in the French bureaucracy were disciples of Saint-Simon and Fourier, and were actively dedicated to applying technical knowledge to social and economic issues.

After 1870 programs were introduced to improve the training of bureaucratic personnel. Recruitment continued to be the province of the ministries, but they were obliged to set forth their personnel requirements in the form of public announcements. Again, the emphasis was on technical training. Yet far more than in Britain, the bureaucracy remained the preserve of the upper bourgeoisie—particularly for those in the so-called *grands corps,* that is, such elite groups as the Council of State (*Conseil d'État*), Finance Inspectorate (*Inspection des Finance*), and the Audit Office or Court of Accounts (*Cour des Comptes*). Loyalty to one's department and corps was the bureaucrat's prime concern; it was induced both by the decentralized nature of recruitment and by the nation's political framework.

The instability of France's regimes and the weakness of its executives made it nearly impossible to give the bureaucracy overall direction. Governments and even individual ministers were relatively short-termed. Too many pressures were placed upon the national government to permit the inception of a workmanlike bureaucratic policy. The structure of departments and field services was to a large extent determined as the result of compromise between conflicting groups rather than the application of any rational criteria; departments continued to work at loggerheads not only with each other but with the government as well. Bureaucrats would bypass their departments in order to negotiate with deputies; deputies, through their committees, would try to persuade bureaucrats to undermine social or economic programs they opposed and to provide favors for their constituents. Lines of bureaucratic authority had a baroque twist that belied the neat organizational charts that the French produced in great profusion.

The higher civil servants continued to be politically conservative; their background and education inclined them to identify themselves with the upper classes, and the widespread practice of using administrative posts as stepping stones to lucrative business positions helped contribute to such identification. Yet conservatism was not the main problem. It is true that traditional biases occasionally led civil servants to impede the implementation of more "radical" programs in the hope that a particular government would fall; from these few cases, the mythology spread that France's transient political regimes were ruled essentially by a conservative bureaucracy. The actual circumstances, however, were far more complicated. Bureaucrats might be conservative, but in many instances their training and positions made them quite sympathetic to proposals for the modernization and rationalization of French social and economic life. Moreover, many of them agreed with Bismarck that the ruling social and political elites of the nation had a duty to press for the welfare of those who were ruled. There were, then, many higher civil servants interested in reform, but the very structure of the political system prevented them from obtaining the kind of practical support and direction they needed to put their ideas into practice. Further, most civil servants were imbued with the conception of obedience to legally constituted authority, which prevented them from stepping too far out of line.

If the bureaucracy did not rule France, it did indeed run France between the governments that came and went by keeping essential public services in operation. Its conservatism, however, was at least as much a result of the stalemated quality of French political life and the lack of political leadership as it was of individual proclivities.

Those who created the Fourth Republic were eager to eliminate the bureaucratic evils they felt had been rampant in the Third. What occurred, therefore, was that broadly uniform, and more democratic, standards were set up for the recruitment of bureaucrats. Also, a general corps of administrators—that is, generalists on the British model—was established for the purpose of instilling some cohesiveness in the viewpoint of the French bureaucratic elite. On the surface, at least, the reforms were unsuccessful. A certain amount of democratization was achieved, but the middle and upper-middle classes, especially civil-service families, were still most favored as a source of bureaucratic personnel. Nor did the idea of a class of general administrators with an overall perspective really work. Members of the *grand corps* continued to dominate the bureaucracy; both they and the ministries persisted in working at cross purposes. Of greater import, the old pattern of complicated lines of authority involving the executive, the legislature, and the bureaucracy was restored with frustrating consequences.

Yet the outward appearance of failure conveyed by these postwar bureaucratic reforms was rather deceptive: in fact, important changes were taking place, the most significant of which was the rapid replacement of a much older generation of bureaucrats by young cadres. France's large loss of manpower during World War I meant that the nation had skipped a generation; the consequent absence of a sizable middle-age segment in the Fourth Republic bureaucracy, plus the purges attendant upon the liberation of France at the end of World War II, brought very quickly to the top a new generation of skilled bureaucrats— young men trained in the social as well as

the natural sciences, whose outlook was far more "modern" and less ideological than that of their predecessors. Their major concern was to renew France, to create a modern industrial state that at the same time preserved the unique features of French culture. It was during the Fourth Republic, therefore, that some of the boldest and most far-sighted plans for reform were hatched in the bureaucracy. Most of them did not see the light of day, primarily because political pressures prohibited the development of any policies that trod on the toes of powerful interests; yet a certain type of economic planning did come into its own because of the dedication of men like Jean Monnet.

It was not until the Fifth Republic that all the postwar agitation and scheming for bureaucratic reform finally culminated in vast changes in the system. The de Gaulle regime made some marginal modifications in recruitment and training patterns, but its major contribution was to provide a government that could offer leadership. Bureaucratic technicians were brought into the executive first as advisors to cabinet members, and increasingly as ministers. Numerous plans for reform were announced and implemented, and the Fifth Republic gave fairly free rein to bureaucratic initiative. Recent studies have demonstrated, however, that while the Gaullists recruited much of their executive leadership from the high civil service, they also molded the high civil service in their own image. As political loyalty became an increasingly important criterion for advancement through the administrative ranks, administrative influence on politics was matched by politicization of the administration.

STRUCTURE: The principal administrative agencies of the French government are the ministries, which perform the traditional functions of government—relating to such matters as foreign affairs, justice, defense, the interior—and also participate in the control of the public sector of the economy. The formal organization of the great ministries is fairly standardized. Under the minister's leadership, the division of authority is tripartite, consisting of (1) the minister's cabinet, (2) the managerial units (*directions*) of the ministry, and (3) various organs of consultation or control.

The French never devised a post equivalent to that of the British permanent secretary, an impartial civil servant who coordinates the work of a department. Why they did not is related to the whole context of French politics. In the past, many ministries have been a hodgepodge of services whose relation to one another was determined on political rather than administrative grounds. Because the *directions* often recruited their own *corps,* developed their own outlook, and acquired their own powerful friends in Parliament, it became almost impossible to coordinate them.

The ministers themselves could not cope with the problem of overall coordination; as a result they habitually appointed personal political friends to bureaucratic posts and drew upon career civil servants who were sympathetic to their political position. These political ministerial cabinets not only aided the minister in his contacts with the legislature and interest groups, but they also tried, somewhat unsuccessfully, to coordinate the managerial staffs within the ministry.

At first these personal cabinets were almost entirely political, but gradually they became dominated by career civil servants, often members of the *grand corps,* who were sympathetic to the minister's point of view. By the time of the Fourth Republic, some two-thirds of the ministerial cabinets consisted of civil servants. Under the Fifth Republic, of course, many of the ministers themselves have been drawn from the bureaucracy. Bureaucratic or political in their complexion, the cabinets' coordinating efforts were usually checkmated. Line officers generally distrusted members of the minister's cabinet who, when not politicians, were often of a lesser standing and seniority than themselves. Many ministers, of course, made efforts to "colonize" their ministries with officials who were loyal to them, thus hampering the efforts of those who came after. For example, the Interior and Education ministries remained Socialist and Radical fiefs during much of the Fourth Republic, whereas the Foreign Office was monopolized by the Popular Republican Movement (MRP) until 1954. Coordination of the government bureacracy improved considerably under de Gaulle; the regime rationalized the overall structure of the government and brought into high-level posts a large number of men sharing a common outlook. Most importantly, it dominated Parliament. The political-bureaucratic executive structure built during a period of sixteen years under de Gaulle and Pompidou has demonstrated strong and open support for Giscard d'Estaing, and a return to the bureaucratic fragmentation of the Fourth Republic is not likely.

The *directeurs* are most frequently the highest-level permanent officials in a ministry, although even they can be replaced by ministers. They have direct access to the minister, often represent him before parliamentary committees, and have the power to sign ministerial decrees falling within the competence of the minister. Below each *direction* (or the *direction générale* in some ministries), little uniformity of organization exists. Sometimes there are *sous-directions,* which are genuine subdivisions. Sometimes the word *service* is used to designate a subdivision; in other instances, a *service* is a fairly autonomous unit either directly under the personal control of the minister or else comparatively independent. This organizational fragmentation, which somewhat resembles the administrative structure of the United States, is closely related to the traditional weakness of the French executive. Many *directions* have had quasi-independent status. Even within ministries, *directeurs* have fought and negotiated with one another, with members of Parliament, and with ministers in order to obtain approval for particular projects. Nevertheless, there is considerable political cohesiveness among *directeurs,* with the vast majority openly committed to the "government."

Because of the wide responsibilities of the central government, most French ministries have established extensive field or external services. In fact, more than 95 percent of French civil servants are located outside Paris. When the French Revolution destroyed the territorial organization of the old regime, the provinces were replaced by administrative departments which have, until quite recently, remained the major units of territorial administration. In the twentieth century, departments became too small for some administrative activities; many ministries found that a field office in each of the ninety-five departments was excessive and made coordination difficult.[3] Since 1959, however, considerable progress has been made in reorganizing field services to conform with the economic division of France into twenty-one regional areas.

All but three government ministries (Justice, Foreign Affairs, and Information) now have inspectorates to supervise field administration. The structure of inspectorates differs from department to department, but the inspectors general usually fulfill three functions: they supervise the activities of their own department or division, take on special investigative missions at the request of a minister, and, in some cases, participate on advisory councils attached to government departments.

At first the advisory councils themselves were composed almost entirely of civil servants. The most renowned of these was the *Conseil d'État*, which will be discussed in detail later. Advisory councils have proliferated widely in the past hundred years and have tended to draw their membership increasingly from interest groups. They may be concerned with the activities of a department or with only one of its divisions. By 1959 close to half of the ministries had a national advisory council competent to review all aspects of the department's work. Most advisory councils are just that; they assume no responsibility for decisions.

[3] With the recent reorganization of the Paris region, France contains ninety-five metropolitan departments and four overseas departments.

CIVIL SERVICE—RECRUITMENT: From the time of Napoleon, many top-ranking positions in the civil service were filled by young men who had received their training as engineers at the *École Polytechnique* or other engineering schools, and had then moved on to either the civil or the military bureaucracy. Training at the *École Polytechnique* was broadly theoretical, and graduates usually left school with not only a knowledge of the general sciences but also at least some familiarity with philosophy and other humanistic subjects. It was felt that a man so educated, although trained as a technician, could develop a general administrative capacity as he moved up in the ranks of a technical corps to which he might be attached and for which he might eventually assume managerial responsibility. Members of the nontechnical corps, on the other hand, were drawn largely from major law schools; their recruitment was informal and usually based on family connections.

With the founding of the Third Republic, reforms were pushed for improving the training and recruitment procedures for higher-level bureaucrats. The *École Libre des Sciences Politiques* was founded in 1871 to provide for the training of administrators in public law, administration, and economics, and beginning in 1882 Parliament passed a series of laws requiring that both ministries and *corps* standardize recruitment methods and make them public. The reforms, however, were not particularly successful. Recruitment patterns continued to be highly undemocratic, and although the *École Polytechnique* did open its doors to many persons of lower-middle-class background, the fees charged at the *École Libre* precluded the admission of all but the well-to-do, lending a distinctly conservative caste to the bureaucracy.

At the beginning of the Fourth Republic, another series of reform measures was initiated to unify and democratize the civil service. The first established a *Direction générale de la fonction publique*, the top civil-service office; it was directly under the premier, who was given prime responsibility for implementing new laws on civil-service recruitment. In 1946 another law divided the civil service into classes modeled on the British system. Four government-wide categories were created—A, B, C, and D—with the first two corresponding more or less to those of the British administrative and executive classes.

The *École Libre* was incorporated into the University of Paris and lost its right-wing bias in the process. Of greater importance was the creation of the national school of administration, the *École Nationale d'Administration* (ENA). Henceforth, those wishing to enter the equivalent of the British administrative class, either in ministries or one of the *grands corps*, would have to pass through the ENA. Democratization of the civil service would be achieved not only because the fees charged ENA entrants would be nominal, but because admission to the school would be open to both university graduates and civil servants in the French equivalent of the British executive class. The ENA would unify the service, because, for the first time, France would have created a group of general administrators who shared a common educational background. Ministries and corps would no longer be permitted to give their own examinations; rather, a common examination would be given to all ENA students.

All these efforts at reform have been only partially successful. Most ministries still more or less determine their own recruitment, and once a person enters a ministry he usually becomes part of a corps, with all that implies. Nor have the *grands corps* been abolished: they retain their existence, their prestige, and the loyalty of their members, who are still the mandarins of the French bureaucracy. Further, not too many members of the executive class have managed to use the ENA as a means of promotion, and since most students enter the *École* only after graduation from a university, its success in democratizing the bureaucracy has been limited. In fact, the proportion of top-level bureaucrats of middle-class background probably has increased in recent

years, while the ratio of those with a working-class origin has dropped. In the mid-1960's the fathers of more than 40 percent of ENA graduates were also civil servants, almost all higher civil servants (Table 16.3).

The graduates of the ENA share something of a common perspective, and they are beginning to bring to the service a somewhat more comprehensive, national outlook than that which has characterized it in the past. Except for those who are already executive-class bureaucrats, candidates for the ENA must pass an entrance examination and must possess a university degree. Some choice in examination subject matter is permitted, depending on a candidate's preferred branch of service, but more than 75 percent of the grade is based on performance in such fields as economic geography, law, and history. Much of the three-years' training of successful ENA applicants is aimed at creating a common background and orientation for the future leaders of the civil service.

The ENA is first and foremost the training ground for French "civil administrators" in the *grands corps* and a few ministries such as Finance and Interior. Other, less prestigious ministries, such as Agriculture, Labor, and Justice, have been able to recruit relatively few graduates. Lower-level administrative positions, for which a university degree alone is necessary, have attracted fewer and fewer applicants during the past decade. Technical personnel are still recruited for the civil service from the *École Polytechnique* and other specialized schools. Because the French are willing to place scientific personnel in the highest levels of administration, many of these graduates achieve positions of general prominence, especially in the management of nationalized industries. Unlike the British, the French place scant faith in such intangibles as "character" or "experience" in determining admission to the ENA—or promotion later.

· Students entering the *École Polytechnique* and the ENA do not always plan to make the state service a lifetime career. Many of the technical-school graduates go immedi-

TABLE 16.3   FAMILY BACKGROUND OF MEMBERS OF THE GRANDS CORPS
ENTERING FROM ÉCOLE NATIONALE D'ADMINISTRATION,
SERVING IN THE GRANDS CORPS, 1953–1968

Occupation of father	Council of State	Court of Accounts	Finance Inspectorate	Average for Grands Corps [1]
Administration				
A₁ (high)	14%	16%	14%	14%
A₂	22	19	17	19
B	2	7	4	4
C	–	2	1	1
D (low)	–	1	1	1
Total, administration	38%	45%	37%	39%
Artisans and shopkeepers	10	9	13	10
Heads of industrial enterprises	1	7	6	5
Commercial employees	25	15	22	21
Industrial employees	5	6	4	5
Liberal professions	16	16	11	14
Workers	3	1	–	2
Farmers	1	1	7	3
Without profession	1	–	–	1
Total, other than administration	62%	55%	63%	61%

[1] Does not include Foreign Service.

Adapted from Ezra N. Suleiman, *Politics, Power and Bureaucracy in France: The Administrative Elite* (Princeton, N.J.: Princeton University Press, 1974), pp. 87–88. Reprinted by permission of Princeton University Press.

ately into private industry; a substantive number of civil servants, including members of the *grands corps*, later join them, usually at about the age of forty. The large role that the French state has always assumed in the economy has placed these men very much in demand, and they can usually command higher salaries in the business world than in the bureaucratic. There has always been a far closer relationship between the *haut fonctionnaire* and the business community in France than in Britain. Sometimes this liaison has tended to make the bureacracy more conservative, but under the Fourth and Fifth Republics, it has contributed greatly to the lessening of friction between the business community and the government in the area of national planning.

CONTROLS: For the seventy years following the end of the Franco-Prussian war, it was all but impossible for the French cabi-

net, and more especially the premier, to have effective control over the bureaucratic machinery—a result of the weakness of the French executive, not of bureaucratic sabotage.

The legislature did, in some ways, exercise a form of control, but its efforts were directed primarily toward obtaining special favors or blocking the full implementation of particular programs. The Fifth Republic has strengthened executive control of the bureaucracy, but the bureaucracy's continued fragmentation into various corps is still a problem.

In the absence of effective political controls, the number of internal-control mechanisms has proliferated. On the whole, these have been legal rather than organizational in nature—that is, they have been designed to prevent bureaucrats from exceeding their powers and to limit venality; they have not been designed for the purpose of creatively coordinating the state civil-service operation.

Perhaps the most important internal-control agency is the *Conseil d'État*. Under Napoleon its functions, like those of the old *Conseil du Roi* under the Bourbons, were to prepare and edit legislation, draw up decrees, and adjudicate disputes among the ministries. During Napoleon's reign it was clearly the most important legislative and administrative body in France, having, for example, the principal responsibility in drawing up the Napoleonic Codes. Gradually, however, the *Conseil d'État* began to take on a series of other duties. Both the revolutionaries and Napoleon wished to eliminate the interference of the regular courts in the work of the government. The evaluation of administrative acts, therefore, and the protection of the citizen against the excesses of administrative authority were placed in the hands of the administration itself, primarily the *Conseil*. Over the years the authority of the *Conseil* in the judicial sphere expanded, and in 1872, under the Third Republic, it was given the authority to issue final judgments in administrative litigation. Until then, its opinions had been only advisory, with final dispositions resting with the executive.

By the latter years of the Third Republic, it had become quite clear that, as an administrative court, the *Conseil d'État* was doing an excellent job in protecting the rights of French citizens. In fact, it gradually built up a body of case law that made French administrative procedure in that area among the most advanced in the world. As its prestige continued to grow, the *Conseil d'État* attracted more of the best qualified civil-service recruits, and its members became part of the *grands corps*. They were often called to other departments on special missions; their placement within other ministries and the breadth of their experience gave the *Conseil* even more authority than it was legally allotted.

Today, the administrative functions of the *Conseil d'État* involve advice on the drafting of bills and executive decrees. Actually, its legal authority in connection with executive decrees has diminished under the Fifth Republic. In both the Third and Fourth Republics, all decrees issued in pursuance of a law had to be placed before the *Conseil* before taking effect. This is still true, but under the constitution of the Fifth Republic the executive has acquired new powers to issue decrees that have the force of law and are not dependent upon specific legislation passed by Parliament; such decrees, which are called ordinances to differentiate them from regular decrees, do not have to be submitted to the *Conseil*, nor do actions taken by the president in an emergency under the powers granted him in Article 16. Nevertheless, the government often consults the *Conseil* before issuing ordinances; because cases involving ordinances may come before the *Conseil* serving as an administrative court, it seems wise to secure the opinion of its members.

The *Conseil d'État* also advises ministries on administrative problems. A 1963 decree formalized what had been the case for a long time: according to this decree, members of the *Conseil* should be given missions to other departments and should offer the government suggestions for reform. In addition, the *Conseil* supervises local government by insuring that locally elected bodies operate only within their legal limits and carry out the duties they are supposed to perform. It can send investigative task forces to local areas and call the government's attention to problems requiring remedial action.

In its judicial functions, the *Conseil* stands at the head of a system of twenty-three administrative courts. It handles appeals from these lower courts, although it may act as a court of first instance in important cases. As an administrative court, the *Conseil* can annul actions if it finds that they exceed the authority of those making them, that they violate proper procedures, or that they fail to adhere to the spirit of the law. For example, if there were evidence that an administrator had issued a regulation that seemed to benefit him to the detriment of others, or that was otherwise unreasonable, his action could be quashed even if he had acted legally.

The *Conseil d'État* can also offer redress for damage caused by administrative actions. Here the court has gradually widened the range of the state's responsibility for the actions of its agents to a point that goes far beyond British or American practice. Today it is possible to sue a public service whenever it can reasonably be held that its agent was on duty at the time of the alleged injury, even when no fault exists on the part of the service or its agent—unless, of course, the damage was due to the complainant's negligence. For example, persons injured in a running fight between policemen and criminals are compensated. If the police official himself is adjudged partially responsible, the court may order him to share the payment of damages with the state.

There can be no gainsaying the excellent work of the *Conseil* in its administrative, leislative, and judicial functions. An institution that once tended to favor the state over the citizen, it has become increasingly a source of protection for the individual, and its admiration by British and American commentators is not without warrant.

In addition to the *Conseil d'État*, individual citizens also have recourse to the office of an ombudsman. In January, 1973, former premier Antoine Pinay was designated as a "mediator" between individual citizens and the administration.

THE PREFECT: The problem of coordinating the work of the French bureaucracy is complicated by the fact that the central government is totally responsible for tasks that in Britain would be left to local authorities. There is no decentralization of authority, only deconcentration; while various ministries have thier own inspectorates for checking up on the work of field offices, one of the most important posts created for this purpose has been filled by the prefect.

Established by Napoleon I to insure effective control of the bureaucracy by the central government, the prefecture was in some ways a carry-over from the intendancy of the old regime. With the destruction of local autonomy, however, it became far more powerful. Throughout a good part of the nineteenth century, prefects not only examined the performances of the external ministries of all departments and helped maintain internal order, they also helped incumbent politicians win re-election. The prefectures' special sphere of authority gave them a distinctly political cast, so that from time to time, changes in government brought wholesale purges. Nevertheless, because of its importance, the office drew to itself men of exceptional talent, and, in effect, it became one of the *grands corps* of the French state. Even after the rise of municipal councils and popularly elected mayors during the Third Republic, the prefect has remained the most powerful figure in the commune as well as in the department.

The prefect is, above all else, the representative of the state. As such he can, in time of emergency, exercise considerable powers—especially police powers—on his own initiative. He is also the representative of the Interior Ministry, which has direct responsibility for the supervision of local authorities; consequently he serves as the middle link in the chain of bureaucracy that extends from the central administration to the commune. The prefect is responsible for the coordination of all government services, and he reports on the work of field offices and the local government itself. Furthermore, requests made by mayors and local councils are funneled through him to the central government, and technicians from the ministries are required to consult with him on their improvement programs, not only to find out what is politically feasible but also to insure that someone concerned with the interests of the department as a whole has a voice in determining the value of such programs. The prefect is also formally responsible for the supervision of the local authorities in his jurisdiction, yet the relationship between them is usually cooperative rather than antagonistic. Local authorities depend upon the prefect for improvements, but the prefect depends upon their cooperation for

FIGURE 16.2 LINKS BETWEEN CENTRAL AND LOCAL GOVERNMENT IN FRANCE

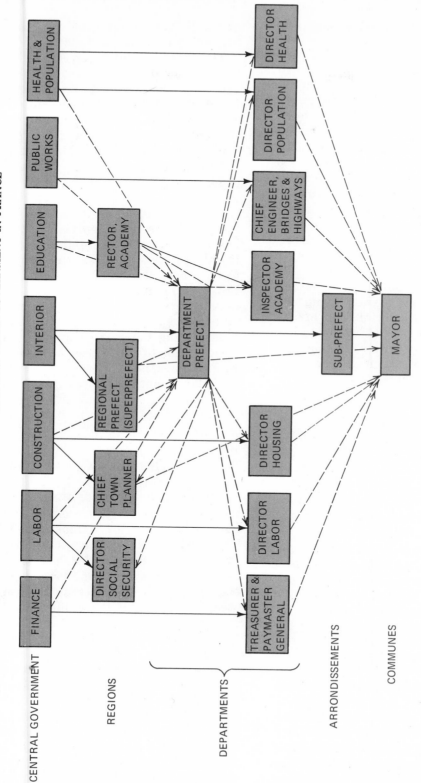

Only some ministries and some external services are shown.

Adapted from F. F. Ridley and Jean Blondel, *Public Administration in France*, rev. ed. (London: Routledge and Kegan Paul, 1969), p. 110, reprinted by permission of Barnes and Noble, Inc. and Routledge and Kegan Paul, Ltd.

keeping order and for helping him maintain his authority.

Fifth Republic France has moved toward restoring the prefect's authority, which had slipped to some extent in the years following World War II. The nation's ninety-five departments always were illogical from the standpoint of officials responsible for administering services. The units are too small, and never have corresponded to natural socioeconomic divisions. The situation has become worse with every decade, making coordination by departmental prefects more and more difficult. Also, despite the assistance of a technical staff, prefects have found themselves unable to deal realistically with problems of a technological nature, with the result that they were being bypassed both by the ministerial field offices and the mayors. Some relief was obtained under decrees issued in 1964; regional prefects (superprefects), who remained responsible also for the administration of a specific department, were provided with increased technical aid and given greater responsibilities in regional economic planning. Their authority in regional development will be strengthened even more by changes that are now taking place. They will have a regional budget and tax power, and will no longer be responsible for a specific department. At the same time, the authority of the departmental prefect has also been augmented. All correspondence between ministries and their field offices relating to the affairs of a department must pass through the prefecture. In effect, the heads of the external services in a department now hold their authority from the prefect rather than from the ministry in Paris.

Under the Fifth Republic, the bureaucracy has come into its own, and some argue that it has become a political arm of the majority. Nevertheless, its members have been vitally helpful in modernizing French society and in lending great impetus to its economic growth. These changes were brought about because younger cadres stepped into important civil-service positions—and because the

de Gaulle regime was able to exercise firm leadership over the bureaucracy.

The major problems faced by the French bureaucracy today are, in some ways, the reverse of those facing the British. The French, for example, have yet to develop an administrative organization that can curb the centrifugal tendencies of the *corps*, especially the *grands corps*. Many of the innovations developed by the Fifth Republic came largely from above, and were the projects of bureaucratic agencies carried through by the executive. These innovations, however, often represented technocratic solutions to what were, in many cases, political problems. Indeed, this seems always to have been the case in France; periods of fairly effective authoritarian leadership have alternated with periods marked by mass movements and political chaos. Indeed, during the Fifth Republic, both tendencies seem to have been accentuated. The French have never developed that capacity to balance authority and participation in policy-making that has traditionally been the hallmark of British politics.

4. THE GERMAN PATTERN

ORIGINS AND DEVELOPMENT: The basis for the modern German civil service was created by Frederick William I and Frederick the Great of Prussia; it was restructed by Baron vom Stein and Prince von Hardenberg in the aftermath of Prussia's defeat by Napoleon. The bureaucracy these men created was a social elite recruited on the basis of competitive examination and dedication both to efficiency and to the principle of autocracy. In the nineteenth century, its competence and integrity brought it tremendous prestige and caused it to be emulated by other countries.

Prussia was the first European nation to accept a large measure of responsibility for seeing to it that the universities produced people with the professional qualifications needed to run a modern state. For general administration, training in law became the normal requirement. But the government also wanted officials with technical qualifications, particularly in the fields of engineering and forestry. Men with professional training, then, were brought into the public service and promoted to top-level administrative positions.

Under the firm guidance of its bureaucrats, Germany made a rapid transition to an industrial society. Theoretically, the bureaucracy was responsible to the monarch and his chief minister, but in practice it made many domestic policy decisions on its own. In treating many political matters as if they were merely questions of administration, the bureaucracy thus became a force that inhibited the development of the German capacity for self-governance. Well into the nineteenth century, moreover, the only checks on the bureaucracy were internal; and when a legislature was incorporated into the Prussian system, many civil-service field officials took on the responsibility of guaranteeing a docile majority by "allowing" themselves to be elected deputies.

The federalism of the Second Reich established national supremacy in the legislative field, but left the administration of the law to the states. Thus, although the Länder, for instance, enforced Reich health laws, administered uniform weights and measures, and collected taxes, the Bundesrat had the authority to issue basic regulations on the uniform execution of the law. The major function of the central administrative offices in Berlin was to draft legislative proposals and to maintain communications with Land ministries. Since most of the Länder had adopted the Prussian administrative pattern and since a good many of their senior civil servants were drawn from the Prussian bureaucracy, personal contacts were close; and in the few cases of major disagreement the Bundesrat could be counted on to iron out differences.

On the state level, the pattern of administration during the Second Reich continued

almost unchanged. Authority moved downward from provincial governors to district officers and Landräte, with additional supervision by the Interior Ministry. After 1872 a certain amount of authority was delegated to self-governing bodies, especially to those on the county level. This meant that the royal official had to share some of his power with a county council and a county committee, but since the Landrat was almost always a local notable, he usually dominated these bodies anyway. In 1875 three tiers of administrative courts were created —district, county, and Land; they came to exercise a degree of independence, and from time to time reversed the decisions of administrative officials. But with most court officials being from the same class and having received the same training as other bureaucrats, conflicts between them were infrequent.

The training of those bureaucrats not in charge of technical services was mostly in law, and though legal training brought out the rights of individuals to equal treatment under the law, it emphasized strict obedience to the state as constituting the supreme legitimate authority. After obtaining a law degree, a prospective bureaucrat served an apprenticeship with a Landrat or district officer and fulfilled his military obligations by service in the reserve. Those admitted to the service were invariably Protestant "gentlemen" of sound "German" instincts, and their training instilled them with loyalty to the service's general ethos. The social position conferred upon them as members of the bureaucracy also contributed to an esprit de corps, and because the sons of bureaucrats so often followed in their fathers' footsteps, the bureaucracy took on the qualities of a closed caste.

The founders of the Weimar Republic moved timidly in the direction of greater centralization. The Weimar constitution provided for the creation of a national field administration for collecting taxes and, by implication, for other purposes as well. The constitution also declared, however, that national laws would be executed by *Land* authorities whenever the federal government failed to take action. In fact, the latter created only two national agencies with their own field services, a Reich Finance Administration and a Reich Unemployment Insurance Authority. The Center Party, which was the cornerstone of most governments of the Weimar years and which was strongly federalist, was instrumental in blocking further measures toward centralization.

It was during the 1920's that the difficulties inherent in Germany's dual system of administration became obvious. The Reich and Prussia were, for the most of the decade, controlled by moderate governments, but many of the *Länder* came under the domination of left-wing or, more often, right-wing regimes. On many occasions, especially with regard to proposed police action against right-wing groups, the *Länder* refused to enforce the law despite pressures from the national government.

The problem was also aggravated by the hostility of upper-level civil servants to the republic itself. Prussia and some of the other states did try to dilute the caste orientation of the bureaucracy by broadening recruitment and lowering educational qualifications. But these reforms were not successful: educational opportunities in Germany at the time were limited, so that the changes were marginal and resulted only in further alienating the permanent officials. The Nazis, of course, completely destroyed the federal structure of the Reich, centralizing all political and administrative authority. Although most bureaucrats went along with the Nazi regime, tensions between the party and the bureaucracy were never satisfactorily resolved. The Nazi Party had never been very successful in enlisting the membership of the administrative elite; these men came mostly from middle- and upper-class families and had spent their lives in bureaucratic security, whereas the Nazi leaders were persons primarily of petit-bourgeois background. To the bureaucratic elite, the party leaders—mostly men whose

lives had been marked by personal disorganization—were bohemians and upstarts. The Nazis viewed with a mixture of resentment and suspicion the bureaucrats whom they had come to dominate. For no matter how politically conservative they might have been, the traditional civil servants insisted upon regular procedures and legal forms. To the party, these forms were a sham; what was needed were dedication to the cause and an inner feeling for the spirit of the German people.

To establish an effective democratic system in postwar Germany, the Allies were convinced that it was necessary to reform the German civil service. All three occupying powers conducted de-Nazification programs, the Americans far more doggedly than either the British or the French. The Americans also placed great importance upon broadening the type of training required for upper-level bureaucrats, including the teaching of social sciences. On the whole, however, the Allies' programs had little lasting impact. Leading Nazis were removed from the service, but the shortage of personnel and the fact that almost every remaining administrator of any importance had been a party member vitiated the effectiveness of their programs. As Germany regained her sovereignty, moreover, the traditional patterns of recruitment were revived.

STRUCTURE: With some significant modifications, the Bonn constitution—the Basic Law—recreated the administrative structure of pre-Nazi Germany. The *Länder* are now again responsible for the execution of federal laws, except where the Basic Law provides otherwise. The postwar constitution specifically permits direct federal administration only in matters pertaining to foreign policy, tax collection, the border police and defense forces, the post office, rail and water transportation, the investigation of subversive activities, and some social-insurance programs. The constitution also permits the federal government to execute new laws when there is an "urgent necessity" for general administration.

In practice, the federal government has established its own agencies in only one field, that of unemployment insurance, though it has also created joint federal-*Land* agencies for the collection of taxes. The *Länder* administer all other domestic programs under federal supervision. This surveillance operates through the Bundesrat, the upper chamber of the Parliament; through informal conferences between federal and state officials; and through the administrative court system, in addition, of course, to regular political channels.

The Bundesrat has, perhaps, the key legal role in federal supervision of *Land* administrative activities. With its consent, the federal government may specify the field organization and the administrative procedures of those state agencies that execute federal laws. The Bundesrat also enacts general administrative regulations, and, with Bundesrat approval, the federal government may dispatch inspectors to *Land* field offices. In practice the Bundesrat has been quite lenient in its supervisory capacity. If a *Land* refuses to comply with federal regulations, however, the federal government possesses the right to apply sanctions with the approval of the Bundesrat. The Bundestag may also appeal to the Federal Constitutional Court for a judgment against a state.

The Basic Law has made the administrative court system completely independent of administrative agencies. The Supreme Administrative Court, whose judges are federal appointees, checks upon *Land* violations of the intent of federal law. The court is the highest body in the bureaucratic hierarchy, and its rulings on disputed questions of administration have tended to accord with the position taken by federal ministries.

Because of the extensive devolution of their administrative authority, German federal offices are much smaller and more compact than their French or even their British counterparts.[4] Most federal ministries are concerned primarily with the preparation of legislation and of ordinances spelling out the rules for its uniform application. Organized along functional lines, they are headed by a political minister and permanent officials who manage the day-to-day affairs of the department. Unlike French ministers, those in Germany do not bring a "political" cabinet into office with them—though they do rely upon the services of political state secretaries who serve as seconds-in-command. Although drawn from the bureaucracy, these men are chosen either for their sympathy with the views of the minister or for their contribution to the political balance of the government. All ministers are also now entitled to parliamentary undersecretaries to help them with both their departmental work and their parliamentary relations.

During the 1950's many ministers did not exercise effective political control over their departments. Often themselves former bureaucrats, they tended to accept the opinions of the permanent career officials who served them, and the influence of the second-echelon officials became such that many interest groups turned directly to them. Perhaps not surprisingly, scandals occurred involving bureaucrats who had received "gifts" from private parties. Ministerial control became somewhat tighter under the Grand Coalition —the majority of cabinet members were fairly strong-minded political figures—and this trend continued under the Brandt regime.

It is true nevertheless that this vertical fragmentation of authority has had a stifling effect on interdepartmental coordination as well as on reform programs desired by the political overseers of public administration. Policy has therefore tended to be reactive rather than creative. Over the years, though, at least three means of overcoming these biases have evolved. Resort has been made to experts from think tanks or universities to suggest technical solutions within a given policy framework. In addition, in some policy areas ministers without portfolio are appointed by the chancellor to carry out special tasks (Egon Bahr, who was

---

[4] Such agencies as the Foreign Ministry, the federal bank, the federal railways, and the federal postal service do have field services.

responsible for Ostpolitik, was such an appointee under Brandt. Finally, increasing resort has been made to transnational forms of collaboration, especially within the context of the European Communities, in order to back up or circumvent Bonn's "thin" bureaucratic structure.

CIVIL SERVICE: To become a permanent member (*Beamte*) of the German civil service means not only a secure position for life and an excellent pension upon retirement; it also means being treated with considerable deference and addressed by one's title (accorded not only to a *Beamte* but to his wife). It should, of course, be pointed out that the term "bureaucracy" has a far wider application in Germany and France than in Britain or the United States. Not only has the state traditionally engaged in a broader variety of activities, but the title "*Beamte*" also applies to judges, teachers, and members of the state railroad and postal systems who carry out managerial functions similar to those of private employees.

In addition to *Beamten*, the administrative services include two other categories of personnel: employees (*Angestellten*) who lack the security of tenure and pension privileges of the *Beamten*, and manual workers (*Arbeiter*). The differences between the *Beamten* and *Angestellten* have steadily diminished over the years; even so, the *Beamten* still command more prestige and hold the highest positions in the civil service.

Most civil-service policy posts, especially those on the federal level, have traditionally been the preserve of those trained in the law. Agencies controlling the railroads and public works, however, are staffed at the top levels by trained engineers. In the Allied program to reform the German civil service after Hitler's defeat, the Americans especially had hoped to bring in people with a social-science background, thus breaking the stranglehold of the law faculties upon the training of bureaucrats. The control of social-science teaching by law faculties blocked this effort, and the Federal Career Officials Act of 1953, followed by state laws modeled

closely upon it, restored the *status quo ante*.[5] The 1953 act and the Civil Service Act of 1961 divide the bureaucracy into three classes, roughly approximating the British and French systems. Recruitment to the "higher" civil service presupposes a university degree. Applicants are chosen on the basis of general examinations and enter a three-year program of in-service training. Success in a second examination at the end of three years leads to a lifetime position in the administrative class. It is rare, however, for entrance into these positions to be gained before the age of twenty-five. For this reason and because of the rather limited educational opportunities and the negligible number of in-service promotions, the German bureaucracy remains very much the domain of older men from the middle and upper-middle classes.

Political leaders today are calling for more extensive training in the social sciences for top-level bureaucrats. Ministries have complained, for example, that they have an embarrassing lack of personnel equipped to deal with other European countries at conferences on topics of common concern. As a result, courses in economics and sociology have been introduced for senior federal bureaucrats, and some states, such as Bavaria, have made arrangements to have their senior civil servants spend part of a year of in-service training at the *École Nationale* in Paris. In 1969 the federal government opened a new academy of public administration to provide further in-service training for senior civil-service personnel.

There are other chips in the encrusted traditions of the civil service. The newer generation of bureaucrats is less likely to stand solely on its dignity, and the deference with which the public once regarded the bureaucracy is slowly eroding. Moreover, Germany, like France and Britain, is finding that many of its best bureaucrats are being lured away from government service by attractive

---

[5] The *Länder* are responsible for the recruitment of their own civil-service personnel; however, the federal government, with the approval of the Bundesrat, has the authority to set general standards.

professional and industrial offers. As in the other two nations, concern has been registered about the growing tendency of German bureaucrats to leave the government at the height of their powers for more lucrative private positions.

CONTROL AND ACCOUNTABILITY: Political controls in Germany, exercised by the federal government through the Bundesrat, have already been described. Like most civil-law countries, Germany has established a general system of specialized administrative courts on both the federal and state levels. The Federal Administrative Court has jurisdiction both as a court of appeal from the supreme administrative courts of the *Länder* and as a court of first and last instance in which other cases are peculiarly "Federal" in nature.

The overall authority of these courts, however, is limited by two factors: (1) civil courts have jurisdiction in cases concerning the value of property appropriated by the government and in cases involving claims against a public authority for damages, and (2) the constitutional courts of the republic and of the various *Länder* have jurisdiction in areas pertaining to the violation of constitutional rights. Nevertheless, the administrative courts have been a liberalizing force in German society; the Supreme Administrative Court, for example, decided in 1955 that the receipt of welfare was a right, and that an administrative decision to refuse welfare benefits could be appealed. It has also decided that it can review a student's grades to determine whether correct examination procedures were followed, and, more importantly, it has widened the grounds on which Germans may refuse to serve in the armed forces. Germany is one of the few countries in which an individual may now gain exemption from military service on moral grounds, without having to base such refusal on transcendental religious beliefs.

17

Economic
and
Social Policy

1. THE EUROPEAN PATTERN

POLITY AND ECONOMY: In feudal Europe, economic behavior was subordinated to problems of community integration and organization. Production and distribution were closely regulated by religio-political norms that defined the "good" society. Even with the development of commercial capitalism and the rise of cities, guilds continued to regulate the price and quality of goods. The new national states went further; during the era of mercantilism every European state engaged in important economic activities, regulating or controlling many aspects of the economy. Seventeenth-century France, for example, supported the creation of chartered, state-controlled companies to exploit the resources of non-European areas, aided the growth of industry by subsidies and the importation of skilled craftsmen, created state industries for the manufacture of tapestries and lace, and encourged the formation of companies, whose operations it then controlled, for the purpose of manufacturing such items as mirrors and tin plate.

As propounded by Hobbes, Locke, and, in mature form, by Adam Smith, classical liberal economic theory argued against such activities by the state. The argument stressed rational self-interest and the market mechanism as the primary means for encouraging economic and social development. The state's business was principally that of enforcing the law, including contracts, and maintaining order; of preventing the growth of monopolistic practices; of engaging in those necessary tasks, such as defense, with which the market system could not cope; and of aiding the poor and indigent who, for some reason not of their own doing, were unable to compete economically. All other areas, it was argued, should be left to private enterprise and the market, for private firms worked more efficiently than either government enterprise or government-controlled enterprise.

These liberal doctrines ("liberal" in the nineteenth century, "classical" in the twentieth) became predominant in Britain (and even more so in the United States, where Britons settled), and it was not until the twentieth century that active governmental intervention in the economy became accepted in that country. On the Continent, in contrast, the older tradition that conceived of economic activity as subordinate to political concerns remained strong. Thus France never went as far as Britain in allowing market mechanisms to direct the allocation of resources. The state continued to subsidize many activities, such as railroad construction, and to operate industries which had long been a source of government revenue. In Germany the impact of liberal economics was even less significant. Feudal and mercantilist attitudes with respect to the state as an economic agent carried over into the modern era, with both national and local governments taking an active part in community development.

SOCIAL WELFARE: As traditional patterns fragment and are succeeded by a market and bureaucratic society, the mutual care inherent in the extensive family is replaced by the public's assuming some responsibility for its citizens, and eventually by extensive social-welfare measures. Thus social-welfare legislation can be seen as the inevitable by-product of advanced economic systems. During the Middle Ages, the Catholic Church was the primary source of charity for the poor. Beginning in the seventeenth century, however, the state began to assume the responsibility for caring for those who could not fend for themselves.

In no European country did public authorities take as large a share of the responsibility as they did in England where, in 1601, the law explicitly recognized the right of every destitute person to relief. The tradition continued throughout the nineteenth century, liberal doctrines notwithstanding, so that by 1911 Britain had laid the foundations for the modern welfare state. By this time Germany also had come to pioneer in this area. Under Bismarck's guidance, a series of acts had been passed which granted benefits for illness, accident, and old age. French developments, in contrast, were far slower, and less comprehensive than those in either Britain or Germany. Bit by bit, legislation ameliorated the lot of the poor, but as late as the 1930's France still lacked a comprehensive welfare system.

2. THE BRITISH PATTERN

THE DRIFT TOWARD PLANNING: When it came to office in 1945, the Labor Party had not yet developed an integrated economic policy. Its nationalization programs and its social-welfare policies were basically stopgap measures designed to eliminate particular evils; they were not part of a comprehensive social and economic plan for the entire country. After an initial period during which it engaged in certain planning ventures, including the preparations of an annual economic survey, the Labor government eschewed overall planning efforts for the economy and limited itself to insuring employment through various Keynesian-inspired fiscal measures and a number of public works projects. Beyond that, the Laborites seemed content to allow the market, with selected interference, to set the direction of the British economy. The Conservatives, though accepting Keynesian economic analysis, when they came to power in 1951 were even cooler toward national planning.

Yet by the early 1960's leaders in both parties were beginning to have second thoughts. They recognized that the problem of Britain's economic stability and growth could not be met by simple reliance upon the market mechanism. The major source for the disquiet was the far more vigorous growth of other European countries in per-capita income, worker productivity, and gross national product. Fiscal controls seemed able to prevent any appreciable amount of unemployment, but they were not enough to resolve long-range problems, especially Britain's declining share of the export market and its unfavorable balance of payments. The Conservative government, therefore, with the example of French planning before it, began thinking about a more systematic approach to economic problems. Among the steps taken by the Macmillan government was the establishment of the National Economic Development Council (NEDC or Neddy), a council made up of representatives from the government, industry, and labor and intended to help formulate economic planning policies.

Not until the Labor Party's victory in 1964, however, did national planning become much more than a concept. Planning was then recognized as a specific function of the government. It was entrusted to a new Department of Economic Affairs, later to be absorbed by the Treasury Department; and a new Department of Technology was created to help solve problems which stood in the way of economic growth. Toward the end of raising the level of productivity, the government enlarged the training facilities for "redundant" workers. It encouraged selected businesses to merge, and it made various financial arrangements with industry to increase technological research and innovations. In an effort to shift workers from the service sector of the economy to the manufacturing—and hence exporting—sector, a "selective employment" tax was levied which fell more heavily on the service sector. The government also divided the country into eleven planning regions, and by means of tax incentives, subsidies, and building-permit regulations became more vigorous in pressing industries to locate in areas of high

unemployment or general economic backwardness, rather than in the south of England.

As perhaps its principal device for solving the nation's economic dilemma, the Wilson government relied upon voluntary wage and price controls as a way to relate wage increases to the growth of productivity. The Macmillan government had earlier begun to encourage the formulation of an incomes policy, but because of trade-union opposition little was accomplished. The Wilson government hoped that it could count upon the goodwill of the trade-union movement to support its efforts for voluntary compliance with the government's wage guidelines, and for a while the hope seemed to be realized. By 1967, however, voluntary measures were proving insufficient, and the government initiated legislation which gave it authority to freeze wages, prices, and dividends. There was a storm of protest within the ranks of the trade unions and the Labor Party, and as a result Wilson announced that he would allow the powers to lapse at the end of 1969; he would once again rely on voluntary restraints.

Shortly after coming to power in 1970, the Heath government began to articulate the ideals of a free-market economy, arguing that state regulation of the economy should be kept to a minimum. Wilson's attempts at an incomes policy were condemned, as were the subsidies which over the years had been paid to the "lame ducks" of industry. Delegates to the 1970 Conservative Conference greeted these pronouncements with wild enthusiasm, since they seemed to signal a break not only with the Socialist policies of the previous six years but also with some of the policies pursued by previous Conservative governments. What was to follow within the next several months dramatically illustrated the superior strength of economic and political realities over ideological dogma. First, Rolls-Royce, long considered the blue chip of British industry, came to the government for financial aid, pleading bankruptcy. Ignoring the logic of its own rhetoric, the government not only agreed to the request, but a year later, in a still more dramatic reversal, announced that it was nationalizing the salvageable portions of the company. Still plagued by the balance-of-payments crisis and convinced of the need to put a halt to the highest rate of inflation in Europe, the Heath government did another complete reversal by imposing a compulsory freeze on wages and prices.

These actions by the Heath government, as well as the subsequent attempts by the Wilson government to work out a system of voluntary wage and price controls, left no doubt that Britain had become a guided economy, an economy still largely sustained by the market mechanism and private ownership, but one in which the government intervenes actively in terms of its conception of the nation's priorities. This fact was dramatically illustrated in 1975 when the Wilson government announced what it called "an approach to industrial strategy." Faced with spiraling inflation and record balance-of-payments deficits, the government stated that it was going to select thirty key industries which would receive government subsidies to stimulate their modernization and development. Explicitly abandoning the traditional priorities of full employment and social welfare expenditures, the Labor Party leader signaled a major shift in national policy.

NATIONALIZATION: For British Socialists, as for their Continental comrades, public ownership of the means of production represented the sine qua non of a Socialist society. When it came to office under Clement Attlee in 1945, the Labor Party brought under public ownership industries that together employed approximately 8 percent of the labor force and provided about 20 percent of the nation's annual capital investment. These industries included the steel, coal, road haulage, railways, and gas industries. The choice of which industries were to be nationalized was dictated by their effect upon the national economy and by the economic conditions prevailing within the industries themselves. In one or two cases the

choice was that of a monopoly that the government deemed unwise to leave in private hands. Public ownership, to be sure, was not a completely new phenomenon in postwar Britain. Telephones had been a state monopoly almost since the beginning, and in 1908 a Liberal government created the Port of London Authority. Between the two world wars, Conservative governments had set up the Central Electricity Board, which is responsible for the nationwide distribution of electrical energy; the British Broadcasting Corporation; the London Passenger Transport Board; and the British Overseas Airways Corporation. Furthermore, most of the industries nationalized after World War II had been gradually coming under public control and regulation anyway. Nationalization, then, did not represent nearly so sharp a break with the past as it might have appeared, and except for the steel industry and long-distance road haulage companies, it did not arouse excessive opposition. With the exception of these two industries, the Conservative Party upon returning to power in 1951 made no attempt to denationalize. The steel industry was again placed largely under public ownership by a Labor government in 1967, and the industry has since remained under public ownership.

In nationalizing industries, the Labor Party opted against bringing them directly under ministerial control. Rather, the government created, on the model of the Port of London Authority, a group of public corporations with six interrelated features: (1) each of them is owned by the state, although it may raise all or some of its capital by issuing bonds to the public; (2) each is created by special law and is not subject to ordinary company law except as provided in the relevant statute; (3) each can sue and be sued, enter into contracts, and acquire property in its own name; (4) each is independently financed, obtaining its funds by borrowing from either the Treasury or the public and deriving its revenue from the sale of goods and services; (5) each is exempt from the forms of parliamentary control that apply to regular government depart-

FIGURE 17.1   NATIONALIZATION OF SECTORS OF THE ECONOMY, 1973

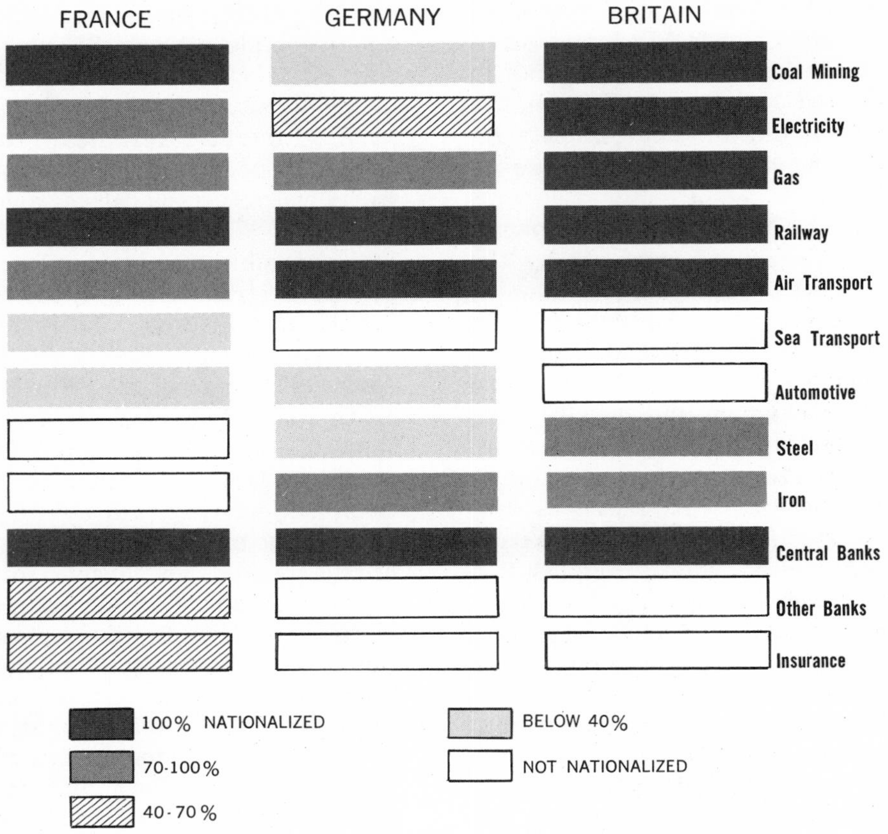

	FRANCE	GERMANY	BRITAIN
Coal Mining	100%	Below 40%	100%
Electricity	70-100%	40-70%	100%
Gas	70-100%	70-100%	100%
Railway	100%	100%	100%
Air Transport	100%	100%	100%
Sea Transport	Below 40%	Not nationalized	Not nationalized
Automotive	Below 40%	Below 40%	Not nationalized
Steel	Not nationalized	Below 40%	70-100%
Iron	Not nationalized	70-100%	70-100%
Central Banks	100%	100%	100%
Other Banks	40-70%	Not nationalized	Not nationalized
Insurance	40-70%	Not nationalized	Not nationalized

Legend:
- ■ 100% NATIONALIZED
- ▨ 70-100%
- ▧ 40-70%
- ▨ BELOW 40%
- □ NOT NATIONALIZED

Adapted from *Decisive Forces in World Economics*
by J. L. Sampedro (New York: McGraw-Hill;
London: Weidenfeld & Nicolson), p. 151. Copyright © 1967 by McGraw-Hill, Inc. Used with permission of McGraw-Hill Book Company.

ments; and (6) the employees of each corporation are not civil servants, but rather are
recruited and paid on terms and conditions
determined by the corporation.

The last four of these characteristics were
intended to give the public corporation the
flexibility of a private enterprise in the conduct of its day-to-day affairs. However, to
guarantee overall public control, the "sponsoring" minister whose area of jurisdiction
relates to the industry nationalized was provided with certain powers. He appoints the
corporation's board or governing body,
which is required to consult with him in de-
vising capital-investment programs and in

formulating plans for training, research,
and education. Any capital the corporation
wishes to raise externally—from the Treasury or from the public—requires the sanction of both the responsible minister and the
Treasury. The minister also receives the
corporation's annual report and financial accounts, which he lays before Parliament.
He may require the corporation to provide
him with any additional information he desires, and, after consultation with its governing board, may issue any general operating directions that appear to him to be in
the public interest. A theoretical distinction
is thus drawn between "day-to-day adminis-

tration," over which the corporation retains its autonomy, and the industry's "general policy," over which the minister exercises more or less continuous supervision. The minister himself is responsible to Parliament only for his statutory functions in connection with the public corporation; consequently, ministers have normally refused to accept responsibility for policies and decisions that are not subject to their intervention.

It is difficult to evaluate the success of Britain's experience with nationalized industries, partly because an evaluation depends in large measure on what standards are used. Even so, most observers would agree that nationalization has not, thus far at least, radically transformed the relation of the worker to his job. Workers in nationalized industries still tend to think of themselves as workers and their employers as bosses, and relations between the two do not seem to differ materially from those in private industry. Nor have the nationalized industries been used as instruments to develop new and imaginative economic policies. It can be argued—and has been, primarily on the left—that this failure, coupled with the failure of nationalization to instill any new attitudes on the part of workers, lies in the fact that the industries have not been fully integrated into a comprehensive system of Socialist, or even semi-Socialist, planning; instead, they have remained subservient to economic goals formulated largely by the needs of a market economy in which the private sector predominates. Critics also argue that the more radical proposals for a workers' democracy, in the form of joint consultation in the setting of policy, have not really been carried out—partly because the structures created toward this end were purposely ill-designed, and partly because the trade unions themselves have not shown any genuine interest in becoming part of management.

It is just about as difficult to determine how successful these industries have been from the point of view of economic efficiency. The difficulties of evaluating performance lie in the very nature of the public corporation. Each of the nationalization acts provided that the price of the nationalized industry's product or services should be sufficient to cover its cost of production, taking into account the good years with the bad. However, no government has been able to decide exactly what this means or how closely such stipulations should be followed. After all, various sectors of the economy are closely interrelated, and industrial activities have side effects which private firms may ignore but which public ones must take into account. For example, one can argue that railroads should be profitable and that rail services running at a loss should be closed down. Yet it has been pointed out that the maintenance of an adequate rail network can promote economic expansion by fostering geographic mobility, and that closing down passenger lines only increases the number of automobiles on the road, resulting in more congestion, more pollution, and more noise. Some of these problems, such as congestion, could be eased by new taxes to build new roads; others, of course, could not be met at all, since they involve a deterioration in the environment which is difficult to correct.

Problems of price and efficiency have been closely tied to another issue: the relations between nationalized industries, the government, and Parliament. The balance between the day-to-day operational independence of an industry and its overall surveillance by the government has raised some touchy problems. In the years immediately following nationalization, the degree of ministerial interference in the operation of an industry was minimal, although it has always varied with the disposition of the particular minister involved, as well as with the government's general policies. Subsequently, however, ministerial intervention increased, and because the statutes did not specify the means of control, the ramifications of this increased intervention were worked out in informal conferences through the "old boy network." At the same time, ministers refused to be held accountable to Parliament for policy decisions taken by an industry's board, on the ground that they were not responsible; yet in actuality, the power of the ministers was and is considerable, especially in view of the relatively short terms of board members.

With government ministries taking the position that they were not accountable for the policy decisions of nationalized industries, more and more parliamentary voices were raised in protest. Parliament wanted some means of securing more adequate information about the industries, at least with regard to policy decisions. The eventual outcome was the formation of a select committee with a fairly broad mandate to investigate matters related to the industries' operation, but its authority was not to encroach upon those ambiguous areas of ministerial responsibility. Reaction to the committee's recommendations has been mixed. Some of its proposals have been partially accepted, but the majority seem to have been ignored. Nevertheless, the committee has served the function of pointing up the present, rather equivocal relationship between a sponsoring minister and the industries under his authority, and it has raised anew the issue of how well the nationalized industries are linked to public policy as a whole. The future seems likely to yield more rather than less ministerial control over the operations of nationalized industries, as well as *more* rather than less acceptance of responsibility by the minister for decisions made by him. This will be especially true if the Labor government carries out its intention, announced in the elections of 1974, to nationalize additional industries that are vital in Britain's struggle to remain economically solvent.

SOCIAL WELFARE: The construction of a modern welfare state in Britain had certainly begun by 1940. Its development had been gradual, and its structure was rather baroque; but a combination of public and private initiative had created a series of institutions to provide at least minimum subsistence for those in need. The experience of World War II and the politics of the first

Labor government altered the structure considerably. The modifications were built on what had gone before, but they were broad enough in scope to constitute a qualitative transformation. The Labor government attempted to model as many social services as possible on a concept of "social insurance" rather than on one of "social welfare"; that is, as many programs as possible would be financed at least partially on the basis of compulsory contributions (premiums) by all citizens.

Basic to the substantiation of this purpose were the Family Allowance Act of 1945, the National Insurance Acts passed in 1946, the National Assistance Act of 1948, and the creation of the National Health Service in the same year. The acts were considerably modified by the Labor Party during its first term of office, and later by the Conservatives, but they provided the structure of the contemporary British welfare state until 1969, when certain significant revisions began to be considered.

The National Insurance Act, applicable to almost everyone over school age, offered substantial coverage for sickness and unemployment, as well as maternity benefits, widows' allowances, and retirement benefits. A second insurance act provided permanent pensions for those incapacitated by industrial accidents. Both acts were supplemented by the National Assistance Act, which fixed on local authorities the responsibility for making accommodations available for the old, the infirm, and any others needing a place to live; it also enjoined local officials to give supplementary aid to persons requiring it, even though those in need were already receiving assistance under insurance programs. Under the Family Allowance Act, weekly benefits were paid out to each family for each child under fifteen, except the first; as amended in 1956, the age limit was raised to eighteen—provided that the child is a full-time student.

With the exception of the National Assistance Act—the provisions of which were altered and redesignated as "supplementary benefits" in 1966—all these measures theoretically dispensed with the concept of need as the basis of aid. Despite the fact that the insurance measures required considerable support from general taxes, they were to be regarded as rights accruing to all persons who paid their premiums.

The Labor government that came to power in 1964 promised to re-examine the entire welfare program with the general aim of extending benefits. Studies had revealed that the benefits actually paid were not sufficient for large numbers of people and that many citizens did not even know of their rights to additional assistance. The hope was to raise the level of retirement benefits and other forms of insurance and to expand the services available to families with serious personal problems.

Although the Wilson government of 1974 did increase some benefits almost immediately, economic difficulties and the uncertainty about just what kinds of revisions were necessary prevented a radical overhaul of the welfare programs. Some Laborites (and Conservatives) urged a return to the principle that aid should be contingent on need, arguing that this would raise the amount of benefits paid. The Labor Party, however, refused to consider this alternative, contending that it would revive the taint of a means test; but the Conservative (Heath) government, thought otherwise, and introduced legislation designed to aid specific groups in need, most notably the chronically disabled and certain low-income families.

Both parties, nonetheless, have continued to be in general agreement over social-welfare policies. In 1969 the Labor government issued a white paper announcing its intention to develop a new national-insurance plan. The proposal, which would supersede the scheme under which workers pay a flat fee and receive a flat pension upon retirement, called for a sliding scale for both contributions and for pension benefits, based

TABLE 17.1 SOCIAL WELFARE EXPENDITURES AS COMPARED TO OTHER GOVERNMENT EXPENDITURES IN GREAT BRITAIN

	Percentages 1951	1972
Social services		
Social security	11.8	18.9
Health and personal social services	10.1	11.8
Education	6.8	12.9
Housing and environmental services		
Housing	6.9	5.3
Environmental services	3.3	4.9
Libraries, museums, and the arts	0.2	0.5
Justice and law	1.4	2.7
Roads and public lighting	1.7	3.4
Transport and communication	2.9	4.4
Commerce and industry	15.3	11.2
Defense and external relations	24.1	12.6
Other expenditure	3.5	2.4
Debt interest	11.8	9.1

Source: Central Statistical Office, *Social Trends,* no. 4 (1973): 187.

upon the amount of wages earned. Two years later the Conservative government's white paper articulated the same basic objectives, although it differed from the previous government's proposal in some important details. The scheme is to be implemented in 1975.

NATIONAL HEALTH SERVICE: Perhaps the major innovation of the Attlee Labor government was the creation of the National Health Service. Its dual purpose was to place all existing health programs—private, local, and national—under one overall authority and to remove the taint of charity from health services by making them freely available to the entire community. The poor, especially, were expected to receive better health care under the program because the expansion of the service, particularly in its public-health aspects, would provide a broader range of facilities.

Responsibility for the National Health Service rests with the secretary of state for social services, who appoints an advisory Central Health Services Council consisting of some forty representatives of the medical profession and different governmental authorities. For descriptive purposes, it is easier to discuss, in order, hospitals and specialists, local-government services, and the general practitioner.

Nearly all hospitals in Britain are now owned by the government and managed by the minister of health. The nation has been divided into twenty hospital regions, most of which have a medical school that serves as center for research and the diffusion of knowledge. Regional hospital boards have had overall responsibility for the development of hospital services in their area, and 450 hospital management committees throughout the country have carried out the actual function of running the hospitals.

Individuals are referred to hospitals for treatment by general practitioners, and most services are free of charge. After a patient is admitted to a hospital, his case is taken over by the staff. Staff medical specialists receive an annual salary and are permitted to maintain a private practice outside the National Health Service; they are also permitted to bring a limited number of their own patients to the hospital on a fee-paying basis.

The services of general practitioners have been administered by 160 local executive councils. A list of available physicians is published in each local area; patients are free to choose any physician they wish, subject to his consent and to a prescribed limit on the number of patients any one doctor can have. There is no evidence that patients have found it excessively difficult to obtain the services of a preferred physician, or that physicians have been forced to take patients they do not want. Doctors wishing to work in a particular district, however, may be refused admission if the area is considered to be "overdoctored," even so, because the list of overdoctored locales is widely publicized and because doctors receive financial bonuses for practicing in "underdoctored" areas, the problem of a doctor's ability to practice where he wants to has not been too irksome. Furthermore, the distribution of doctors in the nation is now far more rational than it ever was in the past, although rural areas still lack a sufficient number of doctors.

Finally, local governments have been responsible for the medical care of children under five, and for the prenatal and postnatal care of mothers. They have also undertaken programs of educating the community in the ways of preventive medicine.

A report issued by the Ministry of Health late in 1968 recommended the replacement of the present regional boards, local health authorities, executive committees, and hospital management committees by between forty and fifty area health authorities—less parochial than local authorities, according to the report, yet less remote than regional boards. The report held that the area health authorities would also provide better coordination, linking local health authorities, general practitioners, and hospitals in a unified effort to offer more adequate medical care and a more comprehensive system of preventive medicine. With some modifications, the recommendations began to be implemented in 1973.

On the whole, Britain's National Health Service has been reasonably successful. Whatever complaints doctors may have regarding particular policies, few would care to abolish it; in fact, they find that the elimination of the cash nexus between doctor and patient has yielded more rewards than difficulties. Doctors are paid a standard fee by the government for each patient treated; they also receive an annual expense allowance. Every public opinion poll indicates that the public, too, is relatively satisfied with the program. Hardly anyone believes that the quality of medical attention has deteriorated or that doctors spend more time on the few patients who do pay fees than on those who are treated free of charge.

Nor has the Health Service proved excessively expensive. During the 1950's Britain spent about 4 percent of its national income on health, compared with approximately 4.5 percent for the United States and 4.6 percent for Sweden. The percentage rose during the 1960's, but no faster than in other countries. And despite the forebodings of the more pessimistic, visits to the doctor by "malingerers" have not increased appreciably: the average Briton still visits a physician far less frequently than the average American.

The chief problems of the service, aside from those involving the recurrent arguments about how much doctors should be paid and on what basis, have to do with the fact that insufficient resources have been expended upon it. In spite of its programs since 1960 to construct hospitals and upgrade medical schools, Britain has fallen further behind the United States and Canada in the quality of its medical education and hospital facilities. The result has been a migration of British doctors to the other side of the Atlantic, where facilities and opportunities for specialization are superior and the income a doctor can earn is larger. Unquestionably, without the migration to Britain of medical students from India,

Pakistan, and other of the less developed Commonwealth nations, the "doctor drain" would be even more serious. There are other problems, too, such as the cleavage between the general practitioner and the more highly paid and prestigious specialist who has the facilities of a hospital at his disposal for his fee-paying patients. Also, hospital overcrowding results in waits of up to a year for nonurgent surgery. Aware of these and other problems, the Wilson government, in 1975, appointed a royal commission to examine the working of the National Health Service.

3. THE FRENCH PATTERN

A MIXED ECONOMY: A recent report by the Hudson Institute suggested that the French Gross National Product, which now exceeds the British, would surpass the German GNP by 1985 and that in ten years France would be the most productive economic power in Europe. The report, prepared for the French government just before the 1973 elections, has been widely criticized as overly optimistic, but it provides a vivid contrast to much of the criticism about "backward" France that was written during the fifties. In fact, France underwent from the mid-fifties until 1973 a period of sustained economic growth that has been halted only recently by the world-wide economic recession.

Much of the impulse for this economic upsurge has come from state technocrats whose power derives from the important role of the state in directing and controlling the French economy. Public enterprises in France account for about a third of the total capital investment in the country. The government completely controls or substantially dominates the railroads, the oil industry, the airlines, the production and distribution of gas, electricity, coal, nonferrous ores, and armaments. Within other fields, such as the auto industry, its control of individual firms, such as Renault motor works—the largest producer of motor vehicles in France—has a direct effect upon that particular sector of the economy. Finally, the state pays the salaries of 27 percent of all salaried workers or wage earners (excluding agricultural workers) in France and thus has an enormous influence over salary and wage levels.

In addition to direct participation, the state has an impressive battery of incentives and legal weapons with which to influence growth and expansion. Almost all bank-credit facilities are nationalized, or are under the centralized control of the Bank of France. By determining which firms can and cannot borrow from banks, and which may issue securities, the government can exert great power over private investment. The government can establish price ceilings, as well as price formulas, and it can fix prices directly for the products of any industry or individual firm, a power that it has used to encourage expansion in return for higher price levels. The government has also attempted to influence growth through such means as tax concessions, subsidies, direct loans and loan guarantees. Thus in the French mixed economy, the state possesses, and has used, considerable powers both through the large public sector and through incentives and controls affecting the private sector.

PLANNING: The devastation of France during World War II, coming upon the nation's failure to move ahead economically in the 1920's and 1930's, yielded a consensus among those constituting the core of the Resistance that some form of planning for national reconstruction was absolutely necessary.[1] Their response was to develop a four-year plan and a high-level planning agency, *Commissariat Général du Plan*— CGP (the General Planning Commission), directed by Jean Monnet. The initial plan has been followed by five more plans, and the concept of planning has become an im-

portant part of French economic development and growth.

The planning process involves a close collaboration between representatives of the state and private economic interests in developing commitments toward broad and detailed economic objectives. The process begins with the government submitting to the Economic and Social Council and to Parliament a set of coordinated "major options," which include such items as goals for the overall growth of the GNP, growth by sector (public and private), growth in consumption, investment, and other basic goals such as a stable currency, full employment, and industrial concentration. These options are then submitted to "modernization" commissions consisting of representatives of the Planning Commission, employers, and (for more detailed elaboration) members of the trade-union confederations. In fact, the real work is done in the working groups of the commissions. Guided by the major options, these groups develop a plan of coordinated commitments of private enterprise and public power. In the process, civil servants, and representatives of the Planning Commission, attempt to arbitrate the inevitable conflicts; and the plan is finally accepted by the government and adopted by Parliament.

Ideally, the plan should be virtually self-enforcing. Cooperation assures sales and profits and reduces risks, since the plan is "indicative" of the movement of the French economy over a five-year period. Moreover, through extensive consultation, those most interested have committed themselves in advance. Nevertheless, the state can also resort to numerous incentives and legal weapons in order to enforce the choices and goals outlined in the plan. Thus, in theory, the French planning process combines the attractiveness of prediction with the voluntary cooperation of labor and management, and adds the possibility of considerable state direction.

Early evaluations of the French planning process lauded the plan as the key to French postwar expansion and as a model that could be emulated by other democratic countries.

[1] Of course, the willingness to plan also reflected traditional French attitudes favoring control of the economy by a technical elite—a legacy of the old regime and the peculiar characteristic of revolutionary and postrevolutionary French "scientism."

More recent and more detailed studies, however, have indicated that the plan has been a less important guide for public and private decision making than has been assumed. As business recovered during the fifties, and as succeeding governments cut back on investment in the public sector to control inflation, more initiative in the formulation of plans was taken by a more aggressive private sector. Thus, by the late fifties, the plan had become a tool of private enterprise rather than a tool for structural reform or for the alteration of economic and social priorities. The dialogues of the planning process, it has been argued, encouraged business expansion by facilitating price fixing and market sharing under an official stamp of approval of the plan.

Although de Gaulle referred to the plan as "an ardent obligation" and although planning agencies were in fact strengthened during the early years of the Fifth Republic, in fact the influence of the public sector over the plan continued to decline. The government tended to use the tools at its command to maintain financial stability rather than influence the direction of economic expansion and reorient investment toward social needs. These tools were less effective in any case by the mid-sixties, when the private sector was able to control its own investment through self-financing. In 1969, Premier Jacques Chaban-Delmas pledged to reduce further the direction of the state over economic affairs and to place more initiative in the hands of private enterprise.[2]

A detailed study of the influence of the French process of planning published in 1969 concluded somewhat regretfully that there had been something of a public "myth" about the influence of the plan over the decisions of government and industry, and that in general the plan had gradually lost its influence over both public and private decision-making. Although the plan does influence some of the more general measures that government initiates to shape the economic environment, it has little influence over the

specific actions that the government takes to control individual industries or companies. Furthermore, the influence of the plan over industrial decision-making and industrial strategy for expansion seems to have declined even as the techniques for planning were improving. Faced with the dramatic downturn in the economy in 1975, President Giscard d'Estaing attempted to give new life to the planning process. He announced that he would meet regularly with the planning commissioner and those cabinet ministers responsible for the economy to coordinate economic decision-making. While this presidential initiative recognized the basic weakness in the planning process, it remains to be seen if this is anything more than a symbolic act of government determination to "do something."

Although the planning process has brought businessmen and state technocrats into close collaboration, representatives of trade unions never have had any significant influence over the outcome of the process. All of the trade-union confederations participated in the modernization commissions of the first plan. The CGT (Confédération générale du travail) refused to participate in the elaboration of the second plan, and was refused representation in the third plan. In the discussions of the fourth plan in 1960–61 for the first time, union representatives including those of the CGT were admitted to the working groups where most of the important discussion takes place.

Nevertheless there is good reason for union representatives to regard the present process with distrust; union influence is highly limited, and unions are effectively excluded from the more critical decisions. Labor's role has been described by one civil servant as "largely a matter of public relations." In fact, employers are reluctant to discuss the details of their operations with representatives of organizations they fundamentally distrust. Obviously, labor's relative isolation from the mechanics of economic planning is not calculated to encourage a sense of labor commitment to the outcome. In any case, trade unions have tended to re-

[2] *Le Monde,* September 18, 1969.

gard the plans as an attempt to promote financial stability by holding down wages.

If the plan has been a less accurate guide for government and business than it was previously thought, the reason is not any lack of government tools to promote planning goals; the tools exist, and they have been used extensively, but in a less coherent way then has been assumed. If the planning process has helped to promote more extensive contacts between businessmen and technocrats—contacts that now exist outside of the planning institutions—the process has left labor representatives feeling rather isolated.

REGIONAL PLANNING AND DEVELOPMENT: Paris dominated France long before the Revolution, and this pre-eminence increased during the nineteenth and the first part of the twentieth centuries, partly as a result of the political centralization of French life. The railway network, for political and strategic reasons, was built like a spider's web around Paris; as late as 1938 it took less time to travel the 683 miles from Toulouse to Lyon via Paris, than to go directly, a distance of 340 miles. France's literary and intellectual life became centered in Paris. So, too, were all the big banks. By the end of the Third Republic, a very high proportion of the nation's wealth was concentrated in the Paris area, while elsewhere large parts of the nation became economically and culturally stagnant. It was only after World War II that French leaders began to redress this imbalance, and only under the Fifth Republic that plans to do so have borne fruit.

The development of a comprehensive regional planning policy dates from 1950 when a *Plan nationale d'aménagement du territoire* was drawn up by the Ministry for Reconstruction and Urban Development. The plan included a detailed inventory of regional problems and outlined the needs of those areas in which human and natural resources were poorly utilized. In 1955 and 1956 the government tightened its control over industrial building in Paris and offered subsidies to businesses if they would decentralize

some of their operations. Parliament also authorized development programs for the twenty-two economic regions into which France had been divided for planning purposes. The number of regions was cut to twenty-one in 1960, and a new set of programs for each area was then drafted as part of the fourth national plan.

As work for the fifth plan got under way, regional organization as strengthened. In 1964 regional prefects were created, and *Commissions de développement économique régionale* (CODER) were established to act as official channels through which interests in a particular area could make their views known. A year earlier another institution, the *Délégation à l'aménagement du territoire et à l'action régionale* (DATAR), was founded as the coordinating body for all aspects of regional policy. French planners have tried to exercise as much care as possible in integrating regional plans with the national plan. Initially, they were anxious to extend help to the obviously less developed areas; today, policy encompasses the long-range view of the relationship between the different regional economies, on the one hand, and between them and the national economy, on the other. The principal problem is still the domination of French life by Paris, but the government is encouraging the growth of eight cities (*métropoles d'équilibre*) to counterbalance the attraction of the Paris area.

To implement regional development, outlying areas have been offered several forms of national assistance in addition to business subsidies, including new cultural facilities and new or enlarged universities. In developing regional programs, planners have also attempted to forecast the possible outcome of policies by conducting studies of the French citizenry; some of their research shows that many Parisians would be more than pleased to live in smaller communities, provided anything like the amenities available in the capital were present.

In reforms that were implemented in 1973 and 1974, the input of regional interests and the authority of regional prefects were

MAP 17.1   THE 21 NEW ECONOMIC REGIONS OF FRANCE

Adapted from *Ambasalle de France Information*, No. 67, May, 1975.

TABLE 17.2   THE SUBURBANIZATION OF PARIS

Population

	1962	1968	Change
City of Paris	2,790,000	2,585,000	− 7.4%
Inner suburbs	2,807,000	3,011,000	+ 7.3
Outer suburbs	1,986,000	2,576,000	+29.7
Towns outside the Paris agglomeration	887,000	1,048,000	+18.2
The entire Paris region	8,470,000	9,220,000	+ 8.9

Source: *Liaisons Sociales*, document no. 84/68, September 10, 1968, p. 40.

strengthened. The CODER were replaced by Economic and Social Committees in each of the twenty-one regions, and regional councils—composed of indirectly elected representatives—were established. The new regional councils were given a small tax base and a budget. The regional "superprefect" now has been relieved of his departmental responsibilities and been granted greater authority to coordinate economic development for the entire region. While the CODER were often criticized for their lack of decision-making powers, they were useful points of direct contact between regional interests and government ministries, often by-passing traditional channels through the prefect and parliamentary contacts. The new institutional arrangements do not surrender any real decision-making power to the regional assemblies. These new arrangements do,

MAP 17.2   THE REGIONAL PLAN FOR THE PARIS REGION, 1975

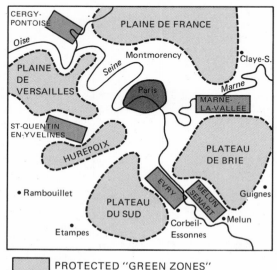

however, increase the points of contact with the administration at the regional level, and augment the power of administrative coordination.

NATIONALIZATION: Under the aegis of more radical governments at the end of World War II, segments of French industry were nationalized, including railroads, electricity, gas, coal, aviation, some insurance companies, some banks and the Renault automobile works. Some were taken over by the government because the then dominant political parties agreed that the "commanding heights" of the economy should be under state control. Some, such as Renault, were nationalized because their owners had collaborated during the war with the Vichy government.

French nationalized companies of a commercial or industrial character have usually taken one of two forms of organization: the "public corporation" and the "mixed economy company." Most of the industries nationalized at the conclusion of World War II became public corporations, although the term "èstablissement public" should not conjure up images of the British model.

Whatever may have been the intention of the original statutes, the distinction between public corporations and ordinary government departments has all but disappeared. The financial autonomy of the corporations has ceased to exist, the power of the boards themselves has been severely circumscribed, and all important corporation decisions are subject to ministerial approval. The chief executives now wield the real power; they are appointed by the government and are frequently drawn from the ranks of the civil service, and the conditions under which other staff members are employed are often similar to those for civil servants.

Today, the boards of public corporations are primarily advisory groups. The key officials are the chairmen and the managing directors. In some industries these posts are combined; when they are separate, the chairmanship is often a part-time position, and the directorship a post of considerably

greater importance. The director is often a former civil servant who maintains close associations with the supervising ministry.

The concept of "mixed economy" industries emerged from the old concessionnaires —companies that were partly private, partly public. In the nineteenth century, local authorities responsible for the organization and control of public-utility services (e. g., local transportation and the distribution of electricity, gas, and water) would often entrust such services to private firms or concessionnaires, but because many had to be operated at a loss, local authorities were forced to participate financially in these services. From this arrangement it was but a short step to the acquisition of part of the capital and a voice in the management. Between the two world wars, the same practice occurred on the national level; the state became deeply involved with railways, shipping, and air transport. It now owns the majority of shares in many utilities and other large companies; as a consequence, it can effectively influence their policy. This control, however, varies: some companies are allowed ample freedom to operate as purely commercial enterprises, while others are as stringently controlled as ordinary public corporations.

Most of the nationalized industries come under the supervision of either the Ministry of Industry, the Ministry of Equipment, or the Ministry of Transport, although the Ministry of the Armed Forces is responsible for the aircraft industry, and financial institutions such as banks and insurance companies are controlled through the Ministry of Economic Affairs and Finance. Because the latter ministry is also responsible for the overall financial coordination of government activity, it helps determine the policies adopted by all public enterprise.

A commissioner for each nationalized industry is appointed by its supervising ministry to represent the government as a whole. Such commissioners may be assigned to all undertakings in which the state has a financial interest; they can attend board meetings and suspend action pending ministerial intervention. In addition to the commissioners, the Ministry of Economic Affairs is represented by controllers, who may also be attached to any undertaking and enjoy a good deal of autonomy; they must be consulted on virtually all financial transactions before any decision by an industry is taken. Prefects, too, have a right to information, and all nationalized industries are subject to regular auditing. Parliamentary control over nationalized industries, however, has fluctuated. It was rather broad during the Fourth Republic, but it has been minimal in the Fifth.

SOCIAL WELFARE: The government that came into power in 1945, in addition to instigating measures on nationalization, wrote into law a series of proposals that fundamentally altered the French social-welfare system. Supplementary laws to strengthen and rationalize the system have been passed since 1958.

Ninety-eight percent of the French working population and their families are now covered by a social-insurance system that is, in principle, self-financing. While the government contributes on behalf of certain categories of people, the program is sustained primarily by graduated contributions. These are made by both employers and employees and vary according to earnings. Social insurance included sickness and health benefits, pensions, family allowances, unemployment compensation, and public assistance. Agricultural workers and self-employed individuals come under a special, separately administered system, and some important occupational groups (civil servants, miners, and railway employees) have a more favorable system of their own. Finally, both employers and employees are now required to contribute small additional amounts to complementary programs covering unemployment and retirement.[3]

[3] For the most recent facts and figures on the French social security system, see *Le Monde*, December 19, 1973, p. 33.

TABLE 17.3   FRENCH SOCIAL WELFARE
EXPENDITURES, 1971

*As percentage of national income,
by major types of coverage*

	1971
Old age, sickness disability	11.4
Sickness and maternity insurance	6.2
Unemployment insurance	.2
Work accident insurance	1.0
Family allowance	3.4
Total	22.2%

Source: Institut National de la Statistique et des Études Économiques, *Annuaire Statistique de la France, 1973* (Paris: INSEE, 1973), p. 550.

The French national health service, which is also administered separately, operates under a "fee reimbursement" plan. The patient chooses and pays the doctor directly, and is reimbursed for 75 percent of the fee. Laboratory fees, prescription drugs, and dental care are reimbursed at a slightly lower rate, but especially expensive treatment, therapy and major surgery are completely reimbursed. There is also an extensive program of mother-and-child protection which includes maternity insurance and a replacement income for a two-week rest period before and after childbirth. The government now maintains some control over doctor's fee scales.

Pensions depend upon the number of years worked and the average earnings during the last ten years of employment. They now average 45 percent of the final salary, and will be about 50 percent in 1975 [4]: an additional 20 percent is provided by the complementary plan. Unemployment insurance is arranged in a similar manner: a fixed sum of about two dollars (plus a dollar for each dependent), with the complementary plan paying up to 40 percent of a worker's salary

[4] This percentage is based on retirement at age sixty-five, and is calculated on the basis of the average pay for the highest paid ten years of work.

for up to a year or more. The unemployment funds also pay for partial unemployment, and in the fall of 1974 began to pay virtually full salaries for a year to workers dismissed because of economic consolidation.

The French social security system now pays quite generous allowances for children. The benefits are graded to favor large families, and additional allowances are paid if the mother does not work. People with large families also receive other benefits such as income-tax rebates, reduced fares on public transportation, and increased pensions. The state also may grant a small rent or home-improvement subsidy. The purpose of the family-allowance program was partly to boost the French birth rate, which indeed rose after the introduction of the program; but the birth rate also increased during the same period in other European countries that did not have a comparable system of allowances, and it has been slowly declining in France since the mid-sixties.

Finally, in conjunction with its social-security program, France, like many other industrial societies, has an extensive system of national assistance known as "social aid." The program involves not only monetary payment to those not covered by insurance, but also government responsibility for orphanages, old people's homes, asylums, and hospitals. This public assistance developed out of the old poor laws and the church endowments. The costs of the program are shared by the state, the department, and the commune.

Despite its multitude of welfare programs, France still has many citizens, generally old people, who have not contributed a sufficient amount to the social-security fund and who are barely able to subsist. For those who have had an occupation, the guaranteed minimum was 3,250 francs per year ($650) in 1971—not a great deal, but a substantial increase over previous years.

4. THE GERMAN PATTERN

PLANNING IN A SOCIAL-MARKET ECONOMY: During the nineteenth century the govern-ments of Prussia and other German states —and, later, of the Empire—helped to create the infrastructure of economic activity by building roads, bridges, canals, and railways. They also promoted industrialization by establishing technical schools, sending people abroad to learn special techniques, encouraging the immigration of foreign craftsmen, and using taxes and subsidies to expand the economy. Although the early years of Weimar brought a slight shift to classical liberal attitudes, the economic chaos of the late 1920's inevitably prompted extensive government intervention in economic activities. The Nazi regime furthered the process, instituting, in line with its corporate ideology, a program of massive state intervention and control. Deficit financing was used for the extensive construction of public works, including the famed autobahns; and business activity was tightly regulated. In 1936 a four-year plan was initiated for the proclaimed purpose of guiding basic production, controlling imports and exports, allocating basic resources, overseeing orders and credit, and strengthening foreign-exchange controls. Until the war necessitated fuller mobilization, however, Nazi economic planning was very much on an *ad hoc* basis.

Many Germans, in their postwar reaction to the Nazi experience, seemed to find a close connection between active government intervention in the economic life of the nation and an authoritarian regime and to have reacted strongly against all forms of government planning and economic control. Under economist Ludwig Erhard, however, the Adenauer government adopted what came to be known as the "social market" policy—the strategy of allowing the market itself to determine basic economic decisions while limiting the function of government to making sure that the market operated as "freely" as possible. In this way, it sought to maximize production while allaying the fears of the Allies and its own people. Many economic controls were lifted and some industries were denationalized. In actuality, the free-market economy involved more intervention by the government than its rhetoric implied. It is true that market forces were given more play in Germany than, say, in France. Nevertheless, it must be borne in mind that the major rules according to which the market "played" were determined by the government.

The general economic policies of the Adenauer regime, as formulated by Erhard, freed the market from "unnecessary" controls but at the same time enforced stricter rules than German industry prior to the Nazis had known in order to insure free competition. Thus, in 1948 price controls came to an end on a wide assortment of products, and the general wage freeze imposed by Occupation authorities was lifted. In 1949 and 1950, rationing was ended for most foodstuffs, although the government continued to regulate food prices through subsidies; by the end of the 1950's, rent controls were being removed. Of perhaps greater significance, the government initiated a program of partly denationalizing such operations as the Volkswagen Automobile Works; Preussag, a huge mining and oil company; and Veba, a state-owned coal, chemicals, and electric-power company.

While all these moves were unquestionably "freeing" the economy, the government was intervening in many other ways to create the competitive order around which the social-market economy was to be built. The Bonn government, for example, levied special taxes and distributed subsidies as it saw fit. The 1951 Investment Aid Act provided for a compulsory loan from the business community of one billion marks to cover, among other things, postwar reconstruction needs in industries producing coal, iron, steel, and energy, including water power. Every business existing in January, 1951, was forced to contribute to the loan. The government, through the 1949 Refugee Aid Measures and the 1953 Federal Expellee Acts, also granted businesses special tax and credit privileges to aid in the resettling of refugees.

Bonn was, in addition, active in the agricultural sector of the economy—subsidizing the production of fertilizer and certain agricultural products, controlling farm prices by regulating imports and exports, and stabilizing these prices by assuring a government market for agricultural produce. It also worked through the use of subsidies to consolidate agricultural holdings and take marginal farms out of production.

The federal government also extensively intervened in the economy, to facilitate the reconstruction of Germany's housing. The Housing Act of 1950 provided government assistance in one form or another for three kinds of construction: subsidized public housing projects for low-income failies, housing projects aided by tax preferences, and privately financed building projects. Under the stimulus provided by the government, some 13 million new dweling units were constructed in Germany between 1949 and 1972; in fact, more dwellings per capita were built in West Germany than in any other Western country.

Furthermore, in line with its economic theory, which gave monetary policy pivotal importance, the West German government has maintained firm control over the supply and flow of money—for example, by giving premium allowances for savings or funds reinvested in the employer's firm and also by regulating the banking and insurance sectors of the economy. But this activity of the government has come much more to the fore in recent years with instabilities in the international money market. The German government has revalued the German mark and the *Bundesbank* (Federal Bank) has also intervened, massively at times, to check the inward and outward flow of money and to stabilize its level in Germany.

Until the recession of 1966–67, the involvement of the German government in the economy was, for the most part, directed toward influencing the market to achieve specific ends. It was not, as in France, based on an overall economic plan involving the control of an extensive public sector. And the social-market policies had in general worked well—West Germany's economy was

TABLE 17.4 HOUSING DIFFERENCES IN GERMANY
ACCORDING TO SOCIAL CLASS

	Percentage owning homes	Average number of rooms per family member	Percentage with bathrooms	Percentage with toilets in their home
Upper-middle class	45	1.07	82	100
Middle-middle class	34	.73	40	81.1
Lower class	17	.55	10	33.3

Adapted from Karl M. Bolte, *Deutsche Gesellschaft im Wandel* (Opladen: Leske, 1967), p. 319.

and still is one of the most dynamic in Western Europe, if not in the world. The recession, however, ended the period of uninterrupted growth for the German economy, and it also brought unprecedented problems —for example, more than 700,000 workers were unemployed in an economy which had long been hungry for labor. Responding to this crisis the Grand Coalition reassessed the economic policies of the government and changed their direction significantly.

Under the Law for Promoting Stability and Growth in the Economy, which was passed in June, 1967, the government has a much more overt and direct role to play in the market. It is now incumbent upon the government to draw up plans projecting expenditures and revenues for five years in order to try to forecast and counteract possible downturns or too rapid expansions in the economy. Moreover, the government can now vary personal and corporate income taxes by as much as 10 percent up or down to counter a particular cycle. A Council for counter-Cyclical Policy was also created which brings together for the first time in a regularized way the federal government, the *Länder*, the *Gemeinde*, and the Central Bank.

As the 1966 recession demonstrated and as the economic turbulence of the 1970's has reaffirmed, the German public is very sensitive to economic dislocations. Despite the fact, for example, that West Germany had the lowest rate of inflation among the major Western nations in 1973, polls indicated that the average German citizen was quite disturbed about inflation and other economic problems—possible unemployment, strikes, and the almost total dependence of Germany upon oil imports. Memories of the catastrophic inflation and depression of the Weimar years are still prevalent, and Germans seem to feel that what they have gained so rapidly can also be taken from them or disappear very quickly. As one might imagine, public opinon surveys continue to show that much of the support which the Federal Republic gets from the average citizen is tied to the performance of the German economy, that the stability of the government is very dependent upon economic well-being. The German government will be needing these controls and perhaps others, too, in the face of the uncertainties of the increasingly interdependent economies of the world.

NATIONALIZATION: As early as the seventeenth century, some of the most highly developed industries in the German states, especially those producing luxuries and armaments, were owned by local princes. Until the end of World War I more and more of these businesses and industrial enterprises were brought under the control of state governments: the breweries of Munich, the porcelain factories of Meissen and Berlin, the tobacco factories of Strassburg. State control of mining and agriculture became even more extensive. It is estimated, in fact, that in 1907 one tenth of all workers in industry, commerce and transportation were employed in the public sector.

The pattern of state intervention continued under the Weimar regime, and was accelerated somewhat during the Nazi period. In postwar Germany some effort was made to divest the state of industrial and commercial holdings, and a majority of shares of the Volkswagen automobile works, for example, were sold to private investors. However, either because customers for shares could not be found, or because of a continued desire to permit the government to influence overall investment patterns, the CDU/CSU never went as far as its rhetoric seemed to indicate it might.

Today, as in most European countries, such services as railroads, telegraphy and telephone, and certain other utilities are owned and operated by the state. In addition, bank services are, to some extent, owned and supplied by the public sector, and the state plays a substantial role in aluminum production, coal, shipbuilding, oil, natural gas and petroleum industries, among others.

SOCIAL WELFARE: In instituting a pioneering social-welfare program, Bismarck was motivated by his desire to draw the teeth of the Socialists as well as by his traditional paternalistic view of the state. The state might be governed by an hereditary elite, but this elite had a moral obligation to take care of the lower classes. Indeed, such responsibility had to be taken on if the power of the German nation was to grow. Nevertheless, Bismarck's welfare program provoked vehement opposition—especially from liberals and progressives who felt that the whole idea would weaken the operation of a free market.

Although Weimar's constitutional fathers continued and even extended the state's welfare commitments, the effects of, first, the inflation and, then, the Great Depression were such as to vitiate the governmental efforts of the republic in this area. The Nazi

regime expanded social-welfare benefits adding stricter regulations of factory conditions, paid vacations at state-run resorts, and the quasi-compulsory collection of goods for the "Aryan" needy.

TABLE 17.5   SOCIAL SECURITY EXPENDITURE AS A PERCENTAGE OF GNP (AT MARKET PRICES), 1966

	1966
Germany	17.4
Britain	15.6
France	16.7
United States	12.3

Adapted from Joachim Wedel, "Social Security and Economic Integration," *International Labour Review* 102 (1970): 593–594; U. S. figures from Ida C. Merriam and Alfred M. Skolnik, *Social Welfare Expenditures Under Public Programs, 1929–1966* (Washington, D.C.: U.S. Department of Health, Education, and Welfare, 1968), p. 192.

As in all Western nations, after World War II social-welfare programs and coverage were considerably expanded. The proponents of neo-liberal ideology (in the classical sense) reluctantly accepted the need for certain forms of social legislation, but still believed that such legislation must be instituted with care lest it reduce individual freedom as well as the individual's "sense of responsibility." As Erhard put it in 1957, the year of great pension reform in Germany:

We reject the welfare state of the socialist variety and the general collectivist maintenance of the citizen not only because this seemingly well meant tutelage of the citizen creates dependence, which in the end breeds only submissiveness and kills the spirit of free citizenship, but also because this kind of self-negation, that is, the surrender of human responsibility, cripples the individual's will to work and must lead to the deterioration of economic performance in general.[5]

[5] Quoted by Gaston V. Rimlinger, "The Economics of Postwar German Social Policy," *Industrial Relations*, 6 (February, 1967), p. 187.

Erhard's pronouncements notwithstanding, the Adenauer government had very little option. Both the dislocation of the postwar years and the demands of the electorate impelled the extension rather than the curtailment of social-welfare measures. What the regime did try to do was to combine social welfare with what it conceived as policies that would not invalidate personal responsibility. German social welfare, therefore, differs somewhat from that which had been adopted in, for example, Britain prior to 1969.

One indication of this diffrence is the social-security legislation of 1957 for old age, permanent disability, and survivorship. A deliberate departure from the old principle of subsistence benefits, the law was intended to allow the insured person to maintain in retirement the relative economic level he had reached during his working life. To this end, the pensions were designed to reflect individual earnings as well as the growth of the national economy. Pension awards are thus made not only on the basis of a complicated computation involving an individual's lifetime earnings in relation to the earnings of others during the same period, but also, after an annual economic review, on the basis of the relation among pensions, the cost of living, and the prevailing wage levels. The aim of the pension scheme was to prevent payments from depreciating as prices rose and to allow retired workers to receive some of the benefits of increasing prosperity. According, old age pensions (along with average wages) rose in value by 150 percent between 1957 and 1970. Retired persons (including farmers and farm laborers, self-employed craftsmen, and professional people, to all of whom social security has been extended) today receive 50 percent or more of their last monthly earnings; there are also special retirement plans for miners and salaried workers which pay even higher benefits. Disability insurance is calculated in much the same way, except that payment comes to approximately two-thirds of the previous year's wages with special provisions for persons with children.

It is true that the public-pension scheme (voluntary industrial plans are also widespread in Germany) aids lower-income persons more than those in the higher-income brackets and is far more generous than comparable programs in other countries. But it is also true that the scheme is basically a horizontal transfer of funds from the young to the old rather than a vertical transfer. It perpetuates income inequalities—and this, in view of the neoliberal emphasis on personal responsibility, was one of the purposes of those who drafted the legislation.

The Federal Republic's commitment to providing economic security for its citizens is reflected in other ways, too. Family allowances were introduced in 1955, and in 1969 more than two million families were receiving aid under this program. Through a program for the promotion of capital formation in the hands of workers, the Federal Republic has since 1961 been granting low-income people special premiums on savings.

In addition, unemployment insurance funds, to which employers and employees contribute equally, provide payments of from thirteen to fifty-two weeks at about half salary, and the Federal Republic has tried hard to prevent technological unemployment and to find jobs for workers. Thus the Federal Employment Office makes payments and grants low-interest loans to workers for a variety of purposes, including the travel expenses of those who are in search of a job, family relocation costs, interview expenses, the maintenance of two households if the job necessitates separation of the family, retraining, vocational guidance and counseling, and physical and mental rehabilitation. Legislation passed in 1969 created an advisory service to help businessmen forecast future needs and create training programs to meet them. The office also subsidizes employers who hire long-term unemployed persons.

German health insurance received its greatest encouragement from Bismarck, and its coverage has gone on being extended ever since. The most recent overhaul of the program occurred under the Insurance Doctors

TABLE 17.6   MEDICAL SERVICES IN EUROPE, 1970–1971

	Doctors		Pharmacists		Hospital beds	
	Number	Persons per doctor	Number	Persons per pharmacist	Number	Persons per bed
Britain	70,122	768	16,732	3,217	508,313	106
France	71,039	721	25,692	1,933	539,700	95
Germany	105,976	561	23,060	2,630	690,236	89

Sources: United Nations *Statistical Yearbook, 1973*, pp. 721–722; Institut National de la Statistique et des Études Économiques, *Annuaire Statistique de la France, 1973* (Paris: INSEE, 1973), p. 76.

Act of 1955; since then, however, although there have been minor changes, moves toward major revisions of the program have thus far been blocked.

The German plan is ostensibly privately run, although regulated by law; it is a program of health insurance rather than a national health service. Its funds come from contributions by both employers and employees, with the federal government contributing only on behalf of unemployed workers. Monies for medical coverage are disbursed through two thousand welfare funds organized either on a specialized basis (for example, by craft) or else by area. The organizations administering the funds are regulated by statute. Each local fund is supervised by a board of directors and a legislative assembly consisting of representatives of employers and those insured. State-level associations coordinate the work of local bodies and, finally, the whole program is coordinated by the Federal Association of Local Sickness Funds.

Physicians licensed to practice are paid by the local Association of Sickness Fund Physicians. Membership in the association is compulsory for all doctors who participate in the national-insurance program. Patients are free to choose any doctors they wish, although doctors practice in specified geographic areas. To receive treatment, the patient presents a voucher, which he obtains each quarter and which is later submitted to the local Association of Sickness Fund Physicians. Except for certain minor charges, medical treatment is free for those insured.

The association tries to recompense doctors in accordance with a standard scale of fees set up in terms of work performed. Doctors police their own membership to reduce the incidence of padded vouchers. Payments do not differentiate sharply between the services of specialists and those of general practitioners—one reason why the proportion of specialists to practitioners in Germany is one of the lowest in Europe. Specialists or not, doctors' salaries compare favorably with those of other professionals, and Germany has one of the highest doctor-to-patient ratios in Europe.

One of the principal weaknesses of the German health-insurance program has been the relative lack of development in group, community, and preventive medicine. In a move to correct this deficiency, the state in 1960 made it possible for insured persons to have regular checkups; it also required that medical-dental checkups be a condition for the free provision of dentures for persons over forty.

In 1971 preventive medicine was given a new push by provisions for the free examination of children under the age of four for certain purposes and free annual cancer examinations for men and women beyond a certain age. However, attempts to broaden the program further or to convert it into a national health-insurance scheme have thus far failed.

Left: German couple. Courtesy German Information Center. *Opposite page:* Chemical industry air liquid plants, Dunkerque, France. Courtesy French Embassy Press & Information Division.

PART FIVE

Some Conclusions

18

The
Future
of
European
Politics

1. THE POLITICS OF EUROPEAN MODERNIZATION

It has become relatively commonplace in recent years for social scientists to discuss political systems in the context of a developmental model. Industrialization, together with the ideologies it generated, marked a fundamental shift in the quality of social and political life, first in Europe and then in other parts of the world. As an aid to explaining the political dynamics of individual nations, scholars have focused their attention increasingly on the tensions of this transition from traditional agrarian societies to modern societies.[1]

[1] The literature of these scholars is extensive. Perhaps the best general collection of essays is that of

According to the framework elaborated by Gabriel Almond and G. Bingham Powell, all political systems are confronted by four problems as they attempt to modernize: state building, nation building, participation, and distribution.[2] State building pertains to

Jason L. Finkle and Richard W. Gable, eds., *Political Development and Social Change*, 2nd ed. (New York: John Wiley & Sons, 1971).

[2] Gabriel A. Almond and G. Bingham Powell, *Comparative Politics: A Developmental Approach* (Boston: Little, Brown & Co., 1966). The model development by Almond has come under increasing criticism recently, only part of which is justified. The most telling points made against it are that: (1) It characterizes as a universal phenomenon something which was initiated by Europe and then spread around the globe, via conquest or imitation. (2) It "ethnocentrically" identifies European patterns of political and social life with "mod-

the creation of institutions that enable the political system to regulate behavior and to extract an increasingly larger volume of resources from the community. Nation building is the process of evolving allegiance to the larger community at the expense of parochial attachments to tribes, villages, or regions. Problems of participation and distribution arise as more and more members of the community demand a voice in the decisions that affect them and what they consider to be a more equitable division of the society's values.

All modernizing nations have faced these problems, and the success (or failure) of their attempts to cope with them has varied widely. Key variables have included the nature of the traditional society, the nature and timing of the modernizing process, the international environment, and such "accidental" factors as the character of political leadership available at crucial historical moments.

It was in Europe that modern society and modern politics first emerged, and the conditions that led to this development, as well as its timing, continue to differentiate European politics from that of other areas of the world. Even when other nations have adopted European ideologies and institutions, through imitation or foreign control, their politics are still clearly distinguishable. For example, the major ideological currents that dominated European politics during the nineteenth century not only caused but reflected the social changes that occurred— and they were uniquely European. European socialists as well as European liberals

drew upon the European heritage, even as they rejected part of it, and European conservatives wanted to preserve what they considered vital elements in that heritage.

Where conservative and liberal movements have developed elsewhere in the world, they have resembled those of Europe; indeed, most liberal movements around the world developed in imitation of the European model. Nonetheless, they have also differed from the European model far more than such movements have differed from each other in various European countries. In Asian and African nations the traditional patterns that conservatives wish to retain are unique, and in only a very few non-European countries has a bourgeoisie emerged that resembles the European entrepreneur in dynamism and organizing ability.

Further there are few countries in the world, aside from those settled by Western Europeans, in which an individualistic tradition like that which sprang from Christianity has had comparable force. Moreover, the timing of change in non-European nations, as well as the fact that it was often induced from the outside, has had a profound impact upon their ideological development. Even Marxism, first transmuted by Soviet leaders to meet Russian needs and conditions, has come to have widely different meanings and consequences in non-European portions of the world—depending on the social culture and structure of the particular society.

European political institutions are also unique in their functioning, because of their derivation. Parliaments evolved through a process of trial and error from feudal institutions, and political parties through a complex interplay of social and political variables that, by and large, have been absent elsewhere. For example, in all three European countries considered in this text the development of mass Socialist parties was related to, and partially dependent on, the development of labor unions of some strength and staying power. True, this circumstance was less true in France than in Germany or Britain because the organizational capacity of French workers was much less than that

ernity." (3) It assumes that modernity is some sort of end point in social development, and, thus, is unable to deal with changes which are taking place in advanced industrial countries. (4) It ignores substantive differences between ways of organizing modern political systems, for example, the differences between socialist and "capitalist welfare" states.

These are telling points, but they can be taken into account, as we have attempted to do, and the model may then still serve as a useful way of organizing a good deal of information about political systems. See Stanley Rothman, "Functionalism and Its Critics," *The Political Science Reviewer* 1 (Fall, 1971), pp. 236–276.

of their German or British counterparts. Yet compared with most "developing" countries, the French working class was highly organized. In most parts of the world left-wing movements have not been based on trade unions, for both the labor movement and the political parties in most non-European nations have lacked organizational capacity. Where the left has triumphed it has been largely because its opponents were less well organized than it was, and its lack of a solid trade-union base (among other factors) has caused it to differ considerably from the European left.

Within an overall European framework, the politics and political institutions of Britain, France, and Germany clearly reflect different combinations of essentially the same European variables. Britain, in part because of its island position, developed a relatively effective state organization and sense of national community quite early in the modern period. Calvinist sects played a significant role in social and political development, and the intermingling of traditional and modern institutions enabled Britain, in comparison with her neighbors, to deal reasonably effectively with many of the problems attendant upon the early stages of modernization. The fact that social change in Britain was sparked by the society itself (and that Britain was first in making social innovations) muted the demand for radically induced political change and softened the edges of social conflict.

The British example was partly responsible for the rise of French nationalism and for the drive to modernize in France, although, in a broadly comparative perspective, French social structure and culture were more conducive to change than that of most non-European nations. In France, change was initiated by a native intelligentsia acting upon a rigid social system. This led to revolutionary upheaval and political fragmentation, a fragmentation that continues to bedevil France in the twentieth century and has left old problems unresolved even as new ones have manifested themselves. The ideological character of French politics and the

nature and failings of French parliamentary institutions over most of the modern period have reflected and contributed to this fragmentation. Added to the problems France has faced is the persistence of traditional orientations deriving from the failure of the Reformation, traditional orientations that have affected the thinking and action even of those who claimed to be most opposed to them.

In Germany the timing and pace of modernization were also important. Modernization was initiated by a conservative upper class, to which the German bourgeoisie deferred, and it occurred under the aegis of a religious cultural orientation that emphasized the controlling and authoritarian aspects of the Christian tradition. The late achievement of unity and the problem of boundaries prompted an intense nationalism that, when frustrated, contributed to the surfacing of a regressive and barbaric regime. Other factors involved included the lack of a genuine tradition of liberal individualism (as compared with that of France and Britain) and the disorganization of social life after World War I.

All three nations experienced fundamentalist reactions to modernization to one degree or another. In Germany these took their sharpest form. As in Britain and France, political forces and institutions in Germany stemmed from a feudal heritage, though they were transformed by the particular features of the German pattern of development. The experience of the Nazi regime and World War II marked an abrupt break with the past, but as our analysis in this volume indicates, many features of the past are still present in German politics and political institutions.

In his discussion of British politics, Almond suggests that British development was relatively peaceful because the British were able to deal with the problems of growth one at a time. France and Germany, on the other hand, were forced to deal with several of them at the same time. In an important sense he is right, though he does not tell us why this was so. To understand why it was so we need a dynamic, historical analysis that is comparative in focus. And this is what we have tried to offer in this book.

In doing so we have attempted to demonstrate that the patterns found in most of the important aspects of the political and social life of these three nations can be related to the overall nature of their development, reflecting basic social changes and contributing to them. Thus, in dealing with the role of the state in economic planning, we pointed out that because British economic development proceeded from below, so to speak, the British could afford to regard the political mechanism primarily as a gyroscope, helping to steer the society; they saw less need than the French or the Germans to use it as a means for inducing or blocking economic change and development. To take another example, the role and nature of bureaucracy in all three nations are best understood when related to overall growth patterns. In Britain, France, and Germany the bureaucracy was considered a legitimate upper class form of service to the community. Britain, because she lacked social cleavages as sharp as those in France or Germany, was the only one of the three to establish a civil service that could truly serve different masters relatively impartially. Moreover, the British could rely on a bureaucracy of generalists because the political system was considered to have somewhat limited functions. In France and Germany, however, in rather different ways, efforts were made to create a technocratic elite that could control the direction of the nation's development.

All the above is, of course, prologue. Since World War II, and with increasing rapidity, new challenges have arisen, and old battles are being fought on new terrain. Until the early 1960's some of the internal issues that had divided Germany and France in earlier periods seemed to have been at least partially resolved, or on their way to being resolved. In recent years both countries (though France more than Germany) have found themselves torn by new divisions and confronted with new crises. Nor have the British been immune to these. Since

World War II many of their traditional virtues have become handicaps, and while the upheavals of the late 1960's were rather milder in England than on the Continent (or than in the United States), the British are now facing a series of crises which portend a new period of strain and attempted adjustment.

Interestingly enough, as new problems have emerged the traditional differences among the three nations seem less significant. Indeed, social and cultural differences between European and other avanced industrial nations also appear to be diminishing. It does begin to look as if we are on the verge of creating a world culture in which, despite some differences, we face common problems and dilemmas. It is a world culture whose major features have been shaped by the rapid advance of technology, an advance that has accelerated so fast in the past twenty years that more and more scholars are now talking about the problems and dilemmas of the immediate future as those of post-industrial society.[3]

2. THE POLITICS OF POST-INDUSTRIAL SOCIETY

Any attempt to outline the probable course of West European politics in "the post-industrial" era is an extremely hazardous undertaking, and the wise man, like the Delphic Oracle, will couch his prognostications in language sufficiently ambiguous to allow several interpretations. Nevertheless, a number of points seem clear. As already noted, the three Western European nations studied in this volume are becoming more and more alike. Their cultural and structural variations are receding and more and more often they are responding in the same way to the same stimuli. This convergence

[3] A short discussion of the history of the phrase will be found in Daniel Bell, *The Coming of Post Industrial Society* (New York: Basic Books, 1973), pp. 33–40.

is partly the result of the social changes generated by advanced industrialization; yet it stems as well from the revolutions in transportation and mass communications. And unless something happens that is as extraordinary as it is unforeseen, this trend is likely to continue. We strongly suspect that it will eventually lead to greater economic and even political unity.

If we ignore, for the moment, pressures from other political systems and their possible consequences, certain additional trends also seem irreversible. It seems reasonable to expect, for example, that poverty in the traditional sense will be eliminated in the next twenty or thirty years in Britain, France, and Germany; that income inequality among various social strata will be reduced, and also that the social-welfare functions of the state will be considerably expanded. The state will assume far more responsibility for national and urban planning, and for two reasons: new demands will force the community to reorganize its resources in order to provide for a better social environment, and the arts, education, and leisure will come to replace the production of goods as individual and community goals. Trends toward income equality will accelerate primarily because of the redistributive effects of social policy. The commitment to greater equality is a continuing and growing force among large sectors of the new European middle class, and the political mobilization of the "relatively poor" has created pressures that are unlikely to diminish. Of course, the current concern with eliminating the remaining pockets of poverty and with reducing income inequalities can be partly attributed to the fact that for the first time in human history a substantial majority of the population in most European nations is well above the traditional poverty line.

It is also difficult to escape the conclusion that the major productive assets of the community will ultimately come under public ownership. We do not foresee the emergence of a Socialist society in the Marxist sense in the near future. Certain forms of property—homes, for example—will undoubtedly remain in private hands; and we cannot conceive of a society without conflict and hence without the need for political authority. What we do foresee in the next fifty to seventy-five years, however, is the end of a capitalist market economy in most European countries.

One reason for the decline in the capitalist market system is the dwindling importance of material goods and the headway made by those sectors of the economy that provide services. Associated with this changeover is the growing influence of a professional class in the mass media and in education, science, and the arts that has little stake in the existing system of productive relationships. A second reason for the decline of the capitalist market system lies in the need to control future technology in the interest of a rationally planned environment. In the past, technological development has proceeded largely on the basis of estimates of consumer demand and marketability by individual, privately controlled enterprises. This is less and less true in Western Europe, where governments are becoming more and more responsible for the creation of new technologies.

Uncontrolled technological development is, of course, no longer feasible; the world has become too interdependent and its technology too advanced. Until recently, the negative ecological side effects of new industrial or consumer products could be largely ignored—or, perhaps, corrected after the fact. In the future the community will have to control the development of such products, taking into account their possible repercussions on the social organization of the community and its natural environment. For instance, the unplanned growth of automobile production and use has yielded not only high levels of air pollution, but national transportation grids that are extremely inefficient. All advanced societies will have to plan transportation networks, determine what kind of vehicles will be produced and in what numbers, and control, or at least direct technical innovation in this field.[4]

One caveat should be noted here. Thus far Socialist command economies have not demonstrated any real superiority over capitalist market economies in planning resource use, as the Soviet example indicates.[5] Clearly, public ownership of the major instruments of production will not, in itself, solve the problems just noted, though it seems to us that public ownership will make it easier to solve them.

A third reason for the decline of the capitalist market system is that wages and profits will eventually no longer serve as the spur for fulfilling those tasks that must be completed if the community is to survive. As recent developments have already begun to indicate, segments of the population of technologically advanced societies have ceased to be motivated merely by the desire for more money; this trend is likely to accelerate in those societies that guarantee at least a minimum of welfare for all their members.

Other forms of incentives, then, will have to be developed. Positions in industrial management will have to offer, for example, the promise of direct community service in addition to income, an offer that is more difficult to extend in a capitalistic economic system. The fact is that a large middle class has been created for which the acquisition of material goods is less central than it was in an earlier generation. The "dirty" jobs of the community may have to be fulfilled on the basis of compulsory requirements for public service, such as some form of compulsory national service corps. The creation of European welfare states, the products themselves of affluence, has reduced the force of those economic impera-

tives that drove people to work at these "dirty" jobs. The decline of capitalism in Europe will stem, not as Marx thought, from its inability to deal with the problem of poverty, but rather from its success in having coped with it.

The future, in short, will require increased national—and international—planning and control if new problems are to be dealt with effectively. New methods for gathering, processing, and communicating information, too, will become necessary, and more effective forms of organization will have to be created. Without much question, such developments will entail the continued growth of national bureaucracies and the increasing centralization of political decision-making.

Some see in these developments the threat of an increasingly dehumanized, computer-run society, in which opportunities for initiative and self-development are curtailed. They feel that this trend to bureaucratization can and must be thwarted by restoring "community control" and by decentralizing government functions. Both their assumptions and their conclusions seem dubious. In densely populated, extremely complex, technologically advanced societies, there is simply no substitute for centralized bureaucratic organizations. The location, design, and control of transportation networks, industry, amenities, health-care facilities, and even schools cannot be left to local communities because decisions on any of these matters affect a far larger number of individuals than those directly involved. In any future Socialist society with overall national planning (even with extensive reliance upon market mechanisms) the necessity for more centralized supervision and control will be greater than in most contemporary capitalist market economies. Imagine the results if every community continued to have the right to determine how it disposed of sewage along major waterways, or to decide whether or not it should provide adequate education for schoolchildren—or set up integrated or segregated schools. Each of these issues has profound implications for the larger so-

[4] A recent discussion of the use of social indicators for purposes of planning in these areas will be found in Andrew Shonfield and Stella Shaw, eds., *Social Indicators and Social Policy* (London: William Heinemann, 1972).

[5] See Marshall I. Goldman, "Growth and Environmental Problems of Non-Capitalist Nations," *Challenge* 16 (July–August, 1973): pp. 45–52.

ciety, though they may not be immediately apparent. It is one of the intellectual quirks of our time that while we have become increasingly aware of the fact that our earth is one ecosystem, many groups are stepping up their demands for autonomy in making decisions that are likely to affect so many others.

To be sure, efforts will have to be made to devolve control where possible and to insure that bureaucratic organizations do not become overly authoritarian. Furthermore, there is no gainsaying the argument that centralized control is more impersonal than decisions made on the local level, and that mistakes made by giant organizations can have widely disastrous consequences. These problems must be dealt with; they cannot be wished away.

On the positive side, of course, centralization and bureaucratic organization can serve to expand opportunities and options. A national transportation network might be a highly bureaucratic operation, but intelligent national and regional decisions may be the only alternative to high levels of pollution and almost total chaos in the area of transporting goods and individuals. National policies for land use can frustrate individuals in particular communities, but in the end they are likely to insure a more satisfying environment for most citizens by preventing urban sprawl and preserving some amenities.

Despite the legitimate concern with problems of bureaucratization, it remains true that the options available to most citizens today are far greater than they were in the past. Traditional communities tended to stifle deviants and to limit individual freedom. Tolerance for variations in life-style seems likely to grow, although just how far without incurring social disorganization is a matter of some dispute.[6]

6 See Bertram Gross, *The Managing of Organizations*, 2 vols. (New York: Free Press, 1964), pp. 280–409 and pp. 807–837; Victor C. Ferkiss, *Technological Man* (New York: George Braziller, 1969); and Alvin Toffler, *Future Shock* (New York: Random House, 1970).

The dominant role that the government will come to assume in both economic and social planning will, thus, require the establishment of a new balance between individual rights and community needs. We see no great difficulty here. For the foreseeable future, we do not think that traditional parliamentary forms will be replaced, although they may be supplemented by other institutions. Proposals for legislative chambers based on functional representation have a long history and some form of representation of this kind may be put into practice in the future. Technocrats will probably exert more and more influence on the making of policy, but there is every reason to expect that they can be held in check; it seems likely, for instance, that legislators will seek more assistance from experts and that a greater number of lawmakers will be drawn from professions other than law.

The Western European population itself is becoming more knowledgeable on public-policy matters, and, as income and educational levels rise, it will unquestionably be better able to express opinions on what it wants. Our ability to educate is advancing with each new decade, and we may be on the verge of breakthroughs in the biological sciences that will revolutionize man's capacity to learn. Thus, we do not see the need for the replacement of democratic participation in Western Europe by an intellectual "meritocracy" of one kind or another. Nor do we fear or hope this will happen.

Assuredly, the nature of European society in the future will depend largely on those in the business of creating and communicating ideas. As the impact of policies upon individuals becomes more indirect and complicated, personal experience will become a less and less satisfactory guide for judging public policy. For the middle class and the working class, the media and the university are replacing direct experience and even peer groups as sources of notions about what is happening in the world and how to deal with its problems. And the media are becoming more centralized and national in scope. They have, in fact, acquired considerable influence over public attitudes, and this influence is likely to become still greater.[7]

Partly as a result of the expanding power of the media, and the university, we can expect continuing changes in the party systems of European nations. The age of the disciplined mass party seems to be passing. Though bureaucratic party organizations will continue to fulfill certain functions, they may be more easily bypassed in the future by candidates who can temporarily mobilize groupings of middle-class activists and effectively use the mass media. Indeed, personal charisma, albeit of a different type from what we have known hitherto, seems likely to become an even more important criterion for political advancement. There are, obviously, dangers in this development. Dynamic political leaders have a tendency to draw upon intense emotional commitments, and their failure to satisfy aspirations can lead to volatile alternations between "love" and "hate" that are hardly conducive to social stability.

We do not foresee the development of any pure form of "participatory democracy," as defined by the "New Left" of the 1960's in both Europe and the United States. Modern society is too complex for the kind of direct democracy that some members of this political sector envisage. All societies, in the near future at least, will require a structure of authority if any decisions are to be made. Any attempts to replace traditional democratic mechanism with the total participation called for by the New Left could lead only to stasis and frustration—followed by the domination of a charismatic dictator. Intellectuals who believe that complete personal autonomy can be combined with both a heightened sense of community and more effective societal decisions in the contemporary world are deceiving themselves.

The future of European politics as we have outlined it above seems less than revolutionary, and thus far our predictions have

exhibited a cautious optimism. Indeed, in the early 1960's it looked as if the gradual establishment of planned Socialist economies in most West European nations would probably come about without any major revolutionary upheavals or intense ideological heat. Events of the middle and late 1960's, however, raised serious questions in this regard. Clashes over life-style and economic and social issues resulted in a new period of ideological ferment associated with the rejection of conventional political behavior by important segments of middle-class college youth. While the 1970's have been rather less volatile thus far, there is little question that some of the attitudes traditionally associated with successful democratic regimes have eroded somewhat in the countries under study.

The events of these years serve as a reminder that democratic political orders have, historically, been the exception among human beings rather than the rule, and that they are quite fragile. When they have been successful, they have depended on the widespread willingness of the populace to exercise considerable restraint in its demands. Throughout most of history much of mankind has lived under one or another form of authoritarian rule, and the most vociferous champions of "human dignity," once in power, have all too often turned out to be disposed toward circumscribing the freedom of others; many have even been inclined to enlighten their opponents through the very trenchant device of splitting open their heads. The new ferment in advanced industrial societies, along with certain other problems that are becoming increasingly salient, prompts us to name some issues that admit of a more pessimistic prognosis.

The first issue is war. It seems less and less likely that a nuclear holocaust will be touched off by one of the major powers, yet the danger of such an event obviously cannot be discounted. Further, as nuclear arms proliferate, we are faced with the prospect of a battery of "mini-nuclear" powers. Short of a dramatic achievement in defense capabilities that would make nuclear warfare obsolete—an event that appears ex-

---

[7] Elisabeth Noelle-Neumann, "The Spiral of Silence and the Public Opinion Process," Paper delivered at the International Congress of Psychology, Tokyo, August 16, 1972 (Xeroxed).

tremely unlikely to occur—the only permanent solution for peace would seem to lie in some form of world order, another unlikely possibility for the short run. In the immediate future, then, our only hope would appear to rest with the prudence of our political leaders.

The threat of a nuclear holocaust has been with us since 1945, but only in the past seven or eight years has an awareness of the possible consequences of our advanced industrialization in conjunction with our phenomenal population growth been brought starkly to our attention. Some proponents of what one writer calls the "Doomsday Syndrome" have undoubtedly exaggerated the immediacy of the dangers we face: overpopulation, ecological ruination, and the gradual exhaustion of many nonrenewable resources.[8] Nonetheless, these are indeed serious problems. Other civilizations have declined as a result of overexploiting their resource base. The possibility that we will face if not destruction then decay accompanied by violence as competition for scarce resources escalates must not be dismissed. That only a small fragment of the world's population today exploits most of its resources further complicates the issue.

Tensions between the have and have-not nations are mounting as the latter steadily demand as their right a greater share of resources. Whether or not the advanced nations, which include the Soviet Union and Japan, will be willing or able to meet these demands is open to question. Also open to question is whether all or even a majority of "third world" nations will be willing or able to respond to the suggestions from European nations that the world move in the direction of zero population growth. Aside from the religious and cultural aspects of the problem, a large population is still widely considered a source of power. In advanced industrial nations, the drive to zero population growth may eventually bring pressures for compulsory limitations on family size. Potentially, this issue is an extremely explosive one and may well induce further changes in the role played by the family in contemporary society—as well as the traditional role of women.

The "counter-culture" movement of the 1960's brought another issue to the fore. Those associated with it often emphasized the need to reject traditional attitudes toward work and achievement, for the purpose of developing small communities, of the "Gemeinschaft" type, based on the free expression of emotional needs. Some of those who were favorably disposed toward some aspects of the movement or who provided ideological justification for it, saw in the counter-culture movement a repudiation of the rationalistic, scientific *Weltanschauung* that generated industrialization in Europe and a "healthy" turn to aesthetic creativity and more humane levels of existence. More radical proponents predicted a profound metamorphosis in human nature and maintained that genital sexuality would eventually disappear, to be replaced by the polymorphous perversity of infancy. Though their views of the human future were not notable for their clarity, it does seem that to them man's destiny was locked into a completely sensual world in which control over reality would become less important than the satisfaction of those erotic impulses that would permeate every portion of the body; it was to be a world dominated by Eros, and, consequently, free of destructive violence.[9]

Others in the late 1960's and early 1970's foresaw increasing anomy. They anticipated a world in which more and more individuals would seek only personal gratification and turn to drugs in their flight from reali-

---

[8] The literature is enormous and growing. See D. H. Meadows et al., *The Limits to Growth* (New York: Universe Books, 1972); Garrett Hardin, *Exploring New Ethics for Survival* (New York: Viking Press, 1972); John Maddox, *The Doomsday Syndrome* (New York: McGraw Hill, 1973); and Robert Heilbronner, *An Inquiry into the Human Prospect* (New York: W. W. Norton, 1974).

[9] See Herbert Marcuse, *Eros and Civilization* (Boston: Beacon Press, 1955); Norman O. Brown, *Life Against Death* (New York: Random House, 1959) and *Love's Body* (New York: Random House, 1966); Theodore Roszak, *Where The Wasteland Ends: Politics and Transcendence in Post-Industrial Society* (Garden City, N.Y.: Doubleday & Co., 1972).

ty. To some analysts, the counter culture constituted a foretaste of what our future was likely to be.[10]

The past few years seem to have belied the predictions of both "optimists" and "pessimists". The student movement has all but disappeared, in England and Germany, and, in France, for the time being, at least, it seems to have served primarily to strengthen the conventional left, that is, the Communist and Socialist parties.

The movement has not, however, been without its consequences. It did contribute to a general weakening of many traditional attitudes toward sexuality, culture, and politics in the countries in which it arose. And it has intensified a general loss of nerve among political elites in both Europe and America.

A new ethic seems to be emerging among significant segments of the population. In addition to the increased concern about questions of equality and the impact of technology, noted earlier, this new ethic stresses the importance of aesthetic and expressive as against rational and instrumental values. To a certain extent, these new emphases seem quite adaptive, given the problems we face. On the other hand, some of the manifestations of the new sensibility have an

[10] Herman Kahn and Anthony J. Wiener, *The Year 2000* (New York: Macmillan Co., 1967).

odor of decay and seem to promise, (or threaten) a retreat to a kind of narcissism and irrationality which could inhibit us in dealing with our problems and create new and even more serious ones.

The idea of progress has been, despite setbacks, a major current in European history since the beginning of the nineteenth century. But the belief that the human race will move from one triumph to another, despite temporary reversals, may simply be a form of hubris. Protoman developed on this planet about two million years ago, and modern man about forty thousand to fifty thousand years ago. The first agricultural settlements that we know of are about ten thousand years old and the first major civilizations date back about five thousand years. Industrial society is only a few hundred years old. If millennia were minutes, any two-hour television show on the history of mankind could allot only a minute or so to the period since 1700—sixty or eighty seconds in which to stress the huge growth in population and the befouling of the environment. The great dinosaurs died because of changes in climatic conditions. Man's capacity to adapt—a quality that led to the Industrial Revolution—may prove in the long run to have concealed a serious fault, and the history of his dominion over the earth may turn out to be relatively short.

List
of
Abbreviations

ARS   *Action républicain et sociale* (Republican and Social Action)

BBC   British Broadcasting Corporation

BDA   *Bundesvereinigung der Deutschen Arbeitgeberverbände* (Federation of German Employers Associations)

BDI   *Bundesverband der Deutschen Industrie* (Federation of German Industry)

BMA   British Medication Association

BRD   *Bundesrepublik Deutschland* (German Federal Republic)

CDP   *Centre démocratie et progrès* (Center for Democracy and Progress)

CDU   Christlich Demokratische Union (Christian Democratic Union)

CDU/CSU   *Christlich Demokratische Union/ Christlich Soziale Union* (Christian Democratic Union and the Christian Social Union)

CFDT   *Confédération française démocratique du travail* (French Democratic Confederation of Labor)

CFTC   *Confédération française des travailleurs chrétiens* (French Confederation of Christian Workers)

CGP   *Commissariat générale du plan* (General Planning Commission)

CGPF   *Confédération générale de la production française* (General Confederation of French Production)

CGPME   *Confédération générale des petites et moyennes entreprises* (General Confederation of Small and Medium Business)

CGT *Confédération générale du travail* (General Confederation of Labor)

CGT–FO *Confédération générale du travail-Force ouvrière* (General Confederation of Labor-Workers' Force)

CGTU *Confédération générale du travail unifié* (Unified General Confederation of Labor)

CID–UNATI *Comité interprofessionel de défense de l'Union Nationale des travailleurs indépendents* (Interprofessional Committee for the Defense of the National Union of Independent Workers)

CND Committee for Nuclear Disarmament

CNIP *Centre national des indépendents et paysans* (National Center of Independents and Peasants)

CNPF *Conseil national du patronat français* (National Council of French Employers)

CODER *Commissions de développement économique régionale* (Commissions for Regional Economic Development)

DATAR *Délégation à l'aménagement du territoire et à l'action régionale* (Delegation for Integrated Development and Regional Action)

DDR *Deutsche Demokratische Republik* (German Democratic Republic)

DGB *Deutscher Gewerkschaftsbund* (German Federation of Trade Unions)

DIHT *Deutscher Industrie und Handelstag* (German Chamber of Industry and Commerce)

DP *Deutsche Partei* (German Party)

DRP *Deutsche Reichspartei* (German Reich Party)

ECSC European Coal and Steel Community

EEC European Economic Community

EFTA European Free Trade Association

ENA *École nationale d'administration* (National School for Administration)

FBI Federation of British Industries

FDP *Freie Demokratische Partei* (Free Democratic Party)

FEN *Fédération de l'éducation nationale* (Federation of National Education)

FGDS *Fédération de la gauche democrate et socialiste* (Federation of the Democratic and Socialist Left)

FNSEA *Fédération nationale des syndicats d'exploitants agricoles* (National Federation of Farmers' Unions)

FRG Federal Republic of Germany

GDR German Democratic Republic

GMC General Management Committee

GNP gross national product

HMSO Her Majesty's Stationery Office

ILP Independent Labor Party

INSEE *Institut National de la Statistique et des Études Économiques* (National Institute of Statistics and Economic Studies)

ITA Independent Television Authority

JAC *Jeunesse agricole chrétienne* (Christian Agricultural Youth)

JP justice of the peace

KPD *Kommunistische Partei Deutschlands* (German Communist Party)

LPP Liberal Parliamentary Party

MODEF *Mouvement de défense de l'exploitation familiale* (Movement for the Defense of Family Farming)

MP member of Parliament

MRP *Mouvement républicain populaire* (Popular Republican Movement)

NATO North Atlantic Treaty Organization

NEC National Executive Committee

NEDC National Economic Development Council

NFU National Farmers' Union

NPD *National Demokratische Partei Deutschlands* (National Democratic Party of Germany)

NSDAP *Nationalsozialistische Deutsche Arbeiter Partei* (National Socialist German Workers' Party)

NUS National Union of Students

OAS *Organisation de l'armée secrète* (Secret Army Organization)

ORTF *Office de radiodiffusion télévision française* (French Office of Television Broadcasting)

PADOG *Plan d'aménagement et d'organisation générale de la région parisienne* (Plan for the Management and General Organization of the Paris Region)

PCF *Parti communiste francais* (French Communist Party)

PDM *Progrès et démocratie moderne* (Progress and Modern Democracy)

PLP Parliamentary Labor Party

PR proportional representation

PRL *Parti républicain de la liberté* (Republican Party of Liberty)

PS *Parti socialiste* (Socialist Party)

PSU *Parti socialiste unifié* (Unified Socialist Party)

RDI *Reichsverband der Deutschen Industrie* (National Association of German Industry)

RPF *Rassemblement du peuple français* (Rally of the French People)

SDS *Sozialistischer Deutscher Studentenbund* (German Socialist Student Alliance)

SFIO *Section française de l'internationale ouvriére* (French Section of the Worker's International)

SPD *Sozialdemokratsische Partei Deutschlands* (Social Democratic Party of Germany)

SRP *Sozialistische Reichpartei* (Socialist Reich Party)

SS *Schutzstaffel* (guard detachment)

T&GWU Transport and General Workers Union

TUC Trade Union Congress

UDR *Union des démocrates pour la république* (Union of Democrats for the Republic)

UFF *Union et fraternité française* (French Union and Fraternity)

UNEF *Union nationale des étudiants de France* (National Union of French Students)

UNR *Union pour la nouvelle république* (Union for the New Republic)

URP *Union des républicains de progrès pour le soutien au président de la république* (Union of Republicans for Progress for the Support of the President of the Republic)

*

Select Bibliography of Books in English

GENERAL AND COMPARATIVE

Almond, Gabriel A., and Powell, G. Bingham, Jr. *Comparative Politics: A Development Approach.* Boston: Little, Brown & Co., 1966. A systematic presentation of comparative politics from a functionalist and developmental perspective. Rather turgid, but essential for the serious student.

Beer, Samuel H., ed. *Patterns of Government.* 3rd ed. New York: Random House, 1973. Analytic and empirical essays on European government, with separate sections on Britain, France, Germany, and the U.S.S.R.

Dahrendorf, Ralf. *Class and Class Conflict in an Industrial Society.* Stanford, Calif.: Stanford University Press, 1959.

Eckstein, Harry, and Apter, David, eds. *Comparative Politics: A Reader.* New York: Free Press, 1963. The best introduction to the discipline of comparative politics for the mature student.

Huntington, Samuel P. *Political Order in Changing Societies.* New Haven, Conn.: Yale University Press, 1968. Lively discussion on the nature of political development that has the additional merit of avoiding jargon. The only caveat is that the author is a little too taken up with the conditions of order.

Lichtheim, George. *Europe in the Twentieth Century.* New York: Praeger, 1972. An admirably synthesized, thematic portrayal focusing on "trends shaping the totality of events and (the) overriding importance of problems common to the entire culture."

389

Macridis, Roy C., and Brown, Bernard E., eds. *Comparative Politics, Notes and Readings.* 4th ed. Homewood, Ill.: Dorsey Press, 1972. An excellent introduction to comparative politics, mostly European. Second only to Eckstein and Apter in sophistication, and perhaps better suited to the beginner.

PART ONE   THE EUROPEAN IN-HERITANCE

Chapter 1. The Development of Modern Europe

Arendt, Hannah. *The Origins of Totalitarianism.* new ed. New York: Harcourt Brace Jovanovich, 1973. Extremely useful for the origins of National Socialism in Germany.

Baldwin, Summerfield. *The Organization of Medieval Christianity.* New York: Henry Holt, 1929.

Bendix, Reinhard. *Nation Building and Citizenship.* rev. ed. Berkeley and Los Angeles: University of California Press, 1975. A developmental examination of European political systems, with some Asian comparisons. Combines scholarship with clarity.

———, ed. *State and Society: A Reader in Comparative Political Sociology.* Boston: Little, Brown & Co., 1968.

Bloch, Marc. *Feudal Society.* Translated by L. A. Manyon, Chicago: University of Chicago Press, 1961. A classic work by one of the great historians of our time.

Carsten, F. L. *The Rise of Fascism.* Berkeley and Los Angeles: University of California Press, 1969.

Clapham, J. H. *The Economic Development of France and Germany, 1815–1914.* 4th ed. Cambridge: At the University Press, 1936. A classic that still rates attention.

Coulborn, Rushton, ed. *Feudalism in History.* Princeton, N.J.: Princeton University Press, 1956. A comparative study that throws new light on the European variant.

Green, Nathaniel, ed. *Fascism.* New York: Thomas Y. Crowell, 1968.

Green, Robert W., ed. *Protestantism, Capitalism, and Social Science.* 2nd ed. New York: D.C. Heath, 1965. Essays on Weber's hypothesis concerning the relationship between Calvinism and capitalism. An excellent collection.

Hartz, Louis. *The Liberal Tradition in America.* New York: Harcourt, Brace Jovanovich & Co., 1955. What the major differences are between European and American politics and why the Lockean tradition caused them. Important.

Heilbroner, Robert. *The Making of Economic Society.* 2nd ed. Englewood Cliffs, N.J.: Prentice-Hall, 1968. A description of Europe's economic evolution and the problems of the developing countries. Very well done.

Hobsbawn, E. J. *The Age of Revolution, 1789–1848.* New York: New American Library, 1965. A depiction of the transformations of European society brought out by political and economic upheavals culminating in the demise of the feudal order. Stimulating in its sensitivity as to the social impact of change.

Landauer, Carl. *European Socialism.* 2 vols. Berkeley and Los Angeles: University of California Press, 1959. Standard history.

Landes, David S. *The Unbound Prometheus.* Cambridge, Mass.: Harvard University Press, 1969. Nicely written survey of European industrialization in the nineteenth century. Essential.

McNeill, William H. *The Rise of the West: A History of the Human Community.* Chicago: University of Chicago Press, 1963. Outstanding history of the development of Europe within the context of world history. McNeill manages to synthesize a great deal of material without falling into recondite philosophic speculations.

Mosse, George. *Calvinism: Authoritarian or Democratic?* New York: Holt, Rinehart and Winston, 1957.

Nolte, Ernest. *Three Faces of Fascism.* New York: Holt, Rinehart and Winston, 1966. A scholarly work defining the philosophic underpinnings of European fascism.

Palmer, R. R., and Colton, Joel. *A History of the Modern World.* 4th ed. New York: Alfred A. Knopf, 1971. One of the better single-volume histories of Europe.

Reichmann, Eva G. *Hostages of Civilization.* London: Gollancz, 1950. Excellent study of anti-Semitism in Central Europe, with the emphasis on Germany.

Watkins, Frederick M. *The Political Tradition of the West.* Cambridge, Mass.: Harvard University Press, 1948. A penetrating examination of Europe's major ideological trends. Hard to fault.

Wilson, Edmund. *To the Finland Station.* New York: Doubleday & Co., Anchor Books, 1963. A study of European socialism through biographical sketches of some of its leading figures. Well worth reading.

Woodhouse, A. S. P., ed. *Puritanism and Liberty.* Chicago: University of Chicago Press, 1951.

Chapter 2. Great Britain, France, and Germany

Bagehot, Walter. *The English Constitution.* Introduction by Richard H. Crossman. London: Collins, Fontana Library, 1963. A classic. Crossman's introduction argues that the British political system is now "quasi-presidential."

Barraclough, Geoffrey. *The Origins of Modern Germany.* 2nd ed. New York: Barnes & Noble, 1966. A scholarly yet exciting book on the medieval foundations of German politics. Essential for the serious student.

Beer, Samuel H. *British Politics in the Collectivist Age.* New York: Alfred A. Knopf, 1965. A historical interpretation of modern British politics, perceptively interweaving ideological, social, and economic changes.

Bracher, Karl D. *The German Dictatorship: The Origins, Structure, and Effects of National Socialism.* Translated by Jean Steinberg. New York: Praeger, 1970. The best single volume on this period.

Bullock, Alan. *Hitler: A Study in Tyranny.* Rev. ed. New York: Harper & Row, 1962. The best study of Hitler available in English.

Cantor, Norman F., and Werthman, Michael S., eds. *The English Tradition.* 2 vols. New York: Macmillan Co., 1967. Essays by historians with differing perspectives on English history. Excellent.

Carsten, F. L. *The Origins of Prussia.* New York: Oxford University Press, 1954.

Cobban, Alfred. *A History of Modern France.* Rev. ed. New York: George Braziller, 1965. Imaginative study, just a bit diffuse for those without a basic knowledge of France.

―――. *The Social Interpretation of the French Revolution.* Cambridge: At the University Press, 1964. A revisionist critique of Marxist and neo-Marxist views that it was essentially a bourgeois revolution. Indispensable.

Dahrendorf, Ralf. *Society and Democracy in Germany.* New York: Doubleday & Co., 1967. Many fascinating insights, but a poorly written book.

Edinger, Lewis J. *Politics in Germany.* Boston: Little, Brown & Co., 1968. A behavioral analysis, very strong on political culture, interest groups, and political communication; not as strong on institutions.

Ehrmann, Henry W. *Politics in France.* 2nd ed. Boston: Little, Brown & Co., 1971. A behavioral study of French politics. Especially good on political socialization, interest groups, political parties, and political leadership. Well-written, but likely to be somewhat confusing for the beginner.

Gay, Peter. *Weimar Culture: The Outsider as Insider.* New York: Harper & Row, 1968.

Gimbel, John. *A German Community Under American Occupation.* Stanford, Calif.: Stanford University Press, 1961.

Grosser, Alfred. *Germany in Our Time: A Political History of the Postwar Years.* Translated by Paul Stephenson. New York: Praeger, 1971. An insightful, tightly written work which focuses on the functioning of the major politico-legal institutions.

Hadrill, J. W. W., and McManners, John M., eds. *France: Government and Society.* London: Methuen & Co., 1957. A short political history. The essays are uniformly good.

―――. *A History of the English People in the Nineteenth Century.* 6 vols. Translated by E. I. Watkin. New York: Barnes & Noble, 1949–1961. Two classic works by a great French historian.

Harrison, J. F. C., ed. *Society and Politics in England, 1780–1960.* New York: Harper & Row, 1965.

Havinghurst, Alfred F. *Twentieth Century Britain.* 2nd ed. New York: Harper & Row, 1966. A competent history.

Heberle, Rudolf. *From Democracy to Nazism.* New York: Howard Fertig, 1967.

Heidenheimer, Arnold J. *The Governments of Germany.* 3rd ed. New York: Thomas Y. Crowell, 1971.

Hobsbawm, E. J. *Industry and Empire: An Economic History of Britain Since 1750*. London: Weidenfeld & Nicolson, 1968. Knowledgeable, readable interpretation of modern British history by a Marxist.

Hoffman, Stanley. *Decline or Renewal: France Since the 1930's*. New York: Viking Press, 1974.

Holborn, Hajo. *A History of Modern Germany*. 3 vols. New York: Alfred A. Knopf, 1959–1969. Probably the best general history of Germany available in English. Scholarship served appetizingly.

International Council for Philosophy and Humanistic Studies. *The Third Reich*. London: Weidenfeld & Nicolson, 1955. A massive collection of essays on every aspect of Nazi Germany. As in all collections, the contributions are uneven, but some of them are indeed brilliant.

Kafker, Frank A., and Laus, James, eds. *The French Revolution: Conflicting Interpretations*. New York: Random House, 1968. A representative selection of some of the newer, detailed analyses on the Revolution by historians with sociological training. Most of the contributions are intelligent and exciting.

Keir, David Lindsay. *The Constitutional History of Modern Britain Since 1485*. 7th ed. Princeton, N.J.: D. Van Nostrand, 1966. Good standard text.

Lowell, A. Lawrence. *The Government of England*. 2 vols. 3rd ed. New York: Macmillan Co., 1919. A classic study that holds up very well.
Lowie, Robert H. *Toward Understanding Germany*. Chicago: University of Chicago Press, 1954. An analysis by an anthropologist who succeeds in destroying a good many of the highly simplistic myths about pre-Nazi German social structure and culture. Some of the points are stretched rather thin.

Macridis, Roy C. *French Politics in Transition: The Years after De Gaulle*. Cambridge, Mass.: Winthrop Publishers, 1975.

Pinson, Koppel S. *Modern Germany: Its History and Civilization*. 2nd ed. New York: Macmillan Co., 1967. The best single-volume account, with intelligent attention given to social, economic, and political factors.

Remond, Réné. *The Right Wing in France from 1815 to De Gaulle*. Translated by James M. Laux. 2nd Americaned. Philadelphia: University of Pennsylvania Press, 1969. A detailed study of French conservatism that makes all the appropriate distinctions.

Rose, Richard. *Politics in England*. 2nd ed. Boston: Little, Brown & Co., 1974. Especially good on political culture and political behavior.

Schaffner, Bertram. *Father Land: A Study of Authoritarianism in the German Family*. New York: Columbia University Press, 1948. The origins of National Socialism explained through an examination of the German family. There is something to the argument, but it is much too simple and ahistorical.

Schoenbaum, David. *Hitler's Social Revolution*. New York: Doubleday & Co., 1966. Focuses quite clearly on the populist features of the Nazi regime.

Sontheimer, Kurt. *The Government and Politics of West Germany*. Translated by Fleur Donecker. New York: Praeger, 1973.

Stern, Fritz. *The Failure of Illiberalism: Essays on the Political Culture of Modern Germany*. New York: Alfred A. Knopf, 1972.

———. N. Y.:

———.

Thomson, David. *Democracy in France Since 1870*. 4th ed. New York: Oxford University Press, 1964. A model study integrating economic, social and political variables. Beautifully written. It does, however, presuppose some familiarity with French history.

Tocqueville, Alexis de. *The Old Regime and the French Revolution*. Translated by Stuart Gilbert. New York: Doubleday & Co., 1955. The classic study of the origins of the French Revolution.

Webb, R. K. *Modern England*. New York: Dodd, Mead & Co., 1968. Knowledgeable, balanced, one-volume history, extremely useful for the beginning student.

Williams, Philip M. *Crisis and Compromise*. New York: Doubleday & Co., 1966. This is the study of politics in Fourth Republic France. Flawless in its scholarship, sophisticated in its judgements, and superbly written.

———, and Harrison, Martin. *Politics and Society in De Gaulle's Republic*. New York: Doubleday & Co., Anchor Books, 1973.

Wright, Gordon. *France in Modern Times*. Chicago: Rand McNally & Co. 1960. The best one-volume study available in English. The bibliographical essays that accompany each chapter, though already somewhat dated, still have much to recommend them.

PART TWO THE SOCIAL AND CULTURAL BASES OF EUROPEAN POLITICS

Chapter 3. Industrialization and Change

Almond, Gabriel, and Verba, Sidney. *The Civic Culture*. Princeton, N.J.: Princeton University Press, 1963.

Anderson, Robert T., and Anderson, Barbara Gallatin. *Bus Stop for Paris*. New York: Doubleday & Co., 1965. Throws considerable light on the culture of rural France and the changes taking place there.

Bendix, Reinhard. *Work and Authority in Industry*. New York: John Wiley & Sons, 1956. On managerial ideologies in Western Europe and the Soviet Union.

McKenzie, Robert T., and Silver, Allan. *Angels in Marble*. Chicago: University of Chicago Press, 1968. Working-class political attitudes in Britain and how they are changing.

Pye, Lucian, and Verba, Sidney, eds. *Political Culture and Political Development*. Princeton, N.J.: Princeton University Press, 1965.

Runciman, W. G. *Relative Deprivation and Social Justice*. Berkeley and Los Angeles: University of California Press, 1966.

Sampson, Anthony. *The New Anatomy of Britain*. 3rd ed. London: Hodder and Stoughton, 1971. Excellent survey of British social and political life by a journalist; detailed, imaginative, well-written.

United Nations Secretariat of the Economic Commission for Europe. *Incomes in Postwar Europe*. Geneva: United Nations, 1967. The only really detailed study of trends in income distribution.

Waterman, Harvey. *Political Change in Contemporary France: The Politics of an Industrial Democracy*. Columbus, Ohio: Charles E. Merrill, 1969.

Wylie, Laurence. *Chanzeaux: A Village in Anjou*. Cambridge, Mass.: Harvard University Press, 1967.

———. *Village in the Vaucluse*. 2nd ed. Cambridge, Mass.: Harvard University Press, 1964. These two studies are easy to read and vividly portray some of the major features of French small-town culture.

Chapter 4. Sources and Organization of Political Conflict: Social Class

Bain, G. S. *The Growth of White Collar Unionism*. Oxford: Oxford University Press, 1970.

Barber, Bernard, and Barber, Elinor G., eds. *European Social Class*. New York: Macmillan Co., 1965. Essays concerning historical changes in the European class structure. The introductory essay is particularly useful.

Bloch, Marc. *French Rural History*. Translated by Janet Sondheimer. Berkeley and Los Angeles: University of California Press, 1966. A basic work on the subject.

Braunthal, Gerald. *The Federation of German Industry in Politics*. Ithaca, N.Y.: Cornell University Press, 1965. A good description of channels of influence in Germany from a plural politics perspective.

Dahrendorf, Ralf. *Society and Democracy in Germany*. New York: Doubleday & Co., 1967.

Ehrmann, Henry W. *Organized Business in France*. Princeton N.J.: Princeton University Press, 1957. Massively documented, beautifully done.

Goldthorpe, John H., Lockwood, David, Bechhofer, Frank, and Platt, Jennifer. *The Affluent Worker*. 3 vols. New York: Cambridge University Press, 1968–1969.

Granick, David. *The European Executive*. New York: Doubleday & Co., 1962.

Grebling, Helga. *History of the German Labour Movement*. Oxford: O. Wolff, 1969.

Hamilton, Richard F. *Affluence and the French Worker in the Fourth Republic*. Princeton, N.J.: Princeton University Press, 1967.

Heidenheimer, Arnold J., and Langdon, F. C. *Business Associations and the Financing of Political Parties*. The Hague: M. Nijhoff, 1968.

Huszar, George B., ed. *The Intellectuals: A Controversial Portrait*. Glencoe, Ill.: Free press,

1960. Stimulating collection of essays attacking, defending, and defining the role of intellectuals in society, with a number of studies of their position and influence in various countries. Unfortunately, no common theme is developed.

Manchester, William. *The Arms of Krupp, 1587–1968.* Boston: Little, Brown & Co., 1968.

Mingay, Gordon E. *English Landed Society in the Eighteenth Century.* London: Routledge & Kegan Paul, 1963.

Nordlinger, Eric A. *The Working-Class Tories.* Berkeley and Los Angeles: University of California Press, 1967.

Pelling, Henry. *A Histroy of British Trade Unionism.* New York: St. Martin's Press, 1963. A capable, scholarly job.

Postan, M. M. *An Economic History of Western Europe, 1945–1964.* London: Metheun & Co., 1967. Thorough, well-written examination of postwar economic and social changes.

Thompson, Edward P. T. *The Making of the English Working Class.* New York: Random House, Pantheon Books, 1964. A powerfully written book on the impact of industrialization. Slightly overstated, but compelling even so.

Vogl, Frank. *German Business after the Economic Miracle.* London: Macmillan & Co., 1973.

Webb, Sidney, and Webb, Beatrice. *The History of Trade Unionism.* London: Longmans Green & Co., 1920. The classic history of the English trade-union movement in the nineteenth and early twentieth centuries.

Willey, Richard J. *Democracy in the West German Trade Unions: A Reappraisal of the "Iron Law."* Beverly Hills, Calif.: Sage Publications, 1971.

Wright, Gordon. *Rural Revolution in France.* Stanford, Calif.: Stanford University Press, 1964.

Chapter 5. Sources and Organization of Political Conflict: Religious, Ethnic, and Regional Differences

Bosworth, William. *Catholicism and Crisis in Modern France.* Princeton, N.J.: Princeton University Press, 1961. Detailed survey of the role of the Catholic Church in Fourth Republic France, with extensive discussion of the MRP. Rather dry, but very useful.

Burrell, Sidney A., ed. *The Role of Religion in Modern European History.* New York: Macmillan Co., 1964.

Deakin, Nicholas. *Color and the British Electorate.* New York: Praeger, 1965.

Enloe, Cynthia H. *Ethnic Conflict and Political Development.* Boston: Little, Brown & Co., 1973.

Ferris, Paul. *The Church of England.* New York: Macmillan Co., 1963.

Fitzsimmons, M. A., ed. *The Catholic Church Today: Western Europe.* Notre Dame, Ind.: University of Notre Dame Press, 1969.

Hales, E. E. Y. *Revolution and Papacy: 1769–1846.* New York: Doubleday & Co., 1960.

Hanham, H. J. *Scottish Nationalism.* London: Basil Blackwell, 1969.

Hayward, Jack. *The One and Indivisible French Republic.* New York: W. W. Norton & Co., 1973.

Helmreich, Ernst C., ed. *A Free Church in a Free State.* Boston: D.C. Heath, 1964.

Hill, Clifford. *Immigration and Integration.* London: Permagon Press, 1970.

Jackson, John A. *The Irish in Britain.* London: Routledge & Kegan Paul, 1963.

Kellas, James G. *The Scottish Political System.* Cambridge: At the University Press, 1972.

Lewy, Guenter. *The Catholic Church and Nazi Germany.* New York: McGraw-Hill, 1964.

Martin, David. *A Sociology of English Religion.* New York: Basic Books, 1967.

Morin, Edgar. *The Red and the White.* Translated by A. M. Sheridan-Smith. New York: Pantheon, 1970.

———. *Rumour in Orleans.* Translated by Peter Green. New York: Pantheon Books, 1971. A study of regional change, modernization, and anti-Semitism.

Mosse, George L. *Germans and Jews.* New York: Howard Fertig, 1970.

Rose, E. J. B., ed. *Colour and Citizenship.* Oxford: Claredon Press, 1969. The single best review of race relations in Britain. Incorporates information contained in other studies.

Rose, Richard. *Governing without Consensus: An Irish Perspective.* London: Faber, 1971. An impressive study of the attitudes of Catholics and Protestants in troubled Northern Ireland.

Schonber, H. *Germans from the East. A Study of Their Migration, Resettlement and Subsequent Group History.* The Hague: M. Nijhoff, 1970.

Schram, Stuart R. *Protestantism and Politics in France.* Paris: Alecon, 1954.

Spotts, Frederic. *The Churches and Politics in Germany.* Middletown, Conn.: Wesleyan University Press, 1973. The major part of Mr. Spotts's book describes how the authority and influence of the churches in 1945 was gradually undermined by new forces and attitudes in Germany.

Chapter 6. Sources and Organization of Political Conflict: Youth

Ali, Gariq, ed. *The New Revolutionaries.* New York: William Morrow & Co., 1969. Essays by European student radicals.

Brown, Bernard. *The French Revolt: May, 1968.* New York: McCaleb-Seiles Co., 1970.

————. *Protest in Paris: Anatomy of a Revolt.* Morristown, N.J.: General Learning Press, 1974.

Crawley, Harriet. *A Degree of Defiance: Students in England and Europe Now.* London: Weidenfeld & Nicolson, 1969.

Eisenstadt, S. N. *From Generation to Generation.* Glencoe, Ill.: Free Press, 1956. Basic appraisal of the problem of generations in primitive and modern societies. Tough going, but exceptionally rewarding.

Feuer, Lewis S. *The Conflict of Generations.* New York: Basic Books, 1969. A sweeping view of student rebellion that does not ignore historical and comparative perspectives. The author's premises and prejudices, stemming from his own involvement, detract from the book's overall merit, but there is so much good material here, and the quality of writing so superior, that Feuer deserves careful attention.

Fields, Belden. *Student Politics in France.* New York: Basic Books, 1970. A study of the French student union, UNEF.

Laqueur, Walter. *Young Germany.* New York: Basic Books, 1962.

Lipset, S. M., and Altbach, Philip G. *Student Politics and Higher Education in the United States: A Selected Bibliography.* St. Louis: United Ministries in Higher Education, 1968.

————. *Students in Revolt.* Boston: Houghton Mifflin Co., 1969.

Martin, David, ed. *Anarchy and Culture: The Problem of the Contemporary University.* London: Routledge & Kegan Paul, 1969. Some wonderful and witty essays on English higher education.

Maschmann, Melita. *Account Rendered.* New York: Abelard-Schuman, 1967. A German woman's autobiographical explanation of why she was so "blind" as to join the Nazi youth movement. Compelling and highly relevant.

Spender, Stephen. *The Year of the Young Rebels.* New York: Random House, 1968. A warmly sympathetic (although not uncritical) overview of student rebellion in Europe and the United States.

"Students Protest," special issue of *The Annals of the American Association of Political and Social Sciences.* May, 1971.

Touraine, Alain, *The May Movement: Revolt and Reform.* Translated by Leonard F. X. Mayhew. New York: Random House, 1971.

Chapter 7. Agents of Political Socialization: The Family, The Schools, and the Mass Media

Aries, Philippe. *Centuries of Childhood: A Social History of the Family.* Translated by Robert Baldick. New York: Alfred A. Knopf, 1962.

Barker, Rodney. *Education and Politics, 1900–1951: A Study of the Labour Party.* Oxford: Oxford University Press, 1972. The Labor Party's non-Marxist, reformist posture as reflected in its educational policies.

Blumler, J. G., and McQuail, Denis. *Television in Politics.* Chicago: University of Chicago Press, 1969.

Central Advisory Council for Education in England. The Newsom Report. *Half our Future.* London: HMSO, 1963.

————. The Plowden Report. *Children and Their Primary Schools.* London: HMSO, 1967.

Clark, James M. *Teachers and Politics in France.* Syracuse, N.Y.: Syracuse University Press, 1967.

Clausen, John, ed. *Socialization and Society.* Boston: Little, Brown & Co., 1968.

Comparative Political Studies. Special issue on political socialization. July, 1970.

Crozier, Michel. *The Stalled Society.* New York: Viking Press, 1971.

Goode, William J. *World Revolution and Family Patterns.* New York: Free Press, 1963. Synthesis of studies on the family in different cultures. Among the best books on the subject.

Hoggart, Richard. *The Uses of Literacy: Changing Patterns in British Mass Culture.* New York: Oxford University Press, 1957.

Hood, Stuart. *A Survey of Television.* London: William Heinemann, 1967.

Hornby, Nathan. *The Press in Modern Society.* London: F. Muller, 1965.

Kerr, Anthony. *Universities of Europe.* London: Bowes & Bowes, 1962.

Merrill, John C. *The Elite Press.* New York: Pitman Publishing Corp., 1968.

Parkinnson, Michael. *The Labour Party and the Reorganization of Secondary Education, 1918–1965.* London: Routledge & Kegan Paul, 1970.

Paulu, Burton. *Radio and Television Broadcasting on the European Continent.* Minneapolis: University of Minnesota Press, 1967.

Political and Economic Planning. *Citizenship and Television.* London: Political and Economic Planning, 1967. A useful, general discussion of television's political impact.

Robbins Report. *Higher Education.* 5 vols. Cmnd. 2154. London: HMSO, 1963.

Schoenbaum, David. *The Spiegel Affair.* New York: Doubleday & Co., 1968.

Seymour-Ure, Colin. *The Press, Politics and the Public.* London: Methuen & Co., 1968. Standard academic discussion.

Thomas, Harford. *Newspaper Crisis.* Zurich: International Press Institute, 1967. On the problems facing the British press.

Wakeford, John. *The Cloistered Elite: A Sociological Analysis of the English Boarding School.* London: Macmillan & Co., 1969.

Wedall, E. G. *Broadcasting and Public Policy.* London: Michael Joseph, 1968.

Whale, John. *The Half-Shut Eye: Television and Politics in Britain and America.* London: Macmillan & Co., 1969.

Wilkinson, Rupert. *Gentlemanly Power: British Leadership and the Public School Tradition.* New York: Oxford University Press, 1964. A good supplement to Weinberg.

PART THREE   POLITICAL PARTIES

Chapter 8.   The European Pattern

Caute, David. *The Left in Europe Since 1789.* World University Library Series. New York: McGraw-Hill, 1966.

Dahl, Robert A., ed. *Political Oppositions in Western Democracies.* New Haven, Conn.: Yale University Press, 1966.

Di Palma, Giuseppe. *Mass Politics in Western Societies.* New York: Free Press, 1970. A thoughtful study on the problem of participation in modern democracies.

Duverger, Maurice. *Political Parties.* 2nd rev. ed. Translated by Barbara and Robert North. London: Methuen & Co., 1959. A work, now classic, that has generated considerable reaction. Limited by the fact that the categories developed are derived primarily from the European experience, but still useful.

Epstein, Leon. *Political Parties in Western Democracies.* New York: Praeger, 1967. Still the best comparative survey available.

Henig, Stanley, ed. *European Political Parties: A Handbook.* New York: Praeger Publishers for Political and Economic Planning, 1969. A country-by-country treatment of party organization in eleven European countries. A valuable guide.

Hermens, F. A. *Democracy or Anarchy?* Notre Dame, Ind.: University of Notre Dame Press, 1941. A formidable attack on proportional representation as contributing to the delinquency of government and the rise of extremist political movements. Overstated and slightly shrill.

La Palombara, Joseph, and Weiner, Myron, eds. *Political Parties and Political Development.* Princeton, N.J.: Princeton University Press, 1966.

Lijphart, Arend, ed. *Politics in Europe: Comparisons and Interpretations,* Englewood Cliffs, N.J.: Prentice-Hall, 1969.

Lipset, Seymour Martin. *Political Man: Essays in the Sociology of Democracy.* New York: Doubleday & Co., 1959.

————. *Revolution and Counterrevolution.* New York: Basic Books, 1968. Both of these books are collections of Lipset essays on contemporary politics. As usual, the author exhibits his knack for assembling a mass of fugitive statistical evidence to make his points. Invaluable.

————, and Rokkan, Stein, eds. *Party Systems and Voter Alignments.* New York: Free Press, 1967.

Mackie, Thomas T., and Rose Richard. *The International Almanac of Election History.* New York: Free Press, 1974.

Michels, Robert. *Political Parties.* Translated by Eden and Cedar Paul. New York: Crowell-Collier, 1962. First-rate study of the German Social Democratic Party just before World War I; raises some significant theoretical issues.

Milnor, A. J. *Elections and Political Stability.* Boston: Little, Brown & Co., 1969.

Ostrogorski, M. *Democracy and the Organization of Political Parties.* 2 vols. Edited and abridged by Seymour Martin Lipset. New York: Quadrangle Books, 1964. Classic study of British and American political parties in the late nineteenth century. Lipset's introduction to this edition is also commendable.

Paterson, William E., and Campbell, Ian. *Social Democracy in Postwar Europe.* New York: Macmillan Co., 1974. A pithy explication of the common dimensions of democratic socialism in Europe, including relations with communist parties, composition of party support, ideology, and domestic and foreign policies.

Pitkin, Hanna F. *The Concept of Representation.* Berkeley and Los Angeles: University of California Press, 1967.

————, ed. *Representation.* New York: Atherton Press, 1969.

Rae, Douglas, W. *The Political Consequences of Electoral Laws.* Rev. ed. New Haven, Conn.: Yale University Press, 1971.

————, and Taylor, Michael. *The Analysis of Political Cleavages.* New Haven, Conn.: Yale University Press, 1970.

Rose, Richard, ed. *Electoral Behavior: A Comparative Handbook.* New York: Free Press, 1974.

Chapter 9. The British Party System

Blondel, Jean. *Voters, Parties, and Leaders.* Baltimore: Penguin Books, 1964. Sociological analysis of the composition of local parties, the bases of party support, and patterns of leadership. Well-written and informative.

Butler, David E., and Pinto-Duschinsky, Michael. *The British General Election of 1970.* New York: St. Martin's Press, 1971. The eighth in the series on general elections.

————, and Stokes, Donald. *Political Change in Britain: Factors Shaping Electoral Choice.* College edition. New York: St. Martin's Press, 1971. Many surprising findings are reported in this pioneering study of electoral attitudes. Required reading for serious students.

Harris, Nigel. *Competition and the Corporate Society: British Conservatives, the State and Industry, 1945–1964.* London: Methuen & Co., 1972. A good account of the Conservatives as a pragmatic party.

Janosik, Edward G. *Constituency Labour Parties in Britain.* New York: Praeger, 1968.

Kitzinger, Uwe. *The Second Try: Labour and EEC.* London: Pergamon Press, 1969.

Leonard, Richard Lawrence. *Elections in Britain.* Princeton, N.J.: D. Van Nostrand, 1968.

McKenzie, Robert T. *British Political Parties.* 2nd ed. New York: St. Martin's Press, 1963. Remains the definite work, although the stress on essential similarities between the Conservatives and Labor parties is overdone.

Ranney, Austin. *Pathways to Parliament: Candidate Selection in Great Britain.* Madison: University of Wisconsin Press, 1965. Exhaustive and solid, yet written with style and humor.

Rasmussen, Jorgen Scott. *Retrenchment and Revival: A Study of the Contemporary British Liberal Party.* Tucson: University of Arizona Press, 1964.

Rose, Richard. *Influencing Voters: A Study in Campaign Rationality.* New York: St. Martin's Press, 1967. An analysis of campaign strategies based primarily on Britain's 1964 elections.

Rush, Michael. *The Selection of Parliamentary Candidates.* London: Nelson, 1969.

Chapter 10.   The French Party System

Brower, Daniel R. *The New Jacobins: The French Communist Party and the Popular Front.* Ithaca, N.Y.: Cornell University Press, 1968.

Campbell, Peter. *French Electoral Systems and Elections Since 1789.* 2nd ed. London: Faber & Faber, 1965. Good, short history that also discusses the development of parties.

Charlot, Jean. *The Gaullist Phenomenon.* New York: Praeger, 1971.

Fejto, François. *The French Communist Party and the Crisis of International Communism.* Cambridge, Mass.: MIT Press, 1967.

Green, Nathanael. *Crisis and Decline: The French Socialist Party in the Popular Front Era.* Ithaca, N.Y.: Cornell University Press, 1969.

Hartley, Anthony. *Gaullism: The Rise and Fall of a Political Movement.* New York: Outerbridge & Lazard, 1972.

Johnson, Richard. *The French Communist Party Versus the Students.* New Haven, Conn.: Yale University Press, 1972.

Kriegel, Annie. *The French Communists: Profile of a People.* Translated by Elaine P. Halperen. Chicago: University of Chicago Press, 1972. The best study of the French Communist party in French or English, except for the author's as yet untranslated 2nd edition of the same book.

Lacouture, Jean. *De Gaulle.* Translated by Francis K. Price. New York: New American Library, 1966. A first-rate biography, probably the best in English.

MacRae, Duncan. *Parliament, Parties, and Society in France: 1946–1958.* New York: St. Martin's Press, 1967. A close analysis of political and parliamentary behavior during the Fourth Republic, relying on complicated statistical techniques. The author destroys, or at least weakens, many myths about French politics. Tough going, but worth serious attention.

Simmons, Harvey, G. *French Socialists in Search of a Role.* Ithaca, N.Y.: Cornell University Press, 1970.

Williams, Philip. *French Politicians and Elections, 1951–1969.* New York: Cambridge University Press, 1970.

Wilson, Frank. *The French Democratic Left, 1963–1969.* Stanford, Calif.: Stanford University Press, 1971.

Chapter 11.   The German Party System

Balfour, Michael. *West Germany.* New York: Praeger, 1968.

Berlau, A. Joseph. *The German Social Democratic Party, 1914–1921.* New York: Columbia University Press, 1949.

Chalmers, Douglas A. *The Social Democratic Party of Germany.* New Haven, Conn.: Yale University Press, 1964.

Childs, David. *From Schumacher to Brandt: The Story of German Socialism, 1945–65.* Oxford: Pergamon Press, 1966. Solid. Leftist.

Comparative Politics. Vol. 2. July, 1970. Special issue on German elections of 1969.

Conradt, David P. *The West German Party System.* Beverly Hills, Calif.: Sage Publications, 1972.

Nyomarkay, Joseph. *Charisma and Functionalism in the Nazi Party.* Minneapolis: University of Minnesota Press, 1967.

Roth, Guenter. *The Social Democrats in Imperial Germany.* Totowa, N.J.: Bedminster Press, 1963.

Schellenger, Harold Kent, Jr. *The SPD in the Bonn Republic: A Socialist Party Modernizes.* The Hague: M. Nijhoff, 1968. An absorbing account of the SPD's change in tactics, style and philosophy in its adaptation to the evolution of Germany's mass, consumer society after World War II.

Schorske, Carl E. *German Social Democracy, 1905–1917.* New York: Russell & Russell, 1955.

PART FOUR THE PROCESS OF GOVERNMENT

Chapter 12.   Parliaments, Executives, Interest Groups: The European Pattern

Blondel, Jean. *Comparative Legislatures.* Englewood Cliffs, N.J.: Prentice-Hall, 1973.
Castles, Francis G. *Pressure Groups and Political Culture: A Comparative Study.* New York: Humanities Press, 1967.

Christoph, James B., and Brown, Bernard, eds. *Cases in Comparative Politics.* Boston: Little, Brown & Co., 1969.

Dahl, Robert A., ed. *Regimes and Opposition.* New Haven, Conn.: Yale University Press, 1973.

Dogan, Mattei, and Rose, Richard, eds. *European Politics: A Reader.* Boston: Little, Brown & Co., 1971.

Edinger, Lewis J., ed. *Political Leadership in Industrialized Societies.* New York: John Wiley & Sons, 1967. Though the book lacks a common focus, many of these essays are interesting either as case studies or for their theoretical insights.

Lijphart, Arend, ed. *Politics in Europe: Comparisons and Interpretations.* Englewood Cliffs, N.J.: Prentice-Hall, 1969.

Loewenberg, Gerhard, ed. *Parliaments: Change or Decline?* Chicago: Aldine-Atherton, 1971. A useful collection of essays.

Riker, William H. *Federalism: Origin, Operation, Significance.* Boston: Little, Brown & Co., 1964.

Sawyer, Geoffrey. *Modern Federalism.* London: C. A. Watts, 1969.

Chapter 13. Cabinet Government in Britain

Amery, Leopold. *Thoughts on the Constitution.* 2nd ed. Oxford: Claredon Press, 1956.

Barker, Anthony, and Rush, Michael. *The Member of Parliament and His Information.* London: George Allen & Unwin, 1970. A useful survey of MP attitudes.

Berkeley, Humphrey. *The Power of the Prime Minister.* New York: Random House, 1969.

Butt, Ronald. *The Power of Parliament.* London: Constable & Co., 1967. Excellent study of Parliament, by an author who denies that its power has declined as much as some critics assert.

Chapman, Brian. *British Government Observed: Some European Reflections.* London: George Allen & Unwin, 1963. A sharp, readable critique of the functioning of British government; weakened by overstatement.

Chester, D. N., and Bowring, Nona. *Questions in Parliament.* New York: Oxford University Press, 1962.

Coombes, David. *The Member of Parliament and the Administration.* London: George Allen & Unwin, 1966.

Crick, Bernard. *The Reform of Parliament.* 2nd ed. London: Weidenfeld & Nicolson, 1967.

Instructive critique with some concrete suggestions for reform.

Crossman, R. H. S. *The Myths of Cabinet Government.* Cambridge, Mass.: Harvard University Press, 1972. Provocative insights by a former Labor minister.

Dicey, Albert V. *Introduction to the Study of the Law of the Constitution.* 10th ed. New York: St. Martin's Press, 1959.

Finer, Samuel F. *Anonymous Empire.* 2nd ed. New York: Humanities Press, 1966. The role of interest groups in British society. Highly sophisticated.

Grainger, J. H. *Character and Style in English Politics.* Cambridge: At the University Press, 1969.

Great Britain, Select Committee on Nationalized Industries. *Ministerial Control of the Nationalized Industries.* 3 vols. H.C. 371–I, II, III. London: HMSO, 1968.

Hanser, Charles J. *Guide to Decision: The Royal Commission.* Totowa, N.J.: Bedminster Press, 1965.

Hanson, A. H., and Crick, Bernard, eds. *The Commons in Transition.* London: Collins, 1970.

Jackson, Robert J. *Rebels and Whips: An Analysis of Dissension, Discipline and Cohesion in British Political Parties Since 1945.* New York: St. Martin's Press, 1968.

Jennings, Ivor. *Cabinet Government.* 3rd ed. New York: Cambridge University Press, 1969.

————. *Parliament.* 2nd ed. New York: Cambridge University Press, 1957.

King, Anthony, ed. *The British Prime Minister: A Reader.* London: Macmillan & Co., 1969.

Lieber, Robert. *British Politics and European Unity: Parties, Elites, and Pressure Groups.* Berkeley and Los Angeles: University of California Press, 1970.

MacKintosh, John P. *The British Cabinet.* 2nd ed. London: Stevens & Sons, 1968. Readable, well-researched introduction to the evolution and structure of contemporary cabinet government; it also notes the decline of parliamentary influence on public policy. Open to argument, perhaps, but worth reading.

Martin, Kingsley. *The Crown and the Establishment.* Baltimore: Penguin Books, 1963. Highly irreverent history of the English monarchy, by a former editor of *The New Statesman*. Enjoyable, but not to be swallowed whole.

Nicholson, Max. *The System*. New York: McGraw-Hill, 1967. An impassioned assault upon most British institutions. Overstated and occasionally wrong-headed, but always fascinating.

Pollard, A. F. *The Evolution of Parliament*. London: Longmans Green & Co., 1920. A durable classic.

Putnam, Robert D. *The Beliefs of Politicians: Ideology, Conflict and Democracy in Britain and Italy*. New Haven, Conn.: Yale University Press, 1973.

Richards, Peter G. *Honourable Members: A Study of the British Backbender*. 2nd ed. New York: Hillary House, 1964.

UNESCO. *Decisions and Decision Makers in the Modern State*. Paris: UNESCO, 1967.

Walker, Patrick G. *The Cabinet*. London: Jonathan Cape, 1970. A denial of the "presidential government" thesis by a former minister.

Walkland, S. A. *The Legislative Process in Great Britain*. London: George Allen & Unwin, 1968. A brief, behavioral treatment of Parliament.

Chapter 14. France: From Parliamentary to Presidential Government

Andrews, William G. *French Politics and Algeria: The Process of Policy Formation, 1954–1962*. New York: Appleton-Century-Croft, 1962.

Avril, Pierre. *Politics in France*. Translated by John Ross. Baltimore: Penguin Books, 1969.

Hayward, Jack. *The One and Indivisible French Republic*. New York: W. W. Norton and Co., 1973.

Hoffman, Stanley. *Decline or Renewal: France Since the 1930's*. New York: Viking Press, 1974.

Leites, Nathan. *On the Game of Politics in France*. Stanford, Calif.: Stanford University Press, 1959.

———. *The Rules of the Game in Paris*. Translated by Derek Coltman. Chicago: University of Chicago Press, 1969.

MacRae, Duncan Jr. *Parliament, Parties and Society in France: 1946–1958*.

Macridis, Roy C. *French Politics in Transition: The Years After De Gaulle*. Cambridge, Mass.: Winthrop Publishers, 1975.

Melnik, Constatin, and Leites, Nathan. *The House Without Windows: France Selects a President*. Evanston, Ill.: Row, Peterson & Co., 1958.

Suleiman, Ezra N. *Politics, Power and Bureaucracy in France: The Administrative Elite*. Princeton, N.J.: Princeton University Press, 1974.

The best recent work on the bureaucracy and the political process.

Williams, Philip M. *Crisis and Compromise: Politics in the Fourth Republic*. London: Longmans Green & Co., 1964.

———. *French Parliament, 1958–1967*. London: George Allen & Unwin, 1968. Short, penetrating look at the parliament in Fifth-Republic France. Easily the best thing available in English.

———, and Harrison, Martin. *Politics and Society in De Gaulle's Republic*. New York: Doubleday & Co., Anchor Books, 1973.

Chapter 15. Parliamentary Government in Germany

Braunthal, Gerard. *The West German Legislative Process*. Ithaca, N.Y.: Cornell University Press, 1972.

Carsten, F. L. *Princes and Parliaments in Germany: From the Fifteenth to to the Eighteenth Century*. New York: Oxford University Press, 1959.

King-Hall, Stephen, and Ullman, Richard K. *German Parliaments: A Study of the Development of Representative Institutions in Germany*. London: Hansard, 1954.

Loewenberg, Gerhard. *Parliament in the German Political System*. Ithaca, N.Y.: Cornell University Press, 1967. The definitive work in English on the Bonn parliament. It has the added value of offering interesting comparisons with other countries.

Mayntz, Renate, and Scharpf, Fritz W. *Policy-Making in the German Federal Bureaucracy*. New York: Elsevier, 1975. An exploration in systems-analytical terms of decisional bottlenecks. Suggestive.

Safran, William. *Veto-Group Politics: The Case of Health Insurance Reform in West Germany*. San Francisco: Chandler Publishing Co., 1967.

Wells, Roger, H. *The States in West German Federalism.* New York: Bockman, 1961.

Chapter 16.   Bureaucracy and the Political System

Armstrong, John A. *The European Administrative Elite.* Princeton, N.J.: Princeton University Press, 1973.

Barker, Sir Ernest. *The Development of Public Service in Western Europe, 1660–1930.* Oxford: Claredon Press, 1944.

Brown, R. G. S. *The Administrative Process in Britain.* New York: Barnes & Noble, 1971. An analysis by a former civil servant: critical of the Fulton Report.

Campbell, G. A. *The Civil Service in Britain.* 2nd ed. London: Duckworth & Co., 1965.

Chapman, Brian. *The Profession of Government: The Public Service in Europe.* 3rd ed. London: George Allen & Unwin, 1966. Fairly orthodox approach, but the product of scrupulous scholarship and extremely well written.

Chapman, R. A. *The Higher Civil Service in Britain.* London: Constable & Co., 1970.

Coombes, David. *The Member of Parliament and the Administration.* London: George Allen & Unwin, 1966.

———. *Politics and Bureaucracy in the European Community.* Beverly Hills, Calif.: Sage Publications, 1970.

Crozier, Michel. *The Bureaucratic Phenomenon.* Chicago: University of Chicago Press, 1964. French, British and American public and private bureaucracies compared; together with some interesting observations about the impact of political culture on the functioning of bureaucratic systems.

De Smith, S. A. *Judicial Review of Administration Action.* New York: Oceana, 1959.

Diamant, Alfred. "The French Administrative System: The Republic Passes but the Administration Remains." In *Toward the Comparative Study of Public Administration,* edited by William J. Siffin. Bloomington: Indiana University Press, 1957. A classic essay on the French bureaucratic system.

Fry, Geoffrey. *Statesman in Disguise: The Changing Role of the Administrative Class of the British Home Civil Service, 1853–1970.* London: Macmillan & Co., 1969.

Great Britain, Committee on the Civil Service, 1966–1968. *The Civil Service.* Cmnd. 3638. 5 vols. London: HMSO, 1968.

Heclo, Hugh and Wildavsky, Aaron. *The Private Government of Public Money: Community and Policy Inside British Politics.* Berkeley and Los Angeles: University of California Press, 1974.

Heady, Ferrel, *Public Administration.* Englewood Cliffs, N.J.: Prentice-Hall, 1966. The focus is comparative. Short and sharp.

Jacob, Herbert. *German Administration Since Bismarck.* New Haven, Conn.: Yale University Press, 1963. Easily the best recent study in English of the German bureaucracy.

Johnson, Nevil. *Parliament and Administration.* London: George Allen & Unwin, 1966.

MacKenzie, W. J. M., and Grove, J. W. *Central Administration in Britain.* 2nd ed. London: Longmans Green & Co., 1969.

Morstein-Marx, Fritz. *The Administrative State.* Chicago: University of Chicago Press, 1957. Traditional analysis of the nature of bureaucracy, in which the author carries his immense erudition lightly. Still serves the reader well.

Ridley, F. F. *Specialists and Generalists.* London: George Allen & Unwin, 1968.

———, and Blondel, Jean. *Public Administration in France.* 2nd ed. London: Routledge & Kegan Paul, 1969. Extraordinary scholarship and scope of coverage have so overshadowed a fairly routine approach to the subject matter that the book is required reading for the earnest student.

Rosenberg, Hans. *Bureaucracy, Aristocracy, and Autocracy: The Prussian Experience, 1660–1815.* Cambridge, Mass.: Harvard University Press, 1958. The origins of the German bureaucracy and its impact upon Prussian and, later, German politics. Basic.

Sharp, Evelyn. *The Ministry of Housing and Local Government.* London: George Allen & Unwin, 1969. The best in the series on Whitehall departments, now called Ministry of Environment.

Suleiman, Ezra N. *Power Politics and Bureaucracy in France: The Administrative Elite.* See Ch. 14.

Chapter 17. Economic and Social Policy

Aldcroft, Derek H. *British Railways in Transition.* New York: St. Martin's Press, 1969.

Ambassade de France, Service de Presse et d'Information. *Social Security and National Health Insurance in France.* New York, 1973.

Ardagh, John. *The New France.* London: Penguin Books, 1973.

Arndt, Hans-Joachim. *West-Germany: Politics of Non-Planning.* Syracuse, N.Y.: Syracuse University Press, 1966.

Bailey, Richard. *Managing the British Economy.* London: Hutchinson & Co., 1968.

Barry, E. Eldon. *Nationalization in British Politics.* Stanford, Calif.: Stanford University Press, 1965.

Beckerman, Wilfred, ed. *The Labour Government's Economic Record, 1965–1970.* London: Duckworth & Co., 1972.

Blaug, Mark. *Social Services for All?* Fabian Tract no. 383. London: Fabian Society, 1968. Cartwright, Ann. *Patients and their Doctors: A Study of General Practice.* New York: Atherton Press, 1967.

Caves, Richard E., ed. *Britain's Economic Prospects.* Washington, D.C.: Brookings Institution, 1968.

Coates, R. J. *The Making of the Welfare State.* New York: Longmans Green & Co., 1966.

Dahl, Robert A., and Lindblom, Charles E. *Politics, Economics and Welfare.* New York: Harper & Bros., 1953. A basic work on the political economy of planning. Difficult going for the beginning student.

Denton, Geoffrey, Forsyth, Murray and MacLennan, Malcolm. *Economic Planning and Policies in Britain, France and Germany.* New York: Praeger, 1969. An excellent, comparative study for the intelligent layman.

Gilpin, Robert G., Jr. *France in the Age of the Scientific State.* Princeton, N.J.: Princeton University Press, 1968.

Gregg, Pauline. *The Welfare State.* Amherst: University of Massachusetts Press, 1969.

Hancock, M. Donald, and Gideon Sjoberg. *Politics in the Post-Welfare State: Responses to the New Individualism.* New York: Columbia University Press, 1972.

Hanson, A. H., ed. *Nationalization: A Book of Readings.* London: George Allen & Unwin, 1963.

Harris, Nigel. *Competition and the Corporate Society: British Conservatives, The State and Industry, 1945–1964.* London: Methven & Co., 1972.

Heclo, Hugh. *Modern Social Politics in Britain and Sweden: From Relief to Income Maintenance.* New Haven, Conn.: Yale University Press, 1974.

Heidenheimer, Arnold J., Hugh Heclo, and Carolyn Tech Adams. *Comparative Public Policy.* New York: St. Martin's Press, 1975.

Kidron, Michael. *Western Capitalism Since the War.* London: Weidenfeld & Nicolson, 1968.

Lutz, Vera. *Central Planning for the Market Economy: An Analysis of the French Theory and Experience.* London: Longmans Green & Co., 1969.

Lynch, Matthew Joseph, and Raphael, Stanley S. *Medicine and the State.* Springfield, Ill.: Charles C. Thomas, 1963.

McArthur, John H. and Scott, Bruce R. *Industrial Planning in France.* Boston: Harvard Graduate School of Business Administration, 1969.

Roemer, Milton J. *The Organization of Medical Care Under Social Security.* Geneva: International Labor Office, 1969.

Rose, Richard, ed. *Policy-Making in Britain.* New York: Free Press, 1969.

Schnitzer, Martin. *East and West Germany: A Comparative Economic Analysis.* New York: Praeger, 1972.

Schorr, Alvin L. *Social Security and Social Services in France.* Washington, D.C.: U.S. Government Printing Office, 1965.

Shanks, Michael, ed. *The Lessons of Public Enterprise.* London: Jonathan Cape, 1963. Essays on major issues facing the nationalized industries. Still quite useful.

Vernon, Raymond, ed. *Big Business and the State: Changing Relations in Western Europe.* Cambridge, Mass.: Harvard University Press, 1974. An excellent volume embodying the most recent research on the political imperative to control and protect large-scale, high technology industry.

Willey, Richard J. *Democracy in the West German Trade Unions*. Beverly Hills, Calif.: Sage Publications, 1971.

*

Index

END OF VOLUME